# MATHEMATICAL MODELS OF DISTRIBUTION CHANNELS

**INTERNATIONAL SERIES IN QUANTITATIVE MARKETING**

**Series Editor:**
Jehoshua Eliashberg
The Wharton School
University of Pennsylvania
Philadelphia, Pennsylvania USA

**Other books in the series:**

*Chakravarty, A. and Eliashberg, J.*
Managing Business Interfaces:
Marketing, Engineering, and Manufacturing Perspectives

*Zaccour, G.*
Differential Games in Marketing

*Wind ,Yoram (Jerry) and Green, Paul E.*
Marketing Research and Modeling:
Progress and Prospects

*Erickson, Gary M.:*
Dynamic Models of Advertising Competition, 2$^{nd}$ Ed

*Hanssens, D., Parsons, L., and Schultz, R.*:
Market Response Models:
Econometric and Time Series Analysis, 2$^{nd}$ Ed

*Mahajan, V., Muller, E. and Wind, Y.*:
New-Product Diffusion Models

*Wierenga, B. and van Bruggen, G.*:
Marketing Management Support Systems:
Principles, Tools, and Implementation

*Leeflang, P., Wittink, D., Wedel, M. and Naert, P.*:
Building Models for Marketing Decisions

*Wedel, M. and Kamakura, W.G.*:
Market Segmentation, 2nd Ed

*Wedel, M. and Kamakura, W.G.*:
Market Segmentation

*Nguyen, D.*:
Marketing Decisions Under Uncertainty

*Laurent, G., Lilien, G.L., Pras, B.*:
Research Traditions in Marketing

*Erickson, G.*:
Dynamic Models of Advertising Competition

*McCann, J. and Gallagher, J.*:
Expert Systems for Scanner Data Environments

*Hanssens, D., Parsons, L., and Schultz, R.*:
Market Response Models:
Econometric and Time Series Analysis

*Cooper, L. and Nakanishi, M.*:
Market Share Analysis

# MATHEMATICAL MODELS OF DISTRIBUTION CHANNELS

*by*

**Charles A. Ingene**
*University of Mississippi*

**Mark E. Parry**
*University of Virginia*

KLUWER ACADEMIC PUBLISHERS

Charles A. Ingene
University of Mississippi
329 Holman Hall
Oxford, MS 38677
cingene@bus.olemiss.edu

Mark E. Parry
University of Virginia
Darden School of Business
Charlottesville, VA 22906
parrym@darden.virginia.edu

Library of Congress Cataloging-in-Publication Data

A C.I.P. Catalogue record for this book is available from the Library of Congress.

Ingene, Charles A.
mathematical models of distribution channels
Includes index.

ISBN 1-4020-7163-9 e-ISBN 0-387-22790-3 Printed on acid-free paper.



Printed in the United States of America.

9 8 7 6 5 4 3 2 1 SPIN 11311577

springeronline.com

**Dedications:**

To my wife and son, Daphne and Ulysses
— Charles A. Ingene

To my father and mother, Arthur and Patricia
— Mark E. Parry

## Contents

## List of Figures

## List of Tables

# Preface

*"Problems worthy of attack; prove their worth by fighting back."*

## 1 IN THE BEGINNING

We began this monograph with what seemed to be a straightforward, three-part task. Our intention was to (i) review the (limited) analytical literature on distribution channels, (ii) restate all models using a common mathematical terminology, and (iii) draw inferences on how demand, costs, wholesale-price policies, and channel structures affect channel performance (i.e., prices, quantities, consumers' surplus, and the level and distribution of channel profit). Our *expectation* was that the then current state-of-the-art was well developed, but that differences in symbolic notation made it difficult to understand why minor modifications of model assumptions left one model's conclusions virtually intact but radically altered the conclusions drawn from a second, seemingly similar model.

We also hoped to gain an understanding of why the analytical marketing science literature overwhelmingly argued that an appropriate wholesale-price policy induces channel coordination (thus potentially making all channel participants better off than they would be without coordination) while the behavioral and practical literatures just as overpoweringly reported empirical indications of ongoing channel conflict that suggested a lack of coordination.

A review of the empirical literature revealed no egregious errors that could account for the apparent absence of widespread coordination. Indeed, the evidence suggests that businesses put significant effort into trying to diminish channel conflict, but with limited success. Because the prescription from the modeling literature is clear-cut—an appropriately specified wholesale price maximizes channel profit and (inferentially) minimizes channel conflict—our review led us to wonder if theorists were improperly analyzing their models. Working through multiple analytical models revealed the unsurprising conclusion that marketing scientists make few algebraic errors. This implied the impossible; these literatures could not both be correct while reaching mutually inconsistent conclusions. As all good academic detectives know, "when you have eliminated the impossible, whatever remains, however improbable, must be the truth" (Doyle 1890, p. 172). One of the approaches had to be in error. We made four deductions: (1) an old stand-by, the bilateral-monopoly model, did not generate results that were compatible with the empirical evidence, (2) its companion, the identical-competitors model, had similar problems, (3) the absence of fixed costs from existing models was neither realistic nor innocuous, and (4) the fundamental prescription, "coordinate the channel," might be wrong.

These deductions encouraged us to focus on developing a set of logically consistent, interwoven theories that contain much of the extant literature as special cases, including the bilateral-monopoly model and the identical-competitors model. We explicitly modeled non-negative fixed costs, thereby including zero fixed costs as a special case. We also required our theories to permit, but not to force, coordinated channel outcomes. In our pursuit of theories with these characteristics, we gained a greater appreciation of the words of the great $20^{th}$ century mathematician Paul Erdös, who said: "Problems worthy of attack; prove their worth by fighting back" (Hoffmann 1998, p. 77). We also became more conscious the wisdom of the $4^{th}$ century (BC) historian Herodotus: "Haste in every business brings failures" (Bartlett 1968, p. 86a). Our task was more arduous than we expected, so we slowed our pace and fought the mathematical and conceptual battles that emerged in our path. This monograph is the result.

## 2 TOWARD A UNIFYING THEORY OF DISTRIBUTION CHANNELS

Our overarching objective in this monograph is to contribute toward the creation of a *Unifying Theory of Distribution Channels* that will facilitate a common awareness in the marketing science profession of how *choices* about modeling the Channel Environment and Channel Structure affect *deductions* about Channel Strategy and Channel Performance. We use the term "Unifying Theory" to convey the idea of a framework that meets four basic criteria.

1. First-Principles: channel members should be modeled as rational, economic actors who engage in maximizing behavior.
2. Empirical-Evidence: models should be in broad conformity with the actual operation of distribution channels.
3. Nested-Models: simpler models should be embedded as special cases within more complex models.
4. Strategic-Endogeneity: all aspects of Channel Strategy and many elements of Channel Structure should be endogenously determined within distribution-channels models as the optimal outcome of channel members' actions.

Adhering to these Criteria should enable modelers, working independently, to advance the marketing science professions' comprehension of distribution-channels theory and practice by building on each other's work. We believe that advancement by independent construction is impossible *if*:

- Channel members are modeled as *not* being self-interested, for then we cannot compare their (effectively random) actions across our models.
- Models are developed that have little relation to reality, for then our models cannot inform us about channel practice.
- Models are not nested, for then we cannot assess the implications of adding a layer of complexity to our models.
- Channel Strategy is imposed on our models, for then we cannot determine if Channel Performance is optimal within the context of the model.

In short, if we as academic researchers adhere to similar modeling criteria, we can collectively construct a comprehensive understanding of distribution channels, for each model will be a piece of a common puzzle. But, if we each speak in our unique tongues, our research efforts will develop pieces of different puzzles that cannot be joined to form a meaningful picture of distribution channels. In the final Chapter of this monograph we offer several suggestions for future research that build upon these criteria.

## 3 CHANNEL MYTHS AND DISTRIBUTION-CHANNELS MODELING

We believe this monograph makes *progress* toward a Unifying Theory of Distribution Channels by developing a "meta-model" that meets our four criteria. Our meta-model generates a wealth of insights into distribution channels, including the revelation of eight *Channel Myths* that have impeded distribution-channels research. We use the term "Channel Myth" to characterize beliefs that are almost universally held by analytical modelers, but whose significance seems not to have been widely grasped. Indeed, these eight Channel Myths are so common that they are rarely cited as assumptions. Note that, because Myths seem reasonable, their misleading nature can be difficult to comprehend; in the words of John Maynard Keynes "the difficulty lies, not in the new ideas, but in escaping the old ones, which ramify . . . into every corner of our minds" (1935, p. viii).

We classify the Channel Myths into three categories: Modeling Myths, Strategic Myths, and Meta-Myths. We identify four *Modeling Myths* that circumscribe the ways in which channel models are constructed. We also identify two *Strategic Myths* that relate to inferences about optimal behavior. Their deductions are accurate within the carefully delimited spheres of specific models, but are inaccurate outside those realms.

Central to our thesis are two *Meta-Myths* that distort the way in which channel problems are perceived. The essence of the *Bilateral-Monopoly* and the *Identical-Competitors Meta-Myths* is the belief that simple, easy to manipulate models generate results that are first-order approximations of what would be obtained from more complex models. Meta-Myths have Modeling and Strategic dimensions. As Modeling Myths they discourage analyses of richer models; as Strategic Myths they encourage managerial advice in domains that are far removed from the models that generated the advice.

By moving beyond bilateral monopoly and identical competitors, our models reveal that a great deal of what is known about distribution channels is a special case that conceals far more than it reveals. The Strategic and Modeling Myths also play a major role in our work, as we show in all the following Chapters. Indeed, our eight Channel Myths form a leitmotif that runs through this monograph.

## 4 ACADEMIC STUDY

Some material in this monograph has appeared in *Marketing Science*, *Marketing Letters*, and the *Journal of Retailing*; however, this book is much more than a compilation of previously presented research. Our published "building blocks" have been extensively reworked to incorporate substantial knowledge that has been gained since their appearance. More importantly, some 80 percent of the text is completely new material.

To facilitate the use of this book by those who may be approaching a detailed study of distribution-channels models for the first time, we have constructed our argument sequentially. To ease its use in the classroom, either as a primary text or as a supplement to journal articles, we have made each Chapter as self-contained as possible. While this leads to a slight redundancy across Chapters, it also means that few Chapters must be read in their presented order. The exceptions are Chapters 8-11. Chapter 8 may be of limited comprehensibility without having first read Chapters 5-7 (in any order). Chapters 9 and 10 build on Chapter 8. Finally, Chapter 11 relies on Chapters 5-7 and Chapter 10. The other Chapters may be approached in any order.

## Acknowledgements

First and foremost we acknowledge the friendship and support of the series editor, Professor Jehoshua ("Josh") Eliashberg of The Wharton School, University of Pennsylvania. Without his initial, and especially his continuing, encouragement this monograph would not have been attempted. Gratitude is also expressed to our sequential, "hands-on" editors at Kluwer Academic Publishers: Julie Kaczinski Barr and David Cella. We were blessed by their patience, and their classical schooling, for like Josh they conformed to a (possibly apocryphal) dictum attributed to Plato, "Never discourage anyone who continually makes progress, no matter how slow."

Second, we thank the copyright holders for permission to reproduce some material that originally appeared in *Marketing Science* (the Institute for Operations Research and the Management Sciences), *Marketing Letters* (Kluwer Academic/Plenum Publishers), and the *Journal of Retailing* (New York University).

Third, we gratefully acknowledge the tireless efforts of Melanie Jones of the University of Virginia. Her hard work has brought our tortured prose closer to conformity with generally accepted communication standards.

We salute those friends who have patiently listened to us, and often debated with us, many technical aspects of modeling distribution channels. Their wisdom has enhanced our thinking. A gigantic Thank You! to John Conlon, Anne Coughlan, Eitan Gerstner, Jim Hess, Pat Kaufmann, Kyu Lee, Paul Messinger, Greg Shaffer, Rick Staelin, and many others; and a very special appreciation to Chan Choi for providing insightful comments on the penultimate draft.

We each owe a special thank you to those who introduced us to logical and creative thought. Ingene acknowledges the guidance of his dissertation chair Martin J. Beckmann, now Professor Emeritus (Economics) at Brown University and Professor Emeritus (Mathematics) at Technische Universität München, who instilled an appreciation of mathematical logic as a tool of economic analysis, and Louis P. Bucklin, now Professor Emeritus (Marketing) at the University of California at Berkeley, for his persuasive argument on applying analytical reasoning to distribution-channels research.

Parry acknowledges his dissertation chair, Professor Frank M. Bass, Eugene C. McDermott University of Texas System Professor of Management at the University of Texas at Dallas, who shaped his approach to the mathematical modeling of marketing problems, and Professor Ram Rao, Professor of Marketing and Founders Professor at the University of Texas at Dallas, for his perspectives on game theory and the modeling of channel behavior.

Chapter 1

# A Commentary on Distribution-Channels Modeling

*"Gallia est omnis divisa in partes tres"*[1]

## 1 INTRODUCTION

The marketing science literature on distribution channels originated with nearly simultaneous studies of (i) competition between channels and (ii) cooperation within a bilateral-monopoly channel.[2] The literature that analyzes competition is divided into three parts, or streams: inter-channel competition, inter-manufacturer competition, and inter-retailer competition. The first stream involves the relationship between competitive intensity and a manufacturer's decision to vertically integrate, or to sell through an independent retailer, given competition from a rival, identical channel.[3] The second stream concerns the link between channel structure and a monopolistic retailer's sourcing of products from independent, identical manufacturers.[4] The third stream tackles the impact of the environment on the performance and strategy of a channel comprised of a monopolistic manufacturer selling to independent, differentiated retailers.[5] The bilateral-monopoly channel, which remains a focal point of the literature, is a special case of all three streams.

Our *modeling goal* in this monograph is to elaborate the third stream of the literature by developing and analyzing a set of interrelated models. Our *strategic goal* with this monograph is to contribute to the development of a *Unifying Theory of Distribution Channels* that combines the three competitive streams and the bilateral-monopoly model. The significance of our strategic goal arises from the conflicting assumptions—and conflicting managerial recommendations—that characterize existing channels models. We believe these conflicts, which impede knowledge development, can be reconciled by the consistent application of four modeling criteria. Before introducing these criteria, we describe the assumptions that differentiate the three competitive streams and that make our four modeling criteria important.

All models of distribution channels are concerned with assessing at least some elements of Channel Performance (prices, quantities, consumers' surplus, channel profit, and the distribution of channel profit). However, different models inevitably feature varied assumptions about the Channel Environment, Channel Structure, and Channel Strategy. The Channel

Environment includes factors that are relevant to the decision-makers whose actions are being modeled, but that are beyond their control. The modeler's choices about these factors are necessarily *exogenous* to the model. Channel Structure concerns phenomena that may or may not be outside managerial control, depending on the channel and the phenomenon that is being modeled; that is, they may be *exogenous* or *endogenous* to the model. Channel Strategy involves variables that are inherently within the control of a model's decision-makers; strategic variables are intrinsically *endogenous* to the model, although they are not always endogenously modeled. A few comments will clarify our distinctions.

Channel-Environment Assumptions fall into three categories. The *Channel-Demand Assumption* specifies the nature of demand that is faced by the channel. Linear demand is the most common assumption, but general demand, rectangular demand, and constant-elasticity demand have also been assumed.[6] The *Channel-Costs Assumption* specifies costs incurred by the channel. Positive per-unit variable costs of distribution and production are often assumed (although zero costs are not uncommon), while fixed costs are typically ignored.[7] A corollary of the channel-demand and channel-costs assumptions is the degree to which competitors are differentiated. The most common approach (competitors that face equal demand and the same cost) generates *identical competitors*. Only the inter-retailer stream of research has employed a heterogeneous-competitors model in which identical competitors are embedded as a special case. The *States-of-Nature Assumption* specifies the number of states-of-nature faced by a channel. Uncertainty has been considered, but certainty is the prevalent assumption.

Channel-Structure Assumptions lie in four areas. The *Inter-Channel Competition Assumption* specifies the nature of competition among channels. Research that addresses inter-channel competition has been based on bilateral-monopolists that operate as Nash competitors.[8] However, because most research on inter-manufacturer and inter-retailer competition has focused on a single channel, this assumption has largely been irrelevant. The *Vertical Channel-Relationship Assumption* specifies the nature of cooperation between members at different levels of a distribution channel. A channel may be modeled as vertically integrated, so one decision-maker controls all channel decisions, or channel levels may be modeled as independent, but linked through a Stackelberg or a Nash game. The *Horizontal Channel-Relationship Assumption* specifies the nature of competition within a level of the channel. For example, a two-retailer model may assume Nash competition or that one retailer is a Stackelberg leader. The *Product-Resale Assumption* specifies whether a firm is allowed to resell a product to its horizontal competitor(s). Horizontal resale does not seem to have attracted the attention of marketing scientists. Channel Structure is typically treated as exogenous.[9]

There are four categories of Channel-Strategy Assumptions. The *Channel-Breadth Assumption* specifies the number of players at each level of the channel. It is common to assume one or two players, but N competitors have also been modeled. The *Wholesale-Price Assumption* states the price strategy used by manufacturers; common options include a one-part tariff, a two-part tariff, a quantity-discount schedule, and a menu of two-part tariffs. The *Category-Management Assumption* specifies the number of products that are produced (or distributed) by each channel member *and* the scope of analysis for setting each product's price; options range from individually pricing a product to collectively pricing the entire product line. The *Marketing-Mix Assumption* specifies the marketing-mix elements used by each channel member to influence demand. Virtually all models include price; other marketing-mix elements have been studied less frequently. Marketing scientists often model the elements of Channel Strategy as exogenous, presumably for convenience. In this monograph we break with "tradition" by modeling channel breadth and the wholesale-price strategy as endogenous variables.[10]

It is clear that there is no set of assumptions that is uniformly agreed upon by marketing scientists. It is also clear that some common assumptions entail treating strategic categories, and endogenous structural areas, as if they were exogenous. Modelers may choose such treatment purposefully, with an *understanding* that the model's findings are only valid in a partial equilibrium context. However, modelers may also make such treatment for convenience, with a *faith* that the model's deductions are valid over a broader milieu. We believe that this faith has bred a set of erroneous beliefs that permeate the profession.

A study of the literature reveals that different modeling assumptions lead to different results and (often) conflicting managerial recommendations. Determining the causes of these variations is often difficult, because models from different streams (and often those within a stream) typically differ on more than one underlying assumption. Thus our over-arching strategic goal in this monograph is to describe and illustrate a process for integrating the marketing science literature on distribution channels. We believe that such integration is critical for a complete understanding of the ways in which modeling decisions regarding the Channel Environment, Channel Structure and Channel Strategy affect Channel Performance. Accordingly, this monograph is our contribution toward the development of a *Unifying Theory of Distribution Channels*.

In Chapter 12 we specify in detail the elements of a Unifying Theory. Here we highlight four essential criteria that emerge from that discussion.

1. ***The First-Principles Criterion.*** A Unifying Theory should be consistent with first principles so that decisions reflect the rational, maximizing behavior of economic actors. Thus the demand curve facing consumer-oriented firms should be derived from a meaningful

utility function while the demand curve facing business-oriented firms should be derived from their customers' profit functions. This criterion should ensure that analyses are logically consistent.

2. ***The Empirical-Evidence Criterion.*** A Unifying Theory should be in broad harmony with the empirical evidence as to how channels of distribution actually operate. This criterion should ensure that models do not spawn suggestions that are irrelevant or managerially dubious.
3. ***The Nested-Models Criterion.*** A Unifying Theory should contain simpler models as special cases that are nested within more complex models (Moorthy 1993). This criterion should generate research that *systematically* builds on previous research; it should also simplify the challenge of understanding how adding layers of complexity (i.e., variables) alters Channel Performance within a model.
4. ***The Strategic-Endogeneity Criterion.*** A Unifying Theory should endogenously determine a model's important strategic decisions and should assess the Performance implications of these choices. In particular, a Unifying Theory should endogenously establish:
   - Each channel member's optimal price strategy;
   - Each channel member's optimal product-line length;
   - Each channel member's optimal level for all non-price elements of the marketing mix;
   - The optimal channel breadth (i) from the channel leader's viewpoint in a Stackelberg game or (ii) from the perspective of all channel participants in a Nash game; and
   - The optimality of channel coordination (i) from the leader's viewpoint in a Stackelberg game or (ii) from the perspective of all channel participants in a Nash game.

   This criterion should ensure that models lead to an *endogenous determination of all elements of Channel Strategy and their consequent impacts on Channel Performance.* We believe that much of the literature imposes strategic assumptions and performance standards that should be endogenously determined in an over-arching meta-model. We offer evidence for our opinion in later Chapters.

We believe that this monograph makes substantial *progress* toward a Unifying Theory by developing a meta-model[11] that meets these four essential criteria. Our meta-model, which is introduced in sub-Section 1.3 of this Chapter, offers a wealth of insights into distribution channels, of which the most fundamental is that the optimality of channel coordination does not extend past the simplistic bilateral-monopoly and identical-competitors models. Because this result is so basic to our research and so contrary to prevailing wisdom in marketing science, we provide a brief overview of our concerns about coordination.

## 1.1 Channel Coordination and Bilateral-Monopoly Models: Conceptualization

The argument in favor of channel coordination is direct and *seems* persuasive: "if channel profit can be maximized through enhancing distributive efficiency, then the profit can be allocated among channel participants to make all of them at least as well off as they would be in the absence of coordination."[12] This argument is predicated on economic models of *bilateral monopoly*.[13] While such models have a venerable history, their relevance to the study of distribution channels should not be accepted without critical evaluation. From an empirical perspective, if bilateral monopoly is a reasonable analogue of reality, or if reality can be viewed as if it were a series of bilateral monopolies, then channels should be modeled as bilateral monopolies. From a theoretical perspective, *even if* bilateral monopoly is a poor analogue of reality, by the principle of Occam's razor we should use a bilateral-monopoly model if it leads to the same predictions as more complex models.[14] But if complex models generate conclusions that differ from those obtained with bilateral-monopoly models (and we will show that they do), then Occam's simplicity principle is insufficient for determining whether a simple or a complex model is superior. Instead, marketing scientists must consider how well the simple and complex models conform to the evidence.

In subsequent Chapters we apply the Strategic-Endogeneity Criterion and find that the bilateral-monopoly model yields implications that are distinct from those obtained in more complex models. According to the Empirical-Evidence Criterion, the choice between conflicting models should be resolved by comparing the fit of each model's assumptions with the real world. We argue in the next sub-Section that the assumptions underlying the bilateral-monopoly model are inconsistent with the empirical evidence.

## 1.2 Channel Coordination and Bilateral-Monopoly Models: Evidence

Virtually all marketers agree that the bilateral-monopoly model does not accurately describe reality; few manufacturers serve only one retailer, but many manufacturers serve multiple, non-identical retailers. The same is true, although to a less dramatic degree, for industrial distribution. If, however, the multiple-retailers problem can be reformulated as a set of unrelated bilateral monopolies—*if the manufacturer can cut separate deals with each retailer*—then the conclusions of the bilateral-monopoly model extend to a multiple-retailers model; additional complexity is then unnecessary and undesirable.

We believe that the multiple-retailers problem should *not* be reformulated as a series of unrelated bilateral monopolies. There are strong reasons to believe that separate deals are *not* cut between a manufacturer and each of its retailers. Survey evidence suggests that manufacturers regard retailer-specific pricing arrangements as unattractive due to substantial administrative, bargaining and contract development costs (Lafontaine 1990; Battacharyya and Lafontaine 1995). Additionally, legal restraints on channel pricing discourage the widespread use of separate deals, at least in the United States.[15] In short, price discrimination is generally impermissible[16] in the presence of retail-level competition and is impractical even in the absence of retailer competition. In reality, *manufacturers treat retailers comparably* by offering common wholesale-price schedules to their retailers.[17] Thus an application of the Empirical-Evidence Criterion suggests that, in general, competing-retailer models should assume *comparable treatment of retailers*.

From a modeling standpoint, there is no need to rely on the questionable tactic of separate deals to achieve coordination. Feasible and legally permissible wholesale-price policies exist that will coordinate every dyad of a multiple-retailers channel without the need for separate deals. The mathematics of coordination is straightforward. The final decision-maker in the channel will set its price equal to the channel's profit-maximizing price provided *its* marginal cost equals the *channel's* marginal cost. This decision will reverberate through the channel, causing *every* marketing mix variable under the control of *any* channel member to be set at its coordinating level (Jeuland and Shugan 1983). The practical task of achieving coordination reduces to equating the marginal cost faced by each decision-maker to the marginal cost incurred by the channel.

Despite a variety of coordinating mechanisms suggested in the literature, there is little evidence that a typical distribution channel is actually coordinated. Indeed, the overwhelming indication from the academic and practical channels literatures is that intra-channel conflict over marketing mix decisions—conflict that ought *not* to occur in a coordinated channel—is chronic and pervasive. Why is coordination less common than is implied by conventional wisdom, a wisdom based on the bilateral-monopoly model? A theoretical possibility may be that channel coordination is not in the best interest of one or more key decision-makers in models that go beyond bilateral monopoly.[18] In later Chapters we explore this issue by constructing analytical models that permit us to evaluate the relative benefits of channel coordination and non-coordination. Consistent with the Nested-Models Criterion, each of our models is derived from a single meta-model, which we introduce in the next sub-Section.

## 1.3 Beyond Channel Coordination and Bilateral-Monopoly Models: The Single-Manufacturer Meta-Model

This monograph is devoted to various analyses of a distribution channel consisting of a single manufacturer selling one product through one, two, or "N" retailers. We consider cases in which the retailers are in competition with each other and cases in which they are not in competition because they have exclusive territories. We primarily address models of full information, characterized by a single state-of-nature, but we also tackle the case of asymmetric information with multiple states-of-nature. In all our models the manufacturer is *restricted*, by legal and/or practical considerations, to treat retailers (or states-of-nature) comparably. The import of this simple, realistic restriction is that *channel coordination often is not in the interest of the manufacturer*—despite the fact that feasible and legally permissible channel-coordinating wholesale-price policies are available for use by the manufacturer in all our models.

We are able to compare our results with those reached by earlier researchers because we embed the bilateral-monopoly model as a special case within our models. One strong conclusion that emerges from our analysis is that coordination is in the manufacturer's interest only over a limited set of *parametric values*. Our parametric dimensions encompass (a) the intensity of competition, (b) the magnitude of competition at the same level of the channel (as measured by market shares), and (c) the retailers' fixed-cost ratios.

The complete range of competitive intensity is typically included in bilateral-monopoly analyses of distribution channels; we conform to the norm on this dimension. Models that have gone beyond bilateral monopoly typically have addressed the special case of *identical competitors* that, by definition, have equal market shares. In contrast, we allow market shares to range from zero to one. One of our key discoveries is that channel coordination is always optimal for the manufacturer if market shares are equal, but is frequently disadvantageous for the manufacturer otherwise.

Fixed costs have rarely been addressed in the literature on channels,[19] possibly because their role in bilateral-monopoly models is limited to the participation constraint.[20] Fixed costs fill the same function in a multiple-retailers model but, when the retailers are not identical, fixed costs affect the distribution of channel profit and may also affect optimal prices and quantities via their impact on the optimal wholesale-price policy. In fact, fixed costs emerge as pivotal variables in our analysis. We show that the difference between competitors' fixed costs is a key component in determining the optimality of channel coordination. We find that, unless competitors' fixed costs differ substantially, it is in the manufacturer's interest to coordinate a multiple-retailers channel only when the retailers are identical competitors.

The crucial factor driving these results is the realistic assumption of *comparable treatment*, for this limits the manufacturer's ability to extract profit from the retailers—whether they are in competition or not. Our central conclusion is that while channel coordination can be optimal, there are a wide range of parametric values over which it is *not* optimal; our models enable us to demarcate specific limits to the optimality of coordination. These results lead us to a strong conclusion: because coordination is *always* optimal in the bilateral-monopoly model and the identical-competitors model, these models are *inappropriate* for assessing whether coordination is optimal in other channel settings. More generally, we suspect that neither of these special-case models is appropriate for modeling distribution channels because they distort conclusions that would be reached in models of heterogeneous competitors.

The remainder of this Chapter unfolds in the following manner. In the next Section we enumerate a set of Myths that arose from the early distribution-channels literature and that continue to influence thinking about channels from both a modeling and a strategic perspective. We will argue that these Myths developed through the generalization of results obtained from the analyses of bilateral-monopoly models. The Myths have persisted because scholars have failed to nest existing models within more general models like the one-manufacturer meta-model described above. In Section 3 we provide an overview of the fundamental assumptions used in subsequent Chapters, while Section 4 sets forth our plan of attack for the monograph.

# 2 CHANNEL MYTHS[21]

We believe that progress in distribution-channels research has been obstructed by well-intentioned analyses that are based on questionable theoretical foundations. We hope that the analyses presented in this book will replace these foundations by putting to rest a number of *Channel Myths* that have shaped the analytical modeling of distribution channels, circumscribed the scope of these models, and tainted the resulting managerial advice. We use the term "Channel Myth" to emphasize the extent to which problematic beliefs have become so ingrained in the collective consciousness of marketing scientists that they appear to be uncritically accepted. We believe that a frank discussion of these Myths is essential for progress to be made in the field.[22]

Channel Myths arose through the widespread, uncritical acceptance of a modeling method or a strategic recommendation. We find it helpful to distinguish three kinds of Myths. A *Modeling Myth* is a belief that circumscribes how models are constructed. A *Strategic Myth* is a belief that is accurate within a specific model, but that is mistakenly thought to apply outside the carefully delimited realm of that model. A *Meta-Myth* is an over-arching belief that has both Modeling and Strategic dimensions; a Meta-Myth colors how scholars approach a problem.

*Table 1.1.* Myths in the Distribution-Channels Literature

| Channel Myth | Description | Chapters |
|---|---|---|
| *Bilateral-Monopoly Meta-Myth** | The bilateral-monopoly model is not a distortion of more complex channel models. | 2-5, 9, 12 |
| *Identical-Competitors Meta-Myth** | There is no distortion due to assuming intra-level competitors to be identical. | 2, 3, 6-9, 11, 12 |
| *Fixed-Cost Modeling Myth** | The manufacturer-optimal wholesale-price is independent of fixed costs at retail. | 2-10, 12 |
| *Channel-Breadth Modeling Myth* | There is no distortion associated with assuming a constant channel breadth. | 3, 4, 10, 12 |
| *Aggregate-Demand Modeling Myth* | The partial derivative with respect to the cross-price effect of the demand curve accurately assesses the effect of a change in competition. | 11, 12 |
| *Multiple-Retailers/ Multiple States-of-Nature Modeling Myth* | Inferences about channel performance that are drawn from a bilateral-monopoly model with multiple-states-of-nature are indistinguishable from inferences deduced from a multiple-retailers model under a single state-of-nature. | 4, 12 |
| *Channel-Coordination Strategic Myth** | Channel coordination maximizes total channel profit; this profit can be allocated between channel members to make them all better off. | 2-5, 7-10, 12 |
| *Double-Marginalization Strategic Myth* | Channel coordination is incompatible with members at *both* levels of the channel having positive per-unit margins; they cannot both set their prices above their own marginal costs. | 2, 5, 12 |

* These Myths are briefly described in this Chapter.

Table 1.1 sets out eight Channel Myths that we address in this monograph. Column two provides a brief description of the Myth and column three cites Chapters in which the Myth is discussed. Here we overview the Meta-Myths, one Modeling Myth, and one Strategic Myth; remaining Myths are discussed in subsequent Chapters. We will show that none of the Myths is innocuous; research that incorporates a Meta-Myth, or one or more Modeling Myths, inevitably generates academic inferences that are misleading relative to research that does not include the Myth(s). Similarly, a model that includes a Meta-Myth, or one or more Strategic Myths, can generate instructions for optimal managerial behavior that conflict with good business practice.

The *Bilateral-Monopoly Meta-Myth* has had an enormous impact on distribution-channels scholarship. Its modeling dimension entails a belief that bilateral-monopoly models capture the essence of more complex models; thus it has discouraged investigation of richer models. Its strategic dimension involves a belief that managerial recommendations that are proper in a true bilateral monopoly generally apply in other channel structures.

The *Identical-Competitors Meta-Myth*, which also has modeling and strategic dimensions, has been just as consequential in its effect on distribution-channels scholarship. Its modeling dimension entails a belief that modeling competitors as if they were identical is non-distorting relative to models in which competitors are non-identical. Its strategic dimension entails the belief that managerial conclusions drawn from identical-competitors' models can be generalized to situations in which the competitors are differentiated. These Meta-Myths have discouraged evaluating richer models.

We will repeatedly show in this monograph that these two Meta-Myths are mutually reinforcing, and that they are at the heart of the Modeling and Strategic Myths listed in Table 1.1. To establish the mythic nature of these beliefs, and in conformity with the Nested-Models Criterion, we develop models that incorporate bilateral monopoly and identical competitors as special cases. We illustrate our approach in Figure 1.1, which describes the possible competitive scenarios in a two-retailer market. The horizontal axis measures the market share of the $j^{th}$ competitor. On the far left the $j^{th}$ firm has a zero market share, so the $i^{th}$ firm controls the entire market; on the far right the $j^{th}$ firm owns the total market. This axis is of unit length. The vertical axis measures the intensity of competition. Through a standardization process that is described in Chapters 5-10, this axis is also of unit length. At the bottom of the Figure the firms are not in competition; at the top they are perfectly substitutable in consumers' eyes.

Because bilateral monopoly entails no retail competition, it must be represented by the bottom axis of the ***unit-square*** that is depicted in Figure 1.1. We represent the bilateral-monopoly model by the solid circle in the lower left corner where the $i^{th}$ firm has 100 percent of the market.[23] The identical-competitors model, whether of intra-channel or inter-channel competition, is denoted by the vertical line at equal market shares. Because the models we explore in this book incorporate the *entire* unit-square,[24] the bilateral-monopoly model and the identical-competitors model are subsumed within our models.

The *Fixed-Cost Modeling Myth* holds that a channel member's optimal price policy is independent of the level of fixed cost at another level of the channel. We prove throughout the following Chapters that the absolute difference in the competing retailers' fixed costs affects the manufacturer's optimal wholesale-price policy.

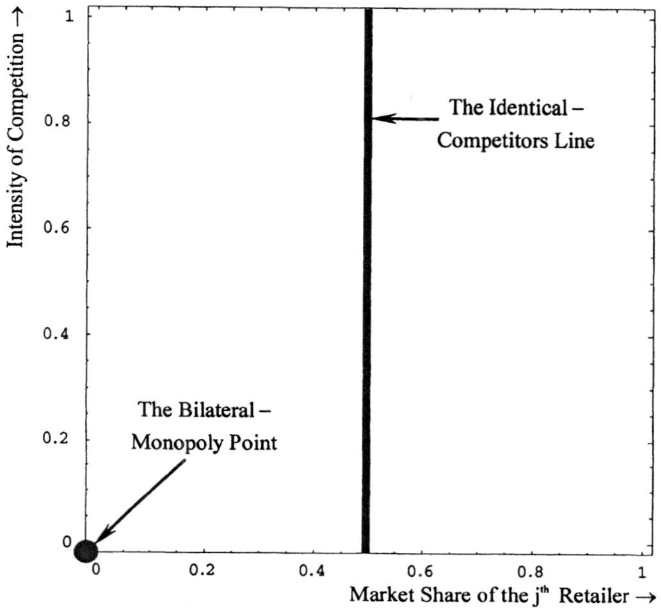


*Figure 1.1:* The Bilateral-Monopoly Model and the Identical-Competitors Model: Subsets of Our Model

The *Channel-Coordination Strategic Myth* leads academics to recommend that managers should coordinate their channels. We show throughout this monograph that seeking channel coordination is often *not* good advice.[25] Subsidiary components of this Myth are that (a) coordination permits a decentralized channel to match the profit generated by a vertically-integrated system and (b) channel profit can be allocated such that all channel members prefer coordination to non-coordination. We prove that (a) may be inaccurate when channel breadth is endogenous and (b) is true only under restrictive parametric values.

In summary, each of our eight myths has contributed to a distorted view of distribution channels from a modeling and/or a strategic perspective. These Channel Myths are neither deliberate nor malicious deceptions; they are merely errors of logic that have impeded the marketing science profession's search for a true understanding of distribution channels. In the words of President John F. Kennedy, "the great enemy of truth is very often not the lie—deliberate, contrived and dishonest—but the myth—persistent, pervasive and unrealistic."[26]

# 3 OUR FUNDAMENTAL ASSUMPTIONS

In this monograph we analyze several sub-models of a meta-model that is characterized by a single manufacturer, producing one product, selling through one or more retailers that utilize price as the only element of their marketing mix. In terms of Channel Strategy, we adhere to our Strategic-Endogeneity Criterion by comparing our results across the sub-models; this enables us to endogenously determine what level of channel breadth, and which wholesale-price strategy, are optimal for the manufacturer. In the final Chapter we discuss potential extensions that address issues of category-management and non-price aspects of the marketing mix.

Consistent with the analytical literature on distribution channels, we assume that all decision-makers are rational profit-maximizers. Although conventional wisdom holds that maximizing channel profit is best for the manufacturer (and the retailers), it is our endogenous determination of the optimality of channel coordination that enables us to prove that, when multiple retailers are treated comparably, coordination need not be in the manufacturer's interest. The fundamental reason is that comparable treatment places limits on the possible extent of profit reallocation within the channel.

## 3.1 Assumptions about the Channel Environment

From a modeling perspective, our models encompass three kinds of Channel-Environment Assumptions: those that are related to demand, those that concern costs, and those that relate to the degree of certainty faced by channel participants. In this monograph we evaluate both general and linear demand. We consider non-negative variable costs at retail and at manufacturer, and we also assess the impact of fixed costs. We assume certainty in the bulk of our analyses (i.e., a single *state-of-nature*). However, to investigate uncertainty, we evaluate multiple states-of-nature in Chapter 4. Our modeling decisions merit explanation.

**Channel-Demand Assumptions**: Our analyses in Chapters 3 and 4 use a *general demand curve* $Q = Q(p)$; we assume that it is downward sloping in price and that it meets the second-order conditions for a profit maximum. This formulation generates powerful, broadly applicable results. However, generalizability comes at a price: the solutions cannot be stated in closed form; and they sometimes lack an immediate intuitive explanation.

Because interpretability is important to us, we switch to a *linear demand curve* in later Sections of Chapter 4 and in all subsequent Chapters. Marketing scientists often characterize consumer demand as linear in price. The reason is practical, yet leads to an elegant result: linearity provides the analytical tractability that is crucial for obtaining closed-form solutions and the robustness that is required for confidence in the results. The need for tractability should be clear, but the need for robustness requires a few words of explanation.

Recall that linear demand generates positively-sloped *price*-reaction functions between members at a level of the channel (i.e., horizontally) and negatively-sloped *margin*-reaction functions between members at different levels of the channel (i.e., vertically). Thus the $i^{th}$ retailer's optimal response to a decrease in its (horizontal) rival's price is to lower its own price, but the optimal response to an increase in the manufacturer's *margin* is to lower its own *margin*. These seem to be eminently reasonable responses. Retailers seldom respond to a competitive price cut by raising their own prices, nor do they typically respond to an increase in manufacturer margins by raising their own margins.[27] Moreover, Lee and Staelin (1997) have proven that, in terms of vertical channel-relationships, linearity does not distort the results obtained with non-linear demand curves, as long as those demand curves are compatible with negatively-sloped margin-reaction functions. As a result, we believe our decision to use linear demand is both reasonable and practical.[28]

Demand curves for consumer goods should be consistent with economic principles of utility maximization. In the Appendix to this Chapter we maximize a representative consumer's utility function subject to the consumer's budget constraint, thereby proving that our system of demand equations satisfies the First-Principles Criterion. Here we simply state our linear-demand system for the case of two, competing retailers:

$$\begin{aligned} Q_i &= A_i - bp_i + \theta p_j \\ Q_j &= A_j - bp_j + \theta p_i \end{aligned} \tag{1.3.1}$$

Equations (1.3.1) should look familiar to those versed in the channels literature, for these curves, or variants of them, have been employed by many authors. In equations (1.3.1) the $p_k$ ($k \in (i,j)$) terms are prices, the $Q_k$ terms are quantities, and the $A_k$ terms are the base level of demand at zero prices (we sometimes call the $A_k$ term the "attractiveness" of the $k^{th}$ retailer). Note that the retailers face different levels of demand if $A_i \neq A_j$. The term "b" denotes own-price sensitivity while the term "$\theta$" denotes cross-price sensitivity. The cross-price effects in this linear system are identical across the demand curves; this is a general property of utility-derived demand that is independent of linearity.

**Channel-Cost Assumptions**: We assume that the manufacturer incurs a constant per-unit production cost C that is retailer independent and that the $k^{th}$ retailer sustains a constant per-unit distribution cost $c_k$, $k \in (i,j)$. The distribution-channels literature typically standardizes these values to zero, although $C > 0$ and $c_i = c_j \equiv c > 0$ appear occasionally. Either a difference in demand *or* a difference in costs is sufficient to guarantee non-identical rivals.

We model both differences while noting that the identical-competitors model can be assessed at any stage of the analysis by setting $A_i = A_j$ and $c_i = c_j$.

We also assume that the manufacturer incurs a fixed cost $F \geq 0$, while each retailer sustains its own, unique fixed cost $f_i \geq 0$. These costs can be interpreted as actual overhead expenses or as *opportunity costs*. With the latter interpretation $f_i$ is the minimal dollar profit the $i^{th}$ retailer must earn to be willing to sell the product. In conformity with the Empirical-Evidence Criterion, we stress that manufacturers and retailers *do* incur real fixed costs that are volume independent. They also have opportunity costs: they could choose to produce/sell a different product that would also generate profit for them. We will show that the difference in retailers' fixed costs plays a critical role in determining if channel coordination is in the manufacturer's interest. Broadly speaking, coordination is manufacturer non-optimal if $f_i = 0 = f_j$.

## 3.2 Assumptions about Channel Structure

Our sub-models share many commonalities regarding Channel Structure. From a modeling perspective, three categories of Channel-Structure Assumptions are important: those between a manufacturer and its retailers, those between competitors at the same level of a channel, and those between channels. In this monograph we evaluate both a vertically-integrated channel and a decentralized channel with the manufacturer as the Stackelberg leader. Horizontally we consider a Nash game between retailers. Because we assume a single manufacturer, there is no inter-channel competition. We do not allow product-resale between competitors for the reasons spelled out in association with the Horizontal Channel-Relationship Assumptions below.

**Vertical Channel-Relationship Assumptions**: In a *Vertically-Integrated System* all channel profit accrues to the unified entity. Thus the decision-maker will take the necessary actions to maximize channel profit. Implementation may involve centralized control by a single decision-maker, or it may entail decentralized control with transfer pricing to ensure proper decisions at all channel levels. In either case, a vertically-integrated system defines the performance (the retail prices, quantities, consumers' surplus, and the profits earned by all channel members) of a coordinated channel; as such it provides a baseline against which alternative approaches may be judged.

The core of our analysis is based on a *vertical, manufacturer Stackelberg leadership* game in which the manufacturer sells directly to the retailers; in this regard we follow a lengthy history of analytical channel models. Such games have two advantages. First, they are compatible with an endogenous allocation of channel profit between the manufacturer and *any* number of retailers, whether there is intra-level competition or not. Second, they are compatible with wholesale-price policies that do, or do not, lead to channel coordination. In these games each retailer seeks to maximize its own profit, while the manufacturer takes the retailers' margin-reaction curves into account in its own maximization process—which may focus on channel profit or on its own profit.

We do not consider a vertical-Nash game for two reasons. First, the distribution of channel profit is *exogenously* determined in such a game; that is, channel profit is assigned to channel members by an arbitrary allocation process, such as bargaining (Jeuland and Shugan 1983). From a modeling standpoint, an inability to allocate channel profit endogenously is contrary to our goal of assessing the conditions under which coordination is, or is not, optimal. Second, from a managerial perspective, horizontal competitors cannot negotiate a joint profit allocation with their common manufacturer without (a) violating antitrust provisions against collusion and (b) confronting their own intra-level profit-allocation arguments that can only be resolved by a decision rule that is, in a modeling sense, arbitrary. Regardless of the value of a Nash game in a bilateral-monopoly model, a vertical-Nash game with intra-level competition cannot facilitate an identification of the conditions under which channel coordination is optimal.

We do not consider a channel with a retailer Stackelberg leader for three reasons. First, Lee and Staelin (1997) offer a compelling argument that such a game is ultimately unstable due to potential moral hazard by retailers. Second, because they are distinct entities, competing retailers need not treat their common manufacturer comparably. Yet without comparable treatment we have two bilateral monopolies in which (i) both dyads are coordinated and (ii) the channel-profit distribution is endogenously indeterminate (Edgeworth 1897). Third, real-world retailers that appear to be Stackelberg leaders are usually supplied by more than one manufacturer; thus they should be analyzed with a multiple-manufacturer meta-model.

**Horizontal Channel-Relationship Assumptions**: We utilize a *horizontal Nash game* to assess models of competing retailers *who purchase directly from the manufacturer*. An alternative is a horizontal Stackelberg game in which the retail leader (the $i^{th}$ firm) considers the effect of its price on the price charged by its follower (the $j^{th}$ firm). The net result is that the $i^{th}$ (the $j^{th}$) retailer obtains larger (smaller) sales and greater (lower) profit than it would in a Nash game. In other respects the horizontal Nash and Stackelberg games play out in the same way, *provided* both retailers purchase from the manufacturer. Neither retailer has an incentive to be a Stackelberg follower, nor does the game contribute much to our knowledge of distribution channels. Thus we do not consider a horizontal Stackelberg game.

A game in which horizontal product resale is allowed evolves in a different way from a game in which such resale is forbidden, because the reseller (either the $i^{th}$ or the $j^{th}$ retailer) can use a two-part tariff to obtain all profit from the purchaser. There is a basic indeterminacy in such a game because neither retailer is willing to purchase from its rival. In addition, the vertical, manufacturer Stackelberg leader could extract all of the reseller's profit with its own two-part tariff, so a horizontal-resale game degenerates to a game of sequential bilateral monopolies in which the manufacturer gains all channel profit. It follows that the manufacturer will always prefer channel coordination if intra-level product resale is permitted. Thus allowing resale offers limited insight relative to standard bilateral-monopoly models. Horizontal product resale is also inconsistent with the empirical evidence that few retailers regularly buy from a rival.

All of this suggests that a meta-model of one manufacturer and multiple retailers should disallow product resale and should be fashioned either as (i) a vertically-integrated system or (ii) as a manufacturer Stackelberg leadership game vertically and a Nash game horizontally. This conclusion holds regardless of the number of products, the number of states-of-nature, or the specific marketing-mix elements featured in the model.

## 3.3 Assumptions about Channel Strategy

Our models are predicated on two kinds of assumptions about channel strategy: those related to channel breadth and those concerning wholesale-price policy. Our models do not incorporate two other facets of channel strategy—the non-price marketing-mix elements and category-management decisions—but we do address these issues in our discussion of future research in Chapter 12.

**Channel-Breadth Assumptions**: We employ a range of channel breadths throughout this monograph. In Chapter 3 we treat channel breadth as an endogenous variable. In Chapter 4 breadth is held constant at one retailer as we investigate the optimal number of states-of-nature to serve; we term this "temporal breadth." In Chapters 5-9 we hold channel breadth constant at two (competing) retailers, but in Chapter 10 we return to the theme of optimal breadth by endogenously determining the parametric values under which the manufacturer will prefer to serve a single retailer rather than two competing retailers. In Chapter 11 we investigate both these models. We will prove that the channel breadth and wholesale-price decisions are interdependent.

**Wholesale-Price Assumptions**: In this book we examine four wholesale-price policies: (1) a general wholesale-price scheme, (2) a quantity-discount schedule, (3) a two-part tariff, and (4) a menu of two-part tariffs. In Chapter 3 we employ the *general form* $W(Q)$ in which the wholesale price is a function (increasing, constant, or decreasing) of the quantity ordered. In Chapter 5 we introduce a *linear quantity-discount schedule* $(W - wQ)$ to obtain closed-form solutions (the capital "W" is the maximal per-unit price and the small "w" is the quantity-discount rate). This functional form appears again in Chapters 8-11.

Managers often implement quantity-discount schedules as two-part tariffs (Oren, Smith and Wilson 1982). In Chapters 3-11 we employ various *two-part tariffs* to advance our analyses; we write them as $\{W, \phi\}$, where "W" is the (quantity-invariant) per-unit wholesale-price and "$\phi$" is the fixed fee. Two-part tariffs are relatively common in franchising. Less obviously, a two-part tariff is a manifestation of a "step-function" quantity discount in which a retailer pays one per-unit wholesale price for purchases below the threshold quantity, and a lower per-unit price for units in excess of the threshold. A two-part tariff is also interpretable as a rebate schedule in which the retailer pays a constant per-unit wholesale price for all units purchased, but receives an end-of-period rebate on purchases above a pre-specified minimum.

In Chapters 7-11 we investigate a *menu of two-part tariffs*, writing it as $\tau \equiv [\tau_i, \tau_j]$, where $\tau_k \equiv \{W_k, \phi_k\}$, $k \in (i, j)$. With a menu the retailer has the option of selecting (i) a tariff (say $\tau_i$) that consists of a lower fixed fee and a higher per-unit wholesale-price, or (ii) a tariff $(\tau_j)$ that carries a higher fixed fee but a lower per-unit wholesale-price.

We will prove that any of the three explicit wholesale-prices—a quantity-discount schedule, a two-part tariff, or a menu of two-part tariffs—may be manufacturer profit-maximizing when demand is linear, depending on the specific cost and demand parameters faced by the channel. The endogenously-determined, optimal wholesale-price strategy is revealed in Chapters 8-10.

In the case of N *non-competing* retailers, channel coordination is possible with a properly specified two-part tariff. This statement does not hold when the N retailers compete. Instead, coordination requires an $(N+1)-$part tariff *or* a menu of N two-part tariffs. We will prove that a properly specified two-element menu or linear quantity-discount schedule (a 3-part tariff) will coordinate a channel consisting of one manufacturer and two competing retailers.

## 4 OUR PLAN FOR THE MONOGRAPH

We close this Chapter with an overview of coming Chapters. Table 1.2 offers a tabular summary of the plan of the monograph. We also highlight some of the key findings presented in each Chapter.

In Chapter 2 we lay the foundation for subsequent Chapters by reviewing the bilateral-monopoly model and then describing and numerically illustrating the four Myths described earlier in this Chapter. In Chapters 3-11 we present a series of models that satisfy the Nested-Models Criterion by incorporating the bilateral-monopoly model and the identical-competitors model (when relevant) as special cases. Consistent with the Empirical-Evidence Criterion, we also constrain the manufacturer to offer a single wholesale-price schedule (or a common menu) to all of its retailers.

## 4.1 Models without Competition

In Chapter 3 we address the issue of *channel breadth* by modeling a manufacturer that sells through multiple, *non*-competing retailers. To maximize the applicability of our results we employ a general demand curve. We obtain endogenous solutions for total channel profit, the division of profit between manufacturer and each retailer, and the channel breadth that is optimal for the manufacturer. We determine that the condition for channel coordination to be manufacturer-optimal has a knife-edge property; this suggests that it is rarely optimal for the manufacturer to coordinate a channel consisting of multiple, non-competing retailers.

In Chapter 4 we address the issue of *temporal coverage* by modeling a bilateral monopoly in which the retailer has information that is unavailable to the manufacturer. This asymmetric information enables the retailer to make its price decision in each time period on the basis of the realized state-of-nature. In contrast, the manufacturer must commit to a wholesale price without knowing the true state-of-nature (i.e., the true magnitude of demand and actual per-unit costs at retail). We begin our analysis with a demand curve $Q = Q(p)$ that yields general results. Then we switch to a linear demand curve and two states-of-nature ("high" or "low" demand). We prove, for both the general and the linear demand curves, that the manufacturer will *not* seek channel coordination *unless* (i) one state-of-nature is served or (ii) the retailer incurs a fixed cost of non-distribution in a state-of-nature. Even when one or both of these conditions is satisfied, we show that coordination is not always optimal for the manufacturer. We also show that decentralization decreases temporal coverage: for many combinations of parametric values, the decentralized channel serves fewer states-of-nature than does the vertically-integrated system.

*Table 1.2.* Our Plan for the Monograph

| | Chapter | Demand | Meta-Model* M / R / Ω | Wholesale-Price Policy** | Key Themes |
|---|---|---|---|---|---|
| | 2 | Linear | | | Myths Illustrated |
| Without Competition | 3 | General | 1 / N / 1 | General, 2-PT | Channel Breadth |
| | 4 | General & Linear | 1 / 1 / N & 1 / 1 / 2 | 2-PT | Temporal Coverage |
| With Competition | 5 | Linear | 1 / 2 / 1 | VI, QD, 2-PT | Seeking Channel Coordination |
| | 6 | Linear | 1 / 2 / 1 | SS | Manufacturer-Optimal Non-Coordination |
| | 7 | Linear | 1 / 2 / 1 | Menu | Ensuring Channel Coordination |
| | 8 | Linear | 1 / 2 / 1 | QD, SS, Menu | Coordination vs. Non-Coordination: Analytics |
| | 9 | Linear | 1 / 2 / 1 | QD, SS, Menu | Coordination vs. Non-Coordination: Graphics |
| Changes in Competition | 10 | Linear | 1 / 2 / 1 & 1 / 1 / 1 | QD, SS, Menu | Channel Breadth |
| | 11 | Linear | 1 / 2 / 1 & 1 / 1 / 1 | VI, QD, SS, Menu | Competitive Substitutability |
| | 12 | | | | Summary |

* Meta-Model abbreviations: M ≡ number of manufacturers = 1, R ≡ number of retailers (1, 2, or N), and Ω ≡ number of states-of-nature (1, 2, or N).

** Wholesale-Price Policy abbreviations: 2-PT ≡ two-part tariff, VI ≡ Vertically-Integrated Pricing, QD ≡ Quantity-Discount Schedule, SS ≡ sophisticated Stackelberg two-part tariff, and Menu ≡ Menu of two-part tariffs.

These Chapters establish that even a modest extension of the bilateral-monopoly model, whether it is to multiple, non-competing retailers or to multiple states-of-nature,[29] is generally sufficient to destroy channel coordination as a vehicle for maximizing manufacturer profit. These two Chapters also demonstrate that fixed costs at retail have considerable impact. In the multiple-retailers model these costs affect channel breadth through the retailers' participation constraints, and when fixed costs are unequal they also affect the distribution of channel profit and the manufacturer-optimal wholesale-price policy. In the multiple states-of-nature model they influence the distribution of channel profit, the decision to distribute (or not to distribute) in a state-of-nature, and the existence of the channel.

## 4.2 Models with Competition

Given the complexity of our analyses with general demand curves, we turn to linear demand in Chapters 5-11. The resulting analyses are still complex, but linearity of demand enables us to obtain closed-form solutions and to ease the challenge of intuitively interpreting the results (at least relative to interpreting the results from a general demand curve). In Chapters 5-9 we address the issue of inter-retailer competition under the assumption of constant channel breadth (one manufacturer selling to two retailers).

In Chapter 5 we show that a properly specified quantity-discount schedule will coordinate a two-retailer channel, but that a two-part tariff *cannot* coordinate the channel, even when the per-unit wholesale-price equals the manufacturer's marginal cost. What may be surprising is that several non-coordinating tariffs are manufacturer-preferred to the channel-coordinating quantity-discount schedule over a wide range of parametric values. From this we infer that a channel-coordinating wholesale-price policy may be inferior to many non-coordinating policies.

In Chapter 6 we devise a "sophisticated Stackelberg" two-part tariff that is the envelope of all possible two-part tariffs; it is obtained by simultaneously choosing a per-unit wholesale-price and a fixed fee. In contrast, an ordinary—a "naïve"—Stackelberg tariff focuses on the choice of a per-unit wholesale-price while treating the fixed fee as a "residual" that extracts all profit from the less profitable retailer. The sophisticated Stackelberg two-part tariff has a special property: it coordinates a bilateral-monopoly channel, or an identical-competitors channel, but no other channel. In contrast, a naïve Stackelberg tariff cannot coordinate *any* channel.

In Chapter 7 we develop a channel-coordinating menu of two-part tariffs. Because each retailer is free to select its most profitable tariff from the menu, there is a potential for "defection" to a tariff intended for another retailer. We prove that (i) the channel cannot be coordinated when defection occurs and (ii) coordination without defection is always possible with an appropriately specified set of fixed fees. We also show that coordination often is not in the manufacturer's interest because, over some parametric values, it must sacrifice too much profit to ensure coordination.

A surprising aspect of all three wholesale-price policies (quantity-discount, sophisticated Stackelberg, and menu) is that each leads to three "Zones" that are themselves endogenously defined in terms of the intensity and magnitude of competition. The following statements hold for each of these policies. Only in one Zone does the manufacturer extract all profit from *both* retailers. In the two remaining Zones the manufacturer extracts all profit from *only one* retailer. In these latter Zones it is the manufacturer's inability to obtain all channel profit that makes the channel-coordinating quantity-discount schedule and the channel-coordinating menu potentially sub-optimal for the manufacturer.

In Chapter 8 we analytically describe the conditions under which each of the following pricing policies is manufacturer preferred to the other options: (i) the channel-coordinating, linear quantity-discount schedule, (ii) the channel-coordinating menu of two-part tariffs, and (iii) the channel *non-*coordinating, sophisticated Stackelberg two-part tariff. Our analysis hinges on an understanding of the relationships among the nine pricing Zones that collectively characterize the three pricing policies. We prove that, over a wide range of differences in the retailers' fixed costs, the non-coordinating, sophisticated Stackelberg two-part tariff is the optimal strategy for the manufacturer. To keep this Chapter to a manageable length, we present a complementary graphical analysis in Chapter 9.

## 4.3 Models of Changes in Competition

In Chapter 10 we return to the issue of channel breadth by exploring the effect of a change in the number of competitors. We compare the manufacturer profit generated by (i) a channel in which two retailers compete and (ii) a channel that serves only one retailer, but in which the second retailer is a potential entrant. To guarantee comparability across models, we apply our Nested-Models Criterion. Specifically, we take the necessary modeling steps to ensure that aggregate demand is not diminished by dropping one retailer—even though the actual quantity sold is decreased. We find that, when the retailers' fixed costs are approximately equal, the "serve two retailers" option is unattractive *unless* market shares are relatively equal. This statement holds for each of the three wholesale-price policies sketched above.

In Chapter 11 we investigate the effects on all of our variables, across all our sub-models from Chapters 5-10, of an exogenous change in inter-retailer substitutability. We first demonstrate that conventional approaches to this issue generate misleading results. We then introduce a new method of analyzing the effect of a change in competitive substitutability that relies on our First-Principles Criterion. This method overcomes the theoretical and practical difficulties of alternative methods. Our results contribute to a fuller understanding of many of the complex results obtained in Chapters 8 and 9.

In Chapter 12 we offer a synopsis of our results, expand our discussion of the Modeling Criteria for creation of a Unifying Theory of Distribution Channels, and address the potential unification of the various parts of the marketing science literature on distribution channels. We also provide a number of suggestions for future research, many of which focus on competitive-channels models that incorporate multiple-products and non-price elements of the marketing mix.

# 5 INTRODUCTORY COMMENTARY

As we look at the wealth of marketing science models dealing with channel competition, we see a literature that, like Gaul, is divided into three parts: inter-channel competition, inter-manufacturer competition, and inter-retailer competition. Yet the empirical evidence is that these topical areas are *interrelated* parts of a single whole, for channels compete, each channel has competing manufacturers, and each manufacturer sells through competing retailers. Thus, like Caesar, we seek the unification of three parts. Our call for a Unifying Theory of Distribution Channels is based on the conviction that there is limited benefit to developing pieces of a puzzle without a process for integrating those pieces. Similarly, there is little value to developing models that are so riddled with Channel Myths that prescriptions based on these models may be misleading or even erroneous. It is our hope that this monograph will contribute toward the creation of a Unifying Theory of Distribution Channels, and that other scholars will join us in facilitating its realization, so that collectively we may completely understand the enigma that is distribution channels.

# 6 APPENDIX[30]

In this Appendix we derive the set of linear demand equations (1.3.1) from first principles. We work with consumer products—meaning that aggregate demand is implicitly embedded in the utility function of a representative consumer. Demand for a business product would be derived in the same manner, but from the profit function of a representative business.

Deriving a linear demand system requires that the representative consumer's utility function be of the form:[31]

$$\mathcal{U} \equiv \sum_{\kappa}\left(\mathcal{A}_{\kappa}Q_{\kappa} - \mathcal{B}_{\kappa}(Q_{\kappa})^{2}/2\right) - \mathcal{T}Q_{i}Q_{j} \quad \kappa \in (h,k),\; k \in (i,j) \qquad (1.A.1)$$

The $Q_{\kappa}$ terms denote quantities purchased of the $\kappa^{th}$ product, $\kappa$ either the focal good (the $k^{th}$ product) or a composite commodity (the $h^{th}$ product); these products are demand-*independent*. The $k^{th}$ product is sold by both the $i^{th}$ and $j^{th}$ retailers; hence these retailers are demand-*interdependent*.[32] We model inter-retailer substitutability (or independence) as $\mathcal{T} > 0$ (or $\mathcal{T} = 0$).[33] Utility (1.A.1) increases at a decreasing rate provided $\mathcal{A}_{k}, \mathcal{B}_{k} > 0$. Only function (1.A.1), or monotonic transformations of it, is compatible with a linear-demand system.

Our representative consumer maximizes:

$$\max_{Q_h, Q_i, Q_j} \mathcal{V} \equiv \mathcal{U} + \lambda\left[Y - \sum_{\kappa} p_{\kappa}Q_{\kappa}\right] \quad \kappa \in (h,k),\; k \in (i,j) \qquad (1.A.2)$$

In this maximization expression the term Y is income, $p_{\kappa}$ is the per-unit price for the $\kappa^{th}$ product/$k^{th}$ retailer, $\lambda$ is the marginal utility of income, and the bracketed term is the consumer's budget constraint.

Taking the requisite first-order conditions and solving yields the demand system for the focal product:

$$\begin{aligned} Q_i &= \left(\frac{\left[\mathcal{B}_j\mathcal{A}_i - \mathcal{T}\mathcal{A}_j\right] - \lambda\mathcal{B}_j p_i + \lambda\mathcal{T}p_j}{\mathcal{B}_i\mathcal{B}_j - \mathcal{T}^2}\right) \\ Q_j &= \left(\frac{\left[\mathcal{B}_i\mathcal{A}_j - \mathcal{T}\mathcal{A}_i\right] - \lambda\mathcal{B}_i p_j + \lambda\mathcal{T}p_i}{\mathcal{B}_i\mathcal{B}_j - \mathcal{T}^2}\right) \end{aligned} \qquad (1.A.3)$$

$$Q_h = \left(\frac{\mathcal{A}_h - \lambda p_h}{\mathcal{B}_h}\right) \qquad (1.A.4)$$

Because equation (1.A.4) represents a product that is demand-independent of the focal product, we do not discuss it further.

In order to simplify our analysis we henceforth set $\mathcal{B}_i = \mathcal{B}_j \equiv \mathcal{B}$. This states that the rate of change of marginal utility of the $k^{th}$ product purchased from the i[th] retailer is equal to the rate of change of marginal utility of the k[th] product purchased from the j[th] retailer. Since the same product is being purchased, this seems to be a relatively innocuous assumption. With it the second order conditions for utility maximization reduce to $\mathcal{B} > \mathcal{T}$. Positive demand intercepts (the terms in square brackets) at both retailers requires:

$$(\mathcal{B}/\mathcal{T}) > (\mathcal{A}_j/\mathcal{A}_i) > (\mathcal{T}/\mathcal{B}) \tag{1.A.5}$$

Inequality (1.A.5) defines limits to the utility function's parameters that must be met for an interior solution to be obtained.

Now make the substitutions:

$$\begin{aligned} A_i &\equiv (\mathcal{B}\mathcal{A}_i - \mathcal{T}\mathcal{A}_j)/(\mathcal{B}^2 - \mathcal{T}^2) > 0, \\ A_j &\equiv (\mathcal{B}\mathcal{A}_j - \mathcal{T}\mathcal{A}_i)/(\mathcal{B}^2 - \mathcal{T}^2) > 0, \\ b &\equiv \lambda\mathcal{B}/(\mathcal{B}^2 - \mathcal{T}^2) > 0, \text{ and} \\ \theta &\equiv \lambda\mathcal{T}/(\mathcal{B}^2 - \mathcal{T}^2) > 0 \end{aligned} \tag{1.A.6}$$

Using (1.A.6) we can rewrite demand (1.A.3) more compactly, and more familiarly, as:

$$\begin{aligned} Q_i &= A_i - bp_i + \theta p_j \\ Q_j &= A_j - bp_j + \theta p_i \end{aligned} \tag{1.A.7}$$

This replicates equations (1.3.1) in the body of this Chapter.[34] Note that the equalization of the own-price terms of the demand curves is the inherent result of equalizing the rate of change of marginal utility of the k[th] product across retail outlets.

In light of Spengler's comments concerning the effect of vertical integration on consumer well-being (1950), we point out that the demand system (1.A.7) can be used to calculate consumers' surplus (the difference between price paid and maximum willingness to pay, aggregated over units purchased). Consumers' surplus for the i[th] retailer is:

$$\begin{aligned} CS_i &= \int_{\ddot{p}_i^*}^{(a+\theta\ddot{p}_j^*)/b} (a - bp_i + \theta\ddot{p}_j^*)\,dp_i \\ &= \frac{b}{2}\left(\frac{(a+\theta\ddot{p}_j^*)}{b} - \ddot{p}_i^*\right)^2 \\ &= \frac{(\ddot{Q}_i^*)^2}{2b} \end{aligned} \tag{1.A.8}$$

In equation (1.A.8) the terms $\ddot{p}_i^*$ and $\ddot{p}_j^*$ are the optimal prices for whichever wholesale-price policy is under investigation and $\ddot{Q}_i^*$ is their associated quantity. Consumers' surplus from the i[th] retailer rises with the amount that is purchased. Total consumers' surplus is merely the sum $CS \equiv CS_i + CS_j$.

# Notes

[1] "All Gaul is divided into three parts" are Gaius Julius Caesar's opening words in *Comentarii De Bello Gallico* (58 B.C.). For a modern translation see Wiseman and Wiseman (1980).
[2] We refer to the work of McGuire and Staelin (1983) and Jeuland and Shugan (1983) respectively.
[3] Early examples of this literature are McGuire and Staelin (1983, 1986), Coughlan (1985), and Coughlan and Wernerfelt (1989). All of them involve competition between bilateral-monopoly channels.
[4] An early example of this literature is (Choi 1991).
[5] Examples include our own work (Ingene and Parry 1995a, 1995b, 1998, 2000).
[6] We fully recognize that managers can *influence* demand through their use of the marketing mix. Our point is that there is an exogenous level of demand, based on tastes, income, and the prices of other goods, that provides a base from which firms attempt to affect demand with the marketing mix.
[7] It is possible to specify some costs as endogenous. For example, in a dynamic model, variable production costs might decline with increases in cumulative volume.
[8] Competing channels could be organized as a Stackelberg leader-follower model, at least theoretically.
[9] McGuire and Staelin (1983) modeled the vertical channel-relationship as endogenous. The horizontal channel-relationship could be endogenous in principle. For example, should a manufacturer employ one retailer that operates two stores or should it sell through two independent retailers, each operating one store? The other Channel-Structure Assumptions could be addressed in a similar manner.
[10] Category management can also be endogenously modeled (Coughlan and Ingene 2002), as can the marketing mix (see Chapter 12). We do not address multiple products or non-price elements of the marketing mix in this monograph.
[11] We use the term meta-model to denote a set of models that are interrelated. We develop several models in this monograph that are based on a single manufacturer that produces a single product; we call this a "one manufacturer, one product" meta-model. To illustrate our concept of the Nested-Models Criterion, a set of models of one manufacturer producing $N$ products is a "one manufacturer" meta-model; our "one manufacturer, one product" meta-model is nested as a special case within the "one manufacturer" meta-model.
[12] For an historical perspective on the importance of distributive efficiency see Stewart and Dewhurst (1939). Marketing scientists and economists have devoted considerable effort to devising methods of maximizing, and of allocating, channel profit. Maximizing suggestions have included vertical integration (Spengler 1950), collusive concords (Henderson and Quandt 1971), exclusive dealing (Rey and Tirole 1986), resale price maintenance (Rey and Tirole 1986), quantity-discounts (Jeuland and Shugan 1983), and two-part tariffs (Moorthy 1987). In short, there have been a variety of structural and wholesale-price proposals for achieving coordination. Profit-allocation proposals have focused on bargaining agreements (Henderson and Quandt 1971; Jeuland and Shugan 1983).
[13] A bilateral monopoly is defined as a single seller interacting with a single buyer. It is the simplest of all possible channel models and is commonly presented as one manufacturer selling through one retailer. Early analyses investigated such topics as channel power (Pigou 1908, Bowley 1928), the policy implications of vertical integration (Morgan 1949, Spengler 1950), and collusive incentives (Henderson and Quandt 1971), amongst other issues.
[14] The first principle of Occam's razor is *simplicity*: if competing theories generate the same predictions, the simpler of the theories should be preferred. The second (often overlooked) principle is *reality*: empirical evidence should not be ignored in theory construction. In

combination, these principles argue that we should prefer the simplest theory that is compatible with the essential evidence. By so doing, we obtain a parsimonious understanding of reality.

[15] Section 2(a) of the Robinson-Patman Act "... prohibits sellers from charging different prices to different buyers for similar products where the effect might be to injure, destroy, or prevent competition, in either the buyers' or sellers' markets" (Monroe 1990, p. 394).

[16] An exception is wholly-owned subsidiaries.

[17] A manufacturer may use several wholesale-price schedules, each intended for a set of retailers. As long as at least one set comprises multiple, non-identical retailers our core point holds: separate deals are not cut with all *individual* retailers.

[18] Another possibility is that the cost of achieving coordination is greater than its benefits; this is an empirical issue which we do not consider. If this is the case, then analytical modelers can contribute to channel practice by studying the properties of uncoordinated channels. A similar view has been espoused by Lee and Staelin (1997). We assess uncoordinated as well as coordinated channels in this monograph.

[19] The primary exception is our work (Ingene and Parry 1995b, 1998, 2000), although Desiraju and Moorthy (1997) do introduce an *optional* fixed cost.

[20] Academic researchers are understandably interested in the properties of a functioning channel; determining that high costs make a channel unviable is hardly news. Thus fixed costs are typically ignored.

[21] A myth is defined by *Webster's Ninth New Collegiate Dictionary* as "a popular belief or tradition that has grown up around something, *an unfounded or false notion*" (italics added for emphasis).

[22] Some of our own published work has perpetuated the Aggregate-Demand Modeling Myth; see Table 1.1 for an outline of this Myth and Chapters 5 and 11 for details about it.

[23] We could also depict a bilateral-monopoly model based on the $j^{th}$ competitor by a circle in the lower right corner.

[24] Fixed costs can be depicted by a third dimension rising from the page. This dimension can also be standardized to unit length. In Chapters 5-10 we deal with the resulting "unit cube."

[25] One of the most difficult aspects of coming to grips with the Channel Myths is that they are based on approaches and/or inferences that are valid for the model in which they were developed. In the case at hand, channel coordination really is manufacturer-optimal in a *pure* bilateral monopoly (i.e., one manufacturer, one retailer, one product, one state-of-nature).

[26] This quotation is from the commencement address given by President Kennedy at Yale University on June 11, 1962; it was cited at www.bartleby.com/66/1/32401.html.

[27] This is a subtle point, for the margin-response differs from the price-response. A retailer typically will raise its price in response to a higher wholesale-price; however, it is generally not profit-maximizing to pass along 100% (or more) of its cost increase to customers.

[28] An alternative formulation that sometimes appears in the marketing literature is the constant-elasticity demand curve (Moorthy and Fader 1988). It has negatively sloped price-reaction functions horizontally and positively sloped margin-reaction functions vertically, phenomena that we find intuitively unappealing. We do not believe that there is substantial empirical evidence that the $i^{th}$ firm's *optimal* response to a *decrease* in its rival's price is to *increase* its own price. The constant-elasticity demand curve is also incompatible with a closed-form solution in a model in which channel structure is more complex than bilateral monopoly. Another alternative is the rectangular demand curve. We also find this curve unappealing for channels research specifically because it treats demand as being insensitive to price.

[29] Multiple can be a very large number; two retailers or two states-of-nature is sufficient to ensure the possible sub-optimality of channel coordination.

[30] We are indebted to Professor Greg Shaffer for discussions on deriving linear demand.

[31] We fully develop the logic of a representative consumer in Chapter 11, sub-Sections 3.1 and 3.2. Until Chapter 11 we *could* regard the demand system (1.3.1) as empirically based since its theoretical foundation is not utilized for any analysis in Chapters 4-10. Accordingly, in this Appendix we merely sketch the logic as a refresher for those familiar with demand derivation.

[32] This explanation suggests (for example) two Ford dealers. An alternative model would involve a pair of competing products (Ford and Chevrolet) either sold through rival retailers—the interpretation of the McGuire and Staelin model (1983, 1986)—or sold through a single retailer—the interpretation of the Choi model (1991). The expanded Choi model (1996) requires notation for two products, each being sold through two retailers.

[33] Complementarity would be modeled as $\mathcal{T} < 0$; we consider only substitutability $(\mathcal{T} > 0)$ and demand independence $(\mathcal{T} = 0)$.

[34] The product that is dependent-independent could be written in compressed notation as: $Q_h = A_h - b_h p_h$ where $A_h \equiv \mathcal{A}_h / \mathcal{B}_h$ and $b_h \equiv \lambda / \mathcal{B}_h$.

Chapter 2

# The Bilateral-Monopoly Model and Channel Myths

*"It is not once nor twice but times without number that the same ideas make their appearance in the world."*

## 1 INTRODUCTION

A *bilateral monopoly* consists of two vertically-dependent firms: an upstream supplier (a "monopolist") that sells *all* its output to a downstream buyer (a "monopsonist") that acquires *all* its supply of an essential input from the monopolist. Their relationship is symmetric. Both have market power, and neither can survive without the other; therefore, the firms "necessarily deal with each other, negotiate and conclude contracts, [and] settle prices and quantities" (Machlup and Taber 1960, p. 104).

Today there is wide acceptance that, within a bilateral monopoly, channel profit-maximization requires incentives that align the individual interests of each channel member with the interests of the channel. This conclusion seems immediately obvious today, but the route economists followed to reach this awareness was neither obvious nor immediate. Bilateral-monopoly models raised a number of subtle issues that engaged many of the finest economic intellects for the better part of a century. Their discussions focused on (1) vertical relations between monopolist and monopsonist, (2) profit distribution between upstream and downstream firms, and (3) methods of achieving channel profit-maximization.

In recent years marketing scientists have developed new models to analyze inter-channel competition, inter-manufacturer competition, and inter-retailer competition. The influence of the *bilateral-monopoly model* on this research appears in two ways: some of its assumptions have been used as the basis for the creation of competitive models, and some of its inferences have been thought to extend to competitive models. However, the process of exporting assumptions and inferences from one model to another can have unexpected consequences. Consider two examples:

1. A retailer's fixed cost does not affect channel performance in a bilateral-monopoly model; thus, a modeling decision to ignore fixed cost is seen as an innocuous simplification.

2. Channel-profit maximization is a prerequisite for manufacturer profit maximization in a bilateral-monopoly model; thus, strategic advice to managers to seek channel coordination is seen as good counsel.

We will prove that fixed costs *do* affect performance in competitive models: a decision not to model fixed costs trivializes the results of models that are richer than is the bilateral-monopoly model. We will also prove that channel-profit maximization is often incompatible with maximizing manufacturer profit in competitive models: a decision to persuade managers to seek channel coordination is frequently bad advice. Accordingly, we call a widespread (but erroneous) belief in the innocuousness of an assumption a "Modeling Myth" and a common (but mistaken) belief that an accurate deduction in one model can be extended to more general models a "Strategic Myth." In later Sections we provide additional examples of both types of myths.

In the next Section, we briefly describe the key facets of the early bilateral-monopoly literature in economics and in marketing science; and we review issues that have bedeviled analyses of distribution channels for over a century, including questions about channel relationships, channel profit-incentives, and the allocation of channel profit. Our core conclusion is that only a multi-part tariff can coordinate a bilateral-monopoly channel while generating an analytically determinate distribution of channel profit. In the third Section we develop the mathematical foundation for the models of distribution channels that we employ in this monograph. In the fourth Section we provide several simple, numerical examples as preliminary evidence of the Channel Myths. We offer a commentary on the implications of our analysis in the final Section.

## 2 THE BILATERAL-MONOPOLY MODEL: THE EARLY LITERATURE[1]

Scholars have understood that bilateral monopolists *ought* to set price and quantity to maximize total economic satisfaction (aggregate *ophelimity*[2]) at least since the analysis by Edgeworth (1881). Yet economists struggled to reconcile the obvious logic of channel coordination with the countervailing logic of monopolistic self-interest. In this Section we touch on the highlights of the early economics literature to illustrate that even geniuses toiled to grasp complex concepts; that giants of the profession debated subtle points for many years; and that strongly held beliefs were sometimes proven to be incorrect. This is important, for it indicates that early analyses do not always stand the test of time, and that beliefs can be sincerely held for many years without being valid. It is precisely this phenomenon that helps to account for the persistence of Channel Myths.

We also reference the early marketing literature on distribution channels to underscore the tension between the bilateral-monopoly model that is a foundation for most analytical research in distribution channels and the observation that actual channels are best characterized as monopolistically competitive. It is a divergence between what is modeled and what is observed that is at the heart of the Channel Myths broached in Chapter 1.

## 2.1 The Early Economics Literature

Early economists disagreed on the ability of independent monopolists to behave as a single decision-maker would; that is, to reproduce the results of a vertically-integrated system. In the classical example of an iron ore miner and a steel smelter, it was clear that an integrated entity would choose the steel price that would maximize joint profits. It was also clear that *if* independent monopolists set the same price, they would sell the same quantity of steel, mine the same tonnage of iron ore, and generate the same joint profits. The interesting question was "Would independent firms set the same price?" This simple question became an extensively-investigated, intellectual conundrum.

Pigou (1908) argued that bilateral monopolists *should* maximize joint profits and that there *should* be a wholesale price ("W") that "both parties . . . [would] consider to represent a draw" (p. 216). To Pigou, this wholesale price would lie halfway between (i) the W that transferred all profit to the miner and (ii) the W that transferred all profit to the smelter. But "should" is not "would"; the question remained as to whether bilateral monopolists would behave as Pigou thought they should.

Bowley (1928) explored three bilateral-monopoly variations:

1. The miner and smelter combine to operate as an integrated firm;
2. The smelter dictates W while the miner determines the amount of iron ore to be quarried; or,
3. The miner dictates W while the smelter determines the amount of iron ore to be purchased.

Variation 1 defines a benchmark level of joint profit, but does not address the division of profit needed to achieve integration. Variations 2 and 3 are Stackelberg models in which the leader (the smelter in the former, the miner in the latter) specifies a wholesale price and the follower chooses its profit-maximizing quantity given the wholesale price.[3] These variations, which produce definitive profit distributions, lead to lower output and profit than with integration.

Tintner (1939) argued that wholesale prices generated by Variations 2 and 3 "determine 'the range' within which the price of iron ore will fall." The precise location of W within this range depended on "the bargaining power of the two monopolists;" as a result, bilateral monopoly contains "an essential indeterminacy" (p. 267). Morgan (1949) concluded that neither firm "will be able to set the price, each one trying to outwit the other . . . but once the price is agreed upon or set by arbitration or by government, . . . output . . . will clearly settle" between the lower of the Stackelberg solutions and the joint optimum (p. 377).

For forty years economists debated the logical outcomes of the bilateral-monopoly model. Points of contention included prices, output, channel profit, and the division of that profit among the participants, but the essential problem underlying all of these disputes was the basic indeterminacy of the bilateral-monopoly model. Fellner (1947) tried to resolve this issue by noting that Stackelberg solutions avoid an indeterminate profit distribution; thus, they could be seen as equivalent to "all-or-nothing" offers in which a buyer purchases all the quantity tendered at a specific price, or it purchases nothing. By extension, negotiation that linked particular prices to specific quantities would have the same beneficial effect since "whenever price offers relate to definite quantities, the all-or-none clause is implicit in these offers and in the contracts based on them" (p. 525).[4] While Fellner's approach helped to narrow the search for a solution, it left unanswered the questions of which "all-or-nothing" offer would be made, and by whom.

Spengler (1950) attempted to resolve the indeterminacy issue by arguing that merging the bilateral monopolists was in the public interest. He reasoned that a merger yields the integrated result, thereby increasing total channel profit and raising consumers' surplus. Spengler's approach implicitly shifts the profit-distribution negotiation to an unresolved merger negotiation in which the firms must agree on how much each contributes to the value of the merged firm.

Nash (1950) transformed the indeterminacy issue by modeling the monopolists as simultaneous players, neither one knowing the other's decision in advance. The result is a stable solution that does not maximize channel profits. Thus, the Nash equilibrium avoids the indeterminacy issue but fails to resolve the original issue raised by Bowley's analysis: is it possible to design a wholesale-price mechanism within a bilateral monopoly that will reproduce the results of a vertically-integrated system?

In sum, there were two key concerns of the early bilateral-monopoly literature in economics. First, a well-specified profit distribution between upstream and downstream firms required a vertical relationship (Stackelberg or Nash) that was incompatible with joint profit maximization. Second, the methods of reaching channel-profit maximization entailed bargaining, merger, arbitration, or governmental intervention; the profit distribution could not be *endogenously* determined, even with a written agreement between firms. Ironically, all of this had been foreseen by Edgeworth, who wrote "contract without competition is indeterminate" (1881, p. 20). We will see that adding intra-level competition to the model eliminates the indeterminacy that plagued early analyses.

## 2.2 The Early Marketing Literature

The preceding review, although necessarily incomplete, captures the flavor of early economic analyses that reflected contemporary concerns about the impact of mergers, acquisitions, cartels, and resulting antitrust enforcement in the manufacturing sector. In contrast, early marketing studies were concerned with the distribution sector of the economy, including the movement of finished goods from manufacturers, through retailers, and on to consumers. Hawkins (1950) stated:

> Although marketing [deals] extensively with price problems and policies, it can scarcely be said that the study of marketing has developed any price theory . . . few, if any, principles have evolved. *Nor has the marketing literature on price policy received much illumination from economic theory.* One reason is that much of the marketing material has been in the field of retail pricing, an area that has been ignored by orthodox economic theory (p. 179; emphasis added).

Hawkins believed that marketers should apply the theory of monopolistic competition to the study of vertical-price relationships; even situations in which manufacturer and retailer were both powerful were best described as "monopsonistic-competitive buyers confronting a monopolistic-competitive seller" (1950, p. 189). Contrasting Hawkins' observations with Edgeworth's words suggests that introducing competition may be an avenue for eliminating the indeterminacy of the distribution of profit in a coordinated channel.

Today marketing has a price theory; marketing scientists have published many models that address optimal pricing in distribution channels. Some research, like that of Jeuland and Shugan (1983) and Moorthy (1987) focused on methods of achieving coordination within a bilateral-monopoly model. As insightful as it was, it did not provide an endogenous resolution for the distribution of channel profit. Other research, like McGuire and Staelin (1983, 1986) and Choi (1991, 1996) concentrated on determinate profit distributions within a competitive setting. As innovative as this research was, it did not allow channel profit maximization; further, it modeled competitors as identical.

The modern analytical channels literature is commonly based on a bilateral-monopoly model or an identical-competitors model. Since neither bilateral monopoly, nor identical competitors, is common in retailing (almost every retailer has at least one differentiated competitor), authors apparently believe that deductions from these models extend to models of differentiated competition. One of the primary purposes of this monograph is to determine the validity of this belief. We start our discovery process by clearly stating the bilateral-monopoly model and its implications; later we address identical competitors.

# 3 THE BILATERAL-MONOPOLY MODEL: FORMAL ANALYSES

In this Section we organize our formal analysis of a bilateral-monopoly model across four channel relationships: a vertically-integrated system, manufacturer Stackelberg leadership, retailer Stackelberg leadership, and Nash equilibrium. In Chapter 1 we discussed eight Channel Myths; here we indicate where we think several of the Channel Myths originated. We stress that neither the modeling decisions nor the strategic inferences of the bilateral-monopoly model are incorrect in its context. It is the extension of these decisions and inferences to multiple-competitors models that causes the Channel Myths to arise.

## 3.1 The Bilateral-Monopoly Model: Assumptions

We make six fundamental assumptions:

1. Each channel member maximizes its own profit;
2. There are constant, non-negative variable costs of production (C) and distribution (c);
3. Fixed costs of production (F) and distribution (f) are non-negative;
4. Each channel member has full information about demand and costs;
5. There is certainty of variables and functional forms; and
6. Consumer preferences are captured by a linear, downward-sloping demand curve that is demand-independent from any other product; we write it as:

   $$Q = A - bp \qquad (2.3.1)$$

   "Q" denotes quantity, "p" denotes price, "A" is the quantity intercept at a zero price, and "b" is the price sensitivity of demand.

Assumptions 1, 4, and 5 are consistent with those commonly employed by marketing scientists who study bilateral-monopoly models. Assumptions 2 and 3 deviate from the common practice; variable costs are often standardized to zero and fixed costs are typically ignored.[5] Setting these variables to zero in the following analyses will reproduce the usual results. Finally, we employ a linear demand curve for two reasons: it enables us to obtain *closed-form* solutions and it can be extended to multiple, competing retailers.[6]

## 3.2 The Bilateral-Monopoly Model: A Vertically-Integrated System

In this sub-Section we derive the optimal price $(p^*)$, quantity $(Q^*)$, and profit $(\Pi_I^*)$ of a channel that is vertically integrated under two scenarios: (1) corporate headquarters specifies the retail price and (2) the pricing decision is left to the manager of the retail outlet. Because a vertically-integrated system generates the maximum profit that can be achieved by a bilateral monopoly, the performance of this system provides a benchmark for evaluating the performance of an independent manufacturer-retailer channel.

### 3.2.1 A Centralized, Vertically-Integrated System

The centralized approach sketched here is consistent with a combined firm that is created by a merger (Spengler 1950). The vertically-integrated system (denoted by the subscript $_I$) maximizes profit:

$$\max_{p} \quad \Pi_I = (p - c - C)Q - f - F \tag{2.3.2}$$

Quantity demanded is given by (2.3.1). The profit-maximizing quantity is:

$$Q^* = b\left[(A/b) - (c + C)\right]/2 \tag{2.3.3}$$

The vertically-integrated system sells one-half the quantity that would be sold if price equaled marginal cost. (We use asterisks to denote optimality.)

The optimal price is:

$$p^* = \left[(A/b) + (c + C)\right]/2 \tag{2.3.4}$$

Simple manipulation reveals that the channel margin is:

$$\mu^* \equiv (p^* - c - C) = Q^*/b \tag{2.3.5}$$

Consistent with intuition, quantity and margin are increasing functions of the product's attractiveness (A) and decreasing functions of variable costs (c and C) and price sensitivity (b). Fixed costs have no impact on these equilibrium solutions, a point noted at least 75 years ago (Bowley 1928, p. 657). This may be the origin of what we call the Fixed-Cost Modeling Myth.

Profit of the vertically-integrated system is obtained by inserting (2.3.3) and (2.3.5) into (2.3.2); this yields:

$$\Pi_I^* = \left( \frac{(Q^*)^2}{b} - f - F \right) \equiv R^* - f - F \tag{2.3.6}$$

We define $R^*$ as the *net revenue* of the vertically-integrated system; it is total revenue minus total variable costs; we will make extensive use of the $R^*$ term in this Chapter. The vertically-integrated system will exist provided the reservation price $(A/b)$ exceeds total variable costs (see (2.3.3)) *and* provided fixed costs are not so high as to cause the channel to lose money (see (2.3.6)). Equation (2.3.6) is our mathematical depiction of Edgeworth's "maximum ophelimity" (1881).

For completeness, we note that consumers' surplus is:

$$CS^* = R^*/2 \tag{2.3.7}$$

(The fraction ½ occurs because demand and costs are modeled as linear.)

### 3.2.2 A Decentralized, Vertically-Integrated System

The decentralized alternative to centralized control of price requires the specification of a *transfer price* "T" at which the manufacturing arm conveys output to the wholly-owned retail outlet. Given T, the manager of the retail outlet maximizes:

$$\max_p \quad \pi = (p - c - T)(A - bp) - f \tag{2.3.8}$$

Taking the derivative of (2.3.8) with respect to p and solving yields the channel-optimal price $p^*$ defined in (2.3.4) *if and only if* the transfer price is:

$$T^* = C \tag{2.3.9}$$

Given the optimal transfer price (2.3.9), the profit of the manufacturing arm in the integrated system is non-positive:

$$\Pi = -F \tag{2.3.10}$$

In contrast, the retail outlet earns a profit:

$$\pi^* = R^* - f \tag{2.3.11}$$

Because a fraction $\phi \le \pi^*$ can be returned to headquarters, the pair $\{T^*, \phi\}$ is equivalent to a two-part tariff.

## 3.3 The Bilateral-Monopoly Model: Stackelberg Leadership

We now turn to the classic model of bilateral monopoly, in which an upstream firm (the "manufacturer") sells to an independent downstream firm (the "retailer"). We consider Stackelberg leadership by the manufacturer, and then by the retailer. We prove that the leader's performance is unaffected by the leader's identity, and similarly for the follower's performance. Thus channel performance (price, quantity, total profit, and consumers' surplus) is unaffected by who leads. The distribution of channel profit is endogenously determined in this model. As noted by Edgeworth (1897), simple Stackelberg leadership cannot achieve the profit of a vertically-integrated system.

### 3.3.1 Manufacturer Stackelberg Leadership

In the second stage of the game, the retailer chooses a price to maximize its profit, given the prices of all factor inputs, including the constant per-unit wholesale price ( $W_L$ ) charged by the manufacturer. (We denote this game by the subscript $_L$ for "manufacturer leader.") The follower's maximand is:

$$\max_{p_L} \quad \pi_L = (p_L - c - W_L)Q_L - f \tag{2.3.12}$$

Quantity demanded is given by equation (2.3.1). We obtain the retailer's price-reaction function by differentiating (2.3.12) with respect to $p_L$:

$$\hat{p}_L = \left[ p^* + (W_L - C)/2 \right] \equiv p^* + \left( \hat{M}_L / 2 \right) \tag{2.3.13}$$

The term $\hat{M}_L$ is the manufacturer's margin. (The caret above a variable denotes a Stackelberg value.)

The retailer's quantity-reaction function is:

$$\hat{Q}_L = Q^* - b\left( \hat{M}_L / 2 \right) \tag{2.3.14}$$

The retailer sets the channel profit-maximizing price, and sells the channel optimal quantity, if and only if the manufacturer sets a zero margin.

Because the manufacturer's sole source of revenue is its per-unit earnings, it nets $-F$ if it sells at cost. This is obviously an unacceptable outcome. Thus, in the first stage of the game, a profit-maximizing manufacturer sets $\hat{W}_L$ given the retailer's quantity-reaction function (2.3.14):

$$\max_{W_L} \quad \Pi_L = \left( \hat{W}_L - C \right)\hat{Q}_L - F \tag{2.3.15}$$

The manufacturer's optimal margin is equal to the optimal channel margin:

$$\hat{M}_L^* \equiv \left(\hat{W}_L^* - C\right) = \mu^* \tag{2.3.16}$$

From (2.3.13), (2.3.14), and (2.3.16) we obtain the optimal quantity, retail margin ( $\hat{m}_L^*$ ), and channel margin under manufacturer leadership:

$$\hat{Q}_L^* = Q^* / 2 \tag{2.3.17}$$

$$\hat{m}_L^* \equiv \left(p_L^* - c - \hat{W}_L^*\right) = \mu^* / 2 \tag{2.3.18}$$

$$\hat{\mu}_L^* = 3\mu^* / 2 \tag{2.3.19}$$

Finally, retail profit ( $\hat{\pi}_L^*$ ), manufacturer profit ( $\hat{\Pi}_L^*$ ), channel profit ( $\hat{\Pi}_L^{C*}$ ), and consumers' surplus ( $\hat{CS}_L^*$ ) are:

$$\hat{\pi}_L^* = \left(\frac{R^*}{4} - f\right) \tag{2.3.20}$$

$$\hat{\Pi}_L^* = \left(\frac{R^*}{2} - F\right) \tag{2.3.21}$$

$$\hat{\Pi}_L^{C*} \equiv \left(\hat{\pi}_L^* + \hat{\Pi}_L^*\right) = \frac{3R^*}{4} - f - F \tag{2.3.22}$$

$$\hat{CS}_L^* = \left(\frac{3R^*}{8}\right) = \frac{3CS^*}{4} \tag{2.3.23}$$

Relative to a vertically-integrated system, channel profit is lower by $(R^* / 4)$ and consumers' surplus is reduced by $(R^* / 8)$. These shortfalls occur because the leader chooses a wholesale price to maximize its own, rather than channel, profit; this choice induces the retailer to set a retail price that is higher than the price offered by a vertically-integrated system. In the literature, this is called the "double-marginalization" problem (Gerstner and Hess 1995). Consequently, quantity and channel profit are below their channel-optimal levels. These results are the origin of what we call the Channel-Coordination Strategic Myth (profit is less than attained by a vertically-integrated system (see (2.3.22))) and the Double-Marginalization Strategic Myth (both channel members have positive margins (see (2.3.16) and (2.3.18))).

### 3.3.2 Retailer Stackelberg Leadership

Now let the retailer be the Stackelberg leader. (We denote this game with a subscript $_F$ for "manufacturer follower.") To solve this game we rewrite the profit and demand expressions in terms of retailer (m) and manufacturer (M) margins:

$$m_F \equiv (p_F - c - W_F)$$
$$M_F \equiv (W_F - C) \tag{2.3.24}$$

We write demand (2.3.1) as:

$$Q_F = A - b(c + C + m_F + M_F) \tag{2.3.25}$$

The manufacturer's maximand for the second stage of the game is:

$$\max_{M_F} \quad \Pi_F = M_F Q_F - F \tag{2.3.26}$$

Using the same methodology employed in the preceding sub-Section, we obtain the manufacturer's margin-reaction and quantity-reaction functions:

$$\hat{M}_F \equiv (\hat{W}_F - C) = \mu^* - (\hat{m}_F / 2) \tag{2.3.27}$$

$$\hat{Q}_F = Q^* - (b\hat{m}_F / 2) \tag{2.3.28}$$

The retailer Stackelberg leader faces the optimization problem:

$$\max_{m_F} \quad \pi_F = \hat{m}_F \hat{Q}_F - f \tag{2.3.29}$$

Maximization of this expression, followed by the appropriate substitution reveals that margins and profit at each level of the channel are:

$$\hat{m}_F^* = \mu^* = \hat{M}_L^* \tag{2.3.30}$$

$$\hat{M}_F^* = (\mu^* / 2) = \hat{m}_L^* \tag{2.3.31}$$

$$\hat{\pi}_F^* = \left(\frac{R^*}{2} - f\right) \tag{2.3.32}$$

$$\hat{\Pi}_F^* = \left(\frac{R^*}{4} - F\right) \tag{2.3.33}$$

These values are the mirror image of those obtained with manufacturer Stackelberg leadership; that is, the leader obtains the same margin and net revenue regardless of whether channel leadership is upstream or downstream.

Channel Performance values are:

$$\hat{\mu}_F^* = (3\mu^* / 2) = \hat{\mu}_L^* \tag{2.3.34}$$

$$\hat{Q}_F^* = (Q^* / 2) = \hat{Q}_L^* \tag{2.3.35}$$

$$\hat{\Pi}_F^{C*} \equiv (\hat{\pi}_F^* + \hat{\Pi}_F^*) = \left(\frac{3R^*}{4} - f - F\right) = \hat{\Pi}_L^{C*} \tag{2.3.36}$$

$$\hat{CS}_F^* = (3R^* / 8) = \hat{CS}_L^* \tag{2.3.37}$$

Channel Performance is unaffected by the leader's identity.

### 3.3.3 Commentary on Stackelberg Leadership

The preceding sub-Sections demonstrate that the lion's share of channel net revenue is earned by the Stackelberg leader. The reason is that the leader has the foresight to envision how its channel partner will react in response to its actions while the follower is blind to how its own behavior affects the leader's decision. Asymmetric prescience yields a well-defined quantity, retail price, channel profit, and channel profit distribution; it eliminates the ambiguity of potential outcomes with which early economists struggled. But Stackelberg leadership fails as a channel-organizing strategy in two regards.

First, Stackelberg leadership cannot achieve the profit *or* consumers' surplus results of a vertically-integrated system. These facts caused Morgan (1949) to suggest arbitration or government intervention. Second, Stackelberg equilibrium relies on "the extreme supposition that [one monopolist] is perfectly intelligent and foreseeing, [while the other] . . . 'cannot see beyond his nose'" (Edgeworth 1897, p. 125).

An alternative approach supposes that the two channel members reach an agreement, perhaps by face-to-face negotiations. It is clear that increasing output to the channel-optimal level adds $R^*/4$ in net revenue above that obtained with Stackelberg equilibrium. Thus the core bargaining question concerns the distribution of channel profit. At least one early writer argued that the range of bargaining outcomes would be bounded by $R^*/4$ and $3R^*/4$, because no channel member would accept a profit less than it could obtain as the Stackelberg follower (Tintner 1939); however, this solution does not eliminate the fundamental indeterminacy of profit distribution. Another early scholar argued for an equal distribution of the gains generated by moving to the vertically-integrated solution (Pigou 1908). This solution depends on the starting points of the negotiations ($\hat{Q}_L^*$ and $\hat{Q}_F^*$). As there is no obvious, endogenous answer to the bargaining problem, Edgeworth regarded the profit distribution as "a throw of a die loaded with villainy" (1881, p. 50).

## 3.4 The Bilateral-Monopoly Model: Nash Equilibrium

We now turn to a Nash game in which the firms simultaneously seek to maximize their own profits. (We use the subscript $_N$ to denote the Nash game.) The relevant maximands are:

$$\max_{M_N} \quad \Pi_M^N = M_N Q_N - F \tag{2.3.38}$$

$$\max_{m_N} \quad \pi_M^N = m_N Q_N - f \tag{2.3.39}$$

where $Q_N \equiv (A - b(c + C + m_N + M_N))$. Simultaneously solving the first order conditions yields the margins:

$$M_N^* = (2\mu^*/3) = m_N^* \tag{2.3.40}$$

These margins are mutually consistent: if the retailer first announces that it will choose $m_N^*$, the manufacturer still chooses $M_N^*$. Similarly, if the manufacturer first announces its choice of $M_N^*$, the retailer still chooses $m_N^*$.

Each channel member claims an equal share of channel profit:

$$\pi_N^* = \left(\frac{4R^*}{9} - f\right) = \Pi_N^* \tag{2.3.41}$$

Because the channel margin is greater than its optimal level, we find that output, channel profit, and consumers' surplus are lower than in the vertically-integrated system:

$$\mu_N^* = 4\mu^*/3 \tag{2.3.42}$$

$$Q_N^* = 2Q^*/3 \tag{2.3.43}$$

$$\Pi_N^{C*} \equiv (\pi_N^* + \Pi_N^*) = \frac{8R^*}{9} - f - F \tag{2.3.44}$$

$$CS_N^* = 4R^*/9 \tag{2.3.45}$$

Note that once again double marginalization precludes channel coordination.

Bargaining that leads to the jointly optimal solution can generate up to an additional $R^*/9$ in net revenue over the Nash equilibrium. *If* this marginal profit is equally distributed between manufacturer and retailer, then each obtains net revenue $R^*/2$; this is precisely what each would gain as a Stackelberg leader. It follows that bargaining from Nash equilibrium can enable both channel members to gain the benefits of Stackelberg leadership without the risk of economic warfare. This profit distribution is compatible with Pigou's call for an equal distribution of the gains from trade (1908).

A comparison of profit equations (2.3.21), (2.3.32), and (2.3.41) reveals that the profit of a Stackelberg leader exceeds the profit earned under a Nash equilibrium by $R^*/18$; in turn, the Nash profit exceeds that of the Stackelberg follower by $7R^*/36$. Thus the Nash equilibrium solution is an attractive option for a Stackelberg follower in the following sense: the follower could pay the leader $R^*/18$ to adopt Nash equilibrium, it would thereby improve its own profit by $5R^*/36$.

## 3.5 The Bilateral-Monopoly Model: Achieving Channel Coordination

Channel coordination, which has the potential to benefit all channel members, can be achieved if two conditions are satisfied. First, the wholesale price must induce the retailer to set the channel-profit maximizing retail price. This requires that the per-unit wholesale price (W) be equal to the marginal cost of production (C). Second, the distribution of channel profit must be acceptable to both monopolists. No one-part tariff can simultaneously satisfy both conditions; therefore, W = C is unacceptable because it gives zero net revenue to the manufacturer. Marketing scientists have proposed methods of handling this problem.

### 3.5.1 The Channel-Coordinating Quantity-Discount Schedule

Jeuland and Shugan (1983) argued that a properly-specified quantity-discount schedule will ensure that output equals the vertically-integrated quantity. They proposed the following wholesale-price schedule:[7]

$$\begin{aligned}\lambda(Q) &\equiv C+\alpha(p-c-C)+\phi/Q \\ &= C+\alpha(p-c-C)+\phi/(A-bp)\end{aligned} \tag{2.3.46}$$

We term $\lambda(Q)$ a three-part tariff because it consists of a constant per-unit fee C, a variable per-unit fee $\alpha(p-c-C)$, and a fixed fee $\phi$. With this quantity-discount schedule, the retailer's profit maximand is:

$$\begin{aligned}\max_{p_\lambda}\ \pi_\lambda &= (p_\lambda - c - W(Q))Q - f \\ &= (1-\alpha)(p_\lambda - c - C)Q - \phi - f\end{aligned} \tag{2.3.47}$$

It is easy to show that, given the wholesale-price schedule (2.3.46), price, quantity, and channel profit are identical to their vertically-integrated values. In conformity with the marketing science literature, we use the term *channel coordinating* to describe any wholesale-price strategy that causes every channel member to set its managerial control variables at a level identical to those set by a vertically-integrated system.

Profits under quantity-discount schedule (2.3.46) are:

$$\pi_{\lambda^*} = (1-\alpha)R^* - \phi - f \tag{2.3.48}$$

$$\Pi_{\lambda^*} = \alpha R^* + \phi - F \tag{2.3.49}$$

Both channel members require non-negative profits, so the profit allocation parameters $\alpha$ and $\phi$ are bounded:

$$\left((1-\alpha)R^* - f\right) \geq \phi \geq \left(F - \alpha R^*\right) \tag{2.3.50}$$

$$\left(\frac{R^* - f - \phi}{R^*}\right) \geq \alpha \geq \left(\frac{F - \phi}{R^*}\right) \tag{2.3.51}$$

Figure 2.1 illustrates these bounds. The manufacturer (retailer) captures all channel profit at each point on the upper (lower) iso-profit line. The convex set delimited by this parallelogram contains all possible distributions that are compatible with the constraint $1 \geq \alpha \geq 0$.[8] Because an infinite number of $\{\alpha, \phi\}$ pairs satisfy these constraints, the distribution of channel profit distribution is indeterminate. Note also that a negative $\phi$ defines a payment from the manufacturer to the retailer (e.g., a slotting allowance).

All the points within the parallelogram shown in Figure 2.1 represent acceptable profit distributions *if* the alternative is channel non-existence. However, many of these channel-coordinating points leave one channel member worse off than it would be in a Stackelberg or a Nash game. Specifically, in a manufacturer Stackelberg leader game, both channel members are better off if and only if:

$$\left(\frac{3 - 4\alpha}{4}\right) > \Phi^* > \left(\frac{1 - 2\alpha}{2}\right) \tag{2.3.52}$$

In this inequality, we define $\Phi^* \equiv \phi / R^*$ as the fixed fee payment as a percent of the net revenue of a coordinated bilateral monopoly.

In a retailer Stackelberg leader game the bounds are:

$$\left(\frac{1 - 2\alpha}{2}\right) > \Phi^* > \left(\frac{1 - 4\alpha}{4}\right) \tag{2.3.53}$$

Finally, in a Nash game the bounds are:

$$\left(\frac{5 - 9\alpha}{9}\right) > \Phi^* > \left(\frac{4 - 9\alpha}{9}\right) \tag{2.3.54}$$

The left-hand inequalities in (2.3.52)-(2.3.54) define the conditions under which channel coordination increases retailer profit, while the right-hand inequalities define the corresponding conditions for the manufacturer. In all three instances, the specified bounds indicate the range of solutions for which channel coordination increases the profit of both channel members; nonetheless, the actual distribution of channel profit remains indeterminate.

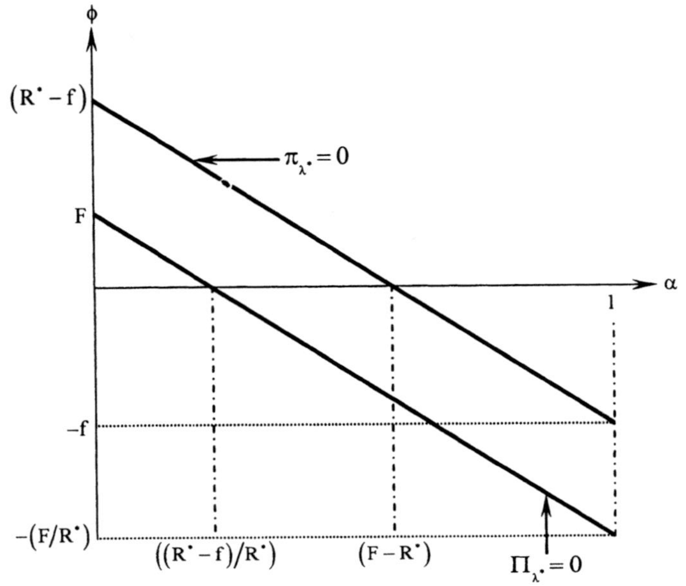


Legend:

$R^{*}$ ≡ Net revenue of a coordinated channel;

F ≡ Fixed cost at manufacture;

f ≡ Fixed cost at retail;

$\Pi_{\lambda^*}$ ≡ Manufacturer profit;

$\pi_{\lambda^*}$ ≡ Retailer profit;

$\phi$ ≡ The fixed fee; and

$\alpha$ ≡ The channel margin sharing ratio.

*Figure 2.1.* Channel Profit Distribution with a Quantity-Discount Schedule

### 3.5.2 Channel Coordination, Collusive Contracts, and Commitment

Moorthy (1987) observed that a three-part tariff is unnecessary to achieve channel coordination. Because the terms $\alpha$ and $\phi$ only affect the distribution of channel profit, it is redundant to have both terms. It is possible to set one of them equal to zero and use the other to ensure any desired profit allocation. For example, setting $\alpha = 0$ yields the two-part tariff $\{C, \phi\}$, where $\phi$ satisfies (2.3.50). Graphically, this tariff corresponds to the portion of the parallelogram that coincides with the $\phi$ – axis. Similarly, setting $\phi = 0$ yields the two-part tariff $\{C, \alpha\}$ where $\alpha$ satisfies (2.3.51).

It *seems* that tariffs $\{C, \phi\}$ and $\{C, \alpha\}$ should be equally effective for coordinating the channel. However, the latter tariff is subject to potential abuse by the downstream firm. To demonstrate this, we assume the manufacturer and retailer agree to a "collusive contract" that embeds either the two-part tariff $\{C, \phi\}$ *or* the tariff $\{C, \alpha\}$, where $\alpha$ is the manufacturer's share of the net revenue of the vertically-integrated channel ($R^*$), and $\phi$ is the value of that share expressed in dollars ($\phi = \alpha R^*$).

Is it in the retailer's interest to abide by the terms of either contract? First, suppose that the contract features the channel-coordinating two-part tariff $\{C, \phi\}$, which has a per-unit fee C and a fixed fee $\phi$. This tariff leads to the retail margin:

$$m_{Col} = (p_{Col} - c - W) \equiv (p_{Col} - c - C) \tag{2.3.55}$$

(The subscript $_{Col}$ denotes a collusive value.) The retailer's maximand is:

$$\max_{p_{Col}} \quad \pi_{Col} = (p_{Col} - c - C)(A - bp_{Col}) - \phi - f \tag{2.3.56}$$

The retailer maximizes its profits by selecting the channel-optimal price $p^*$. The resulting profits are given by (2.3.48) and (2.3.49), evaluated at $\alpha = 0$. This analysis confirms that a properly-specified two-part tariff coordinates a channel (Moorthy 1987).

Second, suppose that the contract features the tariff $\{C, \alpha\}$, where $\alpha$ has been selected to generate the same profit for the manufacturer ($\phi$) as the tariff $\{C, \phi\}$. The tariff $\{C, \alpha\}$ implies a wholesale price of:

$$W_{Col} = \left[C + \alpha\mu^*\right] = \left[C + \alpha(p^* - c - C)\right] \tag{2.3.57}$$

*If* the retailer sets the price $p^*$, profits are:

$$\pi^*_{Col} = (1 - \alpha)R^* - f \tag{2.3.58}$$

$$\Pi^*_{Col} = \alpha R^* - F \tag{2.3.59}$$

This is the optimal outcome under the quantity-discount schedule when $\phi = 0$ (contrast (2.3.58) and (2.3.59) with (2.3.48) and (2.3.49)). It is also the same outcome generated by the tariff $\{C, \phi\}$ when $\phi = \alpha R^*$.

Can the retailer gain even higher profit by violating the channel-coordinating intent of the negotiation that is based on $\{C, \alpha\}$? The answer is "Yes." The retailer will set a price above $p^*$ unless there is a binding contract to preclude deviation from $p^*$. To see this write the retailer's maximand:

$$\max_{p_{Col}} \quad \pi_{Col} = (p_{Col} - c - W_{Col})Q_{Col} - f \tag{2.3.60}$$

subject to:

$$Q_{Col} \equiv A - b(c + C + m_{Col} + \alpha(p_{Col} - c - C)) \tag{2.3.61}$$

There is a fundamental difference between maximands (2.3.47) and (2.3.60). In the former (the three-part tariff) case, the profit share $\alpha$ is based on the *realized* channel margin—a variable partially under the retailer's control. In the latter case, the profit share $\alpha$ is a *predetermined number* specified in the contract between the manufacturer and the retailer. The retailer's actual price decision has no impact on this number. Effectively, the actual margin is a variable to be optimized; the coordinated margin is a parameter that is considered in optimizing the retailer's actual margin.

It is easy to show that the retailer's optimal price is:

$$\hat{p}^*_{Col} = p^* + (\alpha\mu^*/2) \geq p^* \tag{2.3.62}$$

Thus margins and outputs are:

$$\hat{m}^*_{Col} = [(2-\alpha)\mu^*/2] \leq \mu^* \tag{2.3.63}$$

$$\hat{M}^*_{Col} = \alpha\mu^* \geq 0 \tag{2.3.64}$$

$$\hat{Q}^*_{Col} = [(2-\alpha)Q^*/2] \leq Q^* \tag{2.3.65}$$

It is clear from (2.3.65) that the channel-coordinated output ($Q^*$) is produced if and only if $\alpha = 0$; that is, if the manufacturer sells at cost. This result is often summarized by the statement that *double-marginalization* precludes channel coordination.

Profit levels are:

$$\hat{\pi}^*_{Col} = ([(2-\alpha)^2 R^*/4] - f) \geq \pi^*_{Col} \tag{2.3.66}$$

$$\hat{\Pi}^*_{Col} = ([\alpha(2-\alpha)R^*/2] - F) \leq \Pi^*_{Col} \tag{2.3.67}$$

$$\hat{\Pi}^{C*}_{Col} = ([(4-\alpha^2)R^*/4] - f - F) \leq \Pi^{C*} \tag{2.3.68}$$

The equalities in (2.3.62)-(2.3.68) hold if and only if $\alpha = 0$.

Expressions (2.3.66)-(2.3.68) provide unambiguous evidence that the retailer can enhance its profit, at the expense of the manufacturer and the channel, by *not* setting the channel optimal price except in the special case of $\alpha = 0$.[9] A wholesale offer to sell *any quantity* at a price $\hat{W}_{Col} > C$ enables the retailer to enhance its own profit by purchasing less than the channel-coordinating quantity ($\hat{Q}^*_{Col} < Q^*$). Without a legally-binding commitment to prevent this outcome, a mechanism is needed to ensure that the retailer does purchase $Q^*$. The channel-coordinating outcome can be guaranteed by an "all-or-nothing" agreement with a minimum-order quantity of $Q^*$ units:

$$W_{Col} = \begin{cases} (C + \alpha\mu^*) & \text{if } Q \geq Q^* \\ \infty & \text{otherwise} \end{cases} \tag{2.3.69}$$

The step-function (2.3.69) ensures that the bilateral monopolists achieve the channel-coordinating solution (Fellner 1947). This mechanism is unnecessary with a two-part tariff $\{C, \phi\}$ or with a three-part tariff $\{C, \alpha, \phi\}$, because these tariffs generate first-order conditions that are identical to the first-order condition of a vertically-integrated system.

### 3.5.3 Indeterminacy of Channel-Profit Distribution

In the preceding discussion we assumed that the manufacturer and retailer had determined the distribution of channel profit through negotiation. While this solution to the profit distribution problem has been advocated by some scholars (e.g., Tintner 1937; Jeuland and Shugan 1983), we find it unsatisfactory for two reasons. First, as we have seen, some negotiated wholesale-price policies (like $\{C, \alpha\}$) are subject to abuse by the second mover. Second, even if abuse is not an issue—as with the two-part tariff $\{C, \phi\}$, the three-part tariff $\{C, \alpha, \phi\}$, and the step-function (2.3.69)—an exogenously-imposed "negotiated" agreement is, from the modeler's perspective, inherently arbitrary. Because a major goal of this monograph is to determine if channel coordination is optimal for all channel members, *we* cannot capriciously impose a profit distribution by appealing to an unspecified "negotiation between the channel members."

The alternative to negotiation is for one channel member to make an "all-or-nothing" offer (Fellner 1947). We believe this is a superior approach for two reasons. First, manufacturers typically treat retailers comparably (Lafontaine 1990). A direct method of ensuring comparable treatment is to make the same all-or-nothing offer to *all* potential retail partners. Second, such an offer can be derived from profit-maximizing behavior. Because we assume that each retailer's fixed cost includes an opportunity cost of channel participation, an all-or-nothing offer does *not* mean that one or more retailers earn zero accounting profit. An acceptable wholesale-price plan ensures channel participation by allowing each retailer to cover its opportunity cost.

# 4 KEY CHANNEL MYTHS ILLUSTRATED

We begin this Section by reviewing several methods of organizing vertical-channel relationships in a simple bilateral-monopoly model. Then we extend the model to include multiple retailers. This enables us to demonstrate that several important results from the bilateral-monopoly model do not generalize beyond bilateral monopoly. This returns us a topic raised in Chapter 1: Channel Myths that shape the modeling of multiple-retailer channels, or that limit the strategic advice given to practicing managers. Like all myths, each Channel Myth contains a kernel of truth, because each is based on inferences or approaches that are valid in their original context. In the analytical distribution channels literature, almost every Channel Myth can be traced to the bilateral-monopoly model. In this Section we use simple, numerical examples to illustrate the key Channel Myths. Our examples demonstrate that several widely-held beliefs do not bear careful scrutiny. Our assessment is rigorously supported by theoretical analyses in later Chapters.

## 4.1 The Bilateral-Monopoly Model Illustrated

A bilateral monopoly consists of a manufacturer ($M_1$) that sells a product exclusively to one retailer ($R_1$). Their dependency is mutual, because $R_1$ buys an essential input only from $M_1$. In the simplest version of the bilateral-monopoly model:

- There is one retailer decision variable (the retail price);
- There is one manufacturer decision variable (the wholesale price);
- There is full information about costs and demand available to both channel members;
- There is a one-period channel relationship; and
- There is no variable and no fixed cost of production or distribution (that is, $C = 0 = c$ and $F = 0 = f$ ).

We relax the final assumption later in this Section. For illustrative purposes, the retailer faces demand curve (2.3.1) in which $b = 1$ and $A = 150$; thus:

$$Q = 150 - p, \qquad (2.4.1)$$

"Q" denotes the quantity demanded and "p" denotes the retail price.

### 4.1.1 The Vertically-Integrated System

To determine the channel-optimal price, quantity, and profit, we model a vertically-integrated system that sets its retail price to maximize total channel profit. The maximand is:

$$\max_{p} \quad \Pi_I = p(150 - p) \tag{2.4.2}$$

The channel-optimal price $(p^* = \$75)$ leads to output $Q^* = 75$ and total channel profit $\Pi_I^* = \$5{,}625$. We will use these values to evaluate the performance of the decentralized channels analyzed below. The vertically-integrated results can be attained with centralized control or through a decentralized system in which the optimal transfer-price is equal to the marginal cost of production $(T^* = \$0)$.

### 4.1.2 An Independent Manufacturer-Retailer Dyad: A One-Part Tariff

Whether a decentralized channel achieves the same total profit as a vertically-integrated system depends on the manufacturer's wholesale-price policy. We begin our analysis with the simple case of a constant per-unit wholesale-price W. Profit maximands for manufacturer and retailer are:

$$\begin{aligned} &\max_{W} \quad \Pi = W(150 - p) \\ &\max_{p} \quad \pi = (p - W)(150 - p) \end{aligned} \tag{2.4.3}$$

If the vertical-channel relationship is organized as a Stackelberg leadership game, the channel earns 75 percent of the profit of a vertically-integrated system. In a Nash game the channel earns nearly 90 percent of vertically-integrated profit. Full details are presented in Table 2.1.

Although neither Stackelberg game coordinates the channel, this does not mean a channel-coordinating price does not exist. When the manufacturer is the leader, coordination requires a zero manufacturer margin $(W^* = \$0)$. With retailer leadership, coordination requires a zero retail margin $(p^* = W)$. In both cases, channel profits are maximized only when the leader earns zero profit. A comparable analysis generates the same conclusion under a Nash game: coordination requires one of the channel members to accept a zero margin. Because no channel member will voluntarily accept this, *no one-part tariff* can induce a Stackelberg leader or a Nash competitor to set a channel-coordinating margin. These results are often summarized in the statement that both channel members setting positive margins—*double-marginalization*—is incompatible with channel coordination. A subsidiary observation is that fixed costs at the retail and manufacturing levels have no impact on the channel-optimal price or quantity, but they do affect profit at each channel level. Fixed costs also affect each channel member's participation constraint.

*Table 2.1.* Performance of a Bilateral-Monopoly Channel

| | Vertically-Integrated System* | Manufacturer Stackelberg Leadership | Retailer Stackelberg Leadership | Nash Equilibrium |
|---|---|---|---|---|
| Wholesale Price | *$0* | $75.00 | $37.50 | $50.00 |
| Retail Price | $75.00 | $112.50 | $112.50 | $100.00 |
| Quantity | 75 | 37.5 | 37.5 | 50 |
| Manufacturer Margin | *$0* | $75.00 | $37.50 | $50.00 |
| Retail Margin | *$75* | $37.50 | $75.00 | $50.00 |
| Channel Margin | $75.00 | $112.50 | $112.50 | $100.00 |
| Manufacturer Profit | *$0* | $2,812.50 | $1,406.25 | $2,500.00 |
| Retail Profit | *$5,625.00* | $1,406.25 | $2,812.50 | $2,500.00 |
| Channel Profit | $5,625.00 | $4,218.75 | $4,218.75 | $5,000.00 |
| Profit Percentage** | 100% | 75% | 75% | 88.8% |

* Italicized values in this column are for a *decentralized*, vertically-integrated system.
** Values in this row are the percent of vertically-integrated profit obtained under the vertical relationship detailed in the column.

Figure 2.2 illustrates the relationship among the vertically-integrated channel and these three decentralized channels. The vertical axis measures manufacturer profit ($\Pi$), the horizontal axis measures retailer profit ($\pi$). Point **N** denotes profits that result from the Nash game {$2,500, $2,500}. Points **L** and **F** denote the manufacturer Stackelberg leader and follower games. Points on the diagonal iso-profit line define profit combinations that sum to the vertically-integrated level of $5,625. The benefits of coordination can be read from this Figure. In a Nash game, both channel members would benefit from a wholesale-price policy that moved them from **N** to the line-segment (B, D) that defines the set of acceptable bargaining outcomes (the contract curve). Similarly, with manufacturer Stackelberg leadership, both channel members would benefit by a move from **L** to the line segment (A, C). When the manufacturer is the follower, both channel members would benefit by a move from **F** to the line segment (C, E). Each game has a contract curve which consists of those points representing an allocation of the gains from coordination that makes both channel members better off. Because the end points of the curve are defined by the profits earned by each channel member in the absence of negotiation, each of the three games generates a different contract curve. We now discuss mechanisms that can enable the channel members to reach the relevant contract curve.

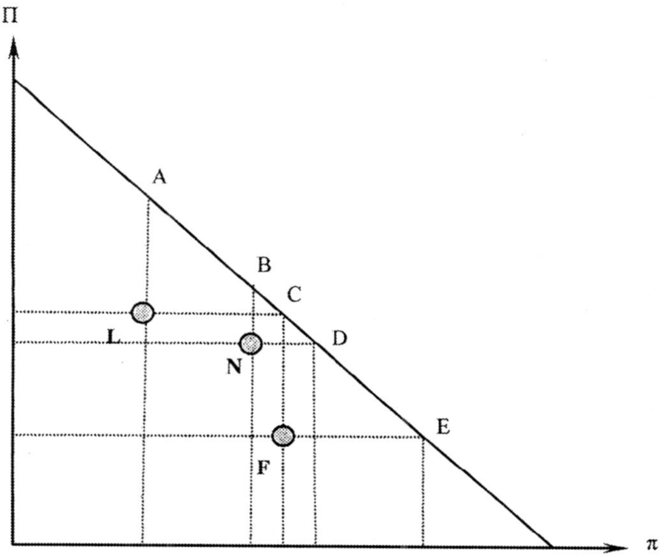


Legend:
Each point is defined in terms of profits $\{\Pi, \pi\}$:

$A \equiv \{\$4{,}218.75, \$1{,}406.25\}$

$B \equiv \{\$3{,}125, \$2{,}500\}$

$C \equiv \{\$2{,}812.50, \$2{,}812.50\}$

$D \equiv \{\$2{,}500, \$3{,}125\}$

$E \equiv \{\$1{,}406.25, \$4{,}218.75\}$

$\mathbf{L} \equiv \{\$2{,}812.50, \$1{,}406.25\}$

$\mathbf{N} \equiv \{\$2{,}500.00, \$2{,}500.00\}$

$\mathbf{F} \equiv \{\$1{,}406.25, \$2{,}812.50\}$

*Figure 2.2.* Potential Benefits from Channel Coordination

### 4.1.3 An Independent Manufacturer-Retailer Dyad: Fixed Fee Tariffs

The marketing science literature describes two ways to coordinate a decentralized, bilateral-monopoly channel. Jeuland and Shugan (1983) proposed a quantity-discount schedule and Moorthy (1987) suggested a two-part tariff. We focus on the former, because it contains the latter as a special case. In our simple example the Jeuland-Shugan scheme[10] is:

$$\lambda(Q(p)) = \alpha p + \phi/(150 - p). \tag{2.4.4}$$

The term "$\alpha$" is the revenue-sharing parameter and "$\phi$" is the fixed fee. Faced with this quantity-discount schedule, the retailer sets $p^*_{QD} = \$75$, yielding manufacturer, retailer, and channel profits:

$$\Pi^{*}_{QD} = (\alpha)\$5,625 + \phi \tag{2.4.5}$$

$$\pi^{*}_{QD} = (1-\alpha)\$5,625 - \phi \tag{2.4.6}$$

$$\Pi^{C*}_{QD} = \$5,625 = \Pi^{*}_{I} \tag{2.4.7}$$

From equation (2.4.7), the schedule (2.4.4) coordinates the channel; so does a two-part tariff, as can be seen by setting $\alpha = 0$ in (2.4.5)-(2.4.7).

The terms $\alpha$ and $\phi$ are constrained by the necessity that both players must be better off than they would be without coordination. This requires an evaluation of the profit associated with coordination versus the profit obtained from a Nash or a Stackelberg game (i.e., from points **N**, **L**, or **F** in Figure 2.2). In the case of the Nash game the revenue-sharing ($\alpha$) and fixed fee ($\phi$) relationship must be:

$$(0.556-\alpha) \geq \Phi \geq (0.444-\alpha) \tag{2.4.8}$$

The term $\Phi \equiv (\phi/\$5,625)$ is the fixed fee as a percent of the net revenue of the coordinated channel. In (2.4.8) the left-hand constraint must be met to ensure that the retailer is no worse off than in a Nash game; the right-hand constraint serves the same purpose for the manufacturer. In a manufacturer Stackelberg leader game the relationship must be:

$$(0.75-\alpha) \geq \Phi \geq (0.5-\alpha) \tag{2.4.9}$$

For the retailer Stackelberg leader game we obtain:

$$(0.5-\alpha) \geq \Phi \geq (0.25-\alpha) \tag{2.4.10}$$

We note that the constraints for a two-part tariff can be obtained from (2.4.8)-(2.4.10) by setting $\alpha = 0$. A subsidiary observation is that fixed costs further limit the acceptable values of $\alpha$ and $\phi$.

In summary, a properly specified two-part (or three-part) tariff will coordinate a bilateral-monopoly channel. Within well-defined limits, both channel members can be made better off through coordination than they would be by playing a Nash or a Stackelberg game. We now turn to the critical issue of whether the fundamental results of the bilateral-monopoly model extend to the case of multiple competitors at the retail level.

## 4.2 The Bilateral-Monopoly Meta-Myth

The bilateral-monopoly model is the basis of an enormous volume of research by economists and marketing scientists. By the principle of Occam's razor,[11] a bilateral-monopoly model is appropriate for analyzing channel issues if it exemplifies a real-world setting *or* if it leads to the same predictions as more complex models. Real-world markets are rarely bilateral monopolies. Thus, we believe the popularity of the bilateral-monopoly model reflects *an unstated but commonly-held belief* that the model is an innocuous, simplifying variant of more complex models. We prove repeatedly through this book that this faith in the bilateral-monopoly model is misplaced; therefore, we call this belief the *Bilateral-Monopoly Meta-Myth.*[12]

To understand the origin of this Meta-Myth, recall that bilateral monopoly entails a monopolist selling to a monopsonist in a single dyadic relationship. It *appears* reasonable to infer that a manufacturer serving N independent retailers has N *independent* dyadic relationships. This view, which is depicted by Figure 2.3, is appropriate *if and only if* each dyad can (and should) be treated as if it is completely independent from other dyadic relationships. Such independence requires not only that the retailers *not* be direct competitors, but also that the manufacturer "cut separate deals" with each non-identical retailer. Survey evidence suggests that individually tailored deals are not widespread due to administrative, bargaining and contract development costs (Lafontaine 1990). Further, legal restraints discourage separate deals, at least in the United States.[13] In short, price discrimination is generally impermissible in the presence of retail competition and is inordinately expensive even without intra-level competition. For these reasons, manufacturers tend *to treat retailers comparably.*[14] Whether offering a common wholesale-price schedule arises from cost concerns or legal constraints, commonality means that the manufacturer has N *interdependent* relationships as depicted in Figure 2.4.

We will prove that channel coordination is not always in the interest of every channel member when there are multiple retailers, whether or not they are competitors. Thus "coordinate the channel" is not necessarily good strategic advice outside a bilateral-monopoly channel. We will also prove that retailer fixed costs influence the optimal wholesale-price strategy. By extension, the wholesale-price policy affects the quantity sold and the total profit earned by the channel. It has an impact on the distribution of profit between channel levels and on the profit distribution between competitors within a specific level of the channel. In short, a decision *not* to model fixed costs generates performance results that are a shadow of the richness that we see in practice, and that we are able to derive from a model of multiple, *non-identical* competitors. We stress "non-identical" because the common practice of modeling rivals as identical competitors also conceals a wealth of insights that are obtained with non-identical competitors. We term these three beliefs the *Channel-Coordination Strategic Myth*, the *Fixed-Cost Modeling Myth*, and the *Identical-Competitors Meta-Myth*. We illustrate these myths in the remainder of this Section. Each of them is rigorously developed later in this monograph.

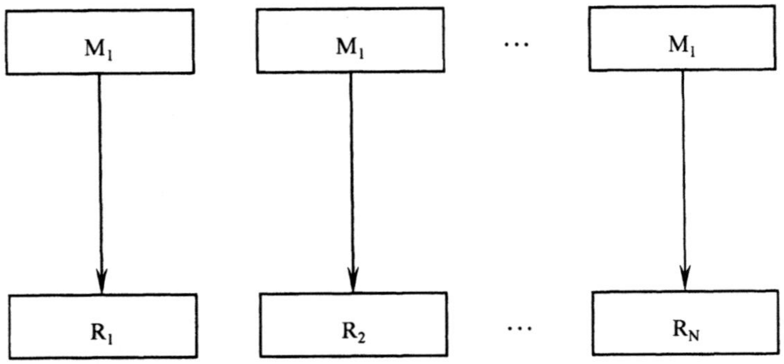


*Figure 2.3.* One Manufacturer Serving N-Retailers: Separate Wholesale-Price Deals

Legend for *Figures 2.3* and *2.4*:

$M_1$ ≡ The manufacturer

$R_1$ ≡ Retailer 1

$R_2$ ≡ Retailer 2

$R_N$ ≡ Retailer N

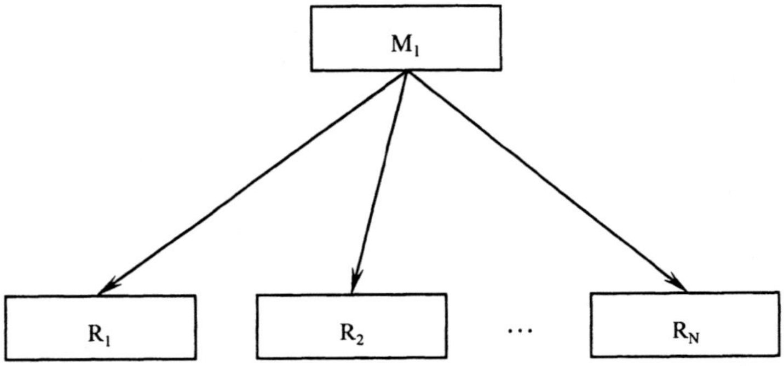


*Figure 2.4.* One Manufacturer Serving N-Retailers: Comparable Treatment

## 4.3 The Channel-Coordination Strategic Myth

A widely accepted belief in the analytical channels literature is that maximizing channel profit can benefit every channel member. This statement is accurate in a bilateral-monopoly channel, and appears to be reasonable within any channel, because it involves dividing up the "largest possible pie." Because this belief *need not hold* when the manufacturer serves competing retailers, we call it the *Channel-Coordination Strategic Myth*. To illustrate this Myth, consider competing retailers who face *asymmetric demand*:

$$\begin{aligned} Q_i &= 150 - p_i + .5p_j \\ Q_j &= 100 - p_j + .5p_i, \end{aligned} \tag{2.4.11}$$

In the demand system (2.4.11), $p_i$ and $p_j$ denote the prices charged by the $i^{th}$ and $j^{th}$ retailers. The cross-price effect is equal across competitors but the intercept terms are unequal; the retailers are not identical. We discuss the outcome of assuming identical competitors in sub-Section 4.5.

We now evaluate four wholesale-price policies that a manufacturer Stackelberg leader might employ in dealing with these retailers: (i) a two-part tariff that *seeks* to maximize *channel* profit, (ii) a two-part tariff that maximizes *manufacturer* profit, (iii) a quantity-discount schedule that maximizes *channel* profit, and (iv) a menu of two-part tariffs that maximizes *channel* profit.[15] The two-part tariffs (i) and (ii) *cannot* coordinate a channel composed of non-identical competitors, while a quantity-discount schedule or a menu *will coordinate* the channel provided they are properly specified.

### 4.3.1 Non-Coordinating Tariffs

We start by considering a two-part tariff that is designed to maximize *channel* profit; we term this a *second-best* tariff in Chapter 5. Its performance is detailed in the third and fourth columns of Table 2.2. The second-best tariff duplicates the results of a vertically-integrated system only in the trivial case of identical competitors; otherwise it generates less channel profit than does the integrated channel. (For comparative purposes, the first and second columns of Table 2.2 display the results of a vertically-integrated system.)

Consider a two-part tariff that is designed to maximize *manufacturer* profit; we term it a *sophisticated Stackelberg* tariff in Chapter 6. The fifth and sixth columns of Table 2.2 present its results. Wholesale and retail prices are higher, and quantities are lower, than with the second-best tariff. Despite this, the manufacturer's profit is \$100 higher, although channel profit is \$100 lower. This \$200 swing is borne entirely by the $i^{th}$ retailer. From the manufacturer's perspective, the sophisticated Stackelberg two-part tariff is the best of all possible two-part tariffs.

*Table 2.2.* Competing Retailers: Manufacturer Profits under Various Two-Part Tariffs

| | A Vertically-Integrated System | | A *Channel* Profit-Maximizing Two-Part Tariff | | A *Manufacturer* Profit-Maximizing Two-Part Tariff | |
|---|---|---|---|---|---|---|
| | $i^{th}$ Retailer | $j^{th}$ Retailer | $i^{th}$ Retailer | $j^{th}$ Retailer | $i^{th}$ Retailer | $j^{th}$ Retailer |
| Wholesale-Price* | *$58.33* | *$66.67* | $62.50 | | $77.50 | |
| Fixed Fee | — | — | $2,756.25 | | $2,256.25 | |
| Retail Price | $133.33 | $116.67 | $135.00 | $115.00 | $145.00 | $125.00 |
| Quantities | 75 | 50 | 72.5 | 52.5 | 67.5 | 47.5 |
| Retailer Profits* | *$5,625.00* | *$2,500.00* | $2,500.00 | $0.00 | $2,300.00 | $0.00 |
| Manufacturer Profit* | *$7,708.33* | | $13,325.00 | | $13,425.00 | |
| Channel Profit | $15,833.33 | | $15,825.00 | | $15,725.00 | |

* Italicized values denote a ***decentralized***, vertically-integrated system; these values are zero in a centrally-managed system.

A two-part tariff cannot coordinate a channel of competing, non-identical retailers. From the manufacturer's perspective, the sophisticated Stackelberg two-part tariff $\{W = \$77.50,\ \phi = \$2,256.25\}$ that seeks to maximize manufacturer profit is superior to the second-best two-part tariff $\{W = \$62.50,\ \phi = \$2,756.25\}$ that seeks to maximize channel profit.

### 4.3.2 Coordinating Tariffs

Coordinating a channel with competing, non-identical retailers entails an effective per-unit wholesale price that differs across competitors. One method of coordination is a linear *quantity-discount schedule*; we develop this schedule in Chapter 5. The first and second columns of Table 2.3 display this schedule's performance, while the sophisticated Stackelberg results are reproduced in the third and fourth columns for comparative purposes. Although the quantity-discount schedule coordinates the channel, manufacturer profits are nearly \$200 lower than they are with the sophisticated Stackelberg tariff. This establishes that there are parametric values for which coordinating a channel with a quantity-discount schedule is *not* in the manufacturer's best interest.

*Table 2.3.* Competing Retailers: Manufacturer Profits with a Quantity-Discount Schedule or a Two-Part Tariff

| | A *Channel* Profit-Maximizing Quantity-Discount Schedule* | | A *Manufacturer* Profit-Maximizing Two-Part Tariff | |
|---|---|---|---|---|
| | $i^{th}$ Retailer | $j^{th}$ Retailer | $i^{th}$ Retailer | $j^{th}$ Retailer |
| Wholesale Price | $W^{QD} = \$83.33$ and $w^{QD} = 0.17$ | | \$77.50 | |
| Fixed Fee | \$2,083.33 | \$2,083.33 | \$2,256.25 | |
| Retail Price | \$133.33 | \$116.67 | \$145.00 | \$125.00 |
| Quantities | 75 | 50 | 67.5 | 47.5 |
| Retailer Profits | \$2,604.67 | \$0.00 | \$2,300.00 | \$0.00 |
| Manufacturer Profit | \$13,229.17 | | \$13,425.00 | |
| Channel Profit | \$15,833.33 | | \$15,725.00 | |

* $W^{QD}$ is the maximum per-unit wholesale price; $w^{QD}$ is the rate at which the per-unit fee declines.

An alternative method of coordinating a channel with competing, non-identical retailers involves a *menu of two-part tariffs*; we develop this menu in Chapter 7, while offering an illustration in Table 2.4 below. Both elements of the menu must have a per-unit component ($W_k^*$) that is uniquely designed for a retailer; there must be a tariff element $\tau_k \equiv \{W_k^*, \phi_k\}$, $k \in (i, j)$ that is designed for the k<sup>th</sup> retailer. The channel will only be coordinated if the $i^{th}$ retailer selects the $i^{th}$ element of the menu, and if the $j^{th}$ retailer selects the $j^{th}$ element. Because the competitors are profit maximizers, they will choose the appropriate element of the menu if and only if it is in their own interest. We prove in Chapter 7 that there are fixed fees ($\phi_i$ and $\phi_j$) which guarantee that each competitor chooses the menu element that ensures coordination.

When both retailers choose the "right" tariff, the $i^{th}$ retailer earns net revenue of \$5,625 and the $j^{th}$ retailer earns \$2,500. To maximize its own profits, the manufacturer extracts as much of the retailers' profit as possible through its fixed fee choices. From the manufacturer's perspective the best menu is the one that enables it to extract all channel profit $\{\tau_i^*, \tau_j^*\}$, where:

- $\tau_i^* \equiv \{W_i^*, \phi_i^*\} = \{\$58.33, \$5{,}625\}$
- $\tau_j^* \equiv \{W_j^*, \phi_j^*\} = \{\$66.67, \$2{,}500\}$.

The channel will be coordinated and the manufacturer will extract all profit from the channel if the $i^{th}$ retailer chooses the $i^{th}$ tariff and the $j^{th}$ retailer chooses the $j^{th}$ tariff. The first and second columns of Table 2.4 report the behavioral values that would result *if* each retailer chose the right tariff.

But retailers are free to select either tariff from the menu. Given our parametric values, both retailers prefer the $j^{th}$ tariff. The $i^{th}$ retailer "defects" to the $j^{th}$ tariff because it earns \$2,556.79 *more* than it does by selecting tariff $\tau_i^*$ (see columns three and four of Table 2.4). To prevent defection, the manufacturer must modify the menu. Because a change in the per-unit fees ensures non-coordination, the only way to prevent defection and preserve coordination is to adjust the fixed fees (we prove this point in Chapter 7). If the manufacturer were to increase the fixed fee component of the $j^{th}$ tariff to make that option less attractive to the $i^{th}$ retailer, the $j^{th}$ retailer would lose money, so it would not participate in the channel. The manufacturer's only option is to *reduce* the fixed fee component of the $i^{th}$ tariff to remove the incentive for defection.

*Table 2.4.* Competing Retailers: A Menu of Two-Part Tariffs and the Defection Problem

| | Both Retailers Choose the "Right" *Unmodified* Menu | | Both Retailers Choose the j$^{th}$ Menu Option | | Both Retailers Choose The "Right" *Modified* Menu | |
|---|---|---|---|---|---|---|
| | i$^{th}$ Retailer | j$^{th}$ Retailer | i$^{th}$ Retailer | j$^{th}$ Retailer | i$^{th}$ Retailer | j$^{th}$ Retailer |
| Wholesale-Price | $58.33 | $66.67 | $66.67 | $66.67 | $58.33 | $66.67 |
| Fixed Fee | $5,625.00 | $2,500.00 | $2,500.00 | $2,500.00 | $3,068.21 | $2,500.00 |
| Retail Price | $133.33 | $116.67 | $137.78 | $117.78 | $133.33 | $116.67 |
| Quantities | 75 | 50 | 71.11 | 51.11 | 75 | 50 |
| Retailer Profits | 0 | 0 | $2,556.79 | $112.35 | $2,556.79 | 0 |
| Manufacturer Profit | $15,833.33 | | $13,148.15 | | $13,276.54 | |
| Channel Profit | $15,833.33 | | $15,817.33 | | $15,833.33 | |

To prevent defection, the fixed fee $\phi_i$ must be reduced by $2,556.79 (the amount that the $i^{th}$ retailer earns by defecting). This adjustment results in the following modified menu $\{\tau_i^M, \tau_j^*\}$:

- $\tau_i^M \equiv \{\$58.33, \$3{,}068.21\}$
- $\tau_j^* \equiv \{\$66.67, \$2{,}500\}$.

The modified menu $\{\tau_i^M, \tau_j^*\}$ retains the same $j^{th}$ tariff as the "best" menu. Columns 5 and 6 of Table 2.4 present the outcome of the modified menu. The channel is coordinated and manufacturer profit is $13,276.54. Menu modification to prevent defection increases manufacturer profits by about $130, although the manufacturer still earns $150 less than it would with the sophisticated Stackelberg tariff.

We have demonstrated that, for specific parametric values, the manufacturer prefers a non-coordinating, sophisticated Stackelberg tariff to a channel-coordinating menu, or to a channel-coordinating quantity-discount schedule, or to any other non-coordinating two-part tariff. This result, which is surprising given the near-sacred status accorded to coordination in the channels literature, occurs because the comparable treatment of competitors limits the manufacturer's ability to redistribute profit via the fixed fee(s).[16] Because the manufacturer can be better off in a non-coordinated channel than in a coordinated one, the notion that channel coordination is always preferred by all channel members is a myth. We refer to it as the *Channel-Coordination Strategic Myth*. At the same time, we stress that there are parametric values for which the manufacturer is better off by coordinating the channel, either with a quantity-discount schedule or with a menu of two-part tariffs. We rigorously develop the conditions under which the manufacturer prefers coordination to non-coordination in Chapter 8.

## 4.4 The Fixed-Cost Modeling Myth

There is a belief, based in the bilateral-monopoly model, that fixed costs have no impact on the profit-maximizing price. This belief dates at least to Bowley (1928). To understand its origin, again consider demand (2.4.1). Given zero fixed costs (denoted as "$f = 0$"), the vertically-integrated system earns $5,625. System profit declines dollar-for-dollar as f increases, but the optimal price is *unaffected*. Fixed cost only matters if it is so great that the channel loses money, causing the channel to cease to exist. In a bilateral monopoly with a manufacturer and an independent retailer, changes in fixed cost have no impact on the per-unit wholesale price; however, with a two-part or three-part tariff, a sufficiently high fixed cost compels the manufacturer to decrease its fixed fee ($\phi$) to ensure the retailer's channel participation. These results have led to a belief that fixed costs never affect the retail price: we call this belief the *Fixed-Cost Modeling Myth.*

When there is inter-retailer competition, the per-unit wholesale price does depend on the difference in retailers' fixed costs, as we prove in Chapter 6 for the sophisticated Stackelberg tariff. We use our ongoing demand example (2.4.11) to illustrate. We find:

$$\begin{aligned} \$2{,}300 > (f_i - f_j) \quad &\Rightarrow \quad W = \$77.50 \\ \$2{,}300 \le (f_i - f_j) \le \$2{,}700 \quad &\Rightarrow \quad W = \$77.50 - \$30.00(\omega) \\ (f_i - f_j) > \$2{,}700 \quad &\Rightarrow \quad W = \$47.50 \end{aligned} \tag{2.4.12}$$

The variable $\omega$ is defined as: $1 \ge \omega \equiv (f_i - f_j - \$2{,}300)/\$2{,}700 \ge 0$. In this example, the manufacturer-optimal wholesale price declines continuously over the range $\$2{,}300 \le (f_i - f_j) \le \$2{,}700$; thus, retail prices and quantities vary over this range, as do total profit and its distribution. Table 2.5 provides illustrative details at two levels of fixed cost differences: \$0 and \$2,400. Note that an increase in the fixed cost of the more profitable (here, the $i^{th}$) retailer solely lowers that retailer's profit until its fixed cost is so great that the $i^{th}$ retailer is on the verge of withdrawing from the channel. Only then does the manufacturer have an incentive to cut the wholesale price and the fixed fee to avoid violating the $i^{th}$ retailer's participation constraint. Due to comparable treatment, both retailers benefit from this adjustment since both of them pay the same per-unit and fixed fees.

We emphasize that the preceding example, which may appear counter-intuitive, is *not* unique. It illustrates the general principle that fixed costs can influence channel pricing decisions when retailers compete. We elaborate this point in considerable detail in our competing-retailer models of Chapters 5-9. In addition, we discuss how fixed costs affect channel breadth, both in the presence of inter-retailer competition (Chapter 10) and in its absence (Chapter 3).

*Table 2.5.* Competing Retailers: Manufacturer Profits with a Sophisticated Stackelberg Tariff and Retail-Level Fixed Costs

| | $f_i = \$0$ and $f_j = \$0$ | | $f_i = \$2,400$ and $f_j = \$0$ | |
|---|---|---|---|---|
| | $i^{th}$ Retailer | $j^{th}$ Retailer | $i^{th}$ Retailer | $j^{th}$ Retailer |
| Wholesale Price | $77.50 | | $70.00 | |
| Fixed Fee | $2,256.25 | | $2,500.00 | |
| Retail Price | $145.00 | $125.00 | $140.00 | $120.00 |
| Quantities | 67.5 | 47.5 | 70 | 50 |
| Retailer Profits | $2,300.00 | $0.00 | $0.00 | $0.00 |
| Manufacturer Profit | $13,425.00 | | $13,400.00 | |
| Channel Profit | $15,725.00 | | $13,400.00 | |
| Coordinated Channel Profit | $15,833.33 | | $13,433.33 | |

## 4.5 The Identical-Competitors Meta-Myth

Models of intra-level competition traditionally focus on the effect of a change in the number of competitors (i.e. $1,2,...,N$). This leads naturally to a desire to exclude other factors that might confound the "numerical" effect. As a result, it is typical to model competitors as being identical in all respects. Unfortunately, the identical-competitors approach has carried over to models in which the issue is not the number of rivals, but the effect of the degree of competition at a constant channel breadth (McGuire and Staelin 1983, 1986; Choi 1991, 1996; Trivedi 1998). This indicates a belief that a model of multiple, *non*-identical competitors would generate the same performance as does the identical-competitors model. Provided this belief is correct, Occam's razor tells us that the simpler model should be employed. But careful scrutiny reveals that this is a misplaced belief, for the identical-competitors model yields results that are trivial compared to those generated by a *non*-identical-competitors model, although they are virtually equivalent to those derived from a bilateral-monopoly model.

To see this, consider the case of competing retailers who face a demand system that is an equal intercepts version of (2.4.11):

$$\begin{aligned} Q_i &= 100 - p_i + .5p_j \\ Q_j &= 100 - p_j + .5p_i \end{aligned} \qquad (2.4.13)$$

We assume that all variable and fixed costs are zero. The retailers are identical in all respects, with identical demand and identical (zero) costs.

A vertically-integrated system sets $p_i^* = p_j^* = \$100$, both retail outlets sell 50 units, and the channel earns \$10,000 profit. These results are summarized in the first and second columns of Table 2.6. With one exception, they are identical to those obtained in bilateral monopoly when the *single* retailer faces demand $Q = 100 - p$. The sole exception is the optimal transfer price; it is \$0 in a bilateral-monopoly model and is \$50 in the identical-competitors model. This difference reflects the demand externality in the competing-retailers model. The per-unit fee recognizes that the demand curve facing a retailer is a function of the price charged by its rival.

The popularity of the identical-competitors model is at least partially due to similarities between its results and those of the bilateral-monopoly model. Another factor that contributes to the widespread use of identical-competitors models is that it is easier to solve mathematical models with identical competitors. We believe that these considerations should be less important than the observation that the results of an identical-competitors model have a knife-edge property: the results *only hold* when the competitors are *exactly identical*.

*Table 2.6.* Identical Competitors with No Fixed Costs

| | A Vertically-Integrated System | | A *Manufacturer* Profit-Maximizing Two-Part Tariff | |
|---|---|---|---|---|
| | $i^{th}$ Retailer | $j^{th}$ Retailer | $i^{th}$ Retailer | $j^{th}$ Retailer |
| Wholesale-Price | *\$50.00** | *\$50** | \$50 | |
| Fixed Fee | — | — | \$2,500 | |
| Retail Price | \$100 | \$100 | \$100 | \$100 |
| Quantities | 50 | 50 | 50 | 50 |
| Retailer Profits | *\$2,500** | *\$2,500** | \$0 | \$0 |
| Manufacturer Profit | *\$5,000** | | \$10,000 | |
| Channel Profit | \$10,000 | | \$10,000 | |

* Italicized values denote a *decentrally*-managed, vertically-integrated system; these values are zero in a centrally-managed system.

The third and fourth columns of Table 2.6 demonstrate that a sophisticated Stackelberg tariff coordinates an identical-competitors channel (it also coordinates a bilateral-monopoly channel); but it cannot coordinate a model with non-identical competitors (see Table 2.3 for an example). For the record, a naïve Stackelberg tariff will not coordinate *any* channel.

The assumption of identical competitors has dissuaded modelers from exploring the effect of asymmetry on marketing decisions. Given the asymmetric demand system (2.4.11), the manufacturer *often* prefers a non-coordinating, sophisticated Stackelberg tariff to channel coordination with a menu of two-part tariffs (Table 2.4) or with a quantity-discount schedule (Table 2.3). We prove in Chapter 8 that a manufacturer's preference for non-coordination depends on the intensity of competition and on the difference in the retailers' market shares (i.e., retailer heterogeneity).

To illustrate this statement, consider the simple case of different fixed costs. Let $f_i = \$2,600$ and $f_j = \$0$. Table 2.7 reports the performance of a vertically-integrated system (first and second columns), a menu (third and fourth columns), and the sophisticated Stackelberg tariff (fifth and sixth columns).

*Table 2.7.* Competing Retailers: Asymmetric Fixed Costs ($f_i$ = \$2,600 and $f_j$ = \$0)

| | A Vertically-Integrated System | | A Modified Channel-Coordinating Menu | | A *Manufacturer* Profit-Maximizing Two-Part Tariff | |
|---|---|---|---|---|---|---|
| | $i^{th}$ Retailer | $j^{th}$ Retailer | $i^{th}$ Retailer | $j^{th}$ Retailer | $i^{th}$ Retailer | $j^{th}$ Retailer |
| Wholesale-Price | *$58.33** | *$66.67** | $58.33 | $66.67 | $55.00 | |
| Fixed Fee | — | — | $3,025.00 | $2,500.00 | $3,025.00 | |
| Retail Price | $133.33 | $116.67 | $133.33 | $116.67 | $130.00 | $110.00 |
| Quantities | 75 | 50 | 75 | 50 | 75 | 55 |
| Retailer Profits | *$3,025.00** | *$2,500.00** | $0.00 | $0.00 | $0.00 | $0.00 |
| Manufacturer Profit | *$7,708.33** | | $13,233.33 | | $13,200.00 | |
| Channel Profit | $13,233.33 | | $13,233.33 | | $13,200.00 | |

* Italicized values denote a decentralized, vertically-integrated system; these values are zero in a centrally-managed system.

Now compare the results of Table 2.7 with results reported in earlier Tables that were derived under the assumption $f_i = \$0 = f_j$. Specifically, compare:

- The vertically-integrated results reported in Tables 2.2 and 2.7;
- The menu results reported in Tables 2.4 and 2.7; and
- The sophisticated Stackelberg results reported in Tables 2.3 and 2.7.

Wholesale and retail prices, as well as quantities, of a vertically-integrated system and of the channel-coordinating menu are unaffected by the illustrated differences in retailer fixed costs. More generally, the external performance characteristics of a *coordinated* channel are unaffected by the level of fixed costs *provided* channel breadth remains constant. However, fixed costs do influence the distribution of profit. The manufacturer is able to extract all profit from both retailers with the menu when $(f_i - f_j) = \$2,600$. This is impossible at any $(f_i - f_j) < \$2,556.79$. The manufacturer acquires all channel profit only when defection is not a problem; that is, if $(f_i - f_j) \geq \$2,556.79$. Up to that level the impact of an increase in $f_i$ falls exclusively on the $i^{th}$ retailer. (Chapter 8 provides a complete description of the ways in which changes in $(f_i - f_j)$ influence the profitability of each channel member.)

Under the sophisticated Stackelberg tariff, the difference in fixed costs influences retail quantities as well as retail and wholesale prices. As $(f_i - f_j)$ increases from \$0 to \$2,600, channel profit declines by \$2,600, but manufacturer profit declines by only \$225. As with the menu, the $i^{th}$ retailer bears most of the impact of its fixed-cost increase. In fact, the $i^{th}$ retailer suffers all the fixed cost increase up to \$2,300, with the manufacturer absorbing an increasing portion of the rise in fixed costs above this level. For the first \$100 increase in $f_i$ above \$2,300, the manufacturer's profit falls by \$25; the next \$100 reduces manufacturer profit by \$75, and then by \$125. These reductions in manufacturer profit reflect the ever-rising subsidy necessary to ensure channel participation by both retailers.

Finally, the manufacturer prefers the sophisticated Stackelberg tariff to either the menu or the quantity-discount schedule at all values of the $i^{th}$ retailer's fixed cost up to $f_i = \$2,543.69$. When the fixed costs of the $i^{th}$ retailer exceed \$2,543.69, the manufacturer prefers the menu. This example illustrates the following principle, which we will formally establish in later Chapters: when retailers are not identical, the optimal wholesale-price strategy depends on the demand conditions facing the retailers and on their variable and fixed costs. The assumption of identical competitors prevents marketing scientists from evaluating the potentially substantial impact of asymmetry on marketing decisions. We show in later Chapters that the identical-competitors assumption yields results that are trivial when evaluated against the range of possibilities that arise under asymmetric competition. Thus the belief that an identical-competitor model is a reasonable approximation of a model with asymmetric competitors is a Myth, one that we refer to as the *Identical-Competitors Meta-Myth*.

# 5 COMMENTARY

A careful reading of the extensive literature on *bilateral-monopoly models* reveals a small number of repeating themes. Foremost among them is the belief that "channel coordination" can benefit both channel members through the sharing of maximal channel profit. Determining how to achieve coordination occupied some of the finest economic minds for an extended period; it has recently attracted substantial attention among marketing scientists. The core challenge for early economists was that, with a constant per-unit wholesale price but no fixed fee, vertical-channel relationships which led to channel coordination entailed a profit distribution that was inherently arbitrary from the modeler's perspective. Conversely, vertical-channel relationships that led to a definitive profit distribution did not coordinate the channel. Economists and marketing scientists eventually completed their quest by deducing that a multi-part tariff can permit coordination with a definitive profit distribution.

A second repeating theme is the belief that fixed costs can be safely ignored, probably because they have a minimal impact in a bilateral-monopoly model. A third theme is that bilateral-monopoly models can be tweaked (supposedly "at no loss of generality") to address complex issues related to competition between channels, manufacturers, and retailers. A fourth theme is that an identical-competitors model, or a model with passive "fringe" competitors, can be used to assess intra-level rivalries between manufacturers or retailers, again "at no loss of generality." The continual recurrence of the same themes calls to mind the words of Aristotle, "It is not once nor twice but times without number that the same ideas make their appearance in the world."[17]

An unfortunate consequence of this repetitive cycle of mutually reinforcing bilateral-monopoly and independent-competitors models is that a set of beliefs have arisen that do not generalize beyond the realms within which they were fashioned. We discovered these beliefs, which we term Channel Myths, because we have taken an approach to modeling that entails adhering to four elementary modeling criteria: "first principles," "empirical evidence," "nested models," and "strategic endogeneity." The first-principles criteria ensured that our results would be logically consistent. The empirical-evidence criteria drove our realistic development of models of multiple, non-identical retailers that are comparably treated by the upstream firm.[18] The nested-models criteria enabled us to make ready comparisons across models. The strategic-endogeneity criteria encouraged us to solve for the optimal level of variables that are under managerial control, but that have routinely been treated as exogenous by many researchers.

Modeling non-identical retailers has enabled us to develop a series of analytical models that extend our comprehension of distribution channels. Our proofs in the following Chapters reveal that much of what is known about distribution channels is valid in a bilateral-monopoly model but is *not* robust to the inclusion of a second, non-identical retailer. An example is the widespread belief that channel coordination is in the best interest of all channel members. We demonstrated in this Chapter, via simple, numerical illustrations, that the manufacturer often prefers non-coordination even though coordination is both legal and feasible. The efficacy of coordination is a myth; we call it the Channel-Coordination Strategic Myth. We also showed that modeling competitors as identical (the Identical-Competitors Meta-Myth), or *not* modeling fixed costs (the Fixed-Cost Modeling Myth), induce serious distortions in the results that are obtained. Collectively, these Myths point to the bilateral-monopoly model as a limited source of inspiration for analytical, distribution channels research but as a rich source of misdirection. In the words of Artemus Ward, "It ain't so much the things we don't know that get us into trouble. It's the things we do know that just ain't so."[19] We hope that, by the end of this monograph, readers will have an excellent grasp of what we actually now know about distribution channels.

## Notes

[1] The concept, but not the term, dates from Cournot (1838); he focused on "complementary monopolists" who sold in fixed proportions. Thus the monopoly producer of zinc and the monopoly producer of copper form a "bilateral monopoly" as they sell their outputs to competitive producers of brass. The fact that zinc and copper are used in specific, fixed proportions is critical, for it ensures that neither monopolist can gain volume from the other via a price cut. It is in both their interests to act in concert so as to maximize their combined profit. The modern notion of "successive monopolists" seems to be due to Jevons (1871). The classic example involves a sole miner of iron ore who sells to the single smelter of steel; neither party can survive without the other. Fixed proportions are not required, but they are commonly assumed.

[2] To understand the concept of "ophelimity" we turn to Pareto: "We will say that the members of a collectivity enjoy *maximum ophelimity* in a certain position when it is impossible to find a way of moving from that position very slightly in such a manner that the ophelimity enjoyed by each of the individuals of that collectivity increases or decreases. That is to say, any small displacement in departing from that position necessarily has the effect of increasing the ophelimity which certain individuals enjoy, and decreasing that which others enjoy; of being agreeable to some, and disagreeable to others" (1906). The "position" to which Pareto refers is a point on the contract curve. These are the set of economically efficient points defined by equality of marginal rates of substitution between two goods or equality of marginal rates of technical substitution between two inputs. The "marginal rates" terminology is well-known by those who studied Edgeworth-Bowley box diagrams in undergraduate economics classes.

[3] In Stackelberg equilibrium the monopolists move sequentially with the leader going first. Implicit in the mathematics is that the leader has perfect foresight as to the follower's response to the leader's action; but the follower "cannot see beyond his nose." This contrasts with the tâtonnement process of Cournot equilibrium in which duopolists make their quantity decisions simultaneously.

[4] A monotonically decreasing quantity-discount schedule is *implicitly* an all-or-nothing offer since each quantity is associated with a unique price. A two-part tariff is not an all-or-nothing offer since it specifies a wholesale price, but not an associated quantity.

[5] Constant costs are common in the marketing science literature on distribution channels. The reason is that the focus is on appreciating the effects of channel structure rather than discerning the effect of non-constant returns to scale. We demonstrate in Section 4 below, and prove in Chapters 3-11, that zeroing out fixed costs dramatically distorts results. We relax the fifth assumption in Chapter 4.

[6] Alternative demand curves that are compatible with closed-form solutions are constant elasticity (Moorthy and Fader 1990) and rectangular. The latter eliminates price sensitivity, a feature that seems incompatible with the frequent price-promotions that are known to characterize much of retailing. Some shortcomings of the former were discussed in Chapter 1, endnote 24. To those comments we add that constant-elasticity demand is incompatible with closed-form solutions when there is more than one participant at any level of the channel.

[7] We have altered the Jeuland-Shugan notation to conform to our notation.

[8] In principle $\alpha$ could be set outside the unit interval; then the acceptable range of $\{\alpha, \phi\}-$values would be bounded by parallel lines stretching from $+\infty \to -\infty$ on the $\phi-$dimension. Profit distribution would be indeterminate in the acceptable range.

[9] When $\alpha = 1$, the profits (2.3.66)-(2.3.68) replicate the results of a manufacturer Stackelberg leadership game. When $\alpha = 2/3$, the Nash results arise. Retailer Stackelberg leadership cannot be reproduced from the wholesale-price schedule (2.3.57).

[10] A quantity-discount schedule is a three-part tariff; its first part is marginal production cost (C). In our illustration $C = 0$, so in our compressed notation this schedule is $\{0, \alpha, \phi\}$.

[11] By convention, the rule first developed by William of Ockham (1288-1347) is known as *Occam*'s razor. We have been unable to ascertain the reason for the existence of two spellings of his name.

[12] Our use of the term *Meta-Myth* denotes a belief which is so powerful that it colors the way in which a problem is viewed. A Meta-Myth circumscribes how modelers construct models *and* encourages extending insights beyond the carefully delimited realm of a specific model within which they are accurate. Meta-Myths encompass both Modeling Myths and Strategic Myths.

[13] Section 2(a) of the Robinson-Patman Act "... prohibits sellers from charging different prices to different buyers for similar products where the effect might be to injure, destroy, or prevent competition, in either the buyers' or sellers' markets" (Monroe 1990, p. 394).

[14] A manufacturer may use several wholesale-price schedules, each intended for a set of retailers. As long as a set comprises multiple, non-identical retailers our core point holds: separate deals are *not* cut with individual retailers; that is, retail outlets.

[15] Since a non-collusive Nash equilibrium will not coordinate the channel, we do not investigate it here.

[16] There is also a limit on the fixed fee that is imposed by the retailer's "participation constraint."

[17] This quotation is from Aristotle's *On the Heavens*; the translation is by Heath (1931, p. 205).

[18] The empirical evidence criterion conforms to Occam's second principle (realism). We also conform to Occam's first principle (simplicity) by confining our analyses to two competitors.

[19] Charles Farrar Brown (1834-1867), a humorist who wrote under the *nom de plume* of Artemus Ward, was a columnist for the *Cleveland Plain Dealer*; and then an editor for *Vanity Fair* and *Punch*. The quotation is from *Encyclopedia Britannica*.

# Channels without Competition

*"If a man will begin with certainties, he shall end in doubts;*
*but if he will be content to begin with doubts, he shall end in certainties."*

In Chapters 3 and 4 we examine two generalizations of the bilateral-monopoly model that assume one or more retailers with exclusive territories.[1] The model in Chapter 3 assumes multiple retailers and demand certainty; that is, each retailer faces a single state-of-nature. In contrast, the model in Chapter 4 features a single retailer that confronts multiple states-of-nature. Thus, the models in this Segment of the monograph—to borrow from the language of science fiction—focus on separate dimensions of the space-time continuum.

Together the models in this Segment permit us to examine the impact on manufacturer profits of variations in (i) geographic channel breath and (ii) temporal channel breadth. These models also allow us to illustrate several Strategic and Modeling Myths that have arisen in the marketing science literature on distribution channels:

- The Channel-Coordination Strategic Myth;
- The Channel-Breadth Modeling Myth;
- The Multiple-Retailers/Multiple States-of-Nature Modeling Myth;
- The Fixed-Cost Modeling Myth;
- The Bilateral-Monopoly Meta-Myth; and
- The Identical-Competitors Meta-Myth.

The *Channel-Coordination Strategic Myth* is actually a set of beliefs or sub-Myths involving the consequences of channel coordination for the level of channel profits, the division of those profits, and design of the manufacturer's wholesale-price policy. The Profit-Maximization sub-Myth is the belief that a coordinated channel replicates the profit of a vertically-integrated system. We show in Chapter 3 that a vertically-integrated system encompasses more retail outlets than does a manufacturer/independent-retailers channel. Although a multiple-retailers channel can be coordinated, a channel-coordinating wholesale-price policy does not reproduce the profit of a vertically-integrated system because it does not lead to the same channel breadth. A comparable analysis holds for Chapter 4.

The Profit-Allocation sub-Myth is the belief that channel profit can be (re)allocated to make all members of the channel better off than they would be without coordination. We show in Chapter 3 that comparable treatment of multiple retailers places limits on profit reallocation. We also show in

Chapter 4 that uncertainty imposes limits on the manufacturer's ability to extract profit from the retailer.

The Channel-Pricing sub-Myth is the belief that a properly specified wholesale-price policy (a quantity-discount schedule, a quantity-surplus schedule, or a two-part tariff) will coordinate the channel. We prove in both Chapters that only a properly specified two-part tariff is compatible with coordination in the presence of comparable treatment of multiple, non-competing retailers or multiple states-of-nature.

The *Channel-Breadth Modeling Myth* is a belief that exogenous specifications of channel breadth do not affect substantive conclusions drawn from a model. In this Segment of the monograph, we prove that the manufacturer's optimal wholesale-price policy cannot be separated from the manufacturer's channel-breadth decision. As a result, the pricing implications generated by the bilateral-monopoly model cannot be generalized to the models examined in Chapters 3 and 4.

The *Multiple-Retailers/Multiple States-of-Nature Modeling Myth* is the belief that the models of Chapters 3 and 4 are mirror images. A simple illustration proves that this is not the case. In a multiple-retailer model the profitability of the $j^{th}$ retailer is independent of the pricing decisions of the $i^{th}$ retailer, because the retailers do not compete. However, in a multiple states-of-nature model, the retail profit earned in the $i^{th}$ state-of-nature can be used to subsidize losses in the $j^{th}$ state-of-nature. We show in Chapter 4 that such losses—which are to be expected in some states-of-nature—are tolerated specifically because they are offset by the net revenues attained in more prosperous states-of-nature.

The *Fixed-Cost Modeling Myth* is the belief that the manufacturer-optimal wholesale price is independent of fixed costs at retail. We prove in Chapter 3 that fixed costs have a substantial impact on the channel's geographic breadth. In Chapter 4 we show that fixed costs affect a channel's temporal breadth and a manufacturer's optimal wholesale price.

The *Bilateral-Monopoly Meta-Myth* is the belief that a bilateral-monopoly model is a non-distorting simplification of more complex models. We prove quite emphatically that this is not the case. In fact, the standard bilateral-monopoly results collapse under the slightest pressure, whether from the introduction of a second (non-competing) retailer or a second (non-competing) state-of-nature. We conclude that a continued reliance on bilateral-monopoly models will block the attainment of an accurate and comprehensive understanding of distribution channels.

The *Identical-Competitors Meta-Myth* is the belief that a model with competitors who are identical is a non-distorting simplification of models that are more complex. We prove that this is not the case. The standard identical-competitors results fail to go through once two competitors are distinguished even to a slight degree. Here, too, we conclude that a continued faith in identical-competitors models will interfere with gaining a full understanding of distribution channels.

We did not grasp these Myths when we began this monograph; indeed, we believed that fixed costs did not matter and that bilateral monopoly was a broadly acceptable modeling approach. It was the analyses presented in this Segment that raised doubts in our minds. Once we were comfortable with our doubts, we became convinced that these and many other widely-held beliefs were wrong and should be identified as Myths. In the words of Sir Francis Bacon, "If a man will begin with certainties, he shall end in doubts; but if he will be content to begin with doubts, he shall end in certainties" (1605; quoted in Devey 1902, p.8).

## Notes

[1] In Chapters 5-9 we cover the case of non-exclusive territories and the associated issue of the degree of inter-retailer competition.

Chapter 3

# Multiple (Exclusive) Retailers[1]

*"It is not from the benevolence of the butcher, the brewer, or the baker, that we expect our dinner, but from their regard to their own interest."*

## 1 INTRODUCTION

In this Chapter we extend the bilateral-monopoly model to the case of a single manufacturer that may sell through *any* number of retailers. This extension enables us to explore the manufacturer's *channel-breadth* decision and to identify those bilateral-monopoly results[2] that generalize to a channel with multiple retailers. The analysis in this Chapter is a logical extension of the bilateral-monopoly model described in Chapter 2.

The decision to serve more than one retailer immediately raises two questions. First, how many retailers should the manufacturer serve? Second, should retail territories be exclusive, in which case retailers do not compete, or overlapping, in which case they do compete? Because the presence of inter-retailer competition may change the implications of adding retailers to the channel, we begin by assuming exclusive territories. Thus we focus exclusively on the issue of channel breadth in this Chapter and address inter-retailer competition in Chapters 5-11.[3]

The model presented in this Chapter will resolve six basic questions:

(1) Can all manufacturer/independent-retailer dyads be coordinated if they are all treated comparably?

(2) Is there more than one wholesale-price policy that will coordinate multiple, independent dyads?

(3) Does coordination of every independent-retailer dyad replicate the channel profit attained by a vertically-integrated system?

(4) Is the manufacturer's profit maximized by coordinating all independent-retailer dyads?

(5) Do any independent retailers earn a positive profit? If so, is the profit distribution between channel members endogenously determined?

(6) What is the manufacturer-optimal channel breadth; that is, how many independent retailers should distribute the manufacturer's product?

Before turning to our formal analysis, we consider how the bilateral-monopoly model would answer each question. If the results of this single-retailer model generalize to the case of multiple retailers, we should find that:

1. All manufacturer/independent-retailer dyads can be coordinated.
2. A quantity-discount schedule, a two-part tariff or a quantity-surplus schedule can coordinate each dyad, provided the schedules are properly specified.
3. Coordination maximizes channel profit because it replicates *all* the results of a vertically-integrated system.
4. The manufacturer can extract all economic profit from every retailer provided it offers a "take-it-or-leave-it" wholesale-price policy; hence its own profit will be maximized by coordination.
5. The division of channel profit between manufacturer and retailer is endogenously indeterminate, regardless of whether the channel members negotiate over terms-of-trade or the manufacturer makes a "take-it-or-leave-it" offer.[4]

These tentative answers, which are based on the bilateral-monopoly model, clearly apply when the manufacturer offers a unique wholesale price to each retailer. However, there is empirical evidence that the number of wholesale-price schedules offered by a manufacturer is typically less than the number of retailers served by that manufacturer. The reasons for limited offerings relate to administrative, bargaining, and contract development costs (Lafontaine 1990; Battacharyya and Lafontaine 1995), negative goodwill toward the manufacturer,[5] as well as information acquisition costs and transaction costs (Rey and Tirole 1986).[6] In practice such costs may exceed the manufacturer's potential profit from using differentiated wholesale-price schedules.

We model the manufacturer as treating its retailers comparably by offering all of them the same wholesale-price schedule. This assumption bears directly on the applicability of the insights derived from the bilateral-monopoly model. In particular, we will show that neither a quantity-surplus nor quantity-discount schedule can coordinate a multiple-retailer channel when there are multiple, non-identical retailers. In contrast, a two-part tariff with a zero per-unit wholesale margin does coordinate the channel. However, we will prove that the profit-maximizing manufacturer generally rejects a zero-margin, channel-coordinating tariff in favor of a non-coordinating tariff with positive margin (although a negative margin tariff is also possible).

The decision to offer all retailers a common wholesale-price schedule has three important consequences. First, the manufacturer can extract all profit only from the marginal retailer(s); all others earn a positive economic profit. Second, comparable treatment removes indeterminacy from the division of dyadic profit between the manufacturer and its retailers; there is a specific, endogenously-specified division of every dyad's total profit. Third, comparable treatment complicates the manufacturer's channel-breadth decision. For example, an adjustment in the wholesale price designed to induce one more retailer (the $n^{th}$) to participate in the channel alters the profit that the manufacturer can obtain from the other $(n-1)$ participating retailers. We prove that the profit-maximizing manufacturer operates a channel with fewer retailers than does a vertically-integrated system; thus the performance of a vertically-integrated system *cannot* be replicated by a channel with a manufacturer selling to independent retailers. Surprisingly, there are even some demand curves for which coordination of an independent-retailer channel does not maximize channel profit, and in which channel profit cannot be allocated in a manner which ensures that all channel members prefer coordination to non-coordination.

This Chapter is organized in the following manner. In Section 2 we describe the assumptions underlying our model and we establish baseline results from a vertically-integrated system. In Section 3 we derive the wholesale-price schedule that maximizes channel profit. In Section 4 we derive the wholesale-price schedule that maximizes manufacturer profit. We then show that channel and manufacturer interests generally diverge. Each Section includes a numerical example to illustrate our mathematical results. The final Section provides a summary and observations on the channels literature. Technical definitions are presented in the Appendix.

# 2 THE VERTICALLY-INTEGRATED SYSTEM

In the previous Chapter we derived the retailer price that maximizes channel profit in a vertically-integrated system. We then evaluated several wholesale-price policies in terms of their ability to reproduce the retail price and quantity results obtained by such a channel. In a similar way we will, in this Chapter, use the price decisions of a vertically-integrated system selling through multiple retail outlets as a benchmark for evaluating the decisions of a decentralized manufacturer serving multiple independent retailers. We start with a model consisting of one manufacturer and a number (to be determined) of retail outlets. Because the single decision-maker controls all choice variables—and has sole claim to channel profit—the decision-maker's objective is maximization of channel profit.

## 2.1 Assumptions

We make the following assumptions:

1. Every retail outlet has an exclusive territory.
2. There is no resale of merchandise between retail outlets.
3. There is certainty of variables and functional forms.

4. All decision makers engage in profit-maximizing behavior.
5. Retail demand functions are characterized by the general formulation:

$$Q_i = Q_i(p_i) \tag{3.2.1}$$

subject to:

$$\frac{dQ_i(p_i)}{dp_i} \equiv Q_i'(p_i) < 0 \tag{3.2.2}$$

$$\frac{d^2Q_i(p_i)}{dp_i^2} \equiv Q_i''(p_i) < \left( \frac{2[Q_i'(p_i)]^2}{Q_i(p_i)} \right) \tag{3.2.3}$$

By virtue of Assumption 1, actions taken by the $i^{th}$ retail outlet have no impact on the demand facing other retailers; that is, there is no inter-retailer competition. Assumption 2 precludes a retailer engaging in "diverting" by re-selling merchandise to another vendor at the same level of the channel. Assumptions 3 and 4 are common in the literature; they require no elaboration. Assumption 5 assigns to each retailer a unique downward-sloping demand curve (3.2.2) that satisfies the second-order conditions for a maximum (3.2.3).

## 2.2 Profit Maximization and Optimal Channel Breadth

Let $\Pi_I$ denote the total profit of the integrated system and let $N_I$ be the actual number of retail outlets. The manager of the vertically-integrated system maximizes:

$$\max_{N_I, p_i} \Pi_I = \sum_{i=1}^{N_I} \{(p_i - c_i - C)Q_i(p_i) - f_i\} - F \tag{3.2.4}$$

In expression (3.2.4) the terms C and $c_i$ denote the constant, average variable costs of the manufacturing arm and the $i^{th}$ retail outlet; similarly, F and $f_i$ are their respective fixed costs. We define the latter's fixed costs to include an adequate rate of return (i.e. an opportunity cost) such that the $i^{th}$ retail outlet is shuttered if and only if it loses money. A similar comment holds for fixed costs associated with manufacturing. Note that retail outlets are allowed to have different costs and unique demand schedules that reflect differences in local competitive, demographic, and environmental conditions.

Maximizing profit with respect to $p_i$ yields $N_I$ first-order conditions of the form:

$$\frac{d\Pi_I}{dp_i} = 0 = Q_i(p_i) + (p_i - c_i - C)Q_i'(p_i) \tag{3.2.5}$$

(Inequality (3.2.3) ensures that second-order conditions for a maximum are met.) In order to simplify our presentation we define the price elasticity of demand at the i[th] retail outlet as:

$$\eta_i \equiv -p_i Q_i' / Q_i > 0 \tag{3.2.6}$$

By using definition (3.2.6) in conjunction with equation (3.2.5) we obtain:

$$p_i^* = \frac{(c_i + C)\,\eta_i^*}{(\eta_i^* - 1)} \qquad \text{s.t. } p_i^* > 0 \tag{3.2.7}$$

Optimality is denoted with an asterisk. Optimal prices rise with increases in costs $(c_i, C)$ but fall with increases in elasticities. Prices generally vary across retail outlets due to differences in per-unit costs of distribution $(c_i)$ and demand elasticities $(\eta_i^*)$.

Insertion of (3.2.7) into profit equation (3.2.4) yields the profit of the vertically-integrated manufacturer:

$$\Pi_I^* = \sum_{i=1}^{N_I} \left\{ \left( \frac{p_i^* Q_i^*(p_i^*)}{\eta_i^*} \right) - f_i \right\} - F \equiv \sum_{i=1}^{N_I} g_i^* - F \tag{3.2.8}$$

We define $g_i^*$ as the net profit contribution of the i[th] retail outlet after accounting for its fixed and opportunity costs.

With regard to channel breadth, we observe that a profit-maximizing, vertically-integrated system will operate an outlet if and only if the outlet's profit contribution $g_i^*$ is positive. Rank all potential outlets by their profit contributions such that:

$$g_1^* \geq g_2^* \geq \cdots \geq g_{N_I^*}^* \geq 0 > g_{N_I^*+1}^* \cdots \tag{3.2.9}$$

A total of $N_I^*$ retail outlets meet the non-negative profit contribution criterion; thus $N_I^*$ is the optimal number of outlets in a vertically-integrated system.

## 2.3 Channel Coordination with Transfer Pricing

The preceding analysis assumes that the manufacturer's central office dictates retail prices. An alternative approach allows the manager of each retail outlet to set prices "independently" in response to a transfer price charged by the manufacturing arm of the integrated system. Each retail manager then maximizes:[7]

$$\max_{p_i} \pi_i = (p_i(T_i) - c_i - T_i) Q_i(p_i(T_i)) - f_i \tag{3.2.10}$$

We write price ($p_i$) as a function of the transfer price ($T_i$), because the retail manager's price decision reflects the wholesale price charged by the central office. Manipulation of the first-order condition reveals:

$$p_i^* = \frac{(c_i + T_i)\eta_i}{(\eta_i - 1)} \tag{3.2.11}$$

Transfer pricing yields the same channel performance as centralized pricing when expressions (3.2.7) and (3.2.11) are equal; this requires $T_i^* = C$. Thus profit maximization in a decentralized system of N non-competing retail outlets requires a common transfer price that is equal to marginal production cost (C). Intuitively, profit maximization in a vertically-integrated system requires every retail outlet to set its marginal revenue $[p_i + Q_i(p_i)/Q_i'(p_i)]$ equal to the dyad's full marginal cost $(c_i + C)$. Because $W = C$ is the requirement for coordination in a bilateral monopoly, this result may seem trivial. We stress its importance for two reasons. First, it extends the bilateral result to the case of multiple retailers that are comparably treated. Second, as we will show in Chapter 5, $T_i^* \neq C$ when the retail outlets are in competition.

Given an optimal transfer price, each retail outlet generates profit of:

$$\pi_i^* = g_i^* \tag{3.2.12}$$

We observe that some amount $\phi_i \leq g_i^*$ can be transferred to corporate headquarters with no impact on the performance of the decentrally-managed retail outlet. Because the transfer-pricing mechanism applies to pricing decisions in an vertically-integrated system, the profit transfer $\phi_i$ may legally differ by retail outlet. Note that the pair $\{T_i^*, \phi_i\} = \{C, \phi_i\}$ takes the form of the two-part tariff described by Moorthy (1987). For this reason, we will use the transfer pricing mechanism to evaluate alternative pricing schemes both in this Chapter and in later Chapters that examine inter-retailer competition.

## 2.4 A Theoretical Illustration

In this sub-Section we provide a theoretical illustration of the results derived above. In the next sub-Section we illustrate our results with specific parametric values. To maintain tractability we assume that the $i^{th}$ potential retail outlet faces a linear-demand curve of the form:[8]

$$Q_i = A_i - bp_i \equiv (A - i\alpha) - bp_i \tag{3.2.13}$$

In equation (3.2.13) the term "i" denotes the $i^{th}$ retailer. Demand across outlets differs only by the intercept term $(A - i\alpha)$.

It is easy to show that the quantity sold by the i[th] vertically-integrated retail outlet is:

$$Q_i^* = \left( \frac{(A - i\alpha) - b(c + C)}{2} \right) \tag{3.2.14}$$

Note that we set $c_i = c$ for all retail outlets; this simplifies our illustrations without materially distorting our results. In order to focus on differences between the retail outlets we recast (3.2.14) in terms of the volume that is common to all retail outlets. That common volume is:

$$Q^* \equiv \left( \frac{A - b(c + C)}{2} \right) \tag{3.2.15}$$

Thus we can rewrite the i[th] retailer's output as:

$$Q_i^* = \left( Q^* - \frac{i\alpha}{2} \right) \tag{3.2.16}$$

Similarly, the channel margin and profit contribution of the i[th] outlet are:

$$\mu_i^* = \left( \frac{Q^* - i\alpha/2}{b} \right) \tag{3.2.17}$$

$$g_i^* = \frac{(Q^* - i\alpha/2)^2}{b} - f_i \tag{3.2.18}$$

The retail price is merely $p_i^* = (\mu_i^* - c - C)$.

It is now simple to show that total profit for the vertically-integrated system is:

$$\begin{aligned} \Pi_I^*(N) &= \sum_{i=1}^{N} g_i^* - F \\ &= \frac{N}{24b} \left\{ \begin{matrix} 24(Q^*)^2 - 12(N+1)\alpha Q^* \\ +(N+1)(2N+1)\alpha^2 \end{matrix} \right\} - \sum_{i=1}^{N} f_i - F \end{aligned} \tag{3.2.19}$$

The expression $\Pi_I^*(N)$ denotes vertically-integrated profit given that N retail outlets are used.

Because N must be an integer, its optimal value must meet the following condition:

$$\{\Pi_I^*(N) - \Pi_I^*(N-1)\} \geq 0 > \{\Pi_I^*(N+1) - \Pi_I^*(N)\} \tag{3.2.20}$$

Expression (3.2.20) states that, for N to be a maximum, increasing the number of outlets from $(N-1)$ to N must not decrease profit, but a further increase in number of outlets to $(N+1)$ must lower total profit.

To determine optimal channel breadth we compare $\Pi_I^*(N)$ with the profit obtained from utilizing $(N-1)$ or $(N+1)$ retail outlets. Performing this exercise reveals:

$$\left[\Pi_I^*(N)-\Pi_I^*(N-1)\right]=\frac{\left(Q^*-N\alpha/2\right)^2}{b}-f_N \tag{3.2.21}$$

$$\left[\Pi_I^*(N+1)-\Pi_I^*(N)\right]=\frac{\left(Q^*-(N+1)\alpha/2\right)^2}{b}-f_{N+1} \tag{3.2.22}$$

Note in each case that the marginal profit of adding an additional retailer is a function of the marginal retailer's fixed costs. In what follows we assume that this pair of equations satisfies the relationship defined by expression (3.2.20).

Setting (3.2.21) equal to zero and solving yields optimal channel breadth as:

$$N_I^* = \text{Integer}\left(2\left(Q^*-\sqrt{bf_N}\right)/\alpha\right) \tag{3.2.23}$$

Note that the value of $N_I^*$ must be rounded down to an integer. Even when $N_I^*$ is an integer, an adjustment may be required, because the output of the $(N_I^*)^{th}$ retail outlet is:

$$Q_{N_I^*}^* = \sqrt{bf_{N_I^*}} \tag{3.2.24}$$

When fixed costs are zero, the outlet has no sales, which violates our assumption that each outlet has positive sales $(Q_N^* > 0)$. Thus when $f_N = 0$, the actual, optimal number of outlets is (i) the integer component of (3.2.23) if $N_I^*$ is not an integer or (ii) $(N_I^*-1)$ if $N_I^*$ is an integer but $Q_N^* = 0$. To simplify subsequent discussions of our Theoretical Illustrations, we set $f_i \equiv f \ \forall \ i \in (1,\infty)$; that is, we restrict each outlet to having the same value of f, which is the sum of the retailer's fixed and opportunity costs.

## 2.5 A Numerical Illustration

To illustrate the functional form used in Section 2.4 we assign to the parameters the following numerical values:

$$A = 101,\ \alpha = 1,\ c_i = \$10 = C, \text{ and } f_i = \$0 \ \forall \ i \in \left(1,(N+1)\right) \tag{3.2.25}$$

Thus demand faced by the $i^{th}$ retail outlet is:

$$Q_i = \left(101-i\right)-bp_i \tag{3.2.26}$$

It follows that the common level of output is:

$$Q^* = (50.5 - 10b) \tag{3.2.27}$$

Using the substitution (3.2.27) in the defining equations (3.2.14), (3.2.17), and (3.2.18) reveals that the price, quantity, and profit contribution of the $i^{th}$ vertically-integrated retail outlet are:

$$\begin{aligned} p_i^* &= \left[(101-i)+20b\right]/2b \equiv \left[Q^* - 0.5i + 20b\right]/b \\ Q_i^* &= \left[(101-i)-20b\right]/2 \equiv \left(Q^* - 0.5i\right) \qquad \text{s.t. } Q_i^* > 0 \\ g_i^* &= \left[(101-i)-20b\right]^2/4b \equiv \left(Q^* - 0.5i\right)^2/b \end{aligned} \tag{3.2.28}$$

Combining (3.2.23) with (3.2.27) gives the optimal number of retail outlets for a vertically-integrated channel:

$$N_I^* = (101 - 20b) \tag{3.2.29}$$

The optimal number of outlets declines with increases in the slope of the demand curve (b). In addition, quantity and profit contribution also decline as b increases, and profit contribution falls with increases in fixed costs.

To illustrate these results, let $b = 1$, which implies that $N_I = 81$. However since the $81^{st}$ outlet has zero sales the optimal number of viable, vertically-integrated retail outlets is $N_I^* = 80$. Total profit of the integrated firm is \$43,470, and the profit contributions of the individual retail outlets ranges from \$0.25 to \$1,600. We present results for other values of the slope parameter b in Section 4, Table 3.1. That Table shows that an increase in b—an increase in price sensitivity—decreases the number of retail outlets and channel profit.

# 3 CHANNEL COORDINATION WITH INDEPENDENT RETAILERS

A channel dyad is said to be coordinated if the independent retailer sets a retail price that maximizes dyadic profit. Dyadic coordination occurs if the manufacturer sets a wholesale price that causes the retailer's full marginal cost to equal the dyad's total marginal cost. In this Section we seek a single wholesale-price schedule that simultaneously coordinates all the dyads.

We model the relationships between a manufacturer and its N independent retailers (N to be determined) as a set of independent, two-stage games. In the first stage the manufacturer offers a single wholesale-price schedule to all retailers on a "take-it-or-leave-it" basis. In the second stage each retailer decides whether to participate in the channel and, if it does participate, what retail price to charge consumers. This price determines the quantity each retailer orders and, consequently, its profit.

To retain as much generality as possible we define the wholesale-price schedule as $W(Q_i(p_i))$; thus we allow the per-unit wholesale price to be a function of the quantity demanded by a retailer. This is compatible with a quantity-discount schedule (Jeuland and Shugan 1983), a two-part tariff (Moorthy 1987), or a quantity-surplus schedule (Moorthy 1987).

## 3.1 The Second Stage of the Game: The Typical Retailer's Pricing Decision

To determine the optimal solution we first solve for a typical retailer's pricing decision in the second stage of the game. The $i^{th}$ retailer's profit function is:

$$\max_{p_i} \pi_i = \left[p_i - c_i - W\left(Q_i\left(p_i\right)\right)\right]Q_i\left(p_i\right) - f_i \tag{3.3.1}$$

The first-order condition for profit maximization is:

$$\frac{d\pi_i}{dp_i} = 0 = \begin{pmatrix} Q_i\left(p_i\right) - W'Q_i'\left(p_i\right)Q_i\left(p_i\right) \\ +\left[p_i - c_i - W\left(Q_i\left(p_i\right)\right)\right]Q_i'\left(p_i\right) \end{pmatrix} \tag{3.3.2}$$

where:

$$W' \equiv \left(\frac{dW\left(Q_i\left(p_i\right)\right)}{dQ_i\left(p_i\right)}\right) \tag{3.3.3}$$

and $Q_i'(p_i)$ is defined at expression (3.2.2). The optimal price $\hat{p}_i$ is:

$$\hat{p}_i = \frac{\left[c_i + W + W'Q_i'\left(\hat{p}_i\right)\right]\hat{\eta}_i}{\left(\hat{\eta}_i - 1\right)} \tag{3.3.4}$$

The hats ("^") in this and subsequent equations denote optimal values in the independent-retailers case *given* the wholesale-price schedule $W(Q_i(p_i))$.

## 3.2 The First Stage of the Game: The Manufacturer's Wholesale-Price Decision

We now turn to the first stage of the game. Our objectives are (i) to devise a wholesale-price schedule that is common to all retailers *and* that coordinates every dyad, and (ii) to maximize the manufacturer's profit by optimizing the number of retailers who participate in the channel.

To coordinate the channel, the $i^{th}$ retailer's first-order condition (3.3.2) must be equal to the vertically-integrated retail outlet's first-order condition (3.2.5). This will only occur if the retailer's marginal purchase cost

$(W + W'Q_i(p_i))$ equals the manufacturer's marginal production cost (C) at the optimal output level ($Q_i^*$).

### 3.2.1 Coordination: Determining the Per-Unit Wholesale Price

A wholesale-price schedule that is common to all retailers and that generates coordination for *all* participating retailers, no matter their demand schedules or costs, is the two-part tariff:[9]

$$W(Q_i(p_i)) = \left( C + \frac{\phi_C}{Q_i(p_i)} \right) \equiv \{C, \phi_C\} \tag{3.3.5}$$

In (3.3.5) the term $\phi_C$ is the fixed fee. We denote the schedule (3.3.5) as $\{C, \phi_C\}$. It differs from the wholesale-price schedule $\{C, \phi_i\}$ that would transfer profit from a wholly owned retail outlet to the headquarters of a vertically-integrated system, because the fixed fee $\phi_C$ is *common* to all independent retailers. In contrast, the fixed fee $\phi_i$ differs by retail outlet in a vertically-integrated system. The schedule $\{C, \phi_i\}$ is infeasible if retailers are independent, because it violates the constraint which requires that the manufacturer treat retailers comparably. (The rationale for this constraint is spelled out in Chapter 1 and in the Introduction to this Chapter.) Thus we focus on the common wholesale-price schedule $\{C, \phi_C\}$ as defined by expression (3.3.5).

Because $[W + W'Q_i(p_i)] = C$, we can rewrite the price equation (3.3.4) as:

$$\hat{p}_i^* = \left( \frac{(c_i + C)\,\hat{\eta}_i^*}{\hat{\eta}_i^* - 1} \right) \tag{3.3.6}$$

To obtain the i[th] retailer's profit, we insert expressions (3.3.5) and (3.3.6) into equation (3.3.1), which yields:

$$\hat{\pi}_i^* = \left( \frac{\hat{p}_i^* Q_i^*(\hat{p}_i^*)}{\hat{\eta}_i^*} - f_i \right) - \phi_C \equiv \hat{g}_i^* - \phi_C = g_i^* - \phi_C \tag{3.3.7}$$

The i[th] retailer will voluntarily participate in the channel only when $\hat{\pi}_i^* \geq 0$.

We now state our observation in propositional form:

**Proposition 1:** An independent retailer that purchases goods from a manufacturer at a constant per-unit cost C will charge the same price and will sell the same quantity as it would if it were a retail outlet in a vertically-integrated system. Thus the two-part tariff given by equation (3.3.5) maximizes profit from each participating dyad; that is, each channel dyad is fully coordinated.

**Proof:** Insert the wholesale-price schedule (3.3.5) into the i[th] retailer's profit function (3.3.1). The result is:

$$\pi_i = (p_i - c_i - C)Q_i(p_i) - f_i - \phi_C \tag{3.3.8}$$

This generates the same first-order condition for the i[th] retailer as equation (3.2.4). **QED**

**Corollary 1**: Neither a monotonic quantity-discount schedule nor a monotonic quantity-surplus schedule will coordinate a channel consisting of one manufacturer that sells through N non-competing retailers.

**Proof**: The marginal wholesale price for each retailer must equal the quantity-invariant per-unit production cost (C). Because retailers face different demand schedules and have different costs, their marginal revenues equal C at different outputs. For this reason, neither a monotonic quantity-discount nor a monotonic quantity-surplus wholesale-price schedule is compatible with a marginal wholesale cost that is equal to C at *all* output levels. **QED**

### 3.2.2 Channel Breadth: Determining the Optimal Fixed Fee

While the magnitude of the fixed fee ($\phi_C$) affects neither retail prices nor quantities, it does determine whether a retailer will participate in the channel; that is, it affects channel breadth. Participation occurs if and only if $(g_i^* - \phi_C) \geq 0$. The larger is $\phi_C$, the lower is the number of retailers who voluntarily participate in the channel. Thus the number of participants $N_C$ is a non-increasing function of $\phi_C$:

$$N_C \equiv N_C(\phi_C), \qquad \frac{\delta N_C}{\delta \phi_C} \leq 0 \tag{3.3.9}$$

"δ" denotes the rate of change in the number of retailers (a discrete variable).

A channel-coordinating manufacturer sets its per-unit wholesale price equal to its constant marginal production cost. As a result, the manufacturer's sole source of revenue is $\phi_C$:

$$\Pi = N_C(\phi_C)\phi_C - F \tag{3.3.10}$$

Because expression (3.3.10) is a function of a discrete variable, it has several interesting properties.

When $\phi_C = 0$, channel breadth is identical to that obtained in vertically-integrated case $(N_C^* = N_I^*)$, but manufacturer profit is negative $(-F)$. Therefore, the manufacturer will not offer the tariff $\{C, \phi_C\} = \{C, 0\}$. As $\phi_C$ rises, manufacturer profit rises until a retailer "drops out" of the channel. At this point the manufacturer's profit falls discontinuously. A further increase in $\phi_C$ again raises manufacturer profit until another retailer drops out. This pattern continues until we reach a unique fixed fee (call it $\overline{\phi}_C$) such that no retailers remain in the channel. The value of $\overline{\phi}_C$ is identical to the pre-fixed fee profitability of the most-profitable (the 1st) retailer ($\overline{\phi}_C = g_1^*$). At this fixed fee level manufacturer profit is again $-F$. Thus the manufacturer's profit function iteratively increases and declines, so that it resembles a serrated-edge parabola as in Figure 3.1. The profit-maximizing manufacturer will always choose to be on a point of this saw-tooth surface by extracting all profit from the "marginal" retailer—leaving it with revenue just sufficient to cover all its costs, including its opportunity cost.

Consistent with Assumption 4, the manufacturer will select the fixed fee $\phi_C$ maximizes its own profit, which is given by equation (3.3.10).[10] Thus the optimal value of $\phi_C$ satisfies:

$$\frac{\delta\Pi}{\delta\phi_C} = N_C\left(\phi_C^*\right) + \phi_C^*\left(\frac{\delta N_C\left(\phi_C^*\right)}{\delta\phi_C^*}\right) \leq 0 \qquad (3.3.11)$$

Because the number of retailers must be an integer, it may not be possible to set $\delta\Pi_M / \delta\phi_C$ precisely equal to zero. For this reason, we characterize the optimum as $\delta\Pi_M / \delta\phi_C \leq 0$.[11]

We now define the elasticity $\varepsilon_C^*$ as the percentage change in the number of retailers participating in the channel with respect to a percentage change in the fixed fee:

$$\varepsilon_C^* \equiv -\left(\frac{\phi_C^*}{N_C\left(\phi_C^*\right)}\right)\left(\frac{\delta N_C\left(\phi_C^*\right)}{\delta\phi_C^*}\right) \qquad (3.3.12)$$

Using this definition, equation (3.3.11) can then be rewritten as:

$$N_C^*\left(\phi_C^*\right)\left(1-\varepsilon_C^*\right) \leq 0 \qquad (3.3.13)$$

Manufacturer profit maximization—subject to the constraint of coordinating all participating dyads—requires $\varepsilon_C^* \geq 1$, which occurs at the fixed fee $\phi_C^*$. This leads to a second proposition:

**Proposition 2**: The number of independent retailers choosing to participate in a channel will not exceed, and will generally be less, than the number of retail outlets operated by a vertically-integrated system ($N_I^* \geq N_C^*$).

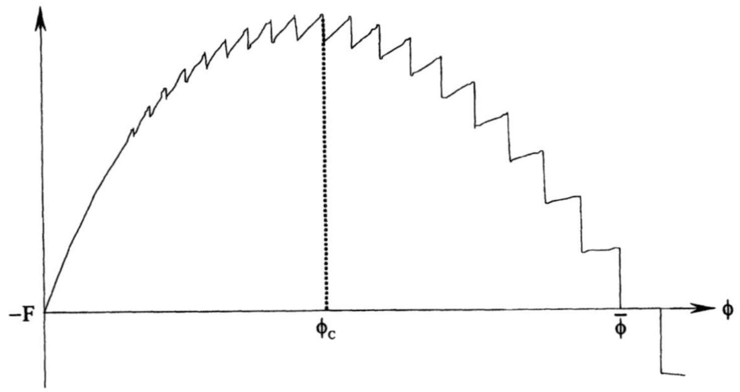


Legend:
$\phi_C \equiv$ The fixed fee component of a channel-coordinating tariff;
$\bar{\phi} \equiv$ The fixed fee at which no independent retailer will participate in the channel;
$F \equiv$ The manufacturer's fixed cost; and
$\Pi \equiv$ The manufacturer's profit $\equiv N_C(\phi_C)\phi_C - F$.

*Figure 3.1.* Manufacturer Profit as a Function of the Fixed Fee

**Proof**: Recall that $N_I^*$ satisfies:

$$g^*_{N_I^*} \geq 0 > g^*_{N_I^*+1} \tag{3.3.14}$$

But in the independent retailer case $N_C^*$ satisfies:

$$g^*_{N_C^*} \geq \phi_C^* > g^*_{N_C^*+1} \tag{3.3.15}$$

If the $(N_C^* + 1)^{st}$ independent retailer does not participate in the channel because the fixed fee is positive rather than zero (i.e., if $\phi_C^* > g^*_{N_C^*+1} > 0$), then $N_C^* < N_I^*$. In contrast, if the $(N_C^* + 1)^{st}$ independent retailer would not participate in the channel even if the fixed fee were zero (that is, if $\phi_C^* = 0 > g^*_{N_C^*+1}$), then the independent channel and the vertically-integrated system would have the same number of retail outlets $(N_C^* = N_I^*)$. **QED**

**Corollary 2.1**: The performance of a coordinated, manufacturer/independent-retailer channel may be lower than the performance of a vertically-integrated system.

**Proof**: Although a retail outlet/independent retailer that participates in both coordinated channels has the same retail price and quantity in both channels, the aggregate performance of the channel with the larger number of retail establishments is superior because it generates a greater total output. **QED**

**Corollary 2.2**: A wholesale-price strategy involving a two-part tariff that is common across retailers fully determines the distribution of channel profit among the manufacturer and the participating retailers.

**Proof**: With a common fixed fee each retailer that participates in the channel nets $(g_i^{*}-\phi_c^{*}) \geq 0$. The manufacturer obtains the remaining channel profit $(\Pi_C^{*} - \sum(g_i^{*}-\phi_c^{*}))$. **QED**

**Observation 2.2**: Corollary 2.2 establishes that a manufacturer Stackelberg leadership game, unlike a Nash game, eliminates the need for an exogenous decision rule to assign channel profit provided there are multiple retailers in the channel.

Figure 3.2 illustrates Proposition 2. The line labeled $g_i^{*}$ depicts the relationship between retail net revenue (profit prior to paying the fixed fee) and the number of retailers.[12] The intersection of $g_i^{*}$ with the horizontal axis defines the number of retail outlets utilized by a vertically-integrated system $(N_I^{*})$. The line labeled $\delta\phi_C$ depicts the marginal relationship between $\delta(N_C\phi_C)/\delta\phi_C$ and the number of independent retailers. The intersection of $\delta\phi_C$ with the horizontal axis occurs at $\varepsilon_C^{*} = 1$; this defines the coordination-constrained number of independent retailers ($N_C^{*}$). The $g_i^{*}$ value at $N_C^{*}$ retailers defines the optimal, coordination-constrained fixed fee $\phi_C^{*}$. This is precisely the fixed fee that leaves the marginal (the $N_C^{*th}$) retailer with zero economic profit.

Intuitively, the vertically-integrated channel operates all retail outlets that generate a non-negative profit contribution. In contrast, independent retailers join the channel if and only if they themselves realize a non-negative profit *after paying* the fixed fee $\phi_C^{*}$. As a consequence, retail profit levels range from zero for the marginal retailer up to $(g_i^{*} - \phi_C)$ for the most-profitable retailer. Therefore the actual distribution of total profit from each dyad is fully determined. (An interesting variation of the preceding analysis occurs when an independent retailer operates multiple outlets. Details are provided in the Appendix to this Chapter.)

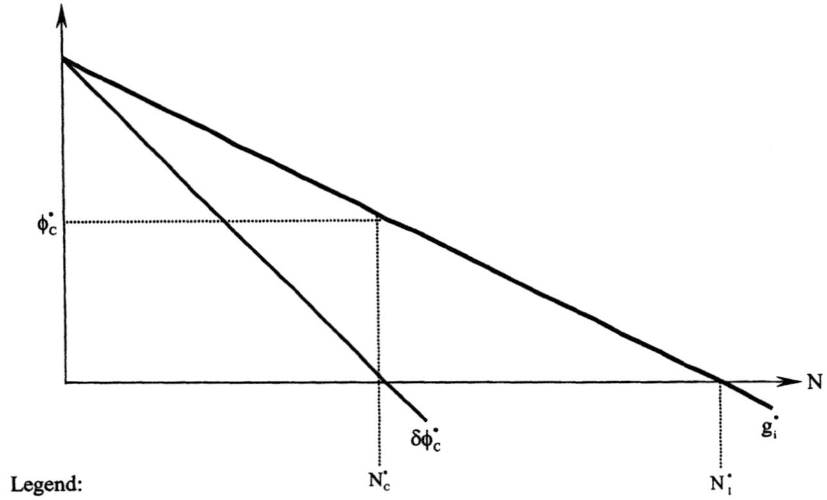


Legend:

$N_C^*$ ≡ The number of retailers with a channel-coordinating tariff;

$N_I^*$ ≡ The number of retailers in a vertically-integrated channel;

$g_i^*$ ≡ The $i^{th}$ retailer's profit prior to paying the fixed fee;

$\phi_C^*$ ≡ The fixed fee component of a channel-coordinating tariff; and

$\delta\phi_C^*$ ≡ The fixed fee change required to compensate for a \$1 change in the per-unit fee.

*Figure 3.2.* Proposition 2 Illustrated:
The Relationship between the Number of Channel Participants and the Fixed Fee

## 3.2 A Theoretical Illustration

We illustrate these results with the illustrative demand curve (3.2.13) used in the previous Section. Given channel coordination with the two-part tariff $\{C, \phi_C\}$, all participating retailers behave exactly as they would if they were part of a vertically-integrated system. The value of $\phi_C$ is equal to the profit of the marginal retailer. Using the approach detailed in equations (3.3.10) and (3.3.11), we find that manufacturer profit equals the number of independent retailers served times the profit of the marginal (the $N_C^{*th}$) retailer. Thus manufacturer profit is:

$$\Pi = N_C \left( \frac{\left(2Q^* - \alpha N_C\right)^2}{4b} - f \right) \tag{3.3.16}$$

In this expression $Q^*$ is defined by (3.2.15). From equation (3.3.16) we see that the manufacturer-optimal channel breadth is:

$$N_C^* = \text{Integer}\left( \frac{4Q^* - 2\sqrt{(Q^*)^2 + 3bf}}{3\alpha} \right) \tag{3.3.17}$$

If fixed costs differ across retailers, the relevant f in the two preceding equations is the fixed cost of the marginal retailer, this is the $N_C^{th}$ firm. We now turn to a numerical illustration of these results.

## 3.3 A Numerical Illustration

Using the same illustrative demand curve and parametric values described earlier (including zero fixed costs), we obtain $\phi_C^* = \$729$, $N_C^* = 27$, and manufacturer profit of $19,683. Channel profit is $30,710.25 while retailer profit ranges from $0 to $871 (after paying the fixed fee). We observe that, although the individual channel dyads are coordinated, channel breadth is narrower than it is in the vertically-integrated system described in Section 2.5. This reflects the theoretical results presented above.

## 3.4 Summary

We have shown that the two-part tariff $\{C, \phi_C^*\}$ maximizes channel profit subject to the constraint of inducing all participating, independent retailers to set channel-coordinating retail prices. This tariff generally leads to a channel of narrower breadth than would occur with vertical integration because the independent retailers must pay a fixed fee for participating in the channel; the retail outlets of a vertically-integrated system do not face this expense. The fixed fee determines the distribution of channel profit between the manufacturer and its retailers with the actual profit division varying by dyad. Only the least-profitable retailer earns a zero economic profit; all others obtain a positive economic rent.

We have proven (at equation (3.3.5)) that neither a single quantity-discount schedule of the form suggested by Jeuland and Shugan (1983), nor a quantity-surplus schedule as suggested by Moorthy (1987), can coordinate a channel comprising one manufacturer and multiple, exclusive retailers.

# 4 MANUFACTURER PROFIT-MAXIMIZATION WITH INDEPENDENT RETAILERS

In this Section we determine whether the manufacturer can obtain a higher profit with a *non*-coordinating two-part tariff $\{W^*, \phi_W^*\}$ than with the coordinating two-part tariff $\{C, \phi_C^*\}$. This analysis is important for two reasons. First, if a *non*-coordinating two-part tariff $\{W^*, \phi_W^*\}$ is manufacturer-optimal, then the bilateral-monopoly principle of dyadic coordination does not extend to a multiple-retailer channel. Second, the manufacturer that prefers a non-coordinating two-part tariff may also prefer a channel breadth that is narrower or wider than the optimal channel breadth under the channel-coordinating two-part tariff.

We divide our analysis in three steps. First, we specify the independent retailer's profit-maximizing response to *any* two-part tariff $\{W, \phi_W\}$. Second, we derive the manufacturer profit-maximizing two-part tariff $\{\hat{W}, \phi_{\hat{W}}\}$ subject to the constraint that precisely $N_C^*$ retailers participate in the channel. That is, we determine if the manufacturer can attain a higher profit with the same number of retailers by offering a non-coordinating tariff $\{\hat{W}, \phi_{\hat{W}}\}$ rather than a coordinating tariff $\{C, \phi_C^*\}$. Third, we relax our constraint on the number of retailers and derive the manufacturer's unconstrained profit-maximizing two-part tariff (it is denoted as $\{W^*, \phi_W^*\}$). While our sequential approach may appear cumbersome, it will help to clarify what would otherwise be a complex set of mathematical conditions.

## 4.1 Retailer Behavior

The i[th] retailer, paying the two-part tariff $\{W, \phi_W\}$, maximizes:

$$\max_{p_i} \pi_i(W, \phi_W) = [p_i(W) - c_i - W] Q_i(p_i(W)) - f_i - \phi_W \tag{3.4.1}$$

In (3.4.1) the term $p_i(W)$ denotes the profit-maximizing retail price, given the wholesale price W. The first-order condition for profit maximization yields a retail price of:

$$p_i(W) = \frac{(c_i + W)\eta_i^W}{(\eta_i^W - 1)} \tag{3.4.2}$$

The term $\eta_i^W$ is demand elasticity evaluated at $p_i(W)$.[13] The i[th] retailer's profit is:

$$\pi_i(W,\phi_W) = \left(\frac{p_i(W)Q_i^W(p_i(W))}{\eta_i^W} - f_i\right) - \phi_W \equiv g_i^W - \phi_W \qquad (3.4.3)$$

The $i^{th}$ retailer participates in the channel if and only if it obtains non-negative profit $(g_i^W \geq \phi_W)$.

## 4.2 Manufacturer Profit Maximization: Constrained Maximization[14]

In this sub-Section we derive a two-part tariff $\{\widehat{W},\phi_{\widehat{W}}\}$ that maximizes manufacturer profit subject to the constraint of retaining precisely $N_C^*$ independent retailers as channel members. (The "flattened hat" above the wholesale price ($\widehat{W}$) denotes this constraint.) We begin by noting that setting $W \neq C$ affects the profitability of every retailer. On one hand, when $W > C$ each retailer earns less than it would at $W = C$; to retain all $N_C^*$ retailers requires a compensating decrease in the fixed fee $(\phi_{\widehat{W}} < \phi_C^*)$. On the other hand, when $W < C$, retailer profit increases, so the manufacturer must raise the fixed fee to keep exactly $N_C^*$ retailers as channel members. Thus the twin goals of manufacturer profit maximization and retention of the least-profitable (the $N_C^{*th}$) retailer as a channel member requires that any alteration in the wholesale price from its initial value of C be accompanied by a compensating change in the fixed fee.

We start by defining the fixed fee that retains the $N_C^{*th}$ retailer. Rank the retailers by their net profit (given $W \neq C$) while heeding the retention requirement:

$$g_1^{\widehat{W}} > g_2^{\widehat{W}} > \cdots > g_{N_C^*}^{\widehat{W}} = \phi_{\widehat{W}} > g_{N_C^*+1}^{\widehat{W}} > \cdots \qquad (3.4.4)$$

To define the requisite compensating change in the fixed fee we totally differentiate the $N_C^{*th}$ retailer's profit equation (3.4.1) and invoke the retailer's first-order condition:

$$\left(\partial\pi_{N_C^*}^{\widehat{W}} / \partial p_i\right) dp_i = 0 = -Q_{N_C^*}^{\widehat{W}}\, d\widehat{W} - d\phi_{\widehat{W}} \qquad (3.4.5)$$

By rearranging terms we obtain:

$$\frac{d\phi_{\widehat{W}}}{d\widehat{W}} = -Q_{N_C^*}^{\widehat{W}} \qquad (3.4.6)$$

Expression (3.4.6) defines the fixed fee adjustment that is necessary to compensate for a marginal change in the per-unit wholesale price so that the marginal—the least-profitable—retailer breaks even.

Given the preceding analysis the manufacturer's total profit from serving $N_C^*$ retailers is composed of a per-unit payment (a markup or markdown from cost C) and a fixed-fee payment:

$$\max_{W} \Pi(\widehat{W}) = (\widehat{W} - C)\sum_{i=1}^{N_C^*} Q_i^{\widehat{W}} + N_C^* \phi_{\widehat{W}} - F \tag{3.4.7}$$

In equation (3.4.7) the quantity term is defined as $Q_i^{\widehat{W}} \equiv Q_i(p_i(\widehat{W}))$. Equation (3.4.7) is a function of a single variable $\widehat{W}$ because the fixed fee is determined by the constraint of retaining $N_C^*$ retailers in the channel. Maximizing (3.4.7) while substituting $-Q_{N_C^*}^{\widehat{W}^*}$ for $d\phi_{\widehat{W}} / d\widehat{W}$ yields:

$$\frac{d\Pi(\widehat{W})}{d\widehat{W}} = 0 = \sum_{i=1}^{N_C^*} Q_i^{\widehat{W}^*} + (\widehat{W}^* - C)\sum_{i=1}^{N_C^*} \frac{dQ_i^{\widehat{W}^*}}{d\widehat{W}^*} - N_C^* Q_{N_C^*}^{\widehat{W}^*} \tag{3.4.8}$$

In this expression the asterisks denote optimal values.

Algebraic manipulation reveals that the optimal wholesale markup is:

$$(\widehat{W}^* - C) = \left( \frac{(1 - S_{N_C^*} N_C^*)}{E_{N_C^*} - (1 - S_{N_C^*} N_C^*)} \right) C \tag{3.4.9}$$

In (3.4.9) $S_{N_C^*}$ is the *marginal* retailer's share of total unit sales and $E_{N_C^*}$ is the aggregate derived demand elasticity of sales with respect to a change in the per-unit fee—evaluated at the optimal value $\widehat{W}^*$. (Equation (3.A.3) and equation (3.A.4) of the Appendix formally define these terms.)

The manufacturer's profit-maximizing two-part tariff $\{\widehat{W}^*, \phi_{\widehat{W}^*}^*\}$ is defined by equations (3.4.4) and (3.4.9). It has been derived under the assumption that precisely $N_C^*$ retailers participate in the channel. What remains to be seen is the relationship between this wholesale-price schedule and the channel-coordinating schedule $\{C, \phi_C^*\}$.

## 4.3 A Comparison of $\{\widehat{W}^*, \phi^*_{\widehat{W}^*}\}$ and $\{C, \phi^*_C\}$

Equation (3.4.9) defines the relationship between $\hat{W}^*$ and C. This equation, which appears to be complex, has a relatively straightforward interpretation. To simplify our presentation we assume that the denominator is positive $[E_{N^*_C} - (1 - S_{N^*_C} N^*_C)] > 0$.[15] When $(1 - S_{N^*_C} N^*_C) = 0$, it immediately follows that $\hat{W}^* = C$. This result, which mimics that obtained in the preceding Section, occurs if the least-profitable retailer's share of total channel sales ($S_{N^*_C}$) equals the average retailer's share of total channel sales $(1/N^*_C)$; clearly $(1 - S_{N^*_C} N^*_C) = 0$ in the special case of $N^*_C = 1$. Thus the bilateral-monopoly model is embedded as a special case in the model examined here. In addition, equation (3.4.9) extends the bilateral-monopoly wholesale price result to the case of multiple, non-competing retailers under a very restrictive assumption: the least-profitable retailer's share of total channel sales exactly equals the average retailer's share. While the tariff $\{C, \phi^*_C\}$ does maximize manufacturer profit in this special case, in general $S_{N^*_C} \neq 1/N^*_C$, so $\{C, \phi^*_C\}$ typically is non-optimal for the manufacturer.

In the "normal" case, the least-profitable retailer has a below average share of sales $(1/N^*_C > S_{N^*_C})$. Under this scenario there is a positive markup $(\widehat{W}^* > C)$ but a smaller compensating fixed fee $\phi^*_{\widehat{W}^*}$ relative to $\phi^*_C$. The increase in the manufacturer's profit due to the positive per-unit markup more than compensates for the lower fixed fee if $(1 - S_{N^*_C} N^*_C) > 0$.

We compare profit for the manufacturer across the two regimes $\{C, \phi^*_C\}$ and $\{\widehat{W}^*, \phi^*_{\widehat{W}^*}\}$ by inserting their optimal values in (3.3.10) and (3.4.7) respectively to reveal:

$$\left(\widehat{W}^* - C\right)\sum_{i=1}^{N^*_C} Q_i^{\widehat{W}^*} > N^*_C\left(\phi^*_C - \phi^*_{\widehat{W}^*}\right), \quad \text{s.t. } S_{N^*_C} < 1/N^*_C \tag{3.4.10}$$

Now consider the possibility that $(1 - S_{N^*_C} N^*_C) < 0$. In this case the manufacturer loses money on each unit sold $(\widehat{W}^* < C)$,[16] but these losses are more than offset by a larger fixed fee $(\phi^*_{\widehat{W}^*} > \phi^*_C)$. Direct comparison of the two tariff regimes gives:

$$N^*_C\left(\phi^*_{\widehat{W}^*} - \phi^*_C\right) > 0 > \left(\widehat{W} - C\right)\sum_{i=1}^{N^*_C} Q_i^{\widehat{W}^*} \quad \text{s.t. } S_{N^*_C} > 1/N^*_C \tag{3.4.11}$$

In summary, if $1/N_C^* \neq S_{N_C^*}$ the manufacturer generally obtains greater profit, while serving the same number of retailers $(N_C^*)$, by offering the constrained optimal tariff $\{\widehat{W}^*, \phi_{\widehat{W}^*}^*\}$ rather than by offering the channel-coordinating tariff $\{C, \phi_C^*\}$. These results lead to a third proposition:

**Proposition 3**: A manufacturer, selling through multiple, exclusive retailers who are comparably treated, generally will *not* coordinate the channel, because it can make more money without coordination than it can with coordination.

**Proof**: If coordination were in the manufacturer's interest the manufacturer-optimal wholesale price $(\widehat{W}^*)$ would equal the channel-coordinating wholesale price (C). Coordination occurs only in the special case in which equation (3.4.9) equals zero. This happens *only* when the least-profitable retailer in the channel sells the same volume as the average retailer. When this condition does not hold, the manufacturer will not coordinate the channel. Thus coordination has a knife-edge property—it holds only at a single point. **QED**

**Corollary 3**: The manufacturer will coordinate a bilateral-monopoly channel or a channel in which all retailers are identical (i.e., in which they have identical demand and identical costs).

**Proof**: With multiple, *identical competitors* all retailers are of average size and all are equally profitable (that is, all of them are marginal retailers). In a bilateral-monopoly channel the one retailer is identical to itself. **QED**

## 4.4 A Theoretical Illustration

We illustrate these results using the theoretical demand curve of equation (3.2.13). The manufacturer's task is to maximize its own profit (3.4.7) subject to retaining $N_C^*$ independent retailers as channel participants. To achieve this end the manufacturer must know each retailer's response function to the wholesale price it faces. This response function is:

$$Q_i\left(\widehat{W}\right) = \left(Q^* - \frac{i\alpha}{2} - \frac{b\left(\widehat{W} - C\right)}{2}\right) \tag{3.4.12}$$

Using expression (3.4.8) in conjunction with (3.4.12) reveals that the constrained optimal per-unit margin for the manufacturer is:

$$\left(\widehat{W}^* - C\right) = \frac{\left(N_C^* - 1\right)\alpha}{2b} \tag{3.4.13}$$

Given this wholesale price, the marginal retailer's profit is:

$$\hat{\pi}^{*}_{N^{*}_{C}} = \frac{\left[4Q^{*} - \left(3N^{*}_{C} - 1\right)\alpha\right]^{2}}{16b} - f \tag{3.4.14}$$

Thus the manufacturer can extract exactly $\hat{\phi}^{*}_{N^{*}_{C}} = \hat{\pi}^{*}_{N^{*}_{C}}$ from all $N^{*}_{C}$ participating retailers. Because the manufacturer earns a positive margin on every unit sold and extracts a fixed fee from every retailer, manufacturer profits are:

$$\hat{\Pi}^{*}\left(\hat{W}^{*}\right) = \left(\frac{N^{*}_{C}}{16b}\right)\begin{pmatrix} 16\left(Q^{*}\right)^{2} - 16\alpha N^{*}_{C}Q^{*} \\ +\left[5\left(N^{*}_{C}\right)^{2} - 2N^{*}_{C} + 1\right]\alpha^{2} \end{pmatrix} - N^{*}_{C}f - F \tag{3.4.15}$$

Finally, channel profit is:

$$\hat{\Pi}^{*}_{C}\left(\hat{W}^{*}\right) = \left(\frac{N^{*}_{C}}{48b}\right)\begin{pmatrix} 48\left(Q^{*}\right)^{2} - 24\alpha\left(N^{*}_{C} + 1\right)Q^{*} \\ +\left[\left(N^{*}_{C}\right)^{2} + 12N^{*}_{C} - 1\right]\alpha^{2} \end{pmatrix} - N^{*}_{C}f - F \tag{3.4.16}$$

We now provide a numerical illustration of these results.

## 4.5 A Numerical Illustration

Continuing with the same assumptions used in Section 2.5, we consider the case of a manufacturer that seeks to maximize its own profit subject to utilizing the channel-coordinating number of independent retailers ($N^{*}_{C} = 27$). In this case the $i^{th}$ retailer pays a wholesale price of $\hat{W}$. We obtain the following expressions for retail price, quantity, and profit:

$$\begin{aligned} p_{i}(\hat{W}) &= \left[\left(101 - i\right) + b\left(10 + \hat{W}\right)\right]/2b \\ Q_{i}(\hat{W}) &= \left[\left(101 - i\right) - b\left(10 + \hat{W}\right)\right]/2 \qquad \text{s.t. } Q_{i}(\hat{W}) > 0 \\ g_{i}(\hat{W}) &= \left[\left(101 - i\right) - b\left(10 + \hat{W}\right)\right]^{2}/4b. \end{aligned} \tag{3.4.17}$$

The profit-maximizing manufacturer, constrained by $N_{\hat{W}} = N^{*}_{C}$, opts for a wholesale price $\hat{W}$ to maximize equation (3.4.7). The optimal $\hat{W}^{*}$ is \$23 when $b = 1$. Given this wholesale price, the fixed fee is less than before: $\phi^{*}_{\hat{W}^{*}} = \$420.25 < \$729.00 = \phi^{*}_{C}$.

By altering the terms of the two-part tariff wholesale price, the manufacturer is able to increase its profit from \$19,683 to \$20,823.75. However, channel profit declines from \$30,710.25 to \$29,569.50. Retailer profit ranges from \$0 to \$702 (after paying the fixed fee). In this numerical example the manufacturer's profit is \$1,140.75 higher *without* coordination than it is with coordination but channel profit is \$1,140.75 lower. Of course, this means that the retailers are collectively worse off by \$2,281.50. This clearly demonstrates that there are conditions under which all channel members do not prefer coordination.

## 4.6 Manufacturer Profit Maximization: Unconstrained Maximization

We have seen that a two-part tariff $\{\widehat{W}^*, \phi^*_{\widehat{W}^*}\}$ generates greater manufacturer profit than does the channel-coordinating schedule $\{C, \phi^*_C\}$ while inducing the same number of independent retailers to participate in the channel. We now relax the constraint that precisely $N^*_C$ retailers must be served and seek the unconstrained profit maximum for the manufacturer. To denote this case we drop the flattened hat above the W. We write the manufacturer's profit as:

$$\max_{W,\phi_W} \Pi(W,\phi_W) = (W - C)\sum_{i=1}^{N_W} Q_i^W + N_W\phi_W - F \tag{3.4.18}$$

where $Q_i^W \equiv Q_i(p_i(W))$ and $p_i(W)$ is defined by equation (3.4.2). In this unconstrained case, a two-part tariff affects manufacturer profit in five ways. (1) The wholesale price W affects how much the manufacturer earns on each unit sold. (2) W also affects the volume $Q_i^W$ purchased by each retailer. (3) W influences whether a specific retailer participates in the channel, and thus influences the number of retailers $N_W$ that participate in the channel. (4) The fixed fee $\phi_W$ obviously affects the common amount paid by each retailer. (5) The fixed fee $\phi_W$ also affects the number of retailers who participate in the channel.

Extending the logic of the previous sub-Section, we simultaneously solve for the optimal values of W and $\phi_W$. Taking the derivative of profit equation (3.4.18) with respect to W, and using condition (3.4.6), we obtain:

$$(W - C) = \left(\frac{\left(1 - S_{N_W} N_W\right)}{E_{N_W} - \left(1 - S_{N_W} N_W\right)}\right) C \tag{3.4.19}$$

Equation (3.4.19) differs from equation (3.4.9) in that the latter is defined for $N^*_C$ retailers, while the current equation holds for any number $N_W$ of retail outlets. Thus $N_W$ is a function of $W$.

We now evaluate the effect of a change in $\phi_W$ on profit. The relevant derivative is:

$$\frac{\delta\Pi(W,\phi_W)}{\delta\phi_W}=\left(\begin{array}{c}\left[\sum_{i=1}^{N_W^*}Q_i^W\frac{\delta W}{\delta N_W}+(W-C)\frac{\delta\Sigma Q_i^W}{\delta N_W}\right]\frac{\delta N_W}{\delta\phi_W}\\+\left(N_W+\phi_W\frac{\delta N_W}{\delta\phi_W}\right)\end{array}\right)\leq 0 \quad (3.4.20)$$

The expression in parentheses on the RHS is the impact of a change in $\phi_W$ on the fixed fee; it is comparable to expression (3.3.10). Because a change in $\phi_W$ may affect the number of participating retailers [the bracketed expression], equation (3.4.20) is the discrete analogue of a derivative of a continuous function. Discreteness implies that it may not be possible to set $\delta\Pi_M/\delta\phi_W$ precisely equal to zero; thus, we characterize the optimum as $\delta\Pi_M/\delta\phi_W\leq 0$.

Converting equation (3.4.20) to an elasticity format yields:

$$N_{W^*}^*\phi_{W^*}^*\left(1-\varepsilon_{W^*}^*\right)+[\mathbf{A}]\leq 0 \qquad \text{where:} \qquad (3.4.21)$$

$$[\mathbf{A}]\equiv-\varepsilon_{W^*}^*\left[\begin{array}{c}(W^*-C)E\left\{\Sigma Q_i^{W^*},N_{W^*}^*\right\}\\+W^*E\left\{W^*,N_{W^*}^*\right\}\end{array}\right]\sum_{i=1}^{N_{W^*}^*}Q_i^{W^*} \qquad (3.4.22)$$

The non-bracketed expression in (3.4.21) is a transformation of $d(N_W\phi_W)/d\phi_W$. It reflects the marginal impact of a change in $\phi_W$ on the fixed fee component of manufacturer profit; it is analogous to the condition derived for the channel coordinating $\phi_C^*$ in equation (3.3.12).

The three elasticity expressions in definition (3.4.22) are themselves defined in the Appendix at (3.A.5)-(3.A.7). The elasticity of the number of independent retailers with respect to a change in $N_W$ is $\varepsilon_{W^*}^*$; it is comparable to the channel-coordinating elasticity defined at (3.3.11) and is positive. The elasticity of total sales with respect to a change in the number of independent retailers is $E\{\Sigma Q_i^{W^*},N_{W^*}^*\}$; it is also positive. Finally, $E\{W^*,N_{W^*}^*\}$ is the elasticity of W with respect to a change in the number of independent retailers; its sign is indeterminate. (Asterisks signify evaluation at the optimal values of W and $N_W$.)

The bracketed expression [A] in (3.4.22) is a transformation of $d[(W-C)\Sigma Q_i^W]/d\phi_W$; it has not appeared previously. [A] reflects the marginal impact of a change in the fixed fee on the volume-driven component of manufacturer profit. The first term inside the [brackets] is the volume-driven change in the manufacturer's net revenue resulting from a change in the number of participating retailers; its sign, like the sign of $(W^{*}-C)$, depends on the marginal (the least-profitable) retailer's sales volume relative to the average-size retailer's sales volume. The second term inside the [brackets] is the change in manufacturer revenue resulting from a change in $W^{*}$ due to a change in channel breadth; it has an indeterminate sign.

The optimal wholesale price $W^{*}$ is defined as the solution to:

$$\left(W^{*}-C\right)=\left(1-S_{N_W^{*}}N_{W^{*}}^{*}\right)C\Big/\left(E_{N_{W^{*}}^{*}}-\left(1-S_{N_{W^{*}}^{*}}N_{W^{*}}^{*}\right)\right) \qquad (3.4.23)$$

The profit-maximizing two-part tariff $\{W^{*},\phi_{W^{*}}^{*}\}$ must simultaneously satisfy equations (3.4.21) and (3.4.23). These equations are related to ones derived earlier in this Chapter. Equation (3.4.23) is the unconstrained analogue to (3.4.9), which specified the profit-maximizing value of W given $N_W = N_C^{*}$, and equation (3.4.21) is the unconstrained analogue to (3.3.12).

To understand equation (3.4.23) we first consider the special case of $1/N_{W^{*}}^{*} = S_{N_W^{*}}$. In this special case the marginal retailer has unit volume exactly equal to average unit sales for all participating retailers so $W^{*} = C$. The bracketed expression [**A**] in equation (3.4.21) is zero, and all of the manufacturer's revenue is derived from the fixed fee.[17] As we established in Section 3.3, in this channel-coordinating situation the manufacturer maximizes its profit by setting a fixed fee of $\phi_C^{*}$, thereby inducing $N_C^{*}$ retailers to participate in the channel. Thus the tariffs $\{W^{*},\phi_{W^{*}}^{*}\}$ and $\{C,\phi_C^{*}\}$ are identical when $1/N_{W^{*}}^{*} = S_{N_W^{*}}$. Although all dyads are coordinated, channel breadth is narrower than in a vertically-integrated system.

In the more general case $1/N_{W^{*}}^{*} \neq S_{N_W^{*}}$, $W^{*} \neq C$ and the bracketed expression [**A**] may be positive, zero, or negative. Little can be said definitively about the relationship between $N_W^{*}$ and $N_C^{*}$ or the relationship between $\phi_W^{*}$ and $\phi_C^{*}$. We use Figure 3.3 to illustrate this ambiguity graphically. In this Figure the term $g_i^{*}$ depicts retailer net revenue from a coordinated solution; the term $g_i^{W^{*}}$ depicts retailer net revenue from unconstrained, uncoordinated maximization. The curve labeled [**A**], which corresponds to expression (3.4.22), has been drawn as positive. The lines labeled $\delta\phi_W^{*}$ and $\delta\phi_C^{*}$ depict the marginal relationship between profit that is due to the fixed fee ($\delta(N_W\phi_W)/\delta\phi_W$) and profit that is due to channel breadth ($\delta(N_C\phi_C)/\delta\phi_C$). (For comparative purposes we lightly reproduce the curves from Figure 3.2.)

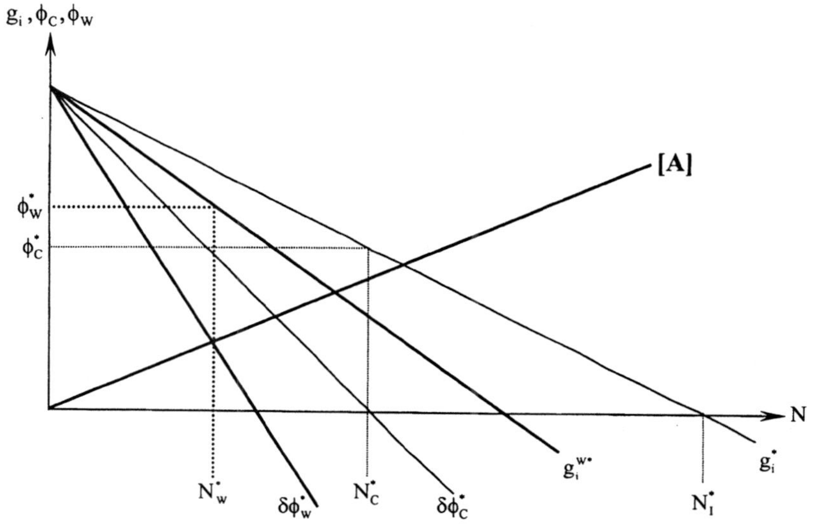


Legend:

$N^*_W$ ≡ The number of retailers when the manufacturer uses a profit-maximizing tariff;

$N^*_C$ ≡ The number of retailers when the manufacturer uses a channel-coordinating tariff;

$N^*_I$ ≡ The number of retailers in a vertically-integrated channel;

$\phi^*_W$ ≡ The fixed fee component of a manufacturer profit-maximizing tariff;

$\phi^*_C$ ≡ The fixed fee component of a channel-coordinating tariff;

$g^*_i$ ≡ The i[th] retailer's pre-fixed fee profit with a channel-coordinating tariff;

$g_i^{W^*}$ ≡ The i[th] retailer's pre-fixed fee profit with a manufacturer profit-maximizing tariff;

[**A**] ≡ The marginal impact of a change in the fixed fee on the volume-driven component of the manufacturer profit; and

$\delta\phi^*_C$ ($\delta\phi^*_W$) ≡ Changes in the fixed fee needed to offset a change in the per-unit fee.

*Figure 3.3.* Profit Maximization When $W^* > C$ is Optimal

To understand the relationship between $N^*_W$ and $N^*_C$ suppose, $S_{N^*_W} < 1/N^*_{W^*}$. Thus $W^* > C$ and the curve $g_i^{W^*}$ lies below the curve $g^*_i$. The intersection of $\delta\phi_W$ with the horizontal axis occurs at $\varepsilon^*_{W^*} = 1$. The intersection of $\delta\phi_W$ with [**A**] defines the optimal number of independent retailers $N^*_{W^*}$, and the value of $g_i^{W^*}$ at $N^*_{W^*}$ determines the manufacturer-optimal fixed fee $\phi^{*}_{W^*}$. Figure 3.3 illustrates the case of $\phi^{*}_{W^*} > \phi^{*}_{C}$ and $N^{*}_{W^*} < N^{*}_{C}$.

Now suppose $1/N^{*}_{W^*} > S_{N^*_W}$, which implies that $W^* < C$ and $[\mathbf{A}] < 0$. In this situation a graph would show $g_i^{W^*}$ above $g^{*}_{i}$. while $[\mathbf{A}] < 0$. The optimum would occur in the fourth quadrant and $N^{*}_{W^*}$ would be greater than $N^{*}_{C}$, but the fixed fee could be higher or lower than the coordinated fixed fee.

Despite the ambiguities outlined above, we may make the following definitive statements. First, if $W^* > C$, $\phi^{*}_{W^*} \geq \phi^{*}_{C}$ implies $N^{*}_{W^*} < N^{*}_{C}$. Second, if $W^* > C$, then $N^{*}_{W^*} \geq N^{*}_{C}$ implies $\phi^{*}_{W^*} < \phi^{*}_{C}$. Third, if $W^* < C$, then $N^{*}_{W^*} > N^{*}_{C}$ and $\phi^{*}_{W^*} > \phi^{*}_{C}$. To say more requires specific functional forms.

## 4.7 A Theoretical Illustration

We return to the illustrative demand curve (3.2.14), but assume now that the manufacturer jointly maximizes its profit over the per-unit fee *and* the fixed fee. We obtain the following values:

$$N^{*}_{W} = \text{Integer}\left( \frac{16Q^* + 2\alpha - \sqrt{\begin{pmatrix} 16(Q^*)^2 + 64\alpha Q^* \\ -11\alpha^2 + 240bf \end{pmatrix}}}{15\alpha} \right) \quad (3.4.24)$$

$$\left(W^* - C\right) = \frac{\left(N^{*}_{W} - 1\right)\alpha}{2b} \quad (3.4.25)$$

Note that the wholesale markup is of the same form in the unconstrained case (3.4.25) and the constrained case (3.4.13). They differ only in terms of the number of retailers engaged in distribution, which is $N^{*}_{W}$ here and $N^{*}_{C}$ in the previous case. The fixed fee also has the same form:

$$\phi^{*}_{W} = \frac{\left[4Q^* - \left(3N^{*}_{W} - 1\right)\alpha\right]^2}{16b} - f \quad (3.4.26)$$

In both instances the similarity of forms is due to the identical optimization procedure used by the independent retailers.

The manufacturer's and the channel's profit can be expressed as:

$$\Pi^*(W^*,\phi^*) = \frac{N_w^*}{16b}\begin{pmatrix} 16(Q^*)^2 - 16\alpha N_w^* Q^* \\ +\left[5(N_w^*)^2 - 2N_w^* + 1\right]\alpha^2 \end{pmatrix} - N_w^* f - F \qquad (3.4.27)$$

$$\Pi_C^*(W^*,\phi^*) = \frac{N_w^*}{48b}\begin{pmatrix} 48(Q^*)^2 - 24\alpha(N_w^* + 1)Q^* \\ +\left[(N_w^*)^2 + 12N_w^* - 1\right]\alpha^2 \end{pmatrix} - N_w^* f - F \qquad (3.4.28)$$

We now provide a specific numerical illustration.

## 4.8 A Numerical Illustration

We numerically analyze the case of the manufacturer seeking to maximize its own profit *without* the constraint that $N_W = N_C^*$. W is chosen to maximize $(W - C)\Sigma Q_i^W + N_W \phi_w$. Under the assumptions that are detailed in Section 2.5, we obtain a per-unit wholesale price $W^* = \$25.50$, a fixed fee $\phi_{W^*}^* = \$280.56$ and a channel breadth $N_{W^*}^* = 32 > 27 = N_C^*$. The tariff {\$25.50, \$280.56} yields \$21,130 in manufacturer profit, which is greater than the \$19,683 earned in the constrained maximization case. Retailer profit ranges from \$0 to \$759.50 (after paying the fixed fee) while channel profit *rises* to \$32,042. These differences reflect the increase in channel breadth relative to the constrained maximization case analyzed in Section 4.5.

All numerical results described in this Chapter are summarized in Tables 3.1 and 3.2, for various values of the slope parameter b. As the Tables illustrate, the greater is the slope of demand, the lower are (1) the optimal wholesale price, (2) the optimal fixed fee, and (3) the optimal number of channel participants. For this family of demand curves, $W^* > C$, $\phi_{W^*}^* < \phi_C^*$, and $N_{W^*}^* \geq N_C^*$. Manufacturer profit rises under a properly-specified, non-coordinating wholesale price strategy. Channel profit is also larger, because optimal non-coordination increases channel breadth.[18]

We now state our final proposition.

**Proposition 4**: There are demand curves for which coordination of a decentralized channel generates lower channel profit and lower manufacturer profit than does *not* coordinating a channel with independent retailers.

**Proof**: Tables 3.1 and 3.2 summarize numerical results calculated from demand curve (3.2.26) for each wholesale-price regimes investigated in this Chapter. To illustrate, we focus on the case of $b = 1$ (the general results hold for all acceptable values of b). The channel-coordinating two-part tariff

$\{C, \phi_C^*\}$ yields channel profit that is \$1,331.75 lower than is generated by the manufacturer-optimal two-part tariff $\{W^*, \phi_{W^*}^*\}$. The coordinating tariff also yields manufacturer profit \$1,447 lower than is earned by the optimal, non-coordinating tariff.

**Corollary 4**: When retail fixed costs are positive, a coordinated channel with independent retailers generally does not earn the same channel profit as does a vertically-integrated system.

**Proof**: Coordination requires that the manufacturer sell at its per-unit cost. Thus it relies on a fixed fee for its revenue. This fixed fee cannot expand, and will generally reduce, the number of retail distributors. Tables 3.1 and 3.2 demonstrate that the vertically-integrated system has more retail outlets than does a decentralized channel—whether or not the latter is coordinated.

**Corollary 5**: The effects of manufacturer profit maximization depend on whether channel breadth is held constant at its coordinated level or is allowed to vary.

**Proof**: We see from Tables 3.1 and 3.2 that the two-part tariff $\{C, \phi_C\}$ generates higher channel profit than the non-coordinating, manufacturer-profit-maximizing two-part tariff $\{\hat{W}^*, \phi_{\hat{W}^*}^*\}$. However, when channel breadth is allowed to vary, the non-coordinating two-part tariff $\{W^*, \phi_{W^*}^*\}$ generates *higher* channel profit than does either the non-coordinating tariff $\{\hat{W}^*, \phi_{\hat{W}^*}^*\}$ or the coordinating tariff $\{C, \phi_C\}$. This profit increase occurs because the uncoordinated channel has five more retailers than does the coordinated channel. Further, the retailers benefit when channel breadth is allowed to vary because channel expansion raises the profits of all retailers who would have participated in the narrower channel; however, they are harmed by non-coordination when channel breadth is held constant. **QED**

**Proof**: We see from Tables 3.1 and 3.2 that the two-part tariff $\{C, \phi_C\}$ generates higher channel profit than the non-coordinating, manufacturer-profit-maximizing two-part tariff $\{\hat{W}^*, \phi_{\hat{W}^*}^*\}$. However, when channel breadth is allowed to vary, the non-coordinating two-part tariff $\{W^*, \phi_{W^*}^*\}$ generates *higher* channel profit than does either the non-coordinating tariff $\{\hat{W}^*, \phi_{\hat{W}^*}^*\}$ or the coordinating tariff $\{C, \phi_C\}$. This profit increase occurs because the uncoordinated channel has five more retailers than does the coordinated channel. Further, the retailers benefit when channel breadth is allowed to vary because channel expansion raises the profits of all retailers who would have participated in the narrower channel; however, they are harmed by non-coordination when channel breadth is held constant. **QED**

*Table 3.1.* Profit Implications of Channel Coordination:
The Impact of Changes in the Slope Parameter b

| Slope Parameter | The Vertically-Integrated System | | The *Channel-Coordinating* Two-Part Tariff $\{C, \phi_C^*\}$ | | | |
|---|---|---|---|---|---|---|
| b | $N_I^*$ | $\Pi_I^*$ | $N_C^*$ | $\phi_C^*$ | $\Pi^*$ | $\Pi_C^*$ |
| 0.5 | 90 | \$123,532.50 | 30 | \$1860.50 | \$55,815.00 | \$86,627.50 |
| 1.0 | 80 | \$43,470.00 | 27 | \$729.00 | \$19,683.00 | \$30,710.25 |
| 2.0 | 60 | \$9,226.25 | 20 | \$210.13 | \$4,202.50 | \$6,458.75 |
| 3.0 | 40 | \$1,845.00 | 14 | \$60.75 | \$850.50 | \$1,328.25 |
| 4.0 | 20 | \$179.38 | 7 | \$12.25 | \$85.75 | \$128.19 |
| 4.5 | 10 | \$21.39 | 4 | \$2.72 | \$10.89 | \$16.33 |

$N_I^*$ ≡ The number of retail outlets with a vertically-integrated channel;
$N_C^*$ ≡ The number of retailers with a channel-coordinating tariff;
$\phi_C^*$ ≡ The fixed fee component of the channel-coordinating tariff;
$\Pi_I^*$ ≡ Channel profit in a vertically-integrated channel;
$\Pi^*$ ≡ Manufacturer profit with a channel-coordinating tariff; and
$\Pi_C^*$ ≡ Channel profit with a channel-coordinating tariff.

*Table 3.2.* Profit Implications of Alternative Price Strategies: The Impact of Changes in the Slope Parameter b

| Slope Parameter | The Manufacturer's *Constrained* Profit-Maximizing Two-Part Tariff $\{\tilde{W}^*, \phi^*_{\tilde{W}}\}$ with $N^*_C$ Retailers | | | | | The Manufacturer's *Unconstrained* Profit-Maximizing Two-Part Tariff $\{W^*, \phi^*_W\}$ | | | | |
|---|---|---|---|---|---|---|---|---|---|---|
| b | $N^*_C$ | $\tilde{W}^*$ | $\phi_{\tilde{W}^*}$ | $\Pi^{\tilde{W}^*}$ | $\Pi_C^{\tilde{W}^*}$ | $N^*_{W^*}$ | $W^*$ | $\phi^*_{W^*}$ | $\Pi_M^{W^*}$ | $\Pi_C^{W^*}$ |
| 0.5 | 30 | $39.00 | $1081.13 | $58,968.75 | $83,473.75 | 36 | $45.00 | $703.13 | $59,962.50 | $91,042.50 |
| 1.0 | 27 | $23.00 | $420.25 | $20,823.75 | $29,569.50 | 32 | $25.50 | $280.56 | $21,130.00 | $32,042.00 |
| 2.0 | 20 | $14.75 | $124.03 | $4,428.13 | $6,233.13 | 24 | $15.75 | $81.28 | $4,503.75 | $6,803.75 |
| 3.0 | 14 | $12.17 | $34.99 | $899.79 | $1,278.81 | 16 | $12.50 | $25.52 | $908.33 | $1,361.67 |
| 4.0 | 7 | $10.75 | $7.56 | $89.69 | $124.25 | 8 | $10.88 | $5.62 | $90.62 | $132.55 |
| 4.5 | 4 | $10.33 | $1.69 | $11.39 | $15.84 | 4 | $10.33 | $1.69 | $11.39 | $15.84 |

$N^*_C$ ≡ The number of retailers with a channel-coordinating tariff.
$N^*_W$ ≡ The number of retailers with a manufacturer profit-maximizing tariff.
$\tilde{W}^*$ ≡ The per-unit component of a constrained profit-maximizing tariff.
$W^*$ ≡ The per-unit component of a manufacturer profit-maximizing tariff.
$\phi^*_{\tilde{W}}$ ≡ The fixed fee component of a constrained profit-maximizing tariff.
$\phi^*_W$ ≡ The fixed fee component of a manufacturer profit-maximizing tariff.
$\Pi_M^{W^*}$ ≡ Manufacturer profit with a manufacturer profit-maximizing tariff.
$\Pi_C^{W^*}$ ≡ Channel profit with a manufacturer profit-maximizing tariff.

## 4.9 Summary

We have shown that when the manufacturer is a Stackelberg leader, offering its goods to independent retailers on a "take-it-or-leave-it" basis, the manufacturer generally does not maximize its profit by setting a wholesale price that coordinates the channel. The manufacturer can often obtain a higher profit by offering an optimal, non-coordinating tariff $\{\mathrm{W}^*, \phi^*_{\mathrm{W}^*}\}$ than by offering the channel-coordinating tariff $\{\mathrm{C}, \phi^*_{\mathrm{C}}\}$. Channel coordination is only optimal when (1) the channel consists of a single retailer or (2) the least-profitable retailer sells the same quantity as the average-size retailer. (The latter case will occur if all the retailers are identical.) Our illustrative demand curve showed that, due to differences in channel breadth, coordination may actually lead to lower channel profit than does unconstrained manufacturer profit maximization of a decentralized channel.

# 5 COMMENTARY

In this Chapter have we investigated a channel consisting of a single manufacturer that sells its product through multiple, independent retailers with exclusive territories. Our analysis generated several conclusions that go well beyond, and often conflict with, the oft-repeated recommendation to "coordinate the channel." We now comment on our results.

## 5.1 Commentary on Coordination

We made five fundamental points related to coordinating a multiple-retailer channel. (1) All channel dyads will be coordinated provided (a) the independent retailers have exclusive territories and (b) the wholesale-price schedule is a two-part tariff in which the per-unit fee is set equal to the manufacturer's marginal production cost. This extends Moorthy's (1987) observation concerning the efficacy of a two-part tariff for a single-retailer channel. However, a quantity-discount schedule of the type employed by Jeuland and Shugan (1983) *cannot* coordinate all the dyads of our multi-dyadic channel, nor can a monotonic quantity-surplus schedule. (2) If the manufacturer coordinates the channel, the fixed fee is its sole source of revenue. (3) The fixed fee determines the number of profit-maximizing, independent retailers who are willing to participate in the channel. Participation occurs voluntarily if and only if the retailer covers its fixed and opportunity costs. (4) The number of participating retailers is generally less than the number that would be utilized by a vertically-integrated system. Thus it is generally *not* possible to replicate the full results of a vertically-integrated system via a channel-coordinating two-part tariff with independent retailers. As a consequence, consumers' surplus will usually be lower in the independent, coordinated channel, because some consumers who would have been served by a vertically-integrated system will not be served by an independent system. (5) The fixed fee endogenously determines the distribution of channel profit between the manufacturer and its retailers. Each retailer realizes a different profit level; only the "marginal" retailer does not obtain a profit in excess of its opportunity cost. Our consideration of the breadth of a coordinated channel eliminates the mathematical indeterminacy of channel profit distribution which characterizes bilateral-monopoly models that are structured as Nash games.

## 5.2 Commentary on Non-Coordination

In Chapter 1 we established four criteria designed to enhance the creation of a Unifying Theory of Distribution Channels. In this Chapter we demonstrated the value of three of those criteria—Empirical Evidence, Nested Models, and Strategic Endogeneity. In particular, we endogenously assessed the validity of two aspects of Channel Strategy that are commonly accepted in the analytical marketing science literature: a belief that channel coordination is optimal for all channel members and a belief that channel breadth can safely be assumed *a priori*.

We found that channel coordination is optimal for the manufacturer under two special conditions: if the least-profitable retailer sells the same volume as the average retailer, or if all the retailers face identical demand and have identical costs. The empirical evidence is that the former condition will be met only by happenstance, while the latter condition cannot be said to be true even for franchised firms once we recognize that there are geographic variations in demographic and socio-economic factors. Accordingly, we nested identical competitors within our model as a special case.

Our decision to explicitly consider non-coordinating pricing schemes yielded two results that are important from the broader perspective of the channel modeling literature. First, it is generally not profit maximizing for the manufacturer to establish a wholesale-price policy that coordinates retailer behavior. The optimal two-part tariff wholesale-price policy $\{W^*, \phi^*_{W^*}\}$ generates greater manufacturer profit than does the channel-coordinating two-part tariff. Moreover, the optimal per-unit fee $W^*$ may be greater or less than marginal production cost C, and the optimal fixed fee $\phi^*_{W^*}$ may be less or greater than the channel-coordinating fee $\phi^*_C$. (The specific relationship between $W^*$ and C is presented in equation (3.4.19) above.) Second, with independent retailers, manufacturer-optimal channel breadth may be broader or narrower than the breadth of a coordinated channel.

Our numerical examples illustrate scenarios in which the objective of manufacturer profit maximization actually yields *greater* channel profit than does maximizing profit subject to a coordination constraint. The reason is that in our example more retailers participate in an uncoordinated channel than in an independent, coordinated channel. When retailers are treated comparably, channel coordination is a second-best solution from the manufacturer's perspective.

## 5.3 Commentary on Five Channel Myths

To provide a final perspective on the results presented in this Chapter, we refer the reader once again to the Channel Myths introduced in Chapter 1. In this Chapter we have provided evidence suggesting that five widely-held beliefs are Myths. These Myths are:

- The Channel-Breadth Modeling Myth;
- The Fixed-Cost Modeling Myth;
- The Channel-Coordination Strategic Myth;
- The Bilateral-Monopoly Meta-Myth; and
- The Identical-Competitors Meta-Myth.

First, we have proven that the manufacturer-optimal wholesale-price *is* dependent on channel breadth. In particular, the output of the least-profitable retailer, relative to the output of the average retailer, determines the manufacturer's optimal per-unit wholesale price. Further, channel breadth itself pivots on both the per-unit price and the fixed fee. This suggests that channel breadth should be modeled as an endogenous variable. We will have more to say on this subject in Chapter 10.

Second, we have proven that the retailers' fixed costs have a substantial impact on the results obtained, for they directly affect each retailer's channel participation decision and indirectly determine which retailer is the least profitable. Further, it is the existence of a fixed cost of operation, which may be interpreted as an opportunity cost, which ensures that a channel comprised of independent retailers will be narrower than a vertically-integrated channel.

Third, we have proven that channel coordination does not always maximize manufacturer profit. Only if the marginal and the average retailer produce the same output do coordination and manufacturer maximization coincide; otherwise the interests of the manufacturer and the channel diverge.

We have also shown that a two-part tariff will coordinate the multiple retailers channel, which is something that neither a quantity-discount nor a quantity-surplus schedule can do.

Fourth, the preceding observations demonstrate that prescriptions drawn from a simple bilateral-monopoly channel of one manufacturer selling one product through one retailer that faces one state-of nature are *not* robust to the slight modification of adding one or more non-identical retailers. We will see this lack of robustness again in Chapter 4, where we explore a model with multiple states-of-nature.

Fifth, we have also seen that the results found with identical retailers replicate the results obtained with a bilateral-monopoly model. That is to say, identical-competitors and bilateral-monopoly models are mutually reinforcing; but they are also similarly distorting of the results deduced from more realistic models.

## 5.4 Summary Commentary

For twenty years marketing scientists have accepted the conventional wisdom that channel coordination will benefit manufacturers, retailers, and consumers. Part of the appeal of this recommendation is its equation of self-interest with altruistic behavior. In this Chapter we have shown that this equation is false: channel coordination is not in the self-interest of the manufacturer. This conflict between altruism and self-interest brings to mind the words of Adam Smith, who wrote, "It is not from the benevolence of the butcher, the brewer, or the baker that we expect our dinner, but from their regard to their own interest" (1796, Book I, Chapter II, paragraph 2). It is the self-interests of the manufacturer and its retail partners that should determine whether we model a channel as coordinated or uncoordinated. For this reason, we have modeled channel members who are concerned with their own self-interest, who do not rely on the benevolence of others for their profit, and who are as *mathematically* distinct as the butcher, the brewer, or the baker. In this Chapter our approach has produced strikingly counter-intuitive results relative to conventional wisdom. We will show that even more profound results arise once we permit inter-retailer competition.

# 6 APPENDIX

In this Appendix we discuss the implications of an independent retailer owning multiple outlets. We also provide formal definitions for the elasticities used in the text.

## 6.1 Ownership of Multiple Outlets

In the analysis in Section 3 of this Chapter, every retail store pays a per-unit wholesale price of $[C + \phi_C^{*} / Q_i(p_i)]$. An alternative result obtains when an independent retailer, operating multiple outlets, pays the tariff $\{C, \phi_C^{*}\}$—that is, when a single fixed fee is spread across multiple stores. In this situation the i[th] retailer, having J stores, maximizes:

$$\max_{p_{ij}} \pi_i = \sum_{j=1}^{J} \left[ \left( p_{ij} - c_{ij} - C \right) Q_{ij}\left( p_{ij} \right) \right] - f_{ij} - \phi_C^{*} \tag{3.A.1}$$

Solving for $p_{ij}^{*}$ and inserting into equation (3.A.1) yields:

$$\pi_i^{*} = \sum_{j=1}^{J} g_{ij}^{*} - \phi_C^{*} = g_i^{*} - \phi_C^{*} \tag{3.A.2}$$

The i[th] retailer will sell the manufacturer's product through all stores meeting the condition $g_{ij}^{*} \geq 0$ so long as $g_i^{*} \geq \phi_C^{*}$. (If the latter condition is not met the i[th] retailer will not participate in the channel.) When a retailer operates a large number of stores, the per-store fixed fee approaches zero. If all stores selling the manufacturer's product belong to a small number of large chains, then the average per-unit wholesale-price approaches C and $N_C^{*}$ approaches $N_I^{*}$.

## 6.2 Definitions of Key Elasticities

In the following definitions, asterisks signify that each variable is evaluated at the optimal values of W and $\phi_W$. The term $S_{N_C^{*}}$ is the marginal (i.e., the least profitable) retailer's share of total unit sales. It is defined as:

$$S_{N_C^{*}} \equiv \frac{Q_{N_C^{*}}^{\tilde{W}^{*}}}{\sum_{i=1}^{N_C^{*}} Q_i^{\tilde{W}^{*}}} > 0 \tag{3.A.3}$$

The term $E_{N_C^*}$ is the total (derived) demand elasticity of unit sales with respect to a change in the per-unit fee W, evaluated at its optimal value $\widehat{W}^*$. It is defined as:

$$E_{N_C^*} \equiv -\left(\frac{\widehat{W}^*}{\sum_{i=1}^{N_C^*} Q_i^{\widehat{W}^*}}\right)\left(\frac{d\left(\Sigma Q_i^{\widehat{W}^*}\right)}{d\widehat{W}^*}\right) > 0 \qquad (3.A.4)$$

The term $\varepsilon_W^*$ is the elasticity of the number of independent retailers with respect to a change in the fixed fee $\phi_{W^*}^*$. It is defined as:

$$\varepsilon_{W^*}^* \equiv -\left(\frac{\phi_{W^*}^*}{N_{W^*}^*}\right)\left(\frac{\delta N_{W^*}^*}{\delta \phi_{W^*}^*}\right) > 0 \qquad (3.A.5)$$

The term $E\{\Sigma Q_i^{W^*}, N_{W^*}^*\}$ is the elasticity of total sales with respect to a change in the number of independent retailers. It is defined as:

$$E\left\{\Sigma Q_i^{W^*}, N_{W^*}^*\right\} \equiv \left(\frac{N_{W^*}^*}{\sum_{i=1}^{N_W^*} Q_i^{W^*}}\right)\left(\frac{\delta\left(\Sigma Q_i^{W^*}\right)}{\delta N_{W^*}^*}\right) > 0 \qquad (3.A.6)$$

The term $E\{W^*, N_{W^*}^*\}$ is the elasticity of W with respect to a change in the number of independent retailers. It is defined as:

$$E\{W^*, N_{W^*}^*\} \equiv \frac{N_{W^*}^*}{W^*}\frac{\delta W^*}{\delta N_{W^*}^*} \gtrless 0 \qquad \text{as } W^* \gtrless C \qquad (3.A.7)$$

# Notes

[1] This Chapter is based upon our *Journal of Retailing* paper: "Coordination and Manufacturer Profit Maximization: The Multiple Retailer Channel," (Ingene and Parry 1995). There is a substantial amount of material in this Chapter that was not in that paper. Material that overlaps with our original paper is reprinted by permission of the copyright holder (New York University).

[2] We showed in Chapter 2 that there are four key results of a bilateral-monopoly model. (1) Channel coordination can be achieved without vertical integration. (2) Greater consumers' surplus is generated by coordination than by non-coordination. (3) Coordination maximizes channel profit. Thus both manufacturer and retailer benefit provided they can agree on a mutually acceptable division of channel profit. (4) The ultimate division of profit between channel members is mathematically indeterminate.

[3] We hold channel breadth constant in Chapters 5-9 in order to focus purely upon the competitive issue. In Chapters 10 and 11 we combine these two topics.

[4] To see this, recognize that any fixed fee is endogenously arbitrary.

[5] We are indebted to Henry ("Skip") Kotkins, Jr., President, Skyway Luggage, for this point.

[6] Rey and Tirole (1986) also examine a channel model with exclusive territories (for the special case of two retailers). They utilized a two-part tariff with equal treatment of the retailers.

[7] We assume away principal-agent coordination problems; thus our result is the highest achievable profit from a vertically-integrated system. Note that different transfer prices at wholly-owned retailers are legally permissible.

[8] The $i^{th}$ retailer's demand curve is a parallel, vertical transformation of the $(i-1)^{th}$ retailer's demand curve; that is, all demand curves have the same slope. Murphy (1977) utilized a similar set of demand curves.

[9] Moorthy (1987) showed that in a bilateral-monopoly channel many wholesale prices—including quantity-discount schedules and quantity-surplus schedules—will coordinate the channel. The basic rules are that (1) marginal cost (MC) must equal marginal revenue (MR) and (2) MC must intersect MR from below. The same pair of rules applies in a multiple-retailers channel. However, unless the retailers are identical, no *monotonic* quantity-discount or quantity-surplus schedule will coordinate all dyads. Only a two-part tariff can achieve coordination, and it does so only when the marginal wholesale price is equal to the manufacturer's marginal cost of production (C).

[10] Jeuland and Shugan (1983) have argued that, in the case of a single retailer, the value of $\phi_C$ can be determined through negotiations between the manufacturer and the retailer. However, as we saw in our review of the early economics literature, negotiation generates an indeterminacy of the ultimate distribution of channel profit. With multiple retailers there are also logistical problems associated with negotiations, not the least of which is the simple reality that a positive fixed fee ($\phi_C$) excludes those potential channel participants for whom $g_i^* > 0 > g_i^* - \phi_C$. In brief, no positive fixed fee can please all potential retailers.

[11] The second derivative of $N_C(\phi_C)$ must be compatible with the second-order conditions.

[12] To simplify drawing this Figure, we have treated the ordered profit-sequence $g_1^*, g_2^*, \cdots$ as if it were linear and continuous. Of course, it need not be linear and it is not continuous—although if N is large the continuity assumption induces no meaningful distortion. Note that it does have to be monotonically non-increasing given the profit ranking (3.2.9).

[13] Comparing equations (3.3.6) and (3.4.2) reveals $W \gtrless C \cdots \Rightarrow p_i(W) \gtrless p_i^*$, $\eta_i^W \gtrless \eta_i^*$, and $Q_i(p_i(W)) \lesseqgtr Q_i^*(p_i^*)$.

[14] This sub-Section builds on the work of Walter Oi (1971).

[15] If $[E_{N_C^*} - (1 - S_{N_C^*} N_C^*)] < 0$, the results for $1/N_C^* \neq S_{N_C^*}$ below are reversed, but the reasoning is the same.

[16] The "marginal" (the $N_C^{*th}$) retailer is defined as the least profitable retailer; the "average" retailer is defined as the one that sells an average quantity.

[17] To see this, note that when $W^* = C$, $E\{W^*, N_{W^*}^*\} = 0$. See the Appendix at equation (3.A.7) for details.

[18] In the extreme case of $b > 4$, the integer constraint on number of retailers yields equality between $N_{W^*}^*$ and $N_C^*$. Because channel breadth is unaffected by non-coordination in this case, total channel profits do decrease. Finally, for the specified demand curve, the channel cannot exist profitably if $b \geq 5$ under any of the investigated wholesale-price schemes, including vertical integration.

# Chapter 4

# Multiple (Exclusive) States-of-Nature[1]

*"Even though work stops, expenses run on."*

## 1 INTRODUCTION

In Chapter 2 we reviewed a single-period, bilateral-monopoly model with complete certainty. In Chapter 3 we extended our analysis to a single-period model of multiple (non-competing) retailers with complete certainty. In this Chapter we examine a multi-period, bilateral-monopoly model under uncertainty, which we model by assuming multiple-states-of-nature. Because the states-of-nature are not in competition, the multiple-states-of-nature model is a variation of our multiple-retailers model. The latter model enabled us to decide which *spatially-distinct* retailers to serve; this model enables us to determine which *temporally-distinct* states-of-nature to serve.[2] The models of Chapters 3 and 4 provide *complementary* perspectives on the breadth of channel coverage in the absence of competition. However, there is a key distinction between the multiple-retailers and the multiple-states-of-nature models. In the former model, the $i^{th}$ retailer's profit does not affect the $j^{th}$ retailer's channel-participation decision. In the latter model, profit in the $i^{th}$ state-of-nature can affect the retailer's distribution decision in the $j^{th}$ state-of-nature. Thus channel breadth may differ across these two models.

Because only one state-of-nature can be realized at a time, there is *a priori* uncertainty about the outcome of managerial actions taken before a time period's actual state-of-nature is revealed. The model presented in this Chapter will illuminate the subtleties associated with this uncertainty by answering three basic questions:

(1) Can a single wholesale-price policy induce coordination across *every* state-of-nature?

(2) If the answer to (1) is "yes," is it in the manufacturer's interest *to coordinate* the channel in all states-of-nature?

(3) *Should* the manufacturer set a wholesale-price schedule that causes the retailer to serve the same states-of-nature that are served by a vertically-integrated system?

Before turning to our formal analysis, we consider how the bilateral-monopoly model would answer each of these questions. If the results of a single-retailer, single state-of-nature model generalize to the case of a single-retailer, multiple-states-of-nature model, we should find that:

1. The manufacturer can set a wholesale-price policy that coordinates all states-of-nature.
2. It is in the manufacturer's interest to coordinate the channel in all states-of-nature.
3. The manufacturer should set its wholesale price to cause the retailer to serve all states-of-nature.

These conclusions, which are simple generalizations of the results obtained from the bilateral-monopoly model, *assume* that the manufacturer has complete information about all cost and demand conditions in all time periods; however, both intuition and evidence suggest that manufacturers often have less information about these conditions than do retailers. We will show that incorporating *informational asymmetry* into the bilateral monopoly-model changes many conclusions drawn from the certainty-equivalent model.

Before turning to our formal analysis, we highlight three critical features of our model: (1) the *duration* of the channel relationship; (2) the *retailer's fixed cost* associated with each state-of-nature; and (3) the presence of *informational asymmetry*. The first has implications for *channel existence*; the second influences the retailer's *product distribution decision*; and the third differentially affects the *marketing decisions* made by the manufacturer and the retailer.

**Duration:** We model the channel as a *time-invariant*, multiple-states-of-nature, repeating game. With time-invariance, the channel faces the same demand, costs, and state-of-nature probabilities every time period (that is, at each *re-order opportunity*), although the *realized* state-of-nature differs across time periods. Because the game repeats, a wholesale price that ensures channel existence in one period ensures channel existence in all periods.

**Fixed Costs:** We model the retailer as incurring quantity-independent costs that derive from three sources. (1) *Dyad-specific assets* that are required for channel participation; these costs are incurred in every time period whether or not distribution occurs. (2) If distribution does occur in a time period, the retailer faces an *opportunity cost* that reflects the profit it could have earned from the next-best use of its scarce resources. (3) If distribution does *not* occur in a time period, making alternative use of its scarce resources imposes a *switching cost* on the retailer. In order to maintain full generalizability, we model these fixed costs as being non-negative. We will prove that fixed costs affect the retailer's *product-distribution* decision.

**Informational Asymmetry:** We model channel members as being fully informed about demand and cost conditions and the probability of every state-of-nature at the start of the game; that is, they initially have identical information. However this information is *incomplete* because the channel members do not know which state-of-nature will occur in each time period.

*Before* each time period's true state-of-nature is revealed, the retailer and the manufacturer commit to channel participation,[3] and the manufacturer commits to a wholesale-price schedule.[4] Because parametric values are time-invariant, repeated plays of the game do not generate additional information. If commitments were re-evaluated each time period *prior* to the realization of the actual state-of-nature, (a) both players would join the channel and (b) the manufacturer would offer the same wholesale-price schedule. An expectation of non-negative profit guarantees channel existence by ensuring the integrity of each channel member's commitments.[5]

*After* the true state-of-nature is revealed, the independent retailer decides if it will *distribute* the manufacturer's product in the revealed state-of-nature. If the distribution decision is "yes," the retailer makes *marketing decisions* about the elements of its marketing mix. Distribution occurs in a particular state-of-nature if and only if the retailer will be at least as well off by distributing as it would be if it did not distribute. The retailer's distribution and marketing decisions are made with full information in each time period. In contrast, the manufacturer's wholesale-price decision is made under uncertainty; that is, the channel members have *asymmetric information.*

In sum, the model of this Chapter assumes that both manufacturer and retailer commit to channel participation. Further, the manufacturer commits to a wholesale-price schedule that is valid over multiple time periods. In each time period the retailer learns the true state-of-nature and *then* decides whether to distribute the product. If distribution occurs, the retailer selects its marketing-mix variables (here confined to price), which determine the quantity sold and the profit realized by both channel members.

We describe our assumptions in Section 2 and establish the baseline results of a vertically-integrated, full-information channel in Section 3. We derive an independent retailer's reaction to a wholesale-price policy in Section 4. In Section 5 we present the manufacturer's profit-maximizing wholesale-price schedule subject to the constraint of channel coordination. In Section 6 we derive the manufacturer's profit-maximizing wholesale-price schedule subject to a constraint that all states-of-nature are served. We analytically and numerically compare the manufacturer's profit from these two wholesale-price schemes in Section 7. We conclude with a discussion of our results and a commentary on the Myth that the multiple-retailers model is an alternative to a multiple-states-of-nature model.

# 2 ASSUMPTIONS OF THE MODEL

We model a distribution channel that is organized either as a vertically-integrated system consisting of a manufacturing arm and a single retail outlet *or* as an independent manufacturer-retailer dyad. In this Section we specify the assumptions common to both channel structures.

In a general version of the multiple-states-of-nature model, there are N mutually-exclusive states-of-nature, one of which is realized in each time period. These states, denoted $\boldsymbol{\Omega}\ [\equiv(\Omega_1,\Omega_2,...,\Omega_N)]$, occur with probability $\boldsymbol{\rho}\ [\equiv(\rho_1,\rho_2,...\rho_N)\ \text{s.t.}\ \Sigma\rho_i=1]$. We make seven assumptions:

1. There is *informational asymmetry* in a manufacturer/independent-retailer dyad.
2. All channel participants incur non-negative *fixed costs*.
3. All parameters of the model are *time-invariant*.
4. All decision-makers have *full knowledge of all parametric values*.
5. All decision-makers are *risk-neutral*.
6. All decision-makers are *profit-maximizers*.
7. *Demand* varies across states-of-nature, but is always linear and downward sloping; in the $i^{th}$ state-of-nature demand is:

$$Q_i=(A_i-bp_i) \tag{4.2.1}$$

Assumption 1 captures the intuitively appealing notion that a retailer generally has better information about the state-of-nature in the current time period than does a manufacturer; an obvious reason is that it is closer to end users.[6] Although both participants are aware of the possible states-of-nature and their probabilities ($\Omega$ and $\rho$) when they commit to channel existence, the state-of-nature associated with a specific time period is unknowable when the manufacturer offers a wholesale-price schedule. However, the retailer knows the actual state-of-nature when it makes its distribution and marketing decisions. A *vertically-integrated system* also commits to channel existence with the limited information contained in $\Omega$ and $\rho$; but it knows the actual state-of-nature prior to making its distribution, marketing and (if retail pricing decisions are decentralized) transfer-pricing decisions.

Assumption 2 recognizes the presence of fixed business expenses that are incurred in every time period if the channel exists, but that are avoided if the channel does not exist. The manufacturer incurs a *fixed cost* ($F\geq 0$) associated with its production facilities whether or not distribution occurs. The retailer incurs three types of fixed costs. First, in every period the retailer incurs a dyad-specific asset cost ($f_{asset}\geq 0$) that enables the retailer to maintain its ability to distribute the product. Second, in time periods in which it offers the manufacturer's product for sale, the retailer incurs an opportunity cost of distribution ($f_{dist} \geq 0$). Third, in time periods in which the manufacturer's product is *not* offered for sale, the retailer incurs a fixed expense of un-stocking merchandise from display and re-stocking it when distribution resumes ($f_{stock} \geq 0$).[7] In short, the retailer's fixed cost depends on its distribution decision. By distributing the manufacturer's product the retailer incurs the fixed cost ($f_A \equiv (f_{asset} + f_{dist}) \geq 0$), and by rejecting distribution the retailer incurs the fixed cost ($f_R \equiv (f_{asset} + f_{stock}) \geq 0$), where the subscript $_A$ denotes the retailer's agreement to distribute the product and the subscript $_R$ denotes its refusal. (Note that, in a vertically-integrated system, F is incurred by the production arm while $f_A$ and $f_R$ are incurred by the retail outlet.)

Assumption 3 states that demand, channel costs, and the probability distribution $\rho$ are constant over time; only the realized state-of-nature differs across time periods. Because Assumptions 4 and 5 are conventional, we do not discuss them. Under Assumption 6, channel existence requires both channel members to expect non-negative profit; thus the channel exists if and only if $E[\pi] \equiv E[\Sigma_i \rho_i \pi_i] \geq 0$ and $E[\Pi] \equiv E[\Sigma_i \rho_i \Pi_i] \geq 0$ (or $E[\Pi^*_{VI}] \geq 0$). Assumptions 2 and 6 imply that distribution occurs in states-of-nature in which the retailer's profit ($\pi_i$) equals or exceeds its profit from non-distribution ($\pi_i \geq -f_R$). In Assumption 7, $A_i$ is the maximal level of demand in the $i^{th}$ state-of-nature and the slope parameter "b" denotes price sensitivity.

# 3 THE VERTICALLY-INTEGRATED SYSTEM

In this Section we first derive the retail prices and quantities that are optimal for a vertically-integrated system. We then identify the states-of-nature served by this system. Because the vertically-integrated system faces no uncertainty when making its *pricing* decision, the results of this Section constitute an "informed-baseline" for evaluating the decentralized-channel results derived later in this Chapter.

## 3.1 Profit Maximization

If distribution occurs in the $i^{th}$ state-of-nature, profit maximization leads to the optimal values of price, quantity, channel margin, and profit:

$$p_i^* = \left[\frac{A_i + b(c_i + C)}{2b}\right] > 0 \qquad (4.3.1)$$

$$Q_i^* = \left[A_i - b(c_i + C)\right]/2 > 0 \qquad (4.3.2)$$

$$\mu_i^* \equiv \left(p_i^* - c_i - C\right) = \left[\frac{A_i - b(c_i + C)}{2b}\right] = \left(\frac{Q_i^*}{b}\right) > 0 \tag{4.3.3}$$

$$\Pi_i^* = \left(\frac{(Q_i^*)^2}{b} - f_A - F\right) \equiv \left(R_i^* - f_A - F\right) \equiv \left(g_i^* - F\right) > 0 \tag{4.3.4}$$

These equations incorporate the per-unit variable costs of *production* (C) and *distribution* ($c_i$); $\Pi_i^*$ and $R_i^*$ indicate profit and net revenue[8] in the $i^{th}$ state-of-nature; and $g_i^*$ denotes the profit contribution in the $i^{th}$ state after allowing for the fixed distribution cost $(f_A)$. Note that the variable distribution cost is modeled as state-of-nature dependent, as is the maximal level of demand.

If distribution does *not* occur in the $j^{th}$ state-of-nature, the vertically-integrated system's profit is:

$$\Pi_j^* = -\left(f_R + F\right) \tag{4.3.5}$$

Combining (4.3.4) and (4.3.5) enables us to rank profit across the N states-of-nature:

$$g_1^* > g_2^* > \cdots g_{n^*}^* \geq -f_R > g_{n^*+1}^* > \cdots g_N^* \tag{4.3.6}$$

This ranking is equivalent to a statement that demand (evaluated at cost) is:

$$(A_1 - b(c_1 + C)) > (A_2 - b(c_2 + C)) > \ldots > (A_N - b(c_N + C)) \tag{4.3.7}$$

Distribution will only occur in the $n^*$ states-of-nature that generate sufficient revenue to ensure a lower loss than would occur in the absence of distribution. Hence the *expected profit* of a vertically-integrated system is:

$$\begin{aligned} E\left(\Pi_{VI}^*\right) &= \left[\sum_{i=1}^{n^*} \rho_i \Pi_i^* - \sum_{j=(n^*+1)}^{N} \rho_j \Pi_j^*\right] \\ &= \left[\sum_{i=1}^{n^*} \rho_i \left(R_i^* - f_A\right) - \sum_{j=(n^*+1)}^{N} \rho_j f_R - F\right] \end{aligned} \tag{4.3.8}$$

The vertically-integrated system exists if and only if $E(\Pi_{VI}^*) \geq 0$.

## 3.2 An Example with Two States-of-Nature

To illustrate the conditions under which the vertically-integrated system does *not* serve all states-of-nature, as well as those conditions for which the channel does not exist, let there be two states-of-nature ($\Omega_1$ and $\Omega_2$) that occur with probabilities $\rho$ and $(1-\rho)$, respectively.

The vertically-integrated system compares profit from serving two states-of-nature with profit from serving either the $1^{st}$ or the $2^{nd}$ state:

$$E(\Pi_1^* + \Pi_2^*) - E(\Pi_1^*) = (1-\rho)[R_2^* - (f_A - f_R)]$$
$$E(\Pi_1^* + \Pi_2^*) - E(\Pi_2^*) = \rho[R_1^* - (f_A - f_R)] \quad (4.3.9)$$

Without loss of generality, we assume that the high-demand state is $\Omega_1$, which implies that $R_1^* > R_2^*$.

### 3.2.1 The Vertically-Integrated System: Temporal Coverage

A vertically-integrated system may serve (a) both states-of-nature, or (b) only the high-demand state-of-nature, or (c) no state-of-nature (i.e., the channel may not exist). Both states are served if and only if:

$$\rho(R_1^* - f_A) + (1-\rho)(R_2^* - f_A) - F \geq 0$$
$$\text{and} \quad R_1^* > R_2^* > (f_A - f_R) \quad (4.3.10)$$

The first line states that the expected profit of a vertically-integrated system must be non-negative when both states-of-nature are served. The second line of (4.3.10) says that the system must make more money serving both states-of-nature than it would by not serving the low-demand state. (The system may lose money in the low-demand state; the second line of (4.3.10) merely limits the magnitude of the loss.)

Only the high-demand state is served if:

$$\rho(R_1^* - f_A) - (1-\rho)f_R - F \geq 0$$
$$\text{and} \quad R_1^* > (f_A - f_R) > R_2^* \quad (4.3.11)$$

The first line states that the expected profit of a vertically-integrated system must be non-negative if only the high-demand state-of-nature is served. The second line of (4.3.11) says that the vertically-integrated system generates positive profit by serving the high-demand state *and* earns more money (or loses less money) by *not* serving the low-demand state than it would by serving it. The vertically-integrated system does not exist if neither (4.3.10) nor (4.3.11) holds.

To clarify the impact of the vertically-integrated system's decision on temporal completeness, we divide our analysis into two parts: we first determine the optimal number of states-of-nature given channel existence, and then we use this analysis to determine whether the channel will exist. *If* the channel exists, it serves both states-of-nature when $R_2^* > (f_A - f_R)$ and it serves a single state when $R_2^* < (f_A - f_R)$. We define the *Complete/ Incomplete-Coverage Boundary* as the set of $(f_A - f_R)$ values that satisfy:

$$R_2^* = (f_A - f_R) \quad (4.3.12)$$

When this condition holds, the vertically-integrated system is indifferent between serving one or both states-of-nature. Equality (4.3.12) defines two Zones: a *Complete-Coverage Zone* and an *Incomplete-Coverage Zone*.

When $R_2^* > (f_A - f_R)$, there is complete coverage *or* no state-of-nature is served. Manipulating the first line of (4.3.10), we find that complete coverage is preferred when the probability of the high-demand state ($\rho$) exceeds the minimum value $\rho_{12}^{VI}$:

$$\rho \geq \left( \frac{F + f_A - R_2^*}{R_1^* - R_2^*} \right) \equiv \rho_{12}^{VI} \qquad (4.3.13)$$

The subscript $_{12}$ in the term $\rho_{12}^{VI}$ (as well as the subscript $_1$ in the term $\rho_1^{VI}$ of the following equation) denotes the states-of-nature served by the channel. We call $\rho_{12}^{VI}$ the *Complete/Zero-Coverage Boundary*. Intuitively, condition (4.3.13) holds when the low-demand state generates a net revenue ($R_2^*$) that is small relative to the fixed costs of distribution ($f_A$) and production (F).

When $R_2^* < (f_A - f_R)$, the system serves the high-demand state *or* the channel does not exist. Manipulating the first line of (4.3.11) reveals that the high-demand state is served if its probability satisfies:

$$\rho \geq \left( \frac{F + f_R}{R_1^* - (f_A - f_R)} \right) \equiv \rho_1^{VI} \qquad (4.3.14)$$

We call $\rho_1^{VI}$ the *Incomplete/Zero-Coverage Boundary*. The channel cannot exist if the denominator of $\rho_1^{VI}$ is negative, because a negative denominator implies $R_2^* < R_1^* < (f_A - f_R)$ and $E[\Pi_{VI}^*] < 0$. Even when the denominator of (4.3.14) is positive, there are $\rho$-values for which F and $f_R$ are positive and the channel does not exist.

### 3.2.2 The Vertically-Integrated System: Re-Scaling the Parameters

To illustrate the interaction of the channel breadth issue and channel existence issue, we re-scale our model by defining four terms:[9]

$\mathcal{Q} \equiv (Q_2^* / Q_1^*)$ ≡ The size of the low-demand state *relative* to the high-demand state;

$f_{\mathcal{A}} \equiv (f_A / R_1^*)$ ≡ The fixed cost of distribution relative to the net revenue earned in the high-demand state;

$\varphi \equiv (f_R / f_A)$ ≡ The fixed cost of not distributing the product relative to the fixed cost of distribution; and

$\mathcal{F} \equiv (F / R_1^*)$ ≡ The fixed cost of production expressed as a proportion of the net revenue earned in the high-demand state.

Each of these re-scaled terms lies in the unit interval. Because $Q_2^*$ is defined as the low-demand state, $Q_2^* < Q_1^*$ and therefore $\mathcal{Q} < 1$. The retailer can only generate a non-negative expected profit when $f_A \leq R_1^*$, which implies $f_{\mathcal{A}} \leq 1$. In our numerical analyses we assume that the fixed cost of distribution is no greater than the fixed cost of non-distribution ($f_R \leq f_A$), which implies that $\varphi \leq 1$. (Note that our mathematics are completely general; $\varphi$ can take on any non-negative value.) Finally, when the vertically-integrated system serves only the high demand state, its participation constraint requires that $(F + f_A) \leq R_1^* \rightarrow F \leq R_1^*$, which implies that $(\mathcal{F} + f_{\mathcal{A}}) \leq 1$ and $\mathcal{F} \leq 1$.

### 3.2.3 The Vertically-Integrated System: Theoretical Effects

Given this re-scaling of the parameters, the boundary conditions ((4.3.12)-(4.3.14)) can be re-written as:

$$\mathcal{Q}^2 = (1-\varphi) f_{\mathcal{A}} \equiv \delta^{VI} \geq 0 \tag{4.3.15}$$

$$\rho_{12}^{VI} = \left( \frac{\mathcal{F} + f_{\mathcal{A}} - \mathcal{Q}^2}{1 - \mathcal{Q}^2} \right) \leq 1 \tag{4.3.16}$$

$$\rho_1^{VI} = \left( \frac{\mathcal{F} + \varphi f_{\mathcal{A}}}{1 - (1-\varphi) f_{\mathcal{A}}} \right) \geq 0 \tag{4.3.17}$$

Recall that (4.3.15) defines the Complete/Incomplete-Coverage Boundary; we label its RHS as $\delta^{VI}$. Complete coverage occurs if $\mathcal{Q}^2 > \delta^{VI}$. Expression (4.3.16) defines the critical $\rho -$value for which there is complete coverage *or* the channel does not exist; this is the Complete/Zero-Coverage Boundary. Expression (4.3.17) is the critical $\rho -$value that defines the Incomplete/Zero-Coverage Boundary. These re-scaled boundary conditions are functions of five terms: relative outputs ($\mathcal{Q}$), the probability of the high-demand state ($\rho$), and the three fixed cost measures of production ($\mathcal{F}$), of distribution ($f_{\mathcal{A}}$), and of non-distribution relative to distribution ($\varphi$). In the following analysis we use two-dimensional graphs in $\langle \rho, \mathcal{Q} \rangle -$space to illustrate how changes in the fixed-cost ratios $\mathcal{F}$, $f_{\mathcal{A}}$ and $\varphi$ affect the breadth of coverage offered by the vertically-integrated system.

An examination of expression (4.3.15) reveals that the value of $\delta^{VI}$ rises with $f_{\mathcal{A}}$, falls with $\varphi$, and is independent of both $\rho$ and $\mathcal{F}$. Thus $\delta^{VI}$ defines a horizontal line in $\langle \rho, \mathcal{Q} \rangle -$space. The effects of changes in key model parameters on the Complete/Zero-Coverage Boundary are:

$$\frac{\partial \rho_{12}^{VI}}{\partial f_{\mathcal{A}}} = \frac{\partial \rho_{12}^{VI}}{\partial \mathcal{F}} = \left(\frac{1}{1-Q^2}\right) > 0$$

$$\frac{\partial \rho_{12}^{VI}}{\partial Q} = \left(\frac{2Q\left(1-f_{\mathcal{A}}-\mathcal{F}\right)}{\left(1-Q^2\right)^2}\right) \geq 0 \tag{4.3.18}$$

$$\partial \rho_{12}^{VI} / \partial \varphi = 0$$

Similarly, the effects of changes in key model parameters on the Incomplete/ Zero-Coverage Boundary are:

$$\frac{\partial \rho_{1}^{VI}}{\partial f_{\mathcal{A}}} = \left(\frac{\varphi+(1-\varphi)\mathcal{F}}{\left(1-(1-\varphi)f_{\mathcal{A}}\right)^2}\right) > 0$$

$$\frac{\partial \rho_{1}^{VI}}{\partial \mathcal{F}} = \left(\frac{1}{\left(1-(1-\varphi)f_{\mathcal{A}}\right)}\right) > 0 \tag{4.3.19}$$

$$\frac{\partial \rho_{1}^{VI}}{\partial \varphi} = \left(\frac{f_{\mathcal{A}}\left(1-f_{\mathcal{A}}-\mathcal{F}\right)}{\left(1-(1-\varphi)f_{\mathcal{A}}\right)^2}\right) \geq 0$$

$$\partial \rho_{1}^{VI} / \partial Q = 0$$

In summary, an increase in $\mathcal{F}$ raises the $\rho-$values that define the Complete/Zero-Coverage Boundary and the Incomplete/Zero-Coverage Boundary, but has no effect on the Complete/Incomplete-Coverage Boundary. This last statement follows directly from the substitution of $\delta^{VI}$ in equation (4.3.15). An increase in $f_{\mathcal{A}}$ also raises both $\rho-$values, as well as $\delta^{VI}$. In contrast to these straightforward results, the effects of a change in $\varphi$ are more complex. A rise in $\varphi$ lowers the $\rho-$value that defines the Complete/ Incomplete-Coverage Boundary, raises the $\rho-$value that defines the Incomplete/Zero-Coverage Boundary, and has no effect on the Complete/ Zero-Coverage Boundary. A change in $Q$ increases the $\rho-$value that defines the Complete/Zero-Coverage Boundary, but has no effect on the Incomplete/Zero-Coverage Boundary or the Complete/ Incomplete Coverage Boundary.

Intuitively, we have shown that an increase in either $\mathcal{F}$ or $f_{\mathcal{A}}$ raises the minimum probability of the high-demand state that is necessary to ensure channel existence. An increase in $f_{\mathcal{A}}$ also increases the fixed-cost difference required to ensure that both states-of-nature are served, while an increase in $\varphi$ lowers the fixed-cost difference needed to ensure that both states-of-nature are served.

### 3.2.4 The Vertically-Integrated System: Numerical Effects

To gain further insight into the decisions of the vertically-integrated channel, we turn to numerical analysis. We describe the system-optimal strategy for all possible values of ρ and $Q$ under four Scenarios that are defined by the values of $f_{\mathcal{A}}$ and φ. Our Scenarios are:

| **Scenario:** | **1** | **2** | **3** | **4** |
|---|---|---|---|---|
| $f_{\mathcal{A}}$ | 0 | .25 | .25 | .25 |
| φ | 0 | 0 | .5 | 1.0 |

There is no fixed cost of distribution in Scenario 1. We include this "extreme" Scenario because the literature largely ignores fixed costs. In Scenario 2 the fixed cost of distribution is 25 percent of net revenues in the high-demand state, but there is no fixed cost of non-distribution (i.e., there is no stocking expense and no fixed-asset expense). This Scenario allows us to investigate the effect of an opportunity cost of distribution in the absence of any fixed cost of non-distribution. In Scenario 3 the fixed cost of non-distribution is set at one-half the fixed cost of distribution. Finally, in Scenario 4 the fixed costs of distribution and non-distribution are equal. (Because the qualitative impact of changes in $\mathcal{F}$ mirror the impact of changes in $f_{\mathcal{A}}$, we set $\mathcal{F}=0$ in all four Scenarios.) Taken together, these Scenarios illustrate the ways in which variations in retail-level fixed costs influence the vertically-integrated system's decisions concerning channel existence and breadth of channel coverage. (To depict our Scenarios graphically, we plug the relevant values of $f_{\mathcal{A}}$ and φ into equation (4.3.15)).

**Scenario 1** ($f_{\mathcal{A}} = 0 = \varphi$): The vertically-integrated system always serves both states-of-nature because $\delta^{VI} = 0$ (implying complete coverage) while the channel-existence constraint is never binding ($\rho_{12}^{VI} < 0$). This Scenario illustrates the general principle that coverage is comprehensive in the absence of fixed costs.

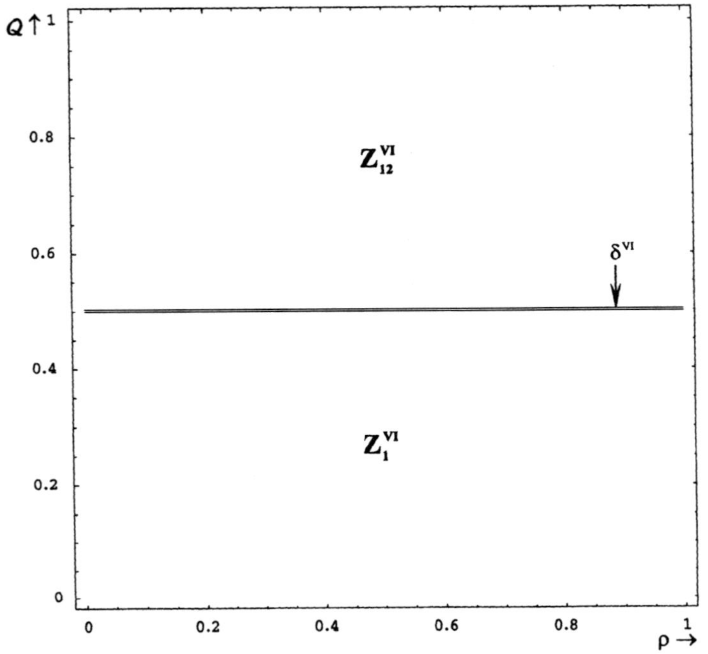


Legend:

$Z_1^{VI} \equiv$ The vertically-integrated system serves the high-demand state-of-nature;

$Z_{12}^{VI} \equiv$ The vertically-integrated system serves both states-of-nature; and

$\delta^{VI} \equiv$ The Complete/Incomplete Coverage Boundary.

*Figure 4.1.* The Vertically-Integrated System's Optimal Strategy When $f_{\mathcal{A}} = 0.25, \varphi = 0$

**Scenario 2** $(f_{\mathcal{A}} = 0.25, \varphi = 0)$: Figure 4.1 depicts the vertically-integrated system's strategy in this Scenario. The channel serves both states-of-nature when $Q \geq \sqrt{\delta^{VI}} = \frac{1}{2}$; otherwise it serves only the high-demand state. We denote the Complete-Coverage Zone as $\mathbf{Z}_{12}^{VI}$ (the superscript $^{VI}$ denotes the vertically-integrated system and the subscript $_{12}$ indicates that both states-of-nature are served). Similarly, we denote the Incomplete-Coverage Zone as $\mathbf{Z}_1^{VI}$ (the subscript denotes that only the high-demand state—state 1—is served). Neither channel-existence constraint is binding in this Scenario, so the vertically-integrated system always serves at least one state-of-nature.

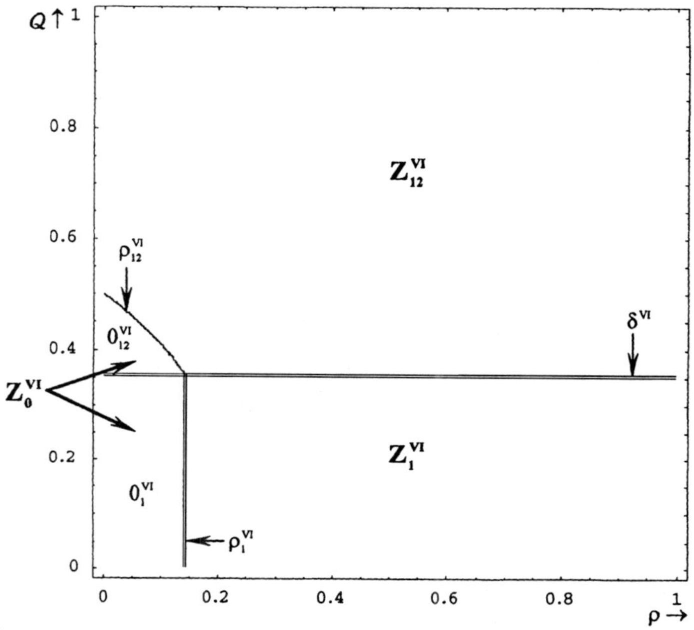


Legend:

$0^{VI}_{1} \equiv$ The channel does not exist: the condition for serving the high-demand state is violated;

$0^{VI}_{12} \equiv$ The channel does not exist: the condition for serving both states-of-nature is violated;

$Z^{VI}_{0} \equiv$ The channel does not exist in this portion of parameter space;

$Z^{VI}_{1} \equiv$ The vertically-integrated system serves the high-demand state-of-nature; and

$Z^{VI}_{12} \equiv$ The vertically-integrated system serves both states-of-nature.

*Figure 4.2.* The Vertically-Integrated System's Optimal Strategy When $f_{\mathfrak{A}} = 0.25, \varphi = 0.5$

**Scenario 3** $(f_{\mathfrak{A}} = .25, \varphi = .5)$: Figure 4.2 shows the vertically-integrated system's strategy in this Scenario. The Complete/Incomplete-Coverage Boundary is $Q = \sqrt{\delta^{VI}} = \sqrt{1/8} \cong 0.354$. Above this horizontal line both states-of-nature are served *provided* that the channel exists; below this line only the high-demand state is served (again, *provided* the channel exists).

Channel non-existence can occur in lieu of complete *or* incomplete coverage. In the former case the channel-existence constraint satisfies:

$$\rho^{VI}_{12} = \left( \frac{1 - 4Q^2}{4(1 - Q^2)} \right) < 1 \qquad (4.3.20)$$

This Complete/Zero-Coverage Boundary intersects the $\langle\rho=0\rangle$ – axis at $Q=\frac{1}{2}$ and curves downward, meeting $\delta^{VI}$ at $\rho=\frac{1}{7}$.

In Figure 4.2 the area below and to the left of the $\rho_{12}^{VI}$ – boundary, and the area above $Q\cong 0.354$, is a Zero-Coverage *sub*-Zone ($0_{12}^{VI}$). A second Zero-Coverage *sub*-Zone ($0_{1}^{VI}$) lies below $Q\cong 0.354$ and to the left of the Incomplete/Zero-Coverage Boundary (4.3.14), which is defined by the equation $\rho_1^{VI}=\frac{1}{7}$. We label the set of parameter values for which the channel does not exist the *Zero-Coverage Zone* and denote it by the symbol $Z_0^{VI}$ (the subscript $_0$ indicates that no state-of-nature is served). By definition, Zone $\mathbf{Z_0^{VI}}$ is the union of the two Zero-Coverage *sub*-Zones ($0_1^{VI}\cup 0_{12}^{VI}$).[10]

**Scenario 4** $(f_{\mathcal{A}}=0.25,\varphi=1)$: Figure 4.3 depicts the vertically-integrated system's strategy for this Scenario. The Complete/Incomplete-Coverage Boundary is $\delta^{VI}=0$, so both states-of-nature are served *provided* the channel exists. From equation (4.3.20), which defines the relevant channel-existence constraint, the Complete/Zero-Coverage Boundary ($\rho_{12}^{VI}$) is a curve sweeping from the $\langle\rho=0\rangle$ – axis at $Q=\frac{1}{2}$ to the $\langle Q=0\rangle$ – axis at $\frac{1}{4}$. To the left of the $\rho_{12}^{VI}$ – boundary the channel does not exist (Zone $\mathbf{Z_0^{VI}}$), while to its right the channel serves both states (Zone $\mathbf{Z_{12}^{VI}}$).

### 3.2.5 The Vertically-Integrated System: The Impact of Fixed Costs

We draw three conclusions from the preceding analysis. First, the vertically-integrated system only provides complete coverage if there are no fixed costs of distribution or production. Second, the vertically-integrated system does not exist over some $\langle\rho,Q\rangle$ – range if there is a fixed cost of *non*-distribution. Third, the greater is the divergence between the fixed costs of distribution and non-distribution, the larger is the Incomplete-Coverage Zone and the smaller is the Zero-Coverage Zone.

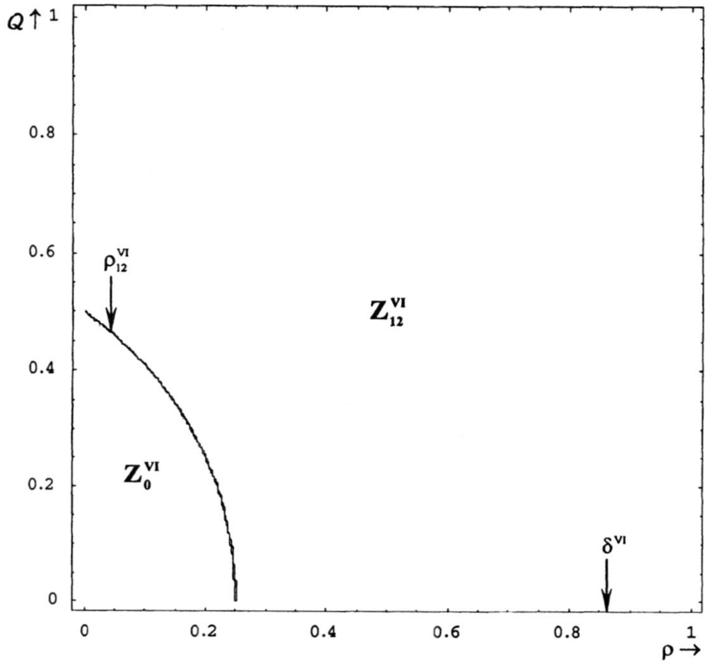


Legend:

$\delta^{VI} \equiv$ The Complete/Incomplete Coverage Boundary;

$Z_{12}^{VI} \equiv$ The vertically-integrated system serves both states-of-nature; and

$Z_{0}^{VI} \equiv$ The channel does not exist: the condition for serving both states-of-nature is violated.

*Figure 4.3.* The Vertically-Integrated System's Optimal Strategy
When $f_{\mathscr{A}} = 0.25, \varphi = 1$

# 4 AN INDEPENDENT RETAILER

In this Section we determine an independent retailer's optimal actions given the manufacturer's wholesale-price schedule. We model the link between the dyadic members as a four-stage game. In the first stage the manufacturer commits to a wholesale-price schedule. In the second stage the retailer decides whether or not to participate in the channel. (This is the second stage because the retailer cannot calculate its expected profit without knowing the wholesale price it will pay). In the third stage the retailer learns the actual state-of-nature and decides if it will distribute the product. In the final stage the retailer sets its profit-maximizing price and determines its order-quantity. The third and fourth stages are played repeatedly, while the first and second stages constitute a one-time game.

## 4.1 Retailer Profit-Maximization

We begin by solving for the retailer's decisions in the fourth stage of the game—given that the manufacturer's wholesale-price policy consists of a single, two-part tariff.[11] *If* the retailer distributes in the $i^{th}$ state-of-nature, it purchases $Q_i$ units from the manufacturer for $WQ_i + \phi$ (W is the per-unit charge and $\phi$ is the fixed fee). The retailer maximizes:

$$\max_{p_i} \pi_i = (p_i - c_i - W)(A_i - bp_i) - f_A - \phi \tag{4.4.1}$$

Solving the first-order condition derived from (4.4.1) yields the optimal price as a function of W:

$$\hat{p}_i = \left[\frac{A_i + b(c_i + W)}{2b}\right] = p_i^* + \frac{(W - C)}{2} \tag{4.4.2}$$

Substituting (4.4.2) into (4.2.1) gives the optimal order-quantity:

$$\hat{Q}_i = \left[\frac{A_i - b(c_i + W)}{2}\right] = Q_i^* - \frac{b(W - C)}{2} \tag{4.4.3}$$

Equations (4.4.2) and (4.4.3) summarize the profit-maximizing retailer's response given the manufacturer's choice of W. When $W > C$ the retail price will be greater, and the quantity will be lower, than in a full-information channel. Thus channel coordination across *all* states-of-nature requires $W = C$, which means that double marginalization is incompatible with channel coordination in this model, just as it is in the bilateral-monopoly model. Moreover, a manufacturer that pursues coordination with a one-part tariff will lose money. A two-part tariff of the form $\{C, \phi\}$ is the simplest wholesale-price policy that coordinates the channel while yielding a positive profit for the manufacturer.

We now turn to the third stage of the game. If the retailer distributes in the $i^{th}$ state-of-nature, its profit is:

$$\hat{\pi}_i^A = \left(\frac{(\hat{Q}_i)^2}{b} - f_A\right) - \phi \equiv (\hat{R}_i - f_A) - \phi \equiv \hat{g}_i - \phi \tag{4.4.4}$$

(The superscript $^A$ denotes that the retailer *agrees* to distribute the product.) *If* the retailer *refuses* to distribute in the $i^{th}$ state-of-nature (denoted by the superscript $^R$), retail profit is:

$$\hat{\pi}_i^R = -f_R \leq 0 \tag{4.4.5}$$

A comparison of (4.4.4) with (4.4.5) reveals that the independent retailer distributes the manufacturer's product in the i[th] state-of-nature when:

$$\left(\hat{R}_i - f_A - \phi\right) \geq -f_R \tag{4.4.6}$$

The retailer will refuse to distribute in the i[th] state-of-nature if this inequality is violated, because the non-distribution option (the RHS) yields a smaller loss than distribution (the LHS).

## 4.2 Asides on Temporal Breadth

The preceding analysis has important implications for the channel's temporal breadth. We comment first on a subtle but important distinction between the channel breadth observed in the vertically-integrated system and that observed in the decentralized channel. We then discuss an important difference between the multiple-retailers model of Chapter 3 and the multiple-states-of-nature, decentralized channel model of the present Chapter.

### 4.2.1 A Vertically-Integrated System *versus* an Independent Dyad

The vertically-integrated system serves the i[th] state-of-nature if:

$$R_i^* - \left(f_A - f_R\right) \geq 0 \tag{4.4.7}$$

This expression merely states that a state-of-nature is served (assuming the channel exists) provided the decision-maker earns at least as much money by serving the state as it would make by not serving that state-of-nature.

In contrast, the independent retailer serves the i[th] state-of-nature (assuming the channel exists) if and only if:

$$\hat{R}_i - \left(f_A - f_R\right) \geq \phi \tag{4.4.8}$$

Contrasting (4.3.9) with (4.4.6), we see that $R_i^* \geq \hat{R}_i$, with the equality holding only when the channel is coordinated (i.e., when $W = C$). Because $\phi > 0$ in an independent dyad, it follows that a coordinated, independent dyad does not offer temporal coverage that is as comprehensive as that provided by a vertically-integrated system. This result echoes our observation in Chapter 3 that a channel consisting of multiple, independent-retailers can never be more *spatially* comprehensive than is a vertically-integrated system.

### 4.2.2 Multiple Retailers *versus* Multiple States-of-Nature

In the multiple-retailers' model the channel-participation criterion is:

$$g^*_{N_c^*} \geq \phi_c^* > g^*_{N_c^*+1} \tag{3.3.14}$$

In the multiple-states-of-nature model the same criterion is:

$$\hat{g}^{*}_{\hat{n}^{*}-x} \geq \left(\phi^{*}_{\hat{n}^{*}-x} - f_{R}\right) > \hat{g}^{*}_{\hat{n}^{*}-(x+1)} \,. \tag{4.4.9}$$

In the former case participation occurs provided the i[th] retailer's profit (after its fixed cost) is at least as great as the fixed fee that it pays. In the latter case the i[th] state-of-nature must generate a profit at least as great as the fixed fee *minus* the fixed cost that would have been incurred had distribution not occurred. Stated differently, in the former model a retailer avoids a *fixed payment* ($\phi^{*}_{C}$) by not participating in the channel. In the latter model the retailer avoids a fixed payment but incurs a fixed cost of non-participation ($f_R$). This is the *critical distinction* between the two models. It means that, when $f_R > 0$, conclusions drawn from one model do not apply to the other model. We term the failure to recognize this distinction the "Multiple-Retailers/Multiple States-of-Nature Modeling Myth."

## 4.3 The Participation Decisions

In the second stage of the game the retailer decides if it will participate in the channel on a continuing basis. Participation requires that the retailer earn non-negative *expected* profit. Let the subscripts "i" and "j" denote the states-of-nature in which the retailer agrees and refuses to distribute the manufacturer's product. Then expected profit is:

$$\begin{aligned} E[\pi] &\equiv \sum_{i} \rho_i \left(\hat{R}_i - f_A - \phi\right) - \sum_{j} \rho_j f_R \\ \text{s.t.} &\quad \left(\sum\nolimits_i \rho_i + \sum\nolimits_j \rho_j\right) = 1 \end{aligned} \tag{4.4.10}$$

Expected profit is non-negative when the retailer's expected net revenue from distribution ($\Sigma_i \rho_i \hat{R}_i$), minus its expected fixed costs of distribution ($\Sigma_i \rho_i f_A$) and non-distribution ($\Sigma_j \rho_j f_R$), must be at least as great as its expected fixed fee payments to the manufacturer ($\Sigma_i \rho_i \phi$).

In the first stage of the game the manufacturer's participation decision is based on the sign of its expected profit:

$$E[\Pi] \equiv \sum_{i} \rho_i \left((W - C)\hat{Q}_i + \phi\right) - F \tag{4.4.11}$$

Channel existence requires that $E[\Pi] \geq 0$. This necessitates that revenue earned from merchandise ($\Sigma_i \rho_i (W - C)\hat{Q}_i$) and from the fixed fee ($\Sigma_i \rho_i \phi$) compensate for the fixed production cost (F) incurred in all states-of-nature.

In the next Section we investigate the manufacturer's optimal behavior subject to the constraint that it offers channel-coordinating schedules. In Section 6 we allow the manufacturer to maximize its profit without the constraint of channel coordination. In Section 7 we determine which of these policies is preferred by the manufacturer.

# 5 THE CHANNEL-COORDINATING TARIFFS

In this Section we seek a manufacturer profit-maximizing two-part tariff subject to the constraint that the tariff be *channel-coordinating*. Coordination requires that the per-unit fee equal the manufacturer's per-unit production cost ( $W = C$ ). Thus the manufacturer depends on the fixed fee for revenue in excess of its own variable cost. To obtain a closed-form solution for the profit that the manufacturer can extract from the retailer, we focus on the simple multiple-states-of-nature Scenario that was developed in Section 3: two states-of-nature $\Omega_1$ and $\Omega_2$ with probabilities $\rho$ and $(1-\rho)$. We rank the states in order of profitability, so that $\hat{g}_1 > \hat{g}_2$ and $Q_1^* > Q_2^*$.[12]

## 5.1 A Comprehensive Fixed Fee: Extracting the Retailer's Entire Expected Profit

We begin by determining if a manufacturer can employ a two-part tariff $\{C, \phi\}$ that extracts the retailer's entire *expected* profit while ensuring distribution in both states-of-nature. Expected profit over both states is:

$$E[\pi] \equiv E[\pi_1 + \pi_2] = \left( \frac{\rho(Q_1^*)^2}{b} + \frac{(1-\rho)(Q_2^*)^2}{b} - f_A \right) - \phi \\ \equiv \left(\rho R_1^* + (1-\rho) R_2^* - f_A\right) - \phi \tag{4.5.1}$$

If the retailer's expected profit *prior* to paying the fixed fee is non-positive, the channel will not exist. Assuming that the channel does exist, the fixed fee that extracts all profit from the retailer is:

$$\phi^{All} = \left(\rho R_1^* + (1-\rho) R_2^* - f_A\right) \tag{4.5.2}$$

$\phi^{All}$ is positively related to $Q_1^*$, $Q_2^*$, and the likelihood of the high-demand state ($\rho$), and is inversely related to the retailer's fixed distribution cost ( $f_A$ ).

Because the tariff $\{C, \phi^{All}\}$ generates an expected retail profit of zero, it may *appear* that the retailer would accept this contract. However, because the retailer makes its distribution decision knowing the true state-of-nature, this decision is driven by its *actual* profit. The retailer's profit (after paying the fixed fee) for an *agree* decision in the first state-of-nature is:

$$\pi_1^A\Big|_{\{C,\phi^{All}\}} = (1-\rho)(R_1^* - R_2^*) \equiv (1-\rho)\Delta > 0 \quad (4.5.3)$$

In inequality (4.5.3) we define the net revenue difference between the two states-of-nature as $\Delta \equiv (R_1^* - R_2^*) > 0$; the positive sign follows from our decision to rank states-of-nature by their profitability. Retailer profit for a *refuse* decision in the first state-of-nature is:

$$\pi_1^R\Big|_{\{C,\phi^{All}\}} = -f_R \le 0 \quad (4.5.4)$$

Given the tariff $\{C,\phi^{All}\}$, the retailer *always* distributes under $\Omega_1$.

With the less favorable state-of-nature $\Omega_2$ we reach a more complex conclusion. Retail profit under both distribution options is negative:

$$\begin{aligned} \pi_2^A\Big|_{\{C,\phi^{All}\}} &= -\rho\Delta < 0 \\ \pi_2^R\Big|_{\{C,\phi^{All}\}} &= -f_R \le 0 \end{aligned} \quad (4.5.5)$$

The retailer prefers to distribute the manufacturer's product[13] provided the probability of the high-demand state satisfies:

$$\rho \le (f_R / \Delta) \quad (4.5.6)$$

This condition merely says that the retailer will distribute in the low-demand state if the probability of $\Omega_2$ (i.e., $(1-\rho)$) is sufficiently high.

In summary, given the channel-coordinating wholesale-price schedule $\{C,\phi^{All}\}$, the retailer distributes the product under both states-of-nature when $(\rho\Delta - f_R) \le 0$. This decision generates zero expected profit for the retailer, while expected profit for the manufacturer ($\Pi$ with no subscript) and the channel ($\Pi$ with a subscript $_C$) are:

$$E\left[\Pi^{AA}\right]\Big|_{\{C,\phi^{All}\}} = E\left[\Pi_C^{AA}\right]\Big|_{\{C,\phi^{All}\}} = \phi^{All} - F \quad (4.5.7)$$

(The superscript $^{AA}$ (for *agree-agree*) denotes the retailer's agreement to distribute in both states-of-nature.) When $(\rho\Delta - f_R) \le 0$, the tariff $\{C,\phi^{All}\}$ is *manufacturer-optimal*, because the manufacturer's profit equals that obtained by the vertically-integrated system.[14]

If $(\rho\Delta - f_R) > 0$, the retailer *agrees* to distribute under $\Omega_1$ but *refuses* to do so under $\Omega_2$. Given this decision, expected profits are:

$$E\left[\pi^{AR}\right]\Big|_{\{C,\phi^{All}\}} = (1-\rho)(\rho\Delta - f_R) > 0 \quad (4.5.8)$$

$$E\left[\Pi^{AR}\right]\Big|_{\{C,\phi^{All}\}} = \rho\phi^{All} - F \quad (4.5.9)$$

$$E\left[\Pi_C^{AR}\right]\Big|_{\{C,\phi^{All}\}} = \rho(R_1^* - f_A) - (1-\rho)f_R - F \quad (4.5.10)$$

(The superscript notation $^{AR}$ (for *agree-refuse*) denotes this case.)

The retailer's refusal to distribute in the low-demand state when $\rho > (f_R / \Delta)$ raises four basic questions for the manufacturer:

1. Is there a different fixed fee (call it $\phi^{AA}$) that maximizes manufacturer profit subject to the constraints that the channel is coordinated and the retailer distributes the product in *both* states-of-nature?
2. Is $\phi^{AII}$ the manufacturer-optimal fixed fee when distribution *only* occurs in the high-demand state-of-nature or is there another fixed fee (call it $\phi^{AR}$) that yields a higher expected profit for the manufacturer?
3. Assuming $\phi^{AA}$ and $\phi^{AR}$ exist, for what parametric values should the manufacturer use fixed fees $\phi^{AII}$, $\phi^{AA}$, or $\phi^{AR}$?
4. Under what parametric values will the channel not exist?

We now address these questions over the probability range $\rho > (f_R / \Delta)$.

## 5.2 An Alternative Fixed Fee: Distributing in Both States-of-Nature

To guarantee distribution in both states of nature, the manufacturer must ensure that the retailer loses *less* money by distributing the product in $\Omega_2$ than it does by refusing to distribute. To maximize its own profit while guaranteeing distribution in both states-of-nature, the manufacturer must extract sufficient rent in the low-demand state to leave the retailer just willing to distribute the product. The resulting fixed fee is necessarily less than $\phi^{AII}$, so it leaves the retailer with positive profit in the high-demand state.

Formally, the tariff that maximizes manufacturer profit while ensuring Complete Coverage is $\{C, \phi^{AA}\}$, where $\phi^{AA}$ satisfies:

$$\phi^{AA} \equiv \left(R_2^{\bullet} - (f_A - f_R)\right) \tag{4.5.11}$$

This fixed fee, which follows directly from the retailer's distribution constraint (4.4.6), is independent of the probability distribution of the states-of-nature. Retail profits by state-of-nature and distribution option are:

$$\pi_1^A\Big|_{\{C,\phi^{AA}\}} = \Delta - f_R > 0 \quad \text{and} \quad \pi_1^R\Big|_{\{C,\phi^{AA}\}} = -f_R \le 0 \tag{4.5.12}$$

$$\pi_2^A\Big|_{\{C,\phi^{AA}\}} = -f_R \le 0 \quad \text{and} \quad \pi_2^R\Big|_{\{C,\phi^{AA}\}} = -f_R \le 0 \tag{4.5.13}$$

Because $\Delta > \rho\Delta > f_R$, it follows from (4.5.12) that the retailer distributes in $\Omega_1$. Distribution occurs in $\Omega_2$ because the "accept" and "reject" options yield identical profits for the retailer (we break ties in favor of distribution).

From the preceding analysis, expected profit levels are:

$$E\left[\pi^{AA}\right]\Big|_{\{C,\phi^{AA}\}} = \rho\Delta - f_R > 0 \tag{4.5.14}$$

$$E\left[\Pi^{AA}\right]\Big|_{\{C,\phi^{AA}\}} = \phi^{AA} - F \tag{4.5.15}$$

$$E\left[\Pi_C^{AA}\right]\Big|_{\{C,\phi^{AA}\}} = \phi^{AII} - F \tag{4.5.16}$$

The two-part tariff $\{C,\phi^{AA}\}$ coordinates the channel in both states-of-nature. Because $W = C$ is common to the tariffs $\{C,\phi^{AA}\}$ and $\{C,\phi^{AII}\}$, and because both states-of-nature are served, both tariffs generate the same channel profit, but they produce distinct distributions of that profit among channel members.

## 5.3 An Alternative Fixed Fee: Distributing in a Single State-of-Nature

When $(\rho\Delta - f_R) > 0$, an alternative channel-coordinating approach for the manufacturer is to maximize its own profit when the retailer does *not* distribute in $\Omega_2$. With this alternative the manufacturer extracts as much rent as possible from the retailer in the high-demand state, subject to the constraint that the retailer's expected profit over all states-of-nature is non-negative. We denote the tariff that accomplishes this goal as $\{C,\phi^{AR}\}$. The fixed fee and the resulting expected profits (for retailer, manufacturer, and channel) are:

$$\phi^{AR} = \left[\rho\left(R_1^* - f_A\right) - (1-\rho)f_R\right]/\rho \tag{4.5.17}$$

$$E\left[\pi^{AR}\right]\Big|_{\{C,\phi^{AR}\}} = 0 \tag{4.5.18}$$

$$E\left[\Pi^{AR}\right]\Big|_{\{C,\phi^{AR}\}} = E\left[\Pi_C^{AR}\right]\Big|_{\{C,\phi^{AR}\}} = \left[\rho\left(R_1^* - f_A\right) - (1-\rho)f_R\right] - F \tag{4.5.19}$$

$\phi^{AR}$ is positively related to probability $\rho$. Like $\{C,\phi^{AII}\}$, the tariff $\{C,\phi^{AR}\}$ extracts all expected profit from the retailer, although channel profit is lower when a single state-of-nature is served than when both states are served.

## 5.4 The Manufacturer's Profit-Maximizing, Channel-Coordinating Decision Rule

Each of the preceding tariffs maximizes manufacturer profit under particular $\rho$-values. A comparison of equations (4.5.7), (4.5.9), (4.5.15) and (4.5.19) reveals the *manufacturer-optimal decision rule* given that the manufacturer sets its wholesale price to coordinate the channel:

$$\begin{aligned} (\rho\Delta - f_R) \le 0 &\quad\Rightarrow\quad \{C, \phi^{All}\} \\ (1-\rho)\phi^{AA} \ge (\rho\Delta - f_R) > 0 &\quad\Rightarrow\quad \{C, \phi^{AA}\} \\ (\rho\Delta - f_R) > (1-\rho)\phi^{AA} &\quad\Rightarrow\quad \{C, \phi^{AR}\} \end{aligned} \tag{4.5.20}$$

These *channel-coordinating contingency tariffs* are conditional upon (1) the known probability of each state-of-nature, (2) the revenues generated in those states, (3) the fixed cost of distributing in a state-of-nature, and (4) the fixed cost of refusing to distribute in a state-of-nature.

Tables 4.1 and 4.2 summarize the actual and the expected profits associated with each of the contingency tariffs in (4.5.20). (The final two rows of each Table are discussed in Section 6 below.) These Tables merit two observations. First, if the $\{C, \phi^{All}\}$ tariff is infeasible, then as $\rho$ rises the manufacturer's tariff preference shifts from $\{C, \phi^{AA}\}$ to $\{C, \phi^{AR}\}$; that is, the higher is $\rho$ the more attractive it is for the manufacturer to extract all channel profit in the high-demand state by not serving the low-demand state. Second, neither the manufacturer nor the retailer can cover their fixed costs in the low-demand state under the $\{C, \phi^{AR}\}$ tariff. These theoretical results reinforce a real-world observation: channel members do not "make money" in all economic climates, and when distribution creates a loss, they can sometimes lose *less* money by refusing to distribute under some demand conditions.

### 5.4.1 The Manufacturer's Participation Constraints

The expressions in Tables 4.1 and 4.2 are only valid when all the relevant participation constraints have been satisfied. By construction, each of the three contingency tariffs satisfies the retailer's participation constraint ($E(\pi) \ge 0$). We now evaluate the manufacturer's participation constraint ($E(\Pi) \ge 0$) for each contingency tariff.

For the $\{C, \phi^{All}\}$ tariff, the manufacturer's participation constraint is:

$$(\phi^{All} - F) = (\rho\Delta - f_R + \phi^{AA} - F) \ge 0 \tag{4.5.21}$$

Under the $\{C, \phi^{AA}\}$ tariff, the manufacturer's participation constraint is:

$$(\phi^{AA} - F) \ge 0 \tag{4.5.22}$$

Finally, with the $\{C, \phi^{AR}\}$ tariff, the manufacturer's participation constraint is:

$$(\rho\phi^{AR} - F) = (\rho\Delta - f_R + \rho\phi^{AA} - F) \ge 0 \tag{4.5.23}$$

It is always best for the manufacturer to coordinate the channel, serve both states-of-nature, and reap all channel profit because $\phi^{All} > \phi^{AA}$ and $\phi^{All} > \rho\phi^{AR}$.

*Table 4.1.* Expected Profits with the Channel-Coordinating and Stackelberg Tariffs

| Tariff | Necessary Condition[1] | Fixed Fee | $E(\Pi_c)+F$ | $E(\Pi)+F$ | $E(\pi)$ |
|---|---|---|---|---|---|
| $\{C,\phi^{AII}\}$ | $(\rho\Delta - f_R)\le 0$ | $\phi^{AII}=\left[(\rho\Delta - f_A)+R_2^*\right]$ | $\phi^{AII}$ | $\phi^{AII}$ | 0 |
| $\{C,\phi^{AA}\}$ | $(1-\rho)\phi^{AA}\ge(\rho\Delta - f_R)>0$ | $\phi^{AA}=\left[R_2^* -(f_A - f_R)\right]$ | $\phi^{AII}$ | $\phi^{AA}$ | $(\rho\Delta - f_R)>0$ |
| $\{C,\phi^{AR}\}$ | $(\rho\Delta - f_R)>(1-\rho)\phi^{AA}>0$ | $\phi^{AR}=\left[\dfrac{\rho(R_1^* - f_A)-(1-\rho)f_R}{\rho}\right]$ | $\rho\phi^{AR}$ | $\rho\phi^{AR}$ | 0 |
| $\{\hat{W}^S,\hat{\phi}^S\}$ | $(\rho\Delta - f_R)\ge 2b\delta^2>0$ | $\hat{\phi}^S=\left[\left((Q_2^* - b\delta)^2/b\right)-(f_A - f_R)\right]$ | $\phi^{AII}-b\delta^2$ | $\phi^{AA}+b\delta^2$ | $\begin{pmatrix}(\rho\Delta - f_R)\\ -2b\delta^2\end{pmatrix}\ge 0$ |
| $\{\hat{W}^S,\hat{\phi}^{S\text{-}Adj}\}$ | $2b\delta^2>(\rho\Delta - f_R)>0$ | $\hat{\phi}^{S\text{-}Adj}=\hat{\phi}^S-\left[2b\delta^2-(\rho\Delta - f_R)\right]$ | $\phi^{AII}-b\delta^2$ | $\phi^{AII}-b\delta^2$ | 0 |

[1] To conserve space we define $\Delta\equiv(R_1^* - R_2^*)>0$ and $\delta\equiv\rho(\mu_1^* - \mu_2^*)>0$. Through simple substitution we have $\phi^{AII}=\phi^{AA}+(\rho\Delta - f_R)$.

*Table 4.2.* Manufacturer and Retailer Profits in each State-of-Nature with the Channel-Coordinating and Stackelberg Tariffs

| Tariff | Condition[1] | $\Pi_1 + F$ | $\Pi_2 + F$ | $\pi_1$ | $\pi_2$ |
|---|---|---|---|---|---|
| $\{C, \phi^{AII}\}$ | $(\rho\Delta - f_R) \le 0$ | $\phi^{AII}$ | $\phi^{AII}$ | $(1-\rho)\Delta > 0$ | $0 > -\rho\Delta > -f_R$ |
| $\{C, \phi^{AA}\}$ | $(1-\rho)\phi^{AA} \ge (\rho\Delta - f_R) > 0$ | $\phi^{AA}$ | $\phi^{AA}$ | $(\Delta - f_R) > 0$ | $-f_R$ |
| $\{C, \phi^{AR}\}$ | $(\rho\Delta - f_R) > (1-\rho)\phi^{AA} > 0$ | $\phi^{AR}$ | $0$ | $\dfrac{(1-\rho)f_R}{\rho} \ge 0$ | $-f_R$ |
| $\{\hat{W}^S, \hat{\phi}^S\}$ | $(\rho\Delta - f_R) \ge 2b\delta^2 > 0$ | $\phi^{AA} + \dfrac{(2-\rho)b\delta^2}{\rho}$ | $\phi^{AA} - b\delta^2$ | $\left(\Delta - \dfrac{2b\delta^2}{\rho} - f_R\right) > 0$ | $-f_R$ |
| $\{\hat{W}^S, \hat{\phi}^{S\text{-}Adj}\}$ | $2b\delta^2 > (\rho\Delta - f_R) > 0$ | $\phi^{AII} + \dfrac{(2-3\rho)b\delta^2}{\rho}$ | $\phi^{AII} - 3b\delta^2$ | $-\dfrac{(1-\rho)}{\rho}(2b\delta^2 - \rho\Delta)$ | $(2b\delta^2 - \rho\Delta) > -f_R$ |

[1] To conserve space we define $\Delta \equiv (R_1^* - R_2^*) > 0$ and $\delta \equiv \rho(\mu_1^* - \mu_2^*) > 0$. Through simple substitution we have $\phi^{AII} = \phi^{AA} + (\rho\Delta - f_R)$.

When the manufacturer's "first-best" policy ($\phi^{AII}$) is infeasible because $(\rho\Delta - f_R) > 0$, there are parametric values for which the manufacturer prefers incomplete coverage with the tariff $\{C, \phi^{AR}\}$ and other parametric values for which the manufacturer prefers complete coverage with the tariff $\{C, \phi^{AA}\}$, even though the latter tariff generates a positive profit for the retailer.

To clarify matters, we define four Zones in $\langle \rho, \mathcal{Q} \rangle$ – space. Complete coverage occurs in Zones $\mathbf{Z}_{12}^{AII}$ and $\mathbf{Z}_{12}^{AA}$ (superscripts refer to the wholesale-price policy while the subscript denotes that both states-of-nature are served). These Zones are separated by a boundary ($\rho_{AA}^{AII}$) that is the solution to $(\rho\Delta - f_R) = 0$. Incomplete Coverage occurs in Zone $\mathbf{Z}_1^{AR}$. Zones $\mathbf{Z}_{12}^{AA}$ and $\mathbf{Z}_1^{AR}$ are separated by a boundary ($\rho_{AR}^{AA}$) that is the solution to $(\rho\Delta - f_R) = (1-\rho)\phi^{AA}$. We show below that *Zero Coverage* is also an option.

To facilitate a comparison of the "coordination-constrained" Zones with our earlier "vertically-integrated" Zones, we re-scale our model using the four terms introduced in sub-Section 3.2.2; we reproduce them here:

$\mathcal{Q} \equiv (Q_2^* / Q_1^*)$ ≡ The size of the low-demand state *relative* to the high-demand state;

$f_{\mathcal{A}} \equiv (f_A / R_1^*)$ ≡ The fixed cost of distribution relative to the net revenue earned in the high-demand state;

$\varphi \equiv (f_R / f_A)$ ≡ The fixed cost of not distributing the product relative to the fixed cost of distribution; and

$\mathcal{F} \equiv (F / R_1^*)$ ≡ The fixed cost of production expressed as a proportion of the net revenue earned in the high-demand state.

### 5.4.2 The Coordinated Channel's Zonal Boundaries

Zones $\mathbf{Z}_{12}^{AII}, \mathbf{Z}_{12}^{AA}$, and $\mathbf{Z}_1^{AR}$ are separated by the zonal boundaries $\rho_{AA}^{AII}$ and $\rho_{AR}^{AA}$. In re-scaled terms these boundaries are:

$$\rho_{AA}^{AII} = \left( \frac{\varphi f_{\mathcal{A}}}{1 - \mathcal{Q}^2} \right) \geq 0 \tag{4.5.24}$$

$$\rho_{AR}^{AA} = \left( \frac{\mathcal{Q}^2 - (1 - 2\varphi) f_{\mathcal{A}}}{1 - (1 - \varphi) f_{\mathcal{A}}} \right) \gtrless 0 \tag{4.5.25}$$

Expression (4.5.24) defines a *Full Profit-Extraction Boundary* that delineates sub-Zones within the Complete-Coverage Zone. Above $\rho_{AA}^{AII}$ the manufacturer earns all profit; below $\rho_{AA}^{AII}$ the retailer shares in channel profit.

The critical value $\rho_{AR}^{AA}$ defines the *Complete/Incomplete-Coverage Boundary* that separates the Complete-Coverage Zone and the Incomplete-Coverage Zone. This boundary also serves as a profit distribution boundary; below $\rho_{AR}^{AA}$ the manufacturer gains all channel profit, while above it (and below $\rho_{AA}^{AII}$) retail profit is positive.

The mutually-exclusive Zones $\mathbf{Z}_{12}^{AII}$, $\mathbf{Z}_{12}^{AA}$, and $\mathbf{Z}_{1}^{AR}$ determine the manufacturer's selection of the proper contingency tariff given that the channel exists (i.e., given that the model's parameters satisfy the pertinent manufacturer-participation constraints defined by expressions (4.5.21)-(4.5.23)). Re-scaling the manufacturer-participation constraint associated with $\{C, \phi^{AII}\}$ yields:

$$\left(\phi^{AII} - F\right) = 0 \quad \rightarrow \quad \rho_0^{AII} = \left(\frac{\mathcal{F} + f_{\mathcal{A}} - Q^2}{1 - Q^2}\right) \equiv \rho_{12}^{VI} \qquad (4.5.26)$$

This condition is identical to the *Complete/Zero-Coverage Boundary* derived for the vertically-integrated manufacturer in expression (4.3.16).

In the case of the two-part tariff $\{C, \phi^{AR}\}$, the rescaled participation constraint becomes:

$$\left(\rho\phi^{AR} - F\right) = 0 \quad \rightarrow \quad \rho_0^{AR} = \left(\frac{\mathcal{F} + \varphi f_{\mathcal{A}}}{1 - (1-\varphi) f_{\mathcal{A}}}\right) \equiv \rho_1^{VI} \qquad (4.5.27)$$

This condition is identical to the *Incomplete/Zero-Coverage Boundary* derived for the vertically-integrated system in expression (4.3.17).

Expressions (4.5.26) and (4.5.27) reveal that a vertically-integrated system and a coordination-constrained, decentralized manufacturer face the same tradeoff between coverage and channel non-existence. The explanation for this result is direct: all profits go to one decision-maker under both the $\{C, \phi^{AII}\}$ tariff and the $\{C, \phi^{AR}\}$ tariff. We observe exactly this situation in the vertically-integrated system.

In contrast to these "clean" results, when parametric values induce the manufacturer to offer the two-part tariff $\{C, \phi^{AA}\}$, we find:

$$\begin{aligned} \left(\phi^{AA} - F\right) = 0 \quad \rightarrow \quad Q^2 &= \left(\mathcal{F} + (1-\varphi) f_{\mathcal{A}}\right) \\ &= \left(\mathcal{F} + \delta^{VI}\right) \equiv \delta^{AA} \end{aligned} \qquad (4.5.28)$$

We use the symbol $\delta^{AA}$ in expression (4.5.28) to denote the combination of fixed costs that defines this *Shared-Profit/Zero-Coverage Boundary*. If $F = 0$

(and therefore $\mathcal{F}=0$), expression (4.5.28) replicates (4.3.15). Thus in this special case, the coordination-constrained manufacturer's Shared-Profit/Zero-Coverage Boundary coincides with part of the vertically-integrated system's Complete/Incomplete-Coverage Boundary.

### 5.4.3 The Coordination-Constrained Decision Rule: Theoretical Effects

We now examine the impact of changes in the re-scaled parameters on temporal coverage and channel existence. It follows from condition (4.5.24) that the *Full Profit-Extraction Boundary* ($\rho_{AA}^{All}$) rises with increases in $f_{\mathcal{A}}$, $\varphi$, and $Q$, but is independent of $\mathcal{F}$. The Complete/Incomplete Coverage Boundary ($\rho_{AR}^{AA}$) rises with $\varphi$ and $Q$, is independent of $\mathcal{F}$, and has a complex relationship with $f_{\mathcal{A}}$:

$$\begin{aligned}\frac{\partial\rho_{AR}^{AA}}{\partial f_{\mathcal{A}}} &= \left(\frac{(1-\varphi)Q^2-(1-2\varphi)}{\left(1-(1-\varphi)f_{\mathcal{A}}\right)^2}\right)\gtrless 0 \\ \Rightarrow \quad \frac{\partial\rho_{AR}^{AA}}{\partial f_{\mathcal{A}}} &\gtrless 0 \quad \forall \quad Q^2 \gtrless \left(\frac{1-2\varphi}{1-\varphi}\right)\end{aligned} \tag{4.5.29}$$

An increase in $f_{\mathcal{A}}$ clearly increases $\rho_{AR}^{AA}$ for all $\varphi > \frac{1}{2}$; the reverse is true at sufficiently low values of $\varphi$. For example, in the absence of a fixed cost of non-distribution ($f_R = 0 \rightarrow \varphi = 0$) we find $\partial\rho_{AR}^{AA}/\partial f_{\mathcal{A}} < 0$.

The relevant partial derivatives for the Zero-Coverage Boundaries $\rho_0^{All}$ and $\rho_0^{AR}$ are found at (4.3.18) and (4.3.19), respectively. Finally, an analysis of the Complete/Zero-Coverage Boundary $\delta^{AA}$ reveals that $Q$ rises with increases in $\mathcal{F}$ and $f_{\mathcal{A}}$, is independent of the value of $\rho$, and declines with increases in $\varphi$. With this theoretical background we turn to numerical illustrations of these boundaries in $\langle\rho, Q\rangle$ – space.

### 5.4.4 The Coordination-Constrained Decision Rule: Numerical Effects

To gain further insight into the channel-coordinating contingency tariffs, we turn to numerical analysis. Because changes in the manufacturer's fixed cost (F) do not affect the retailer's distribution decision, we set $F=0$. Under this assumption, the Shared-Profit/Zero-Coverage Boundary reduces to $Q^2=\delta^{AA}=\delta^{VI}$. We now describe the manufacturer's optimal strategy in $\langle\rho, Q\rangle$ – space, given the channel-coordination constraint, for the four Scenarios introduced in Section 3.

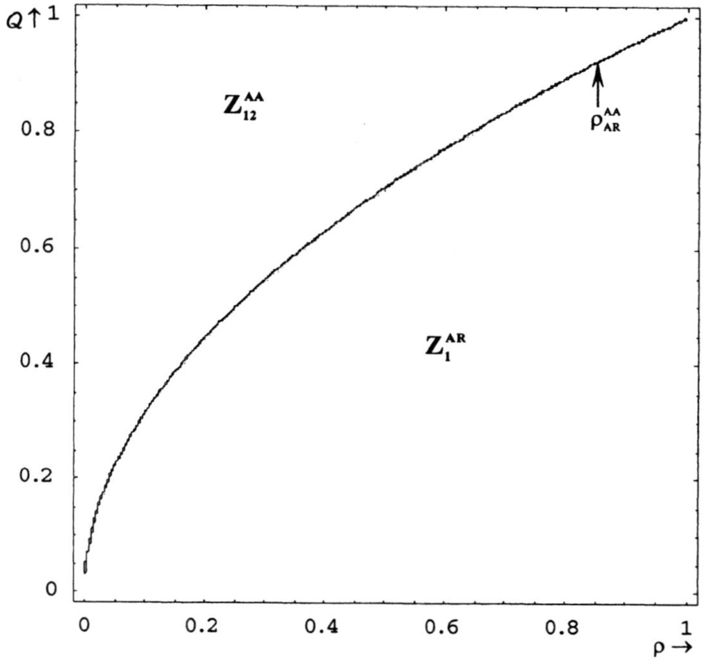


Legend:

$\rho_{AR}^{AA} \equiv$ The Complete/Incomplete Coverage Boundary;

$Z_{12}^{AA} \equiv$ The coordination-constrained manufacturer serves both states-of-nature; and

$Z_{1}^{AR} \equiv$ The coordination-constrained manufacturer only serves the high-demand state.

*Figure 4.4.* The Manufacturer-Optimal, Channel-Coordinating Strategy When $f_{\mathcal{A}} = 0 = \varphi$

**Scenario 1** ($f_{\mathcal{A}} = 0 = \varphi$): Figure 4.4 depicts the manufacturer-optimal, channel-coordinating wholesale-price policy in this Scenario. Because $\rho_{AA}^{All} = 0$, the two-part tariff $\{C, \phi^{All}\}$ is *never* optimal; the manufacturer selects either $\{C, \phi^{AA}\}$ or $\{C, \phi^{AR}\}$. The Complete/Incomplete Coverage Boundary is defined as:

$$\rho_{AR}^{AA} = Q^2 \tag{4.5.30}$$

The $\rho_{AR}^{AA}$ – boundary describes a parabola that intercepts the $\langle \rho = 0 \rangle$ – axis at $Q = 0$ and the $\langle \rho = 1 \rangle$ – axis at $Q = 1$.

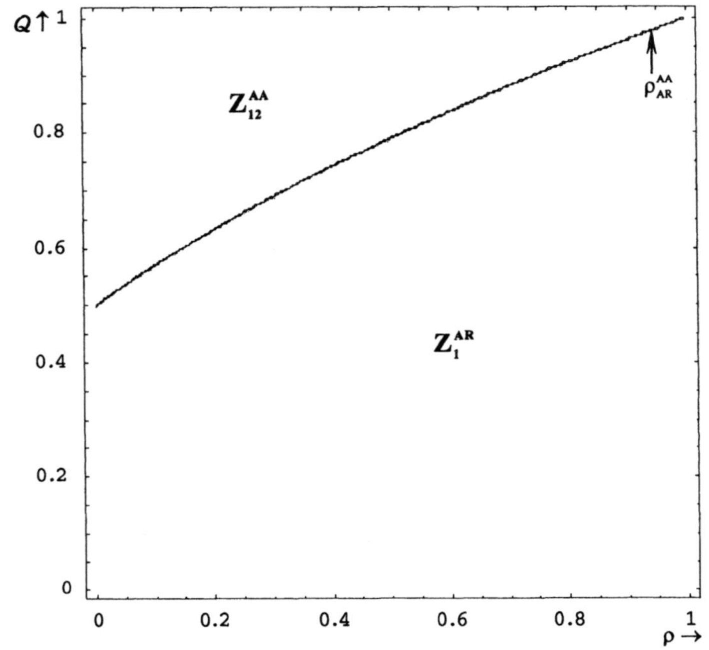


Legend:

$\rho_{AR}^{AA}$ ≡ The Complete/Incomplete Coverage Boundary;

$Z_{12}^{AA}$ ≡ The coordination-constrained manufacturer serves both states-of-nature; and

$Z_1^{AR}$ ≡ The coordination-constrained manufacturer only serves the high-demand state.

*Figure 4.5.* The Manufacturer-Optimal, Channel-Coordinating Strategy When $f_{\mathcal{A}} = 0.25, \varphi = 0$

In Scenario 1 the manufacturer's participation constraints are non-binding in Zone $\mathbf{Z}_{12}^{AA}$ or Zone $\mathbf{Z}_1^{AR}$. As a result, above $\rho_{AR}^{AA}$ the manufacturer sets a wholesale price to serve both states-of-nature, while below $\rho_{AR}^{AA}$ the manufacturer prices to serve only the high-demand state. Recall that the vertically-integrated system always served both states-of-nature in this Scenario. Therefore, channel-decentralization narrows temporal breadth for these (commonly assumed) parametric values.

**Scenario 2** ($f_{\mathcal{A}} = 0.25, \varphi = 0$): Figure 4.5 depicts the manufacturer-optimal, channel-coordinating wholesale-price policy in this Scenario. As in the previous Scenario, because $\rho_{AA}^{AII} = 0$, the two-part tariff $\{C, \phi^{AII}\}$ is *never*

optimal, so the manufacturer offers $\{C,\phi^{AA}\}$ or $\{C,\phi^{AR}\}$. The Complete/ Incomplete Coverage Boundary is defined as:

$$\rho_{AR}^{AA} = (4Q^2 - 1)/3 \qquad (4.5.31)$$

The parabola-shaped boundary (4.5.31) intercepts the $\langle\rho = 0\rangle$ – axis at $Q = 1/2$ and the $\langle\rho = 1\rangle$ – axis at $Q = 1$. Because the manufacturer-participation constraints are not binding, the channel exists at all $\langle\rho, Q\rangle$ – values. Above the $\rho_{AR}^{AA}$ – boundary the manufacturer prices for complete coverage; below this boundary the manufacturer prices to serve only the high-demand state. As the vertically-integrated system served both states when $Q > 1/2$, we again see that channel-decentralization narrows temporal breadth. Finally, comparing Figures 4.4 and 4.5 confirms our theoretical conclusion at inequality (4.5.29): as $f_{\mathcal{A}}$ increases (here from 0 to $1/4$), the $\rho_{AR}^{AA}$ – boundary pivots upward around the point $\langle\rho = 1, Q = 0\rangle$, thereby expanding the Incomplete-Coverage Zone.

**Scenario 3** ($f_{\mathcal{A}} = 0.25, \varphi = 0.5$): Figure 4.6 shows the manufacturer's channel-coordinating wholesale-price policy. The Full Profit-Extraction Boundary is:

$$\rho_{AA}^{AII} = 1/(8[1 - Q^2]) \qquad (4.5.32)$$

This boundary intercepts the $\langle Q^* = 0\rangle$ – axis at $\rho = 1/8$ and the $\langle\rho = 1\rangle$ – axis at $Q = \sqrt{7/8} \simeq 0.935$. The Complete/Incomplete-Coverage Boundary ($\rho_{AR}^{AA}$) satisfies:

$$\rho_{AR}^{AA} = 8Q^2/7 \qquad (4.5.33)$$

This boundary intercepts the $\rho_{AA}^{AII}$ – boundary at $Q = \sqrt{1/8} \cong 0.354$ and the $\langle\rho = 1\rangle$ – axis at $Q = \sqrt{7/8} \simeq 0.935$, but does *not* intercept the $\langle\rho = 0\rangle$ – axis.

We now turn to the (complex) conditions under which the channel does not exist. The Complete/Zero-Coverage Boundary satisfies:

$$\rho_0^{AII} = \rho_{12}^{VI} \equiv (1 - 4Q^2)/(4[1 - Q^2]) \qquad (4.5.34)$$

The $\rho_0^{AII}$ – boundary intercepts the $\langle\rho = 0\rangle$ – axis at $Q = 1/2$; it also intercepts the $\rho_{AA}^{AII}$ – boundary at $Q = \sqrt{1/8} \cong 0.354$.

The Incomplete/Zero-Coverage Boundary in Scenario 3 satisfies:

$$\rho_0^{AR} \equiv \rho_1^{VI} = 1/7 \qquad (4.5.35)$$

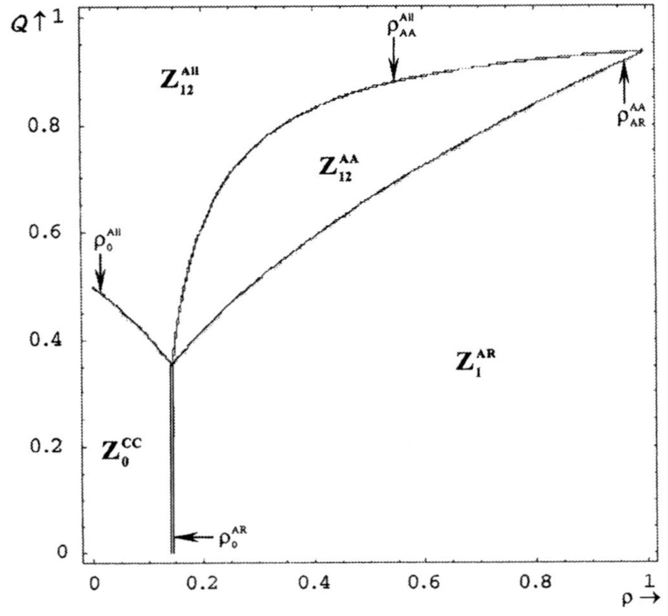


Legend:

$\rho^{All}_{AA} \equiv$ The Shared-Profit Boundary;

$\rho^{AA}_{AR} \equiv$ The Complete/Incomplete Coverage Boundary;

$\rho^{All}_{0} \equiv$ The Complete/Zero-Coverage Boundary;

$\rho^{AR}_{0} \equiv$ The Incomplete/Zero-Coverage Boundary;

$Z^{All}_{12} \equiv$ The coordination-constrained manufacturer serves both states-of-nature, and extracts all expected channel profit;

$Z^{AA}_{12} \equiv$ The coordination-constrained manufacturer serves both states-of-nature but does not obtain all channel profit;

$Z^{AR}_{1} \equiv$ The coordination-constrained manufacturer only serves the high-demand state; and

$Z^{CC}_{0} \equiv$ The coordination-constrained manufacturer serves neither state-of-nature.

*Figure 4.6.* The Manufacturer-Optimal, Channel-Coordinating Strategy When $f_{\mathcal{R}} = 0.25, \varphi = 0.5$

Expressions (4.5.32)-(4.5.35) collectively define the Zones in which coverage occurs. The Complete-Coverage Zone lies (i) above and to the right of the $\rho^{All}_{0}$ – boundary and (ii) above and to the left of the $\rho^{AA}_{AR}$ – boundary.

Within this Zone the Shared-Profit sub-Zone is delineated by the $\rho_{AA}^{All}$ – boundary and the $\rho_{AR}^{AA}$ – boundary. The Incomplete-Coverage Zone lies to the right of the $\rho_0^{AR}$ – line and below the $\rho_{AR}^{AA}$ – boundary. Finally, the Zero-Coverage Zone ($\mathbf{Z}_0^{CC}$) occupies the remainder of $\langle \rho, Q \rangle$ – space (the superscript $^{CC}$ denotes a coordination-constrained channel); it is delineated by the $\rho_0^{All}$ – boundary and the $\rho_0^{AR}$ – boundary.

A visual comparison of Figures 4.2 and 4.6 reveals that the vertically-integrated system offers more complete coverage than does the decentralized channel. Although the Zero-Coverage Zone is the same for these two methods of organizing distribution, the Incomplete-Coverage Zone is larger in the decentralized channel. The reason is that the independent manufacturer cannot extract all profit from the retailer below the Full Profit-Extraction Boundary; therefore the manufacturer finds it advantageous to eliminate distribution in the low-demand space over a non-trivial portion of $\langle \rho, Q \rangle$ – space.

**Scenario 4** ($f_{\mathcal{A}} = 0.25, \varphi = 1$): Figure 4.7 depicts the manufacturer-optimal, channel-coordinating wholesale-price policy in this Scenario. The Full Profit-Extraction Boundary $\rho_{AA}^{All}$ has shifted to the right relative to its location in Figure 4.6. As a result, it now satisfies:

$$\rho_{AA}^{All} = 1/\left(4\left[1 - Q^2\right]\right) \tag{4.5.36}$$

The $\rho_{AA}^{All}$ – boundary intercepts the $\langle Q = 0 \rangle$ – axis at $\rho = \frac{1}{4}$ and the $\langle \rho = 1 \rangle$ – axis at $Q = \sqrt{\frac{3}{4}} \cong 0.866$. The Complete/Incomplete-Coverage Boundary now satisfies:

$$\rho_{AR}^{AA} = Q^2 + \frac{1}{4} \tag{4.5.37}$$

The $\rho_{AR}^{AA}$ – boundary intercepts the $\langle Q = 0 \rangle$ – axis at $\frac{1}{4}$ and the $\langle \rho = 1 \rangle$ – axis at $Q = \sqrt{\frac{3}{4}} \cong 0.866$.

The Complete-Coverage Zone encompasses the areas labeled $\mathbf{Z}_{12}^{All}$ and $\mathbf{Z}_{12}^{AA}$ in Figure 4.7; the Incomplete-Coverage Zone consists of the area labeled $\mathbf{Z}_1^{AR}$. In contrast, recall that in this Scenario the vertically-integrated system offered complete coverage in all three of these zonal areas. Thus, for some parametric values, channel decentralization narrows channel breadth. However, the same, lower-left portion of $\langle \rho, Q \rangle$ – space is not served by the vertically-integrated system and the decentralized channel.

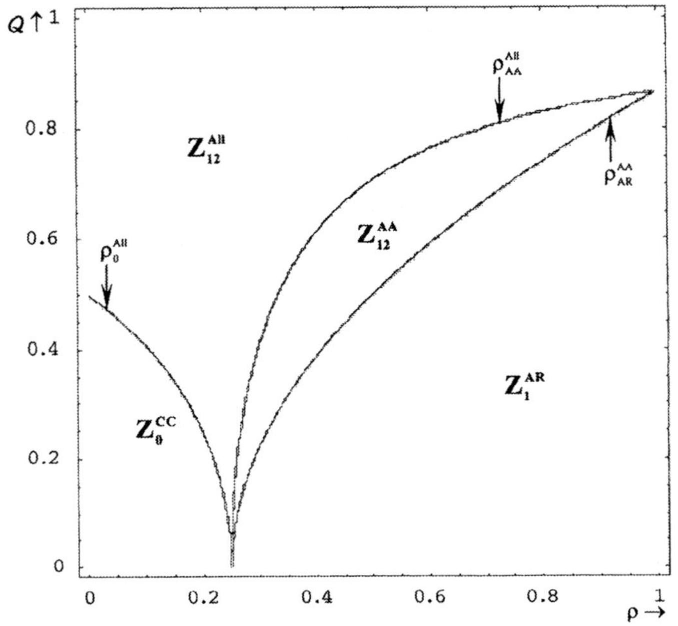


Legend:

$\rho_{AA}^{All} \equiv$ The Shared-Profit Boundary;

$\rho_{AR}^{AA} \equiv$ The Complete/Incomplete Coverage Boundary;

$\rho_0^{All} \equiv$ The Complete/Zero-Coverage Boundary;

$Z_{12}^{All} \equiv$ The coordination-constrained manufacturer serves both states-of-nature, and extracts all expected channel profit;

$Z_{12}^{AA} \equiv$ The coordination-constrained manufacturer serves both states-of-nature but does not obtain all channel profit;

$Z_1^{AR} \equiv$ The coordination-constrained manufacturer only serves the high-demand state; and

$Z_0^{CC} \equiv$ The coordination-constrained manufacturer serves neither state-of-nature.

*Figure 4.7.* The Manufacturer-Optimal, Channel-Coordinating Strategy When $f_{\mathcal{A}} = 0.25, \varphi = 1$

### 5.4.5 The Coordination-Constrained Decision Rule: The Impact of Fixed Costs

We draw three key conclusions from our analysis of the channel-coordinating tariffs derived in this Section. First, conforming to intuition, an increase in the fixed cost of distribution ($f_A$) decreases the set of $\langle \rho, Q \rangle$ – values under which the manufacturer sets a wholesale price that leads to *complete coverage.* Second, increases in the fixed cost of non-distribution ($f_R$) decrease the set of $\langle \rho, Q \rangle$ – values under which there is *incomplete coverage.* Third, increases in the fixed cost of non-distribution ($f_R$) increase the set of $\langle \rho, Q \rangle$ – values for which *the channel does not exist.*

*Incomplete Coverage* occurs whenever the manufacturer's wholesale-price policy causes the retailer to refuse to serve the low-demand state. The decentralized manufacturer prefers incomplete coverage, and establishes its wholesale-price policy accordingly, when $(\rho\Delta - f_R) > (1-\rho)[R_2^\bullet - (f_A - f_R)]$. Simple manipulation of this inequality reveals that, given the decision to maximize channel profit, incomplete coverage is manufacturer-optimal when the probability of the high-demand state satisfies the following condition:

$$\rho > \rho_{AR}^{AA} \equiv \left( \frac{R_2^\bullet - (f_A - 2f_R)}{R_1^\bullet - (f_A - f_R)} \right) = \left( \frac{Q^2 - (1-2\varphi) f_{\mathcal{A}}}{1 - (1-\varphi) f_{\mathcal{A}}} \right) \tag{4.5.38}$$

Inequality (4.5.38) reflects the fact that, when $\rho$ is sufficiently great, it is in the interest of the manufacturer to employ a wholesale-price policy that induces the retailer to serve only $\Omega_1$. The intuitive reason for this is that the manufacturer can obtain all channel profit with the tariff $\{C, \phi^{AR}\}$, but can only earn a portion of channel profit with the tariff $\{C, \phi^{AA}\}$. Notice that incomplete coverage is optimal (for some parametric values) when the cost of non-distribution is zero; that is, $f_R = 0$ implies $\rho_{AR}^{AA} < 1$.

*Channel Non-Existence* occurs whenever a wholesale-price schedule leaves the retailer or the manufacturer with negative expected profit. Given that the manufacturer uses a channel-coordinating strategy, the maximum possible channel profit can be shared between channel members with the two-part tariff $\{C, \phi\}$. Expected channel profit is:

$$E[\Pi_C] = \rho R_1^\bullet + (1-\rho) R_2^\bullet - f_A - F \tag{4.5.39}$$

Applying simple algebra to the expected channel-profit constraint reveals:

$$\rho < \rho_0^{All} = \rho_{12}^{VI} \equiv \left( \frac{F + f_A - R_2^\bullet}{R_1^\bullet - R_2^\bullet} \right) = \left( \frac{\mathcal{F} + f_{\mathcal{A}} - Q^2}{1 - Q^2} \right) \tag{4.5.40}$$

A necessary condition for channel non-existence is that the probability of the high-demand state (ρ) *be less than* $\rho_0^{All}$. This critical probability is negative (and therefore irrelevant) when the fixed costs of production and distribution do not exceed net revenue in the low-demand state. The $\rho_0^{All}$ – value rises with increases in F and $f_A$ and declines with increases in the net revenue of either state-of-nature. (This condition is a restatement of the manufacturer's participation constraint under the wholesale-price policy $\{C, \phi^{All}\}$.)

The maximal ρ – value associated with the manufacturer-participation constraint under the $\{C, \phi^{AR}\}$ tariff is:

$$\rho \leq \rho_0^{AR} = \rho_1^{VI} \equiv \left( \frac{\mathcal{F} + \varphi f_{\mathcal{A}}}{1 - (1 - \varphi) f_{\mathcal{A}}} \right) \tag{4.5.27}$$

In combination, inequalities (4.5.26) and (4.5.27) reveal that the size of the Zero-Coverage Zone depends on the manufacturer's fixed production cost; and on the retailer's fixed costs of distribution and non-distribution.

## 5.5 Commentary on Channel Coordination

We have shown that coordination is possible under all states-of-nature. Specifically, the manufacturer can coordinate the channel by setting a per-unit wholesale price that is equal to its own marginal production cost, in which case the fixed fee is the manufacturer's sole revenue source. We have also shown that there are limits to the manufacturer's rent-extraction ability, because a wholesale-price schedule $\{C, \phi\}$ can generate three responses:

- The retailer may distribute under both states-of-nature;
- The retailer may distribute only under the high-demand state; or
- The retailer may refuse to participate in the channel.

The option chosen by the retailer depends on five factors:

(a) The probability of the high-demand state-of-nature (ρ);

(b) The attractiveness of the low-demand relative to the high-demand states-of-nature ($\mathcal{Q}$);

(c) The retailer's fixed costs of distributing ($f_A$) or not distributing ($f_R$);

(d) The manufacturer's fixed cost of production (F); and

(e) The fixed fee charged by the manufacturer ($\phi$).

Although the manufacturer controls (e) and is aware of (a)-(d), it does not have the power to force the vertically-integrated solution. As a result, the decentralized channel often is of narrower temporal breadth—it serves fewer states-of-nature—than does the vertically-integrated system.

# 6 THE STACKELBERG TARIFFS

In Section 5 we derived three tariffs that maximized manufacturer profit subject to the constraint of channel coordination. As a result, both states-of-nature were not always served: there was incomplete coverage for some parametric values and zero coverage for other values. In this Section we derive three tariffs that maximize manufacturer profit subject to a distribution-constraint that *both* states-of-nature are served.[15] While this Section's tariffs *need not* coordinate the channel, they *may* generate higher manufacturer profit than do the coordinating tariffs. (In Section 7 we test the hypothesis that the manufacturer may prefer own-profit maximization to channel coordination.)

The retailer's decision-making *process* is unaffected by whether the manufacturer's objective is channel coordination or own-profit maximization. With either objective, the retailer determines its optimal price (equation (4.4.2)) and order-quantity (equation (4.4.3)) in the fourth stage of the game, decides if it will distribute the product in the low demand state-of-nature in the third stage (equation (4.4.6)), and makes its channel-participation decision in the second stage (equation (4.4.10)). Because the manufacturer's objective may affect its wholesale-price policy, the objective can have an effect on the retailer's actual decisions. Thus we begin our analysis by discussing the manufacturer's distribution-constrained, profit-maximization problem.

## 6.1 Expected Profit-Maximization by the Manufacturer

The manufacturer sets its wholesale-price strategy to maximize its *expected* profit, subject to the constraint that the retailer distributes in both states-of-nature. To achieve this breadth-of-distribution objective, the manufacturer's wholesale-price policy must satisfy the retailer's participation and distribution constraints, which require (i) non-negative expected profit across all states-of-nature and (ii) profit in the low-demand state that is at least as great as the loss from non-distribution. For the channel to exist, the manufacturer's participation constraint must also be met.

Our approach involves Stackelberg leadership by the manufacturer, with *simultaneous* optimization of both elements of a two-part tariff. To the extent that is possible, when the resulting wholesale-price policy violates the retailer's participation constraint, we adjust the fixed fee to keep the retailer as a channel participant. Even with this adjustment, there are parametric values for which there is zero coverage; our approach merely guarantees that channel non-existence is a mutual decision. (We do not consider the possibility that a channel member may operate at a loss.)

The manufacturer's expected profit is:

$$E(\Pi) = (\hat{W} - C)\left[\rho\hat{Q}_1(\hat{W}) + (1-\rho)\hat{Q}_2(\hat{W})\right] + \hat{\phi} - F \tag{4.6.1}$$

We see in expression (4.6.1) that the manufacturer's earnings come from two sources: (i) selling its product at a (potentially) positive margin and (ii) charging a fixed fee. The term $\hat{Q}_i(\hat{W})$ is the retailer's quantity-reaction function (see (4.4.3)) and the symbol ^ denotes a Stackelberg variable.

### 6.1.1 Full Channel-Profit Extraction with Complete Coverage

We begin our analysis by examining a distribution constraint that extracts the retailer's entire expected profit:

$$\left[\rho\hat{R}_1 + (1-\rho)\hat{R}_2 - f_A - \hat{\phi}\right] = 0 \tag{4.6.2}$$

In this constraint the term $\hat{R}_i \equiv (\hat{Q}_i(\hat{W}))^2 / b,\ i \in (1,2)$ is the retailer's net revenue in the i[th] state-of-nature. Expression (4.6.2) merely states that the retailer earns an expected profit of zero, given the two-part tariff $\{\hat{W}, \hat{\phi}\}$. Maximization of (4.6.1), subject to (4.6.2), leads to a channel coordinating per-unit fee ($\hat{W}^* = C$) and an associated fixed fee ($\hat{\phi}^* = \phi^{All}$) that is defined at (4.5.2). In Section 5 we proved that all profit generated by the channel-coordinating tariff $\{C, \phi^{All}\}$ is obtained by the manufacturer ($E[\Pi_C] = E[\Pi]$ $= (\phi^{All} - F)$). Thus channel-coordination and Stackelberg maximization lead to the same outcomes over the range of parameter values for which the retailer's distribution constraint is met ($\rho \leq f_R / \Delta$).

### 6.1.2 Limited Channel-Profit Extraction with Complete Coverage

Both states-of-nature *will not* be served if the manufacturer offers $\{C, \phi^{All}\}$ when $\rho > f_R / \Delta$. Because the retailer's distribution constraint cannot be violated, the fixed fee must ensure that the retailer's profit from distribution in the low-demand state equals or exceeds its profit from non-distribution. Therefore the proper distribution-constraint is:

$$\left[\hat{R}_2 - (f_A - f_R) - \hat{\phi}\right] = 0 \tag{4.6.3}$$

This constraint is reminiscent of equation (4.5.11), although it leads to the same results only when $\hat{W}^* = C$.

We maximize (4.6.1), subject to constraint (4.6.3), by taking the appropriate partial derivatives and solving the first-order conditions. We find that the manufacturer's optimal margin is:

$$(\hat{W}^S - C) = 2\rho(Q_1^* - Q_2^*)/b = 2\rho(\mu_1^* - \mu_2^*) \equiv 2\delta > 0 \tag{4.6.4}$$

We define $\delta \equiv \rho(\mu_1^* - \mu_2^*) > 0$ as *the probability-weighted difference in the channel-optimal margins* associated with each state-of-nature; and we use the superscript $^S$ to denote the unadjusted Stackelberg pricing variables when $\rho > f_R / \Delta$. Because the wholesale margin $(\hat{W}^S - C)$ is positive,[16] the channel is uncoordinated in both states-of-nature. Note that the margin increases with the output (and the probability) of the high-demand state, but decreases with output in the low-demand state. Substituting (4.6.4) into decision rules (4.4.2) and (4.4.3) yields the following prices and quantities:

$$\hat{p}_i^S = (p_i^* + \delta) > p_i^* \tag{4.6.5}$$

$$\hat{Q}_i^S = (Q_i^* - b\delta) < Q_i^* \tag{4.6.6}$$

Relative to the channel-coordinating unit margin, the margin in (4.6.4) generates a higher retail price and a lower quantity sold. Given the per-unit wholesale price $\hat{W}^S$, we can write retail profit in the i[th] state-of-nature as:

$$\hat{\pi}_i^A\Big|_{\{\hat{W}^S,\hat{\phi}^S\}} = \left[\left((Q_i^* - b\delta)^2/b\right) - f_A - \hat{\phi}\right] \equiv \left[(\hat{R}_i^S - f_A) - \hat{\phi}\right] \tag{4.6.7}$$

However, by refusing to distribute the product, the retailer can earn a profit of $\pi_i^R = -f_R$. Thus the Stackelberg fixed fee that *ensures distribution in the low-demand state* is:

$$\hat{\phi}^S = \left[\left((Q_2^* - b\delta)^2/b\right) - (f_A - f_R)\right] = \left[\hat{R}_2^S - (f_A - f_R)\right] \tag{4.6.8}$$

This fixed fee, which is inversely related to ρ, guarantees a positive economic profit for the retailer in the high-demand state ($\hat{\pi}_1^A = (\Delta - f_R)$) and sufficient revenue in the low-demand state to ensure distribution ($\hat{\pi}_2^A = \hat{\pi}_2^R = -f_R$).

With the tariff $\{\hat{W}^S, \hat{\phi}^S\}$, the manufacturer's expected profit is:

$$\begin{aligned} E[\hat{\Pi}^S] &= (\hat{W}^S - C)\left[\rho\hat{Q}_1^S + (1-\rho)\hat{Q}_2^S\right] + \hat{\phi}^S - F \\ &= \phi^{AA} + b\delta^2 - F \end{aligned} \tag{4.6.9}$$

The manufacturer-optimal, distribution-constrained Stackelberg tariff is $\{\hat{W}^S, \hat{\phi}^S\}$ *provided* it satisfies the retailer's participation constraint:

$$E[\hat{\pi}]\Big|_{\{\hat{W}^S,\hat{\phi}^S\}} = (\rho\Delta - f_R) - (2b\delta^2) \geq 0 \tag{4.6.10}$$

When $(\rho\Delta - f_R) \geq 2b\delta^2 > 0$, the retailer earns a non-negative expected profit by serving both states-of-nature.

### 6.1.3 Full Channel-Profit Extraction: Maintaining Complete Coverage

The retailer's expected profit is *negative* if the manufacturer offers $\{\hat{W}^S, \hat{\phi}^S\}$ when $2b\delta^2 > (\rho\Delta - f_R) > 0$, so the channel will not exist. To retain the retailer as a channel participant, the manufacturer must *adjust* its fixed fee downward by the amount needed to restore retailer's expected profit to zero:

$$\hat{\phi}^{S\text{-}Adj} = \hat{\phi}^S - \left[2b\delta^2 - (\rho\Delta - f_R)\right] \tag{4.6.11}$$

The wholesale price is unaffected by this adjustment, so the distribution-constrained tariff when $2b\delta^2 > (\rho\Delta - f_R) > 0$ is $\{\hat{W}^S, \hat{\phi}^{S\text{-}Adj}\}$. This leads to a manufacturer profit:

$$\begin{aligned} E[\hat{\Pi}^{S\text{-}Adj}] &= (\hat{W}^S - C)\left[\rho\hat{Q}_1^S + (1-\rho)\hat{Q}_2^S\right] + \hat{\phi}^{S\text{-}Adj} - F \\ &= \phi^{All} - b\delta^2 - F \end{aligned} \tag{4.6.12}$$

The net result of this adjustment is that the retailer distributes in both states-of-nature, but earns zero expected profit when the tariff is $\{\hat{W}^S, \hat{\phi}^{S\text{-}Adj}\}$.

### 6.1.4 Limits to Complete Coverage: Infeasible Output

Thus far we have treated output as non-negative in both states-of-nature. This is certainly true when the wholesale price equals marginal production cost, as with the two-part tariff $\{C, \phi^{All}\}$. However, when the wholesale markup is positive $(\hat{W}^S > C)$, there are parametric values that generate zero output in the *low-demand* state-of-nature. By substituting $\delta$ from equation (4.6.4) into equation (4.6.6), we obtain the following alternative expressions for retail quantities:

$$\hat{Q}_1^S = \left[(1-\rho)Q_1^* + \rho Q_2^*\right] > 0 \tag{4.6.13}$$

$$\hat{Q}_2^S = \left[-\rho Q_1^* + (1+\rho)Q_2^*\right] > 0 \quad \forall \quad \boldsymbol{Q} \equiv \left(\frac{Q_2^*}{Q_1^*}\right) > \left(\frac{\rho}{1+\rho}\right) \tag{4.6.14}$$

It follows from Equation (4.6.14) that the low-demand state *cannot be served* for some $\langle\rho, \boldsymbol{Q}\rangle$ – values because the solution $\hat{Q}_2^S \le 0$ is infeasible. Because $\boldsymbol{Q}$ may lie anywhere in the unit interval, depending on the parametric values of demand and variable costs, and because the value $\rho/(1+\rho)$ also lies in the unit interval, $\boldsymbol{Q} \le \rho/(1+\rho)$ occurs for some values of the model's parameters.

## 6.2 The Manufacturer's Distribution-Constrained, Stackelberg Decision Rule

The preceding analysis reveals that the *manufacturer-optimal, distribution-constrained Stackelberg decision rule* is:

$$\begin{aligned} (\rho\Delta - f_R) \leq 0 \qquad & \Rightarrow \quad \{C, \phi^{All}\} \\ 2b\delta^2 > (\rho\Delta - f_R) > 0 \qquad & \Rightarrow \quad \{\hat{W}^S, \hat{\phi}^{S\text{-}Adj}\} \\ (\rho\Delta - f_R) \geq 2b\delta^2 > 0 \quad & \Rightarrow \quad \{\hat{W}^S, \hat{\phi}^S\} \end{aligned} \tag{4.6.15}$$

The contingency tariffs in (4.6.15) are conditional upon (1) the known probability of each state-of-nature, (2) the revenues generated in those states, (3) the channel margins in both states-of-nature, and (4) the fixed cost of refusing to serve a state-of-nature. Equation (4.6.4) defines the value of $\hat{W}^S$ while the fixed fees are defined in equations (4.5.2), (4.6.8), and (4.6.11). Details concerning the profit consequences of these distribution-constrained tariffs are presented in Tables 4.1 and 4.2 above.

Three observations are in order. First, provided $Q > [\rho/(1+\rho)]$, both states-of-nature are served under all the tariffs. Second, the tariffs $\{C, \phi^{All}\}$ and $\{\hat{W}^S, \hat{\phi}^{S\text{-}Adj}\}$ allocate all expected channel profit to the manufacturer, while the retailer earns a positive expected profit under the $\{\hat{W}^S, \hat{\phi}^S\}$ tariff. Third, these contingency tariffs are restricted to parametric values for which both channel members earn a non-negative profit. We have shown that each of the contingency tariffs satisfies the retailer's participation constraint ($E(\pi) \geq 0$). We now consider whether these tariffs also satisfy the manufacturer's participation constraints.

### 6.2.1 The Manufacturer's Participation Constraints

With the tariff $\{C, \phi^{All}\}$ the manufacturer's participation constraint is:

$$\phi^{All} - F \geq 0 \tag{4.6.16}$$

The manufacturer's participation constraint with the $\{\hat{W}^S, \hat{\phi}^{S\text{-}Adj}\}$ tariff is:

$$\phi^{All} - b\delta^2 - F \geq 0 \tag{4.6.17}$$

Under the $\{\hat{W}^S, \hat{\phi}^S\}$ tariff, the manufacturer's participation constraint is:

$$\phi^{AA} + b\delta^2 - F \geq 0 \tag{4.6.18}$$

In all three cases, the satisfaction of the manufacturer's participation constraint ensures that the channel exists.

To identify the parameter sets that satisfy the participation constraints (4.6.16)-(4.6.18), we re-scale these constraints using the four variables introduced in Section 3.2.2 and reproduced here:

$\mathcal{Q} \equiv (Q_2^* / Q_1^*)$ ≡ The size of the low-demand state *relative* to the high-demand state;

$f_{\mathcal{A}} \equiv (f_A / R_1^*)$ ≡ The fixed cost of distribution relative to the net revenue earned in the high-demand state;

$\varphi \equiv (f_R / f_A)$ ≡ The fixed cost of not distributing the product relative to the fixed cost of distribution; and

$\mathcal{F} \equiv (F / R_1^*)$ ≡ The fixed cost of production expressed as a proportion of the net revenue earned in the high-demand state.

### 6.2.2 The Distribution-Constrained Channel's Zonal Boundaries

The manufacturer- and retailer-participation constraints, together with the non-negative output constraint, define five Zones in $\langle \rho, \mathcal{Q} \rangle$ – space. We begin with the three Complete-Coverage Zones, which we denote by $\mathbf{Z}_{12}^{\text{All}}$, $\mathbf{Z}_{12}^{\text{S-Adj}}$ and $\mathbf{Z}_{12}^{\text{S}}$ (superscripts reference wholesale-price policies while the common subscript denotes that both states-of-nature are served). The first pair of Zones are separated by the *Full Profit-Extraction Boundary* $\rho_{\text{S-Adj}}^{\text{All}}$ that solves $(\rho\Delta - f_R) = 0$. The second pair of Zones is partitioned by the *Uncoordinated/Shared-Profit Boundary* $\rho_{\text{S}}^{\text{S-Adj}}$, which is the solution to $(\rho\Delta - f_R) = 2b\delta^2 > 0$.

Zero coverage occurs in two additional Zones that we denote by $\mathbf{Z}_0^{Q_2}$ and $\mathbf{Z}_0^{\text{S}}$ (their common subscript $_0$ denotes that neither state-of-nature is served, the superscript $^{Q_2}$ refers to non-positive output in the low-demand state and the superscript $^{\text{S}}$ refers to the distribution-constrained, Stackelberg channel). In Zone $\mathbf{Z}_0^{Q_2}$ the manufacturer's optimal wholesale-price policy generates an infeasible (a negative) output in the low-demand state. The *Feasible/Infeasible-Output Boundary* is defined by $\rho_0^{Q_2}$, which is the solution to $\mathcal{Q} = \rho/(1+\rho)$. In Zone $\mathbf{Z}_0^{\text{S}}$ the manufacturer's participation constraint is violated. A portion of the Complete/Zero-Coverage Boundary is delineated by $\rho_0^{\text{S}}$, which is defined by equation (4.6.23) below.

These five Zones, which are mutually exclusive and completely exhaustive in $\langle \rho, \mathcal{Q} \rangle$ – space, define the manufacturer-optimal wholesale-price policy, given the constraint of complete or zero temporal coverage. Given these Zonal definitions, we now define the boundaries that separate these Zones. The rescaled value of the *Full Profit-Extraction Boundary* is:

$$\rho_{\text{S-Adj}}^{\text{All}} = \left(\frac{\varphi f_{\mathcal{A}}}{1-Q^2}\right) \equiv \rho_{\text{AA}}^{\text{All}} \geq 0 \tag{4.6.19}$$

The rescaled value of the *Uncoordinated/Shared-Profit Boundary* is:

$$\rho_{\text{S}}^{\text{S-Adj}} = \left((1+Q)-\sqrt{(1+Q)^2 - 8\varphi f_{\mathcal{A}}}\right)\Big/\left(4(1-Q)\right) \tag{4.6.20}$$

The rescaled value of the *Feasible/Infeasible-Output Boundary* is:

$$\rho_0^{Q_2} = Q/(1-Q) > 0 \tag{4.6.21}$$

Re-scaled values of the manufacturer's participation constraints are:

$$\rho_0^{\text{All}} = \left(\frac{\mathcal{F} + f_{\mathcal{A}} - Q^2}{1-Q^2}\right) \equiv \rho_{12}^{\text{VI}} \tag{4.5.26}$$

$$\rho_0^{\text{S-Adj}} = \left(\frac{(1+Q)-\sqrt{(1+Q)^2 - 4\left(\mathcal{F} + f_{\mathcal{A}} - Q^2\right)}}{2(1-Q)}\right) \tag{4.6.22}$$

$$\rho_0^{\text{S}} = \left(\frac{\sqrt{\mathcal{F} + (1-\varphi) f_{\mathcal{A}} - Q^2}}{1-Q}\right) \tag{4.6.23}$$

Expressions (4.5.26), (4.6.22), and (4.6.23) define the three segments of the *Complete/Zero-Coverage Boundary.*

### 6.2.3 The Distribution-Constrained, Stackelberg Decision Rule: Theoretical Effects

We now examine the impact of changes in the re-scaled parameters on temporal coverage and channel existence. We begin with the Complete-Coverage Zones. The value of $\rho_{\text{S-Adj}}^{\text{All}}$ rises with increases in $f_{\mathcal{A}}, \varphi$, and $Q$, but is independent of $\mathcal{F}$. Similarly, the value of $\rho_{\text{S}}^{\text{S-Adj}}$ increases with $\varphi$ and $f_{\mathcal{A}}$, is independent of $\mathcal{F}$, and has a complex relationship with $Q$:

$$\frac{\partial \rho_{\text{S}}^{\text{S-Adj}}}{\partial Q} = \left(\frac{4\varphi f_{\mathcal{A}} - (1+Q) + \sqrt{(1+Q)^2 - 8\varphi f_{\mathcal{A}}}}{2(1-Q)^2\sqrt{(1+Q)^2 - 8\varphi f_{\mathcal{A}}}}\right) \gtrless 0 \tag{4.6.24}$$

Turning to the Zero-Coverage Zones, the Feasible/Infeasible-Output Boundary rises with $Q$ (up to $Q = ½$) and is unaffected by the fixed cost parameters. The Complete/Zero-Coverage Boundary has three segments: $\rho_0^{\text{All}}$, $\rho_0^{\text{S-Adj}}$ and $\rho_0^{\text{S}}$. The relevant partial derivatives for $\rho_0^{\text{All}}$ are presented at (4.3.18). The value of $\rho_0^{\text{S-Adj}}$ rises with $\mathcal{F}$ and $f_{\mathcal{A}}$ , is independent of $\varphi$, and is affected in an ambiguous manner by $Q$:

$$\frac{\partial \rho_0^{\text{S-Adj}}}{\partial Q} = -\left( \frac{\begin{array}{c}(1+Q) - 2(\mathcal{F} + f_{\mathcal{A}} - Q) \\ -\sqrt{(1-Q)^2 - 4(\mathcal{F} + f_{\mathcal{A}} - Q^2)}\end{array}}{(1-Q)^2 \sqrt{(1-Q)^2 - 4(\mathcal{F} + f_{\mathcal{A}} - Q^2)}} \right) \gtrless 0 \qquad (4.6.25)$$

Finally, provided $\rho_0^{\text{S}}$ has a non-imaginary solution, it rises with $\varphi$, $f_{\mathcal{A}}$, $\mathcal{F}$, and $Q$. We now turn to numerical analysis to shed additional light on those parameters with indeterminate signs.

### 6.2.4 The Distribution-Constrained, Stackelberg Decision Rule: Numerical Effects

To gain insight into the distribution-constrained contingency tariffs, we turn to numerical analysis. We depict the manufacturer's optimal strategy in $\langle \rho, Q \rangle$ – space for the four Scenarios used in previous Sections. Consistent with our earlier analyses, we set $\mathcal{F} = 0$.

**Scenario 1** $(f_{\mathcal{A}} = 0 = \varphi)$ **:** Figure 4.8 depicts the manufacturer-optimal, distribution-constrained, wholesale-price policy for Scenario 1. The two-part tariff $\{\text{C}, \phi^{\text{All}}\}$ is *never* manufacturer-optimal because $\rho_{\text{S-Adj}}^{\text{All}} = 0$. The $\{\hat{\text{W}}^{\text{S}}, \hat{\phi}^{\text{S-Adj}}\}$ tariff is also non-optimal for the manufacturer because the boundary $\rho_{\text{S}}^{\text{S-Adj}}$ lies inside Zone $\mathbf{Z}_0^{\text{Q}_2}$. Only two Zones are relevant in this Scenario: Zones $\mathbf{Z}_{12}^{\text{S}}$ and $\mathbf{Z}_0^{\text{Q}_2}$. The Feasible/Infeasible-Output Boundary separating these Zones is:

$$\rho_0^{\text{Q}_2} = Q/(1-Q) \qquad (4.6.21)$$

This boundary intercepts the $\langle \rho = 0 \rangle$ – axis at $Q = 0$ and the $\langle \rho = 1 \rangle$ – axis at $Q = \frac{1}{2}$. Above the $\rho^{\text{Q}_2}$ – boundary the manufacturer offers $\{\hat{\text{W}}^{\text{S}}, \hat{\phi}^{\text{S}}\}$. Below this boundary the channel does not exist, because the Stackelberg wholesale price generates negative output in the low-demand state.

**Scenario 2** $(f_{\mathcal{A}} = 0.25, \varphi = 0)$ **:** Because the graphs of the distribution-constrained Stackelberg wholesale-price policy in Scenarios 1 and 2 are identical, we do not present a separate Figure for Scenario 2.

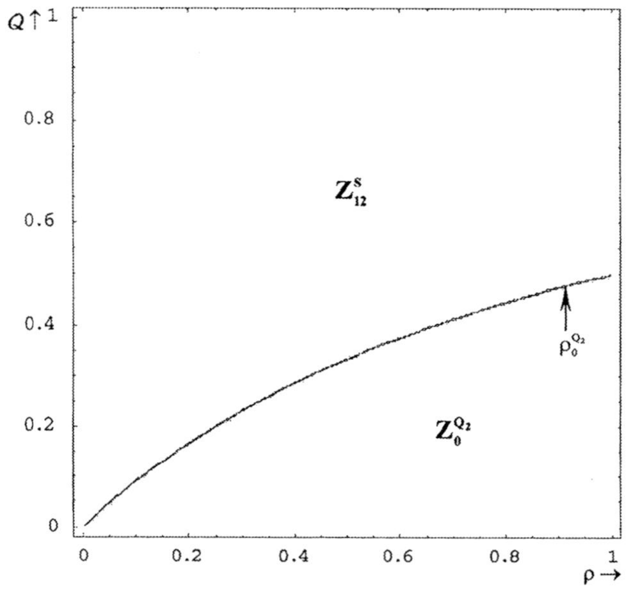


Legend:

$\rho_0^{Q_2}$ ≡ The Feasible/Infeasible-Output Boundary;

$Z_{12}^{S}$ ≡ The distribution-constrained Stackelberg strategy is optimal; and

$Z_0^{Q_2}$ ≡ The Stackelberg strategy generates an infeasible output.

*Figure 4.8.* The Manufacturer-Optimal, Distribution-Constrained Strategy When $f_{\mathfrak{R}} = 0 = \varphi$ and When $f_{\mathfrak{R}} = 0.25, \varphi = 0$

**Scenario 3** ($f_{\mathcal{A}} = 0.25, \varphi = 0.5$): Figure 4.9 shows the manufacturer's optimal, distribution-constrained wholesale-price policy for this Scenario. The Full Profit-Extraction Boundary satisfies:

$$\rho^{\text{All}}_{\text{S-Adj}} = 1/\left(8[1-Q^2]\right) \tag{4.6.26}$$

This boundary intercepts the $\langle Q=0\rangle$ – axis at $\rho = 1/8$ and the $\langle \rho = 1\rangle$ – axis at $Q = \sqrt{7/8} \cong 0.935$. Zone $\mathbf{Z}^{\text{All}}_{12}$ lies above $\rho^{\text{All}}_{\text{S-Adj}}$ when the channel exists.

The Uncoordinated/Shared-Profit Boundary satisfies:

$$\rho^{\text{S-Adj}}_{\text{S}} = \left((1+Q) - \sqrt{Q(2+Q)}\right)/\left(4[1-Q]\right) \tag{4.6.27}$$

This boundary intercepts the $\langle Q=0\rangle$ – axis at $\rho = 1/4$ and the $\langle \rho = 1\rangle$ – axis at $Q = (8+\sqrt{10})/12 \cong 0.930$. In Zone $\mathbf{Z}^{\text{S-Adj}}_{12}$, which lies between these two curves, the manufacturer uses the two-part tariff $\{\hat{W}^{\text{S}}, \hat{\phi}^{\text{S-Adj}}\}$ when the participation and feasible-output constraints are met.

The Feasible/Infeasible-Output Boundary ($\rho^{\text{Q}_2}_0$) of Scenario 3 is given by equation (4.6.21). In addition to its intersections with the $\langle \rho = 0\rangle$ – axis and the $\langle \rho = 1\rangle$ – axis, the $\rho^{\text{Q}_2}_0$ – boundary intersects the $\rho^{\text{S-Adj}}_{\text{S}}$ – boundary at a $\langle \rho, Q\rangle$ – value that is about $\langle 0.172, 0.146\rangle$.[17] Zone $\mathbf{Z}^{\text{S}}_{12}$ lies between the $\rho^{\text{S-Adj}}_{\text{S}}$ – boundary and the $\rho^{\text{Q}_2}_0$ – boundary. Above $\rho^{\text{Q}_2}_0$ there is complete coverage with either the $\{\hat{W}^{\text{S}}, \hat{\phi}^{\text{S-Adj}}\}$ or the $\{\hat{W}^{\text{S}}, \hat{\phi}^{\text{S}}\}$ tariff, *provided* the manufacturer's channel participation constraint is satisfied. Below $\rho^{\text{Q}_2}_0$ the $\{\hat{W}^{\text{S}}, \hat{\phi}^{\text{S}}\}$ and $\{\hat{W}^{\text{S}}, \hat{\phi}^{\text{S-Adj}}\}$ tariffs are infeasible because output is negative in the low-demand state. We label this Zone $\mathbf{Z}^{\text{Q}_2}_0$.

The Zero-Coverage Zone for Scenario 3 is determined by the Feasible/Infeasible Output Boundary *or* by the violation of the manufacturer's channel participation constraint that is given by the Complete/Zero Coverage Boundary, which satisfies:

$$\rho^{\text{All}}_0 = (1-4Q^2)/\left(4[1-Q^2]\right) \tag{4.6.28}$$

The Zero-Coverage Zone is delimited by four $\langle \rho, Q\rangle$ – points: (a) $\langle 0, 1/2\rangle$, (b) $\langle 1/7, \sqrt{1/8}\rangle \cong \langle 0.143, 0.354\rangle$, (c) $\langle 1/7, 1/8\rangle \cong \langle 0.143, 0.125\rangle$, and (d) $\langle 1, 1/2\rangle$. The $\rho^{\text{All}}_0$ – boundary curves from point (a) to point (b) while the $\rho^{\text{Q}_2}_0$ – boundary curves from point (c) to point (d). The vertical line from point (b), through point (c), to the $\langle Q=0\rangle$ – axis is $\rho^{\text{VI}}_1 = \rho^{\text{AR}}_0 (= 1/7)$. This line also appeared in our analysis of the vertically-integrated system (see Figure 4.2). The two sub-zones of the Zero-Coverage Zone are denoted by the symbols $\mathbf{Z}^{\text{S}}_0$ and $\mathbf{Z}^{\text{Q}_2}_0$.

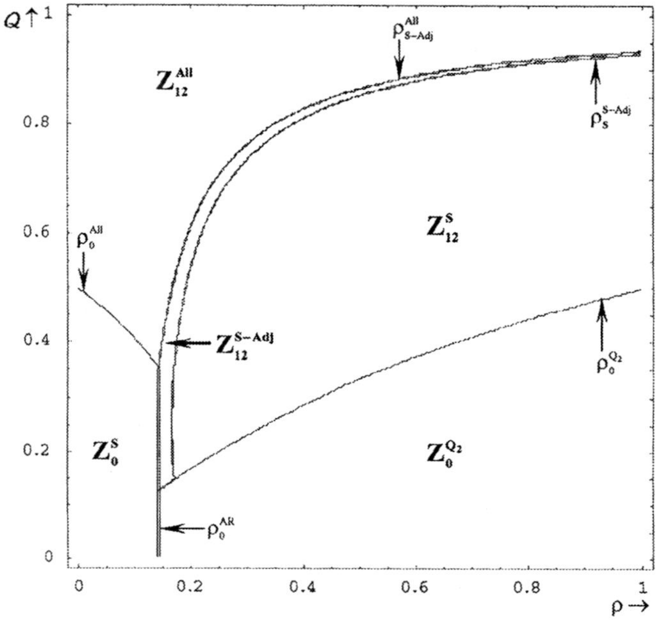


Legend :

$\rho^{All}_{S-Adj} \equiv$ The Coordinated/Uncoordinated Boundary;

$\rho^{S-Adj}_{S} \equiv$ The Uncoordinated/Shared-Profit Boundary;

$\rho^{Q_2}_{0} \equiv$ The Feasible/Infeasible-Output Boundary;

$\rho^{All}_{0} \equiv$ A portion of the Complete/Zero-Coverage Boundary;

$\rho^{AR}_{0} \equiv$ A portion of the Complete/Zero-Coverage Boundary;

$Z^{All}_{12} \equiv$ The channel-coordinating strategy is optimal;

$Z^{S-Adj}_{12} \equiv$ The distribution-constrained, profit-adjusted Stackelberg strategy is optimal;

$Z^{S}_{12} \equiv$ The distribution-constrained Stackelberg strategy is optimal;

$Z^{Q_2}_{0} \equiv$ The Stackelberg-strategy generates an infeasible output in the low-demand state; and

$Z^{S}_{0} \equiv$ The manufacturer's participation constraint with a Stackelberg strategy is violated.

*Figure 4.9.* The Manufacturer-Optimal, Distribution-Constrained Strategy
When $f_{\mathcal{A}} = 0.25, \varphi = 0.5$

**Scenario 4** $(f_{\mathcal{A}} = 0.25, \varphi = 1)$: Figure 4.10 depicts the optimal, distribution-constrained wholesale-price policy for the manufacturer in this Scenario. The Full Profit-Extraction Boundary satisfies:

$$\rho^{\text{All}}_{\text{S-Adj}} = 1/\left(4\left[1 - Q^2\right]\right) \tag{4.6.29}$$

This boundary intercepts the $\langle Q = 0\rangle$ – axis at $\rho = 1/4$ and the $\langle \rho = 1\rangle$ – axis at $Q = \sqrt{3}/2 \cong 0.866$. The Uncoordinated/Shared-Profit Boundary satisfies:

$$\rho^{\text{S-Adj}}_{\text{S}} = \left(\frac{(1+Q) \pm \sqrt{Q^2 + 2Q - 1}}{4(1-Q)}\right) \tag{4.6.30}$$

This boundary intercepts the $\langle \rho = 1\rangle$ – axis at $Q = 1/2$ and at $Q = 5/6 \cong 0.833$. In Zone $\mathbf{Z}^{\text{S}}_{12}$, which lies inside the parabolic-shaped $\rho^{\text{S-Adj}}_{\text{S}}$ – curve, the optimal tariff is $\{\hat{W}^{\text{S}}, \hat{\phi}^{\text{S}}\}$. In Zone $\mathbf{Z}^{\text{S-Adj}}_{12}$, which lies between the curves defined by (4.6.29) and (4.6.30), the manufacturer's optimal tariff is $\{\hat{W}^{\text{S}}, \hat{\phi}^{\text{S-Adj}}\}$, provided the participation and feasible-output constraints are met.

The only relevant Complete/Zero-Coverage Boundary is given by equation (4.6.28). This boundary intercepts the $\langle \rho = 0\rangle$ – axis at $Q = 1/2$ and the $\langle Q = 0\rangle$ – axis at $\rho = 1/4$. Zone $\mathbf{Z}^{\text{S}}_{0}$ lies below $\rho^{\text{All}}_{0}$ while Zone $\mathbf{Z}^{\text{All}}_{12}$ lies between $\rho^{\text{All}}_{0}$ and $\rho^{\text{All}}_{\text{S-Adj}}$.

Zone $\mathbf{Z}^{\text{S-Adj}}_{12}$ is truncated on the bottom by the Feasible/Infeasible-Output Boundary $\rho^{\text{Q}_2}_{0}$ that is defined at (4.6.21). The $\rho^{\text{Q}_2}_{0}$ – boundary intercepts the $\langle \rho = 1\rangle$ – axis at $Q = 1/2$; it intercepts the $\rho^{\text{All}}_{\text{S-Adj}}$ – boundary at $Q = (\sqrt{2} - 1)/2 \cong 0.207$. The distribution-constrained Stackelberg wholesale price generates negative output for the low-demand state in Zone $\mathbf{Z}^{\text{Q}_2}_{0}$.

A comparison of Figures 4.9 and 4.10 suggests that increases in the fixed cost of non-distribution dramatically expand the range of $\langle \rho, Q\rangle$ – values for which the manufacturer must reduce its fixed fee in order to retain the retailer as a channel member.

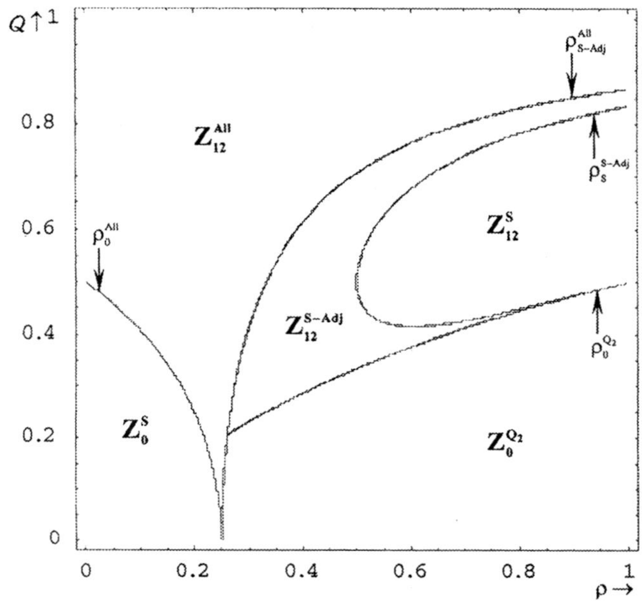


Legend:

$\rho_{S-Adj}^{All} \equiv$ The Coordinated/Uncoordinated Boundary;

$\rho_{S}^{S-Adj} \equiv$ The Uncoordinated/Shared-Profit Boundary;

$\rho_{0}^{Q_2} \equiv$ The Feasible/Infeasible-Output Boundary;

$\rho_{0}^{All} \equiv$ The Complete/Zero-Coverage Boundary;

$Z_{12}^{All} \equiv$ The channel-coordinating strategy is optimal;

$Z_{12}^{S-Adj} \equiv$ The distribution-constrained, profit-adjusted Stackelberg strategy is optimal;

$Z_{12}^{S} \equiv$ The distribution-constrained Stackelberg strategy is optimal;

$Z_{0}^{Q_2} \equiv$ The Stackelberg strategy generates an infeasible output in the low-demand state; and

$Z_{0}^{S} \equiv$ The manufacturer's participation constraint with a Stackelberg strategy is violated.

*Figure 4.10.* The Manufacturer-Optimal, Distribution-Constrained Strategy
When $f_{\mathcal{A}} = 0.25, \varphi = 1$

## 6.3 Commentary on the Stackelberg Tariff

We have established that the channel-coordinating tariff $\{C, \phi^{All}\}$ maximizes manufacturer profit when $(\rho\Delta - f_R) \leq 0$. Thus distribution-constrained Stackelberg optimization is consistent with channel coordination over part of $\langle \rho, Q \rangle$ − space. We have also shown that, when $(\rho\Delta - f_R) > 0$:

- It is in the manufacturer's interest to set a wholesale price in excess of its marginal cost of production ( $\hat{W}^S > C$ ). As a result, the channel is uncoordinated.
- Because $\hat{W}^S > C$, there is a range of values within which there are no sales in the low-demand state.
- As a consequence of these points, the objective of distributing in both states-of-nature cannot be satisfied for all parameter values.

We now compare manufacturer profitability under the channel-coordinating and the constrained Stackelberg contingency tariffs.

# 7 COORDINATION *VS.* MAXIMIZATION

In the two previous Sections we derived the manufacturer's optimal contingency tariffs under (i) a channel-coordination constraint and (ii) an "all-or-nothing" constraint of either complete coverage or zero coverage. These constraints led to different patterns of temporal breadth (coverage across states-of-nature that was complete, incomplete, or non-existent) and dissimilar profit distributions (channel profit went entirely to the manufacturer or it was shared with the retailer). In this Section we solve for the *unconstrained* contingency tariff that maximizes the manufacturer's profit. Our analysis will determine the parametric values for which it is in the manufacturer's interest to set its wholesale-price policy to duplicate the results of a vertically-integrated system, although we defer discussion of such duplication to the next Section. We are motivated to explore this issue by our discovery in Section 5 that a manufacturer/independent-retailer dyad that coordinates the channel does *not* reproduce the Channel Performance of a vertically-integrated system.

We will prove that the unconstrained tariff allows four combinations of temporal breadth and coordination, each of which is optimal for a range of parametric values: (i) complete coverage with coordination, (ii) incomplete coverage with coordination, (iii) zero coverage, and (iv) complete coverage without coordination. We note that combinations (i)-(iii) are *compatible* with a vertically-integrated system, but that these combinations need not occur over the same set of parametric values in an independent dyad.

We begin with a discussion of the parametric values for which the manufacturer can have complete coverage, channel profit maximization, and full channel-profit extraction. We then analyze the manufacturer's choice when parametric values make these goals mutually incompatible. Because the boundary conditions for the contingency tariffs (4.5.20) and (4.6.15) complicate the interpretation of our analytical results, we also offer numerical analyses to clarify the manufacturer's tariff preferences.

## 7.1 Classic Coordination: Channel-Profit Maximization, Full Channel-Profit Extraction and Complete Coverage

In Sections 5 and 6 we derived a tariff—the $\{C,\phi^{All}\}$ tariff—that offers *classic coordination* under some parametric values. By this we mean that the $\{C,\phi^{All}\}$ tariff (i) maximizes channel profit, (ii) enables the manufacturer to extract all channel profit, and (iii) has the *potential* to ensure distribution in all states-of-nature (i.e., *complete coverage*). Whenever this tariff induces complete coverage, the manufacturer will prefer it to any other tariff. We know from (4.5.20) that the $\{C,\phi^{All}\}$ tariff produces complete coverage only when the probability of the high-demand state satisfies:

$$\rho \le \rho_{AA}^{All} = \rho_{S\text{-}Adj}^{All} \equiv \left(\frac{f_R}{R_1^{*} - R_2^{*}}\right) = \left(\frac{\varphi f_{\mathcal{R}}}{1 - Q^2}\right) \tag{4.7.1}$$

The maximal value $\rho_{AA}^{All}$ rises with the fixed cost of non-distribution ($f_R$) and with net revenue in the low-demand state ($R_2^{*}$), but it falls with net revenue in the high-demand state ($R_1^{*}$). The probability $\rho_{AA}^{All}$ is positive if and only if the retailer incurs a fixed cost of non-distribution. Thus classic coordination will never be chosen by the manufacturer when fixed costs are zero. We find this result ironic, given that marketing science articles commonly ignore fixed cost, but regularly prescribe coordination as a meritorious channel objective.

## 7.2 The Manufacturer's Tariff Choice When Classic Coordination Is Unattainable: Theoretical Analysis

When the condition $\rho \le \rho_{AA}^{All}$ is violated, the manufacturer cannot simultaneously coordinate the channel, obtain all channel profit, and ensure coverage of all states-of-nature. Instead, the manufacturer must choose from one of the following alternatives:

1. Coordination with *incomplete* coverage with the tariff $\{C,\phi^{AR}\}$. In this case the manufacturer earns all channel profit.
2. Coordination with *complete* coverage with the tariff $\{C,\phi^{AA}\}$. In this case the manufacturer does not obtain all channel profit.
3. Complete coverage *without* coordination with two possible tariffs:
   (a) The tariff $\{\hat{W}^S,\hat{\phi}^S\}$ which gives the manufacturer all channel profit, and
   (b) The tariff $\{\hat{W}^S,\hat{\phi}^{S-Adj}\}$ which does not give all channel profit to the manufacturer.[18]

A fourth option, zero coverage, arises when none of the preceding options generate positive profit for the manufacturer.

The manufacturer's choice turns on the relative profitability of the coordinating tariffs ($\{C,\phi^{AR}\}$, $\{C,\phi^{AA}\}$) and the non-coordinating tariffs ($\{\hat{W}^S,\hat{\phi}^S\}$, $\{\hat{W}^S,\hat{\phi}^{S-Adj}\}$). In Sections 5 and 6 we identified the conditions under which the manufacturer prefers (i) $\{C,\phi^{AR}\}$ to $\{C,\phi^{AA}\}$ and (ii) $\{\hat{W}^S,\hat{\phi}^S\}$ to $\{\hat{W}^S,\hat{\phi}^{S-Adj}\}$. We are left with four comparisons, each of which is relevant under a set of conditions that are defined in Table 4.3.

Comparison **A** is relevant when the parameters faced by the channel satisfy $0<(\rho\Delta-f_R)<(1-\rho)\phi^{AA}$ and $0<(\rho\Delta-f_R)<2b\delta^2$; in this Situation the manufacturer chooses between the tariffs $\{C,\phi^{AA}\}$ and $\{\hat{W}^S,\hat{\phi}^{S-Adj}\}$. The other Comparisons are read in a similar manner.

*Table 4.3.* Coordination *vs.* Maximization: Relevant Tariff Comparisons

| | | Distribution Constraint | |
|---|---|---|---|
| | | $0<(\rho\Delta-f_R)<2b\delta^2$ | $0<2b\delta^2<(\rho\Delta-f_R)$ |
| Coordination Constraint | $0<(\rho\Delta-f_R)<(1-\rho)\phi^{AA}$ | **A*** $\{C,\phi^{AA}\}\gtrless\{\hat{W}^S,\hat{\phi}^{S-Adj}\}$ | **B** $\{C,\phi^{AA}\}\gtrless\{\hat{W}^S,\hat{\phi}^S\}$ |
| | $0<(1-\rho)\phi^{AA}<(\rho\Delta-f_R)$ | **C** $\{C,\phi^{AR}\}\gtrless\{\hat{W}^S,\hat{\phi}^{S-Adj}\}$ | **D** $\{C,\phi^{AR}\}\gtrless\{\hat{W}^S,\hat{\phi}^S\}$ |

* The symbol $\gtrless$ denotes "preferred by the manufacturer ($\succ$) or *not* preferred by the manufacturer ($\prec$);" it is the preference-version of "greater-or-less-than."

### 7.2.1 The Manufacturer's Profit Comparisons

We now analyze the paired-profit comparisons that determine the manufacturer's optimal wholesale-price strategy. Let $\Pi^{x}$ denote the manufacturer's profit from offering the $x^{th}$ tariff, $x \in (AR, AA, S-Adj, S)$, where $AA \equiv \{C, \phi^{AA}\}$, $AR \equiv \{C, \phi^{AR}\}$, $S-Adj \equiv \{\hat{W}^{S}, \hat{\phi}^{S-Adj}\}$ and $S \equiv \{\hat{W}^{S}, \hat{\phi}^{S}\}$. The four paired-profit comparisons can be written as:

Comparison **A**: $$(\Pi^{AA} - \Pi^{S-Adj}) = b\delta^2 - (\rho\Delta - f_R) \qquad (4.7.2)$$

Comparison **B**: $$(\Pi^{AA} - \Pi^{S}) = -b\delta^2 < 0 \qquad (4.7.3)$$

Comparison **C**: $$(\Pi^{AR} - \Pi^{S-Adj}) = b\delta^2 - (1-\rho)\phi^{AA} \qquad (4.7.4)$$

Comparison **D**: $$(\Pi^{AR} - \Pi^{S}) = (\rho\Delta - f_R) - (1-\rho)\phi^{AA} - b\delta^2 \qquad (4.7.5)$$

We see from (4.7.3) that, in the parameter-space defined by Comparison **B** ($0 < 2b\delta^2 < (\rho\Delta - f_R) < (1-\rho)\phi^{AA}$), the manufacturer always chooses the tariff $\{\hat{W}^{S}, \hat{\phi}^{S}\}$ because it dominates the $\{C, \phi^{AA}\}$ tariff.

To gain further insight into the manufacturer's decision, we re-scale these paired-profit comparisons using the same four variables defined in the preceding Sections. We repeat their definitions here:

- $\mathcal{Q} \equiv (Q_2^{*}/Q_1^{*})$ ≡ The size of the low-demand state *relative* to the high-demand state;
- $f_{\mathcal{A}} \equiv (f_A / R_1^{*})$ ≡ The fixed cost of distribution relative to the net revenue earned in the high-demand state;
- $\varphi \equiv (f_R / f_A)$ ≡ The fixed cost of not distributing the product relative to the fixed cost of distribution; and
- $\mathcal{F} \equiv (F / R_1^{*})$ ≡ The fixed cost of production expressed as a proportion of the net revenue earned in the high-demand state.

The re-scaled values of the paired-profit comparisons (4.7.2)-(4.7.5) are:

Comparison **A**: $$(\Pi^{AA} - \Pi^{S-Adj}) = R_1^{*}\left(\rho^2(1-\mathcal{Q})^2 - \rho(1-\mathcal{Q}^2) + \varphi f_{\mathcal{A}}\right) \qquad (4.7.6)$$

Comparison **B**: $$(\Pi^{AA} - \Pi^{S}) = -R_1^{*}\rho^2(1-\mathcal{Q})^2 < 0 \qquad (4.7.7)$$

Comparison **C**: $$(\Pi^{AR} - \Pi^{S-Adj}) = R_1^{*}\begin{pmatrix} \rho^2(1-\mathcal{Q})^2 - (1-\rho)\mathcal{Q}^2 \\ +(1-\rho)(1-\varphi)f_{\mathcal{A}} \end{pmatrix} \qquad (4.7.8)$$

Comparison **D**: $$(\Pi^{AR} - \Pi^{S}) = R_1^{*}\begin{pmatrix} (1-\rho)\rho + 2\rho^2\mathcal{Q} - (1+\rho^2)\mathcal{Q}^2 \\ +\left[(1-2\varphi) - \rho(1-\varphi)\right]f_{\mathcal{A}} \end{pmatrix} \qquad (4.7.9)$$

Two results follow immediately from these comparisons. First, when the conditions that define Comparison **B** are satisfied, the $\{\hat{W}^S, \hat{\phi}^S\}$ tariff always dominates the $\{C, \phi^{AA}\}$ tariff. Second, when the conditions that define Comparison **A** are satisfied, the $\{\hat{W}^S, \hat{\phi}^{S\text{-}Adj}\}$ tariff dominates the $\{C, \phi^{AA}\}$ tariff when either the fixed cost of distribution or the fixed cost of non-distribution is zero.

A change in distribution costs affect Comparisons **A**, **C**, and **D**. The fixed cost of *distribution* ($f_{\mathcal{A}}$) enhances the relative profitability of the coordination-constrained approach in Comparisons **A** and **C** and has an ambiguous impact in Comparison **D**. The fixed cost of *non-distribution* ($\varphi f_{\mathcal{A}}$) expands the comparative profitability of the coordination-constrained approach in Comparison **A** and has a negative effect in Comparisons **C** and **D**. The fixed production cost $\mathcal{F}$ has no impact on any of these Comparisons.

### 7.2.2 The Manufacturer's Comparison-Specific Zonal Boundaries

In this sub-Section we ascertain the zonal boundaries for each of the Comparisons discussed above. Comparison **A**'s Profit-Equality Boundary is:

$$\rho^{AA}_{S-Adj} = \left( \frac{(1+Q) - \sqrt{(1+Q)^2 - 4\varphi f_{\mathcal{A}}}}{2(1-Q)} \right) \tag{4.7.10}$$

The manufacturer prefers the coordinating tariff $\{C, \phi^{AA}\}$ at $\rho-$values greater than $\rho^{AA}_{S-Adj}$, while at $\rho-$values less than $\rho^{AA}_{S-Adj}$ it prefers the non-coordinating tariff $\{\hat{W}^S, \hat{\phi}^S\}$. There is no profit-equality boundary for Comparison **B** because there is no $\rho-$value for which the manufacturer prefers tariff $\{C, \phi^{AA}\}$ over tariff $\{\hat{W}^S, \hat{\phi}^S\}$.

Comparison **C**'s Profit-Equality Boundary is:

$$\rho^{AR}_{S-Adj} = \left( \frac{\left((1-\varphi)f_{\mathcal{A}} - Q^2\right) + \sqrt{\begin{matrix}\left((1-\varphi)f_{\mathcal{A}} - Q^2\right)^2 \\ -4(1-Q)^2\left((1-\varphi)f_{\mathcal{A}} - Q^2\right)\end{matrix}}}{2(1-Q)^2} \right) \tag{4.7.11}$$

Comparison **D**'s Profit-Equality Boundary is:

$$\rho^{AR}_{S} = \left( \frac{\left(1-(1-\varphi)f_{\mathcal{A}}\right) - \sqrt{\begin{matrix}\left(1-(1-\varphi)f_{\mathcal{A}}\right)^2 \\ -4(1-Q)^2\left(Q^2 - (1-2\varphi)f_{\mathcal{A}}\right)\end{matrix}}}{2(1-Q)^2} \right) \tag{4.7.12}$$

Although the fixed costs of distribution and non-distribution affect the Profit-Equality Boundaries (4.7.10)-(4.7.12), their impacts are not easy to grasp intuitively—even after taking the requisite derivatives. Thus we now turn to a numerical analysis.

## 7.2 The Manufacturer's Tariff Choice When Classic Coordination Is Unattainable: Numerical Analysis

To gain further insight into the manufacturer's optimal wholesale-price strategy, we turn to numerical analysis. We depict the manufacturer's optimal strategy in $\langle\rho,Q\rangle$ – space for the Scenarios used in previous Sections.

**Scenario 1** ($f_{\mathcal{A}} = 0 = \varphi$): From Figures 4.4 and 4.8, we know that the manufacturer's tariff-choice decision comes from the set $\{C,\phi^{AA}\}$, $\{C,\phi^{AR}\}$, and $\{\hat{W}^S,\hat{\phi}^S\}$. Moreover, we know from Comparison **B** that $\{\hat{W}^S,\hat{\phi}^S\}$ always dominates $\{C,\phi^{AA}\}$. Thus in this Scenario the manufacturer chooses between the $\{C,\phi^{AR}\}$ tariff and the $\{\hat{W}^S,\hat{\phi}^S\}$ tariff.

These tariffs generate identical profits for the manufacturer at Comparison **D**'s Profit-Equality Boundary:

$$\rho_S^{AR} = \left(\frac{1-\sqrt{1-4Q^2(1-Q)^2}}{2(1-Q)^2}\right) \tag{4.7.13}$$

The $\rho_S^{AR}$ – boundary intercepts the $\langle\rho=0\rangle$ – axis at $Q=0$ and the $\langle\rho=1\rangle$ – axis at $Q=1$. The non-coordinating, distribution-constrained tariff $\{\hat{W}^S,\hat{\phi}^S\}$ is manufacturer-preferred above $\rho_S^{AR}$ (in Zone $\mathbf{Z}_{12}^S$), and the channel-coordinating tariff $\{C,\phi^{AR}\}$ is preferred below $\rho_S^{AR}$ (in Zone $\mathbf{Z}_1^{AR}$).

A comparison of Figures 4.4 and 4.11 illustrates the impact of the channel-coordination constraint on temporal breadth. In Figure 4.4, the Complete/Incomplete Coverage Boundary was defined as $\rho_{AR}^{AA} = Q^2$. Like $\rho_S^{AR}$, $\rho_{AR}^{AA}$ intercepts the $\langle\rho=0\rangle$ – axis at $Q=0$ and the $\langle\rho=1\rangle$ – axis at $Q=1$; however, Figure 4.11 illustrates that the Complete/Incomplete Coverage Boundary ($\rho_{AR}^{AA}$) lies *just above* Comparison **D**'s Profit-Equality Boundary ($\rho_S^{AR}$). In the thin zone between these boundaries, the $\{C,\phi^{AR}\}$ tariff would be preferred *if* the $\{\hat{W}^S,\hat{\phi}^S\}$ tariff were not available to the manufacturer. By *not* forcing channel coordination, there is a slight increase in the parametric values for which there is complete coverage: temporal breadth is *enhanced* by allowing non-coordination as an optimizing option.

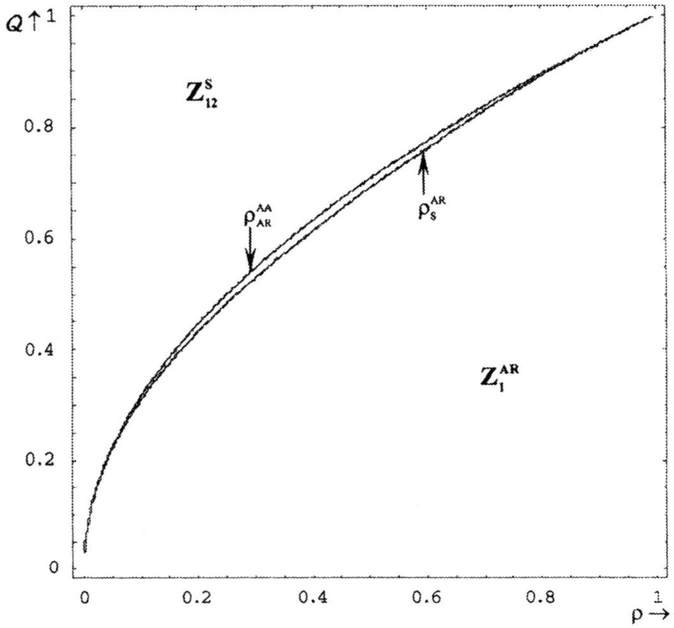


Legend:

$Z^S_{12}$ ≡ The Stackelberg strategy is optimal;

$Z^{AR}_1$ ≡ The incomplete but coordinated-coverage strategy is optimal;

$\rho^{AR}_S$ ≡ The Profit-Equality Boundary in Situation **D**; and

$\rho^{AA}_{AR}$ ≡ The Complete/Incomplete Coverage Boundary (included for comparison).

*Figure 4.11.* The Manufacturer-Optimal Stackelberg Strategy When $f_{\mathcal{A}} = 0 = \varphi$

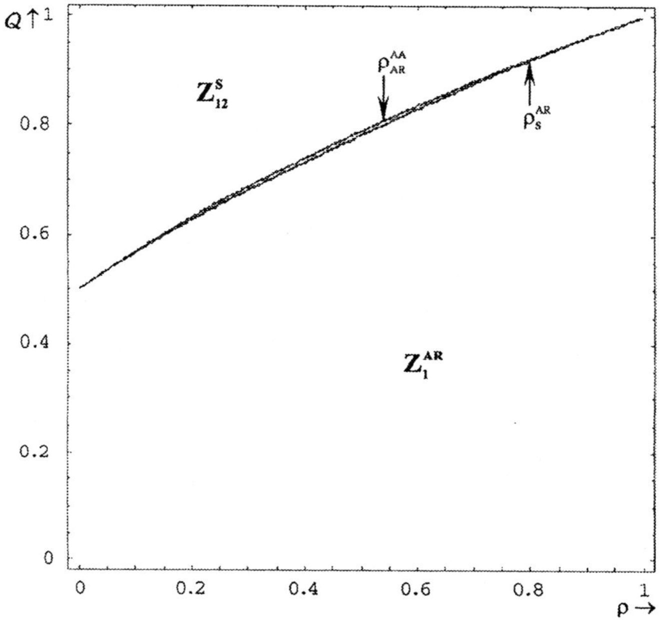


Legend:

$Z^{S}_{12}$ ≡ The Stackelberg strategy is optimal;

$Z^{AR}_{1}$ ≡ The incomplete but coordinated-coverage strategy is optimal;

$\rho^{AR}_{S}$ ≡ The Profit-Equality Boundary in Situation **D**; and

$\rho^{AA}_{AR}$ ≡ The Complete/Incomplete Coverage Boundary (included for comparison).

*Figure 4.12.* The Manufacturer-Optimal Stackelberg Strategy When $f_{\mathfrak{R}} = 0.25, \varphi = 0$

**Scenario 2** ($f_{\mathcal{A}} = 0.25\ \varphi = 0$): The manufacturer chooses either the $\{C, \phi^{AR}\}$ tariff or the $\{\hat{W}^{S}, \hat{\phi}^{S}\}$ tariff. Comparison **D**'s Profit-Equality Boundary is:

$$\rho_{S}^{AR} = \left(3 - \sqrt{9 - 16(1-Q)^2(4Q^2 - 1)}\right) \Big/ \left(8\left[1 - Q^2\right]\right) \tag{4.7.14}$$

(4.7.14) intercepts the $\langle \rho = 0 \rangle$ – axis at $Q = \frac{1}{2}$ and the $\langle \rho = 1 \rangle$ – axis at $Q = 1$. Zone $\mathbf{Z}_{12}^{S}$ lies above $\rho_{S}^{AR}$ and Zone $\mathbf{Z}_{1}^{AR}$ lies below it in Figure 4.12. The rise in $f_{\mathcal{A}}$ lessens temporal breadth by pivoting **D**'s Profit-Equality Boundary clockwise to about the point $\langle \rho = 1, Q = 1 \rangle$.

A comparison of Figures 4.5 and 4.12 illustrates the impact of the channel-coordination constraint on temporal breadth. The Complete/ Incomplete Coverage Boundary of Figure 4.5 is:

$$\rho_{AR}^{AA} = (4Q^2 - 1)/3 \tag{4.5.31}$$

Like $\rho_{S}^{AR}$, this boundary intercepts the $\langle \rho = 0 \rangle$ –axis at $Q = \frac{1}{2}$ and the $\langle \rho = 1 \rangle$ – axis at $Q = 1$. Figure 4.12 illustrates that $\rho_{AR}^{AA}$ lies slightly above $\rho_{S}^{AR}$, although the gap between them is so small that they appear to be one line. The $\{\hat{W}^{S}, \hat{\phi}^{S}\}$ tariff dominates the $\{C, \phi^{AR}\}$ tariff between these boundaries, so the Stackelberg tariff induces slightly more temporal breadth than does the channel-coordinating tariff.

**Scenario 3** ($f_{\mathcal{A}} = 0.25, \varphi = 0.5$): This Scenario, which combines information from Figure 4.6 and Figure 4.9, is illustrated in Figures 4.13. Figure 4.13a is a complete picture of $\langle \rho, Q \rangle$ – space; Figure 4.13b details the complex zonal relationships of this Scenario for a little less than one-percent of $\langle \rho, Q \rangle$ – space.

We begin with the Full Profit-Extraction Boundary. Its value is:

$$\rho_{AA}^{All} = 1 \Big/ \left(8\left[1 - Q^2\right]\right) \tag{4.5.32}$$

This boundary intercepts the $\langle Q = 0 \rangle$ – axis at $\rho = \frac{1}{8}$ and the $\langle \rho = 1 \rangle$ – axis at $Q = \sqrt{\frac{7}{8}} \cong 0.935$. A portion of the Complete/Zero Coverage Boundary is defined as:

$$\rho_{0}^{All} = (1 - 4Q^2)/(4[1 - Q^2]) \tag{4.6.28}$$

This boundary intercepts the $\langle \rho = 0 \rangle$ –axis at $Q = \frac{1}{2}$ and the $\langle Q = 0 \rangle$ – axis at $\rho = \frac{1}{4}$. The $\rho_{AA}^{All}$ – boundary and the $\rho_{0}^{All}$ – boundary meet at $\langle \rho = \frac{1}{7} \cong 0.143$, $Q = \sqrt{\frac{1}{8}} \cong 0.354 \rangle$

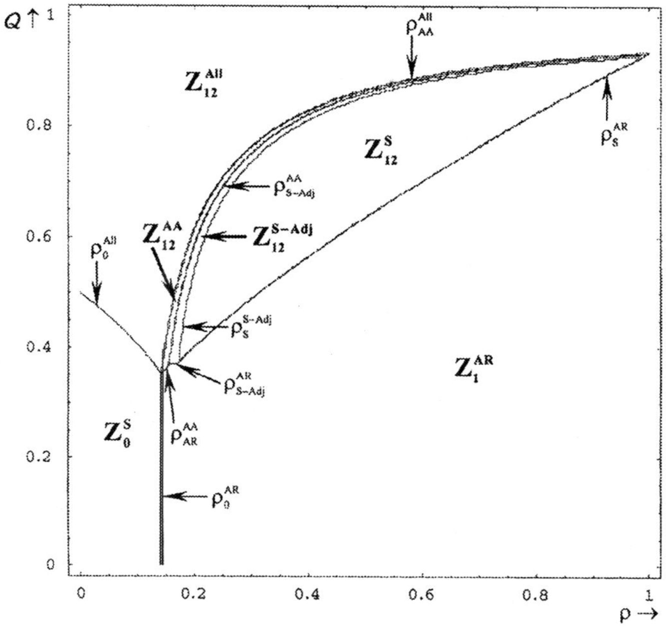


Legend:

$Z_{12}^{All}$ ≡ The channel-coordinating, complete-coverage strategy is optimal;

$Z_{12}^{AA}$ ≡ The channel-coordinating, profit-sharing, complete-coverage strategy is optimal;

$Z_{12}^{S\text{-}Adj}$ ≡ The fixed-fee adjusted Stackelberg strategy is optimal;

$Z_{12}^{S}$ ≡ The Stackelberg strategy is optimal;

$Z_{1}^{AR}$ ≡ The incomplete but coordinated-coverage strategy is optimal;

$Z_{0}^{S}$ ≡ The zero-coverage strategy is optimal;

$\rho_{AA}^{All}$ ≡ The Coordinated/Shared-Profit Boundary;

$\rho_{S}^{S\text{-}Adj}$ ≡ The Uncoordinated/Shared-Profit Boundary;

$\rho_{S\text{-}Adj}^{AA}$ ≡ The Coordinated/Uncoordinated Boundary;

$\rho_{0}^{All}$ ≡ The Complete/Zero-Coverage Boundary;

$\rho_{0}^{AR}$ ≡ The Incomplete/Zero-Coverage Boundary;

$\rho_{AR}^{AA}$ ≡ A portion of the Complete/Incomplete-Coverage Boundary;

$\rho_{S\text{-}Adj}^{AR}$ ≡ The Profit-Equality Boundary in Situation **C**; and

$\rho_{S}^{AR}$ ≡ The Profit-Equality Boundary in Situation **D**.

*Figure 4.13a.* The Manufacturer-Optimal Stackelberg Strategy
When $f_{\mathcal{R}} = 0.25, \varphi = 0.5$

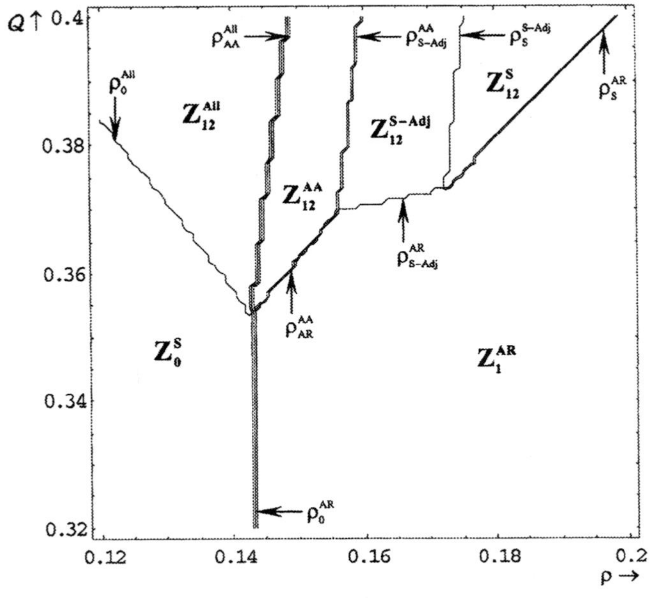


Legend:

$Z_{12}^{All}$ ≡ The channel-coordinating, complete-coverage strategy is optimal;

$Z_{12}^{AA}$ ≡ The channel-coordinating, profit-sharing, complete-coverage strategy is optimal;

$Z_{12}^{S\text{-}Adj}$ ≡ The fixed-fee adjusted Stackelberg strategy is optimal;

$Z_{12}^{S}$ ≡ The Stackelberg strategy is optimal;

$Z_{1}^{AR}$ ≡ The incomplete but coordinated-coverage strategy is optimal;

$Z_{0}^{S}$ ≡ The zero-coverage strategy is optimal;

$\rho_{AA}^{All}$ ≡ The Coordinated/Shared-Profit Boundary;

$\rho_{S}^{S\text{-}Adj}$ ≡ The Uncoordinated/Shared-Profit Boundary;

$\rho_{S\text{-}Adj}^{AA}$ ≡ The Coordinated/Uncoordinated Boundary;

$\rho_{0}^{All}$ ≡ The Complete/Zero-Coverage Boundary;

$\rho_{0}^{AR}$ ≡ The Incomplete/Zero-Coverage Boundary;

$\rho_{AR}^{AA}$ ≡ A portion of the Complete/Incomplete-Coverage Boundary;

$\rho_{S\text{-}Adj}^{AR}$ ≡ The Profit-Equality Boundary in Situation **C**; and

$\rho_{S}^{AR}$ ≡ The Profit-Equality Boundary in Situation **D**.

*Figure 4.13b.* The Manufacturer-Optimal Stackelberg Strategy When $f_{\mathcal{A}} = 0.25, \varphi = 0.5$

Zone $\mathbf{Z}_{12}^{\text{All}}$, within which the channel-coordinating tariff $\{C, \phi^{\text{All}}\}$ is manufacturer-optimal, lies in that portion of $\langle \rho, Q \rangle$ – space that is above both the $\rho_{\text{AA}}^{\text{All}}$ – boundary and the $\rho_0^{\text{All}}$ – boundary. The area that is directly below the $\rho_0^{\text{All}}$ – boundary (which runs from $\langle \rho = 0, Q = \tfrac{1}{2} \rangle$ to $\langle \rho = \tfrac{1}{7}, Q = \sqrt{\tfrac{1}{8}} \rangle$) defines the Zero-Coverage Zone $\mathbf{Z}_0^{\text{S}}$.

All four Comparisons are relevant in the remainder of $\langle \rho, Q \rangle$ – space. Comparison **A**'s Profit-Equality Boundary satisfies:

$$\rho_{\text{S-Adj}}^{\text{AA}} = \left( \frac{(1+Q) - \sqrt{\left(2(1+Q)^2 - 1\right)/2}}{2(1-Q)} \right) \tag{4.7.15}$$

This boundary intercepts the $\langle Q = 0 \rangle$ – axis at $\rho = (\sqrt{2} - 1)/(2\sqrt{2}) \cong 0.146$ and the $\langle \rho = 1 \rangle$ – axis at $Q \cong 0.937$. Recall from (4.7.7) that in Comparison **B**, the Stackelberg strategy dominates the channel-coordinating, complete-coverage, shared-profit strategy.

Comparison **C**'s Profit-Equality Boundary satisfies:

$$\rho_{\text{S-Adj}}^{\text{AR}} = \left( \frac{(1 - 8Q^2) + \sqrt{(31 - 64Q + 40Q^2)(8Q^2 - 1)}}{16(1-Q)^2} \right) \tag{4.7.16}$$

This portion of the Complete/Incomplete-Coverage Boundary intercepts the $\langle \rho = 0 \rangle$ – axis at $Q = \sqrt{\tfrac{1}{8}} \cong 0.353$ and the $\langle \rho = 1 \rangle$ – axis at $Q = 1$.

Comparison **D**'s Profit-Equality Boundary satisfies:

$$\rho_{\text{S}}^{\text{AR}} = \left( \frac{7 - \sqrt{49 - 256Q^2(1-Q)^2}}{16(1-Q)^2} \right) \tag{4.7.17}$$

This portion of the Complete/Incomplete-Coverage Boundary intercepts the $\langle \rho = 0 \rangle$ – axis at $Q = 0$ and the $\langle \rho = 1 \rangle$ – axis at $Q \cong 0.933$.

Before we assign portions of the parameter space to one of the four possible tariffs, we must determine three additional boundaries: the final element of the Complete/Incomplete Coverage Boundary ($\rho_{\text{AR}}^{\text{AA}}$), the Incomplete/Zero-Coverage Boundary ($\rho_0^{\text{AR}}$), and the Uncoordinated/Shared-Profit Boundary ($\rho_{\text{S}}^{\text{S-Adj}}$). These boundaries satisfy:

$$\rho_{\text{AR}}^{\text{AA}} = 8Q^2/7 \tag{4.5.33}$$

$$\rho_0^{\text{AR}} = \tfrac{1}{7} \tag{4.7.18}$$

$$\rho_{\text{S}}^{\text{S-Adj}} = \left( \frac{(1+Q) - \sqrt{Q(2+Q)}}{4(1-Q)} \right) \tag{4.7.19}$$

This Complete/Incomplete Coverage Boundary intercepts the $\langle \rho = 0 \rangle$ – axis at $Q = 0$ and the $\langle \rho = 1 \rangle$ – axis at $Q = \sqrt{7/8} \cong 0.935$ while the Uncoordinated/ Shared-Profit Boundary intercepts the $\langle Q = 0 \rangle$ – axis at $\rho = 1/4$ and the $\langle \rho = 1 \rangle$ – axis at $Q = (8 + \sqrt{10})/12 \cong 0.930$.

Zone $\mathbf{Z}_{12}^{AA}$ forms a narrow, curving ribbon in $\langle \rho, Q \rangle$ – space whose edges are the $\rho_{AA}^{All}$ – boundary (4.5.32), the $\rho_{S-Adj}^{AA}$ – boundary (4.7.15), and the $\rho_{AR}^{AA}$ – boundary (4.5.33). Within this Zone the manufacturer prefers the channel-coordinating tariff $\{C, \phi^{AA}\}$ that causes channel profit to be shared with the retailer. Zone $\mathbf{Z}_{12}^{S-Adj}$ also forms a curving band in $\langle \rho, Q \rangle$ – space that is bounded by the $\rho_{S-Adj}^{AA}$ – boundary (4.7.15), the $\rho_{S-Adj}^{AR}$ – boundary (4.7.16), and the $\rho_{S}^{S-Adj}$ – boundary (4.7.19). In this Zone the manufacturer prefers the channel non-coordinating tariff $\{\hat{W}, \hat{\phi}^{S-Adj}\}$ that directs all channel profit to the manufacturer. Zone $\mathbf{Z}_{12}^{S}$ forms a substantial, lenticular area in $\langle \rho, Q \rangle$ – space that is framed by the $\rho_{S}^{AR}$ – boundary (4.7.17) and the $\rho_{S}^{S-Adj}$ – boundary (4.7.19). Within this Zone the manufacturer prefers the channel non-coordinating tariff $\{\hat{W}, \hat{\phi}^{S}\}$ that shares channel profit with the retailer. Figure 4.13a shows the location of all the Zones.

The preceding three Zones guarantee complete coverage; but there is incomplete coverage in Zone $\mathbf{Z}_{1}^{AR}$, which is bordered by the $\rho_{S-Adj}^{AR}$ – boundary (4.7.16), the $\rho_{S}^{AR}$ – boundary (4.7.17), the $\rho_{AR}^{AA}$ – boundary (4.5.33), and the $\rho_{0}^{AR}$ – boundary (4.7.18). Within this Zone the manufacturer sets a wholesale price $\{C, \phi^{AR}\}$ that coordinates the channel in the high-demand state-of-nature and that steers all profit to the manufacturer.

Focusing on Figure 4.13b, we note that:

1. The $\rho_{S}^{AR}$ – boundary and the $\rho_{S-Adj}^{AR}$ – boundary intersect at $\langle \rho \cong 0.172, Q \cong 0.373 \rangle$;
2. The $\rho_{S-Adj}^{AR}$ – boundary intersects the $\rho_{AR}^{AA}$ – boundary at $\langle \rho \cong 0.156, Q \cong 0.369 \rangle$; and
3. The $\rho_{AR}^{AA}$ – boundary meets the $\rho_{0}^{AR}$ – boundary at $\langle \rho \cong 0.143, Q \cong 0.353 \rangle$.

(This is the point where the $\rho_{0}^{All}$ – boundary intersects the $\rho_{0}^{AR}$ – boundary.) Below the jagged line defined by these points the manufacturer serves only the high-demand state-of-nature and prices to coordinate the channel.

**Scenario 4** $(f_{\mathcal{A}} = 0.25, \varphi = 1)$: This Scenario, which combines information from Figure 4.7 and Figure 4.10, is illustrated in Figure 4.14. Once again we begin with the Full Profit-Extraction Boundary. Its value is:

$$\rho_{AA}^{All} = 1/\left(4\left[1 - Q^2\right]\right) \tag{4.7.20}$$

This boundary intercepts the $\langle Q = 0 \rangle$ – axis at $\rho = 1/4$ and the $\langle \rho = 1 \rangle$ – axis at $Q = \sqrt{3}/2 \cong 0.866$. We also note that the Complete/Zero Coverage Boundary is defined as:

$$\rho_0^{All} = (1 - 4Q^2)/(4[1 - Q^2]) \tag{4.6.28}$$

The $\rho_0^{All}$ – boundary intercepts the $\langle \rho = 0 \rangle$ – axis at $Q = 1/2$ and the $\langle Q = 0 \rangle$ – axis at $\rho = 1/4$.

The remainder of our analysis for this Scenario follows the same pattern as our analysis of Scenario 3. Therefore, to conserve space, we simply focus on the various boundary conditions. Comparison **A**'s Profit-Equality Boundary satisfies:

$$\rho_{S-Adj}^{AA} = \left( \frac{(1 + Q) - \sqrt{Q(2 + Q)}}{2(1 - Q)} \right) \tag{4.7.21}$$

This boundary intercepts the $\langle Q = 0 \rangle$ – axis at $\rho = 1/2$ and the $\langle \rho = 1 \rangle$ – axis at $Q = (1/2 + \sqrt{1/8}) \cong 0.854$. Recall from (4.7.7) that in Comparison **B**, the Stackelberg strategy dominates the channel-coordinating, complete-coverage, shared-profit strategy.

Comparison **C**'s Profit-Equality Boundary for Scenario 4 satisfies:

$$\rho_{S-Adj}^{AR} = Q\left[\left(-Q + \sqrt{4 - 8Q + 5Q^2}\right)/\left(2[1 - Q]^2\right)\right] \tag{4.7.22}$$

The $\rho_{S-Adj}^{AR}$ – boundary meets the $\langle \rho = 0 \rangle$ – axis at $Q = 0$ and the $\langle \rho = 1 \rangle$ – axis at $Q = 1$.

Comparison **D**'s Profit-Equality Boundary is:

$$\rho_S^{AR} = \left( \frac{1 - \sqrt{Q(2 - 5Q + 8Q^2 - 4Q^3)}}{2(1 - Q)^2} \right) \tag{4.7.23}$$

The $\rho_S^{AR}$ – boundary intercepts the $\langle \rho = 1 \rangle$ – axis at $Q = (1/2 + \sqrt{1/8}) \cong 0.854$ and the $\langle Q = 0 \rangle$ – axis at $\rho = 1/2$.

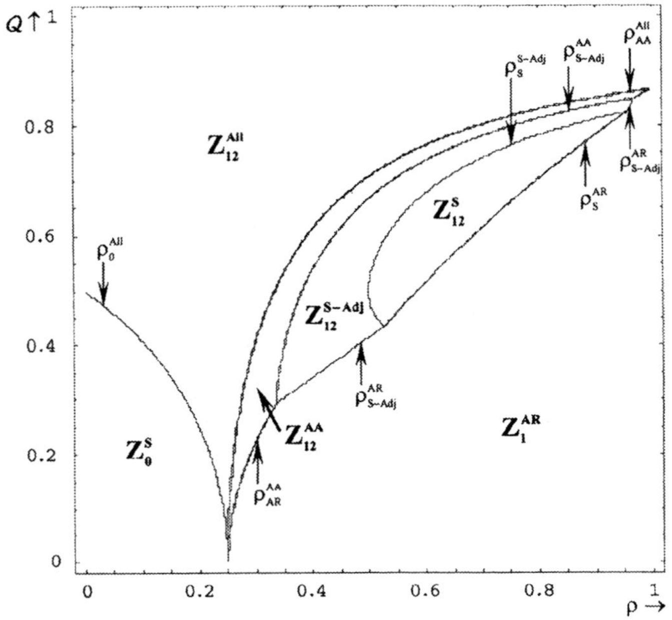


Legend:

$Z_{12}^{All}$ ≡ The channel-coordinating, complete-coverage strategy is optimal;

$Z_{12}^{AA}$ ≡ The channel-coordinating, complete-coverage, shared-profit strategy is optimal;

$Z_{12}^{S-Adj}$ ≡ The fixed-fee adjusted Stackelberg strategy is optimal;

$Z_{12}^{S}$ ≡ The Stackelberg strategy is optimal;

$Z_{1}^{AR}$ ≡ The incomplete but coordinated-coverage strategy is optimal;

$\rho_{AA}^{All}$ ≡ The Full-Profit Extraction Boundary;

$\rho_{S-Adj}^{AA}$ ≡ The Coordinated/Uncoordinated Boundary;

$\rho_{S}^{S-Adj}$ ≡ The Uncoordinated/Shared-Profit Boundary;

$\rho_{0}^{All}$ ≡ The Complete/Zero-Coverage Boundary;

$\rho_{AR}^{AA}$ ≡ A portion of the Complete/Incomplete Coverage Boundary;

$\rho_{S-Adj}^{AR}$ ≡ The Profit-Equality Boundary in Situation **C**; and

$\rho_{S}^{AR}$ ≡ The Profit-Equality Boundary in Situation **D**.

*Figure 4.14.* The Manufacturer-Optimal Stackelberg Strategy When $f_{\mathfrak{R}} = 0.25, \varphi = 1$

Before we assign portions of parameter space to one of the four possible tariffs, we determine two additional boundaries. They are the final element of the Complete/Incomplete Coverage Boundary ($\rho^{AA}_{AR}$) and the Uncoordinated/Shared-Profit Boundary ($\rho^{S-Adj}_{S}$). These boundaries satisfy:

$$\rho^{AA}_{AR} = Q^2 + 1/4 \tag{4.5.37}$$

$$\rho^{S}_{S-Adj} = \left( \frac{(1+Q) \pm \sqrt{Q^2 + 2Q - 1}}{4(1-Q)} \right) \tag{4.7.24}$$

These equations previously appeared as (4.5.37) and (4.6.30), respectively. The $\rho^{AA}_{AR}$ – boundary intercepts the $\langle \rho = 1 \rangle$ – axis at $Q = \sqrt{3}/2 \cong 0.866$ and the $\langle Q = 0 \rangle$ – axis at $\rho = 1/4$. The $\rho^{S}_{S-Adj}$ – boundary meets the $\langle \rho = 1 \rangle$ – axis at $Q = 5/6 \cong 0.833$ and at $Q = 1/2$; it does not touch the $\langle Q = 0 \rangle$ – axis, the $\langle \rho = 0 \rangle$ – axis, or the $\langle \rho = 1 \rangle$ – axis.

It is now straightforward to specify the six Zones, their boundaries, and the wholesale-price strategy related to each Zone. First, the conventional-coordination Zone $\mathbf{Z}^{All}_{12}$, within which the manufacturer collects all channel profit by employing the channel-coordinating tariff $\{C, \phi^{All}\}$, is bordered by the Full Profit-Extraction Boundary ($\rho^{All}_{AA}$) and the Complete/Zero-Coverage Boundary ($\rho^{All}_{0}$).

Second, Zone $\mathbf{Z}^{AA}_{12}$ forms a curving ribbon in $\langle \rho, Q \rangle$ – space. The edges of this Zone are the $\rho^{All}_{AA}$ – boundary (4.7.20), the $\rho^{AA}_{S-Adj}$ – boundary (4.7.21), and the $\rho^{AA}_{AR}$ – boundary (4.5.37). In this Zone the manufacturer uses the channel-coordinating tariff $\{C, \phi^{AA}\}$ that causes channel profit to be shared with the retailer.

Third, Zone $\mathbf{Z}^{S-Adj}_{12}$ forms a broad, curving band in $\langle \rho, Q \rangle$ – space that is framed by the $\rho^{AA}_{S-Adj}$ – boundary (4.7.21), the $\rho^{AR}_{S-Adj}$ – boundary (4.7.22), and the $\rho^{S-Adj}_{S}$ – boundary (4.6.30). In this Zone the manufacturer uses the non-coordinating tariff $\{\hat{W}, \hat{\phi}^{S-Adj}\}$ and obtains all channel profit. Fourth, Zone $\mathbf{Z}^{S}_{12}$ forms a teardrop-shaped area in $\langle \rho, Q \rangle$ – space that is bordered by the $\rho^{AR}_{S}$ – boundary (4.7.23) and the $\rho^{S-Adj}_{S}$ – boundary (4.6.30). In this Zone the manufacturer uses the non-coordinating tariff $\{\hat{W}, \hat{\phi}^{S}\}$ that causes channel profit to be shared with the retailer.

Fifth, there is incomplete coverage in Zone $\mathbf{Z}^{AR}_{1}$, which is bordered by the $\rho^{AR}_{S-Adj}$ – boundary (4.7.22), the $\rho^{AR}_{S}$ – boundary (4.7.23), and the

$\rho_{AR}^{AA}$ – boundary (4.5.37). In this Zone the manufacturer sets a wholesale price $\{C, \phi^{AR}\}$ that coordinates the channel in the high-demand state-of-nature and that steers all profit to the manufacturer. Finally, the Zero-Coverage Zone $\mathbf{Z}_0^S$ is located inside the Complete/Zero-Coverage Boundary ( $\rho_0^{All}$ ).

# 8 COMMENTARY

In this Chapter we investigated a dyadic relationship in which channel members make decisions under uncertainty. Although channel participants are aware of all relevant details about demand, costs, and the probability of every possible state-of-nature, the manufacturer commits to channel participation, and to a wholesale price, without knowing the quantity that will be demanded in each time-period. The retailer's channel-participation decision involves the same uncertainty, but the retailer has full information about demand and its costs before it selects each time-period's price and order quantity (including a zero-order quantity associated with refusing to distribute in a state-of-nature). We believe that modeling *asymmetric information* is consistent with our Empirical-Evidence Criterion, for manufacturers often set their wholesale prices with less information about the demand curve than is available to their retailers.

Our results also depend on the key assumptions of *time-invariant parameters* and positive *fixed costs*. Because we model parameters as time-invariant, the manufacturer offers the same wholesale price in every time-period. Because the realized state-of-nature can vary from one time period to the next, the retailer may make different price and distribution decisions in successive time-periods. In addition, our model assumes that the retailer's decision to distribute the manufacturer's product generates a fixed cost, while a non-distribution decision generates a different fixed cost. These fixed costs play a crucial role in driving our results, as do the probabilities associated with the states-of-nature, the retail demand in each state-of-nature, and the variable costs of the channel members.

## 8.1 Commentary on Coordination: The Vertically-Integrated System

We began our analysis with a model of N states-of-nature. We showed that a vertically-integrated system with full information offers more complete temporal breadth than does a coordinated (but decentralized) channel with asymmetric information. This result is similar to our conclusion regarding channel breadth that we presented in Chapter 3.

We used a model of two states-of-nature and to show that a vertically-integrated system serves all states-of-nature if and only if there are *no* fixed costs of production (F), distribution ($f_A$), or non-distribution ($f_R$). When $f_A > f_R \geq 0$, the vertically-integrated system will either not exist (when $f_R > 0$) or will serve only the high-demand state-of-nature.[19] Recall that the presence of a fixed cost in Chapter 3 was sufficient to create incomplete spatial coverage for a vertically-integrated system. Fixed costs play a similar role in this Chapter, although there are subtleties arising from the distinction between the fixed costs of distribution and non-distribution.

## 8.2 Commentary on Coordination: The Manufacturer/Independent Retailer Channel

Now consider the more interesting case of the manufacturer/independent retailer dyad. We argued in the Introduction to this Chapter that, if the results of a single-retailer, single state-of-nature model generalize to the case of a single-retailer, multiple states-of-nature model, we *should* find that:

(1) The manufacturer can set its wholesale-price policy to coordinate the channel in all states-of-nature;

(2) The manufacturer should set its wholesale-price policy to coordinate the channel in all states-of-nature; and

(3) The manufacturer should set its wholesale-price policy to cause the retailer to serve all states-of-nature that are served by the vertically-integrated system.

We have shown that the first generalization is true. Because states-of-nature are independent, coordination only requires that the manufacturer set its marginal wholesale price equal to its marginal production cost.

We have also shown that the second and third generalizations are false. Although a vertically-integrated system will coordinate any state-of-nature that it serves, it is not optimal for the profit-maximizing manufacturer to behave in the same manner for all parametric values. Moreover, neither a vertically-integrated system nor a decentralized channel will offer complete coverage over all possible parametric values.

We clarify our observations on Channel Strategy by presenting side-by-side comparisons of optimal behavior (i) in a vertically-integrated system (Section 3) and (ii) in an unconstrained, profit-maximizing manufacturer/independent-retailer dyad (Section 7). Our comparisons cover the same Scenarios detailed in our earlier analyses. The vertically-integrated system appears on the left-hand side of Figures 4.15-4.18 and the dyadic channel appears on the right. To simplify our presentation, we label the degree of temporal coverage with subscripts for complete coverage ( $_{12}$ ), incomplete coverage ( $_{1}$ ), and zero coverage ( $_{0}$ ). We use superscripts to indicate a channel that is coordinated ( $^{C}$ ) or uncoordinated ( $^{U}$ ).

Figure 4.15 reveals that, in the absence of any fixed costs, the very act of decentralization is sufficient to cause temporal coverage, and the extent of coordination, to degrade relative to a vertically-integrated system. In fact, in the portion of the right-hand Figure that is labeled $Z_1^C$, only the high-demand state is served. In the portion of the parameter-space where coverage is complete (Zone $\mathbf{Z}_{12}^{U}$), the channel is uncoordinated under decentralization, even though the vertically-integrated system is fully coordinated in the same portion of $\langle \rho, \mathcal{Q} \rangle -$ space. As a result, consumers pay a higher retail price than they would if the channel were organized as a vertically-integrated system.

Figure 4.16 shows that, in the presence of a positive fixed distribution cost, the vertically-integrated system does not serve the low-demand state when the coordinated-output ratio ($\mathcal{Q} \equiv Q_2^* / Q_1^*$) is low. Relative to the vertically-integrated system, the decentralized channel chooses to serve only a high-demand state over a larger portion of $\langle \rho, \mathcal{Q} \rangle -$ space. Moreover, coordination does not occur with complete coverage in a decentralized channel, while a vertically-integrated system is always coordinated.

Comparing Figure 4.17 with Figure 4.16 reveals that the introduction of a fixed cost of non-distribution ( $f_R$ ) changes the manufacturer's strategy in several important ways. A positive $f_R$ (i) creates an area within which there is zero coverage ( $Z_0$ ), (ii) increases the area over which coverage is temporally complete ( $Z_{12}^C$ ), and (iii) induces the independent manufacturer to set its wholesale price to achieve coordination in a part of $\langle \rho, \mathcal{Q} \rangle -$ space. Finally, we note that the vertically-integrated system and the decentralized channel offer zero coverage over the same part of $\langle \rho, \mathcal{Q} \rangle -$ space.

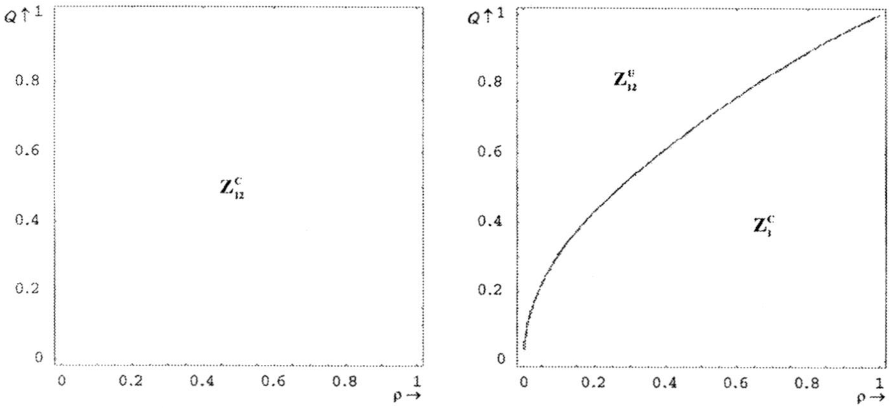


$Z_{12}^{C}$ ≡ Both states-of nature are served and the channel is coordinated;

$Z_{12}^{U}$ ≡ Both states-of nature are served but the channel is *not* coordinated; and

$Z_{1}^{C}$ ≡ Only the high-demand state-of-nature is served and the channel is coordinated.

*Figure 4.15.* The Vertically-Integrated System and the Manufacturer-Optimal Stackelberg Strategy When $f_{\mathfrak{R}} = 0$, $\varphi = 0$

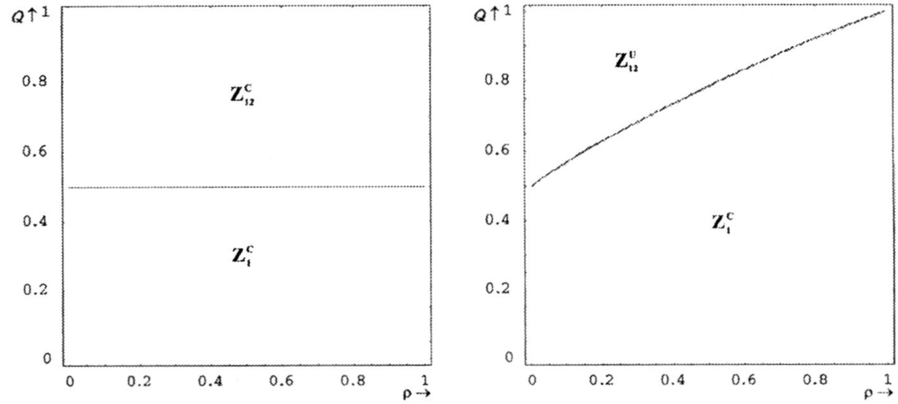


$\mathbf{Z}_{12}^{C}$ ≡ Both states-of nature are served and the channel is coordinated;

$\mathbf{Z}_{12}^{U}$ ≡ Both states-of nature are served but the channel is *not* coordinated; and

$\mathbf{Z}_{1}^{C}$ ≡ Only the high-demand state-of-nature is served and the channel is coordinated.

*Figure 4.16.* The Vertically-Integrated System and the Manufacturer-Optimal Stackelberg Strategy When $f_{\mathcal{R}} = 0.25$, $\varphi = 0$

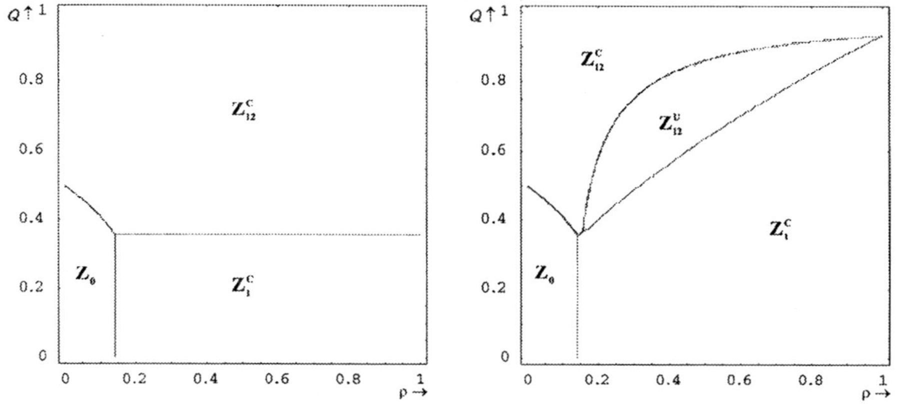


$Z_{12}^{C}$ ≡ Both states-of nature are served and the channel is coordinated;

$Z_{12}^{U}$ ≡ Both states-of nature are served but the channel is *not* coordinated;

$Z_1^{C}$ ≡ Only the high-demand state-of-nature is served and the channel is coordinated; and

$Z_0$ ≡ Neither state-of nature is served.

*Figure 4.17.* The Vertically-Integrated System and the Manufacturer-Optimal Stackelberg Strategy When $f_{\pi} = 0.25$, $\varphi = 0.5$

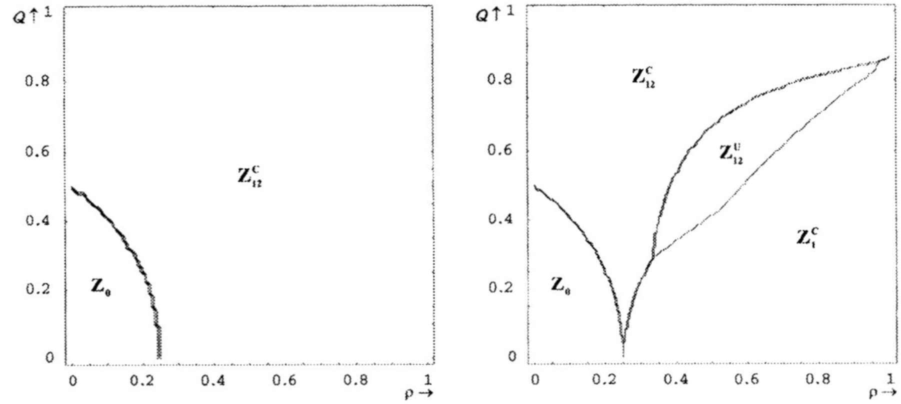


$Z_{12}^C$ ≡ Both states-of nature are served and the channel is coordinated;
$Z_{12}^U$ ≡ Both states-of nature are served but the channel is *not* coordinated;
$Z_1^C$ ≡ Only the high-demand state-of nature is served and the channel is coordinated; and
$Z_0$ ≡ Neither state-of-nature is served.

*Figure 4.18.* The Vertically-Integrated System and the Manufacturer-Optimal Stackelberg Strategy When $f_{\mathfrak{R}} = 0.25$, $\varphi = 1$

Figure 4.18 reveals that, when the fixed costs of distribution and non-distribution are equal, incomplete coverage is eliminated in a vertically-integrated system and is diminished in a decentralized channel. Correspondingly, there is an increase in the portions of the parameter space over which channel coordination is optimal. Further, the Zero-Coverage Zone is again identical across the two forms of channel organization investigated in this sub-Section and is also larger than it was in Figure 4.17. We conclude that increases in the magnitude of the fixed cost of non-distribution (i) increase the extent of zero-coverage and (ii) decrease the extent of temporal incompleteness.

## 8.3 Commentary on Five Channel Myths

In this Chapter we have provided evidence that five widely-held beliefs about distribution channels are Myths. These Channel Myths are:

- The Bilateral-Monopoly Meta-Myth;
- The Channel-Breadth Modeling Myth;
- The Fixed-Cost Modeling Myth;
- The Channel-Coordination Strategic Myth; and
- The Multiple-Retailers/Multiple States-of-Nature Modeling Myth.

The Bilateral-Monopoly Meta-Myth implies that the results of the bilateral-monopoly model generalize to a model with multiple states-of-nature. We have shown that the prescriptions drawn from a simple, bilateral-monopoly model of one manufacturer, selling one product, through one retailer, facing one state-of nature, are *not* robust to the slight modification of adding a second state-of-nature, let alone multiple states-of-nature. This lack of robustness also appeared in Chapter 3, where adding multiple (exclusive) retailers to the bilateral-monopoly model dramatically altered the manufacturer's optimal wholesale-price strategy.

The Channel-Breadth Modeling Myth states that assuming a constant channel breadth is an innocuous modeling assumption. In this Chapter we considered a model with an endogenous temporal breadth (the states-of-nature served). Our results indicate that, depending on the model's parametric values, the channel may distribute in both states-of-nature, in a single state-of-nature, or in no states-of-nature. The point is that, when we treat channel breadth as endogenous, we reach conclusions that are inconsistent with those that are reached under the assumption of constant channel breadth. Thus the belief that modeling channel breadth as exogenous is a Myth. We infer that analyses of multiple states-of-nature models should explore temporal comprehensiveness, just as analyses of multiple-retailer models ought to explore spatial extensiveness.

The Fixed-Cost Modeling Myth states that it is acceptable for modelers to ignore fixed costs. We have proven that the retailer's fixed costs have a substantial impact on the manufacturer's wholesale-price policy and on the retailer's distribution and retail-price decisions. Increases in fixed costs negatively affect the retailer's channel participation decision, but increase the likelihood of complete temporal coverage when the retailer does participate in the channel. We have also shown that a fixed cost of non-distribution is essential for the manufacturer ever to prefer channel coordination.

According to the Channel-Coordination Strategic Myth, all channel members prefer a wholesale-price policy that maximizes channel profits. We have clearly refuted this belief because, for some parametric values, channel profit maximization does not maximize manufacturer profits.

The Multiple-Retailers/Multiple States-of-Nature Modeling Myth asserts that deductions from a multiple states-of-nature model generalize to a model of multiple, exclusive retailers. The analyses presented in Chapters 3 and 4 prove that this belief is incorrect. In the multiple-retailers model of Chapter 3, the profit of the $i^{th}$ retailer has no effect on the actions taken by the $j^{th}$ retailer. In the model examined in this Chapter, the profit obtained in the $i^{th}$ state-of-nature does affect the single retailer's ability to incur losses in the $j^{th}$ state-of-nature; therefore it affects the retailer's channel-participation decision and the retailer's distribution decision in each state-of-nature. "Cross-subsidization," which is an implicit feature of the multiple states-of-nature model, is absent from the multiple exclusive-retailers model because the former model has a single, retail-level decision-maker, while the latter has multiple decision-makers at the retail level.

## 8.4 Summary Commentary

Over 2000 years ago the Roman censor Cato observed that, "Even though work stops, expenses run on."[20] Like Cato, we find it impossible to avoid the empirical evidence that, even when the work of distributing a product has stopped, expenses are incurred to maintain the ability to distribute the product in the future. Thus, the model examined in this Chapter included a "fixed cost of non-distribution." We showed that this cost has a crucial impact both on temporal breadth and on the manufacturer's desire to coordinate the channel. These results, together with those presented in Chapter 3, demonstrate that fixed costs have a major impact on Channel Strategy and Channel Performance. Accordingly, we will incorporate fixed costs in our competing-retailers model, which we introduce in the next Chapter.

# Notes

[1] Appreciation is expressed to John Conlon of the University of Mississippi and to the participants of the 1999 Conference on Competition and Marketing, University of Mainz, for helpful comments on an earlier draft of this Chapter.

[2] Our terminology derives from the fact that only one state-of-nature can be realized in a time period; thus, failure to serve a state-of-nature is equivalent to failure to serve a time period.

[3] Without commitments from both channel members to participate, the channel cannot exist.

[4] This schedule may be imposed ("take-it-or-leave-it") or the result of negotiations (à la Jeuland and Shugan 1983).

[5] In practice, manufacturer credibility may be based on (a) a legally-binding, wholesale-price contract of specified duration, (b) participation in multiple, exclusive dyadic relationships that would be adversely affected by violating a commitment, or (c) a reputation for infrequent wholesale-price changes. Retailer credibility may be based on (a), (b), or (d) an investment in dyad-specific assets that are tangible (e.g., diagnostic equipment unique to one automobile) or intangible (e.g., a training program unique to one manufacturer's product).

[6] Crocker (1983), Rey and Tirole (1986), Blair and Lewis (1994), Desiraju and Moorthy 1997), and probably other authors make similar arguments about the "downstream" firm having greater knowledge than the "upstream" firm.

[7] Because the retailer has agreed to channel participation, the decision not to distribute in a specific time period also includes an implicit decision to re-stock the item when the state-of-nature is favorable. This re-display expense is properly charged to the decision not to distribute because it can be avoided by distributing in every time period.

[8] We define net revenue as total revenue minus total variable cost.

[9] Our re-parameterizations entail no loss of generality; all the original elements of the model are retained: $\mathcal{Q} \equiv Q_j^{*}/Q_i^{*} = [A_j - b(c_j + C)]/[A_i - b(c_i + C)]$ and $f_{\mathcal{A}} \equiv (f_A / R_1^{*}) = bf_A/(Q_1^{*})^2$.

[10] In later Sections of this Chapter we simplify our Figures by suppressing information on the details of the various sub-Zones associated with each Zero-Coverage Zone. However, the basic logic reported in this Section carries over to subsequent Sections.

[11] We restrict our analyses to two-part tariffs for the reasons given in Chapter 3.

[12] In terms of our demand and cost primitives it is equivalent to $(A_1 - A_2) > b(c_1 - c_2)$.

[13] We adopt the rule that in the case of "ties" the retailer will remain open for business.

[14] *If* $f_R = 0$, the condition $(\rho\Delta - f_R) \le 0$ can only be met when $\rho = 0$. The standard bilateral-monopoly result is embedded in our model as is the degenerate case of a single state-of-nature.

[15] Our focus in this Section is on an "all-or-nothing" distribution constraint. Of course, when parametric values dictate incomplete coverage, it is obvious that the manufacturer can do better by using the channel-coordinating tariff $\{C, \phi^{AR}\}$ and collecting all channel profit than it can by not serving the channel at all. It is equally obvious that $\{C, \phi^{All}\}$ plays the same role when there is complete coverage. Thus the real purpose of this Section is to lay the groundwork for a comparison of the distribution-constrained Stackelberg tariffs and the one channel-coordinating tariff that does not enable the manufacturer to obtain all channel profit: $\{C, \phi^{AA}\}$.

[16] Recall that $Q_1^{*} > Q_2^{*}$ by assumption.

[17] The precise $\mathcal{Q}$ – value is $\mathcal{Q} = (\frac{1}{2} - \sqrt{\frac{1}{8}})$.

[18] An apparent fourth choice, incomplete coverage without coordination, can be shown to be strictly manufacturer-profit dominated by the $\{C, \phi^{AR}\}$ tariff.

[19] The parameters that determine no coverage *versus* incomplete coverage are the probability of the high-demand state-of-nature (ρ), the ratio of coordinated output in the low-demand state to the high-demand state ($Q \equiv Q_2^* / Q_1^*$), and the fixed costs cited in this paragraph.

[20] Cato's Latin prose is sometimes translated as "Cessation of work is not accompanied by cessation of expenses;" see Hooper (1934) for one translation.

# Channels with Competition

*"To make a correct conjecture . . . it is necessary to calculate exactly the number of possible cases and then to determine how much more likely it is that one case will occur than another."*

In Chapters 5-9 we present a series of analyses that collectively address one of the central questions in the marketing science literature on distribution: *"Does coordination benefit all channel members when the channel is characterized by intra-level competition?"* An affirmative answer will extend the principle pronouncement of the academic literature—the desirability of intra-channel coordination—to a wider range of channel structures. A negative answer will establish that the value of coordination is restricted to cases of bilateral monopoly. A qualified answer will identify the set of parametric values for which coordination is suitable. Thus this Segment of the monograph will ascertain whether channel modelers should impose coordination, avoid coordination, or clarify the conditions under which coordination is optimal. Unless the answer is positive, the optimality of coordination in any model must be established, not simply assumed.

To evaluate the desirability of coordination, we develop a meta-model of a single manufacturer, selling a single product, under a single state-of-nature, through two retailers. Because we allow the intensity of inter-retailer competition to range from zero to one, our model incorporates the special cases of perfect substitutability and complete independence. This characteristic of our model conforms to our Nested-Models Criterion, which states that simpler models should be embedded in more general models. Because there is evidence that comparable treatment of retailers is the norm (Lafontaine 1990; Battacharyya and Lafontaine 1995), we require our manufacturer to treat its retailers comparably by offering both of them the same set of wholesale-price options. This requirement accords with our Empirical-Evidence Criterion, which states that assumptions should be in broad harmony with how distribution channels operate.

Our technique in Chapters 5-7 is to calculate the consequences of three wholesale-price strategies that have been described in previous research, while in Chapters 8 and 9 we assess the relative attractiveness of these strategies to the manufacturer. Our method follows the advice of Jacob Bernoulli, who wrote that "to make a correct conjecture . . . it is necessary to calculate exactly the number of possible cases and then to determine how much more likely it is that one case will occur than another" (1713).

In Chapter 5 we concentrate on three issues. First, we solve for the channel-optimal prices and quantities in a "vertically-integrated system" (a "VI-system") such as proposed by Edgeworth (1881), Spengler (1950), and many others. The Channel Performance[1] of the VI-system provides the benchmark against which all other wholesale-price strategies must be judged. The decentrally-managed version of the VI-system reveals that the channel-coordinating transfer prices are unequal except in the degenerate case of identical competitors. Thus a simple two-part tariff, which by definition is equal across the rival retailers, cannot coordinate the channel. Moreover, because the manufacturer-optimal two-part tariff generates positive manufacturer and retailer margins, double marginalization is a necessary condition of channel coordination when retailers compete. These points provide the groundwork for our refutation of two Channel Myths: the *Identical-Competitors Meta-Myth* and the *Double-Marginalization Strategic Myth.*[2]

Second, we develop a linear, channel-coordinating quantity-discount schedule (a "QD-schedule") which proves that the absence of vertical control is not an impediment to the maximization of channel profit. Third, we consider three non-coordinating two-part tariffs. Contrary to conventional wisdom, over limited ranges of the difference in the retailers' fixed costs, each non-coordinating tariff generates greater manufacturer profit than does the QD-schedule. These points provide the groundwork for the refutation of two more Channel Myths: the *Channel-Coordination Strategic Myth* and the *Fixed-Cost Modeling Myth.*

In Chapter 6 we formulate what we call a "sophisticated Stackelberg" two-part tariff (an "SS-tariff"), which is the envelope of *all* two-part tariffs that maximize manufacturer profits for at least one possible set of fixed costs at retail. This tariff is created by maximizing manufacturer profits through the simultaneous selection a per-unit wholesale price *and* a fixed fee, subject to the retailers' reaction functions. Both components of the resulting tariff vary continuously over a range of differences in the retailers' fixed costs, although they are constant over other cost ranges. The SS-tariff only coordinates the channel in the degenerate cases of bilateral monopoly or identical retailers. These points provide the groundwork for our refutation of the *Bilateral-Monopoly Meta-Myth*, as well as additional evidence for our refutation of the *Identical-Competitors Meta-Myth*.

In Chapter 7 we devise a channel-coordinating menu (a "menu") of two-part tariffs. We prove that, through a judicious choice of the fixed fees, the manufacturer can ensure that each retailer chooses the appropriate tariff—meaning the tariff that the retailer must choose in order for the menu to coordinate the channel. We also establish that the manufacturer can extract all profit from the channel only over a limited range of the difference in retailers' fixed costs. Outside this range a share of channel profit must be shifted to one of the retailers as the "cost" of ensuring coordination by preventing defection.

In Chapter 8 we combine our analyses from Chapters 5-7 to decide whether the manufacturer should (i) coordinate the channel with either the menu or the QD-schedule or (ii) *not* coordinate the channel with the SS-tariff. We prove that the optimal strategy varies over three parametric dimensions:

- The intensity of competition, calculated as the ratio of cross-price to own-price effects from the demand curve;
- The magnitude of competition, measured as the (volume-based) market share of the $j^{th}$ retailer in the VI-system; and
- The retailers' fixed-cost ratio, expressed as a share of retail net revenue.

All three parametric dimensions are scaled from zero to one.

We prove that non-coordination with the SS-tariff is optimal for the manufacturer over a very wide range of parametric values. For example, when fixed costs comprise less than 70 percent of net revenue, coordination is only manufacturer-optimal at an intensity of competition greater than two-thirds and a magnitude of competition that involves one retailer holding more than a 90 percent market share. But, when the retailers' fixed-cost ratios are very high, channel coordination is manufacturer-preferred. One important exception to these principles arises in the case of identical retailers. In this special case, coordination is always in the manufacturer's interest. Collectively, these results provide further evidence for our rejection of the *Identical-Competitors Meta-Myth*, the *Fixed-Cost Modeling Myth*, and the *Channel-Coordination Strategic Myth*.

In Chapter 9 we supplement the analysis of Chapter 8 with a geometric depiction of the manufacturer's wholesale-price strategy as a function of the three parametric dimensions identified above. In Chapter 9 we build on the graphical approach first introduced in Chapter 4 by using three-dimensional graphs to illustrate the relationships among the three variables that drive the manufacturer's decision.

The essential message of Chapters 5-9 is that, when the channel is characterized by intra-level competition, *channel coordination benefits the manufacturer only under specific, well-defined parametric values of demand and cost.* Thus future analytical models of distribution channels should endogenously determine the optimality of channel coordination, and the optimal wholesale-price strategy, from the perspective of the channel leader in a Stackelberg game or from the perspective of all participants in a Nash game.

## Notes

[1] "Channel Performance" refers to retail prices, quantities, and profit at all channel levels.
[2] Each of the Myths mentioned here was sketched in Table 1.1.

Chapter 5

# Toward a Manufacturer-Optimal Per-Unit Fee: A Channel-Coordinating Quantity-Discount Schedule[1]

*"How wonderful that we have met with a paradox; now we have some hope of making progress."*

## 1 INTRODUCTION

The existence of multiple retailers raises two important issues: channel breadth and inter-retailer competition. In Chapter 3 we examined channel breadth in a model in which exclusive territories ensured an absence of competition. We now turn to overlapping territories, analyzing inter-retailer competition at a constant channel breadth.[2] For expositional ease we focus on two retailers, the minimum necessary to address this topic.

The model presented in this Chapter will resolve three questions:

(1) Can a single wholesale-price policy coordinate *both* channel dyads?

(2) Does coordination of both dyads maximize *channel* profit?

(3) Does coordination of both dyads maximize *manufacturer* profit?

Prior to our formal analysis, we consider how the bilateral-monopoly model would answer these questions. *If* the results of a single-retailer model generalize to the case of two competing retailers, we should find that:

1. Both manufacturer/retailer dyads can be coordinated with a properly specified quantity-discount schedule, quantity-surplus schedule, or two-part tariff.
2. Channel profit will be maximized when both dyads are coordinated.
3. Manufacturer profit will be maximized when both retail competitors are coordinated.

These conclusions, which are simple generalizations of the results found in a bilateral-monopoly model, implicitly assume that (i) the retailers are identical or (ii) the manufacturer can "cut a separate deal" with each retailer. However, as we have argued in earlier Chapters, the first assumption is patently inconsistent with the empirical evidence, while the second assumption contradicts legal and practical constraints on managerial practice. From both an analytic and managerial perspective, the interesting question is not whether coordination is optimal in a model predicated on the unrealistic assumptions of competitors who are identical and/or who are treated differentially by the manufacturer. The interesting question is whether coordination naturally arises in a model of non-identical competitors who are comparably treated. We will show that inter-retailer differentiation is a crucial characteristic of any comprehensive investigation of a multiple-retailers model of a distribution channel.

To this end, we model the manufacturer as offering a single wholesale-price schedule to non-identical competitors. To ascertain the effect of different demand and/or costs, we embed the special case of identical competitors in our model. If conventional wisdom is correct, then the introduction of non-identical retailers will yield the same results that occur in the embedded, identical-competitors model. In fact, we will prove that the assumption of identical competitors distorts the results obtained in a non-identical, competing-retailers model by yielding overly simplified deductions.

We will also show that the assumption of non-identical, competing retailers has important implications for the optimal wholesale-price policy. With inter-retailer competition, a change in one retailer's price induces a change in its rival's price *via* their demand interaction. Any wholesale-price policy that coordinates the channel must account for this demand interaction, which means that the optimal wholesale price must be a function of the parameters of the retail demand curves. This suggests that the bilateral-monopoly approach of setting the wholesale price ($W$) equal to a (common) marginal production cost ($C$) will not be optimal, for $W = C$ ignores this demand-curve interaction.

Finally, we will prove that the difference in fixed costs at retail plays a crucial role in determining the desirability of channel coordination and the optimality of various wholesale-price policies for the manufacturer. Previous researchers have typically not modeled this cost, apparently because they did not view it as a factor that could influence short-run marketing decisions such as pricing. Apart from "wealth effects" in the literature on "decision-making under uncertainty," we are unaware of models in which fixed costs play as vital a role as they do here.

Because the analytical marketing science literature on distribution channels began with a model that employed a quantity-discount schedule to induce coordination (Jeuland and Shugan 1983), we begin by determining whether such a schedule will coordinate a competing-retailers channel. We will show that, under our continuing assumption of comparable treatment of non-identical retailers, there is a channel-coordinating, quantity-discount schedule that duplicates the price and quantity results of a vertically-integrated system. The channel model explored here *can* be fully coordinated.

We will also derive a set of specific two-part tariffs that *cannot* coordinate the channel. In particular, we will examine a simple "sell-at-cost" tariff, a "naïve" Stackelberg[3] tariff, and a "second-best" two-part tariff that approximates, but does not reproduce, the results obtained by a vertically-integrated system. We will demonstrate that there are parametric values for which the manufacturer prefers the sell-at-cost tariff, leaving the channel uncoordinated, rather than achieving coordination with a quantity-discount schedule. We will also show that either the naïve Stackelberg tariff or the second-best tariff may be manufacturer-preferred to the quantity-discount schedule. Thus we prove that—counter to conventional wisdom—channel coordination does *not* maximize manufacturer profit over all possible parametric values.

Our discovery that the manufacturer may prefer not to coordinate the channel is a paradox that raises three questions. First, why should *some* non-coordinating tariffs *sometimes* dominate a channel-coordinating schedule? Second, what exactly are the parametric limits for *any* non-coordinating two-part tariff to be manufacturer-preferred to a quantity-discount schedule? Third, is our observation that non-coordination is preferred for some parametric values generally valid, or is it a fluke related to our use of a linear quantity-discount schedule?

We address the first question by exploring the relationship between the quantity-discount schedule and the three non-coordinating two-part tariffs at various parametric values of demand and costs in this Chapter. In Chapters 6-9 we answer the second and third questions by developing and contrasting two additional wholesale-price policies. In Chapter 6 we develop a fully general two-part tariff that is the envelope of all possible two-part tariffs. This tariff, which we term a "sophisticated" Stackelberg two-part tariff, cannot coordinate the channel. In Chapter 7 we devise a channel-coordinating menu of two-part tariffs.[4] Finally, in Chapters 8 and 9 we contrast all three policies in order to make a definitive comparison between coordination *versus* non-coordination.

We present this Chapter in nine Sections. In Section 2 we describe the assumptions underlying our model. In Section 3 we establish the baseline results of a vertically-integrated system and derive transfer prices that serve as a basis for comparison of the per-unit wholesale component of the two-part tariffs. In Section 4 we examine the behavior of a manufacturer and a pair of independent retailers under a quantity-discount schedule. In Section 5 we address a manufacturer that can use various two-part tariffs to sell to its independent retailers. In Section 6 we compare the resulting prices, outputs, margins, profits and consumer's surplus obtained in Sections 3-5. In Section 7 we contrast profit of the manufacturer under the various wholesale-price strategies explored in this Chapter. In Section 8 we investigate in detail the effect of parametric values on the quantity-discount schedule. We discuss our results in Section 9. Technical details are contained in an Appendix to this Chapter.

# 2 THE MODEL'S ASSUMPTIONS

We model a distribution channel consisting of a single manufacturer selling its product through a pair of competing retailers. Our assumptions are straightforward:

1. Two retail outlets with *non-exclusive territories*;
2. *No resale* of merchandise between retailers;
3. *Certainty* of variables and functional forms;
4. *Profit-maximizing* behavior by all decision-makers; and
5. *Demand functions* that are linear and downward-sloping.

The first assumption enables us to focus upon the issue of inter-retailer competition without having to consider the question of optimal channel breadth. Assumptions 2-4 are carried over from Chapter 3; they require no further justification.

We formalize the fifth assumption with the following demand system:

$$\left.\begin{array}{l} Q_i = A_i - bp_i + \theta p_j \\ Q_j = A_j - bp_j + \theta p_i \end{array}\right\} \quad \text{s.t.} \quad 0 \leq \theta < b. \tag{5.2.1}$$

In this expression $p_k$ denotes the price charged by the $k^{th}$ retailer $k \in (i, j)$. Simpler forms of this demand curve (with $A_k = 1 = b$) have been used by McGuire and Staelin (1983) and Jeuland and Shugan (1988), among others.[5] The intercept term $A_k$ is a measure of the base level of demand facing the $k^{th}$ retailer, which we define to be the quantity demanded when both retailers charge a zero price. The parameter b measures own-price sensitivity and the cross-price parameter $\theta$ measures the sensitivity of one retailer's sales to changes in its rival's price. In the extreme case, $\theta = 0$ and consumers do not switch stores on the basis of price. An increasing number of consumers switch on the basis of price as $\theta \to b$.

# 3 THE VERTICALLY-INTEGRATED SYSTEM

In this Section we examine the pricing decisions of a vertically-integrated system under two organizational structures. In the first we model pricing as centrally determined. In the second we utilize a transfer-pricing scheme to examine decentralized pricing. Our decentralized results reveal the profit contribution from each retail outlet and from the manufacturer; they also uncover the channel-coordinating wholesale and retail markups.

## 3.1 Channel Coordination with Centralized Pricing

Our vertically-integrated system sets prices ($p_i$ and $p_j$) to maximize channel profit ($\Pi_C$). The maximand is:

$$\max_{p_i, p_j} \Pi_I = \begin{Bmatrix} (p_i - c_i - C)(A_i - bp_i + \theta p_j) - f_i \\ +(p_j - c_j - C)(A_j - bp_j + \theta p_i) - f_j \end{Bmatrix} - F \\ \equiv \sum_k \{g_k\} - F \qquad k \in (i, j) \tag{5.3.1}$$

The terms $c_k (f_k)$ and $C(F)$ denote the average variable (the fixed) costs of the $k^{th}$ retail outlet and the manufacturer respectively while $g_k$ is the net profit of the $k^{th}$ outlet. Each retailer has unique demand and cost parameters that reflect variations in local competitive, demographic, and economic conditions.

Solving for optimal prices and quantities yields:

$$p_i^* = \left( \frac{bA_i + \theta A_j + (b^2 - \theta^2)(c_i + C)}{2(b^2 - \theta^2)} \right) > 0 \tag{5.3.2}$$

$$Q_i^* = \left( \frac{A_i - b(c_i + C) + \theta(c_j + C)}{2} \right) > 0 \tag{5.3.3}$$

Second-order conditions for profit maximization are satisfied at these prices and quantities. Consistent with economic intuition, the optimal price is an increasing function of $A_i$, $A_j$, $c_i$, and C; the optimal quantity is an increasing function of its own demand intercept and its rival's cost but is a decreasing function of its own cost and manufacturing cost.

An understanding of equation (5.3.3) is essential, for we use it in every Chapter. The channel-optimal quantity $Q_i^*$ is precisely one-half of the quantity that would be sold with full marginal-cost pricing: (i.e., $p_k = (c_k + C)$). We may express the optimal, vertically-integrated system's margin at the $i^{th}$ retail outlet by using equation (5.3.3) to obtain:

$$\mu_i^* \equiv (p_i^* - c_i - C) = \left[ \frac{bQ_i^* + \theta Q_j^*}{(b^2 - \theta^2)} \right] \tag{5.3.4}$$

We will refer to the pricing strategy specified by equation (5.3.4) as the *vertically-integrated price strategy*.

A comparison of the relative prices, quantities, and margins at the two outlets reveals:

$$p_i^* \gtrless p_j^* \quad \text{as} \quad \left[A_i + (b+\theta)c_i\right] \gtrless \left[A_j + (b+\theta)c_j\right]$$

$$Q_i^* \gtrless Q_j^* \quad \text{as} \quad \left[A_i - (b+\theta)c_i\right] \gtrless \left[A_j - (b+\theta)c_j\right] \qquad (5.3.5)$$

$$\mu_i^* \gtrless \mu_j^* \quad \text{as} \quad Q_i^* \gtrless Q_j^*$$

Demand and cost parameters determine which retail outlet charges the higher price and which one sells more units. Note that it is possible for the higher price outlet to sell a greater volume; however, the larger-volume retailer always generates the greater channel margin.

## 3.2 Channel Coordination with Decentralized Pricing

An alternative to centrally dictated pricing is to allow each retail manager independent price control. Facing a transfer price of $T_i$, the i[th] outlet's manager will maximize:

$$\max_{p_i} \ \pi_i = (p_i - c_i - T_i)(A_i - bp_i + \theta p_j) - f_i \qquad (5.3.6)$$

In light of the resulting reaction function, headquarters can readily establish an optimal transfer price from manufacturer to retailer that will ensure that the i[th] retail manager sets the vertically-integrated profit-maximizing price $p_i^*$. It is easy to show that this optimal transfer-price is:

$$T_i^* = \theta\left(\frac{\theta Q_i^* + bQ_j^*}{b(b^2 - \theta^2)}\right) + C \qquad (5.3.7)$$

We instantly see that, with one exception, the optimal transfer price ($T_i^*$) *must* exceed the marginal cost of production (C). The exception occurs in the absence of inter-retailer competition (i.e., when $\theta = 0$); this limiting case involves a pair of bilateral monopolies that have no demand interaction.[6]

Inserting (5.3.7) in (5.3.6), setting the partial derivatives of the resulting first-order conditions to zero, and jointly solving for prices yields the $p_i^*$ defined at equation (5.3.2). At the prices $p_i^*$ and $p_j^*$ the i[th] retail outlet earns a per-unit margin of:

$$m_i^* \equiv (p_i^* - c_i - T_i^*) = Q_i^* / b$$

Thus the i[th] outlet's profit is:

$$\pi_i^* = m_i^* Q_i^* - f_i = \left[(Q_i^*)^2 / b\right] - f_i \qquad (5.3.8)$$

With transfer pricing the manufacturing arm earns a net profit:

$$\Pi_M^* \equiv \sum_{k=i,j}(T_k^* - C)Q_k^* - F$$

$$= \left( \frac{\theta\left\{\theta(Q_i^*)^2 + 2bQ_i^*Q_j^* + \theta(Q_j^*)^2\right\}}{b(b^2-\theta^2)} \right) - F \tag{5.3.9}$$

Adding the net revenue of the retail outlets (5.3.8) to this value yields the total profit of a vertically-integrated system as:

$$\Pi_I^* = \left( \frac{b(Q_i^*)^2 + 2\theta Q_i^*Q_j^* + b(Q_j^*)^2}{(b^2-\theta^2)} \right) - f_i - f_j - F \tag{5.3.10}$$

To calculate aggregate consumers' surplus generated by a vertically-integrated system, we use the formula (1.A.8) from Chapter 1 to obtain:

$$CS_I^* = \left((Q_i^*)^2 + (Q_j^*)^2\right)\Big/2b \tag{5.3.11}$$

Unsurprisingly, the more consumers purchase, the greater is consumers' surplus. Equations (5.3.10) and (5.3.11) form our baseline measures of channel performance against which all alternative wholesale-price strategies will be judged. Notice that our results are consistent with Spengler's (1950) observation that a vertically-integrated system maximizes both channel profit and consumer's surplus.

## 3.3 Six Comments on Transfer Pricing

The preceding results merit six observations that will help clarify our analysis of coordination in a decentralized channel. First, profit maximization requires management to establish a transfer price (5.3.7) that is *unique* to each retail outlet[7] *unless* the retailers are identical (i.e., $Q_i^* = Q_j^*$) or do not compete (i.e., $\theta = 0$). With competition between non-identical retailers, the optimal transfer price *differs* by retail outlet ($T_i^* \neq T_j^*$). Second, when $\theta > 0$, there is a positive wholesale margin ($T_k^* > C,\ k \in (i,j)$), and positive retail margins ($p_k^* > (c_k + T_k^*)$). Third, coordination of a decentralized channel requires that the marginal wholesale-price paid by the k[th] retailer exactly equal $T_k^*$; no other marginal wholesale-price is compatible with coordination.

Fourth, the retail outlet selling the *lower* quantity pays the *higher* transfer price; that is, ($T_i^* \gtrless T_j^*$ as $Q_i^* \lessgtr Q_j^*$). This relationship is critical, for it means that neither a single two-part tariff, nor a quantity-surplus schedule, can coordinate a competing-retailers channel. Fifth, it follows that coordination of an independent-retailers channel requires a wholesale-price policy that is either a quantity-discount schedule or a menu of two-part tariffs. In the next Section we prove that a quantity-discount schedule can achieve coordination; in Chapter 7 we prove that a properly specified menu of two-part tariffs is channel-coordinating.

Sixth, in the vertically-integrated system an amount $\phi_i \le \pi_i^*$ can be transferred to system headquarters. Thus the pair $\tau_i^* \equiv \{T_i^*, \phi_i\}$ is analogous to a single two-part tariff designed for the i$^{th}$ retail outlet. Because the j$^{th}$ outlet faces a comparable two-part tariff $\tau_j^* \equiv \{T_j^*, \phi_j\}$, it is clear that the pair $\{\tau_i^*, \tau_j^*\}$ is *akin* to a menu. Note, however, that in a vertically-integrated system the retail outlets are *assigned* a specific tariff ($\tau_i^*$ or $\tau_j^*$) while in an independent-retailers channel the retailers must be allowed to select their preferred element from $\{\tau_i^*, \tau_j^*\}$. Only in the latter case does each retailer face a true menu of wholesale-pricing options.

## 4 INDEPENDENT RETAILERS AND A QUANTITY-DISCOUNT SCHEDULE

We model the relationship between the manufacturer and its independent retailers as a two-stage game. In the first stage the manufacturer announces a channel-coordinating quantity-discount schedule that is common to both retailers. In the second stage each retailer determines its profit-maximizing order quantity and retail price in light of its costs, its demand, and its rival's price. For the reasons spelled out in Chapter 1, we treat competitive interaction between the retailers as a Nash pricing game and the relationship between channel levels as a manufacturer Stackelberg leadership game. We focus on a quantity-discount schedule that fully coordinates the channel; this schedule will duplicate the results of a vertically-integrated system.

A profit-maximizing retailer will set a price that is compatible with its marginal cost curve intersecting its marginal revenue curve. Provided the intersection occurs at the channel-optimal quantity, the retailer will settle on a channel-optimal retail price. Profit maximization by both retailers coincides with maximization of channel profit under this condition.

In the case of competing, non-identical retailers *only* a declining marginal wholesale price can coordinate a channel. As we proved above, neither a quantity-surplus schedule nor a two-part tariff (Moorthy 1987) will do. Jeuland and Shugan (1983) have argued that, whatever the wholesale-price mechanism, it may be imposed unilaterally or be determined by negotiation. We place the onus for coordination on the manufacturer,

reasoning that the inter-retailer cooperation necessary for negotiation is impractical as well as illegal under U.S. antitrust laws.[8]

## 4.1 The Retailers' Decisions

We focus on a linear quantity-discount schedule, which is the simplest of the infinite number of negatively-sloped wholesale-price schedules that can coordinate the channel. We choose linearity because it enables us to obtain closed-form solutions. We specify the payment schedule faced by the i[th] retailer as:

$$(W - wQ_i)Q_i + \phi \tag{5.4.1}$$

Under this three-part tariff schedule $\{W, w, \phi\}$ both retailers pay the same fixed fee ($\phi$) but pay a per-unit wholesale price $(W - wQ_k)$ that differs according to the quantity that they purchase.

We begin by solving for retailer decisions in the second stage of the game. Each retailer has a maximand of the form:

$$\max_{p_i} \ \pi_i = \left(p_i - c_i - \left(W - wQ_i\right)\right)Q_i - f_i - \phi \tag{5.4.2}$$

Maximizing each retailer's profit with respect to its own price and jointly solving the first-order conditions yields channel margins ($\bar{\mu}_k \equiv (\bar{p}_k - c_k - C)$) and quantities ($\bar{Q}_i$) as functions of W and w:

$$\bar{\mu}_i = \left( \frac{\begin{array}{l} 2(1-2bw)\left[2b(1-bw)Q_i^* + \theta(1-2bw)Q_j^*\right] \\ +b\left[2b(1-bw)+\theta(1-2bw)\right](W-C) \end{array}}{\left\{4b^2(1-bw)^2 - \theta^2(1-2bw)^2\right\}} \right) \tag{5.4.3}$$

$$\bar{Q}_i = \left( \frac{\begin{array}{l} 2b\left[2b(1-bw)Q_i^* + \theta(1-2bw)Q_j^*\right] \\ -b(b-\theta)\left[(2b(1-bw)+\theta((1-2bw))(W-C)\right] \end{array}}{\left\{4b^2(1-bw)^2 - \theta^2(1-2bw)^2\right\}} \right) \tag{5.4.4}$$

These reaction functions are inputs to the manufacturer's decision process.

## 4.2 The Manufacturer's Decision

We assume that in the first stage of the game the manufacturer chooses W and w to maximize *channel* profit, subject to the price-reaction functions of the game's second stage:

$$\max_{W,w} \ \bar{\Pi}_C = \sum_k \left(\bar{\mu}_k \bar{Q}_k - f_k\right) - F \qquad k \in (i,j) \tag{5.4.5}$$

Taking the first derivatives of (5.4.5), inserting them into the retailers' price-reaction functions (5.4.3), and setting the resulting prices $\overline{p}_i^*$ and $\overline{p}_j^*$ equal to $p_i^*$ and $p_j^*$ yields a pair of equations in the unknowns W and w. Solving these equations yields the optimal, channel-coordinating values:

$$\begin{aligned} W^{QD^*} &= \left( \frac{\theta\left(Q_i^* + Q_j^*\right)}{\left(b^2 - \theta^2\right)} \right) + C \\ w^{QD^*} &= \left( \frac{\theta}{2b\left(b+\theta\right)} \right) \end{aligned} \tag{5.4.6}$$

The superscript $QD^*$ denotes the manufacturer-optimal solution to the quantity-discount schedule. We find that $(W - wQ_k) > 0 \ \forall \ Q_k \leq Q_k^*$.

A linear quantity-discount schedule with these values results in quantities, retail prices and channel profit that replicate those obtained by a vertically-integrated system. The i[th] retailer's per-unit margin is:

$$\begin{aligned} m_i^{QD^*} &\equiv \left(p_i^{QD^*} - c_i - \left(W^{QD^*} - w^{QD^*}Q_i^*\right)\right) \\ &= \left( \frac{(2b+\theta)Q_i^*}{2b\left(b+\theta\right)} \right) \end{aligned} \tag{5.4.7}$$

Net revenue (gross revenue minus per-unit costs) for the i[th] retailer is:

$$R_i^{QD^*} = \left[\left(1 - bw^{QD^*}\right)\left(\left(Q_i^*\right)^2 / b\right)\right] = \left( \frac{2b+\theta}{2\left(b+\theta\right)} \right)\left( \frac{\left(Q_i^*\right)^2}{b} \right) \tag{5.4.8}$$

An independent retailer realizes lower net revenue than does a retail outlet in a vertically-integrated system, because the former pays a higher *average* wholesale price even though both pay the same *marginal* wholesale price.

Equation (5.4.8) implicitly defines the highest fixed fee that can be extracted from the i[th] retailer while retaining it as a channel participant. For *both* retailers to earn non-negative profits, the maximal value of $\phi$ (i.e., $\phi^{QD^*}$) must satisfy both participation constraints:

$$\phi^{QD^*} \equiv \min\left\{ \left(R_i^{QD^*} - f_i\right), \left(R_j^{QD^*} - f_j\right) \right\} \tag{5.4.9}$$

Formulation (5.4.9) demonstrates that the fixed fee is a *residual* extracted from both retailers.

# 5 INDEPENDENT RETAILERS AND A TWO-PART TARIFF

In this Section we explore the implications of the manufacturer utilizing a two-part tariff for its wholesale price-policy. This tariff is a special case of a linear quantity-discount schedule (set $w = 0$ in (5.4.1) to see this). We develop the retailers' general reactions to a two-part tariff and then we illustrate the results with three specific tariff rules: (1) the "sell-at-cost" rule $(W = C)$, (2) the naïve Stackelberg rule, and (3) the "second-best" rule.[9] The first rule is designed to avoid double-marginalization, which is widely-believed to be sub-optimal. We have already shown that this pricing strategy does not coordinate the channel when retailers compete. The second rule follows conventional wisdom regarding optimal pricing under a one-part tariff. This rule also fails to coordinate the channel. The third rule, developed by Ingene and Parry (1995), seeks a two-part tariff that "approaches" coordination. As we have seen, a two-part tariff cannot attain coordination, but the second-best tariff comes as close as possible to the goal given that the manufacturer is constrained to a single two-part tariff.

## 5.1 The Retailers' Decisions

To determine the perfect equilibrium under a two-part tariff we begin by solving for retailer decisions in the second stage of the game. Let the $i^{th}$ retailer purchase $Q_i$ units from the manufacturer for $WQ_i + \phi$, where $W$ is the constant per-unit charge and $\phi$ is the fixed fee. The $i^{th}$ retailer's profit maximand is:

$$\max_{p_i} \ \pi_i = (p_i - c_i - W)(A_i - bp_i + \theta p_j) - f_i - \phi \tag{5.5.1}$$

(The $j^{th}$ retailer's maximand is symmetric.)

Differentiating (5.5.1) with respect to $p_i$ and jointly solving for both retail prices within a Nash equilibrium context yields the optimal retail price $\hat{p}_i$ as a function of W:

$$\hat{p}_i = \left( \frac{2bA_i + \theta A_j + 2b^2 c_i + b\theta c_j + b(2b+\theta)W}{(4b^2 - \theta^2)} \right) \tag{5.5.2}$$

Retail prices reflect demand and cost conditions and the wholesale price. Comparing prices at the two outlets, we obtain:

$$\hat{p}_i \gtrless \hat{p}_j \quad \text{as} \quad (A_i + bc_i) \gtrless (A_j + bc_j) \tag{5.5.3}$$

This condition is *not* the same as the condition for $p_i^* \gtrless p_j^*$ in equation (5.3.5).

Substituting (5.5.2) into (5.2.1) yields quantity $\hat{Q}_i$ as a function of W:

$$\hat{Q}_i = b\left(\frac{2\left(2bQ_i^* + \theta Q_j^*\right) - (b-\theta)(2b+\theta)(W-C)}{\left(4b^2 - \theta^2\right)}\right) \tag{5.5.4}$$

It is easy to show that $\hat{Q}_i \gtrless \hat{Q}_j$ as $Q_i^* \gtrless Q_j^*$ for all values of W. From this simple fact we draw an important conclusion: *no common two-part tariff will change the size ranking of the retailers* from the ranking that occurs in a vertically-integrated system.

Equations (5.5.1), (5.5.2) and (5.5.4) collectively imply that the i[th] retailer's profit is:

$$\hat{\pi}_i = \left(\left[\left(\hat{Q}_i\right)^2 / b\right] - f_i\right) - \phi \equiv \left(\hat{R}_i - f_i\right) - \phi \tag{5.5.5}$$

In expression (5.5.5) the term $\hat{R}_i$ is the net revenue of the i[th] retailer. The maximal value of $\phi$ must satisfy both participation constraints:

$$\max\ \phi \equiv \hat{\phi} = \left\{\min\left(\hat{R}_i - f_i\right), \left(\hat{R}_j - f_j\right)\right\} \tag{5.5.6}$$

Equations (5.5.2) and (5.5.4) summarize the profit-maximizing retailer's response given the manufacturer's choice of W.

## 5.2 The Manufacturer's Choices for a Two-Part Tariff

We now turn to the first stage of the game in which the manufacturer determines its two-part tariff. We focus on three possible criteria for determining the wholesale price:

1. Set $W = C$, the channel-coordinating wholesale-price in the absence of inter-retailer competition. We term this wholesale-price strategy the *sell-at-cost tariff.* This tariff is (i) channel-coordinating and manufacturer profit-optimal in a single dyad channel and (ii) channel-coordinating but manufacturer non-optimal in a channel consisting of multiple, non-competing retailers. (See Chapter 3.)
2. Set W to maximize manufacturer profit. We term this wholesale-price strategy the *naïve Stackelberg tariff.* This tariff is known to be manufacturer-optimal for a single dyad channel when a fixed fee cannot be charged. (See Chapter 2 for details.)
3. Set W to try to maximize *channel* profit. We term this wholesale-price strategy the *second-best tariff* (Ingene and Parry 1995).

From our analysis of the integrated channel, we know that no pricing strategy based on these criteria can coordinate the channel, except when the retailers do not compete, i.e., when $\theta = 0$. However, we will show that all three criteria lead to wholesale-price policies that, under certain parametric values, are more profitable for the manufacturer than is the channel-coordinating quantity-discount schedule derived above.

### 5.2.1 Criterion 1: The Sell-at-Cost Tariff

Under Criterion 1 there is no maximization to perform. Instead, the manufacturer follows the simplistic rule of pricing at marginal cost. Substituting C for W in (5.5.2) and (5.5.4), and making use of (5.3.3), we obtain:

$$\hat{\mu}_i^{W=C} \equiv \left(\hat{p}_i^{W=C} - c_i - C\right) = \left(\frac{2\left(2bQ_i^{*} + \theta Q_j^{*}\right)}{\left(4b^2 - \theta^2\right)}\right) \tag{5.5.7}$$

The i[th] retailer's margin is identical to the channel margin with this Criterion. Quantity sold is:

$$\hat{Q}_i^{W=C} = \left(\frac{2b\left(2bQ_i^{*} + \theta Q_j^{*}\right)}{\left(4b^2 - \theta^2\right)}\right) \tag{5.5.8}$$

Quantity $\hat{Q}_i^{W=C}$ is a weighted average of the channel-optimal quantities $Q_i^{*}$ and $Q_j^{*}$.

Retailer net revenue is $\hat{R}_i^{W=C} = [(\hat{Q}_i^{W=C})^2 / b]$, while manufacturer net revenue is zero. The fixed fee is the lesser of the two retailers' profits. Finally, total channel profit in this case is:

$$\hat{\Pi}_C^{W=C} = \frac{4b\begin{pmatrix} \left(4b^2 + \theta^2\right)\left(Q_i^{*}\right)^2 \\ +8b\theta Q_i^{*} Q_j^{*} \\ +\left(4b^2 + \theta^2\right)\left(Q_j^{*}\right)^2 \end{pmatrix}}{\left(4b^2 - \theta^2\right)^2} - f_i - f_j - F \tag{5.5.9}$$

Marginal-cost pricing is not channel-coordinating because it does not account for the inter-retailer externality implicit in the cross-price term $\theta$. The channel profit-maximizing results are replicated *only* if the retailers do not compete ($\theta = 0$).

### 5.2.2 Criterion 2: The Naïve Stackelberg Tariff

Under Criterion 2 the manufacturer chooses W to maximize its own profit in light of the profit-maximizing behavior of its retailers. Formally, the manufacturer's problem is:

$$\max_{W} \ \Pi_M = \left(W - C\right)\sum\nolimits_k \hat{Q}_k + 2\phi - F, \qquad k \in \left(i, j\right) \tag{5.5.10}$$

subject to (5.5.4). Let the per-unit, manufacturer profit-maximizing wholesale price be denoted as $\hat{W}^*$. It is easy to show that the manufacturer's optimal gross margin is:

$$\left(\hat{W}^* - C\right) = \left(\frac{Q_i^* + Q_j^*}{2(b-\theta)}\right) \tag{5.5.11}$$

Substituting (5.5.11) into (5.5.2) yields the optimal channel margin:

$$\hat{\mu}_i^* = \left(\frac{\left(10b^2 - 7b\theta\right)Q_i^* + \left(2b^2 + 5b\theta - 4\theta^2\right)Q_j^*}{2(b-\theta)\left(4b^2 - \theta^2\right)}\right) \tag{5.5.12}$$

In a similar manner we obtain the i[th] retailer's margin as:

$$\hat{m}_i^* \equiv \left(\hat{p}_i^* - c_i - \hat{W}^*\right) = \left(\frac{(6b-\theta)Q_i^* - (2b-3\theta)Q_j^*}{2\left(4b^2 - \theta^2\right)}\right) \tag{5.5.13}$$

Substituting (5.5.12) into (5.5.4) yields the i[th] retailer's quantity:

$$\hat{Q}_i^* = b\left(\frac{(6b-\theta)Q_i^* - (2b-3\theta)Q_j^*}{2\left(4b^2 - \theta^2\right)}\right) \tag{5.5.14}$$

A simple set of paired comparisons demonstrates that *no* value of $\theta$ will yield $\hat{p}_i^* = p_i^*$ and *none* will yield $\hat{Q}_i^* = Q_i^*$. The inference is obvious: naïve Stackelberg leadership can *never* coordinate a channel with multiple retailers, whether there is inter-retailer competition or not.

The i[th] retailer's unit sales given by (5.5.14) are positive only when the following boundary condition is satisfied:

$$\hat{Q}_i^* > 0 \quad \text{requires} \quad Q_i^* > \left(\frac{2b-3\theta}{6b-\theta}\right)Q_j^* \tag{5.5.15}$$

The parenthetical term on the RHS of (5.5.15) is less than one. There is a symmetric condition for $\hat{Q}_j^* > 0$. These boundary conditions reduce to:

$$\left(\frac{Q_j^*}{Q_i^*}\right), \left(\frac{Q_i^*}{Q_j^*}\right) > \left(\frac{2b-3\theta}{6b-\theta}\right) \tag{5.5.16}$$

The RHS of (5.5.16) ranges from $1/3$ to $-1/5$ as $\theta$ ranges from 0 to $b$. Since naïve Stackelberg leadership is compatible with serving *both* retailers if and only if (5.5.16) is met for *both* ratios on the LHS, each competitor must have at least a 25 percent market share for the naïve Stackelberg manufacturer to serve both retailers when the intensity of competition ($\theta / b$) is near zero; with an intensity greater than $2/3^{rds}$ any market share is acceptable. In the remainder of this Chapter we assume that (5.5.16) is satisfied; our numerical illustrations satisfy these boundary conditions.

The manufacturer's net revenue, prior to collecting the fixed fee, is:

$$\hat{R}^{*}_{M} = \left( \frac{b\left(Q^{*}_{i} + Q^{*}_{j}\right)^{2}}{2(b-\theta)(2b-\theta)} \right) \tag{5.5.17}$$

Retailer net revenue is $\hat{R}^{*}_{i} = [(\hat{Q}^{*}_{i})^{2}/b]$. From the preceding price and quantity values we derive the maximal fixed fee compatible with both retailers' participation constraints:

$$\max\ \phi \equiv \hat{\phi}^{*} = \min\left\{\left(\hat{R}^{*}_{i} - f_{i}\right),\left(\hat{R}^{*}_{j} - f_{j}\right)\right\} \tag{5.5.18}$$

Finally, total channel profit is:

$$\hat{\Pi}^{*}_{C} = \frac{b\begin{pmatrix} \left(28b^{3} - 28b^{2}\theta + 15b\theta^{2} - 6\theta^{3}\right)\left(Q^{*}_{i}\right)^{2} \\ -2\left(4b^{3} - 36b^{2}\theta + 25b\theta^{2} - 2\theta^{3}\right)Q^{*}_{i}Q^{*}_{j} \\ +\left(28b^{3} - 28b^{2}\theta + 15b\theta^{2} - 6\theta^{3}\right)\left(Q^{*}_{j}\right)^{2} \end{pmatrix}}{2(b-\theta)\left(4b^{2} - \theta^{2}\right)^{2}} - f_{i} - f_{j} - F \tag{5.5.19}$$

### 5.2.3 Criterion 3: The Second-Best Tariff

Under Criterion 3 the manufacturer seeks to maximize channel profit, but does so subject to the constraint of both retailers paying the same wholesale price and fixed fee. Thus the manufacturer offers a common two-part tariff $(WQ_{i} + \phi)$ for $Q_{i}$ units. The manufacturer's maximization problem is:

$$\max_{W}\ \Pi_{C} = \sum_{k}\left\{(\hat{p}_{k} - c_{k} - C)\hat{Q}_{k} - f_{k}\right\} - F, \qquad k \in (i,j) \tag{5.5.20}$$

subject to equations (5.5.2) and (5.5.4). Let $\tilde{W}^{*}$ denote the second-best wholesale-price:

$$\tilde{W}^{*} = \left(\frac{\theta}{b}\right)\left(\frac{Q^{*}_{i} + Q^{*}_{j}}{2(b-\theta)}\right) + C \tag{5.5.21}$$

$\tilde{W}^{*}$ lies in the interval $[C, \hat{W}^{*})$ as $\theta$ ranges from 0 to $b$.

Substituting (5.5.21) in (5.5.2) enables us to obtain the i[th] retailer's optimal price:

$$\tilde{p}^{*}_{i} = \left(\frac{(4b-\theta)Q^{*}_{i} + 3\theta Q^{*}_{j}}{2(b-\theta)(2b+\theta)}\right) + c_{i} + C \tag{5.5.22}$$

Thus the i[th] retailer's margin is:

$$\tilde{m}^{*}_{i} = \left(\frac{(4b+\theta)Q^{*}_{i} + \theta Q^{*}_{j}}{2b(2b+\theta)}\right) \tag{5.5.23}$$

Similarly, substituting (5.5.21) into (5.5.4) generates the i[th] retailer's quantity:

$$\tilde{Q}_i^* = \left( \frac{(4b+\theta)Q_i^* + \theta Q_j^*}{2(2b+\theta)} \right) \qquad (5.5.24)$$

The manufacturer's net revenue—prior to collecting the fixed fee—is:

$$\tilde{R}_M^* = \left( \frac{\theta\left(Q_i^* + Q_j^*\right)^2}{2b(b-\theta)} \right) \qquad (5.5.25)$$

It is easy to see that the maximum possible fixed fee that is compatible with retention of both retailers as channel members is:

$$\max\ \phi \equiv \tilde{\phi}^* = \min\left\{\left(\tilde{R}_i^* - f_i\right), \left(\tilde{R}_j^* - f_j\right)\right\} \qquad (5.5.26)$$

We define $\tilde{R}_i^* \equiv [(\tilde{Q}_i^*)^2/b]$. Channel profit in the second-best case is:

$$\tilde{\Pi}_C^* = \frac{\left( \begin{array}{c} \left(8b^2+\theta^2\right)\left[\left(Q_i^*\right)^2 + \left(Q_i^*\right)^2\right] \\ +2\theta(8b+\theta)Q_i^*Q_j^* \end{array} \right)}{2(b-\theta)(2b+\theta)^2} - f_i - f_j - F \qquad (5.5.27)$$

Summarizing our results, $\tilde{W}^* = C$ if and only if retailers do not compete ($\theta = 0$). In this special case the second-best tariff yields channel optimal prices ($\tilde{p}_i^* = p_i^*$), quantities ($\tilde{Q}_i^* = Q_i^*$), and profit ($\tilde{\Pi}_C^* = \Pi_C^*$). These results are not surprising, because the second-best tariff was designed to try to coordinate the channel. What is surprising is that with *identical competitors* ($Q_i^* = Q_j^*$), the second-best and channel-optimal prices and quantities are also identical even though $\hat{W}^* > C$. (To see this, set $Q_i^* = Q_j^*$ in equations (5.3.2) and (5.5.22) for prices and in equations (5.3.3) and (5.5.24) for quantities.)

# 6 COMPARING THE VARIOUS TARIFFS

In the preceding two Sections we solved for a channel-coordinating quantity-discount schedule and three non-coordinating two-part tariffs. In this Section we compare these diverse strategies in terms of their wholesale prices and their associated retail prices, quantities, and margins. We also contrast manufacturer net revenues, channel profits, and consumers' surplus.

## 6.1 Wholesale Prices

We begin by comparing the wholesale prices derived in Sections 4 and 5. We obtain:

$$\hat{W}^* > \left(W^{QD^*} - w^{QD^*}Q_k^*\right) > \tilde{W}^* \geq C \qquad k \in (i,j) \tag{5.6.1}$$

Recall that the term $\hat{W}^*$ ($\tilde{W}^*$) is the wholesale price under the naïve Stackelberg (the second-best) tariff and the term $(W^{QD^*} - w^{QD^*}Q_k^*)$ is the *average* wholesale-price under the quantity-discount schedule.

We also have:

$$\hat{W}^* > T_i^* = \left(W^{QD^*} - 2w^{QD^*}Q_k^*\right) \geq C \qquad k \in (i,j) \tag{5.6.2}$$

$(W^{QD^*} - 2w^{QD^*}Q_k^*)$ is the *marginal* wholesale price with the channel-coordinating quantity-discount schedule. We see that the naïve Stackelberg manufacturer always sets a price that is greater than the channel profit-maximizing wholesale price, which in turn is always at least as great as marginal production cost (C). (The equality signs in (5.6.1) and (5.6.2) hold only for the special case of no inter-retailer competition $(\theta = 0)$.)

A final comparison reveals:

$$T_i^* = \left(W^{QD^*} - 2w^{QD^*}Q_i^*\right) \gtrless \tilde{W}^* \quad \text{as} \quad Q_i^* \lessgtr Q_j^* \tag{5.6.3}$$

The second-best wholesale price always exceeds the channel-coordinating wholesale price for the larger retailer and always falls short of that value for the smaller retailer. Moreover, the *average* transfer-price is equal to the second-best wholesale price:

$$\left(\Sigma T_i^*/2\right) = \tilde{W}^* \tag{5.6.4}$$

Thus the second-best wholesale price is optimal "on average."

## 6.2 Retail Prices

In this sub-Section we contrast retail prices, recognizing that channel margins precisely mirror the price relationships detailed here. Comparing retail prices we find:

$$\hat{p}_i^* > \tilde{p}_i^* \geq \hat{p}_i^{W=C} \tag{5.6.5}$$

We also see that:

$$\hat{p}_i^* > p_i^* \geq \hat{p}_i^{W=C} \tag{5.6.6}$$

A retailer purchasing from a naïve Stackelberg manufacturer sets a price greater than either the second-best price or the price that maximizes channel profit. In turn, each of these prices is at least as great as the price charged by a retailer who purchases at average variable manufacturing costs. (Once again, the equality signs in (5.6.5) and (5.6.6) hold only when $\theta = 0$.)

Comparing the channel-coordinating with the second-best retail prices reveals:

$$p_i^* \gtreqless \tilde{p}_i^* \quad \text{as} \quad Q_i^* \lesseqgtr Q_j^* \tag{5.6.7}$$

In addition the *average* channel-optimal retail price is equal to the average second-best retail price:

$$\Sigma p_i^* = \Sigma \tilde{p}_i^* \tag{5.6.8}$$

Thus the second-best retail price, like the second-best wholesale price, is optimal "on average."

## 6.3 Quantities, Margins, Net Revenues, and Consumers' Surplus

In each scenario the retail margin can be expressed as $(Q_k / b)$ where "$Q_k$" refers to quantity for the k[th] retailer in the relevant scenario. Similarly, retail net revenues are $(Q_i^2 / b)$ and $(Q_j^2 / b)$; while consumers' surplus is $\Sigma(Q_k^2)/2b$. Hence we now turn to the quantity rankings. We find:

$$\hat{Q}_i^* < \tilde{Q}_i^* \le \hat{Q}_i^{W=C} \tag{5.6.9}$$

$$\hat{Q}_i^* < Q_i^* \le \hat{Q}_i^{W=C} \tag{5.6.10}$$

Note that the quantity relationships are the mirror of the retail price relationships set forth above. (Again the equality sign in (5.6.10) holds only when $\theta = 0$.)

Comparing the channel-coordinating quantity with the second-best quantity reveals:

$$Q_i^* \gtreqless \tilde{Q}_i^* \text{ as } Q_i^* \gtreqless Q_j^* . \tag{5.6.11}$$

The relationship between *aggregate* channel outputs for the various tariffs is:

$$\sum \hat{Q}_i^* = \frac{b \sum Q_i^*}{(2b - \theta)} < \sum Q_i^* = \sum \tilde{Q}_i^* \le \frac{2b \sum Q_i^*}{(2b - \theta)} = \sum \hat{Q}_i^{W=C} \tag{5.6.12}$$

Notice that the second-best solution yields the channel-optimal *total* output.

Aggregate consumers' surplus is defined as $CS \equiv \Sigma(Q_i^2 + Q_j^2)/2b$:

$$\widehat{CS}^* < \widetilde{CS}^* < CS^* < CS^{W=C} \tag{5.6.13}$$

These results reflect the total output results (5.6.12), although the different distribution of output between the integrated channel and the second-best tariff tips the consumers' surplus ranking toward the integrated solution.

## 6.4 The Manufacturer's Net Revenue

Comparing the manufacturer's net revenues reveals the patterns:

$$\hat{R}_M^{\bullet} > \tilde{R}_M^{\bullet} > R_M^{\bullet} > \hat{R}_M^{W=C} = 0 \quad (5.6.14)$$

$$\hat{R}_M^{QD^{\bullet}} > \tilde{R}_M^{\bullet} > R_M^{\bullet} > \hat{R}_M^{W=C} = 0 \quad (5.6.15)$$

The relationship between the naïve Stackelberg and the quantity-discount schedules is complex. We obtain:

$$\hat{R}_M^{\bullet} \gtrless \hat{R}_M^{QD^{\bullet}} \quad \Leftrightarrow \quad (b-\theta)\left(\frac{\begin{array}{c}(b^2-\theta^2)(Q_i^{\bullet}+Q_j^{\bullet})^2 \\ -\theta(2b-\theta)Q_i^{\bullet}Q_j^{\bullet}\end{array}}{2b(b^2-\theta^2)(2b-\theta)}\right) \gtrless 0 \quad (5.6.16)$$

The naïve Stackelberg approach dominates the quantity-discount schedule when competition is low (i.e., a low θ); however, this ranking is reversed with high competition (i.e., as $\theta \to b$). We can clarify this result by recognizing the point of equality depends on the retailers' market shares (say $S_j \equiv Q_j^{\bullet}/(Q_i^{\bullet}+Q_j^{\bullet})$) and competitive intensity (say $\chi \equiv \theta/b$). Both $S_j$ and $\chi$ lie in the unit interval. We find:

$$\hat{R}_M^{\bullet} \gtrless \hat{R}_M^{QD^{\bullet}} \quad \Leftrightarrow \quad \left(\frac{1-\chi^2}{\chi(2-\chi)}\right) \gtrless S_j(1-S_j) \quad (5.6.17)$$

What is important is that, in terms of generating net revenue for the manufacturer, there are parametric values at which the naïve Stackelberg policy outperforms the channel-coordinating quantity-discount schedule.[10] This is our first clue that, when we account for the fixed fee, channel coordination may not be in the best interest of the manufacturer.

## 6.5 Channel Profit

Utilizing the preceding prices and quantities enables us to determine channel profit under each of the previously-defined scenarios. Comparing the results with the profit of the vertically-integrated system (equation (5.3.10)), we obtain:

$$\Pi_I^{\bullet} = \Pi_C^{QD^{\bullet}} \geq \tilde{\Pi}_C^{\bullet} \geq \hat{\Pi}_C^{W=C} \quad (5.6.18)$$

Similarly:

$$\Pi_I^{\bullet} = \Pi_C^{QD^{\bullet}} \geq \tilde{\Pi}_C^{\bullet} \geq \hat{\Pi}_C^{\bullet} \quad (5.6.19)$$

The equality part of the "$\geq$" signs in (5.6.18) and (5.6.19) holds when $\theta = 0$.

Our final comparison is between the naïve Stackelberg and the wholesale-at-cost policies:

$$\hat{\Pi}_C^{\bullet} \gtrless \hat{\Pi}_C^{W=C} \text{ as } \chi \gtrless \tfrac{1}{2} \quad (5.6.20)$$

The sell-at-cost wholesale-pricing policy generates greater channel profit at lower levels of competition, while the naïve Stackelberg approach is more profitable at higher levels of competition.

## 6.6 Relative Profits: The Quantity-Discount Schedule *vs.* the Second-Best Tariff

Even though *total* output and *average* prices are equal in the coordinated channel and the second-best cases, total channel profits are not equal. The difference is:

$$\left[\Pi_C^* - \tilde{\Pi}_C^*\right] = \left( \frac{\theta^2 (Q_i^* - Q_j^*)^2}{2(b+\theta)(2b+\theta)^2} \right) \geq 0 \tag{5.6.21}$$

The equality sign holds in the absence of competition *or* in the presence of identical competitors. But, when retailers compete for customers ($\theta \neq 0$), and when channel-optimal retail sales are *unequal* ($Q_i^* \neq Q_j^*$), the coordinated and second-best channel profits are *not* identical. The vertically-integrated system earns more than the decentralized channel, because the former can charge different transfer prices to its retail outlets, while the latter cannot charge wholesale prices to its independent retailers that differ. Similarly, a quantity-discount schedule enables the manufacturer to charge different (but self-selected) marginal costs to its retailers. In contrast, a manufacturer employing a two-part tariff with a constant per-unit fee offers both independent retailers the same average (and marginal) wholesale price. Intuitively, non-identical retailers have an asymmetric influence on each other's sales. A vertically-integrated system can adjust its wholesale-price policy to reflect such asymmetries. In contrast, an independent manufacturer has too few "degrees of freedom" with a two-part tariff; the resulting inability to charge retailer-specific wholesale prices dissipates channel profit.

## 6.7 Summary Comments

We now offer some general comments on the results obtained in this Section, and we provide an illustrative example of the various wholesale-price policies. We start with a demonstration of our results for an illustrative scenario in which the values of the demand intercepts are $A_i = 150$ and $A_j = 100$, the own-price and cross-price slopes are $b = 1.0$ and $\theta = 0.5$, per-unit distribution and production costs are $c_i = c_j = C = \$10$, fixed costs are $f_i = f_j = \$500$, and $F = \$1{,}000$. Table 5.1 catalogs our results.

The "sell-at-cost" and naïve Stackelberg tariffs generate equal channel profit. The naïve Stackelberg policy produces the largest manufacturer net revenue, but this reflects our parametric assumptions: it would fall to second-place behind the quantity-discount schedule at a sufficiently high $\theta$ value. The second-best tariff almost duplicates the coordinated results on most measures. Coordination maximizes channel profit, while the sell-at-cost strategy maximizes consumers' surplus. Finally, sell-at-cost is the top performer on "social welfare" ($\Pi_C + CS$), thereby illustrating the well-known theorem that marginal-cost pricing is in the best interest of society.

Now consider the two limiting cases of near-zero competition and near-perfect inter-retailer competition. In the former case, as $\theta \to 0$ all wholesale-prices, except the naïve Stackelberg, approach marginal production cost (C). Hence, all the policies apart from the naïve Stackelberg generate the same total output, while the naïve Stackelberg solution generates one-half the output of a coordinated channel; this is the standard bilateral-monopoly result. In contrast, as $\theta \to b$, all the pricing policies except sell-at-cost converge. Hence, *if* coordination is the superordinate goal, then at very high or very low levels of competition it may make no practical difference whether the manufacturer selects a coordinating plan or a non-coordinating plan.

*Table 5.1* The Implications of Various Tariffs for Channel Profit[1]

| Variables | Coordinated System[2] | Sell-at-Cost Tariff | Naïve Stackelberg | Second-Best Tariff |
|---|---|---|---|---|
| $T_i^*$ | $63.33 | NA | NA | NA |
| $T_j^*$ | $71.67 | NA | NA | NA |
| W | $86.67 | $10.00 | $125.00 | $67.50 |
| w | 0.17 | NA | NA | NA |
| $p_i$ | $143.33 | $106.67 | $183.33 | $145.00 |
| $p_j$ | $126.67 | $86.67 | $163.33 | $125.00 |
| $\Sigma p_k/2$ | $135.00 | $96.67 | $173.33 | $135.00 |
| $m_i$ | $70.00 | $86.67 | $48.33 | $67.50 |
| $m_j$ | $45.00 | $66.67 | $28.33 | $47.50 |
| $Q_i$ | 70 | 86.67 | 48.33 | 67.5 |
| $Q_j$ | 45 | 66.67 | 28.33 | 47.5 |
| $\Sigma Q_k$ | 115 | 153.33 | 76.67 | 115 |
| $R_i$ | $4,900.00[3] | $7,511.00 | $2,336.11 | $4,556.25 |
| $R_j$ | $2,025.00[3] | $4,444.44 | $802.78 | $2,256.25 |
| $R_M$ | $6,508.33[3] | $0 | $8,816.67 | $6,612.50 |
| CS | $3,462.50 | $5,977.78 | $1,569.44 | $3,406.25 |
| $\Pi_C$ | $11,433.33 | $9,955.56 | $9,955.56 | $11,425.00 |
| SW | $14,895.33 | $15,933.33 | $11,525 | $14,831.25 |

[1] Given $A_i = 150$, $A_j = 100$, $c_j = c_i = C = \$10$, $f_j = f_i = \$500$, $F = \$1000$, $b = 1.0$, $\theta = 0.5$.

[2] Column includes the vertically-integrated system and the quantity-discount schedule—both lead to the same retail prices, quantities, and total channel profit.

[3] These values are for the vertically-integrated system. With the quantity-discount schedule the values are $4,083.33 for the i$^{th}$ outlet, $1,687.50 for the j$^{th}$ outlet, and $7,662.50 for the manufacturing arm.

# 7 THE MANUFACTURER'S PROFIT UNDER THE ALTERNATIVE TARIFFS

We now turn to the ultimate issue raised by this Chapter, which is the manufacturer's preference among the four wholesale-price policies that we have elaborated. Our analysis is driven by the fact that a portion of the manufacturer's profit is derived from a fixed fee that is extracted from both retailers, but that is calibrated to ensure participation by the *less*-profitable retailer. As a result, the manufacturer's profit is affected by the retailers' fixed costs. Due to the importance of fixed costs for the manufacturer-optimal policy, we begin our analysis with a discussion of these costs.

## 7.1 The Retailers' Fixed Costs

To simplify our exposition, we assume that the $i^{th}$ retailer is the larger-volume retailer. When $Q_i^* > Q_j^*$, the $i^{th}$ retailer earns the greater net revenue under all of the tariff policies considered in this Chapter. It follows that, if the retailers have equal fixed costs, then the $j^{th}$ retailer is the less profitable. Accordingly, the fixed fee is equal to the $j^{th}$ retailer's net revenue minus its fixed cost.

Now consider a \$1 increase in the $i^{th}$ retailer's fixed cost ($f_i$). This increase has no effect on manufacturer profitability as long as it does not reverse the retailers' profit ranking. However, there is a critical value of $f_i$ at which the retailers earn equal profits. When $f_i$ exceeds this critical value, the $i^{th}$ retailer will not participate in the channel unless the manufacturer appropriately alters the fixed fee. Note that this critical value is a function of the fixed fee charged by the manufacturer. Retention of both retailers as channel members requires that the fixed fee be diminished dollar-for-dollar as $f_i$ rises above the critical value. Thus manufacturer profit declines by *\$2* for every \$1 increase beyond the critical $f_i$ value. This critical value defines a kink in the manufacturer's profit function (see Figure 5.1). Similar observations hold for changes in the $j^{th}$ retailer's fixed cost.

Each of the wholesale-price policies investigated in this Chapter generates a kink in the manufacturer's profit function when profit is graphed against the difference in the retailers' fixed costs. In the Appendix we prove the existence of specific values of the difference in retailers' fixed costs such that *any* of the preceding two-part tariffs may maximize manufacturer profit.

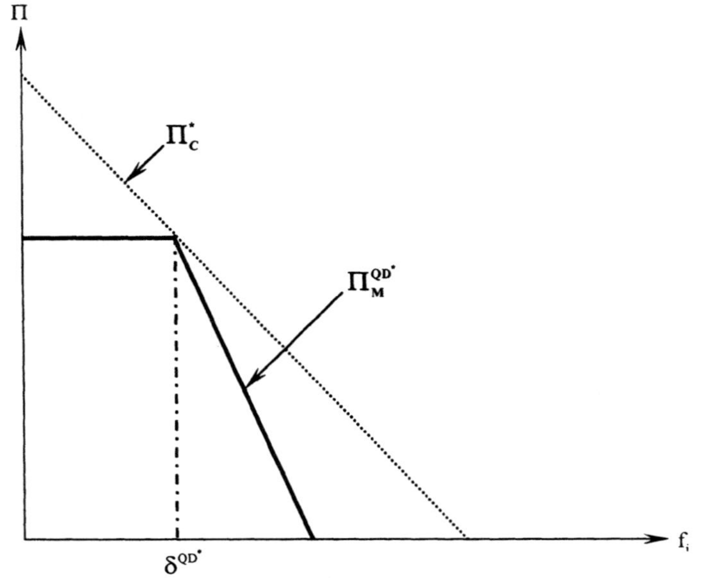


Legend:

$\Pi_C^*$ ≡ Total profit of a coordinated channel;

$\Pi_M^{QD^*}$ ≡ Manufacturer profit with the channel-coordinating quantity-discount schedule; and

$\delta^{QD^*}$ ≡ $f_i$ – value at which the quantity-discount schedule extracts all profit from both retailers.

*Figure 5.1.* Retailers' Fixed Costs and Manufacturer Profitability with a Channel-Coordinating Quantity-Discount Schedule

## 7.2 A Numerical Illustration: Three Scenarios

Here we offer three Scenarios to illustrate that any of the wholesale-price policies investigated in this Chapter may be manufacturer-optimal. The Appendix to this Chapter provides formal proofs of these illustrations. To simplify our discussion, let $\Pi_M^{QD^*}$ denote the manufacturer's profit under a channel-coordinating quantity-discount schedule and let $\Pi_M^{W=C}$, $\hat{\Pi}_M^*$, and $\tilde{\Pi}_M^*$ denote manufacturer profit under, respectively, the sell-at-cost tariff, the naïve Stackelberg, and the second-best tariffs. For all Scenarios we set $A_j = 100$, $c_i = c_j = C = \$10$, $f_j = \$500$, and $F = \$1000$. We allow the i[th] retailer's fixed cost to vary in order to illustrate its critical value (or, in some instances, values). The Scenarios are distinguished by the values of the demand parameters $A_i$, b and $\theta$:

Scenario 1: $A_i = 150$, $b = 1.0$, and $\theta = 0.5$

Scenario 2: $A_i = 230$, $b = 1.0$, and $\theta = 0.5$

Scenario 3: $A_i = 150$, $b = 0.6$, and $\theta = 0.1$

The first Scenario depicts a moderate degree of competition between retailers, combined with the i[th] retailer having a 50 percent greater "base" demand than does the j[th] retailer. In the second Scenario the i[th] retailer has a substantially higher level of base demand. The third Scenario is characterized by significantly less inter-retailer competition than are the first and second Scenarios. Note that, in comparison to those Scenarios, both b and $\theta$ have declined by 0.4 in the third Scenario. This ensures that aggregate demand is equal in Scenarios 1 and 3.

## 7.3 Scenario 1

Given the parametric values cited above, $Q_i^* = 70$ and $Q_j^* = 45$. Manufacturer profit under a naïve Stackelberg tariff is a function of $f_i$:

$$\hat{\Pi}_M^*(f_i) = \begin{cases} \$8,422,22 & \text{if } f_i \le \$2,033.33 \\ \left[\$8,422.22 - 2\left(f_i - \$2,033.33\right)\right] & \text{otherwise} \end{cases} \qquad (5.7.1)$$

The point $f_i = \$2,033.33$ is the critical value associated with the kink in the manufacturer's profit function. At $f_i < \$2,033.33$ the profit function (5.7.1) has a slope of zero, while at $f_i > \$2,033.33$ the function has a slope of $-\$2$. The slope changes at this point because the identity of the less-profitable retailer changes, as we discussed above. A subtlety is that, at values of $f_i > \$2,336.11$, the i[th] retailer earns negative profit even without paying a fixed fee. It follows that retention of both retailers as channel members would require the manufacturer to *pay* a fixed fee to both retailers.

Manufacturer profit under the second-best tariff can be written as a function of $f_i$:

$$\tilde{\Pi}_M^*(f_i) = \begin{cases} \$9,125.00 & \text{if } f_i \le \$2,800.00 \\ \left[\$9,125.00 - 2\left(f_i - \$2,800.00\right)\right] & \text{otherwise} \end{cases} \qquad (5.7.2)$$

As in (5.7.1), the change in slope reflects a change in the identity of the less-profitable retailer. A comparison of equations (5.7.1) and (5.7.2) reveals that the second-best tariff always dominates the naïve Stackelberg tariff.

The manufacturer's profit under the quantity-discount schedule is:

$$\Pi_M^{QD^*}(f_i) = \begin{cases} \$9,037.50 & \text{if } f_i \le \$2,895.83 \\ \left[\$9,037.50 - 2\left(f_i - \$2,895.83\right)\right] & \text{otherwise} \end{cases} \tag{5.7.3}$$

A comparison of the lower line of (5.7.2) and the upper line of (5.7.3) reveals that these profit functions intersect at the point $f_i = \$2,843.75$. The second-best tariff manufacturer profit-dominates the quantity-discount schedule for $f_i \le \$2,843.75$. The quantity-discount schedule maximizes manufacturer profit for $f_i \ge \$2,843.75$.

Finally, we can write the manufacturer's profit function with the sell-at-cost tariff as:

$$\Pi_M^{W=C}(f_i) = \begin{cases} \$6,888.89 & \text{if } f_i \le \$3,566.66 \\ \left[\$6,888.89 - 2\left(f_i - \$3,566.66\right)\right] & \text{otherwise} \end{cases} \tag{5.7.4}$$

A comparison of (5.7.3) and (5.7.4) reveals that the coordinating quantity-discount schedule yields greater manufacturer profit than does the $W = C$ tariff. These results are illustrated in Table 5.2. This Table demonstrates that, for the parametric values of Scenario 1, *either the second-best tariff or the quantity-discount schedule may maximize manufacturer profit.* Which tariff is preferred by the manufacturer depends on the retailers' fixed costs.

The first column in Table 5.2 (as well as Tables 5.3 and 5.4) offers a range of values for $f_i$. Each entry (except $f_i = \$0$) represents either a point of discontinuity in the manufacturer's profit function, or it depicts a point of manufacturer-profit equality between the wholesale-price strategies. We denote the points of profit equality with a $\delta$.

Starting at $f_i = \$0$, we see that manufacturer profit is maximized by using the second-best tariff. All profit values remain constant until $f_i$ reaches the critical value $\$2,033.33$; at this point there is a kink in the manufacturer profit function obtained from the naïve Stackelberg two-part tariff $(\hat{\Pi}_M^*)$. Beyond $f_i = \$2,033.33$, every \$1 increase in $f_i$ leads to a \$1 decrease in the fixed fee paid by both retailers; thus manufacturer profit declines by \$2 for every \$1 increase in $f_i$. Because $\tilde{\Pi}_M^* > \hat{\Pi}_M^*$ at $f_i = \$0$, and because the kink in $\hat{\Pi}_M^*$ occurs at a lower $f_i$ than does the kink in $\tilde{\Pi}_M^*$, the second-best tariff manufacturer profit-dominates the naïve Stackelberg tariff at all $f_i$ values. Similarly, because the sell-at cost tariff generates lower manufacturer profit than does the second-best tariff at $f_i = \$3,566.66$ (the sell-at-cost kink), and because manufacturer profit under both tariffs declines at \$2 for every \$1 increase in $f_i$, the second-best tariff manufacturer profit-dominates the sell-at-cost tariff for all higher values of $f_i$.

*Table 5.2.* Manufacturer Profit across Four Wholesale-Price Schedules Scenario 1: Quantity-Discount or Second-Best May Be Optimal[1]

| Fixed Cost of the $i^{th}$ Retailer | Quantity-Discount Schedule | Sell-at-Cost Tariff | Second-Best Tariff | Naïve Stackelberg Tariff[6] |
|---|---|---|---|---|
| *\$0.00* = $\delta_1^*$ | \$9,037.50 | \$6,888.89 | **\$9,125.00** | \$8,422.22 |
| *\$2,033.33*[2] | \$9,037.50 | \$6,888.89 | **\$9,125.00** | \$8,422.22 |
| *\$2,800.00*[3] | \$9,037.50 | \$6,888.89 | **\$9,125.00** | \$6,888.89 |
| *\$2,843.75*= $\delta_2^*$ | **\$9,037.50** | \$6,888.89 | **\$9,037.50** | \$6,801.39 |
| *\$2,895.83*[4] | **\$9,037.50** | \$6,888.89 | \$8,933.34 | \$6,697.23 |
| *\$3,566.66*[5] | **\$7,695.83** | \$6,888.89 | \$7,591.68 | \$5,355.57 |

**Boldface** entries denote the manufacturer's maximal profit, including the fixed fee, within each row (that is, given the fixed cost of the $i^{th}$ retailer). The column heading then gives the manufacturer's optimal wholesale-price strategy.

[1] Given $A_i = 150$, $A_j = 100$, $c_i = c_j = C = \$10$, $f_j = \$500$, $F = \$1{,}000$, $b = 1.0$, and $\theta = 0.5$.

[2] There is a value $f_i$ = \$2.033.33 that is the point of non-differentiability in the manufacturer profit function under the naïve Stackelberg price strategy. At this point the identity of the less-profitable retailer switches.

[3] There is a value $f_i$ = \$2,800 that is the point of non-differentiability in the manufacturer profit function under the second-best price strategy.

[4] There is a value $f_i$ = \$2,895.33 that is the point of non-differentiability in the manufacturer profit function under the quantity-discount schedule.

[5] There is a value $f_i$ = \$3,566.66 that is the point of non-differentiability in the manufacturer profit function under the sell-at-cost tariff.

[6] When $f_i >$ \$2,336.11, the $i^{th}$ retailer makes a negative profit under the naïve Stackelberg price strategy. Thus the manufacturer must pay a fixed fee to both retailers at higher $f_i$ values.

Turning to a comparison of the second-best tariff and the quantity-discount schedule, we see that the former manufacturer-profit-dominates the latter from $f_i = \$0$ to the $\tilde{\Pi}_M^*$ kink at $f_i = \$2{,}800$. Indeed, profit-equivalence does not occur until $f_i = \$2{,}843.75$. Because the profit kink under the quantity-discount schedule occurs at an even higher value of $f_i$, we find that the manufacturer's profit-maximizing decision rule in Scenario 1 is:

- Use the second-best tariff for all $f_i \le \$2{,}843.75$; and
- Use the quantity-discount schedule for all $f_i \ge \$2{,}843.75$.

We now consider the second Scenario.

## 7.4 Scenario 2

To illustrate the potential optimality of a naïve Stackelberg price strategy, we increase $A_i$ from 150 to 230. Given this change in our parametric values, we now obtain $Q_i^* = 110$ and $Q_j^* = 45$. Manufacturer profit under the naïve Stackelberg tariff is:

$$\hat{\Pi}_M^*(f_i) = \begin{cases} \$15,334.22 & \text{if } f_i \le \$5,873.33 \\ \left[\$15,334.22 - 2((f_i - \$5,873.33)\right] & \text{otherwise} \end{cases} \quad (5.7.5)$$

At $f_i > \$6032.11$ the manufacturer must pay a fixed fee to the retailers if they are both to be retained as channel members. Under the second-best tariff the manufacturer's profit is:

$$\tilde{\Pi}_M^*(f_i) = \begin{cases} \$15,317.00 & \text{if } f_i \le \$8,560.00 \\ \left[\$15,317.00 - 2((f_i - \$8,560.00)\right] & \text{otherwise} \end{cases} \quad (5.7.6)$$

The manufacturer's profit under the channel-coordinating quantity-discount schedule is:

$$\Pi_M^{QD^*}(f_i) = \begin{cases} \$15,037.50 & \text{if } f_i \le \$8,895.83 \\ \left[\$15,037.50 - 2((f_i - \$8,895.83)\right] & \text{otherwise} \end{cases} \quad (5.7.7)$$

Finally, the manufacturer's profit with the sell-at-cost tariff is:

$$\Pi_M^{W=C}(f_i) = \begin{cases} \$9,960.89 & \text{if } f_i \le \$11,246.66 \\ \left[\$9,960.89 - 2(f_i - \$11,246.66)\right] & \text{otherwise} \end{cases} \quad (5.7.8)$$

A comparison of the appropriate profit equations reveals that (i) the naïve Stackelberg and the second-best profit functions intersect at the point $f_i = \$5,881.95$, and (ii) the second-best profit function and the channel-coordinating quantity-discount profit function intersect at the point $f_i = \$8,699.75$. In addition, from the manufacturer's perspective, the channel-coordinating quantity-discount schedule always profit-dominates the sell-at-cost tariff.

Thus, we find that the manufacturer's profit-maximizing decision rule in Scenario 2 is:

- Use the naïve Stackelberg tariff for all $f_i \le \$5,881.95$;
- Use the second-best tariff for all $\$5,881.95 \le f_i \le \$8,699.75$; and
- Use the quantity-discount schedule for all $f_i \ge \$8,699.75$.

These results are illustrated in Table 5.3. A comparison of Table 5.3 with Table 5.2 suggests that the naïve Stackelberg tariff may be optimal in industries with relatively larger differences in base demand across retailers. We now consider the third Scenario.

*Table 5.3.* Manufacturer Profit across Four Price Schedules in Scenario 2: Naïve Stackelberg, Second-Best, or Quantity-Discount May Be Optimal[1]

| Fixed Cost of the i<sup>th</sup> Retailer | Quantity-Discount Schedule | Sell-at-Cost Tariff | Second-Best Tariff | Naïve Stackelberg Tariff[6] |
|---|---|---|---|---|
| *$0.00* | $15,037.50 | $9,960.89 | $15,317.00 | **$15,334.22** |
| *$5,873.33*[2] | $15,037.50 | $9,960.89 | $15,317.00 | **$15,334.22** |
| *$5,881.95*= $\delta_1^*$ | $15,037.50 | $9,960.89 | **$15,317.00** | **$15,317.00** |
| *$8,560.00*[3] | $15,037.50 | $9,960.89 | **$15,317.00** | $9,960.89 |
| *$8,699.75*= $\delta_2^*$ | **$15,037.50** | $9,960.89 | **$15,037.50** | $9,681.39 |
| *$8,895.83*[4] | **$15,037.50** | $9,960.89 | $14,645.33 | $9,289.22 |
| *$11,246.66*[5] | **$11,335.85** | $9,960.89 | $9,943.68 | $4,587.57 |

**Boldface** entries denote the manufacturer's maximal profit, including the fixed fee, within each row (that is, given the fixed cost of the i<sup>th</sup> retailer). The column heading then gives the manufacturer's optimal wholesale-price strategy.

[1] Given $A_i = 230, A_j = 100, c_i = c_j = C = \$10, f_j = \$500, F = \$1,000, b = 1.0,$ and $\theta = 0.5$.

[2] The value $f_i = \$5,873.33$ is the point of non-differentiability in the manufacturer's profit function under the naïve Stackelberg price strategy.

[3] The value $f_i = \$8,560.00$ is the point of non-differentiability in the manufacturer's profit function under the second-best price strategy.

[4] The value $f_i = \$8,895.83$ is the point of non-differentiability in the manufacturer's profit function under the optimal quantity-discount schedule.

[5] The value $f_i = \$11,246.66$ is the point of non-differentiability in the manufacturer's profit function under the sell-at-cost tariff.

[6] When $f_i > \$6032.11$, the i<sup>th</sup> retailer makes a negative profit under the naïve Stackelberg price strategy. Thus the manufacturer must pay a fixed fee to both retailers at higher $f_i$ values.

## 7.5 Scenario 3

To illustrate the potential optimality of sell-at-cost pricing, let $A_i = 150$ as in Scenario 1 but decrease $\theta$ to 0.1 and b to 0.6. Given these parametric values $Q_i^* = 70$ and $Q_j^* = 45$. These quantity values are identical to the ones we observed in Scenario 1; aggregate demand is constant because $(b - \theta)$ is the same for both Scenarios. The manufacturer's profit under the naïve Stackelberg tariff may be written as:

$$\hat{\Pi}_M^*(f_i) = \begin{cases} \$6{,}523.76 & \text{if } f_i \leq \$2{,}912.59 \\ \left[\$6{,}523.76 - 2\left(f_i - \$2{,}912.59\right)\right] & \text{otherwise} \end{cases} \quad (5.7.9)$$

In this Scenario the naïve Stackelberg tariff entails an additional complexity that is not fully captured by equation (5.7.9). The $i^{th}$ retailer makes a negative profit *without* paying a fixed fee when $f_i > \$3{,}067.65$. Retention of both retailers requires the manufacturer to pay a positive fixed fee to both of them at higher $f_i$ values.

The manufacturer's profit under the second-best tariff is:

$$\tilde{\Pi}_M^*(f_i) = \begin{cases} \$7{,}245.71 & \text{if } f_i \leq \$4{,}923.07 \\ \left[\$7{,}245.71 - 2\left(f_i - \$4{,}923.07\right)\right] & \text{otherwise} \end{cases} \quad (5.7.10)$$

The manufacturer's profit under the quantity-discount schedule is:

$$\Pi_M^{QD^*}(f_i) = \begin{cases} \$7{,}222.02 & \text{if } f_i \leq \$4{,}949.40 \\ \left[\$7{,}222.02 - 2\left(f_i - \$4{,}949.40\right)\right] & \text{otherwise} \end{cases} \quad (5.7.11)$$

Manufacturer profit with the sell-at-cost tariff is:

$$\Pi_M^{W=C}(f_i) = \begin{cases} \$6{,}734.31 & \text{if } f_i \leq \$5{,}325.17 \\ \left[\$6{,}734.31 - 2\left(f_i - \$5{,}325.17\right)\right] & \text{otherwise} \end{cases} \quad (5.7.12)$$

A comparison of the relevant profit equations reveals that the naïve Stackelberg tariff is always dominated by the second-best tariff. In addition, the second-best tariff and the quantity-discount schedule generate identical levels of manufacturer profit when $f_i = \$3{,}050.19$, while the quantity-discount and sell-at-cost profit functions generate equal manufacturer profits at the point $f_i = \$3{,}126.69$. We find that the manufacturer's profit-maximizing decision rule in Scenario 3 is:

- Use the second-best tariff for all $f_i \leq \$4{,}934.92$;
- Use the quantity-discount schedule if $\$4{,}934.92 \leq f_i \leq \$5{,}193.26$; and
- Use the sell-at-cost tariff for all $f_i \geq \$5{,}193.26$.

These results appear in Table 5.4.

*Table 5.4.* Manufacturer Profit across Four Wholesale-Price Schedules in Scenario 3: Quantity-Discount, Sell-at-Cost, or Second-Best May Be Optimal[1]

| Fixed Cost of the $i^{th}$ Retailer | Quantity-Discount Schedule | W=C Tariff | Second-Best Tariff | Naïve Stackelberg Tariff[6] |
|---|---|---|---|---|
| *\$2,912.59*[2] | \$7,222.02 | \$6,734.31 | **\$7,245.71** | \$6,523.76 |
| *\$4,923.07*[3] | \$7,222.02 | \$6,734.31 | **\$7,245.71** | \$2,502.80 |
| *\$4,934.92* $= \delta_2^*$ | **\$7,222.02** | \$6,734.31 | **\$7,222.02** | \$2,479.10 |
| *\$4,949.40*[4] | **\$7,222.02** | \$6,734.31 | \$7,193.06 | \$2,450.14 |
| *\$5,193.26* $= \delta_3^*$ | **\$6,734.31** | **\$6,734.31** | \$6,705.34 | \$1,962.42 |
| *\$5,325.17*[5] | \$6,470.49 | **\$6,734.31** | \$6,441.52 | \$1,698.60 |

**Boldface** entries denote the manufacturer's maximal profit, including the fixed fee, within each row (that is, given the fixed cost of the $i^{th}$ retailer). The column heading then gives the manufacturer's optimal wholesale-price strategy.

[1] Given $A_i = 150$, $A_j = 100$, $c_i = c_j = C = \$10$, $f_j = \$500$, $F = \$1,000$, $b = 0.6$, and $\theta = 0.1$.

[2] The value $f_i = \$2,912.59$ is the point of non-differentiability in the manufacturer's profit function under the naïve Stackelberg strategy.

[3] The value $f_i = \$4,923.07$ is the point of non-differentiability in the manufacturer's profit function under the second-best price strategy.

[4] The value $f_i = \$4,949.40$ is the point of non-differentiability in the manufacturer's profit function under the optimal quantity-discount schedule.

[5] The value $f_i = \$5,325.17$ is the point of non-differentiability in the manufacturer's profit function under the sell-at-cost tariff.

[6] When $f_i > (\hat{Q}_i^*)^2/b$ the $i^{th}$ retailer makes negative profits under the naïve Stackelberg price strategy. For our parameters this occurs at $f_i = \$3,067.65$. The manufacturer must pay a fixed fee to both retailers at higher $f_i$ values.

Tables 5.2-5.4 suggest that the naïve Stackelberg policy is attractive when there are substantial differences in the retailers' channel-optimal output levels. The quantity-discount schedule becomes more attractive relative to the second-best tariff as retailers' fixed costs diverge. Selling at cost seems to be attractive only when the degree of competition is low. It appears that, under a wide range of circumstances, the manufacturer does not prefer a channel-coordinating wholesale-price policy. Although coordination maximizes channel profit, profit *cannot* always be reallocated in a way that benefits all channel members. We will return to the theme of the manufacturer-optimal wholesale-price policy in Chapters 8 and 9.

# 8 THE QUANTITY-DISCOUNT SCHEDULE AND RETAILER PROFIT-EXTRACTION

We have shown that there are parametric values for which various channel *non-coordinating* two-part tariffs generate greater manufacturer profit than does a linear, channel-coordinating quantity-discount schedule. Because the latter wholesale-price policy unambiguously creates greater channel profit than does the former, it must be the case that there are parametric values for which the manufacturer is unable to extract all profit from both retailers. In this Section we provide an in-depth examination of the relationship between the quantity-discount schedule, retailer profitability after paying the fixed fee, and key parametric values.[11]

## 8.1 Quantity-Discount Zones

We start with the condition that determines whether or not manufacturer profit equals channel profit; this only occurs when the fixed fee extracts all profit from both retailers. As derived in the Appendix to this Chapter, both retailers make zero profits when:

$$\delta^{QD^*} = \left(f_i - f_j\right) \tag{5.8.1}$$

where $\delta^{QD^*}$ is defined as:

$$\delta^{QD^*} \equiv \left(R_i^* - R_j^*\right) = \left(\frac{(2b+\theta)\left(Q_i^* + Q_j^*\right)\left(Q_i^* - Q_j^*\right)}{2b(b+\theta)}\right) \tag{5.8.2}$$

This condition merely states that, when the difference in the retailers' (coordinated) net revenues is equal to the difference in the retailers' fixed costs, the retailers are equally profitable. Therefore the manufacturer can obtain all channel profit via an optimal choice for its fixed fee. However, if $\delta^{QD^*} > (f_i - f_j)$, then the $j^{th}$ retailer is the less profitable. As a result, the fixed fee can extract all rent from this retailer (who nets zero economic profit), but the $i^{th}$ retailer will earn a positive profit.[12] In a like vein, if $\delta^{QD^*} < (f_i - f_j)$ the $i^{th}$ retailer nets zero profit and the $j^{th}$ retailer earns a positive profit. The manufacturer can always coordinate the channel with the quantity-discount schedule, but it cannot gain all profit from the channel unless (5.8.1) holds. The manufacturer's share of channel profit is lower and the greater is the absolute difference $|\delta^{QD^*} - (f_i - f_j)|$.

For ease of exposition, we use the term Zone $Z_j^{QD^*}$ to denote the range of values within which $\delta^{QD^*} > (f_i - f_j)$ and we refer to the range for which $\delta^{QD^*} < (f_i - f_j)$ as Zone $Z_i^{QD^*}$. The zonal subscripts denote the zero-profit retailer. Only on the boundary line (5.8.1) that divides these Zones is neither retailer profitable. For consistency with discussions in later Chapters, we label this boundary line Zone $Z_{ij}^{QD^*}$.

## 8.2 Zonal Re-Parameterization

Both $\delta^{QD^*}$ and $(f_i - f_j)$ are beyond managerial control in our model. Thus it is important to investigate the relationship between the three Zones defined by these variables and the underlying model parameters. It appears from (5.8.1) and (5.A.3) that there are nine relevant model parameters: $b, \theta, A_i, A_j, c_i, c_j, C, f_i$, and $f_j$. However, we can reduce the number of underlying parameters through judicious substitutions; we have already shown that five of these parameters ($A_i, A_j, c_i, c_j$, and C) can be reduced to the pair $Q_i^*$ and $Q_j^*$, but this reduced set of six ($b, \theta, Q_i^*, Q_j^*, f_i$, and $f_j$.) can be further tightened. We offer the following definitions:

$$\chi \equiv (\theta/b) \tag{5.8.3}$$

$$S_j \equiv Q_j^* / (Q_i^* + Q_j^*) \tag{5.8.4}$$

The variable $\chi$ is the *intensity of competition*; it must lie in the unit interval for second-order conditions to be satisfied $(0 \le \chi < 1)$. The larger is $\chi$, the more substitutable the two retailers are in the eyes of consumers. We will refer to the variable $S_j$, which is measured by the market share of the $j^{th}$ retailer, as the *magnitude of competition*. This variable must lie in the unit interval $(0 \le S_j \le 1)$. The closer the value $S_j$ is to one-half, the more equal are the competitors' outputs.

Through these re-parameterizations we may rewrite $\delta^{QD^*}$ as:

$$\delta^{QD^*} = R_i^* \left[(2+\chi)(1-2S_j)\right] \Big/ \left[2(1-S_j)^2 (1+\chi)\right] \tag{5.8.5}$$

The term $\delta^{QD^*}$ is expressed as a function of the two parameters $\chi$ and $S_j$ and the monotonic shift factor $R_i^*$, which is the net revenue of the $i^{th}$ retailer when the channel is coordinated.

In a like manner we may re-parameterize the retailers' fixed costs as:

$$\mathcal{f}_k \equiv (f_k / R_k^*) \quad \forall \quad k \in (i, j) \tag{5.8.6}$$

The term $f_k$ is the k[th] firm's *fixed-cost ratio* defined as a function of its net revenue. By the participation constraint, this ratio must lie in the unit interval $(0 \le f_k < 1)$. The only exception to this statement arises when the manufacturer pays the retailer to participate in the channel; we do not consider that possibility here. Because we are concerned with the difference in the retailers' fixed costs, we write:

$$(\mathrm{f}_i - \mathrm{f}_j) = \mathrm{R}_i^* \left( \left[ (1-\mathrm{S}_j)^2 f_i - \mathrm{S}_j^2 f_j \right] \Big/ (1-\mathrm{S}_j)^2 \right) \tag{5.8.7}$$

This difference is a function of the parameters $\mathrm{S}_j$, $f_i$, and $f_j$ and the monotonic shift factor $\mathrm{R}_i^*$. Through these re-parameterizations we have legitimately reduced our original nine parameters to four parameters: $\chi$, $\mathrm{S}_j$, $f_i$ and $f_j$.

Due to the inherent complexity of our solutions, we further simplify our graphical illustration of the problem by focusing on an equal fixed-cost ratio: $f_i = f_j \equiv f$. Note that this is *not* the same as assuming $\mathrm{f}_i = \mathrm{f}_j$, *except* in the very special case of identical competitors $(\mathrm{Q}_i^* = \mathrm{Q}_j^*)$.

## 8.3 The Quantity-Discount Zones and Retailers' Profits

The condition on a manufacturer's profit extraction capability is:

$$\begin{aligned} \delta_{\Delta f}^{QD^*} &\equiv \left[ \delta^{QD^*} - (\mathrm{f}_i - \mathrm{f}_j) \right] \Big|_{f_i = f_j} = 0 \\ &= \left( \frac{\mathrm{R}_i^* (1 - 2\mathrm{S}_j)}{2(1+\chi)(1-\mathrm{S}_j)^2} \right) \big( (2+\chi) - 2(1+\chi) f \big) = 0 \end{aligned} \tag{5.8.8}$$

Condition $\delta_{\Delta f}^{QD^*}$ is a function of the parameters $\chi, \mathrm{S}_j$ and $f$, all of which lie between zero and one. These three dimensions define a "unit-cube." Because we have assumed $f_i = f_j \equiv f$, the unit-cube is perfectly symmetric about the $\mathrm{S}_j = ½$ axis. For this reason, we focus our discussion on the *unit half-cube* defined by $(0 \le \chi < 1,\ 0 \le \mathrm{S}_j \le ½,\ 0 \le f \le 1)$. We illustrate our discussion with slices of this unit half-cube taken at various $f$ – values.

Our task is to determine which parametric values are associated with each of the three QD – Zones. There are three possibilities:

- $\delta_{\Delta f}^{QD^*} > 0 \rightarrow$ Zone $\mathrm{Z}_j^{QD^*}$ in which the j[th] retailer nets zero profit;
- $\delta_{\Delta f}^{QD^*} = 0 \rightarrow$ Zone $\mathrm{Z}_{ij}^{QD^*}$ in which both retailers net zero profit; and
- $\delta_{\Delta f}^{QD^*} < 0 \rightarrow$ Zone $\mathrm{Z}_i^{QD^*}$ in which the i[th] retailer nets zero profit.

Zone $Z_{ij}^{QD^*}$ is the boundary that separates Zones $Z_j^{QD^*}$ and $Z_i^{QD^*}$ within the unit half-cube. The locations of this boundary are found by setting the numerator of (5.8.8) equal to zero. There is a trivial solution at $S_j = ½$. At this value the retailers are identical, so the manufacturer can obviously extract all profit from both competitors.

Turning to substantive solutions, conceptually the unit half-cube can be divided into two $f$ – Regions:

- $f$ – **Region 1:** $0 \le f^{QD^*} \le ¾$
- $f$ – **Region 2:** $¾ < f^{QD^*} < 1$

Both $f$ – Regions are determined by the value of:

$$\chi = -2\left(\frac{1-f}{1-2f}\right) \tag{5.8.9}$$

The first $f$ – Region covers $f$ – values that are no greater than ¾; these $f$ – values generate a *non*-positive $\chi$ – values according to the formula defined by (5.8.9). This $f$ – Region corresponds to Zone $Z_j^{QD^*}$ within which the manufacturer is *unable* to extract all rent from the channel, although it does obtain all the profit of the smaller (the $j^{th}$) retailer.

The second $f$ – Region is defined by a positive value of (5.8.9). Since this $\chi$ – value is independent of market share $S_j$; the boundary is a horizontal line in $\langle \chi, S_j \rangle$ – space. The value of $\chi$ is inversely related to the value of $f$, so increases in $f$ yield ever lower $\chi$ – values for the zonal boundary $\delta_{\Delta f}^{QD^*}$.

An illustration is provided in Figure 5.2. At $f = 0.85$ we find:

$$\begin{aligned} \chi < 3/7 &\rightarrow \text{Zone } Z_j^{QD^*} \\ \chi = 3/7 &\rightarrow \text{Zone } Z_{ij}^{QD^*} \\ \chi > 3/7 &\rightarrow \text{Zone } Z_i^{QD^*} \end{aligned} \tag{5.8.10}$$

It is now apparent why the quantity-discount schedule may yield lower manufacturer profit than do various non-coordinating two-part tariffs even though it generates higher channel profit. The quantity-discount schedule allows the manufacturer to extract all channel profit *only* (i) on the vertical axis defined by $S_j = ½$ and (ii) on the line labeled $Z_{ij}^{QD^*}$ in Figure 5.2. Moreover, the latter line only exists when $f^{QD^*} > ¾$.

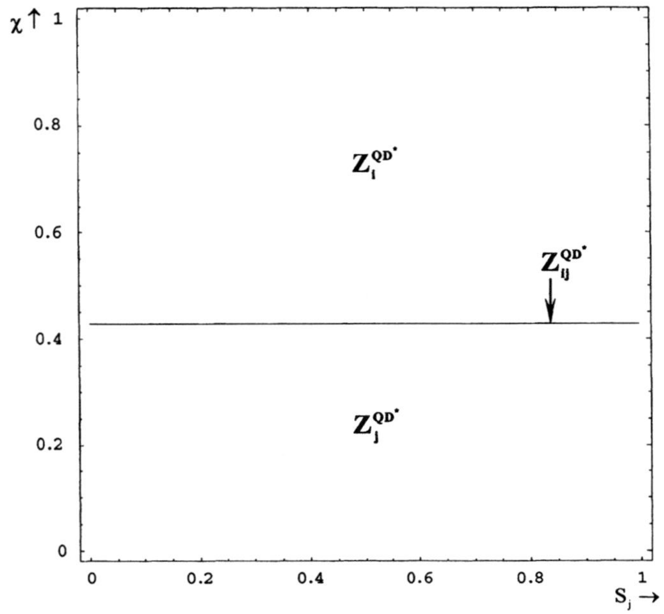


Legend:

$Z_j^{QD^*}$ ≡ The channel-coordinating quantity-discount Zone; in it the j[th] retailer earns zero profit;

$Z_{ij}^{QD^*}$ ≡ The channel-coordinating quantity-discount Zone; in it both retailers earn zero profit (This is the zonal boundary separating $Z_j^{QD^*}$ from $Z_i^{QD^*}$); and

$Z_i^{QD^*}$ ≡ The channel-coordinating quantity-discount Zone; in it the i[th] retailer earns zero profit.

*Figure 5.2.* The Channel-Coordinating Quantity-Discount Zones When $f = 0.85$

We stress that our graphical results are fully general, subject to the caveat that $f_i = f_j$. *Any combination* of parametric values for demand and costs, whether at retail or at manufacture, that generates the same values for our three dimensions ($\chi$, $S_j$, and $f$) will lead to the same level of manufacturer profit. (Our mathematical results are fully general because they encompass all four dimensions.)

# 9 COMMENTARY

In this Chapter we have investigated a two-level channel in which a single manufacturer distributes through a pair of independent, competing retailers. These retailers are treated comparably; the manufacturer offers them both the same wholesale-price schedule. The assumption of comparability, which we use throughout this monograph, is critical to our analyses, for it breaks the tyranny of *de facto* bilateral monopoly that characterizes so much of the literature. We begin our summary of results by discussing the implications of the comparability assumption for models of competing-retailers models. We then relate these results to the analysis of non-competing retailers and the Channel Myths identified in Chapters 1 and 2.

## 9.1 Commentary on a Competing-Retailers Model

We have proven that there exists a *quantity-discount schedule* that will coordinate both channel dyads, thus generating a channel performance that is the same as that produced by a vertically-integrated system. (By "channel performance" we mean prices, quantities, and channel profit.) This schedule is effective because it causes each retailer to pay a unique, *marginal* wholesale price. This leads to each retailer setting its channel-optimal retail price. Coordination occurs because the quantity-discount schedule explicitly considers cross-demand effects; however, this means that both retailers pay a marginal (and an average) wholesale price which exceeds marginal production cost. Because the retailers also sell at a positive markup, we have proven that the coordination of a competing-retailer's channel necessarily entails double marginalization.

In contrast to the quantity-discount schedule, *no common, two-part tariff* can duplicate the channel performance of a vertically-integrated system, except in the trivial cases of identical competitors or non-competing retailers. We have also proven the existence of a "second-best" two-part tariff, common to both retailers, that yields channel coordination "on average." This tariff leads to the same *total* output and the same *average* retail price as in a coordinated channel, although it falls short of the profits attained by the vertically-integrated system because the larger (smaller) retailer's output is reduced (enhanced) relative to the vertically-integrated solution.

Our analyses of several possible wholesale-price policies generated the initially unexpected conclusion that channel coordination, at least with a linear, quantity-discount schedule, need *not* maximize the manufacturer's profit. We showed that, under many parametric values, the manufacturer obtains a higher profit by utilizing one (of several possible) non-coordinating two-part tariffs. The key underlying factor driving our conclusions is comparable treatment; this limits the manufacturer's ability to extract rent from its retailers. Perhaps surprisingly, the quantity-discount schedule places tighter limits on the manufacturer than do the non-coordinating two-part tariffs.

The most important contribution of this Chapter is our demonstration that the difference in retailers' fixed costs affects the manufacturer-optimal wholesale-price strategy. Fixed-cost differences can arise in several ways. First, in a *geographic* sense, the manufacturer-optimal strategy may vary across regions due to differences in real estate costs at retail. For instance, real estate in Manhattan, KS, is considerably less expensive than real estate in Manhattan, NY. Second, in an *industrial* sense, the manufacturer-optimal strategy may vary due to differences in interior designs. For example, the interior fixtures at warehouse clubs are less costly than are those at upscale department stores. Third, in a *temporal* sense, the manufacturer-optimal strategy may change as retailers' fixed costs evolve. To illustrate, an increase in real estate taxes may alter the manufacturer's strategy from a non-coordinating tariff to a channel-coordinating quantity-discount schedule. Regardless of the source of the difference in retailers' fixed costs, these costs have two impacts. First, each retailer's willingness to be a channel member is limited by its unwillingness to operate at a loss; this is the well-understood participation constraint. The higher is a retailer's fixed cost, the less profit there is for the manufacturer to extract rent in the form of a fixed fee.[13] Second, the manufacturer's optimal wholesale-price strategy depends on the *difference* in the fixed costs of the retailers. Depending on the magnitude of this difference, *any* of the wholesale price policies investigated in this Chapter may be optimal.

In terms of the questions we raised in the Introduction to this Chapter, we have shown that *both* competitors can be coordinated with a properly specified quantity-discount schedule. Coordination of both dyads does maximize *channel* profit, but over some parametric values it does not maximize *manufacturer* profit.

## 9.2 Commentary on Multiple-Retailers Models

In Chapter 3 we analyzed a model of multiple retailers who do *not* compete. Some of the results of that Chapter carry over to this Chapter. First, the concept of the manufacturer having a preference for non-coordination echoes a core conclusion of our model of non-competing retailers. As in that model, coordination is manufacturer-optimal if the competing retailers are identical. Second, in the competing-retailers model of this Chapter, we find that *total* channel profit is higher when the manufacturer uses a coordinating wholesale-price strategy instead of a non-coordinating strategy. This result differs from that of Chapter 3, because here we hold channel breadth constant, while in Chapter 3 we allowed channel breadth to vary. The general rule is that non-coordination cannot increase channel profitability when the number of retailers is fixed, but it can improve manufacturer profitability. It is only through an increase in channel breadth that non-coordination has the potential to augment total channel profit. We rigorously prove that this observation generalizes to a competing-retailers model in Chapter 10.

## 9.3 Commentary on Five Channel Myths

This Chapter has demonstrated that several inferences derived from a simple bilateral-monopoly model do not hold in a world of competing retailers. Because many of these inferences appear repeatedly in the marketing science literature on distribution channels, we have referred to them as Myths. The results in this Chapter are relevant to five of these myths.

First, we have proven that a positive markup at both levels of the channel ("double marginalization") is required for channel coordination in a model with competing retailers. This result contrasts sharply with those obtained from either a bilateral-monopoly model or a model with multiple, non-competing retailers. In these latter two cases, only one level of the channel can have a positive margin if the channel is to be coordinated. *The appropriate decision rule for achieving channel coordination is to embrace double marginalization in the presence of competition but to avoid it in the absence of competition.* The widespread belief in the marketing science literature that only one level of the channel should have a positive markup, and that any wholesale-price schedule which avoids double marginalization is channel-coordinating, is a myth; we call it the *Double-Marginalization Strategic Myth.*

The desirability of double marginalization has important implications for the kind of wholesale-price policy that is capable of coordinating a competing-retailers channel. Channel coordination requires that the larger-output competitor pay the lower per-unit marginal wholesale price.[14] An appropriately specified quantity-discount schedule meets this criterion, but neither a two-part tariff nor a monotonic quantity-surplus schedule does.

Second, we have shown that channel coordination does not always maximize manufacturer profit. The reason is that comparable treatment of retailers limits the manufacturer's ability to extract all profit from its retailers. This result shows that the widespread belief in the marketing science literature that channel coordination is always in the best interest of all channel members is a myth; we call it the *Channel-Coordination Strategic Myth.*

Third, we have shown that the difference in fixed costs at retail affects the manufacturer's optimal wholesale-price policy. It follows that the widespread belief that fixed costs only affect the participation constraint is a myth; we call it the *Fixed-Cost Modeling Myth.* This Myth has appeared in Chapters 3 and 4, and it will appear again in each of the following Chapters.

Fourth, we have used several wholesale-price policies to demonstrate that the common assumption of identical competitors leads to results that are compatible with those obtained in a bilateral-monopoly model, but that are *incompatible* with those found when the competitors are not identical. The belief that modeling identical competitors is an innocuous, simplifying assumption is also a myth. We call it the *Identical-Competitors Meta-Myth,* for an identical-competitors model distorts the results of any model of non-identical competitors, and does so in a manner that can be truly significant.

Fifth, we have shown that predictions deduced from a bilateral-monopoly model are generally inaccurate when applied in models with competing retailers; this observation is consistent with the results of preceding Chapters. Because the single-manufacturer, single-retailer, single-product, single state-of-nature model is the most common model in the analytical literature on channels, we believe it is appropriate to label a belief in the generalizability of this approach to modeling distribution a myth; we call it the *Bilateral-Monopoly Meta-Myth.*

## 9.4 Summary Commentary

The most fundamental prescription from the marketing science literature on distribution channels is that coordination will benefit all channel members. Our discovery that several non-coordinating two-part tariffs can overturn the efficacy of coordination is so contrary to received opinion that it may be termed a paradox. Thoughtful analysis reveals that the resolution to this paradox must lie somewhere between two extremes. On the one hand, our discovery may be limited in scope; the consequence of employing a specific, linear quantity-discount schedule to achieve coordination; in short, our finding may not generalize. On the other hand, our discovery may be broadly applicable under a host of scenarios; in brief, it may apply to all models other than the bilateral-monopoly model and the identical-competitor model. As we explore this range of possibilities, we recall the words of Niels Bohr, 1922 Nobel Laureate in Physics, "How wonderful that we have met with a paradox. Now we have some hope of making progress."[15] In the ensuing Chapters we will make considerable progress toward resolving this paradox.

# 10 APPENDIX

This Appendix defines the conditions under which the manufacturer prefers the channel-coordinating quantity-discount schedule, the sell-at-cost two-part tariff, the naïve Stackelberg two-part tariff, or the second-best two-part tariff. Each of these policies has a single "critical value" (defined below) at which the manufacturer obtains all channel profit after payment of the fixed fee ($\phi$). However, at all "non-critical values," one retailer obtains a positive economic profit,[16] while its rival obtains zero economic profit. The manufacturer is limited in its ability to maximize its profit because it cannot control the critical value.

## 10.1 Determining the "Critical Values"

The critical value, dimensioned in dollars, is defined in terms of the *retailers' fixed-cost difference* $(f_i - f_j)$. For expository purposes we discuss the case in which $(f_i - f_j)$ lies below its critical value. Because the *less* profitable (say the j[th]) retailer nets zero economic profit, any increase in $f_j$ must be met with a dollar-for-dollar decrease in the fixed fee. The j[th] retailer will not participate in the channel without this adjustment in $\phi$. Moreover, any increase in the *more* profitable (the i[th]) retailer's fixed cost has no effect on the fixed fee until $f_i$ reaches its "critical value;" at this point the retailers have equal profit. Any further increase in $f_i$ causes the i[th] retailer to become the less-profitable competitor. Thus $\phi$ must decline "dollar-for-dollar" if the i[th] retailer is to continue to participate in the channel.

Whenever the less-profitable retailer's fixed cost increases by \$1, the manufacturer must decrease the fixed fee by \$1 to retain this retailer as a channel member. As a result, the manufacturer's own profit declines by \$2, because the lower fixed fee is paid by *both* retailers. In contrast, an increase in the more profitable retailer's fixed cost has no impact on the manufacturer's profit. Thus there is a kink in the manufacturer's profit function at every "critical value." We now address the determination of these "critical values."

To compare profit across retailers, we start with a set of simple definitions, using the sell-at-cost two-part tariff for illustrative purposes:

$$\begin{aligned}\Delta\hat{\pi}^{W=C} &\equiv \left(\hat{\pi}_i^{W=C} - \hat{\pi}_j^{W=C}\right)\\ &\equiv \left(\hat{R}_i^{W=C} - f_i\right) - \left(\hat{R}_j^{W=C} - f_j\right)\\ &\equiv \left(\hat{R}_i^{W=C} - \hat{R}_j^{W=C}\right) - \left(f_i - f_j\right)\\ &\equiv \left(\hat{\delta}^{W=C}\right) - \left(f_i - f_j\right)\end{aligned} \tag{5.A.1}$$

Expression (5.A.1) merely says that the difference in retailer profit is equal to the difference in their revenues (denoted as $\hat{\delta}^{W=C}$) minus the difference in their fixed costs.

Using this definition we now ask whether the profit difference is positive or negative—that is, we ask which retailer is less profitable. In the case of the $W = C$ tariff we obtain:

$$\Delta\hat{\pi}^{W=C} \gtrless 0 \iff \hat{\delta}^{W=C} = \left(\frac{4b\left(Q_i^* + Q_j^*\right)}{(4b^2 - \theta^2)}\right)\left(Q_i^* - Q_j^*\right) \gtrless \left(f_i - f_j\right) \tag{5.A.2}$$

Similarly, in the cases of the other three tariffs it can be shown that:

$$\begin{aligned}\Delta\pi^{QD^*} \gtrless 0 &\iff \delta^{QD^*} = \left(\frac{(2b+\theta)\left(Q_i^* + Q_j^*\right)}{2b(b+\theta)}\right)\left(Q_i^* - Q_j^*\right) \gtrless \left(f_i - f_j\right)\\ \Delta\tilde{\pi}^* \gtrless 0 &\iff \tilde{\delta}^* = \left(\frac{2\left(Q_i^* + Q_j^*\right)}{(2b+\theta)}\right)\left(Q_i^* - Q_j^*\right) \gtrless \left(f_i - f_j\right)\\ \Delta\hat{\pi}^* \gtrless 0 &\iff \hat{\delta}^* = \left(\frac{2b\left(Q_i^* + Q_j^*\right)}{(4b^2 - \theta^2)}\right)\left(Q_i^* - Q_j^*\right) \gtrless \left(f_i - f_j\right)\end{aligned} \tag{5.A.3}$$

We always define the profit difference as the i[th] retailer minus the j[th] retailer.

Let $Q_i^* > Q_j^* > 0$, so that all the $\delta$ expressions defined above are positive. The preceding expressions describe five "Scenarios:"

$$\begin{aligned}&\textbf{Scenario I:} && \hat{\delta}^{w=c} > \delta^{QD^*} > \tilde{\delta}^* > \hat{\delta}^* > \Delta f\\ &\textbf{Scenario II:} && \hat{\delta}^{w=c} > \delta^{QD^*} > \tilde{\delta}^* > \Delta f > \hat{\delta}^*\\ &\textbf{Scenario III:} && \hat{\delta}^{w=c} > \delta^{QD^*} > \Delta f > \tilde{\delta}^* > \hat{\delta}^*\\ &\textbf{Scenario IV:} && \hat{\delta}^{w=c} > \Delta f > \delta^{QD^*} > \tilde{\delta}^* > \hat{\delta}^*\\ &\textbf{Scenario V:} && \Delta f > \hat{\delta}^{w=c} > \delta^{QD^*} > \tilde{\delta}^* > \hat{\delta}^*\end{aligned} \tag{5.A.4}$$

In expression (5.A.4) we define $\Delta f \equiv (f_i - f_j)$. These Scenarios detail the less profitable retailer under each wholesale-price strategy. This retailer, identified in the next Table, has all its profit extracted by the fixed fee $\phi$.

| Scenarios and Tariffs: Identity of the Less-Profitable Retailer | | | | |
|---|---|---|---|---|
| Scenario | Sell-at-Cost | Quantity-Discount | Second-Best | Naïve Stackelberg |
| I | $j^{th}$ retailer | $j^{th}$ retailer | $j^{th}$ retailer | $j^{th}$ retailer |
| II | $j^{th}$ retailer | $j^{th}$ retailer | $j^{th}$ retailer | $\mathbf{i^{th}}$ retailer |
| III | $j^{th}$ retailer | $j^{th}$ retailer | $\mathbf{i^{th}}$ retailer | $\mathbf{i^{th}}$ retailer |
| IV | $j^{th}$ retailer | $\mathbf{i^{th}}$ retailer | $\mathbf{i^{th}}$ retailer | $\mathbf{i^{th}}$ retailer |
| V | $\mathbf{i^{th}}$ retailer | $\mathbf{i^{th}}$ retailer | $\mathbf{i^{th}}$ retailer | $\mathbf{i^{th}}$ retailer |

## 10.2 Solutions for the "Critical Values"

Determination of the manufacturer-optimal wholesale-price policy requires a set of "side-by-side" comparisons of the manufacturer's profit generated by each policy. Each profit expression contains a term that is dependent on the manufacturer's markup on units sold ($((W-C)\Sigma Q_k \geq 0)$) and a second term that is based on the profit level of the less-profitable retailer ($2\phi$). For a "side-by-side" contrast in which the identity of the less profitable retailer does not differ, the comparison is predicated on $Q_i^*$, $Q_j^*$, $b$ and $\theta$. This is the case for Scenarios **I** and **V**. For Scenarios **II, III,** and **IV** the identity of the less-profitable retailer differs, so the value of $(f_i - f_j)$ also matters. It is this difference that drives the existence of potential "critical values" (labeled as $\delta_k^*$, $k \in (1,2,3)$ in Tables 5.2-5.4). Details are presented in tabular format:

| Scenario | The Manufacturer's Profit Comparisons | Critical δ Value | Parametric Values Determining Profit-Dominance |
|---|---|---|---|
| I | $\tilde{\Pi}_M^* \gtrless \hat{\Pi}_M^* > \Pi_M^{QD^*} > \hat{\Pi}_M^{W=C}$ | NA | $Q_i^*, Q_j^*, b, \theta$ |
| II | $\hat{\Pi}_M^* \gtrless \tilde{\Pi}_M^* > \Pi_M^{QD^*} > \hat{\Pi}_M^{W=C}$ | $\delta_1^*$ | $Q_i^*, Q_j^*, b, \theta$ and $(f_i - f_j)$ |
| III | $\tilde{\Pi}_M^* \gtrless \Pi_M^{QD^*} > \hat{\Pi}_M^*, \hat{\Pi}_M^{W=C}$ | $\delta_2^*$ | $Q_i^*, Q_j^*, b, \theta$ and $(f_i - f_j)$ |
| IV | $\Pi_M^{QD^*} \gtrless \hat{\Pi}_M^{W=C} > \tilde{\Pi}_M^*, \hat{\Pi}_M^*$ | $\delta_3^*$ | $Q_i^*, Q_j^*, b, \theta$ and $(f_i - f_j)$ |
| V | $\Pi_M^{QD^*} \gtrless \hat{\Pi}_M^{W=C} > \tilde{\Pi}_M^*, \hat{\Pi}_M^*$ | NA | $Q_i^*, Q_j^*, b, \theta$ |

To conserve space we simply state our results here. Interested readers who wish to reproduce these results may do so by pursuing the logic described above and below. In Scenario **I** manufacturer profit is maximized by either the naïve Stackelberg or the second-best tariff. In Scenario **II** we obtain a similar result, but which tariff is manufacturer-preferred is partially determined by $(f_i - f_j)$. In Scenario **III** either the quantity-discount schedule or the second-best tariff will be manufacturer-optimal. In Scenarios **IV** and **V** the quantity-discount schedule or the sell-at-cost tariff is manufacturer-preferred. In all five Scenarios the values of $b, \theta, Q_i^*$ and $Q_j^*$ affect the manufacturer's choice of a wholesale-price policy. But, in Scenarios **II-IV** the difference in retailers' fixed costs also matters. In these three Scenarios there may exist a critical value of $f_i$ (call it $f_{in}, n \in (1,2,3)$). In the first case the critical value satisfies:

$$\left(f_{i1} - f_j\right) \geq \tilde{\delta}^* \text{ s.t. } \tilde{\Pi}_M^* = \hat{\Pi}_M^* \tag{5.A.5}$$

We define $\delta_1^*$ as:

$$\delta_1^* \equiv \begin{cases} f_{i1} & \text{if } f_{i1} > 0 \\ 0 & \text{otherwise} \end{cases} \tag{5.A.6}$$

The same logic applies in Scenarios **III** and **IV**.

## 10.3 Manufacturer Profit by Strategy

In this sub-Section we calculate manufacturer profit from the wholesale-price strategies developed above. We also calculate the maximal fixed-cost value for the less profitable retailer if the manufacturer is to obtain non-negative profit. To conserve space we only report the results for the second-best tariff relative to the quantity-discount schedule; results for the other pricing policies can be derived in a similar fashion.

### 10.3.1 The Quantity-Discount Schedule

It is straightforward to show that with a channel-coordinating, linear quantity-discount schedule the manufacturer obtains a profit of:

$$\Pi_M^{QD^*} = \begin{cases} \Pi_C^* - \delta^{QD^*} & \forall \quad \delta^{QD^*} \geq \left(f_i - f_j\right) \\ \Pi_C^* - \delta^{QD^*} - 2\left[\left(f_i - \overline{f}_j\right) - \delta^{QD^*}\right] & \forall \quad \delta^{QD^*} < \left(f_i - f_j\right) \end{cases} \tag{5.A.7}$$

The upper line states that for all fixed-cost differences below the critical value the manufacturer nets the channel profit minus the critical value (which is denominated in dollars). Below this critical value profit declines at two times any fixed cost difference in excess of the critical value.

The manufacturer will participate in the channel only when $\Pi_M^{QD^*} > 0$. The maximum possible fixed cost for the i[th] retailer that is compatible with non-negative manufacturer profit is:

$$\bar{f}_i^{QD^*} = \frac{\left(R_C^* + \delta^{QD^*} - F\right)}{2} + \bar{f}_j \tag{5.A.8}$$

where $\bar{f}_j$ is a constant level of the j[th] retailer's fixed cost and $R_C^*$ is channel net revenue.

In Figure 5.3 the thick line depicts the manufacturer's profit with a channel-coordinating quantity-discount schedule as a function of the i[th] retailer's fixed cost. The dashed line shows channel profit. (For now ignore the points labeled A, B and C.)

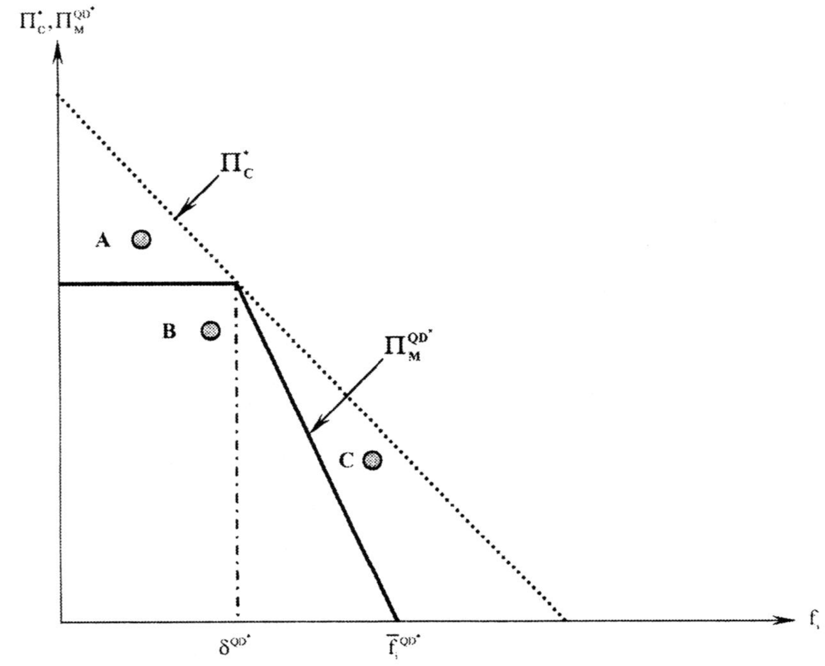


Legend:

$\Pi_C^*$ ≡ Total profit of a coordinated channel;

$\Pi_M^{QD^*}$ ≡ Manufacturer profit with the channel-coordinating quantity-discount schedule;

$\overline{f}_i^{QD^*}$ ≡ The maximum fixed cost for the ith retailer if the manufacturer is to participate in the channel, given that the $j^{th}$ retailer has a fixed cost of $\overline{f}_j$; and

$\delta^{QD^*}$ ≡ $f_i$ – value at which the quantity-discount schedule extracts all profit from both retailers.

*Figure 5.3.* Manufacturer Profit: A Channel-Coordinating Quantity-Discount Schedule *vs.* a Non-Coordinating Two-Part Tariff

### 10.3.2 The Second-Best Tariff

Utilizing the same logic as above, we can show that with a second-best tariff the manufacturer obtains a profit level of:

$$\tilde{\Pi}_M^* = \begin{cases} \tilde{\Pi}_C^* - \tilde{\delta}^* & \forall \;\; \tilde{\delta}^* \geq (f_i - f_j) \\ \tilde{\Pi}_C^* - \tilde{\delta}^* - 2\left[\left(f_i - \overline{f}_j\right) - \tilde{\delta}^*\right] & \forall \;\; \tilde{\delta}^* < (f_i - f_j) \end{cases} \tag{5.A.9}$$

The manufacturer obtains all of channel profit at the kink—which is defined by the critical value.

From (5.A.9) it is apparent that there is a maximum possible value of the i[th] retailer's fixed cost that is compatible with the manufacturer being willing to participate in the channel. This value can be written as:

$$\tilde{f}_i^* = \frac{\left(\tilde{\Pi}_C^* + \tilde{\delta}^* + 2\overline{f}_j\right)}{2} \tag{5.A.10}$$

A similar expression may be derived for the j[th] retailer's fixed cost. An important feature of these terms is that each maximally-allowed fixed cost is defined in terms of its rival's fixed cost.

Now consider Figure 5.3 once again. If we were to draw the manufacturer's profit with a second-best tariff as a function of $f_i$ it would be of the same *form* as the thick line. The "kink" in such a curve would lie inside the coordinated channel profit line, for the second-best tariff does not coordinate the channel. There are three possibilities for the location of this kink relative to the manufacturer's profit line with the quantity-discount schedule. First, it may lie above the horizontal portion of $\Pi_M^{QD^*}$ (represented by point A). In this case there is a range of $(f_i - \overline{f}_j)$ values for which the second-best tariff manufacturer profit-dominates the quantity-discount schedule. Second, it may lie below the horizontal portion of $\Pi_M^{QD^*}$ and to the left of the diagonal segment of this profit function (represented by point B). In this case the quantity-discount schedule manufacturer profit-dominates the second-best tariff. Third, it may lie to the right of the diagonal segment of $\Pi_M^{QD^*}$ (represented by point C). In this case there is a range of $(f_i - \overline{f}_j)$ values for which the second-best tariff manufacturer profit-dominates the quantity-discount schedule.

# Notes

[1] This Chapter builds upon our *Marketing Science* paper (Ingene and Parry 1995). There is a substantial amount of new material in this Chapter. Material that overlaps with our original paper [Ingene, C., M. Parry "Channel Coordination when Retailers Compete" *Marketing Science* **14** (Fall) 1995, pp. 360-377] is reprinted by permission; copyright 1995, the Institute for Operations Research and the Management Sciences, 901 Elkridge Landing Road, Suite 400, Linthicum, MD 21090 USA.
[2] In Chapters 5-9 and 11 we evaluate the "one manufacturer/two competing retailers" model. In Chapters 10 and 11 we compare serving one *versus* two retailers; that is, we investigate inter-retailer competition at *non*-constant channel breadth.
[3] Our terminology "naïve" Stackelberg refers to maximization by choosing the per-unit wholesale-price In Chapter 6 we introduce the concept of a "sophisticated" Stackelberg tariff. The sophisticated Stackelberg tariff entails maximization through the simultaneous choice of the per-unit wholesale-price *and* the fixed fee in a two-part tariff.
[4] One of our goals is to obtain closed-form solutions. A linear quantity-discount schedule meets this goal, a non-linear schedule does not. This raises the possibility that our "non-coordination is preferred..." result is due to linearity. Hence we introduce a fully general, *channel-coordinating* menu of two-part tariffs in Chapter 7 to test the coordination *versus* non-coordination issue.
[5] A more general formulation for demand is $Q_i = Q_i(p_i, p_j)$ s.t. $\partial Q_i/\partial p_j > 0 > \partial Q_i/\partial p_i$. We do not adopt this approach because it precludes obtaining closed-form expressions. In our *Marketing Science* paper (Ingene and Parry 1995) we set $b = 1$. We develop the implications of this decision in detail in Chapter 11; these implications were unrealized in 1995.
[6] Note that this limiting case yields the same result found in Chapter 3: double-marginalization is incompatible with channel coordination *in the absence of inter-retailer competition.*
[7] Different transfer prices are legally permissible in a vertically-integrated system.
[8] We detailed our reasons for modeling manufacturer Stackelberg leadership in Chapter 1.
[9] Our terminology comes from Lipsey and Lancaster (1956-57); they defined a "second-best solution" as the best obtainable solution given an institutional restriction that precludes attaining the optimal (the "first-best") solution. Here the manufacturer-optimal solution would coordinate the channel and extract all profit from both retailers. As we have seen, coordination is not possible when the manufacturer is restricted to offering a single two-part tariff.
[10] Specifically, the quantity-discount schedule generates the higher net revenue for the manufacturer at high $\chi$-values in the vicinity of equal market shares.
[11] We will address the same relationships between the various two-part tariffs in Chapter 6.
[12] Recall that in Chapters 5-9 we restrict our analysis to a constant channel breadth. We consider the consequences of optimizing channel breadth in Chapter 10.
[13] The manufacturer sets a fixed fee that extracts all profit from the less-profitable retailer. The more profitable retailer (in Chapter 3, all the other retailers) generally recognizes a positive profit after paying the fixed fee.
[14] This phenomenon holds for any number of competing retailers; some form of quantity-discount is required for coordination. However, a *linear* schedule is generally unacceptable for more than two competitors.
[15] The quotation is cited by Ponomarev (1993, page 75).
[16] Economic profit is profit in excess of the firm's opportunity cost.

Chapter 6

# The Manufacturer-Optimal Two-Part Tariff[1]

*"Each truth that I found was a rule which helped me to find others."*

## 1 INTRODUCTION

In Chapter 5 we investigated three wholesale-price policies that were variations of non-coordinating two-part tariffs. Given the proper parametric values, each of these tariffs can generate greater manufacturer profit than can a channel-coordinating quantity-discount schedule.[2] That three very different wholesale prices, each determined by fundamentally dissimilar methods, can dominate a channel-coordinating policy suggests that there may be other two-part tariffs that can also outperform a channel-coordinating quantity-discount schedule, at least from the manufacturer's perspective. This realization motivates the research reported here. Our specific goal in this Chapter is to develop a two-part tariff that includes as special cases *all* two-part tariffs that are manufacturer-optimal for some parametric values. Our intention is for this generalized tariff to enable us to identify the manufacturer-optimal two-part tariff and thereby to clarify the relative attractiveness to the manufacturer of seeking coordination *versus* embracing non-coordination.

A shared feature of the two-part tariffs analyzed in Chapter 5 was that their fixed fees were "residuals," defined by the difference between the less-profitable retailer's net revenue (i.e., gross revenue minus variable costs) and its fixed cost. While this handling of the fixed fee is broadly consistent with the two-part tariff pricing literature, it ignores the effect a per-unit wholesale price has on each retailer's net revenue—and thus on the magnitude of the fixed fee that the retailers can afford to pay. Expressed from the price-setter's perspective, the per-unit wholesale price affects the margin earned on each unit sold and the fixed fee paid by all retailers. Thus a manufacturer-optimal two-part tariff should explicitly account for the tradeoff between the wholesale price that is charged and the fixed fee that can be extracted from the retailers. This insight is the basis of the two-part tariff developed here.

Our analysis will address six basic questions within the context of our model of one manufacturer that sells through competing, comparably treated retailers. These questions are:

(1) Is there a unique two-part tariff that maximizes manufacturer profit over all parametric values?

(2) If the answer to (1) is "yes," how are the specific two-part tariffs discussed in Chapter 5 related to the optimal two-part tariff?
(3) Does the difference in retailers' fixed costs $(f_i - f_j)$ systematically affect the *per-unit wholesale price*?
(4) Does $(f_i - f_j)$ systematically affect the optimal *fixed fee*?
(5) Are there *any* parametric values for which a two-part tariff can extract all profit from both retailers?
(6) Can the manufacturer extract all channel profit at all $(f_i - f_j)$ – values, or is the manufacturer's "profit-extraction power" limited?

To answer these questions we derive the optimal wholesale-price policy of a "sophisticated" Stackelberg manufacturer. We use the term "sophisticated" to denote a decision-maker who explicitly considers the *interdependence* between its choice of a per-unit wholesale price and the fixed fee that it can charge. We will prove that every two-part tariff that is manufacturer-optimal for some parametric values is a special case of the sophisticated Stackelberg wholesale-price strategy.

The remainder of the Chapter is organized as follows. In Section 2 we derive the wholesale prices and fixed fees that maximize the profitability of the sophisticated Stackelberg manufacturer selling through independent, competing retailers. In Section 3 we investigate alternative methods of ensuring that neither retailer refuses to participate in the channel. In Section 4 we compare the resulting manufacturer profit with the profit obtained under the alternative two-part tariff wholesale-price policies of Chapter 5.[3] We examine the relationship between the manufacturer's ability to extract profit from the retailers and the parameters of the demand and cost functions in Section 5. In Section 6 we provide a summary and a commentary of the Fixed-Cost Modeling Myth and the Identical-Competitors Meta-Myth. A critical mathematical proof appears in the Appendix.

## 2 OPTIMAL PER-UNIT PRICES AND FIXED FEES: THE BASICS

We model a distribution channel that consists of a single manufacturer selling its product through two competing retailers.[4] The relationship between channel levels is modeled as a two-stage game. In the first stage of the game the manufacturer announces a wholesale-price policy consisting of a per-unit fee and a fixed fee $\{W, \phi\}$. In the second stage each retailer determines its profit-maximizing order quantity and its retail price, given its costs and the demand it faces. In order to ensure comparability across Chapters, we retain the assumptions specified in Chapter 5, Section 2.

We utilize the vertically-integrated results of Chapter 5, Section 3, to assess the performance of the sophisticated Stackelberg wholesale-price strategy relative to the maximum possible channel performance. Because we have already derived the independent retailers' decision rules in Chapter 5, Section 5.1, we move directly to the first stage of the game.

## 2.1 Manufacturer-Stackelberg Leadership

A Stackelberg leader maximizes its own profit ($\hat{\Pi}_M$) subject to the retailers' quantity-reaction functions; this approach is common to "naïve" or "sophisticated" leadership. The difference between these leadership styles lies with the maximization procedure. A naïve leader controls one variable: it *selects* the wholesale price but it *accepts* the fixed fee. A sophisticated leader controls two variables: it simultaneously *selects* the wholesale price *and* the fixed fee.

Note that with competing retailers, a Stackelberg leader faces a *pair* of constraints: both the $i^{th}$ *and* the $j^{th}$ retailer must earn non-negative profit to be willing to participate in the channel. In the following pages we prove that under plausible, well-defined conditions, one of the participation constraints will be violated by the simplest version of the sophisticated Stackelberg tariff. When this occurs the manufacturer must adjust its wholesale-price policy to be able to retain both retailers as channel members. A "semi-sophisticated" leader ensures participation by both retailers solely through manipulation of the fixed fee.[5] The sophisticated Stackelberg leader achieves the same end through a contemporaneous adjustment of the per-unit fee *and* the fixed fee. As a result, the sophisticated leader out-performs the semi-sophisticated leader when either participation constraint would have been violated without an adjustment.

In principle, the pair of retailer participation constraints could be addressed simultaneously; however, for expository purposes we evaluate the manufacturer's maximization problem with respect to each constraint separately. We then confirm that our results are consistent with both constraints. To simplify our exposition, we will assume $Q_i^* > Q_j^*$ throughout this Chapter; this assumption entails no loss of generality.

## 2.2 The Manufacturer's Choice of W Subject to $\hat{\pi}_j^* = 0$

We begin by assuming that the manufacturer structures its two-part tariff to extract all profit from the $j^{th}$ retailer; that is, the $j^{th}$ retailer's participation constraint is strictly binding, while the i[th] retailer's participation constraint may not be binding (i.e., $0 = \hat{\pi}_j^* \le \hat{\pi}_i^*$). We first derive the manufacturer-optimal values for the per-unit wholesale price and the fixed fee given the constraint; then we assess the compatibility of our results with participation by the i[th] retailer. If there are parameters under which the i[th] retailer's profit is negative, we will explore options for retaining that retailer in the channel.

The manufacturer's profit maximand is:

$$\max_{\hat{W},\hat{\phi},\lambda_j} \hat{\Pi}_M = \left( \begin{array}{c} \sum_k \left(\hat{W}(j) - C\right)\left[\hat{Q}_k\left(\hat{W}(j)\right)\right] + 2\hat{\phi}(j) - F \\ +\lambda_j \left( \dfrac{\left[\hat{Q}_j\left(\hat{W}(j)\right)\right]^2}{b} - f_j - \hat{\phi}(j) \right) \end{array} \right), \quad k \in (i,j) \quad (6.2.1)$$

In (6.2.1) the term $[\hat{Q}_k(\hat{W}(j))]$ is the k[th] retailer's quantity-reaction function. This expression is a function of the wholesale price that was defined in equation (5.5.4). The expressions $\hat{W}(j)$ and $\hat{\phi}(j)$ denote the per-unit wholesale price and the fixed fee *given* that the j[th] retailer is the less profitable. A hat ("^") indicates a sophisticated Stackelberg maximization. The (parenthetical) Lagrangian in equation (6.2.1) defines the fixed fee $\hat{\phi}(j)$ which ensures that the j[th] retailer just covers its opportunity cost (i.e., $\hat{\pi}_j^* = 0$).

We take the appropriate derivatives, set them to zero, and simultaneously solve them. This yields three first-order conditions whose solutions identify the optimal fixed fee $\hat{\phi}(j) = [(\hat{Q}_j^2 / b) - f_j]$, the (constrained) number of retailers $\lambda_j = 2$, and the optimal wholesale price:

$$\hat{W}^*(j) = \frac{(2b-\theta)^2\left(Q_i^* - Q_j^*\right) + 2\theta\left(\theta Q_i^* + 2bQ_j^*\right)}{2b(b-\theta)(2b+\theta)} + C \quad (6.2.2)$$

(Asterisks denote optimality.) Given $Q_i^* > Q_j^*$, the wholesale price $\hat{W}^*(j)$ is positive.

Substituting (6.2.2) into the quantity response-function (5.5.4), then inserting the result in the j[th] retailer's profit function (5.5.5), generates the optimal fixed fee:

$$\hat{\phi}^*(j) = \frac{\left[-(2b-3\theta)Q_i^* + (6b-\theta)Q_j^*\right]^2}{4b(2b+\theta)^2} - f_j \quad (6.2.3)$$

The pair (6.2.2) and (6.2.3) defines the two-part tariff $\hat{\tau}^*(j) \equiv \{\hat{W}^*(j), \hat{\phi}^*(j)\}$.[6]

The tariff $\hat{\tau}^*(j)$ was derived subject to a constraint that ensured the j[th] retailer's channel participation. Will the $i^{th}$ retailer also participate in the channel? The answer depends on the $i^{th}$ retailer's participation constraint. Algebraic manipulation of this constraint reveals that the $i^{th}$ retailer will participate in the channel when the difference in retailer fixed costs satisfies the following condition:

$$\left(f_i - f_j\right) \leq \frac{2\left(Q_i^* - Q_j^*\right)\left[3\theta Q_i^* + \left(4b - \theta\right)Q_j^*\right]}{\left(2b + \theta\right)^2} \equiv L^{SS^*} \qquad (6.2.4)$$

Condition (6.2.4) will be violated by *any* $(f_i - f_j)$ that is greater than $L^{SS^*}$. Should the difference in fixed costs fall above this bound, the $i^{th}$ retailer earns negative profits and will refuse to participate in the channel. This violates the fundamental assumption under which the tariff $\hat{\tau}^*(j)$ was derived—channel participation by both retailers. Thus, if $(f_i - f_j) > L^{SS^*}$, we must seek an alternative tariff that retains both retailers in the channel. We begin our search by modifying the Lagrangian constraint.

## 2.3 The Manufacturer's Choice of W Subject to $\hat{\pi}_i^* = 0$

We have derived the manufacturer-optimal two-part tariff under the assumption that the $i^{th}$ retailer participates in the channel. When this assumption is incorrect—that is, when condition (6.2.4) is violated—the manufacturer must use a different two-part tariff. To derive this alternative tariff, we assume that the $i^{th}$ retailer's participation constraint is binding, while the $j^{th}$ retailer's is not binding (i.e., $\hat{\pi}_j^* \geq \hat{\pi}_i^* = 0$). We use the same logic employed in the previous sub-Section, but we reverse the $i^{th}$ and the $j^{th}$ subscripts in the Lagrangian constraint (6.2.1). We then calculate the first-order conditions and proceed in the same manner as above. The resulting wholesale price and fixed fee mimic equations (6.2.2) and (6.2.3) with the $i^{th}$ and $j^{th}$ subscripts reversed.

Despite this symmetry there is a key difference: the wholesale margin $(\hat{W}^*(i) - C)$ will be *negative* at a sufficiently low level of inter-retailer competition (as $\theta \to 0$).[7] This leads to a retail price that is even lower than in a vertically-integrated system. In this extreme case the manufacturer loses money on every unit, but the fixed fee more than compensates the manufacturer for these losses. An abnormally low wholesale price reverberates downstream; it increases retail margins while lowering prices to consumers. The result is higher volume and higher net revenue for both retailers—and thus a higher fixed fee. (For a similar finding in the context of non-competing retailers, see Section 4.3 of Chapter 3).

Using the same logic presented in the previous sub-Section, we note that the two-part tariff $\tau^*(i) \equiv \{\hat{W}^*(i), \hat{\phi}^*(i)\}$ is consistent with the assumed profit relationship $\hat{\pi}_j^* \geq \hat{\pi}_i^* = 0$ if and only if:

$$(f_i - f_j) \geq \frac{2(Q_i^* - Q_j^*)\left[(4b-\theta)Q_i^* + 3\theta Q_j^*\right]}{(2b+\theta)^2} \equiv U^{SS^*} \tag{6.2.5}$$

The term $U^{SS^*}$ is positive by virtue of our expository assumption $Q_i^* > Q_j^*$. Condition (6.2.5) will be violated by all $(f_i - f_j) < 0$ and also by any positive $(f_i - f_j)$ that is sufficiently close to zero.

A simple comparison reveals that, when $Q_i^* > Q_j^*$, the participation constraints have the relationship: $0 < L^{SS^*} < U^{SS^*}$. The difference in retailers' fixed costs $(f_i - f_j)$ may lie below $L^{SS^*}$, above $U^{SS^*}$, or between $L^{SS^*}$ and $U^{SS^*}$. Thus the sophisticated Stackelberg manufacturer faces three "Zones" in $\langle f_i - f_j \rangle$-space. We label these Zones $Z_j^{SS^*}$, $Z_{ij}^{SS^*}$, and $Z_i^{SS^*}$; we define them in the following manner:

$$\begin{aligned} L^{SS^*} &> (f_i - f_j) && \rightarrow \text{Zone } Z_j^{SS^*} \\ L^{SS^*} \leq (f_i - f_j) &\leq U^{SS^*} && \rightarrow \text{Zone } Z_{ij}^{SS^*} \\ (f_i - f_j) &> U^{SS^*} && \rightarrow \text{Zone } Z_i^{SS^*} \end{aligned} \tag{6.2.6}$$

In Zone $Z_j^{SS^*}$, the manufacturer charges the tariff $\hat{\tau}^*(j)$ that was derived under the assumption that $0 = \hat{\pi}_j^* \leq \hat{\pi}_i^*$. In Zone $Z_i^{SS^*}$ the manufacturer charges the tariff $\hat{\tau}^*(i)$ that was derived under the assumption that $\hat{\pi}_j^* \geq \hat{\pi}_i^* = 0$. In both Zones the retailers' profits are compatible with channel participation. Table 6.1 catalogs the prices, quantities and profits for Zones $Z_j^{SS^*}$ and $Z_i^{SS^*}$.

*Table 6.1.* The Sophisticated Stackelberg Tariff: Zone $Z_j^{ss*}$

| | |
|---|---|
| The $i^{th}$ Retailer's Price | $\hat{p}_i^*(j)=\left(\frac{3(2b-\theta)Q_i^*-(2b-5\theta)Q_j^*}{2(b-\theta)(2b+\theta)}\right)+c_i+C$ |
| The $j^{th}$ Retailer's Price | $\hat{p}_j^*(j)=\left(\frac{Q_i^*+Q_j^*}{2(b-\theta)}\right)+c_j+C$ |
| The $i^{th}$ Retailer's Quantity | $\hat{Q}_i^*(j)=\left(\frac{(2b+3\theta)Q_i^*+(2b-\theta)Q_j^*}{2(2b+\theta)}\right)$ |
| The $j^{th}$ Retailer's Quantity | $\hat{Q}_j^*(j)=\left(\frac{-(2b-3\theta)Q_i^*+(6b-\theta)Q_j^*}{2(2b+\theta)}\right)$ |
| Total Quantity | $\sum_k \hat{Q}_k^*(j)=\left(\frac{3\theta Q_i^*+(4b-\theta)Q_j^*}{(2b+\theta)}\right)$ |
| The $i^{th}$ Retailer's Profit | $\hat{\pi}_i^*(j)=2\left(\frac{3\theta(Q_i^*)^2+4(b-\theta)Q_i^*Q_j^*-(4b-\theta)(Q_j^*)^2}{(2b+\theta)^2}\right)-(f_i-f_j)$ |
| The $j^{th}$ Retailer's Profit | $\hat{\pi}_j^*(j)=0$ |
| The Manufacturer's Net Revenue | $\hat{R}_M^*(j)=\left(\frac{3\theta(4b^2-4b\theta+3\theta^2)(Q_i^*)^2+2(8b^3-16b^2\theta+20b\theta^2-3\theta^3)Q_i^*Q_j^*-(16b^3-36b^2\theta+12b\theta^2-\theta^3)(Q_j^*)^2}{2b(b-\theta)(2b+\theta)^2}\right)$ |
| The Manufacturer's Profit | $\hat{\Pi}_M^*(j)=\left(\frac{(4b^2-4b\theta+9\theta^2)(Q_i^*)^2-2(4b^2-16b\theta+3\theta^2)Q_i^*Q_j^*+(20b^2-12b\theta+\theta^2)(Q_j^*)^2}{2(b-\theta)(2b+\theta)^2}\right)-2f_j-F$ |
| Channel Profit | $\hat{\Pi}_C^*(j)=\left(\frac{(4b^2+8b\theta-3\theta^2)(Q_i^*)^2+2(4b^2+5\theta^2)Q_i^*Q_j^*+(4b^2+8b\theta-3\theta^2)(Q_j^*)^2}{2(b-\theta)(2b+\theta)^2}\right)-f_i-f_j-F$ |

**Note**: Results in Zone $Z_i^{ss*}$ are obtained by reversing the $i^{th}$ and $j^{th}$ subscripts above and changing the parenthetical (j)'s to (i)'s.

However, *neither* strategy can be applied in Zone $Z_{ij}^{SS^*}$ without violating the assumption under which that strategy was derived. If the manufacturer charges $\hat{\tau}^*(j)$ in Zone $Z_{ij}^{SS^*}$, the i[th] retailer will earn a negative profit and therefore will not participate in the channel. And, if the manufacturer charges $\hat{\tau}^*(i)$ in Zone $Z_{ij}^{SS^*}$, the j[th] retailer will earn a negative profit and will not participate. The manufacturer must "adjust" its wholesale-price strategy in Zone $Z_{ij}^{SS^*}$ to retain both retailers. We now address this issue.

# 3 ENSURING PARTICIPATION WITH AN OPTIMAL PER-UNIT WHOLESALE PRICE AND FIXED FEE

The need to adjust the wholesale-prices derived in Section 2 is due to the existence of Zone $Z_{ij}^{SS^*}$. Within this Zone each tariff violates one of the retailer participation constraints. We begin our analysis with a discussion of the range of $(f_i - f_j)$ – values over which one retailer abandons the channel. In short, we begin this Section by detailing the "width" of Zone $Z_{ij}^{SS^*}$. We then turn to methods of ensuring participation by both retailers within this Zone.

There are two possible techniques for adjusting the two-part tariffs $\hat{\tau}^*(j)$ and $\hat{\tau}^*(i)$ to guarantee participation by both retailers. One method entails a "semi-sophisticated adjustment" to the wholesale-price policies identified in the previous Section; it is similar to the approach we took in Chapter 4. The other approach involves what we call a "sophisticated adjustment." We describe both methods, and then we contrast the results of the sophisticated adjustment to those obtained in a vertically-integrated system. We conclude with a simple numerical analysis to illustrate our key findings.

## 3.1 The Width of Zone $Z_{ij}^{SS^*}$

We define the width of Zone $Z_{ij}^{SS^*}$ as:

$$\left(U^{SS^*} - L^{SS^*}\right) = \left(\frac{8(b-\theta)\left(Q_i^* - Q_j^*\right)^2}{(2b+\theta)^2}\right) \geq 0 \tag{6.3.1}$$

It is clear from expression (6.3.1) that the width—and thus the importance—of this Zone declines (i) as the intensity of competition approaches one (as $\theta \to b$) and (ii) as the retailers approach equality in their channel-coordinated output levels. In particular, notice that when ($Q_i^* = Q_j^*$) the width of Zone $Z_{ij}^{SS^*}$ is zero. This should not be surprising, because:

$$Q_i^* = Q_j^* \quad \to \quad \hat{W}^*(j) = \hat{W}^*(i) = T_i^* = T_j^* \tag{6.3.2}$$

(We defined the optimal transfer price $T_i^*$ with equation (5.3.7)). When competitors are identical, the optimal manufacturer per-unit price is equal to the optimal wholesale price; a single two-part tariff coordinates the channel and maximizes manufacturer profit for this special case. It follows that the common assumption of identical competitors ($Q_i^* = Q_j^*$) is far from innocuous; it eliminates a major convolution in the manufacturer's pricing policy. We develop the details of this intricacy below.

## 3.2 The Semi-Sophisticated Adjustment

We have identified a pair of two-part tariffs labeled $\hat{\tau}^*(j)$ and $\hat{\tau}^*(i)$. Each comprises a per-unit fee ($\hat{W}^*(j)$ or $\hat{W}^*(i)$) and a fixed fee ($\hat{\phi}^*(j)$ or $\hat{\phi}^*(i)$).[8] We start by solving for the necessary adjustment to $\hat{\tau}^*(j)$, then we calculate the resulting profit for the manufacturer. We then retrace our steps with $\hat{W}^*(i)$ as our baseline. We denote the manufacturer's profit, given the per-unit wholesale price $\hat{W}^*(k)$, $k \in (i, j)$, with the symbol $\hat{\Pi}_M^*(k)$. Because the process examined here adjusts the fixed fee while leaving the per-unit fee unchanged, we refer to this process as a semi-sophisticated adjustment.

With the two-part tariff $\hat{\tau}^*(j)$, the $i^{th}$ retailer's non-negativity profit constraint is *not* binding in Zone $Z_j^{SS^*}$. Thus increases in $f_i$ have no impact on the *manufacturer's* profit, but they do reduce the profit of the $i^{th}$ retailer (and the channel). However, if the manufacturer were to employ the tariff $\hat{\tau}^*(j)$ in Zone $Z_{ij}^{SS^*}$ or $Z_i^{SS^*}$, the $i^{th}$ retailer would earn a negative profit. If the manufacturer wants to use tariff $\hat{\tau}^*(j)$ in these Zones while retaining the $i^{th}$ retailer as a channel member, then the manufacturer must decrease the fixed fee. To be specific, when $(f_i - f_j) > L^{SS^*}$, each \$1 increase in $f_i$ must be accompanied by a \$1 decrease in the fixed fee component of $\hat{\tau}^*(j)$. Every dollar of this adjustment decreases $\hat{\Pi}_M^*(j)$ by \$2, because both retailers pay the same fixed fee. Thus $\hat{\Pi}^{*}_{M}(j)$ is a constant function of $(f_i - f_j)$ in Zone $Z^{SS*}_{j}$ and has a slope of $-\$2$ in Zones $Z^{SS*}_{ij}$ and $Z^{SS*}_{i}$. The *solid* line ("abcd") in Figure 6.1 graphically displays the relationship between $\hat{\Pi}^{*}_{M}(j)$ and $(f_i - f_j)$ at a constant $f_j$. (Please ignore the dashed lines and line thickness for now.)

Now consider the case of the manufacturer charging the two-part tariff $\hat{\tau}^{*}(i)$. Under this wholesale-price strategy, the $i^{th}$ retailer is the less profitable in Zone $Z^{SS*}_{i}$ but the *more-profitable* retailer in Zones $Z^{SS*}_{j}$ and $Z^{SS*}_{ij}$. Any increase in $f_i$ reduces the $i^{th}$ retailer's profit but has no impact on manufacturer profit in Zone $Z^{SS*}_{j}$ or $Z^{SS*}_{ij}$. However, in Zone $Z^{SS*}_{i}$ an increase in $f_i$ must be matched by a \$1 decrease in the fixed fee. Without this adjustment the $i^{th}$ retailer will not participate in the channel. Because the fixed fee is common to both retailers, the value of $\hat{\Pi}^{*}_{M}(i)$ will decline by \$2 for every \$1 increase in $f_i$ inside Zone $Z^{SS*}_{i}$. (In the other Zones the value of $\hat{\Pi}^{*}_{M}(i)$ is invariant with respect to $(f_i - f_j)$). The relationship between $\hat{\Pi}^{*}_{M}(i)$ and $(f_i - f_j)$ is depicted by the *dashed* line ("ecgh") in Figure 6.1. (Please ignore the thickness of the lines for now.)

Profits $\hat{\Pi}^{*}_{M}(j)$ and $\hat{\Pi}^{*}_{M}(i)$ intersect at the midpoint of Zone $Z^{SS*}_{ij}$; we label this point $Z^{SS^*}$; its value is

$$Z^{SS^*} \equiv \left[\left(L^{SS*} + U^{SS*}\right)/2\right] = \left[2\left(Q^{*}_{i} - Q^{*}_{j}\right)\left(Q^{*}_{i} + Q^{*}_{j}\right)/\left(2b + \theta\right)\right] \qquad (6.3.3)$$

When $(f_i - f_j) \le Z^{SS^*}$, the manufacturer prefers the wholesale-price strategy $\hat{\tau}^{*}(j)$; otherwise, the manufacturer prefers $\hat{\tau}^{*}(i)$. This conditional policy is depicted in Figure 6.1 by the *thick* solid and dashed lines ("abcgh) that intersect at $Z^{SS^*}$.

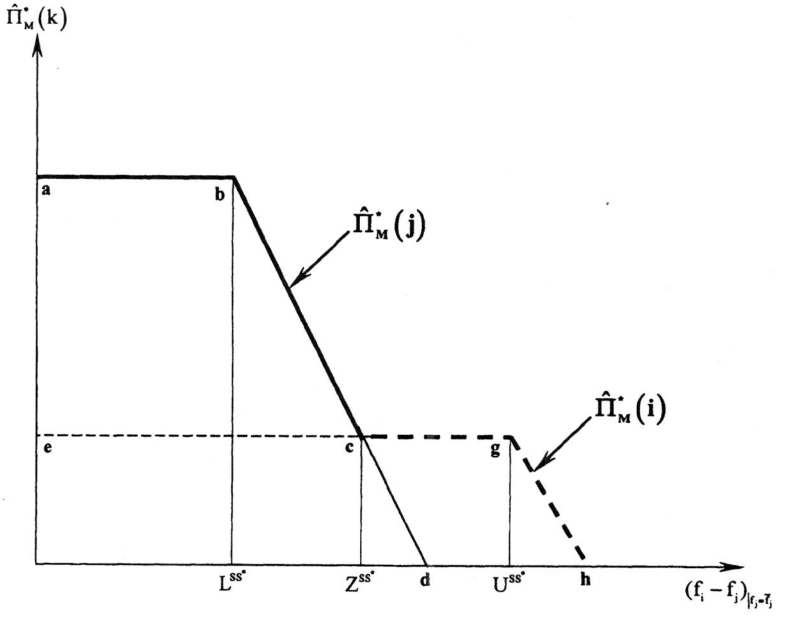


Legend:

$\hat{\Pi}_M(k) \equiv$ Manufacturer profit when the $k^{th}$ retailer's profit constraint is used in the manufacturer's maximand;

$f_k \equiv$ Fixed cost of the $k^{th}$ retailer, $k \in (i, j)$;

$L^{ss^*} \equiv$ Lower bound below which the $i^{th}$ retailer earns a positive profit;

$U^{ss^*} \equiv$ Upper bound above which the $j^{th}$ retailer earns a positive profit; and

$Z^{ss^*} \equiv (L^{ss^*} + U^{ss^*})/2$.

This Figure is drawn for a constant level of $f_j$.

*Figure 6.1.* Manufacturer Profit Given a Semi-Sophisticated Adjustment to the Fixed Fee

In sum, *if* the manufacturer's wholesale-price strategies are confined to $\{\hat{W}^*(j),\hat{\phi}^*(j)\}$ or $\{\hat{W}^*(i),\hat{\phi}^*(i)\}$, then the optimal *semi-sophisticated* wholesale-price strategy is:

$$\begin{aligned}
(f_i - f_j) \le L^{ss^*} \quad &\rightarrow \quad \{\hat{W}^*(j), \hat{\phi}^*(j)\} \\
L^{ss^*} < (f_i - f_j) \le Z^{ss^*} \quad &\rightarrow \quad \{\hat{W}^*(j), [\hat{\phi}^*(j) - \{(f_i - f_j) - L^{ss^*}\}]\} \\
Z^{ss^*} \le (f_i - f_j) \le U^{ss^*} \quad &\rightarrow \quad \{\hat{W}^*(i), \hat{\phi}^*(i)\} \\
(f_i - f_j) \ge U^{ss^*} \quad &\rightarrow \quad \{\hat{W}^*(i), [\hat{\phi}^*(i) - \{(f_i - f_j) - U^{ss^*}\}]\}
\end{aligned} \tag{6.3.4}$$

Expression (6.3.4) states that the optimal per-unit wholesale price is $\hat{W}^*(j)$ if the retailers' fixed-cost difference is less than $Z^{ss^*}$; otherwise the wholesale price should be $\hat{W}^*(i)$. The fixed fee decision is more complex. The fixed fee is $\hat{\phi}^*(j)$ when the fixed-cost difference is less than $L^{ss^*}$. If the fixed-cost difference lies between $L^{ss^*}$ and $Z^{ss^*}$, then the fixed fee is equal to $\hat{\phi}^*(j)$ minus the difference between $(f_i - f_j)$ and $L^{ss^*}$. Thus, there is a dollar-for-dollar decline in the fixed fee as $(f_i - f_j)$ rises from $L^{ss^*}$ to $Z^{ss^*}$. When the fixed-cost difference is greater than $Z^{ss^*}$ but less than $U^{ss^*}$, the fixed fee is $\hat{\phi}^*(i)$. Finally, when the fixed-cost difference exceeds $U^{ss^*}$, the fixed fee is equal to $\hat{\phi}^*(i)$ minus the difference between $(f_i - f_j)$ and $U^{ss^*}$. We again see a dollar-for-dollar decline in the fixed fee as $(f_i - f_j)$ rises above $U^{ss^*}$.

How does this semi-sophisticated Stackelberg pricing policy compare to the "naïve" Stackelberg price policy described in Chapter 5? The wholesale prices can be ranked as:

$$\begin{aligned}
\hat{W}^*(j) \gtrless \hat{W}^* \quad &\text{as} \quad (2b - 3\theta)Q_i^* \gtrless (6b - \theta)Q_j^* \\
\hat{W}^*(i) \gtrless \hat{W}^* \quad &\text{as} \quad (6b - \theta)Q_i^* \gtrless (2b - 3\theta)Q_j^*
\end{aligned} \tag{6.3.5}$$

It can be shown that the fixed fee under a naïve Stackelberg policy must lie between $\hat{\phi}^*(j)$ and $\hat{\phi}^*(i)$. Also, the critical $(f_i - f_j)$-value at which the manufacturer's profit function has a kink occurs between $L^{ss^*}$ and $U^{ss^*}$. In the vicinity of this kink, the naïve Stackelberg strategy generates greater manufacturer profit than does the semi-sophisticated Stackelberg strategy, but the latter is manufacturer profit-dominant elsewhere.[9] Because the naïve approach to leadership dominates the semi-sophisticated strategy for some

$(f_i - f_j)$ – values, it is clear that the semi-sophisticated strategy is *not* globally optimal for the manufacturer. To find a globally optimal strategy, we turn to a more subtle approach for ensuring retailer participation when $(f_i - f_j)$ lies in Zone $Z_{ij}^{SS^*}$.

## 3.3 The Sophisticated Adjustment

The essence of the sophisticated adjustment is *to vary the per-unit fee and the fixed fee simultaneously* within Zone $Z_{ij}^{SS^*}$. Synchronized variation of all elements under managerial control is reminiscent of our result in Chapter 3: the manufacturer selling through N non-competing retailers maximizes its own profit by concurrently adjusting the per-unit fee and the fixed fee.

The optimal wholesale price in Zone $Z_{ij}^{SS^*}$ (given $Q_i^* > Q_j^*$) is:

$$\begin{aligned}\hat{W}^*(\omega) &= \omega\hat{W}^*(i) + (1-\omega)\hat{W}^*(j), \qquad \omega \in (0,1) \\ &= \hat{W}^*(j) - \left(\frac{2\omega(2b-\theta)(Q_i^* - Q_j^*)}{b(2b+\theta)}\right)\end{aligned} \tag{6.3.6}$$

In equation (6.3.6) we define ω as:

$$1 \geq \omega \equiv \left(\frac{(f_i - f_j) - L^{SS^*}}{U^{SS^*} - L^{SS^*}}\right) \geq 0 \quad \forall \quad U^{SS^*} \geq (f_i - f_j) \geq L^{SS^*} > 0 \tag{6.3.7}$$

The value of ω is determined by the difference in retailer fixed costs and by the elements of $U^{SS^*}$ and $L^{SS^*}$ (i.e., b, θ, $Q_i^*$ and $Q_j^*$). Because the definition of ω assumes that $(f_i - f_j)$ lies in the interval defined b $L^{SS^*}$ and $U^{SS^*}$, ω must lie in the unit interval. The midpoint of Zone $Z_{ij}^{SS^*}$ $(Z^{SS^*})$, occurs at $\omega = ½$. Figure 6.2 illustrates relationships among $\hat{W}^*(j)$, $\hat{W}^*(i)$, and $\hat{W}^*(\omega)$, given $Q_i^* > Q_j^*$.

$\hat{W}^*(\omega)$ is a decreasing function of $(f_i - f_j)$, with the rate of decline depending on $S_j \equiv Q_j^*/(Q_i^* + Q_j^*)$. As $S_j \to ½$, $[\partial\hat{W}^*(\omega)/\partial(f_i - f_j)] \to 0$. In the extreme case of identical retailers, there is only one wholesale price (i.e., $\hat{W}^*(j) = \hat{W}^*(i) = \hat{W}^*(\omega)$).

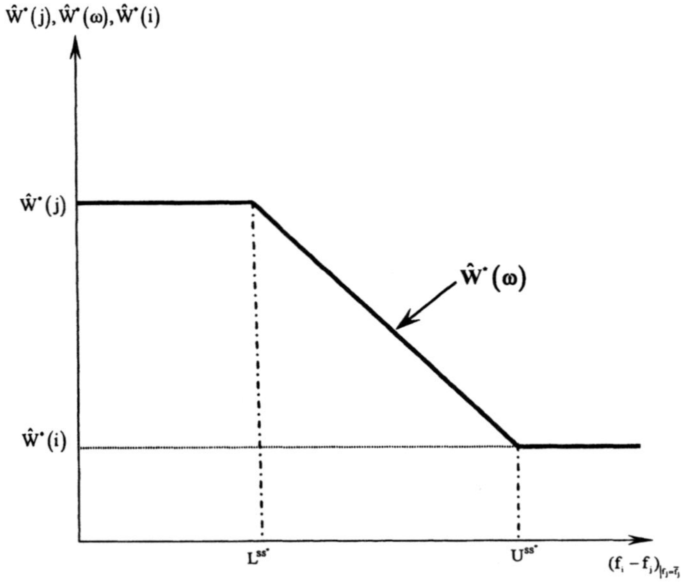


Legend:

$W(\square) \equiv$ Manufacturer-optimal per-unit wholesale-price with a sophisticated Stackelberg tariff;

$f_k$ $\equiv$ Fixed cost of the $k^{th}$ retailer;

$L^{ss^*}$ $\equiv$ Lower bound of the difference in fixed costs (below this bound the $i^{th}$ retailer earns positive profit); and

$U^{ss^*}$ $\equiv$ Upper bound of the difference in fixed costs (above this bound the $j^{th}$ retailer earns positive profit).

This Figure is drawn for a constant level of $f_j$.

*Figure 6.2.* The Sophisticated Stackelberg per-Unit Wholesale Price

The wholesale price (6.3.6) implies that the fixed fee in Zone $Z_{ij}^{SS^*}$ is:

$$\begin{aligned}\hat{\phi}^*(\omega) &= \frac{\left[\hat{Q}_j^*(\omega)\right]^2}{b} - f_j \\ &= \frac{\begin{pmatrix} -(2b-3\theta)Q_i^* + (6b-\theta)Q_j^* \\ +4\omega(b-\theta)(Q_i^* - Q_j^*) \end{pmatrix}^2}{4b(2b+\theta)^2} - f_j \end{aligned} \tag{6.3.8}$$

As $(f_i - f_j)$ increases through Zone $Z_{ij}^{SS^*}$, the fixed fee also increases.

The information in expressions (6.3.6) and (6.3.8) reduces to the sophisticated Stackelberg, wholesale-price decision rule:

$$\left\{\hat{W}^*, \hat{\phi}^*\right\} \equiv \begin{cases} \left\{\hat{W}^*(j), \hat{\phi}^*(j)\right\} & \forall \ L^{SS^*} > (f_i - f_j) \quad \leftrightarrow \ \text{Zone } Z_j^{SS^*} \\ \left\{\hat{W}^*(\omega), \hat{\phi}^*(\omega)\right\} & \forall \ L^{SS^*} \leq (f_i - f_j) \leq U^{SS^*} \quad \leftrightarrow \ \text{Zone } Z_{ij}^{SS^*} \\ \left\{\hat{W}^*(i), \hat{\phi}^*(i)\right\} & \forall \ (f_i - f_j) > U^{SS^*} \quad \leftrightarrow \ \text{Zone } Z_i^{SS^*} \end{cases} \tag{6.3.9}$$

Figure 6.3 illustrates the relationship between the manufacturer's profits and $(f_i - f_j)$ under the sophisticated Stackelberg tariff. In this Figure, the thick, curved line "abgh" depicts *manufacturer* profit. We have also lightly embedded Figure 6.1 in Figure 6.3 to simplify the comparison between the semi-sophisticated adjustment and the sophisticated adjustment.

The sophisticated Stackelberg strategy strictly dominates the semi-sophisticated strategy within Zone $Z_{ij}^{SS^*}$, while the policies are identical in Zones $Z_j^{SS^*}$ and $Z_i^{SS^*}$. Note that the sophisticated strategy extracts all profit from both retailers in Zone $Z_{ij}^{SS^*}$. (The proof of this statement is in the Appendix.) Finally, there is a maximum value of the i[th] retailer's fixed cost that is compatible with channel existence. We denote this value as $\overline{f}_i^{SS^*}$; it is a function of the j[th] retailer's fixed cost $f_j$:

$$\overline{f}_i^{SS^*} = \left(R_C^{SS^*} + U^{SS^*} - F_j\right)/2 \tag{6.3.10}$$

Manufacturer profits are negative when $f_i > \overline{f}_i^{SS^*}$. The value $\overline{f}_i^{SS^*}$ appears in Figure 6.3 as the point "h".

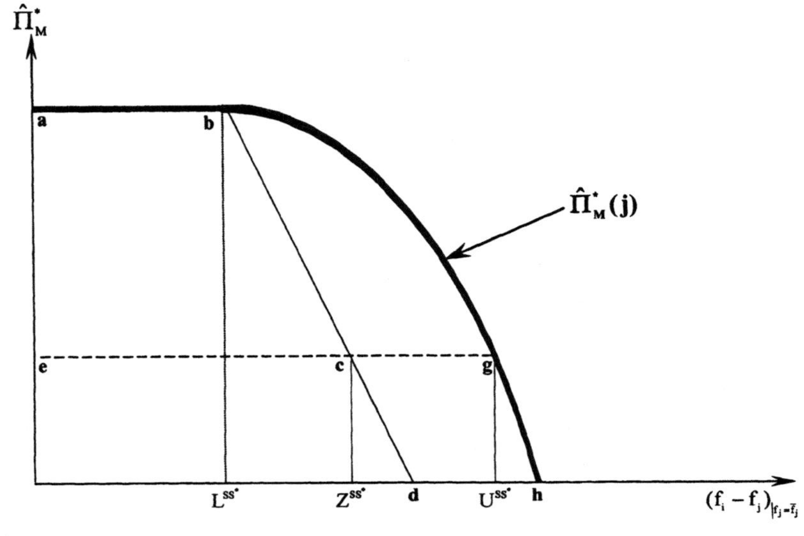


Legend:

$\hat{\Pi}^{ss^*}_M$ ≡ Channel profit when the sophisticated Stackelberg two-part tariff is utilized;

$f_k$ ≡ Fixed cost of the $k^{th}$ retailer, $k \in (i, j)$;

$L^{ss^*}$ ≡ Lower bound below which the $i^{th}$ retailer earns a positive profit;

$U^{ss^*}$ ≡ Upper bound above which the $j^{th}$ retailer earns a positive profit; and

$Z^{ss^*} \equiv (L^{ss^*} + U^{ss^*})/2$.

This Figure is drawn for a constant level of $f_j$.

*Figure 6.3.* Manufacturer Profit with a Sophisticated Stackelberg Two-Part Tariff

A graphical representation of *channel profit* is presented in Figure 6.4; it augments the preceding Figure with information on channel profit in Zones $Z^{ss^*}_i$ and $Z^{ss^*}_j$. For comparative purposes the Figure also depicts the profit of a coordinated channel. Note that *no* Stackelberg strategy can coordinate the channel. Thus the line depicting the total profit of a coordinated channel lies above the sophisticated Stackelberg channel profit line at all $(f_i - f_j)$ – levels. The minimal difference between the profit of a coordinated channel and channel profit with sophisticated Stackelberg pricing occurs at $Z^{ss^*}$, where $\omega = ½$.

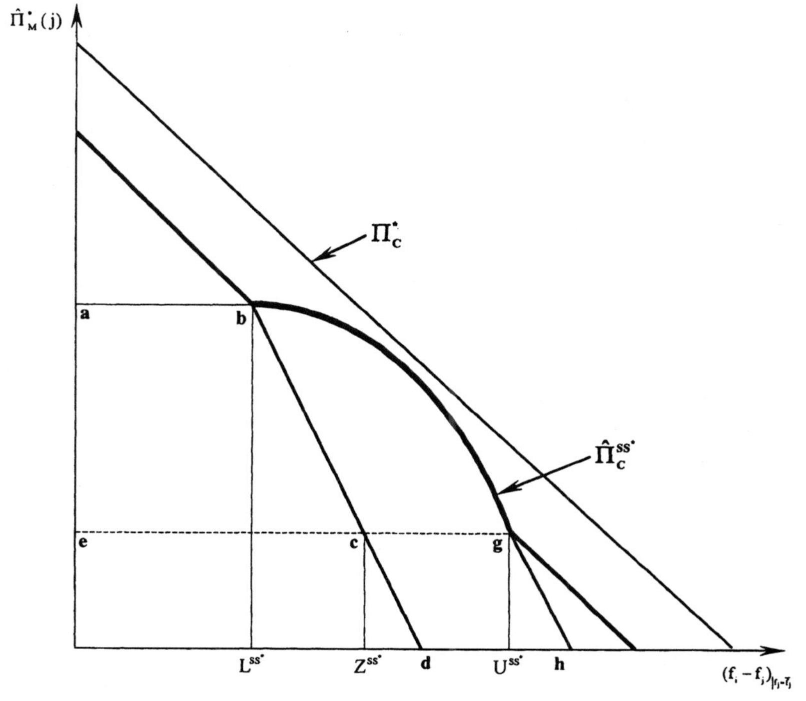


Legend:

$\hat{\Pi}^{ss^*}_M \equiv$ Channel profit when the sophisticated Stackelberg two-part tariff is utilized;

$\Pi_I \equiv$ Channel profit when the channel is coordinated;

$f_k \equiv$ Fixed cost of the $k^{th}$ retailer, $k \in (i, j)$;

$L^{SS^*} \equiv$ Lower bound below which the $i^{th}$ retailer earns a positive profit;

$U^{SS^*} \equiv$ Upper bound above which the $j^{th}$ retailer earns a positive profit; and

$Z^{SS^*} \equiv (L^{SS^*} + U^{SS^*})/2$.

This Figure is drawn for a constant level of $f_j$.

*Figure 6.4.* Channel Profit with a Sophisticated Stackelberg Two-Part Tariff

*Table 6.2.* The Sophisticated Stackelberg Tariff: Zone $Z_{ij}^{SS*}$

| | |
|---|---|
| The i$^{th}$ Retailer's Price | $\hat{p}_i^*(\omega)=\{\hat{p}_i^*(j)-z_\omega\}$ s.t. $z_\omega \equiv \left(\dfrac{2\omega(Q_i^*-Q_j^*)}{(2b+\theta)}\right)$ |
| The j$^{th}$ Retailer's Price | $\hat{p}_j^*(j)=\{\hat{p}_j^*(j)-z_\omega\}$ |
| The i$^{th}$ Retailer's Quantity | $\hat{Q}_i^*(\omega)=(\hat{Q}_i^*(j)+(b-\theta)z_\omega)$ |
| The j$^{th}$ Retailer's Quantity | $\hat{Q}_j^*(\omega)=(\hat{Q}_j^*(j)+(b-\theta)z_\omega)$ |
| The Retailer's Profits | $\hat{\pi}_i^*(\omega)=0=\hat{\pi}_j^*(\omega)$ |
| Manufacturer and Channel Profit | $\hat{\Pi}_M^*(\omega)=\hat{\Pi}_C^*(\omega)=\left\{\hat{\Pi}_C^*(j)+\dfrac{2(1-\omega)(b-\theta)z_\omega^2}{\omega}\right\}$ |

## 3.4 Optimal Quantities, Prices and Profits

Table 6.2 catalogs the quantities sold, prices charged, margins earned and profit obtained in Zone $Z_{ij}^{SS*}$. An interesting point is that the per-unit margin obtained by the smaller (illustratively, the j$^{th}$) retailer is *less* than the per-unit margin realized by the i$^{th}$ retailer in all the Zones. This duplicates the margin ranking in the vertically-integrated system. Similarly, the quantity ranking $(Q_i > Q_j)$ also holds in all three Zones

## 3.5 Comparisons with a Vertically-Integrated System

Table 6.3 compares prices and quantities of a vertically-integrated system with those from an independent manufacturer/retailers model with sophisticated Stackelberg leadership. Given our expository assumption $(Q_i^* > Q_j^*)$, we observe[10] that $\hat{W}^*(j) > T_j^* > T_i^* > \hat{W}^*(i)$. If the difference in the retailers' fixed costs places the sophisticated Stackelberg manufacturer in Zone $Z_j^{SS*}$ $(Z_i^{SS*})$, then the per-unit wholesale-price exceeds (falls short of) the vertically-integrated transfer prices. Within Zone $Z_{ij}^{SS*}$ the wholesale price may lie above, between, or below the vertically-integrated transfer prices.

*Table 6.3.* The Sophisticated Stackelberg Tariff *vs.* the Vertically-Integrated System

| | |
|---|---|
| | $W_i^*, W_j^* \gtrless \hat{W}^*(j)$ as $Q_j^* \gtrless Q_i^*$ |
| | $p_i^* \gtrless \hat{p}_i^*(j)$ as $Q_j^* \gtrless Q_i^*$ |
| Zone $Z_j^{ss^*}$ | $p_j^* \gtrless \hat{p}_j^*(j)$ as $Q_j^* \gtrless Q_i^*$ |
| | $Q_i^* \gtrless \hat{Q}_i^*(j)$ as $Q_j^* \gtrless Q_i^*$ |
| | $Q_j^* \gtrless \hat{Q}_j^*(j)$ as $(2b-3\theta)(Q_i^*-Q_j^*) \gtrless 0$ |
| | $W_i^* \gtrless \hat{W}^*(\omega)$ as $\begin{bmatrix} 4b^2(1-2\omega)-4b\theta\omega \\ -\theta^2(3-4\omega) \end{bmatrix}(Q_i^*-Q_j^*) \gtrless 0$ |
| | $W_j^* \gtrless \hat{W}^*(\omega)$ as $\begin{bmatrix} 4b^2(1-2\omega) \\ +\theta(4b-\theta)(1-\omega) \end{bmatrix}(Q_i^*-Q_j^*) \gtrless 0$ |
| Zone $Z_{ij}^{ss^*}$ | $p_i^* \gtrless p_i^*(\omega)$ as $[2b(1-2\omega)+\theta(3-4\omega)](Q_i^*-Q_j^*) \lessgtr 0$ |
| | $p_j^* \gtrless p_j^*(\omega)$ as $[2b(1-2\omega)+\theta(1-4\omega)](Q_i^*-Q_j^*) \lessgtr 0$ |
| | $Q_i^* \gtrless Q_i^*(\omega)$ as $[2b(1-2\omega)-\theta(1-4\omega)](Q_i^*-Q_j^*) \gtrless 0$ |

**Note:**
Zone $Z_i^{ss^*}$ results may be obtained by reversing the $i^{th}$ and $j^{th}$ subscripts for Zone $Z_j^{ss^*}$.

Given these per-unit wholesale price relationships, it is not surprising to find that a similar relationship holds for retail prices. However, the ω value at which $\hat{p}_i^*(\omega) = p_i^*$ differs from the ω value at which $\hat{p}_j^*(\omega) = p_j^*$:

$$\begin{aligned} \hat{p}_i^*(\omega) &\gtrless p_i^* \quad \text{as} \quad \frac{(2b+3\theta)}{4(b+\theta)} \gtrless \omega \quad \text{and} \\ \hat{p}_j^*(\omega) &\gtrless p_j^* \quad \text{as} \quad \frac{(2b+\theta)}{4(b+\theta)} \gtrless \omega \end{aligned} \tag{6.3.11}$$

By using the expressions in (6.3.11), we can compare the prices paid by consumers who buy from a vertically-integrated system with those who purchase from a decentralized channel with sophisticated Stackelberg leadership by the manufacturer. We find:

$$\begin{aligned} &\hat{p}_i^*(\omega) > p_i^* \text{ and } \hat{p}_j^*(\omega) > p_j^* \quad \forall \quad \omega < \frac{(2b+\theta)}{4(b+\theta)} \\ &\hat{p}_i^*(\omega) > p_i^* \text{ but } \hat{p}_j^*(\omega) < p_j^* \quad \forall \quad \frac{(2b+3\theta)}{4(b+\theta)} > \omega > \frac{(2b+\theta)}{4(b+\theta)} \\ &\hat{p}_i^*(\omega) < p_i^* \text{ and } \hat{p}_j^*(\omega) < p_j^* \quad \forall \quad \frac{(2b+3\theta)}{4(b+\theta)} < \omega \end{aligned} \tag{6.3.12}$$

Depending on the difference in retailers' fixed costs, consumers may be better or worse off under non-coordinating, sophisticated Stackelberg leadership than they are with a coordinated, vertically-integrated system. This deduction runs counter to Spengler's analysis (1950) of the vertical-channel relationship that generates the higher consumers' surplus in a bilateral monopoly.

It is apparent from Table 6.3 that no simple statement describes the relationship between the sophisticated Stackelberg retail quantities and those of a vertically-integrated system, although one principle does emerge. Under the sophisticated Stackelberg tariff, the quantity sold by the more-profitable retailer is greater than what it would sell in a vertically-integrated system. (Mathematically, $Q_i^* > \hat{Q}_i^*(j)$ in Zone $Z_j^{SS*}$ and $Q_j^* > \hat{Q}_j^*(i)$ in Zone $Z_i^{SS*}$.)

## 3.6 A Numerical Illustration

We illustrate the results presented in this Section with the simple numerical example that we have used in earlier Chapters. Let $A_i = 150$, $A_j = 100$, $c_i = c_j = \$10 = C$, $F = \$1000$, $b = 1.0$, $\theta = 0.5$ and $f_j = \$0$. Thus $Q_i^* = 70$, $Q_j^* = 45$, $L^{SS*} = \$2{,}100$ and $U^{SS*} = \$2{,}500$. Optimal transfer prices for a decentrally-organized, vertically-integrated system are $T_i^* = \$67.33$ and $T_j^* = \$71.67$. The sophisticated Stackelberg Zones may be defined entirely in terms of $f_i$:

$$\begin{aligned} &\text{Zone } Z_j^{SS*} \leftrightarrow && \$2{,}100 > f_i \\ &\text{Zone } Z_{ij}^{SS*} \leftrightarrow && \$2{,}100 \le f_i \le \$2{,}500 \\ &\text{Zone } Z_i^{SS*} \leftrightarrow && f_i > \$2{,}500 \end{aligned} \tag{6.3.13}$$

We report the resulting retail prices, quantities and the manufacturer's profit for all three Zones in Table 6.4. (Zone $Z_{ij}^{SS*}$ values are illustrative.) For comparative purposes the same variables are reported for the vertically-integrated system and for a naïve Stackelberg manufacturer—both at the mid-point of Zone $Z_{ij}^{SS*}$. Note that the row labeled $\Pi_C$ is the *actual channel profit*, given $f_i$, for the wholesale-price policy listed at the head of each column, the row labeled $\Pi_C^*$ is *coordinated channel profit*, and the row labeled $\Delta\Pi_C$ is the *difference between the coordinated channel profit and the actual channel profit*. These values coincide only for the vertically-integrated system.

In Zone $Z_j^{SS*}$ the sophisticated Stackelberg wholesale price is $\hat{W}^*(j) = \$82.50$ and the fixed fee is $\hat{\phi}^*(j) = \$1{,}806.25$. This fixed fee extracts all profit from the $j^{th}$ retailer. In Zone $Z_i^{SS*}$ the sophisticated Stackelberg wholesale price is $\hat{W}^*(i) = \$52.50$, but the fixed fee $\hat{\phi}^*(i)$ depends on the profit earned by the less-profitable (the $i^{th}$) retailer—who nets zero profit after paying the fixed fee. Specifically, each dollar increase in $f_i$ above $U^{SS^*}$ reduces the fixed fee by \$1 and manufacturer profit by \$2. The apparent asymmetry between these Zones occurs because we held $f_j$ constant while raising the value of $f_i$. Reversing the roles of $f_i$ and $f_j$ reverses this "asymmetry."

*Table 6.4.* The Sophisticated Stackelberg Tariff: An Illustrative Example

| | Vertically-Integrated System[2] | Naïve Stackelberg Tariff | Sophisticated Stackelberg Tariff[1] | | |
|---|---|---|---|---|---|
| | | | Zone $Z_j^{ss*}$ | Zone $Z_{ij}^{ss*}$ | Zone $Z_i^{ss*}$ |
| $f_i$ | \$2,300.00 | \$2,300.00 | \$2000.00 | \$2300.00 | \$2600.00 |
| $Q_i$ | 70 | 48.33 | 62.5 | 67.5 | 72.5 |
| $Q_j$ | 45 | 28.33 | 42.5 | 47.5 | 52.5 |
| $W^3$ | NA | \$125.00 | \$82.50 | \$67.50 | \$52.50 |
| $p_i$ | \$143.33 | \$183.33 | \$155.00 | \$145.00 | \$135.00 |
| $p_j$ | \$126.67 | \$163.33 | \$135.00 | \$125.00 | \$115.00 |
| $\pi_i$ | *\$2,600.00* | \$0 | \$100 | \$0 | \$0 |
| $\pi_j$ | *\$2,025.00* | \$766.67 | \$0 | \$0 | \$100 |
| $\phi$ | NA | \$36.11 | \$1,806.25 | \$2,256.25 | \$2,656.25 |
| $\Pi_M$ | *\$5,508.33* | \$7,888.89 | \$10,225.00 | \$10,125.00 | \$9,625.00 |
| $\Pi_C$ | \$10,133.33 | \$8,655.56 | \$10,325.00 | \$10,125.00 | \$9,725.00 |
| $\Pi_C^*$ | \$10,133.33 | \$10,133.33 | \$10,433.33 | \$10,133.33 | \$9,833.33 |
| $\Delta\Pi_C$ | \$0 | \$1,477.77 | \$108.33 | \$8.33 | \$108.33 |

**Note:** These results assume $A_i = 150$, $A_j = 100$, $c_i = c_j = C = \$10$, $f_j = 0$, $F = \$1000$, $b = 1.0$, and $\theta = 0.5$.

[1] Values in Zone $Z_{ij}^{ss*}$ are illustrative. Results are shown for $\omega = 0.5$, as is implied by $f_i = \$2,300$. The Zonal boundaries are $L^{ss*} = \$2,100$ and $U^{ss*} = \$2,500$. The kink in the naïve Stackelberg two-part tariff occurs at $f_j = \$1,533.33$.

[2] Values in italics hold for a decentrally-managed, vertically-integrated system.

[3] For the vertically-integrated system the transfer prices are $T_i^* = \$63.33$ and $T_j^* = \$71.67$.

In Zone $Z_{ij}^{SS*}$, which lies between Zones $Z_j^{SS*}$ and $Z_i^{SS*}$, the wholesale price is a linear, decreasing function of $f_i$ (holding $f_j$ constant), while the fixed fee is a linear, increasing function of $f_i$. In this Zone the manufacturer extracts all profit from both retailers because they earn equal net revenues. (This full-profit extraction property is independent of which retailer's fixed-cost parameter is held constant.) Accordingly, manufacturer profit $(\hat{\Pi}_M^*(\omega))$ and channel profit $(\hat{\Pi}_C^*(\omega))$ are identical, although channel profit with sophisticated Stackelberg pricing is less than it is in a vertically-integrated system. At the midpoint of this Zone (at $f_i = \$2,300$), the difference in channel profits between the vertically-integrated system and the sophisticated Stackelberg strategy is at its minimum; in our example, this minimal difference is $[\Pi_I^* - \hat{\Pi}_C^*(\omega)] = \$8.33$. The minimal gap *always* occurs at the zonal midpoint $(Z^{SS^*})$, which is also the point where the divergence between the sophisticated and semi-sophisticated policies is greatest.

In this Section we have shown that, within Zone $Z_{ij}^{SS^*}$, a sophisticated Stackelberg adjustment of the wholesale price and the fixed fee generates greater manufacturer profit than does a semi-sophisticated policy that focuses only on the fixed fee. In the next Section we examine the relationship between the sophisticated Stackelberg pricing strategy and the two-part tariffs examined in Chapter 5.

## 4 ALTERNATIVE TWO-PART TARIFFS: COMPARISONS

Any per-unit wholesale price can be expressed in terms of a specific markup above per-unit production cost. Symbolically this entails setting $W = \upsilon C$, where $\upsilon > 1$. Simple algebraic manipulation reveals that the manufacturer's unit margin, expressed as a percentage of price, is a function of the markup $\upsilon$:

$$M \equiv (W - C)/W \equiv (\upsilon - 1)/\upsilon \qquad (6.4.1)$$

For this reason, we refer to the general formula $W = \upsilon C$ as a *fixed-margin tariff.* When $\upsilon = 1$, we have the "sell-at-cost" price strategy that maximizes channel profit in a bilateral-monopoly model. The other tariffs derived in Chapter 5 can also be expressed in terms of $\upsilon$. We denote the *naïve Stackelberg tariff,* which maximizes manufacturer net revenue, by the symbol $\hat{\upsilon}^*$. Similarly, we denote the *second-best tariff,* which maximizes channel profit, by the symbol $\tilde{\upsilon}^*$.[11]

Every fixed margin tariff necessarily implies the existence of a *critical value* ($\delta^{\upsilon}$) that is defined in $\langle f_i - f_j \rangle$ – space. This critical value can be used to prove that:

- Manufacturer profit is a constant function of $f_i$ for $(f_i - f_j) < \delta^{\upsilon}$;
- Manufacturer profit is equal to channel profit at the critical value $(f_i - f_j) = \delta^{\upsilon}$; and
- Manufacturer profit is declining at the rate of $-\$2$ for $(f_i - f_j) > \delta^{\upsilon}$.

At the critical value $\delta^{\upsilon}$ the manufacturer's profit function is non-differentiable in $(f_i - f_j)$; that is, there is a kink in the function as illustrated in Figures 5.1 and 5.3.

## 4.1 The Fixed-Margin Tariff and $\delta^{\upsilon}$

Under a fixed-margin strategy the manufacturer sets its per-unit wholesale price to earn a pre-specified gross margin per-unit. Net revenue ($R_{\upsilon}$) for the manufacturer is:

$$R_{\upsilon} = \sum_k (\upsilon C - C)\hat{Q}_k(\upsilon C), \qquad k \in (i,j) \tag{6.4.2}$$

The values of the optimal retail and wholesale prices, quantities, and the fixed fee, given a wholesale price of $W = \upsilon C$, are reported in Table 6.5.

With the information in Table 6.5 we can write manufacturer profit as:

$$\Pi_M^{\upsilon} = 2b(\upsilon - 1)\left(\frac{Q_i^* + Q_j^* - (b-\theta)(\upsilon-1)C}{(2b-\theta)}\right)C + 2\hat{\phi}(\upsilon) - F \tag{6.4.3}$$

The single point of non-differentiability in the manufacturer's profit function occurs at:

$$\delta^{\upsilon} = \left(\frac{4b(Q_i^* - Q_j^*)}{(4b^2 - \theta^2)}\right)(Q_i^* + Q_j^* - (b-\theta)(\upsilon-1)C) \tag{6.4.4}$$

We now consider the implications of $\delta^{\upsilon^*}$ occurring in each of the three Zones.

*Table 6.5.* The Fixed-Margin Tariff:
Wholesale Prices, Fixed Fees, and Retail Prices and Quantities

| | |
|---|---|
| The Per-unit Fee | $W^{\upsilon^*} = \upsilon C$ |
| The Fixed Fee | $\phi^{\upsilon^*} = \min\left\{\frac{[Q_i^*(\upsilon)]^2}{b} - f_i, \frac{[Q_j^*(\upsilon)]^2}{b} - f_j\right\}$ |
| The i[th] Price | $p_i^{\upsilon^*} = \frac{(2(2Q_i^* + \theta Q_j^*) + b(2b+\theta)(\upsilon-1)C)}{(4b^2-\theta^2)} + c_i + C$ |
| The i[th] Retailer's Margin | $m_i^{\upsilon^*} = \frac{(2(2Q_i^* + \theta Q_j^*) - (b-\theta)(2b+\theta)(\upsilon-1)C)}{(4b^2-\theta^2)}$ |
| The i[th] Quantity | $Q_i^{\upsilon^*} = b\frac{(2(2bQ_i^* + \theta Q_j^*) - (b-\theta)(2b+\theta)(\upsilon-1))C}{(4b^2-\theta^2)}$ |
| Total Quantity | $\sum_k Q_k^{\upsilon^*} = 2b\frac{((Q_i^* + Q_j^*) - (b-\theta)(\upsilon-1))C}{(2b-\theta)}$ |
| The i[th] Retailer's Profit | $\pi_i^{\upsilon^*} = \frac{(Q_i^{\upsilon^*})^2}{b} - f_i - \phi^{\upsilon^*}$ |

## 4.2 The Fixed-Margin Tariff When $\upsilon C > \hat{W}^*(j)$

If $\upsilon C > \hat{W}^*(j)$, $\delta^\upsilon$ lies in Zone $Z_j^{SS*}$. Comparing manufacturer profits at the point of non-differentiability under the sophisticated Stackelberg and the fixed-margin strategies reveal:

$$\left[\hat{\Pi}_M^*\left(\delta^\upsilon\right) - \Pi_M^\upsilon\left(\delta^\upsilon\right)\right] = \frac{2b^2\left(b-\theta\right)\left(\hat{W}^*\left(j\right) - \upsilon C\right)^2}{\left(2b-\theta\right)^2} > 0 \tag{6.4.5}$$

Manufacturer profit from the sophisticated Stackelberg strategy, denoted by $\hat{\Pi}_M^*(\delta^\upsilon)$, dominates profit from the fixed-margin tariff ($\Pi_M^\upsilon(\delta^\upsilon)$) at the point of non-differentiability. At this point, consider the effect of a *decrease* in $f_i$, holding $f_j$ fixed. Such a decrease has no effect on manufacturer profit under either wholesale-price strategy; thus for all $(f_i - f_j) < \delta^\upsilon$ we must also have $\hat{\Pi}_M^* > \Pi_M^\upsilon$. Now consider the effect of an *increase* in $f_i$ while holding $f_j$ fixed. Manufacturer profit $\Pi_M^\upsilon$ declines at a rate of \$2 for every \$1 increase in $f_i$. In contrast, $\hat{\Pi}_M^*$ does not decrease in Zone $Z_j^{SS*}$, declines at a rate of $\$2(1-\omega)$ in Zone $Z_{ij}^{SS*}$, and declines at a rate of \$2 in Zone $Z_i^{SS*}$. Thus the sophisticated Stackelberg wholesale-price strategy dominates the fixed margin strategy for all $(f_i - f_j)$ – values.

## 4.3 The Fixed-Margin Tariff When $\hat{W}^*(j) > \upsilon C > \hat{W}^*(i)$

If $\hat{W}^*(j) > \upsilon C > \hat{W}^*(i)$, then $\delta^\upsilon$ lies in Zone $Z_{ij}^{SS*}$. A comparison of manufacturer profit under the sophisticated Stackelberg and the fixed-margin price strategies at the point of non-differentiability yields:

$$\left[\hat{\Pi}_M^*\left(\delta^\upsilon\right) - \Pi_M^\upsilon\left(\delta^\upsilon\right)\right] = 0 \tag{6.4.6}$$

At $\delta^\upsilon$ manufacturer profits are identical under these strategies. For a comparison elsewhere, note that a *decrease* in $f_i$ while holding $f_j$ fixed, increases manufacturer profit under the sophisticated Stackelberg price strategy, but has no effect on manufacturer profit under a fixed-margin strategy. Thus for any $(f_i - f_j) < \delta^\upsilon$ we must have $\hat{\Pi}_M^* > \Pi_M^\upsilon$. Now consider an *increase* in $f_i$ (holding $f_j$ fixed). Manufacturer profit $\Pi_M^\upsilon$ declines at a rate of \$2 for every \$1 increase in $f_i$ while $\hat{\Pi}^*_M$ declines at a rate of $\$2(1-\omega)$ in Zone $Z^{SS*}_{ij}$ and at a rate of \$2 in Zone $Z^{SS*}_i$. Therefore the sophisticated Stackelberg policy weakly dominates the fixed-margin strategy.

## 4.4 The Fixed-Margin Tariff When $\upsilon C < \hat{W}^*(i)$

If $\mu C < \hat{W}^*(i)$, then $\delta^\upsilon$ lies in Zone $Z^{SS*}_i$. A comparison of manufacturer profit at this point of non-differentiability yields:

$$\left[\hat{\Pi}^*_M(\delta^\upsilon) - \Pi^\upsilon_M(\delta^\upsilon)\right] = \frac{2b^2(b-\theta)}{(2b-\theta)^2}\left[\hat{W}^*(i) - \upsilon C\right]^2 > 0 \qquad (6.4.7)$$

This result is symmetric to Zone $Z^{SS*}_j$. By the same argument used in sub-Section 4.2, the sophisticated Stackelberg price-strategy dominates any fixed-margin strategy.

## 4.5 Comments

A comparison of the sophisticated Stackelberg wholesale-price strategy with the fixed-margin strategy reveals five major points:

(1) In Zone $Z^{SS*}_{ij}$ the manufacturer's profit function is the *envelope* of an infinite number of fixed-margin manufacturer profit functions, each of which touches the envelope only at the point of non-differentiability. Every possible two-part tariff generates a kinked manufacturer profit function in which the kink itself lies on the envelope.

(2) In Zone $Z^{SS*}_{ij}$ (where $\hat{W}^*(j) > W = \upsilon C > \hat{W}^*(i)$) the sophisticated Stackelberg wholesale-price strategy weakly dominates *all* fixed-margin two-part tariffs. The domination is "weak" because at each point on the envelope there is a specific fixed-margin tariff that duplicates the results of the sophisticated Stackelberg tariff *at that point alone.*

(3) Throughout Zone $Z^{SS*}_{ij}$ the manufacturer *extracts all profit* from both retailers; a fixed-margin strategy is only able to do so at the critical $(f_i - f_j)$ value defined as the point of non-differentiability.

(4) In Zone $Z^{SS*}_j$ (where $W = \upsilon C > \hat{W}^*(j)$) *and* in Zone $Z^{SS*}_i$ (where

$W = \upsilon C < \hat{W}^*(i)$, the sophisticated Stackelberg two-part tariff strictly dominates all possible fixed-margin tariffs.

(5) At the single point $Z^{ss*}$ the sophisticated Stackelberg strategy and the second-best strategy yield identical manufacturer *and* channel profits. At all other points the sophisticated Stackelberg strategy generates higher *manufacturer* profit, even though the second-best strategy yields higher *channel* profit.

# 5 THE SOPHISTICATED STACKELBERG TARIFF AND RETAILER PROFIT-EXTRACTION

We have shown that the sophisticated Stackelberg Zones determine the share of a retailer's profit that the manufacturer can extract. In this Section we examine the way in which underlying parametric values interact to determine the applicability of the three Zones that define the sophisticated Stackelberg tariff.

## 5.1 Zonal Re-Parameterization

We wish to identify the sets of parametric values that lie in each of the three sophisticated Stackelberg Zones $Z_j^{ss^*}$, $Z_{ij}^{ss^*}$, and $Z_i^{ss^*}$. The boundary between Zones $Z_j^{ss^*}$ and $Z_{ij}^{ss^*}$ satisfies $L^{ss^*} = (f_i - f_j)$, while the boundary between Zones $Z_{ij}^{ss^*}$ and $Z_i^{ss^*}$ satisfies $U^{ss^*} = (f_i - f_j)$. (The definitions of $L^{ss^*}$ and $U^{ss^*}$ are given by (6.2.4) and (6.2.5), respectively.) Although this is a six-parameter problem, we proved in Chapter 5, Section 8, that it can be reduced to four dimensions through a simple re-parameterization:

$$\chi \equiv (\theta/b) \tag{6.5.1}$$

$$S_j \equiv Q_j^* / (Q_i^* + Q_j^*) \tag{6.5.2}$$

$$\mathit{f}_k \equiv (f_k / R_k^*) \quad \forall \quad k \in (i, j) \tag{6.5.3}$$

The term $\chi$ is the *intensity of competition*, the term $S_j$ is the *magnitude of competition*, and the term $\mathit{f}_k$ is the k[th] retailer's *fixed-cost ratio*. This re-parameterization has the effect of standardizing several key variables to the unit interval at no loss of generality.

We use these standardized parameters in calculating the boundaries, but we first set $\mathit{f}_i = \mathit{f}_j \equiv \mathit{f}$. As we argued in Chapter 5, this simplifies our analytical task by reducing four dimensions to a three-dimensional "unit-cube." Further, the left-half and the right-half of the unit-cube are symmetric about the plane defining equal market shares (i.e., $Q_i^* = Q_j^*$). As a result, we can confine our analysis to half of the unit-cube.

To simplify our discussion, let $L_{\Delta f}^{SS^*}$ denote the boundary between Zones $Z_j^{SS^*}$ and $Z_{ij}^{SS^*}$, where:

$$\begin{aligned} L_{\Delta f}^{SS^*} &\equiv \left[L^{SS^*} - (f_i - f_j)\right]\Big|_{f_i = f_j} = 0 \\ &= \left(\frac{(1-2S_j)R_i^*}{(1-S_j)^2(2+\chi)^2}\right)\left(6\chi + 8(1-\chi)S_j - (2+\chi)^2 f\right) = 0 \end{aligned} \tag{6.5.4}$$

Similarly, let $U_{\Delta f}^{SS^*}$ denote the boundary between Zones $Z_i^{SS^*}$ and $Z_{ij}^{SS^*}$:

$$\begin{aligned} U_{\Delta f}^{SS^*} &\equiv \left[U^{SS^*} - (f_i - f_j)\right]\Big|_{f_i = f_j} = 0 \\ &= \left(\frac{(1-2S_j)R_i^*}{(1-S_j)^2(2+\chi)^2}\right)\left(2(4-\chi) - 8(1-\chi)S_j - (2+\chi)^2 f\right) = 0 \end{aligned} \tag{6.5.5}$$

Notice that equations (6.5.4) and (6.5.5) both hold when $S_j = ½$.

## 5.2 The Sophisticated Stackelberg Zones and Retailer Profit Extraction

As in Section 8 of Chapter 5, we conserve space by focusing our discussion on the *unit half-cube* defined by $(0 \le \chi < 1,\ 0 \le S_j \le ½,\ 0 \le f \le 1)$. The focus is justified by the fact that, given the assumed equality of the retailers' fixed-cost ratios, the right-hand side of the cube is a mirror-image of the left-hand side. Because equations (6.5.4) and (6.5.5) always hold when $S_j = ½$, the plane defined by $S_j = ½$ always satisfies the boundary conditions $L_{\Delta f}^{SS^*}$ and $U_{\Delta f}^{SS^*}$. What is unclear is whether the interior of the unit half-cube contains one or more additional lines that correspond to $L_{\Delta f}^{SS^*}$ or $U_{\Delta f}^{SS^*}$. We address this question below. We illustrate our results by taking slices of the unit half-cube at various $f$ – values. We call these slices *unit half-squares*; each satisfies $(0 \le \chi < 1,\ 0 \le S_j \le ½)$.

The sophisticated Stackelberg two-part tariff is feasible if and only if both retailers sell a positive quantity when faced with the tariff $\{W(k), \phi(k)\}$,

$k \in (i, j)$. Table 6.1 reveals that, in the unit half-cube, the feasibility constraint is violated when:

$$S_j \leq \frac{(2-3\chi)}{4(2-\chi)} \tag{6.5.6}$$

The $j^{th}$ retailer does not participate in the channel ( $Q_j^*(j) < 0$ ) when its market share falls below this critical value. In fact, constraint (6.5.6) defines a boundary intersecting the $\langle \chi = 0 \rangle$ – axis at $S_j = ½$ and the $\langle S_j = 0 \rangle$ – axis at $\chi = ⅔$. Note that this boundary is independent of the retailers' fixed costs.

We can summarize the relationships among the Zones and their parameters by describing four regions that are defined by the value of the retailer-fixed-cost parameter $f$ :

- $f$ **– Region 1 :** $0 = f^{SS^*}$
- $f$ **– Region 2 :** $0 < f^{SS^*} < ⅔$
- $f$ **– Region 3 :** $⅔ = f^{SS^*}$
- $f$ **– Region 4 :** $⅔ < f^{SS^*} < 1$

The first $f$ – Region is defined by $f = 0$. At this $f$ – value the boundaries $L_{\Delta f}^{SS^*}$ and $U_{\Delta f}^{SS^*}$ correspond to the $S_j = ½$ axis; thus, Zone $Z_j^{SS^*}$ consists of all of the unit half-square except (i) the area lying inside the SS-infeasible Region and (ii) the $S_j = ½$ axis. As a result, provided the SS-tariff is feasible, all profit is extracted from the smaller (the $j^{th}$) competitor. And, on the $S_j = ½$ axis, all profit is extracted from both (identical) competitors.

In the second $f$ – Region, the boundary $L_{\Delta f}^{SS^*}$ intersects the horizontal $\langle \chi = 0 \rangle$ – axis at $S_j = f/2$; thus, as $f \to 0$, $S_j \to 0$ and as $f \to ⅔$, $S_j \to ⅓$. In addition, $L_{\Delta f}^{SS^*}$ intersects the vertical $\langle S_j = 0 \rangle$ – axis at:

$$\chi = \left(3 - 2f - \sqrt{3(3-4f)}\right) \Big/ f \quad \in \quad (0, 1) \tag{6.5.7}$$

The meaning of the parenthetical expression (0,1) is that at $f = 0$ (at $f$ 's lower limit in this $f$ – region) the value of (6.5.7) is $\chi = 0$. Similarly, at $f$ 's upper limit (at $f = ⅔$), the value of the expression is $\chi = 1$. More generally, whenever we use this notation, the first parenthetical number denotes the value of the equation at its lower $f$ – limit and the second parenthetical number denotes the value of the equation at its upper $f$ – limit. This $f$ – Region is illustrated in Figure 6.5 for $f = 0.6$.

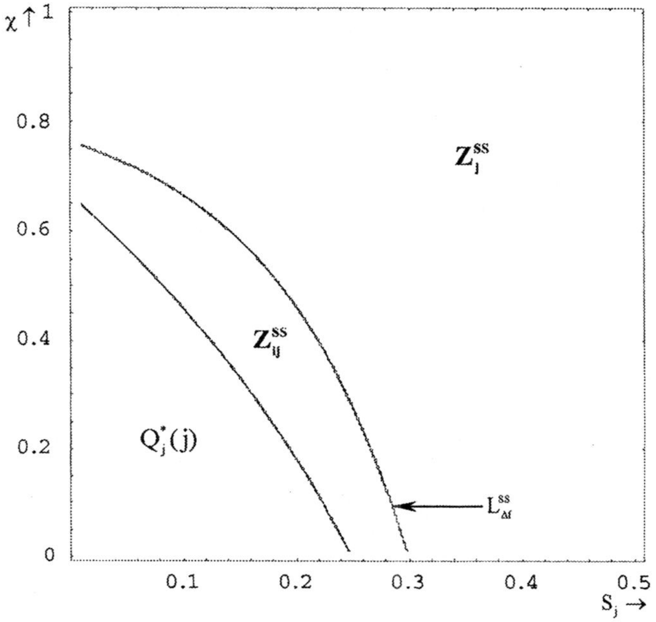


Legend:

$\mathbf{Z}_j^{ss}$ ≡ The Sophisticated Stackelberg Zone in which the $j^{th}$ retailer is the less profitable;

$\mathbf{Z}_{ij}^{ss}$ ≡ The Sophisticated Stackelberg Zone in which the retailers are equally profitable;

$Q_j^*(j)$ ≡ The Sophisticated Stackelberg tariff is infeasible; and

$L_{\Delta f}^{ss}$ ≡ The boundary separating Zones $Z_j^{ss^*}$ and $Z_{ij}^{ss^*}$.

*Figure 6.5.* The Sophisticated Stackelberg Zones
When $f = 0.6$

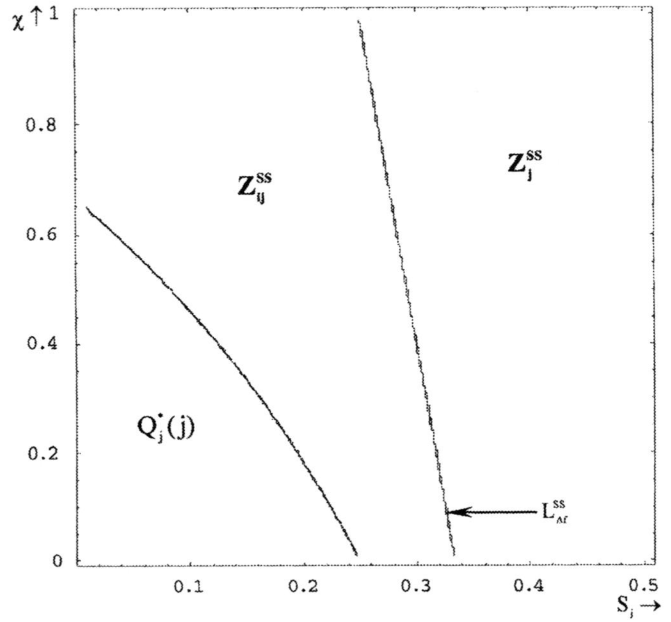


Legend:

$\mathbf{Z}^{ss}_{j}$ ≡ The Sophisticated Stackelberg Zone in which the j[th] retailer is the less profitable;

$\mathbf{Z}^{ss}_{ij}$ ≡ The Sophisticated Stackelberg Zone in which the retailers are equally profitable;

$Q^*_j(j)$ ≡ The Sophisticated Stackelberg tariff is infeasible; and

$L^{ss}_{\Delta f}$ ≡ The boundary separating Zones $Z^{ss^*}_{j}$ and $Z^{ss^*}_{ij}$.

*Figure 6.6.* The Sophisticated Stackelberg Zones
When $f = \frac{2}{3}$

In the third $f$ – Region, $L_{\Delta f}^{ss^*}$ intersects the horizontal $\langle \chi = 0 \rangle$ – axis at $S_j = 1/3$, and the horizontal $\langle \chi = 1 \rangle$ – axis at $S_j = 1/4$. At lower values ($f < 2/3$), $L_{\Delta f}^{ss^*}$ intersects the $\langle S_j = 0 \rangle$ – axis, while at higher values ($f > 2/3$), $L_{\Delta f}^{ss^*}$ intersects the $\langle S_j = 1/2 \rangle$ – axis; there is a jump discontinuity here. Thus $L_{\Delta f}^{ss^*}$ *only* intersects the $\langle \chi = 1 \rangle$ – axis at $f = 2/3$. Figure 6.6 illustrates this result.

In the fourth $f$ – Region, $L_{\Delta f}^{ss^*}$ intersects the horizontal $\langle \chi = 0 \rangle$ – axis at $S_j = f/2$ and the vertical $\langle S_j = 1/2 \rangle$ – axis at:

$$\chi = 2(1-f)/f \tag{6.5.8}$$

$U_{\Delta f}^{ss^*}$ also intersects the vertical $\langle S_j = 1/2 \rangle$ – axis at this $\chi$ – value. In addition, the boundary $U_{\Delta f}^{ss^*}$ intersects the vertical $\langle S_j = 0 \rangle$ – axis at:

$$\chi = \left(-(1+2f) + \sqrt{1+12f}\right)/f \quad \in \quad (1, 0.606) \tag{6.5.9}$$

Figure 6.7 illustrates this $f$ – Region for the case of $f = 0.85$.

In summary, as $f$ increases from 0 to 1, the boundaries $L_{\Delta f}^{ss^*}$ and $U_{\Delta f}^{ss^*}$ migrate through the unit half-square along the following paths. As $f$ rises from zero, $L_{\Delta f}^{ss^*}$ appears in the lower left corner (at $\chi = 0 = S_j$) and moves northeasterly. As $f$ approaches $2/3$, the $\langle S_j = 0 \rangle$ – intercept approaches 1, and the $\langle \chi = 0 \rangle$ – intercept approaches $1/3$. Zone $Z_j^{ss^*}$ is located above $L_{\Delta f}^{ss^*}$; Zone $Z_{ij}^{ss^*}$ is located below it. At the unique value $f = 2/3$, $L_{\Delta f}^{ss^*}$ intersects the $\langle \chi = 0 \rangle$ – axis at $S_j = 1/3$ and the $\langle \chi = 1 \rangle$ – axis at $S_j = 1/4$. Zone $Z_{ij}^{ss^*}$ is now located to the left of $L_{\Delta f}^{ss^*}$ and Zone $Z_j^{ss^*}$ is located to the right.

When $f > 2/3$, $L_{\Delta f}^{ss^*}$ intersects both the $\langle \chi = 0 \rangle$ – axis and the $\langle S_j = 1/2 \rangle$ – axis. As $f$ increases from $2/3$ to 1, the $\langle S_j = 1/2 \rangle$ – intercept decreases from 1 to 0. In addition, $U_{\Delta f}^{ss^*}$ appears at the top of the unit half-square, intersecting both $S_j$ – axes. We find that as $f$ increases from $2/3$ to 1, the $\langle S_j = 0 \rangle$ – intercept decreases from 1 to about 0.606, and the $\langle S_j = 1/2 \rangle$ – intercept decreases from 1 to 0. Within this $f$ – range, Zone $Z_i^{ss^*}$ is located above $U_{\Delta f}^{ss^*}$; Zone $Z_{ij}^{ss^*}$ is located below both $U_{\Delta f}^{ss^*}$ and $L_{\Delta f}^{ss^*}$; and Zone $Z_j^{ss^*}$ is located below $L_{\Delta f}^{ss^*}$.

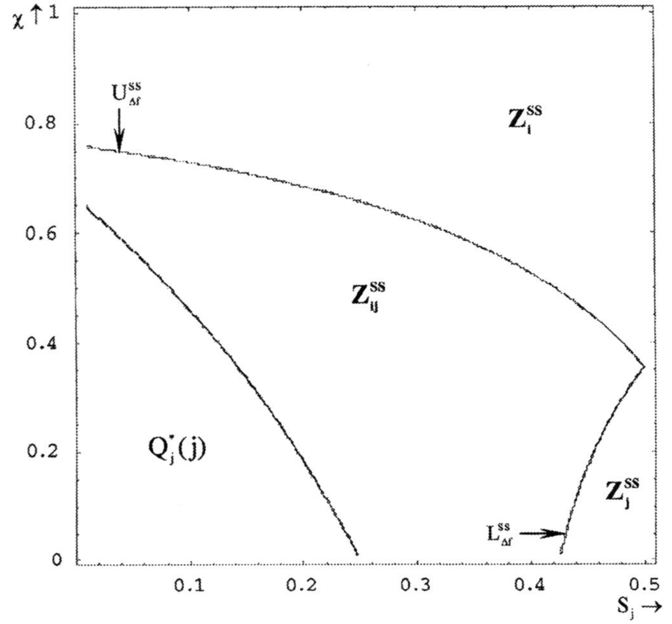


Legend:

$Z_j^{ss}$ ≡ The Sophisticated Stackelberg Zone in which the j[th] retailer is the less profitable;

$Z_{ij}^{ss}$ ≡ The Sophisticated Stackelberg Zone in which the retailers are equally profitable;

$Z_i^{ss}$ ≡ The Sophisticated Stackelberg Zone in which the i[th] retailer is the less profitable;

$Q_j^*(j)$ ≡ The Sophisticated Stackelberg tariff is infeasible;

$L_{\Delta f}^{ss}$ ≡ The boundary separating Zones $Z_j^{ss^*}$ and $Z_{ij}^{ss^*}$; and

$U_{\Delta f}^{ss}$ ≡ The boundary separating Zones $Z_i^{ss^*}$ and $Z_{ij}^{ss^*}$.

*Figure 6.7.* The Sophisticated Stackelberg Zones When $f = 0.85$

## 5.3 The Sophisticated Stackelberg Tariff *versus* the Quantity-Discount Schedule

We now evaluate the parametric values for which the manufacturer earns a greater profit by using the non-coordinating, sophisticated Stackelberg two-part tariff of this Chapter rather than the channel-coordinating quantity-discount schedule of Chapter 5. Because we devote Chapters 8 and 9 to a detailed comparison of these wholesale-price policies (as well as a channel-coordinating menu of two-part tariffs), in this sub-Section we only consider the special case of $f = 0$. Our attention to this special case is justified by the fact that the analytical channels literature typically assumes no fixed costs.

Given this assumption, we find that, from the manufacturer's perspective, the sophisticated Stackelberg tariff dominates the linear, channel-coordinating quantity-discount schedules. This statement holds for *all* values of $\chi$ and $S_j$. (We provide the details of our analysis in Chapters 8 and 9.) We caution that this statement does not hold for all possible values of the retailer- fixed-cost parameters. We will show in Chapters 8 and 9 that, when the $f$ values are sufficiently high, the quantity-discount schedule generates greater profit from the manufacturer at some—but not all—values of $\chi$ and $S_j$.

# 6 COMMENTARY

In this Chapter we derived a "sophisticated Stackelberg" wholesale-price strategy by simultaneously determining the wholesale price and fixed fee that *jointly* maximize manufacturer profit. We proved that the manufacturer prefers this strategy to one that ignores the effect that its wholesale price has on the fixed fee that can be extracted from both retailers.

## 6.1 Commentary on the Sophisticated Stackelberg Tariff

The sophisticated Stackelberg tariff derived in this Chapter has several important characteristics. First, *the per-unit wholesale price depends on the difference in the retailers' fixed costs.* This result contrasts with policies that maximize the manufacturer's net revenue (margin times quantity). Such policies inevitably set a wholesale price that is independent of the retailers' fixed costs.

Second, there is *no single, optimal per-unit wholesale price.* The optimal wholesale price varies across three "Zones" that are defined by the magnitude of the difference in the retailers' fixed costs $(f_i - f_j)$. The wholesale prices are different in Zones $Z_j^{SS*}$ and $Z_i^{SS*}$, although the prices are unaffected by marginal changes in $(f_i - f_j)$. However, in the middle Zone ($Z_{ij}^{SS*}$), the wholesale price is a continuous function of $(f_i - f_j)$. The existence of wholesale-price Zones that are based on fixed-cost differences has not been acknowledged in the marketing science literature, with the exception of the article on which this Chapter builds (Ingene and Parry 1998).

Third, the *optimal fixed fee also varies across Zones*. We have shown that the optimal fixed fee is a monotonically increasing function of $(f_i - f_j)$ in Zone $Z_{ij}^{SS*}$, although it is constant in the other Zones. Fourth, the manufacturer extracts *all profit* from the competitors over the range of retailers' fixed costs defined by Zone $Z_{ij}^{SS*}$. Fifth, the profit which the manufacturer can obtain from any single two-part tariff is equal to the sophisticated Stackelberg profit only at a single, unique value of $(f_i - f_j)$; elsewhere it is lower. Mathematically, the sophisticated Stackelberg tariff is the envelope of all possible two-part tariffs that satisfy the following condition: the per-unit fee lies between the per-unit fee charged in Zone $Z_j^{SS*}$ and the one charged in Zone $Z_i^{SS*}$. Sixth, the sophisticated Stackelberg two-part tariff is the *optimal* (the first-best) wholesale-price strategy given that the manufacturer implements its wholesale pricing strategy with a two-part tariff and treats its retailers comparably.

## 6.2 Commentary on Two Channel Myths

The analysis presented in this Chapter illustrates the ways in which the Fixed-Cost Myth and the Identical-Competitors Meta-Myth diminish the marketing science profession's ability to draw insights from analytical channel models. To see this, suppose we had ignored fixed costs at retail, but had made no other modifications to our model. Given our expository assumption ($Q_i^* > Q_j^*$), we would have found that $U^{SS^*} > L^{SS^*} > 0 \equiv (f_i - f_j)$. Then the manufacturer-optimal solution would be found by decision rule (6.2.6), which leads to a single wholesale price given by equation (6.2.2) and a single fixed fee given by (6.2.3). As a result, the manufacturer would extract all profit from the smaller retailer. Clearly the rich results derived from our model would disappear. This raises the following question: what is the cost to the marketing profession of ignoring retailers' fixed costs?

If one believes that retailers do not incur non-variable costs of operation, and that they do not incur opportunity costs by devoting scarce resources to distributing merchandise, then it is appropriate to build models that ignore fixed costs. But the empirical evidence is that retailers have substantial fixed operating expenses that include real estate, fixtures, utilities, and management. Those who understand retailing also know that some of these expenses are tied to the distribution of specific manufacturer's products. Examples include dedicated tune-up equipment at automobile dealerships, specialized training programs for many high-tech products, and specific areas within a department store that are devoted to a brand. Each of these examples also point up the existence of opportunity costs of financial resources, labor, and physical capital. We iterate that the theoretical results obtained, and the managerial advice offered, are materially affected by excluding retailers' fixed costs. Competing-retailer models that ignore these costs generate incomplete results that capture only a fraction of the insights that emerge when fixed costs are explicitly modeled. The (apparently widespread) belief that ignoring fixed costs is a mere simplifying assumption is a myth; we call it the *Fixed-Cost Modeling Myth.*

The difference in competitor size (as measured by unit volume in an integrated channel) also plays a vital role in our analysis. Suppose we had assumed that our competing retailers were equal sized ($Q^*_= \equiv Q^*_i = Q^*_j$).[12] Under this extreme (but common) assumption of identical competitors, there is a single sophisticated Stackelberg wholesale price that can be found from equation (6.2.2):

$$W^*_= = \left(\theta Q^*_= / b\left(b-\theta\right)\right) + C \tag{6.6.1}$$

We use symbols $Q^*_=$ and $W^*_=$ to denote the special case of equal outputs. In this special case the wholesale price (6.6.1) is invariant with changes in retailers' fixed costs, even when these costs are modeled. The assumption of identical competitors obscures the body of *potential* knowledge about channel strategy, because it reduces the comparable treatment constraint to an irrelevance. Identical competitors are inevitably treated comparably, not because of Robinson-Patman, but because it is in the manufacturer's interest to do so. Because channels are generally characterized by retailers who are of unequal size, and because assuming identical competitors dramatically narrows the insights obtained from a competing-retailer model, we conclude that the belief that competitors can safely be modeled as identical is a myth, one that we call the *Identical-Competitors Meta-Myth.*

## 6.3 Commentary on Stackelberg Models

Our results also have important implications for the way that marketing scientists think about Stackelberg leadership. To see this, consider the simple case of one manufacturer that sells through two retailers who are identical in all respects. Because the manufacturer collects all profit, it should maximize channel profit. Further, because the retailers are identical, a two-part tariff can maximize both manufacturer and channel profits. (The per-unit fee coordinates the channel and the fixed fee extracts all profit.) It is straightforward to prove that a sophisticated Stackelberg manufacturer will set the wholesale-price (6.6.1). In contrast, the naïve Stackelberg manufacturer will set a wholesale price:

$$\hat{W}^* = \left(Q_=^* / (b-\theta)\right) + C \tag{6.6.2}$$

(This value is replicated from (5.5.11) after accounting for $Q_i^* = Q_j^*$.) A clear-cut comparison of (6.6.1) with (6.6.2) reveals that the relationship between the sophisticated Stackelberg and the naïve Stackelberg wholesale margins is:

$$\left(W_=^* - C\right) = \left(\theta Q_=^* / b(b-\theta)\right) < \left(Q_=^* / (b-\theta)\right) = \left(\hat{W}^* - C\right) \tag{6.6.3}$$

Because $\theta < b$, the sophisticated Stackelberg wholesale price is *always less* than the naïve Stackelberg wholesale price, even with identical competitors. More importantly, the sophisticated Stackelberg two-part tariff (6.6.1) is equal to the optimal transfer price given by (5.3.7). Given identical competitors, the channel is fully coordinated by a sophisticated Stackelberg two-part tariff. It follows that the sophisticated approach is a "new and improved" version of the traditional Stackelberg methodology.

## 6.4 Summary Commentary

A basic precept of the marketing science literature on distribution channels is that coordination benefits all channel members. To the extent that this prescription has been evaluated, it has been against the "straw man" of a "naïve" Stackelberg two-part tariff that can never coordinate any channel. We have proven that this naïve tariff is itself one of an infinite number of special cases of a fully comprehensive (a "sophisticated Stackelberg") tariff that is the envelope of all possible two-part tariffs. In addition to being inclusive, the sophisticated Stackelberg tariff is also completely flexible. It coordinates both a bilateral-monopoly channel and an identical-competitors channel, although it cannot coordinate any channel of competing, but non-identical, retailers. In short, the sophisticated Stackelberg tariff is robust across a variety of modeling assumptions. In future Chapters we will extend our examination of robustness in several key directions. Our path reflects the experience of Rene Descartes, who wrote, "I began with the most simple and general, and each truth that I found was a rule which helped me to find others [i.e., other rules]."[13] Descartes comment applies as well to our use of the sophisticated Stackelberg tariff to solve the vexing problem of determining the parametric conditions for which channel coordination is, or is not, optimal for all channel members. Before doing so we must create a worthy, channel-coordinating rival to the (generally) non-coordinating sophisticated Stackelberg two-part tariff. Thus, in the next Chapter, we develop a channel-coordinating menu of two-part tariffs.

# 7 APPENDIX

In this Appendix we prove that retailer profits are zero in Zone $Z_{ij}^{SS*}$ after paying the fixed fee (i.e., $\hat{\pi}_i^*(\omega) = 0 = \hat{\pi}_j^*(\omega)$ ).

We start by defining net revenue for the k[th] retailer:

$$\hat{R}_k^*(\omega) \equiv \frac{\left[\hat{Q}_k^*(\omega)\right]^2}{b} \qquad k \in (i,j) \tag{6.A.1}$$

The j[th] retailer's profit is:

$$\hat{\pi}_j^*(\omega) = \left(\hat{R}_j^*(\omega) - f_j\right) - \hat{\phi}^*(\omega) \tag{6.A.2}$$

Set $\hat{\phi}^*(\omega)$ to extract all rent from the j[th] retailer; thus $\hat{\pi}_j^*(\omega) = 0$ . This leaves the i[th] retailer with a profit of:

$$\hat{\pi}_i^*(\omega) = \left(\hat{R}_i^*(\omega) - f_i\right) - \hat{\phi}^*(\omega) = \left[\hat{R}_i^*(\omega) - \hat{R}_j^*(\omega)\right] - \left(f_i - f_j\right) \tag{6.A.3}$$

We now manipulate the definition of ω to obtain:

$$\left(f_i - f_j\right) = \frac{2\left(Q_i^* - Q_j^*\right)\left(\hat{Q}_i^*(\omega) + \hat{Q}_j^*(\omega)\right)}{\left(2b + \theta\right)} \tag{6.A.4}$$

The RHS of equation (6.A.4) can be shown to be identically equal to $[\hat{R}_i^*(\omega) - \hat{R}_j^*(\omega)]$. Hence after payment of the fixed fee $\hat{\pi}_i^*(\omega) = 0 = \hat{\pi}_j^*(\omega)$ throughout Zone $Z_{ij}^{SS*}$. **QED**

# Notes

[1] This Chapter is based upon our *Marketing Letters* paper: "Manufacturer-Optimal Wholesale Pricing When Retailers Compete" (Ingene and Parry 1998). It includes a substantial amount of material that has been developed since that article appeared. (Kluwer Academic/Plenum Publishers holds the *Marketing Letters* copyright; our material is used with permission.)

[2] See Tables 5.2-5.4.

[3] In Chapters 8 and 9 we compare manufacturer profits from a channel-coordinating quantity-discount schedule (Chapter 5), a sophisticated Stackelberg two-part tariff (Chapter 6), and a menu of channel-coordinating two-part tariffs (Chapter 7).

[4] Throughout this Chapter we assume that the manufacturer serves both retailers. If the difference in retailer profits is large enough, the manufacturer will serve only the more-profitable retailer and will extract all its profit, because the single-retailer model is a bilateral monopoly. We ignore this possibility in Chapters 5-9; however, we devote Chapter 10 to the issue of channel breadth by delineating specific parametric values under which serving a single retailer is manufacturer-profit-optimal.

[5] See equation (5.5.6) for details.

[6] We distinguish the optimized values in the sophisticated Stackelberg case from those in the naïve Stackelberg case through notational differences: $\hat{X}^*(k)$ for the former, $\hat{X}^*$ for the latter, where X denotes any variable and $k \in (i, j)$.

[7] The reason that $(\hat{W}^*(i) - C) < 0 < (\hat{W}^*(j) - C)$ may occur is that we have assumed $Q_i^* > Q_j^*$; reversing the quantity inequality would lead to the manufacturer's margin on sales to the $j^{th}$ retailer potentially being negative.

[8] The values of $\hat{W}^*(i)$ and $\hat{\phi}^*(i)$ can be obtained by switching the $i^{th}$ and $j^{th}$ subscripts in the definitions of $\hat{W}^*(j)$ and $\hat{\phi}^*(j)$—see equations (6.2.2) and (6.2.3), respectively.

[9] We prove this statement rigorously in Section 4 and the Appendix to this Chapter.

[10] See Chapter 5, equation (5.3.7), for the optimal transfer-prices $T_i^*$ and $T_j^*$.

[11] $\hat{\upsilon}^* \equiv \left[1 + \left\{\left(Q_i^* + Q_j^*\right)/\left(2(b-\theta)C\right)\right\}\right]$ and $\tilde{\upsilon}^* \equiv \left[1 + \left\{\theta\left(Q_i^* + Q_j^*\right)/\left(2b(b-\theta)C\right)\right\}\right]$

[12] Equal outputs require the retailers to have equal demand intercepts and equal per-unit costs.

[13] The quotation is from *Discourse on Method,* translated by Lafleur (1950, p. 13).

Chapter 7

# The Channel-Coordinating Menu[1]

*"...in the great chess-board of human society, every single piece has a principle of motion of its own, altogether different from that which the legislator might choose to impress upon it."*

## 1 INTRODUCTION

In this Chapter we continue our investigation of channel performance in the presence of inter-retailer competition. Here we investigate the consequences of the manufacturer utilizing a channel-coordinating menu of two-part tariffs as its wholesale-price policy. Although the manufacturer can customize the menu so that a specific two-part tariff is designed for each retailer,[2] an independent retailer can—and will—select whichever element of the menu it prefers given (i) its demand and cost conditions and (ii) its belief about the tariff chosen by its competitor. Thus a key contribution of this Chapter is our analysis of the feasibility, and the manufacturer profitability, of achieving channel coordination with a more complex wholesale-price schedule than we used in Chapter 5.[3]

The model presented here will resolve five basic questions:

(1) Is it possible to design a menu of two-part tariffs that coordinates the channel *and* that enables the manufacturer to gain all channel profit?

(2) Will a retailer accept the menu element that is intended for it, or will it "defect" to an element of the menu designed for its rival?

(3) If defection occurs is the channel still coordinated?

(4) Is there a menu that will always preclude defection, thereby inducing channel coordination?

(5) What is the distribution of profit between channel members under a channel-coordinating menu?

In this Chapter we derive three important results. First, a menu of two-part tariffs will only coordinate the channel if and only if each retailer selects the tariff that is designed for it (the "right" tariff). Second, through a judicious choice of fixed fees, the manufacturer can always ensure that all retailers will select the "right" tariff. Third, there are parametric values that make it impossible for the manufacturer to extract all channel profit. This raises the possibility that the manufacturer may prefer an alternative, non-coordinating wholesale-price policy. We defer investigation of this prospect to the next Chapter.

The intuitive essence of our analysis is that there is an interaction effect; the $i^{th}$ retailer's selection of one tariff rather than another tariff affects not only its own profit, but also the profit of its rival, the $j^{th}$ retailer. This occurs because the marginal wholesale price paid by the $i^{th}$ retailer affects the price it will charge consumers, and this retail price influences the $j^{th}$ retailer's price through the cross-price term in the $j^{th}$ retailer's demand curve.

We also determine the conditions under which the retailers' tariff choices define an equilibrium outcome. By way of illustration, if the $i^{th}$ retailer selects the $m^{th}$ tariff under the belief that the $j^{th}$ retailer will select the $n^{th}$ tariff, an equilibrium solution requires that the $j^{th}$ retailer actually select the $n^{th}$ tariff under the belief that the $i^{th}$ retailer will select the $m^{th}$ tariff.

This Chapter is organized as follows. Section 2 develops a retailer's decision process when it selects from a menu of two-part tariffs. In Section 3 we assess the manufacturer's choice of the fixed fee for each of the two-part tariffs that compose the channel-coordinating menu. In Section 4 we examine the relationship between the manufacturer's ability to extract profit from the retailers and the parameters of the demand and cost functions. We present a numerical illustration of our results in Section 5. Finally, we offer a discussion and summary in Section 6.

## 2 THE RETAILERS' RESPONSE TO A MENU OF TWO-PART TARIFFS

We proved in Chapter 5 that a vertically-integrated system has a unique pair of profit-maximizing transfer prices ($T_i^*$ and $T_j^*$—see equation (5.3.7)). In the case of an arms-length channel relationship, achieving channel coordination requires that each retailer pay a *per-unit* wholesale price ($W_k^*$, $k \in (i, j)$) that is equal to the channel-coordinating transfer price ($W_k^* = T_k^*$). In contrast, the *fixed fees* do not affect coordination provided they do not drive a retailer from the market, but they do determine the allocation of profit among channel members. For expositional ease we describe a channel-coordinating two-part tariff with the abbreviated notation $\tau_k \equiv \{W_k^*, \phi_k\}$, $k \in (i, j)$; we denote a *menu* of such tariffs as $\{\tau_i, \tau_j\}$.

Because the retailers are Nash competitors, their choices from $\{\tau_i, \tau_j\}$ must be mutually compatible. In fact, the retailers' joint decisions logically yield four Cases:

**Case I:** The i[th] retailer chooses $\tau_j$ and the j[th] retailer chooses $\tau_i$;

**Case II(i):** Both retailers choose $\tau_i$;

**Case II(j):** Both retailers choose $\tau_j$; and

**Case III:** The i[th] retailer chooses $\tau_i$ and the j[th] retailer chooses $\tau_j$.

Only Case III is compatible with channel coordination, because it is the only case in which $W_k^* = T_k^*$, $k \in (i,j)$ (we prove this point below). Thus it is important to understand the conditions under which a retailer will choose the "wrong" tariff. To this end we model the decision process as a three-stage game. In the first stage, the manufacturer devises a menu of two-part tariffs and offers the same menu to each retailer. In the second stage, each retailer selects its preferred menu element, contingent on its belief about what element its rival will select. In the third stage, each retailer sets a consumer price to maximize its profit, given its chosen tariff and the tariff choice of its rival. The first stage entails a manufacturer Stackelberg leadership game. The second stage engages each retailer in assessing its own self-selection constraint, and the third stage involves a Nash equilibrium game.

## 2.1 The Retailer's Profit-Maximizing Price Decision

We begin by analyzing the retailer pricing decisions in the third stage. Let $p_{imn}$ and $Q_{imn}$ denote the price charged and quantity sold by the i[th] retailer, given that it selects the m[th] two-part tariff $\tau_m$ and the j[th] retailer selects the n[th] two-part tariff $\tau_n$ $(m,n \in (i,j))$.[4] Let $\pi_{imn}$ denote profit earned by the i[th] retailer given prices $p_{imn}$ and $p_{jnm}$. The i[th] retailer maximizes:

$$\max_{p_{imn}} \pi_{imn} = \left(p_{imn} - c_i - W_m^*\right)\left(A_i - bp_{imn} + \theta p_{jnm}\right) - f_i - \phi_m, \qquad (7.2.1)$$

where demand is now written as:

$$Q_{imn} = A_i - bp_{imn} + \theta p_{jnm} \qquad (7.2.2)$$

We maximize $\pi_{imn}$ and (the implicit equation) $\pi_{jnm}$ and jointly solve for the optimal retail prices given $W_m^* \equiv T_m^*$ and $W_n^* \equiv T_n^*$:

$$p_{imn}^* = \frac{2b\left(A_i + bc_i + bW_m^*\right) + \theta\left(A_j + bc_j + bW_n^*\right)}{\left(4b^2 - \theta^2\right)} \qquad (7.2.3)$$

$$p_{jnm}^* = \frac{\theta\left(A_i + bc_i + bW_m^*\right) + 2b\left(A_j + bc_j + bW_n^*\right)}{\left(4b^2 - \theta^2\right)} \qquad (7.2.4)$$

Manipulation yields margins for the channel, the manufacturer, and each retailer. We find quantities by inserting the prices into demand curve (7.2.2).

For example, in Case I the $i^{th}$ retailer chooses $\tau_j$ and the $j^{th}$ retailer selects $\tau_i$. We make the necessary substitutions to determine the prices, channel margins and quantities sold:

$$\left(p_{iji}^{*} - c_i - C\right) \equiv \mu_{iji}^{*} = \mu_i^{*} + \left(\frac{\theta\left(Q_i^{*} - Q_j^{*}\right)}{(b+\theta)(2b+\theta)}\right) \tag{7.2.5}$$

$$Q_{iji}^{*} = \frac{2bQ_i^{*} + \theta Q_j^{*}}{(2b+\theta)} = Q_i^{*} - \left(\frac{\theta\left(Q_i^{*} - Q_j^{*}\right)}{(2b+\theta)}\right) \tag{7.2.6}$$

In a comparable fashion we determine quantities for Cases II(i), II(j), and III. These quantities are:

$$\text{Case II(i)}: \qquad Q_{iii}^{*} = Q_i^{*} - \left(\frac{b\theta^2\left(Q_i^{*} - Q_j^{*}\right)}{(b+\theta)\left(4b^2 - \theta^2\right)}\right) \tag{7.2.7}$$

$$\text{Case II(j)}: \qquad Q_{iij}^{*} = Q_i^{*} - \left(\frac{\theta\left(2b^2 - \theta^2\right)\left(Q_i^{*} - Q_j^{*}\right)}{(b+\theta)\left(4b^2 - \theta^2\right)}\right) \tag{7.2.8}$$

$$\text{Case III}: \qquad Q_{iij}^{*} = Q_i^{*} \tag{7.2.9}$$

It is obvious from equations (7.2.6)-(7.2.8) that the channel is not coordinated in Case I, Case II(i) or Case II(j), because these Cases do not result in an output level of $Q_i^{*}$ for the $i^{th}$ retailer—except in the degenerate cases of identical competitors or an absence of competition.

As a technical aside, in Cases II(i) and II(j) the channel is not even coordinated "on average" except in the aforementioned degenerate cases. For example, in Case II(i) total output is:

$$\left[Q_{iii}^{*} + Q_{jii}^{*}\right] = \left[\left(Q_i^{*} + Q_j^{*}\right) - \left(\frac{\theta(b-\theta)\left(Q_i^{*} - Q_j^{*}\right)}{(b+\theta)(2b-\theta)}\right)\right] \neq \left(Q_i^{*} + Q_j^{*}\right) \tag{7.2.10}$$

To obtain (7.2.10) add $Q_{iii}^{*}$ from (7.2.7) to $Q_{jii}^{*}$ from (7.2.8) *after* reversing all subscripts in (7.2.8). Total output in Case II(i) is equal to vertically-integrated output *only* in the trivial situations of (i) identical competitors $(Q_i^{*} = Q_j^{*})$, (ii) perfect substitutability $(b = \theta)$, or (iii) no competition $(\theta = 0)$. In these situations a menu of tariffs is meaningless because $T_i^{*} = T_j^{*}$. Case II(j) is symmetric, so our other analyses ignore these trivial situations.

Channel margins for Cases II(i), II(j), and III are:

Case II(i): $$\mu^*_{iii} = \mu^*_i - \left( \frac{\theta^2 \left( Q^*_i - Q^*_j \right)}{(b+\theta)\left(4b^2 - \theta^2\right)} \right) \tag{7.2.11}$$

Case II(j): $$\mu^*_{iij} = \mu^*_i + \left( \frac{2b\theta \left( Q^*_i - Q^*_j \right)}{(b+\theta)\left(4b^2 - \theta^2\right)} \right) \tag{7.2.12}$$

Case III: $$\mu^*_{iij} = \left( \frac{bQ^*_i + \theta Q^*_j}{\left(b^2 - \theta^2\right)} \right) = \mu^*_i \tag{7.2.13}$$

Only Case III is consistent with channel coordination.

We can see the price-quantity subtleties associated with defection by evaluating the case of $Q^*_i > Q^*_j$. Recall that channel-coordination requires the larger retailer to pay a lower per-unit wholesale price (Chapter 5, Section 3.3). Defection by the j[th] retailer to the tariff intended for the i[th] retailer (Case II(i)) lowers the per-unit cost of the j[th] retailer, which leads that retailer to price below its channel-optimal price. Because retailer demand curves are interdependent, the i[th] retailer also decreases its price, but not enough to prevent its output from declining (even though channel output rises). In contrast, defection by the i[th] retailer (Case II(j)) raises all prices and lowers total output, although the output of the smaller retailer rises.

The level of retailer profit associated with all four Cases can be computed by substituting the appropriate quantity in the following general profit equation:

$$\begin{aligned} \pi^*_{kmn} &= \left[ \left( Q^*_{kmn} \right)^2 / b \right] - f_k - \phi_m \\ &\equiv \left( R^*_{kmn} - f_k \right) - \phi_m \equiv g^*_{kmn} - \phi_m, \quad k \in (i,j) \end{aligned} \tag{7.2.14}$$

The case-dependent levels of retail prices, quantities and profits for the j[th] retailer may be obtained by reversing the i[th] and j[th] subscripts in equations (7.2.5)-(7.2.14). Note that the fixed fee $\phi_m$ is determined in the first stage of the game: it has a maximal value of $g^*_{kmn}$. Any attempt to extract a larger fixed fee will violate the i[th] retailer's participation constraint.

## 2.2 The Retailers' Tariff-Selection Decisions

We now turn to the retailers' tariff choices in the second stage of the game. We impose two conditions. First, the tariff chosen by a retailer must at least weakly dominate the tariff it rejects. Second, the tariffs selected by the i[th] and j[th] retailers must simultaneously represent an equilibrium pair of choices. To illustrate, suppose the i[th] retailer selects $\tau_m$ and the j[th] retailer chooses $\tau_n$. We define an equilibrium set of menu choices as:

$$\pi^*_{imn} > \pi^*_{inn} \quad \text{and} \quad \pi^*_{jnm} > \pi^*_{jmm} \tag{7.2.15}$$

This means that, in equilibrium, neither retailer can increase its profit by choosing the alternative two-part tariff: neither has an incentive to "defect."

Having defined an equilibrium set of menu choices, we now evaluate the four Cases. To this end we adopt the following simplifying notation:

$$\begin{aligned}
&\zeta_1 \equiv \left( \frac{\theta(2b^2-\theta^2)(Q^*_i - Q^*_j)}{b(b+\theta)^2(4b^2-\theta^2)^2} \right) \gtrless 0 \qquad \text{as} \quad (Q^*_i - Q^*_j) \gtrless 0 \\
&\zeta_2 \equiv (8b^3 + 6b^2\theta - 2b\theta^2 - \theta^3) > 0 \\
&\zeta_3 \equiv (8b^3 + 6b^2\theta - 4b\theta^2 - \theta^3) = (\zeta_2 - 2b\theta^2) > 0 \\
&\zeta_4 \equiv \theta(2b^2 + 2b\theta - \theta^2) \geq 0 \\
&\zeta_5 \equiv \theta(2b^2 - \theta^2) = (\zeta_4 - 2b\theta^2) \geq 0
\end{aligned} \tag{7.2.16}$$

These variables have the following relationship: definitions may be ranked as $\zeta_2 > \zeta_3 > \zeta_4 \geq \zeta_5 \geq 0$, where the equalities on $\zeta_4$ and $\zeta_5$ hold only when $\theta = 0$. To simplify our discussion, and at no loss of generality, we henceforth assume that $\zeta_1 > 0$; this is equivalent to the assumption that the $i^{th}$ retailer produces the larger output ($Q^*_i > Q^*_j$). We made the same expository assumption in Chapter 6.

**Case I.** In Case I the $i^{th}$ retailer chooses the tariff $\tau_j$ and the $j^{th}$ retailer chooses the tariff $\tau_i$. This occurs if and only if:

$$\pi^*_{iji} > \pi^*_{iii} \quad \text{and} \quad \pi^*_{jij} > \pi^*_{jjj} \tag{7.2.17}$$

It can be shown that:

$$\pi^*_{iji} > \pi^*_{iii} \quad \Rightarrow \quad \zeta_1\left[\zeta_3 Q^*_i + \zeta_4 Q^*_j\right] < (\phi_i - \phi_j) \tag{7.2.18}$$

$$\pi^*_{jij} > \pi^*_{jjj} \quad \Rightarrow \quad \zeta_1\left[\zeta_4 Q^*_i + \zeta_3 Q^*_j\right] > (\phi_i - \phi_j) \tag{7.2.19}$$

These conditions *cannot* hold simultaneously. To see this compare the LHS's of the two preceding inequalities:

$$(\zeta_3 - \zeta_4)Q^*_i < (\zeta_3 - \zeta_4)Q^*_j \tag{7.2.20}$$

Because $(\zeta_3 - \zeta_4) > 0$, $Q^*_i < Q^*_j$ is required for (7.2.20) to hold. But $Q^*_i < Q^*_j$ contradicts our assumption that $Q^*_i > Q^*_j$.[5] It follows that *Case I cannot represent an equilibrium set of menu choices*, because at least one retailer does not defect to the tariff intended for its competitor.

**Case II(i).** In Case II(i) equilibrium both retailers choose the tariff

$\tau_i$. This occurs if and only if:

$$\pi^*_{iii} > \pi^*_{iji} \quad \text{and} \quad \pi^*_{jii} > \pi^*_{jji} \tag{7.2.21}$$

It can be shown that:

$$\pi^*_{iii} > \pi^*_{iji} \quad \Rightarrow \quad \zeta_1\left[\zeta_3 Q^*_i + \zeta_4 Q^*_j\right] > \left(\phi_i - \phi_j\right) \tag{7.2.22}$$

$$\pi^*_{jii} > \pi^*_{jji} \quad \Rightarrow \quad \zeta_1\left[\zeta_5 Q^*_i + \zeta_2 Q^*_j\right] > \left(\phi_i - \phi_j\right) \tag{7.2.23}$$

Because (7.2.23) is a tighter condition than (7.2.22), both conditions are satisfied when:

$$B_i \equiv \zeta_1\left[\zeta_5 Q^*_i + \zeta_2 Q^*_j\right] > \left(\phi_i - \phi_j\right) \tag{7.2.24}$$

We term $B_i$ the "i[th] boundary condition." When $B_i > (\phi_i - \phi_j)$, both retailers choose tariff $\tau_i$.

**Case II(j).** In Case II(j) equilibrium both retailers choose the tariff $\tau_j$. This occurs if and only if:

$$\pi^*_{ijj} > \pi^*_{iij} \quad \text{and} \quad \pi^*_{jjj} > \pi^*_{jij} \tag{7.2.25}$$

It can be shown that:

$$\pi^*_{ijj} > \pi^*_{iij} \quad \Rightarrow \quad \zeta_1\left[\zeta_2 Q^*_i + \zeta_5 Q^*_j\right] < \left(\phi_i - \phi_j\right) \tag{7.2.26}$$

$$\pi^*_{jjj} > \pi^*_{jij} \quad \Rightarrow \quad \zeta_1\left[\zeta_4 Q^*_i + \zeta_3 Q^*_j\right] < \left(\phi_i - \phi_j\right) \tag{7.2.27}$$

Because (7.2.26) is a tighter condition than (7.2.27), both conditions are satisfied when:

$$B_j \equiv \zeta_1\left[\zeta_2 Q^*_i + \zeta_5 Q^*_j\right] < \left(\phi_i - \phi_j\right) \tag{7.2.28}$$

We term $B_j$ the "j[th] boundary condition." When $B_j < (\phi_i - \phi_j)$, both retailers choose tariff $\tau_j$.

**Case III.** In Case III equilibrium the i[th] retailer chooses the tariff $\tau_i$ and the j[th] retailer chooses the tariff $\tau_j$. This occurs if and only if:

$$\pi^*_{iij} > \pi^*_{ijj} \quad \text{and} \quad \pi^*_{jji} > \pi^*_{jii} \tag{7.2.29}$$

It can be shown that:

$$\pi^*_{iij} > \pi^*_{ijj} \quad \Rightarrow \quad \zeta_1\left[\zeta_2 Q^*_i + \zeta_5 Q^*_j\right] > \left(\phi_i - \phi_j\right) \tag{7.2.30}$$

$$\pi^*_{jji} > \pi^*_{jii} \quad \Rightarrow \quad \zeta_1\left[\zeta_5 Q^*_i + \zeta_2 Q^*_j\right] < \left(\phi_i - \phi_j\right) \tag{7.2.31}$$

For these conditions to hold simultaneously, we must have:

$$B_j \equiv \zeta_1\left[\zeta_2 Q^*_i + \zeta_5 Q^*_j\right] \geq \left(\phi_i - \phi_j\right) \geq \zeta_1\left[\zeta_5 Q^*_i + \zeta_2 Q^*_j\right] \equiv B_i \tag{7.2.32}$$

Provided the difference in fixed fees lies between the i[th] and the j[th] boundary conditions, each retailer will select the tariff intended for it and the channel will be coordinated.

To summarize, we have shown that:

$$\begin{array}{lll} \textbf{Case I} \text{ is } \textit{not} \text{ an equilibrium solution} & & \\ \textbf{Case II(i)} \text{ is an equilibrium solution iff:} & (\phi_i - \phi_j) \geq B_i & \\ \textbf{Case II(j)} \text{ is an equilibrium solution iff:} & B_j < (\phi_i - \phi_j) & (7.2.33) \\ \textbf{Case III} \text{ is an equilibrium solution iff:} & B_j \geq (\phi_i - \phi_j) \geq B_i & \end{array}$$

The equilibrium solution[6] depends on the relative magnitudes of the $i^{th}$ and $j^{th}$ boundary conditions and on the *difference in fixed fees* between the tariffs. The *boundary conditions are exogenous* to the manufacturer,[7] but the manufacturer endogenously determines the fixed fees. These fees must be set to ensure channel coordination. There is, in effect, a "defection constraint" that the manufacturer must satisfy if the channel is to be coordinated. Defection is not a concern provided the difference in fixed fees lies between boundaries $B_i$ and $B_j$; outside these bounds the manufacturer must adjust the fixed fees.

## 3 THE MANUFACTURER'S DECISIONS ON THE FIXED FEES

We now turn to the first stage of the game, in which the manufacturer specifies the elements of a *channel-coordinating* menu of two-part tariffs. Because $W_k^* = T_k^*$ is required for coordination, the manufacturer only needs to determine its profit maximizing fixed fees $\phi_i$ and $\phi_j$, subject to two constraints. First, to ensure retailer participation, the fixed fees must leave the retailers with non-negative profits. Thus $\phi_k$ must satisfy:

$$\phi_k \leq g_k^* \equiv \left\{ \left[ (Q_k^*)^2 / b \right] - f_k \right\} \equiv \left( R_k^* - f_k \right), \qquad k \in (i, j) \tag{7.3.1}$$

Second, because channel coordination is only consistent with Case III equilibrium, the tariffs must be designed to prevent defection. To satisfy the defection constraint while achieving channel coordination, the difference in fixed fees must satisfy:

$$B_j \geq \left( \phi_i - \phi_j \right) \geq B_i \tag{7.3.2}$$

Within the boundaries given by this pair of inequalities, the manufacturer is free to maximize its own profit. We now turn to this topic.

## 3.1 Full Profit Extraction

From the manufacturer's perspective, the *ideal* menu extracts all profit from both retailers while coordinating the channel:

$$\tau^{g^*} = \left\{ \tau_i^{g_i^*}, \tau_j^{g_j^*} \right\}$$
$$\text{s.t.} \quad \tau_k^{g_i^*} \equiv \left\{ W_k^*, \phi_k^* \right\} = \left\{ W_k^*, g_k^* \right\}, \quad k \in (i,j) \tag{7.3.3}$$

If both retailers select the "right" tariff—if the menu (7.3.3) generates Case III equilibrium—then no non-coordinating wholesale-price schedule can manufacturer profit-dominate this channel-coordinating menu. The reason is simple; the manufacturer obtains the total profit of a coordinated channel.

However, if one retailer opts for the "wrong" tariff—if a boundary condition in (7.3.2) is violated—then the channel will not be coordinated, nor will the manufacturer extract all profit from both retailers. Thus a non-coordinating tariff may manufacturer-profit dominate the menu.

We use a two-step process to rewrite the boundary inequality (7.3.2) in terms of the differences in the retailers' fixed costs. First we substitute the definition of the fixed fees of the menu $\tau^{g^*}$ into $(\phi_i - \phi_j)$; that is, we replace $\phi_i$ with $g_i^*$ and $\phi_j$ with $g_j^*$. Second, we replace $g_j^*$ with its definition from (7.3.1). Rearranging terms yields the i$^{th}$ retailer's defection condition:[8]

$$L^{Menu^*} \equiv \frac{\xi_1\left[b\xi_1 Q_i^* + \xi_2 Q_j^*\right]\left(Q_i^* - Q_j^*\right)}{(b+\theta)^2\left(4b^2 - \theta^2\right)^2} > \left(f_i - f_j\right) \tag{7.3.4}$$

A similar analysis of Case II(i) shows that the j$^{th}$ retailer defects if and only if:

$$\left(f_i - f_j\right) > \frac{\xi_1\left[\xi_2 Q_i^* + b\xi_1 Q_j^*\right]\left(Q_i^* - Q_j^*\right)}{(b+\theta)^2\left(4b^2 - \theta^2\right)^2} \equiv U^{Menu^*} \tag{7.3.5}$$

Comparing inequalities (7.3.5) and (7.3.4), and recalling our expository assumption $Q_i^* > Q_j^*$, we find that $U^{Menu^*} > L^{Menu^*} > 0$. Finally, Case III holds if *neither* inequality (7.3.4) nor inequality (7.3.5) holds.

Given the menu $\tau^{g^*} \equiv \{\tau_i^{g^*}, \tau_j^{g^*}\}$, the equilibrium Cases and their consequences can be expressed in terms of three "Zones" in $(f_i - f_j)$ space:

$$\begin{array}{lcl} \text{The i}^{th} \text{ retailer defects to } \tau_j^{g^*} & \Leftrightarrow & \left(f_i - f_j\right) < L^{Menu^*} \\ \text{Neither retailer defects} & \Leftrightarrow & U^{Menu^*} \geq \left(f_i - f_j\right) \geq L^{Menu^*} \\ \text{The j}^{th} \text{ retailer defects to } \tau_i^{g^*} & \Leftrightarrow & U^{Menu^*} < \left(f_i - f_j\right) \end{array} \tag{7.3.6}$$

We have shown that when competing retailers are confronted with the menu choices $\tau^{g^*} = \{\tau_i^{g_i^*}, \tau_j^{g_j^*}\}$ there are three possible outcomes. Either both retailers opt for the two-part tariff $\tau_i^{g_i^*}$ (Case II(i) equilibrium), or both retailers select tariff $\tau_j^{g_j^*}$ (Case II(j) equilibrium), or each retailer accepts the tariff intended for it. Only in the last instance does the menu $\tau^{g^*}$ achieve the goal of channel coordination. The next Table details the connection between the Zones of this Section and the previous Section's Cases:

| Case | Case Boundary Condition | Zone | Zonal Boundary Condition |
|---|---|---|---|
| II(j) | $B_j < (\phi_i - \phi_j)$ | $Z_j^{Menu^*}$ | $(f_i - f_j) < L^{Menu^*}$ |
| III | $B_j > (\phi_i - \phi_j) > B_i$ | $Z_{ij}^{Menu^*}$ | $U^{Menu^*} \geq (f_i - f_j) \geq L^{Menu^*}$ |
| II(i) | $(\phi_i - \phi_j) < B_i$ | $Z_i^{Menu^*}$ | $U^{Menu^*} < (f_i - f_j)$ |

## 3.2 Ensuring Channel-Coordination *via* Adjustment of the Fixed Fees

If the ideal menu—the menu defined in equation (7.2.36)—induces one retailer to defect, the manufacturer must modify the fixed fees to ensure channel coordination. We begin by seeking an understanding of a defector's reasoning. We then use this information to block defection.

To illustrate the process, consider the Case II(j) equilibrium, in which both retailers select the j[th] tariff when offered the menu $\{\tau_i^*, \tau_j^*\}$. If the i[th] retailer does *not* defect, it earns zero economic profit. The reason is that its net revenue minus its fixed cost equals the "ideal" fixed fee $\phi_i^* = [R_i^* - f_i]$. By defecting the i[th] retailer lowers the fixed fee that it pays ($\phi_j^* = [R_j^* - f_j] < \phi_i^*$), but it incurs a higher per-unit fee ($W_j^* > W_i^*$). The change in the per-unit wholesale price reduces the i[th] retailer's net revenue from $R_i^*$ to $\{R_i^* - B_j\}$,[9] but this reduction is more than offset by the savings from the lower fixed fee. As a result, the i[th] retailer's profit rises. Formally we have:

$$\begin{aligned} \pi_{ijj} &\equiv \left(\{R_i^* - B_j\} - f_i\right) - \left[R_j^* - f_j\right] \\ &> \left(R_i^* - f_i\right) - \left[R_i^* - f_i\right] \equiv \pi_{iij} = 0 \end{aligned} \tag{7.3.7}$$

The [bracketed] terms are the relevant fixed fee and the (parenthetical) terms are retailer profits prior to paying the fixed fee. The term in {braces} in the upper line is the $i^{th}$ retailer's net revenue when it defects; the bottom line is its net revenue when it does not defect. Expression (7.3.7) simply states that the retailer's profit due to defection is greater than the zero profit that is earned without defecting.

To ensure coordination the manufacturer must eliminate the $i^{th}$ retailer's incentive to defect. Because adjustments in the per-unit fees preclude coordination, the manufacturer must alter a fixed fee. This approach is reminiscent of the "semi-sophisticated" approach that we took in Chapter 4 and again in Chapter 6, Section 3.2; in both those cases we adjusted the fixed fee while holding the per-unit wholesale price constant.

If the manufacturer were to raise $\phi_j^*$, it would encourage the $j^{th}$ retailer to defect; thus the manufacturer's only option is to reduce $\phi_i^*$. The magnitude of the requisite reduction is implicitly defined by expression (7.3.7). In particular, by defecting the $i^{th}$ retailer pays a lower fixed fee ($\phi_j^*$) *but* sacrifices net revenue of $B_j$. Thus the maximum fixed fee that the manufacturer can extract from the $i^{th}$ retailer without causing defection is $(\phi_j^* + B_j)$. Accordingly, instead of offering $\tau_i^* \equiv \{W_i^*, \phi_i^* = [R_i^* - f_i]\}$ as the $i^{th}$ element of the menu, the manufacturer must offer the alternative tariff $\tau_i^L \equiv \{W_i^*, \phi_i^L = [(R_j^* - f_j) + B_j]\}$. (To calculate the optimal fixed fee $\phi_i^L$, replace $[R_i^* - f_i]$ on the lower line of expression (7.3.7) with a $\phi$. Then set the upper line of (7.3.7) equal to the lower line and solve for $\phi$. The solution is the optimal $\phi_i^L$.) To summarize, in Case II(j) equilibrium, the manufacturer-optimal menu of two-part tariffs is $\{\tau_i^L, \tau_j^*\}$. This menu creates a positive economic profit for the $i^{th}$ retailer and extracts all profit from the $j^{th}$ retailer.[10]

In Case II(i) equilibrium both retailers would select the tariff $\tau_i^*$. Defection by the $j^{th}$ retailer can be prevented if the $j^{th}$ element of the menu is $\tau_j^U \equiv \{W_j^*, \phi_j^U = [(R_i^* - f_i) + B_i]\}$. With this adjustment the tariff intended for the $i^{th}$ retailer ($\tau_i^*$) and the (modified) tariff intended for the $j^{th}$ retailer ($\tau_j^U$) yield the same positive economic profit to the $j^{th}$ retailer:

$$\begin{aligned} \pi_{jii} &\equiv \left(\left\{R_j^* - B_i\right\} - f_j\right) - \left[R_i^* - f_i\right] \\ &= \left(R_j^* - f_j\right) - \left[\left(R_i^* - f_i\right) + B_i\right] \equiv \pi_{jji} > 0 \end{aligned} \qquad (7.3.8)$$

In expression (7.3.8) the upper line is the $j^{th}$ retailer's profit from defecting when the menu is $\{\tau_i^*, \tau_j^*\}$, while the lower line is the profit from *not* defecting when the menu is $\{\tau_i^*, \tau_j^U\}$. The [bracketed] terms are the relevant fixed fee, the (parenthetical) terms are profit before paying the fixed fee; the term in {braces} on the top line is the $j^{th}$ retailer's net revenue when it defects; and the term $B_i$ (which is defined at (7.2.24)) is the net revenue reduction due to defection.[11]

## 3.3 The Channel-Coordinating Menu of Two-Part Tariffs

Because the manufacturer-optimal, channel-coordinating menu of two-part tariffs varies across Zones, profits vary by Zone. Table 7.1 contains the relevant details. In Zone $Z_j^{Menu^*}$ the $j^{th}$ (the less-profitable) retailer earns zero profit, while in Zone $Z_i^{Menu^*}$ the $i^{th}$ retailer earns zero profit. In Zone $Z_{ij}^{Menu^*}$ both retailers earn zero economic profits after paying their fixed fees.

*Table 7.1.* Profit Distribution by Zone

| Zone | Tariff | Channel Profit | Manufacturer Profit | Profit of the $i^{th}$ Retailer | Profit of the $j^{th}$ Retailer |
|---|---|---|---|---|---|
| $Z_j^{Menu^*}$ | $\tau^{L*}$ | $g_i^* + g_j^* - F$ | $2g_j^* + B_j - F$ | $g_i^* - (g_j^* + B_j)$ | 0 |
| $Z_{ij}^{Menu^*}$ | $\tau^*$ | $g_i^* + g_j^* - F$ | $g_i^* + g_j^* - F$ | 0 | 0 |
| $Z_i^{Menu^*}$ | $\tau^{U*}$ | $g_i^* + g_j^* - F$ | $2g_i^* + B_i - F$ | 0 | $g_j^* - (g_i^* + B_i)$ |

Zonal boundaries are defined at expressions (7.3.4)-(7.3.6). The optimal tariffs are defined at (7.3.3) and (7.3.8)-(7.3.10). The $k^{th}$ retailer's profit (prior to the fixed fee) is $g_k^* \equiv ([(Q_k^*)^2/b] - f_k)$. The terms $B_k, (k \in (i,j))$ are defined at expression (7.2.31).

Zonal variations detailed in Table 7.1 reflect the variations in menu elements across Zones. While the per-unit fees ($W_i^*$ and $W_j^*$) are the same in every Zone (a necessary condition for coordination), the fixed fees vary to ensure that both retailers select "their" element of the menu. The specific manufacturer-optimal menu and the fixed fees charged are shown by Zone in

Table 7.2. Thus an appropriately specified menu of two-part tariffs can coordinate the channel *regardless* of the actual difference in retailers' fixed costs, provided the channel participation constraints are not violated.

*Table 7.2* Zones, Menus and Fixed Fees

| Zone | Menu | Zonal Definitions | Fixed Fees | |
|---|---|---|---|---|
| | | | $i^{th}$ Retailer | $j^{th}$ Retailer |
| $Z_j^{Menu^*}$ | $\tau^{L^*} \equiv \{\tau_i^{L^*}, \tau_j^{g_j^*}\}$ | $L^{Menu^*} > (f_i - f_j)$ | $[(R_j^* - f_j) + B_j]$ | $R_j^* - f_j$ |
| $Z_{ij}^{Menu^*}$ | $\tau^{g^*} \equiv \{\tau_i^{g_i^*}, \tau_j^{g_j^*}\}$ | $L^{Menu^*} \le (f_i - f_j) \le U^{Menu^*}$ | $R_i^* - f_i$ | $R_j^* - f_j$ |
| $Z_i^{Menu^*}$ | $\tau^{U^*} \equiv \{\tau_i^{g_i^*}, \tau_j^{U^*}\}$ | $(f_i - f_j) > U^{Menu^*}$ | $R_i^* - f_i$ | $[(R_i^* - f_i) + B_i]$ |

Figure 7.1 illustrates the "cost" of coordination in Zones $Z_j^{Menu^*}$ and $Z_i^{Menu^*}$. The manufacturer's profit is depicted by the solid line that is (i) horizontal in Zone $Z_j^{Menu^*}$, (ii) declining at the rate of \$1 for every \$1 increase in the fixed cost of the i[th] retailer in Zone $Z_{ij}^{Menu^*}$, and (iii) declining at a "two-for-one" rate in Zone $Z_i^{Menu^*}$. The logic behind this pattern is as follows. In Zone $Z_j^{Menu^*}$ the manufacturer's profit does not vary with changes in the i[th] retailer's fixed cost; an increase in $f_i$ simply lowers the profit of the i[th] (the more-profitable) retailer. Manufacturer profit declines at a constant rate ($\partial\Pi_M^{Menu^*}/\partial f_i = -\$1$) in Zone $Z_{ij}^{Menu^*}$ because a \$1 increase in $f_i$ lowers the fixed fee in tariff $\tau_i^*$ by \$1, but does *not* affect the fixed fee in tariff $\tau_j^*$. In Zone $Z_i^{Menu^*}$ an increase in $f_i$ decreases the profit of the i[th] (now the less-profitable) retailer. Consequently, the manufacturer must adjust the fixed fee to prevent the j[th] retailer from defecting *and* the i[th] retailer from not participating in the channel; thus $\partial\Pi_M^{Menu^*}/\partial f_i = -\$2$. (The effect of a change in $f_j$ is symmetric.) Finally, the dotted/solid/dotted straight line that declines at a one-for-one rate is the total profit of the coordinated channel.

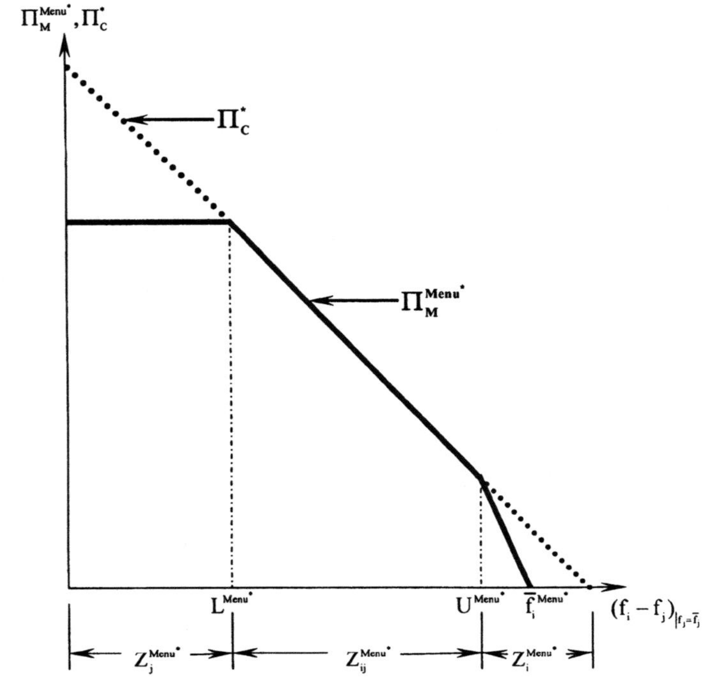


Legend:

$\Pi_M^{Menu^*}$ ≡ The manufacturer's profit from the Menu;

$\Pi_C^*$ ≡ Total (coordinated) channel profit with the Menu;

$L^{Menu^*}$ ≡ Lower bound below which the i[th] retailer earns a positive profit;

$U^{Menu^*}$ ≡ Upper bound above which the j[th] retailer earns a positive profit; and

$Z_k^{Menu^*}$ ≡ Zonal boundaries; $k \in (j, ij, i)$.

*Figure 7.1.* Manufacturer Profit across Zones with a Menu of Two-Part Tariffs

## 3.4 Fixed Costs and Channel Existence

When the manufacturer offers a channel-coordinating menu of tariffs, there are situations in which the channel earns a positive profit, but the manufacturer earns a negative profit. Because the manufacturer correctly forecasts its losses, it will refuse to serve the channel. To identify these situations, we note that manufacturer profit in Zone $Z_i^{Menu^*}$ is equal to channel profit at the Zonal boundary minus the reduction in the fixed fee associated with $(f_i - f_j)$ being beyond the boundary. Channel profit at the boundary is net revenue $(R_C^{\bullet})$ minus all fixed costs, evaluated at $U^{Menu^*}$. We find:

$$\begin{aligned}\left(\Pi_M^{Menu^*} \middle| f_j = \bar{f}_j\right) &= \left(R_C^{\bullet} - f_i - \bar{f}_j - F\right) - 2\left\{\left(f_i - \bar{f}_j\right) - U^{Menu^*}\right\} \\ &= \left(R_C^{\bullet} - U^{Menu^*} - 2\bar{f}_j - F\right) - 2\left\{\left(f_i - \bar{f}_j\right) - U^{Menu^*}\right\} \\ &= \left(R_C^{\bullet} + U^{Menu^*} - 2f_i - F\right)\end{aligned} \qquad (7.3.9)$$

where $\bar{f}_j$ denotes a fixed value of $f_j$. The second line of (7.3.9) is manufacturer profit after the substitution $f_i = \bar{f}_j + U^{Menu^*}$.[12] The maximum permissible value for the i^th^ retailer's fixed cost that is compatible with the manufacturer serving the channel is:

$$\bar{f}_i^{Menu^*} \equiv \left(R_C^{\bullet} + U^{Menu^*} - F\right)/2 \qquad (7.3.10)$$

A decentralized, coordinated channel can generate a positive channel profit and yet *not* create sufficient profit for the manufacturer to participate in the channel. In particular, channel profit is positive for all $f_i$ such that:

$$f_i \le \left(R_C^{\bullet} - \bar{f}_j - F\right) \equiv \hat{f}_i^{Menu^*} \qquad (7.3.11)$$

Comparing (7.3.10) with (7.3.11) reveals:

$$\bar{f}_i^{Menu^*} \gtrless \hat{f}_i^{Menu^*} \quad \text{as} \quad F \gtrless \left(R_C^{\bullet} - U^{Menu^*} - 2\bar{f}_j\right) \qquad (7.3.12)$$

Thus when $\bar{f}_i^{Menu^*} < f_i < \hat{f}_i^{Menu^*}$, a vertically-integrated system will distribute the product, but a decentralized channel will not, because the manufacturer's participation constraint is violated. Table 7.3 summarizes the retail fixed cost values that are consistent with channel existence:

*Table 7.3.* The Manufacturer's Participation Constraint: Conditions on Channel Existence *vs.* Non-Existence

| Limits on $f_i$ (given $f_j = \bar{f}_j$) | Vertically-Integrated System | Decentralized System |
|---|---|---|
| $f_i > \bar{f}_i^{Menu^*},\ \hat{f}_i^{Menu^*}$ | Non-Existence | Non-Existence |
| $\hat{f}_i^{Menu^*} > f_i > \bar{f}_i^{Menu^*}$ | Existence | Non-Existence |
| $\hat{f}_i^{Menu^*} > \bar{f}_i^{Menu^*} > f_i$ | Existence | Existence |

The existence of a manufacturer's participation constraint brings to mind our discussion in Chapter 3, where we observed that an independent channel contains fewer retailers than does a vertically-integrated system. Here channel breadth is held constant, but the acceptable level of fixed cost at retail diverges from that observed in a vertically-integrated channel. We illustrate this phenomenon in the next Section.

# 4 A NUMERICAL ILLUSTRATION

In this Section we provide a brief numerical example of the three Zones discussed in Section 3. We then illustrate the impact of fixed costs on channel existence. To simplify comparisons for the reader, we again use the values $A_j = 100$, $c_i = c_j = C = \$10$, $f_i = \$500$, and $F = \$1000$. The Scenarios are distinguished by the values assigned to parameters $A_i$, $\theta$ and $b$:

Scenario 1: $A_i = 150$, $\theta = 0.5$ and $b = 1.0$

Scenario 2: $A_i = 230$, $\theta = 0.5$ and $b = 1.0$

Scenario 3: $A_i = 150$, $\theta = 0.1$ and $b = 0.6$

Recall that Scenario 3 has the same level of aggregate demand as Scenario 1, but a lower intensity of inter-retailer competition.

## 4.1 Scenario 1

Scenario 1 depicts a moderate intensity of competition between the retailers, with the $i^{th}$ retailer having a base level of demand 50 percent greater than the demand of the $j^{th}$ retailer. Under this Scenario's assumptions, Table 7.4 gives information on fixed fees and profits across the three Menu Zones. The first column depicts Zone $Z_j^{Menu^*}$ at zero fixed cost for the $i^{th}$ retailer. The second and third columns detail the *minimal* and *maximal* values of $f_i$ that are compatible with Zone $Z_{ij}^{Menu^*}$. The last column is \$1 into Zone $Z_i^{Menu^*}$.

As can be seen from Table 7.4, the manufacturer-optimal fixed fee for the $i^{th}$ retailer ($\phi_i^*$) is constant throughout Zone $Z_j^{Menu^*}$, but declines at the rate of \$1 for every \$1 increase in $f_i$ thereafter. Thus the $i^{th}$ retailer's profit is unaffected by the magnitude of $f_i$ in Zone $Z_j^{Menu^*}$. Outside of this Zone, any increase in $f_i$ reduces the $i^{th}$ retailer's profit and requires a compensating adjustment in the fixed fee, thereby reducing the manufacturer's profit.

*Table 7.4.* The Channel-Coordinating Menu of Tariffs: Scenario 1

| | $Z_j^{Menu^*}$ | $Z_{ij}^{Menu^*}$ | $Z_{ij}^{Menu^*}$ | $Z_i^{Menu^*}$ |
|---|---|---|---|---|
| $f_i$ | \$0.00 | \$2,845.68 | \$3,009.88 | \$3010.88 |
| $\phi_i^{Menu^*}$ | \$2,054.32 | \$2,054.32 | \$1,890.12 | \$1,889.12 |
| $\phi_j^{Menu^*}$ | \$1,525.00 | \$1,525.00 | \$1,525.00 | \$1,524.00 |
| $\pi_i^{Menu^*}$ | \$2,845.68 | \$0.00 | \$0.00 | \$0.00 |
| $\pi_j^{Menu^*}$ | \$0.00 | \$0.00 | \$0.00 | \$1.00 |
| $\Pi_M^{Menu^*}$ | \$9,087.65 | \$9,087.65 | \$8,923.45 | \$8,921.45 |
| $\Pi_C^{Menu^*}$ | \$11,933.33 | \$9,087.65 | \$8,923.45 | \$8,922.45 |
| $f_i + \Pi_C^{Menu^*}$ | \$11,933.33 | \$11,933.33 | \$11,933.33 | \$11,933.33 |

This Table assumes: $A_i = 150, A_j = 100, c_i = c_j = C = \$10, f_j = \$500, F = \$1000$, $b = 1.0$, and $\theta = 0.5$; this yields $W_i^* = \$63.33$ and $W_j^* = \$71.67$ while $Q_i^* = 70$ and $Q_j^* = 45$.

Similarly, $\phi_j^*$ is constant throughout Zone $Z_j^{Menu^*}$ and Zone $Z_{ij}^{Menu^*}$, but declines at the rate of \$1 for every \$1 increase in $f_i$ within Zone $Z_i^{Menu^*}$. The $j^{th}$ retailer makes no profit in the first two Zones, but makes a positive profit in Zone $Z_i^{Menu^*}$. The reason is that both retailers receive a reduced fixed fee in this last Zone. The reduction reflects the manufacturer's desire to (i) retain the $i^{th}$ retailer as a channel member and (ii) prevent the $j^{th}$ retailer from defecting to the tariff intended for the $i^{th}$ retailer.

The net result of these effects is that, as $f_i$ increases, manufacturer profit is constant throughout Zone $Z_j^{Menu^*}$, declines at a dollar-for-dollar rate in Zone $Z_{ij}^{Menu^*}$, and declines at a rate of *two*-dollars-for-*one*-dollar in Zone $Z_i^{Menu^*}$. In contrast, channel profit is reduced by one dollar for every one-dollar increase in $f_i$. Finally, we note that the sum of the $i^{th}$ retailer's fixed cost and channel profit is a constant.

*Table 7.5.* The Channel-Coordinating Menu of Tariffs: Scenario 2

| | $Z_j^{Menu^*}$ | $Z_{ij}^{Menu^*}$ | $Z_{ij}^{Menu^*}$ | $Z_i^{Menu^*}$ |
|---|---|---|---|---|
| $f_i$ | \$0.00 | \$8,452.79 | \$9,562.77 | \$9,563.77 |
| $\phi_i^{Menu^*}$ | \$3,647.21 | \$3,647.21 | \$2,537.23 | \$2,536.23 |
| $\phi_j^{Menu^*}$ | \$1,525.00 | \$1,525.00 | \$1,525.00 | \$1,524.00 |
| $\pi_i^{Menu^*}$ | \$8,452.79 | \$0.00 | \$0.00 | \$0.00 |
| $\pi_j^{Menu^*}$ | \$0.00 | \$0.00 | \$0.00 | \$1.00 |
| $\Pi_M^{Menu^*}$ | \$15,480.54 | \$15,480.54 | \$14,370.56 | \$14,368.56 |
| $\Pi_C^{Menu^*}$ | \$23,933.33 | \$15,480.54 | \$14,370.56 | \$14,369.56 |
| $f_i + \Pi_C^{Menu^*}$ | \$23,933.33 | \$23,933.33 | \$23,933.33 | \$23,933.33 |

This Table assumes: $A_i = 230, A_j = 100, c_i = c_j = C = \$10, f_j = \$500, F = \$1000,\ b = 1.0,$ and $\theta = 0.5$; this yields $W_i^* = \$76.67$ and $W_j^* = \$98.33$ while $Q_i^* = 110$ and $Q_j^* = 45$.

## 4.2 Scenarios 2 and 3

Scenarios 2 and 3 are materially different from Scenario 1. In Scenario 2, the i[th] retailer has a higher level of base demand. In Scenario 3 there is a substantially lower level of inter-retailer competition, but the same level of base demand as in Scenario 1. Tables 7.5 and 7.6 present information on these Scenarios. Both Tables offer a profit picture that is fundamentally similar to that presented in Table 7.4. In all three scenarios, the profit patterns across the Zones are the same. We conclude that, while the parameters of demand $(A_i,\ A_j,\ b \text{ and } \theta)$ and cost $(c_i, c_j, \text{and } C)$ affect (i) wholesale and retail prices, (ii) unit sales, and (iii) Zonal boundaries, it is the difference in fixed costs that determines which Zone is relevant for creating the specific two-part tariffs that compose the channel-coordinating menu.

*Table 7.6.* The Channel-Coordinating Menu of Tariffs: Scenario 3

| Zone: | $Z_j^{Menu^*}$ | $Z_{ij}^{Menu^*}$ | $Z_{ij}^{Menu^*}$ | $Z_i^{Menu^*}$ |
|---|---|---|---|---|
| $f_i$ | \$0.00 | \$4,883.15 | \$5,020.44 | \$5,021.44 |
| $\phi_i^{Menu*}$ | \$3,283.51 | \$3,283.51 | \$3,146.23 | \$3,145.23 |
| $\phi_j^{Menu*}$ | \$2,875.00 | \$2,875.00 | \$2,875.00 | \$2,874.00 |
| $\pi_i^{Menu*}$ | \$8,452.79 | \$0.00 | \$0.00 | \$0.00 |
| $\pi_j^{Menu*}$ | \$0.00 | \$0.00 | \$0.00 | \$1.00 |
| $\Pi_M^{Menu*}$ | \$7,288.27 | \$7,288.28 | \$7,150.99 | \$7,148.99 |
| $\Pi_C^{Menu*}$ | \$12,171.43 | \$7,288.28 | \$7,150.99 | \$7,149.99 |
| $f_i + \Pi_C^{Menu*}$ | \$12,171.43 | \$12,171.43 | \$12,171.43 | \$12,171.43 |

This Table assumes: $A_i = 150$, $A_j = 100$, $c_i = c_j = C = \$10$, $f_j = \$500$, $F = \$1000$, $b = 0.6$, and $\theta = 0.1$; this yields $W_i^* = \$26.19$ and $W_j^* = \$32.14$ while $Q_i^* = 70$ and $Q_j^* = 45$.

## 4.3 Fixed Costs and Channel Existence Once Again

In Section 3 we proved that, when the manufacturer uses a channel-coordinating menu of two-part tariffs, there are some conditions under which the channel does not exist because the manufacturer earns negative profits. We focus on Scenario 1 to illustrate the manufacturer's participation constraint. In this Scenario the channel-coordinating quantities are $Q_i^* = 70$ and $Q_j^* = 45$, and channel net revenues are $R^* = \$13,433.33$. A vertically-integrated system will exist provided its total fixed costs do not exceed $R^*$.

Given this result, what is the maximum level of fixed costs $(F)$ that the independent manufacturer can incur before it refuses to participate in the channel? Intuitively the answer is $(\$13,433.33 - f_i - f_j)$, but this is *incorrect*.

Participation is predicated, not on channel net revenues, but on manufacturer profitability, which in turn depends on the manufacturer's ability to extract retailer profit through fixed fees. As we now know, the relevant elements of the menu depend on which Zone is applicable. For Scenario 1, we find $L^{Menu^*} = \$2{,}345.68$ and $U^{Menu^*} = \$2{,}509.88$. Manufacturer profit is equal to channel profit *only* if the retailer's fixed cost difference $(f_i - f_j)$ lies between these upper and lower values. Outside this fixed-cost difference the largest acceptable fixed cost for the manufacturer is less than $(R^* - f_i - f_j)$.

Clearly the best case situation for the manufacturer that is compatible with being in Zone $Z_{ij}^{Menu^*}$ occurs when $f_i = \$2{,}345.68$ and $f_j = \$0$. In this situation we find $\Pi_M^{Menu^*} = \Pi_C^{Menu^*} = \$11{,}087.65 - F$. It immediately follows that if $\$13{,}433.33 \geq F > \$11{,}087.65$, a vertically-integrated system will serve the channel, but an independent manufacturer will not.

This result is based on extracting all rent from the channel. Can the manufacturer incur a higher fixed cost if it is unable to obtain the totality of channel profit? Channel profits are maximized when $f_i = f_j = 0$, which places the manufacturer-optimal wholesale-price policy in Zone $Z_j^{Menu^*}$. For this level of retailer fixed costs, we obtain the following results:

$$\begin{aligned} \Pi_C^{Menu^*} &= \$13{,}433.33 - F, \\ \Pi_M^{Menu^*} &= \$11{,}087.65 - F, \\ \pi_i^{Menu^*} &= \$2{,}345.68, \text{ and} \\ \pi_j^{Menu^*} &= \$0. \end{aligned} \tag{7.4.1}$$

We again see that the manufacturer's participation constraint requires that $F < \$11{,}087.65$. The bottom line is that, even when channel breadth is held constant, a vertically-integrated system can tolerate higher fixed costs than can a manufacturer that serves independent retailers.

Finally, notice that different fixed costs have different impacts on the distribution of channel profits. To see this, consider the case in which $f_i = f_j = F = \$0$. A \$1 increase in any of these costs lowers channel profit by \$1. At the same time:

- A \$1 increase in F decreases manufacturer profit by \$1;
- A \$1 increase in $f_i$ decreases the $i^{th}$ retailer's profit by \$1; and
- A \$1 increase in $f_j$ (i) has no effect on the $j^{th}$ retailer's profit, (ii) lowers the manufacturer's profit by *\$2*, and (iii) *raises* the $i^{th}$ retailer's profit by \$1.

The first two results are intuitively obvious, the third is not. Holding channel breadth constant requires that a cost increase at the *less*-profitable retailer be compensated by an equal fixed fee reduction for that retailer. However, comparable treatment of competitors means that both retailers receive the same compensation.[13] It follows that the $i^{th}$ retailer's best-case situation is for the $j^{th}$ retailer to have fixed costs that are substantial, but not so great as to induce the manufacturer to narrow its channel breadth by dropping the $j^{th}$ retailer (because this would enable the manufacturer to extract all profit from the remaining—the $i^{th}$—retailer).

# 5 THE CHANNEL-COORDINATING MENU AND RETAILER PROFIT-EXTRACTION

We have shown that three menu Zones determine whether or not the manufacturer can, by offering a menu of tariffs, simultaneously maximize channel profit and extract all economic profit from each retailer. In this Section we examine the way in which demand and cost parameters interact to determine the applicability of the three Zones that define the channel-coordinating menu of tariffs.

## 5.1 Zonal Re-Parameterization

We wish to identify the sets of parametric values that lie in each of the three Menu Zones $Z_j^{Menu^*}$, $Z_{ij}^{Menu^*}$, and $Z_i^{Menu^*}$. The boundary between Zones $Z_j^{Menu^*}$ and $Z_{ij}^{Menu^*}$ satisfies $L^{Menu^*} = (f_i - f_j)$, while the boundary between Zones $Z_{ij}^{Menu^*}$ and $Z_i^{Menu^*}$ satisfies $U^{Menu^*} = (f_i - f_j)$. (The definitions of $L^{Menu^*}$ and $U^{Menu^*}$ are given by (7.3.4) and (7.3.5), respectively.) Although this is a six-parameter problem, we proved in Chapter 5, Section 8, that it can be reduced to four dimensions through a simple re-parameterization:

$$\chi \equiv (\theta/b) \tag{7.5.1}$$

$$S_j \equiv \left(Q_j^* / \left(Q_i^* + Q_j^*\right)\right) \tag{7.5.2}$$

$$f_k \equiv \left(f_k / R_k^*\right) \quad \forall \quad k \in (i,j) \tag{7.5.3}$$

The term $\chi$ is the *intensity of competition*, the term $S_j$ is the *magnitude of competition*, and the term $f_k$ is the $k^{th}$ retailer's *fixed cost ratio*. This re-parameterization has the effect of standardizing key variables to the unit interval at no loss of generality. We also set $f_i = f_j \equiv f$; this reduces our analytical task to a three-dimensional "unit-cube" whose left-half and right-half are symmetric about the equal market shares plane ($Q_i^* = Q_j^* \rightarrow S_j = \frac{1}{2}$).

To simplify our discussion, let $L_{\Delta f}^{Menu^*}$ denote the boundary between Zones $Z_j^{Menu^*}$ and $Z_{ij}^{Menu^*}$. The value of $L_{\Delta f}^{Menu^*}$ is:

$$L_{\Delta f}^{Menu^*} \equiv \left[ L^{Menu^*} - \left(f_i - f_j\right) \right]\Big|_{f_i = f_j} = 0$$

$$= \left(ZZ^{Menu^*}\right) \begin{pmatrix} \left(4 + 2\chi - \chi^2\right) \begin{pmatrix} \left(4 + 2\chi - \chi^2\right)\left(1 - S_j\right) \\ + \left(4 + 6\chi - \chi^2 - 2\chi^3\right) S_j \end{pmatrix} \\ - \left(1 + \chi\right)^2 \left(4 - \chi^2\right)^2 f \end{pmatrix} = 0 \quad (7.5.4)$$

where:

$$\left(ZZ^{Menu^*}\right) \equiv \left( \frac{\left(1 - 2S_j\right) R_i^*}{\left(1 + \chi\right)^2 \left(4 - \chi^2\right)^2 \left(1 - S_j\right)^2} \right) \geq 0 \quad (7.5.5)$$

The equality in definition (7.5.5) holds only for the special case of $S_j = \frac{1}{2}$. Similarly, let $U_{\Delta f}^{Menu^*}$ denote the boundary between Zones $Z_i^{Menu^*}$ and $Z_{ij}^{Menu^*}$:

$$U_{\Delta f}^{Menu^*} \equiv \left[ U^{Menu^*} - \left(f_i - f_j\right) \right]\Big|_{f_i = f_j} = 0$$

$$= \left(ZZ^{Menu^*}\right) \begin{pmatrix} \left(4 + 2\chi - \chi^2\right)\left(4 + 6\chi - \chi^2 - 2\chi^3\right)\left(1 - S_j\right) \\ + \left(4 + 2\chi - \chi^2\right)^2 S_j - \left(1 + \chi\right)^2 \left(4 - \chi^2\right)^2 f \end{pmatrix} = 0 \quad (7.5.6)$$

The two-dimensional boundaries $L_{\Delta f}^{Menu^*}$ and $U_{\Delta f}^{Menu^*}$ curve through three-dimensional $\langle \chi, S_j, f \rangle$ – space.

## 5.2 The Channel-Coordinating Menu and Retailer Profit Extraction

As in Section 8 of Chapter 5, we conserve space by focusing our discussion on the *unit half-cube* defined by $(0 \leq \chi < 1,\ 0 \leq S_j \leq \frac{1}{2},\ 0 \leq f \leq 1)$. Our focus is justified by the fact that the right-hand side of the cube is a mirror-image of the left-hand side. The plane defined by $S_j = \frac{1}{2}$, which is a boundary of the unit half-cube, always satisfies the boundary conditions defined by $L_{\Delta f}^{Menu^*}$ and $U_{\Delta f}^{Menu^*}$. (This statement follows directly from equation

(7.5.5).) What remains unclear is whether the interior of the unit half-cube contains one or more additional lines that correspond to $L_{\Delta f}^{Menu^*}$ and/or $U_{\Delta f}^{Menu^*}$. We address this question below, and illustrate our results, with slices of the unit half-cube taken at various $f$ values. We denote these slices as the *unit half-square* $(0 \le \chi < 1,\ 0 \le S_j \le 1/2)$.

The relationships among the Menu Zones and their underlying parameters are delimited by *seven regions* that are themselves defined by the value of the retailers' fixed-cost ratio $f$. These regions are:

- **$f$ – Region 1:** $0 \le f < 0.672572,$
- **$f$ – Region 2:** $0.672572 \le f < 25/36 \approx 0.694444$
- **$f$ – Region 3:** $25/36 \le f < 0.820105$
- **$f$ – Region 4:** $0.820105 \le f < 5/6 \approx 0.833333$ (7.5.7)
- **$f$ – Region 5:** $5/6 \le f < 0.967638$
- **$f$ – Region 6:** $0.967638 \le f < 35/36 \approx 0.972222$
- **$f$ – Region 7:** $35/36 \le f < 1$

The $f$ – values that delineate these Regions are defined by the fact that a boundary condition ($L^{Menu^*}$ and/or $U^{Menu^*}$) intersects, or becomes tangent to, one of the edges of the unit half-square. To clarify what would otherwise be a complex presentation, we introduce simplifying notation for the locations of these intersections and tangencies in Table 7.7.

*Table 7.7.* Intercepts of the Boundary Conditions with the Edges of the Unit Half-Square

| | |
|---|---|
| □ $\chi_U^{LMenu^*}(0)$ | $\equiv$ The *upper* intersection of $L_{\Delta f}^{Menu^*}$ with the $\langle S_j = 0\rangle$ – axis; |
| □ $\chi_L^{LMenu^*}(0)$ | $\equiv$ The *lower* intersection of $L_{\Delta f}^{Menu^*}$ with the $\langle S_j = 0\rangle$ – axis; |
| □ $\chi_U^{LMenu^*}(1/2)$ | $\equiv$ The *upper* intersection of $L_{\Delta f}^{Menu^*}$ with the $\langle S_j = 1/2\rangle$ – axis; |
| □ $\chi_L^{LMenu^*}(1/2)$ | $\equiv$ The *lower* intersection of $L_{\Delta f}^{Menu^*}$ with the $\langle S_j = 1/2\rangle$ – axis; |
| □ $\chi_U^{UMenu^*}(0)$ | $\equiv$ The *upper* intersection of $U_{\Delta f}^{Menu^*}$ with the $\langle S_j = 0\rangle$ – axis; |
| □ $\chi_L^{UMenu^*}(0)$ | $\equiv$ The *lower* intersection of $U_{\Delta f}^{Menu^*}$ with the $\langle S_j = 0\rangle$ – axis; |
| □ $\chi_U^{UMenu^*}(1/2)$ | $\equiv$ The *upper* intersection of $U_{\Delta f}^{Menu^*}$ with the $\langle S_j = 1/2\rangle$ – axis; |
| □ $\chi_L^{UMenu^*}(1/2)$ | $\equiv$ The *lower* intersection of $U_{\Delta f}^{Menu^*}$ with the $\langle S_j = 1/2\rangle$ – axis; |
| □ $S_j^{LMenu^*}(1)$ | $\equiv$ The intersection of $L_{\Delta f}^{Menu^*}$ with the $\langle \chi = 1\rangle$ – axis; and |
| □ $S_j^{UMenu^*}(1)$ | $\equiv$ The intersection of $U_{\Delta f}^{Menu^*}$ with the $\langle \chi = 1\rangle$ – axis. |

$f$ – **Region 1**: For the range $0 \le f < 0.672572$, the two boundaries $L_{\Delta f}^{Menu^*}$ and $U_{\Delta f}^{Menu^*}$ coincide with the $S_j = ½$ axis. Within this range, Zone $Z_j^{SS^*}$ consists of the entire interior of the unit half-square; this means that the manufacturer can extract all profit from the smaller (the j[th]) competitor. In the remaining cases ($f > 0.672572$), the unit half-square contains an internal boundary that separates Zone $Z_j^{Menu^*}$ from Zone $Z_{ij}^{Menu^*}$. We now turn to these other $f$ – Regions.

$f$ – **Region 2**: When $0.672572 \le f < {}^{25}\!/_{36}$, $L_{\Delta f}^{Menu^*}$ appears inside the unit half-square as a parabola that intersects the $\langle S_j = 0\rangle$ – axis twice. The interior of the area created by this parabola and the $\langle S_j = 0\rangle$ – axis constitutes Zone $Z_{ij}^{Menu^*}$. When $f$ is at its minimal value in this $f$ – Region, the parabola is a single point on the $\langle S_j = 0\rangle$ – axis; but, as $f$ increases from 0.672572 to ${}^{25}\!/_{36}$, the ends of the parabola separate: $\chi_U^{LMenu^*}(0)$ rises from 0.798223 to 1 and $\chi_L^{LMenu^*}(0)$ declines from 0.798223 to 0.579796. Figure 7.2 illustrates this $f$ – Region for $f = 0.68$ (slightly above the lowest value for $f$ – Region 2).

$f$ – **Region 3**: When ${}^{25}\!/_{36} \le f < 0.820105$, the boundary $L_{\Delta f}^{Menu^*}$ continues to intersect the $\langle S_j = 0\rangle$ – axis at $\chi_L^{LMenu^*}(0)$. However, the upper intersection intersects the $\langle \chi = 1\rangle$ – axis. Accordingly, we use the notation $S_j^{LMenu^*}(1)$ to depict the $S_j$ – value at which this occurs. An increase in $f$ from ${}^{25}\!/_{36}$ to 0.820105 lowers the value of $\chi_L^{LMenu^*}(0)$ from 0.579796 to 0.236908, and raises the value of $S_j^{LMenu^*}(1)$ from zero to 0.452378. The area above $L_{\Delta f}^{Menu^*}$ is Zone $Z_{ij}^{Menu^*}$, and the area below is Zone $Z_j^{Menu^*}$. Figure 7.3 illustrates this $f$ – Region for $f = ¾$; this is about halfway through $f$ – Region 3.

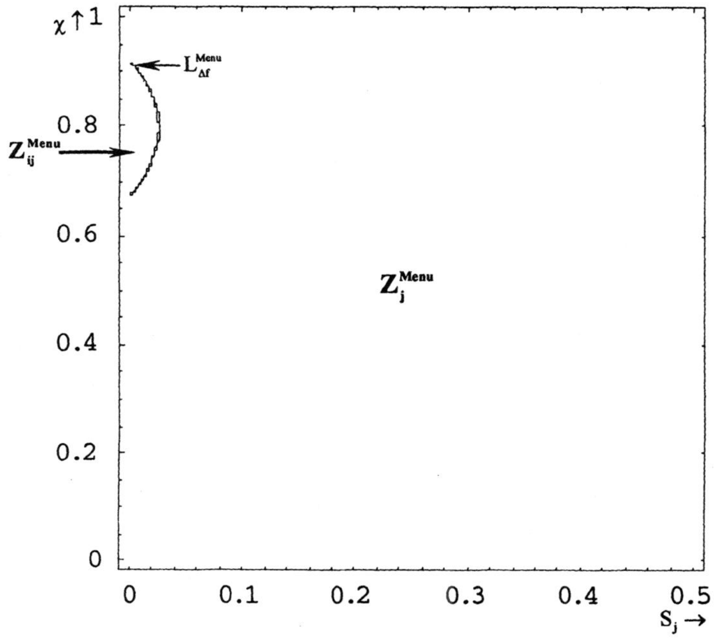


Legend:

$Z_j^{Menu}$ ≡ The Menu Zone within which the j[th] retailer is the less profitable;

$Z_{ij}^{Menu}$ ≡ The Menu Zone within which both retailers net zero profit; and

$L_{\Delta f}^{Menu}$ ≡ The boundary separating $Z_j^{Menu}$ and $Z_{ij}^{Menu}$.

*Figure 7.2.* The Channel-Coordinating Menu Zones
When $f = 0.68$

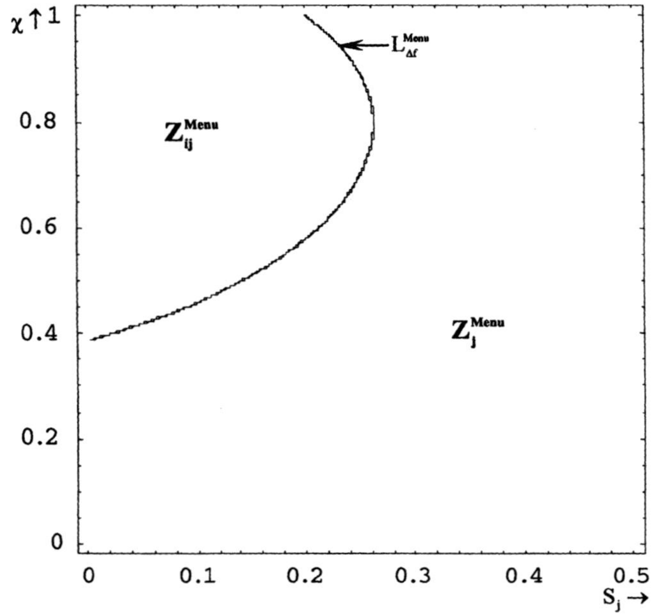


Legend:

$Z_j^{Menu}$ ≡ The Menu Zone within which the j[th] retailer is the less profitable;

$Z_{ij}^{Menu}$ ≡ The Menu Zone within which both retailers net zero profit; and

$L_{\Delta f}^{Menu}$ ≡ The boundary separating $Z_j^{Menu}$ and $Z_{ij}^{Menu}$.

*Figure 7.3.* The Channel-Coordinating Menu Zones When $f = 3/4$

$f$ **– Region 4**: When $0.820105 < f \le 5/6$, both $L_{\Delta f}^{Menu^*}$ and $U_{\Delta f}^{Menu^*}$ are in the interior of the unit half-square. (Figure 7.4 illustrates this $f$ – Region for $f = 0.827$.) We begin by describing the location of $L_{\Delta f}^{Menu^*}$. An increase in $f$ from 0.082015 to $5/6$ lowers the value of $\chi_L^{LMenu^*}(0)$ from 0.236908 to 0.214035. And, when $f = 0.820105$, the rightmost point on $L_{\Delta f}^{Menu^*}$ is tangent to the $\langle S_j = 1/2 \rangle$ – axis at $\chi = 0.798223$. As $f$ increases further, $L_{\Delta f}^{Menu^*}$ intersects the $\langle S_j = 1/2 \rangle$ – axis at points denoted as $\chi_U^{LMenu^*}(1/2)$ and $\chi_L^{LMenu^*}(1/2)$. As $f$ increases from 0.820105 to $5/6$, $\chi_U^{LMenu^*}(1/2)$ rises from 0.798223 to 1 and $\chi_L^{LMenu^*}(1/2)$ declines from 0.798223 to 0.579796.

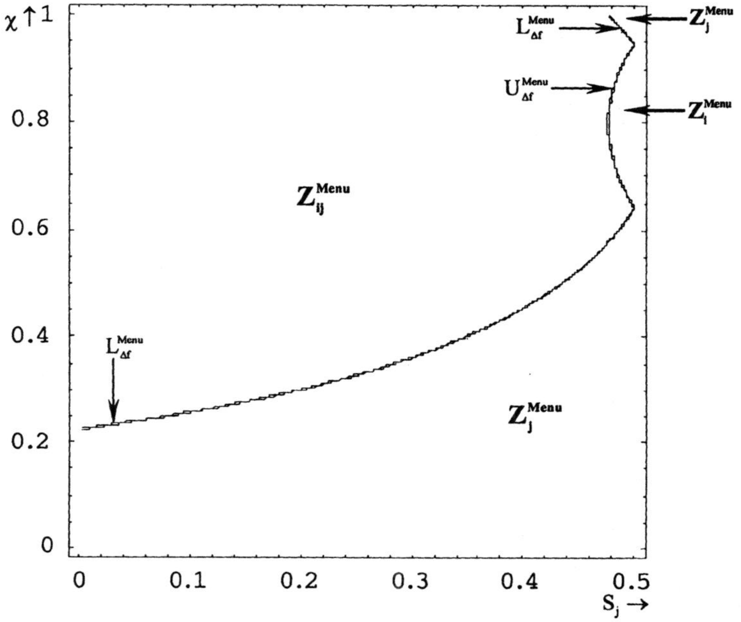


Legend:

$Z_j^{Menu}$ ≡ The Menu Zone within which the j[th] retailer is the less profitable;

$Z_{ij}^{Menu}$ ≡ The Menu Zone within which both retailers net zero profit;

$Z_i^{Menu}$ ≡ The Menu Zone within which the i[th] retailer is the less profitable;

$L_{\Delta f}^{Menu}$ ≡ The boundary separating $Z_j^{Menu}$ and $Z_{ij}^{Menu}$; and

$U_{\Delta f}^{Menu}$ ≡ The boundary separating $Z_{ij}^{Menu}$ and $Z_i^{Menu}$.

*Figure 7.4.* The Channel-Coordinating Menu Zones
When $f = 0.827$

Intercepts $\chi_U^{UMenu^*}(\frac{1}{2})$ and $\chi_L^{UMenu^*}(\frac{1}{2})$ define intersections of $U_{\Delta f}^{Menu^*}$ with the $\langle S_j = \frac{1}{2}\rangle$ – axis. At $f = 0.820105$, $U_{\Delta f}^{Menu^*}$ is tangent to the $\langle S_j = \frac{1}{2}\rangle$ – axis at $\chi = 0.798223$. As $f$ increases, $U_{\Delta f}^{Menu^*}$ e the interior of the unit half-square, intersecting the $\langle S_j = \frac{1}{2}\rangle$ – axis at $\chi_U^{UMenu^*}(\frac{1}{2})$ and $\chi_L^{UMenu^*}(\frac{1}{2})$. The area inside the parabola defined by $L_{\Delta f}^{Menu^*}$ corresponds to Zone $Z_i^{Menu^*}$. Zone $Z_j^{Menu^*}$ is located in a small triangular-shaped area in the upper right-hand corner of the graph and in a larger area along the bottom of the Figure.

$f$ – **Region 5**: When $\frac{5}{6} < f \leq 0.967638$, $L_{\Delta f}^{Menu^*}$ intersects the $\langle S_j = 0 \rangle$ – axis at $\chi_L^{LMenu^*}(0)$ and the $\langle S_j = \frac{1}{2} \rangle$ – axis at $\chi_L^{LMenu^*}(\frac{1}{2})$. Increases in $f$ have the effect of shifting $L_{\Delta f}^{Menu^*}$ down. The area below $L_{\Delta f}^{Menu^*}$ corresponds to Zone $Z_j^{Menu^*}$, while the area immediately above the boundary is Zone $Z_j^{Menu^*}$.

When $\frac{5}{6} < f \leq 0.967638$, $U_{\Delta f}^{Menu^*}$ continues to intersect the $\langle S_j = \frac{1}{2} \rangle$ – axis at $\chi_L^{UMenu^*}(\frac{1}{2})$. When $f = \frac{5}{6}$, the upper boundary of $U_{\Delta f}^{Menu^*}$ intersects the $\langle S_j = \frac{1}{2} \rangle$ – axis at $\chi = 1$. Thus $U_{\Delta f}^{Menu^*}$ intersects the $\langle \chi = 1 \rangle$ – axis at $S_j^{UMenu^*}(1)$. As $f$ increases from $\frac{5}{6}$ to 0.967638, $S_j^{UMenu^*}(1)$ declines from ½ to $S_j \cong 0.017$.

Figure 7.5 offers an illustration of this $f$ – Region for $f = 0.9$, which is located about halfway through this $f$ – Region. Note that the area below $L_{\Delta f}^{Menu^*}$ corresponds to Zone $Z_j^{Menu^*}$; the area above $U_{\Delta f}^{Menu^*}$ corresponds to Zone $Z_i^{Menu^*}$; and the area between $L_{\Delta f}^{Menu^*}$ and $U_{\Delta f}^{Menu^*}$ corresponds to $Z_{ij}^{Menu^*}$.

$f$ – **Region 6**: When $0.967638 < f \leq \frac{35}{36}$, increases in $f$ continue to shift $L_{\Delta f}^{Menu^*}$ (and therefore the $\langle S_j = \frac{1}{2} \rangle$ – intercept of $U_{\Delta f}^{Menu^*}$) down. If $f = 0.967638$, $U_{\Delta f}^{Menu^*}$ is tangent to the $\langle S_j = 0 \rangle$ – axis at point $\chi = 0.798223$. As a result, if $0.967638 < f \leq \frac{35}{36}$, $U_{\Delta f}^{Menu^*}$ intersects the $\langle S_j = 0 \rangle$ – axis at two points; we denote them as $\chi_U^{UMenu^*}(0)$ and $\chi_L^{UMenu^*}(0)$. As $f$ increases from 0.967638 to $\frac{35}{36}$, $\chi_U^{UMenu^*}(0)$ increases from 0.798223 to 1, while $\chi_L^{UMenu^*}(0)$ decreases from 0.798223 to 0.579796.

Figure 7.6 illustrates this $f$ – Region for $f = 0.969$. Note that Zone $Z_{ij}^{Menu^*}$ is now located in two different parts of the unit half-square a small triangular-shaped area in the upper left-hand corner of the graph and a larger area that stretches horizontally across the middle of Figure 7.6.

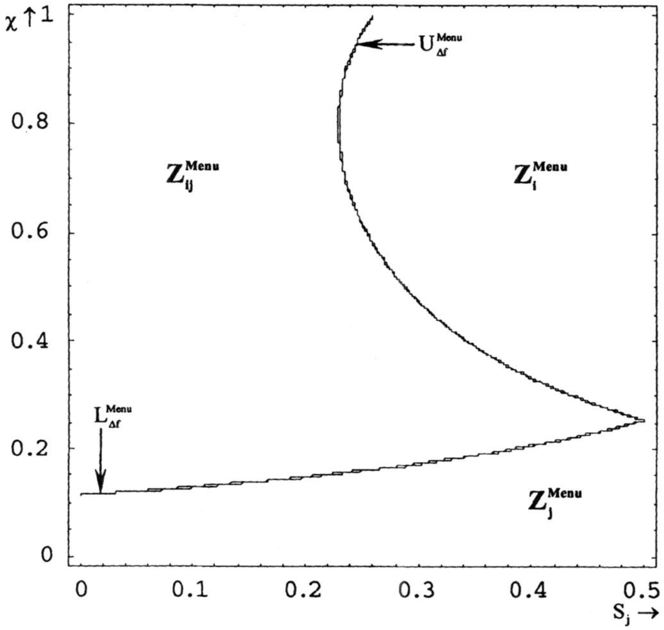


Legend:

$\mathbf{Z}_j^{Menu}$ ≡ The Menu Zone within which the j[th] retailer is the less profitable;

$\mathbf{Z}_{ij}^{Menu}$ ≡ The Menu Zone within which both retailers net zero profit;

$\mathbf{Z}_i^{Menu}$ ≡ The Menu Zone within which the i[th] retailer is the less profitable;

$L_{\Delta f}^{Menu}$ ≡ The boundary separating $Z_j^{Menu}$ and $Z_{ij}^{Menu}$; and

$U_{\Delta f}^{Menu}$ ≡ The boundary separating $Z_{ij}^{Menu}$ and $Z_i^{Menu}$.

*Figure 7.5.* The Channel-Coordinating Menu Zones
When $f = 0.9$

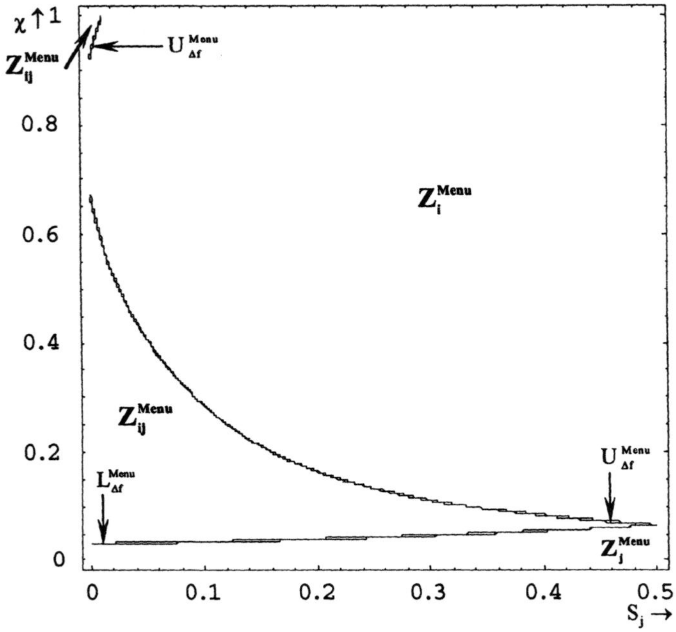


Legend:

$Z_j^{Menu}$ ≡ The Menu Zone within which the j[th] retailer is the less profitable.

$Z_{ij}^{Menu}$ ≡ The Menu Zone within which both retailers net zero profit.

$Z_i^{Menu}$ ≡ The Menu Zone within which the i[th] retailer is the less profitable.

$L_{\Delta f}^{Menu}$ ≡ The boundary separating $Z_j^{Menu}$ and $Z_{ij}^{Menu}$.

$U_{\Delta f}^{Menu}$ ≡ The boundary separating $Z_{ij}^{Menu}$ and $Z_i^{Menu}$.

*Figure 7.6.* The Channel-Coordinating Menu Zones
When $f = 0.969$

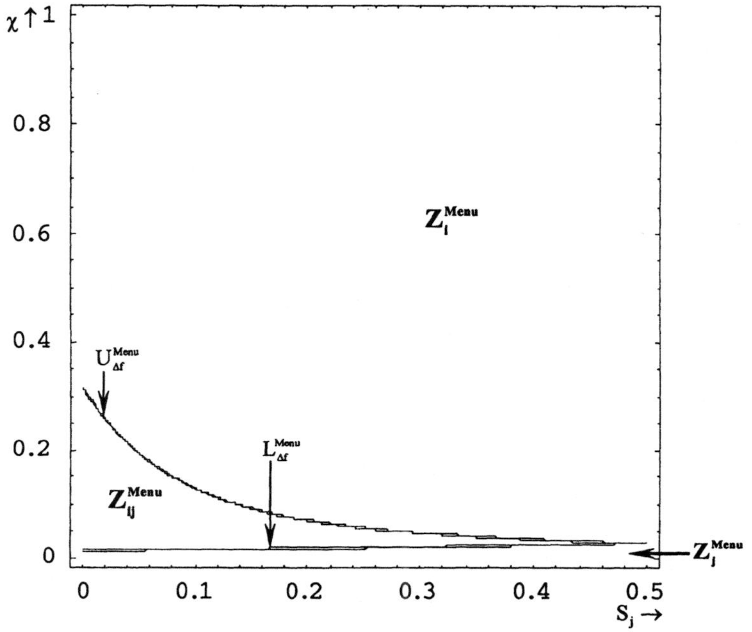


Legend:

$Z_j^{Menu}$ ≡ The Menu Zone within which the j[th] retailer is the less profitable.

$Z_{ij}^{Menu}$ ≡ The Menu Zone within which both retailers net zero profit.

$Z_i^{Menu}$ ≡ The Menu Zone within which the i[th] retailer is the less profitable.

$L_{\Delta f}^{Menu}$ ≡ The boundary separating $Z_j^{Menu}$ and $Z_{ij}^{Menu}$.

$U_{\Delta f}^{Menu}$ ≡ The boundary separating $Z_{ij}^{Menu}$ and $Z_i^{Menu}$.

*Figure 7.7.* The Channel-Coordinating Menu Zones
When $f = 7/12$

$f$ – **Region** 7: Within the $f$ – range $35/36 < f \leq 1$, increases in $f$ continually shift $L_{\Delta f}^{Menu^*}$ down. As a consequence, as $f \rightarrow 1$, $L_{\Delta f}^{Menu^*}$ approaches the $\langle \chi = 0 \rangle$ – axis. $U_{\Delta f}^{Menu^*}$ also shifts down, with the $\langle S_j = 1/2 \rangle$ – intercept of $U_{\Delta f}^{Menu^*}$ approaching 0 as $f$ rises to its maximal value of 1. Figure 7.7 illustrates this $f$ – Region at its midpoint.

In summary, the results of these seven $f$ – Regions indicate that there are three conceptually distinct sectors that occur as $f$ ranges from 0 to 1. First, at relatively low $f$ – values (below 0.67), the manufacturer can capture all channel profit only over a small portion of the unit half-square because it cannot extract all profit from the *large-volume* retailer. Second, at moderate $f$ – values (between 0.67 and 0.82), the manufacturer can extract all rent from the channel over most parametric values that are consistent with a relatively high degree of competition. Third, at high $f$ – values (above 0.82), the area within which the manufacturer can extract all channel profit is restricted to a narrow band that shifts downward within the unit half-square as $f$ increases. Here it is an inability to extract all economic profit from the *small-volume* retailer that limits the manufacturer's profitability.

# 6 COMMENTARY

In this Chapter we derived a channel-coordinating menu of two-part tariffs. Although this policy maximizes channel profit, it limits the manufacturer's flexibility. Because the menu is designed to ensure coordination, the manufacturer cannot adjust the per-unit fees in response to a change in the fixed fee that is required to prevent defection. In Chapter 3 we saw that it is the ability to make these per-unit fee adjustments that leads to a globally-optimal, non-coordinating wholesale-price strategy for the manufacturer when retailers do not compete. This result leads us to speculate that, when retailers do compete, a non-coordinating wholesale-price policy like the sophisticated Stackelberg tariff may dominate a less flexible, channel-coordinating wholesale-price policy like the menu of tariffs explored in this Chapter, or the channel-coordinating quantity-discount schedule of Chapter 5. This speculation is our motivation for the analyses presented in Chapters 8 and 9.

## 6.1 Commentary on a Channel-Coordinating Menu

We have established the existence of a channel-coordinating menu that reproduces the performance of a vertically-integrated system in a channel with a manufacturer that sells through independent, competing retailers. The vertically-integrated results *only* obtain when each retailer selects the "right" tariff, meaning the tariff that the manufacturer intended. But a retailer's objective is not to select the "right" tariff; it is to select the tariff that will maximize its own profit. Either retailer may defect from the "right" tariff, but we have shown that, in equilibrium, no more than one of them does so.

To ensure the "right" choice by the retailers, the fixed fee components of the tariff must satisfy certain conditions. When these conditions are violated, one retailer will "defect" from the tariff designed for it in favor of the tariff intended for its rival. Should defection occur, retail prices and outputs for *both* retailers will deviate from their coordinated values and, for some parametric values, total channel profit will be less than the profit generated by the single, second-best tariff described in Chapter 5.

While the manufacturer may adjust the fixed fee components of the menu to guarantee that defection never occurs, the adjustment comes at the expense of sharing profit with the retailer who would otherwise defect. A comparison of Table 7.2 with Table 5.1 (both based on the same parametric values) reveals that, when $0 \le f_i \le \$2,818.67$, the second-best tariff yields greater profit for the manufacturer than does a channel-coordinating menu. This simple example illustrates the fact that it is not always in the manufacturer's profit-maximizing interest to coordinate the channel with a menu of tariffs, even though it is always possible to do so.[14]

## 6.2 Commentary on Three Channel Myths

Consistent with the analyses presented in earlier Chapters, we found that retailer fixed costs play a critical role in the design of this channel-coordinating wholesale-price policy. The significance of retailer fixed costs extends beyond the retailer participation constraints, because the difference in these costs helps to determine the maximum fixed fees that can be charged without inducing defection. It is clear from Table 7.1 that, when retailer fixed costs are zero, the larger retailer obtains an economic profit, while the smaller volume retailer cannot earn any profit. Similarly, the manufacturer cannot extract all profit from the channel in the absence of fixed costs at retail that are sufficiently, but not excessively, different.

These results demonstrate yet again that the decision to model a channel without considering retailers' fixed costs generates a result that is a trivial case of a more general model. In addition to the retail-level costs discussed above, we have seen that fixed costs at manufacturer level can lead to channel non-existence under parametric values that would be compatible with a vertically-integrated system distributing the product. In brief, we have shown that the belief that fixed costs can be safely disregarded is a myth, one that we have termed the *Fixed-Cost Modeling Myth.*

A separate issue involves the assumption of identical competitors. Under this assumption, the manufacturer charges the same two-part tariff to each retailer, so the concept of a menu is irrelevant. Further, as we noted in the last Chapter, this single two-part tariff coordinates the channel and extracts all profit from both retailers. An identical-competitors assumption reduces the complex analysis of this Chapter to an inconsequential extension of the bilateral-monopoly model. Clearly the belief that the identical-competitors assumption is a harmless modeling simplification is a myth, one that we have termed the *Identical-Competitors Meta-Myth.*

Finally, we note that re-allocating profit among channel members relies on the existence of a fixed fee. We have proven that in the case of a menu there are distinct limits to the difference in fixed fees that can be charged if a channel-coordinating equilibrium is to be attained (see equation (7.2.32)). In fact, we have shown that there are conditions under which a vertically-integrated system will exist but a decentralized channel will not. Thus the belief that the profit of a coordinated channel can always be allocated to benefit all channel members is a myth; we call it the *Channel-Coordination Strategic Myth.*

## 6.3 Summary Commentary

Given our assumption of comparable treatment of retailers, no manufacturer can command its channel partners to behave in particular ways. In Chapter 3 the manufacturer could not direct the "marginal," non-competing retailer to participate in the channel; the manufacturer had to motivate participation with a modification of the fixed fee and the per-unit charge. In Chapter 4 the manufacturer could not command the single retailer to distribute in the low-demand state-of-nature; the manufacturer had to motivate distribution with a modification of the wholesale price. In this Chapter the manufacturer could not order its retailers to select the "right" tariffs; the manufacturer had to motivate the desired choices with an adjustment of the fixed fee. In each case, the retailer is concerned with its own profit maximization; the manufacturer must construct a wholesale-price policy that recognizes this constraint. This principle is consistent with the observations of Adam Smith, who wrote, "in the great chess-board of human society, every single piece has a principle of motion of its own, altogether different from that which the legislator might choose to impress upon it" (1759). Neither our manufacturer, nor Smith's legislator, can dictate the behavior of others, for they hold a countervailing power, even though the channel captain may prefer unquestioning acceptance of its dictates.

In the next Chapter we formally compare the channel-coordinating menu, and the channel-coordinating quantity-discount schedule, with the sophisticated Stackelberg two-part tariff under the complete range of fixed costs differences. This will be a critical test of coordination as an objective for the manufacturer. Regardless of the outcome, it should be recognized that there are distinct limits to the use of the channel-coordinating wholesale-price policies analyzed here in a channel containing more than two retailers. We can state definitively that the linear, quantity-discount schedule does not generalize to three or more retailers. We strongly suspect, but have not yet proven, that the separating equilibrium that is necessary to prevent what we have termed "defection" from the "right" element of a menu breaks down in the presence of more than two retailers. The sophisticated Stackelberg two-part tariff appears to be more robust than either of these channel-coordinating strategies. If, with two competing retailers, the manufacturer prefers—over many parametric values—a non-coordinating wholesale-price strategy to a strategy that coordinates the channel, the manufacturer serving three or more competitors is unapt to regard coordination as an attractive option.

# Notes

[1] Earlier versions of Chapters 7 and 8 appeared in a combined form in our *Journal of Retailing* paper, "Is Channel Coordination All It Is Cracked Up to Be?" (Ingene and Parry 2000). An earlier—and much less detailed—version of Chapter 7 went through the *Marketing Science* review process but, due to space limitations, was deleted from the final version of our paper "Channel Coordination When Retailers Compete" (Ingene and Parry 1995). This Chapter includes a substantial amount of material that has not appeared previously. (New York University holds the *Journal of Retailing* copyright; our material is used with permission.)

[2] Because all elements of the menu are available to all retailers, and because a retailer may select whichever element it desires, a menu satisfies U.S. legal requirements. We are indebted to Professor Patrick Kaufmann for sharing his expertise on antitrust law with us.

[3] In Chapter 8 we directly compare Chapter 6's sophisticated Stackelberg results with the menu results of this Chapter. Thus the next Chapter provides a thorough test of profit maximization versus channel coordination.

[4] The first subscript references the retailer, the second subscript references that retailer's tariff choice, and the third subscript refers to its rival's tariff choice.

[5] If $Q_i^* < Q_j^*$, the term $\zeta_1$ is negative, leading to the same logical inconsistency.

[6] Strictly speaking, retailers are indifferent between Case III and Case II(i) when the equality with $B_i$ holds. Similarly, the retailers are indifferent between Case III and Case II(j) when the equality with $B_j$ holds. We assign the equality conditions to Case III for ease of presentation. In effect, we break ties in favor of coordination.

[7] The boundary conditions are functions of $b, \theta, Q_i^*$ and $Q_j^*$. In turn, $Q_i^*$ and $Q_j^*$ are functions of the model parameters $b$, $\theta$, $A_i$, $c_i$, $c_j$ and $C$.

[8] In (7.3.4) and (7.3.5) we use the definitions:

$$\xi_1 \equiv (4b^2 + 2b\theta - \theta^2) > 0 \qquad \text{and}$$

$$\xi_2 \equiv (4b^3 + 6b^2\theta - b\theta^2 - 2\theta^3) = b\xi_1 + 2\theta(2b^2 - \theta^2) > 0.$$

[9] See (7.2.28) for the definition of $B_j$.

[10] In the modified menu $\{\tau_i^L, \tau_j^*\}$, the tariff intended for the i[th] retailer ($\tau_i^L$) and the tariff intended for the j[th] retailer ($\tau_j^*$) generate equal profit for the i[th] retailer. We break such "ties" in favor of the channel-coordinating solution.

[11] A comparison of the reduction in net revenues due to defection shows that $B_j > B_i > 0$ for our illustrative $Q_i^* > Q_j^*$.

[12] Recall that at the zonal boundary $(U^{Menu^*} = (f_i - \overline{f}_j))$.

[13] See Table 7.2 entitled "Zones, Menus and Fixed Fees" above. The retailers select different elements from the same menu. The prospect of defection drives an equal adjustment to the fixed fees.

[14] Analogous results can be obtained for the other two-part tariffs analyzed in Chapter 5.

# Chapter 8

## Coordination *versus* Maximization: Theoretical Analyses[1]

*"The whole is more than the sum of its parts."*

## 1 INTRODUCTION

In the three previous Chapters we investigated a set of wholesale-price strategies under the assumption that the manufacturer treats its competing retailers comparably. In Chapter 5 we developed a channel-coordinating quantity-discount schedule, but we proved that for some parametric values any of three specific, non-coordinating two-part tariffs could manufacturer profit-dominate this schedule. In Chapter 6 we established the existence of an envelope of all possible two-part tariffs and we proved that this "sophisticated Stackelberg" tariff cannot coordinate a channel composed of competing, non-identical retailers. From this we deduce that, for some parametric values, the manufacturer prefers the non-coordinating sophisticated Stackelberg tariff to the channel-coordinating quantity-discount schedule. In Chapter 7 we proved the existence of a channel-coordinating menu of two-part tariffs and described the implications of this menu for manufacturer profits.

In this Chapter we evaluate the relative performance of these three wholesale-price schedules at a constant channel breadth. Our analysis attends to a core question of analytical channels research: *Does the profit-maximizing manufacturer prefer to use a channel-coordinating wholesale-price strategy?* In the process of answering this question, we address three subsidiary questions:

(1) Under what parametric values does the quantity-discount schedule manufacturer profit-dominate the sophisticated Stackelberg tariff?

(2) Under what parametric values, if any, does the quantity-discount schedule manufacturer profit-dominate the menu of two-part tariffs?

(3) Under what parametric values, if any, does the sophisticated Stackelberg policy manufacturer profit-dominate the menu?

We will prove analytically, and will demonstrate numerically, that there are parametric values for which the manufacturer reaps the greatest profit by using a linear quantity-discount schedule. We will also prove that there are other parametric values that cause the manufacturer to prefer a menu of two-part tariffs. Both of these policies coordinate the channel, so it is unsurprising that they are sometimes preferred by the manufacturer. What may be surprising, given the insights derived from bilateral-monopoly models, is that the manufacturer favors the non-coordinating, sophisticated Stackelberg wholesale-price strategy over an absolute majority of all possible parametric values. In short, whether the manufacturer should coordinate the channel is not a philosophical question; it is a parametric question. We will show that four parametric dimensions determine the manufacturer's optimal wholesale-price policy. These dimensions are the *intensity of competition*, the *magnitude of competition*, and each retailer's *fixed-cost ratio*. These are the same parameters that governed the zonal boundaries developed in earlier Chapters. Here we relate the zones to manufacturer profit from each strategy.

We organize the Chapter as follows. In Section 2 we briefly review the three wholesale-price policies developed in Chapters 5-7. In Section 3 we analytically derive the conditions under which each policy may be optimal for the manufacturer. In Section 4 we elaborate our understanding of the parametric dimensions that determine which wholesale-price policy is optimal for the manufacturer. In Section 5 we offer several numerical illustrations of our analytical results. In the final Section we discuss our results and offer observations about the analytical modeling literature on distribution channels. An Appendix incorporates important technical details of our analysis.

## 2 THE THREE WHOLESALE-PRICE POLICIES

To make this Chapter self-contained, we begin by briefly summarizing key elements of the analyses in Chapters 5-7. Our overview emphasizes important *similarities* among the three wholesale-price policies. As in earlier Chapters, we write *as if* the $i^{th}$ retailer is always the larger ($Q_i^* > Q_j^*$). This convention, which we adopt for expository purposes, does not limit our conclusions in any way: the $i^{th}$ retailer's market share can range from zero to one in all of our analytical work.

### 2.1 A Channel-Coordinating Quantity-Discount Schedule

The $i^{th}$ retailer's profit under a linear, channel-coordinating quantity-discount schedule is:

$$\pi_i^{QD^*} \equiv R_i^{QD^*} - f_i - \phi^{QD} = \left(\frac{2b+\theta}{2(b+\theta)}\right) R_i^* - f_i - \phi^{QD} \qquad (8.2.1)$$

We first presented this definition at equation (5.4.8). In expression (8.2.1) the term $R_i^*$ is defined as $(Q_i^*)^2/b$; it is the $i^{th}$ retailer's "net revenue" (revenue net of all variable costs) when the channel is coordinated.

Given our decision to hold channel breadth constant,[2] the size of the fixed fee is constrained by the necessity of retaining both retailers as channel participants:

$$\phi^{QD^*} = \min\left\{\left(R_i^{QD^*} - f_i\right), \left(R_j^{QD^*} - f_j\right)\right\} \tag{8.2.2}$$

Expression (8.2.2) is a restatement of equation (5.4.9). A profit-maximizing manufacturer will extract the maximum possible fixed fee; this will leave the *less*-profitable retailer with zero economic profit.

The identity of the less-profitable retailer depends on the net revenues, and the fixed costs, of the competitors. Using Equation (5.4.8), the difference in net revenues is:

$$\delta^{QD^*} \equiv \left(R_i^{QD^*} - R_j^{QD^*}\right) = \frac{(2b+\theta)\left(Q_i^* - Q_j^*\right)\left(Q_i^* + Q_j^*\right)}{2b\left(b+\theta\right)} \tag{8.2.3}$$

If the larger-volume (the $i^{th}$) retailer is the more-profitable competitor, then $\delta^{QD^*} > (f_i - f_j)$ and the fixed fee extracts all profit from the $j^{th}$ retailer: $\phi^{QD^*} = (R_j^{QD^*} - f_j)$. However, for any set of demand and cost parameters, there exist $(f_i - f_j)-$values such that $(f_i - f_j) > \delta^{QD^*}$. When this occurs the $i^{th}$ retailer is less profitable, so the fixed fee extracts all its profit: $\phi^{QD^*} = (R_i^{QD^*} - f_i)$. When retailer profits are equal, $\delta^{QD^*} = (f_i - f_j)$ and the fixed fee extracts all profit from both retailers. In light of the preceding, we define three "Zones" in $\langle f_i, f_j \rangle -$space:

$$\begin{aligned} \delta^{QD^*} &> \left(f_i - f_j\right) &\rightarrow\quad &\text{Zone } Z_j^{QD^*} \\ \delta^{QD^*} &= \left(f_i - f_j\right) &\rightarrow\quad &\text{Zone } Z_{ij}^{QD^*} \\ \delta^{QD^*} &< \left(f_i - f_j\right) &\rightarrow\quad &\text{Zone } Z_i^{QD^*} \end{aligned} \tag{8.2.4}$$

The zonal subscript indicates the retailer that earns zero profit *after* paying the fixed fee. This is the $j^{th}$ retailer in Zone $Z_j^{QD^*}$, both retailers in Zone $Z_{ij}^{QD^*}$, and the $i^{th}$ retailer in Zone $Z_i^{QD^*}$.

The impact of a change in $f_i$ on *manufacturer* profit varies by Zone:

$$\begin{aligned} \partial\Pi_M^{QD^*}\left(f_i, f_j\right)/\partial f_i &= \$0 \qquad \forall \quad \left(f_i - f_j\right) < \delta^{QD^*} \\ \partial\Pi_M^{QD^*}\left(f_i, f_j\right)/\partial f_i &= -\$2 \qquad \forall \quad \left(f_i - f_j\right) > \delta^{QD^*} \end{aligned} \tag{8.2.5}$$

(Changes in $(f_i - f_j)$ have a symmetric impact on manufacturer profit across the Zones.) At values of $(f_i - f_j)$ below $\delta^{QD^*}$, an increase in $f_i$ lowers the profit of the *more* profitable retailer; therefore it has *no* effect on the fixed fee. At $(f_i - f_j)-$values above $\delta^{QD^*}$, retention of the i[th] retailer requires that a \$1 increase in $f_i$ be matched by a compensating \$1 *decrease* in the fixed fee to prevent the i[th] retailer from abandoning the channel. Both retailers pay the same fixed fee, so the profit of the j[th] retailer rises by \$1. As a result, manufacturer profit declines by \$2. Note that, although the quantity-discount schedule given by equations (5.4.6) and (5.4.9) coordinates the channel at *all* $(f_i - f_j)-$values, it allows the manufacturer to obtain all channel profit *only* at the $(f_i - f_j)-$values defined by $\delta^{QD^*} = (f_i - f_j)$.

Equation $\delta^{QD^*} = (f_i - f_j)$ defines a discontinuity—a kink—in the manufacturer's profit function. The points that satisfy this discontinuity, which we have labeled Zone $Z_{ij}^{QD^*}$, form a *line* in $\langle f_i, f_j \rangle-$space. A glance at (8.2.3) shows that the sign of the difference in the retailers' net revenue ($\delta^{QD^*}$) can be expressed in terms of channel-coordinated output levels:

$$\delta^{QD^*} \gtreqless 0 \quad \text{as} \quad Q_i^* \gtreqless Q_j^*. \tag{8.2.6}$$

When market shares are equal, $\delta^{QD^*} = 0$ and Zone $Z_{ij}^{QD^*}$ applies. In this case the manufacturer can extract all channel profit with the quantity-discount schedule. More generally, Zone $Z_{ij}^{QD^*}$ applies *only* when the retailers earn equal profits under the channel-coordinating quantity-discount schedule; this is when the retailers' fixed-cost difference equals their revenue difference, irrespective of their market shares.

## 2.2 The Sophisticated Stackelberg Two-Part Tariff

We derived the sophisticated Stackelberg two-part tariff in Chapter 6 and showed that the elements of this tariff also vary across three Zones. These zones, which we first presented in expression (6.2.6), are:

$$\begin{array}{rl} (f_i - f_j) < L^{SS^*} & \rightarrow \text{ Zone } Z_j^{SS^*} \\ U^{SS^*} \geq (f_i - f_j) \geq L^{SS^*} & \rightarrow \text{ Zone } Z_{ij}^{SS^*} \\ U^{SS^*} < (f_i - f_j) & \rightarrow \text{ Zone } Z_i^{SS^*} \end{array} \tag{8.2.7}$$

Once again the zonal subscript indicates which retailer earns zero profit after payment of the fixed fee. Retailer net revenue differs by Zone because the per-unit wholesale price differs across zones (see equations (6.2.2) and (6.3.4) for details). This net revenue is a continuously variable function of $(f_i - f_j)$ in Zone $Z_{ij}^{SS^*}$. Accordingly, the fixed fee also differs by zone (see equations (6.2.3) and (6.3.8)).

The upper ($U^{SS^*}$) and lower ($L^{SS^*}$) zonal boundaries are defined by equations (6.2.4) and (6.2.5), respectively.[3] If the coordinated outputs are equal, both boundaries are identically zero; in this special case Zone $Z_{ij}^{SS^*}$ reduces to the equal-market-shares line in $\langle f_i, f_j \rangle$ – space.

For the reason given in regard to the quantity-discount schedule, the impact of a change in $f_i$ on *manufacturer* profit varies by Zone. We find:

$$\begin{aligned}
\partial \Pi_M^{SS^*}(f_i,f_j)/\partial f_i &= \$0 && \forall \quad (f_i - f_j) < L^{SS^*} \\
\$0 \le \partial \Pi_M^{SS^*}(f_i,f_j)/\partial f_i &= -\$2(1-\omega) && \forall \quad U^{SS^*} \ge (f_i - f_j) \ge L^{SS^*} \\
\partial \Pi_M^{SS^*}(f_i,f_j)/\partial f_i &= -\$2 && \forall \quad U^{SS^*} < (f_i - f_j)
\end{aligned} \tag{8.2.8}$$

Changes in $f_j$ have a symmetric impact on manufacturer profit across Zones. (The value of $\omega$ is defined at (6.3.7); it lies within the unit interval.)

## 2.3 The Channel-Coordinating Menu of Tariffs

In Chapter 7 we derived the channel-coordinating menu of two-part tariffs. Again there are three Zones; they are defined as:

$$\begin{aligned}
(f_i - f_j) < L^{Menu^*} &\rightarrow \quad \text{Zone } Z_j^{Menu^*} \\
U^{Menu^*} \ge (f_i - f_j) \ge L^{Menu^*} &\rightarrow \quad \text{Zone } Z_{ij}^{Menu^*} \\
U^{Menu^*} < (f_i - f_j) &\rightarrow \quad \text{Zone } Z_i^{Menu^*}
\end{aligned} \tag{8.2.9}$$

Equations (7.3.4) and (7.3.5) define the upper ($U^{Menu^*}$) and lower ($L^{Menu^*}$) zonal boundaries, while Table 7.2 of Chapter 7 reports the optimal fixed fees.

The impact of a change in $f_i$ on *manufacturer* profit varies by Zone:

$$\begin{aligned}
\partial \Pi_M^{Menu^*}(f_i,f_j)/\partial f_i &= \$0 && \forall \quad (f_i - f_j) < L^{Menu^*} \\
\partial \Pi_M^{Menu^*}(f_i,f_j)/\partial f_i &= -\$1 && \forall \quad U^{Menu^*} \ge (f_i - f_j) \ge L^{Menu^*} \\
\partial \Pi_M^{Menu^*}(f_i,f_j)/\partial f_i &= -\$2 && \forall \quad U^{Menu^*} < (f_i - f_j)
\end{aligned} \tag{8.2.10}$$

The effect of a change in $f_j$ is symmetric.

## 2.4 Summary

We have shown that each of the three wholesale-price policies examined in the preceding Chapters can be expressed in terms of three Zones defined in $\langle f_i, f_j \rangle$ – space. Corresponding Zones share important properties. First, within the "$Z_j$ – Zones" the manufacturer extracts the total economic profit of the $j^{th}$ retailer (but not of the $i^{th}$ retailer). Moreover, a change in $f_i$ does not affect the manufacturer's profit, but a \$1 increase in $f_j$ costs the manufacturer \$2.

Second, the "$Z_i$ – Zones" are mirror images of the "$Z_j$ – Zones." In these Zones the manufacturer garners the total profit of the $i^{th}$ retailer (but not of the $j^{th}$ retailer). Further, a change in $f_j$ does not affect the manufacturer's profit, but a \$1 increase in $f_i$ decreases manufacturer profits by \$2.

Third, in the "$Z_{ij}$ – Zones" the manufacturer extracts all profit from the channel. In the case of the quantity-discount schedule this "Zone" is only a line in $\langle f_i, f_j \rangle$ – space that separates the other two Zones, but zonal width is substantive for the other wholesale-price policies. In the case of the menu, a \$1 increase in $f_i$ decreases manufacturer profits by \$1; but in the case of the sophisticated Stackelberg tariff, a \$1 increase in $f_i$ decreases manufacturer profits by between \$0 and \$2, with the precise amount depending on the difference in the retailers' fixed costs.

Within the context of our model, the manufacturer cannot affect the zonal boundaries (they are *exogenous*), nor can it influence the *exogenous* value of $(f_i - f_j)$. What is *endogenous* for the manufacturer is its choice of a wholesale-price policy. In deciding which of the three strategies to adopt, the manufacturer must contrast profitability across these strategies for a specific $(f_i - f_j)$ – value.

Modelers must make a more general comparison; our task is to identify the manufacturer-optimal wholesale-price policy at *every possible* $(f_i - f_j)$ – value. Three observations simplify this complex task.

***Observation 1***: When $(f_i - f_j)$ lies in Zone $Z_{ij}^{QD^*}$ or $Z_{ij}^{Menu^*}$, the manufacturer prefers a channel-coordinating wholesale-price strategy because this gives the manufacturer all channel profit.

***Observation 2***: If a wholesale-price policy is manufacturer-optimal at a *single* $(f_i - f_j)$ – value that lies in the three $Z_i$ – Zones, then that policy is manufacturer-optimal at *all* $(f_i - f_j)$ – values that lie in the three $Z_i$ – Zones. The reason is that changes in $f_i$ have no effect on manufacturer profit in the $Z_i$ – Zones.

***Observation 3***: If a wholesale-price policy is manufacturer-optimal at a *single* $(f_i - f_j)$ – value that lies in the three $Z_j$ – Zones, then that policy is manufacturer-optimal at *all* $(f_i - f_j)$ – values that lie in the three $Z_j$ – Zones. The reasoning is analogous to that of *Observation 2*.

Given these Observations, we are left with two tasks. First, we must determine which Zone is relevant for each wholesale-pricing strategy for every $(f_i - f_j)$ – value. Second, if one of the rules cited above does not apply to a particular $(f_i - f_j)$ – value, we must identify the strategy that generates the greatest profit for the manufacturer. We now turn to these tasks.

# 3 THE MANUFACTURER'S CHOICE OF AN OPTIMAL WHOLESALE-PRICE STRATEGY: THEORETICAL FOUNDATIONS

We now analytically answer the core question: "Is it more profitable for the manufacturer to coordinate, or not to coordinate, the channel?"

## 3.1 The Relationship among Zonal Boundaries

To assess the manufacturer's preferences among the wholesale-price policies, we must know which profit comparisons to make. For example, suppose that a particular value of $(f_i - f_j)$ lies in the sophisticated Stackelberg Zone $Z_i^{SS^*}$. To determine the relative optimality of the profit generated by the sophisticated Stackelberg Tariff at this $(f_i - f_j)$ – value, we must also identify the quantity-discount zone that contains this $(f_i - f_j)$ – value and the menu zone that contains this value. This requires an understanding of the relationships among the nine Zones described in Section 2.

The Zones are defined by five boundary conditions that we have labeled $L^{Menu^*}$, $U^{Menu^*}$, $L^{SS^*}$, $U^{SS^*}$ and $\delta^{QD^*}$. We show in the Appendix that, when $Q_i^* > Q_j^*$, four Zonal Scenarios are possible:[4]

$$\begin{array}{llllllllll}
\textbf{Scenario 1:} & L^{SS^*} & < & L^{Menu^*} & < \delta^{QD^*} & < & U^{Menu^*} & < & U^{SS^*} & \\
\textbf{Scenario 2:} & L^{SS^*} & < & L^{Menu^*} & < \delta^{QD^*} & \gtrless & U^{SS^*} & < & U^{Menu^*} & \\
\textbf{Scenario 3:} & L^{SS^*} & < & U^{SS^*} & < L^{Menu^*} & < & \delta^{QD^*} & < & U^{Menu^*} & \\
\textbf{Scenario 4:} & L^{SS^*} & < & U^{SS^*} & < \delta^{QD^*} & < & L^{Menu^*} & < & U^{Menu^*} &
\end{array} \tag{8.3.1}$$

In the first three Zonal Scenarios, the channel-coordinating quantity-discount schedule is a special case of the channel-coordinating menu of two-part tariffs, because $L^{Menu^*} < \delta^{QD^*} < U^{Menu^*}$. Both policies maximize channel profit, but the former enables the manufacturer to obtain all channel profit only at a single $(f_i - f_j)$ – value ($\delta^{QD^*}$), while the menu accomplishes this feat over a range of $(f_i - f_j)$ – values that includes $\delta^{QD^*}$. Only in Scenario 4 does the quantity-discount schedule dominate the menu for some $(f_i - f_j)$ – values.

We can reduce the apparent complexity of the Scenario definitions in (8.3.1) by focusing on the three boundary relationships that change across Scenarios. The sign of $(U^{SS^*} - L^{Menu^*})$ distinguishes the first two Scenarios from the remaining two. In addition, the sign of $(U^{SS^*} - U^{Menu^*})$ distinguishes Scenarios 1 and 2, while the sign of $(\delta^{QD^*} - L^{Menu^*})$ distinguishes Scenarios 3 and 4. In Table 8.1 we use the signs of these differences to define the four Scenarios succinctly.

Each boundary line separating two successive Scenarios is a function of two zonal-boundary parameters. In particular, along each boundary line the difference between two zonal-boundary parameters is zero:

$$\begin{array}{lll}
\textbf{Scenarios 1 and 2} & \Leftrightarrow & \Delta^{USS}_{UMenu} \equiv \left[\left(U^{SS*} - U^{Menu^*}\right) = 0\right] \\
\textbf{Scenarios 2 and 3} & \Leftrightarrow & \Delta^{USS}_{LMenu} \equiv \left[\left(U^{SS*} - L^{Menu^*}\right) = 0\right] \\
\textbf{Scenarios 3 and 4} & \Leftrightarrow & \Delta^{\delta QD}_{LMenu} \equiv \left[\left(\delta^{QD^*} - L^{Menu^*}\right) = 0\right]
\end{array} \tag{8.3.2}$$

We show in the Appendix that these differences are a function of $b, \theta, Q_i^*, \text{and} Q_j^*$ (see equations (8.A.2), (8.A.3), and (8.A.8)). Through the same re-parameterization[5] used in Chapters 5-7, we can reduce these basic parameters to *two* dimensions: $S_j \; (\equiv Q_j^* / (Q_i^* + Q_j^*))$ and $\chi \, (\equiv \theta / b)$.

*Table 8.1.* Zonal Scenario Definitions Given $Q_i^* > Q_j^*$

| | $L^{Menu^*} < \delta^{QD^*}$ ? | $L^{Menu^*} < U^{SS^*}$ ? | $U^{Menu^*} < U^{SS^*}$ ? |
|---|---|---|---|
| **Scenario 1** | Yes | Yes | Yes |
| **Scenario 2** | Yes | Yes | No |
| **Scenario 3** | Yes | No | No |
| **Scenario 4** | No | No | No |

In the trivial cases of the bilateral-monopoly model ($\theta = 0$) and the identical-competitors model ($S_j = \frac{1}{2}$), all three Scenario boundaries in (8.3.2) are simultaneously met. In addition, for any specific value of $S_j < \frac{1}{2}$, there exist unique values of $\chi$ such that $\Delta^{USS}_{UMenu} = 0$ or $\Delta^{USS}_{LMenu} = 0$ or $\Delta^{\delta QD}_{LMenu} = 0$. These $\chi$ values are implicitly defined by the following equations:

$$S_j = S^{USS}_{UMenu} \equiv \left( \frac{16 - 8\chi - 36\chi^2 + 6\chi^3 + 15\chi^4 - 4\chi^5}{32 - 16\chi - 64\chi^2 + 20\chi^3 + 28\chi^4 - 10\chi^5} \right) \leftrightarrow \Delta^{USS}_{UMenu} = 0 \quad (8.3.3)$$

$$S_j = S^{USS}_{LMenu} \equiv \left( \frac{16 + 8\chi - 28\chi^2 - 6\chi^3 + 11\chi^4 - 2\chi^5}{32 + 16\chi - 48\chi^2 - 4\chi^3 + 20\chi^4 - 6\chi^5} \right) \leftrightarrow \Delta^{USS}_{LMenu} = 0 \quad (8.3.4)$$

$$S_j = S^{\delta QD}_{LMenu} \equiv \left( \frac{16 + 8\chi - 16\chi^2 - 8\chi^3 + 3\chi^4 + \chi^5}{32 + 16\chi - 24\chi^2 - 8\chi^3 + 4\chi^4} \right) \leftrightarrow \Delta^{\delta QD}_{LMenu} = 0 \quad (8.3.5)$$

Let the set of $\langle \chi, S_j \rangle$ – pairs that satisfy $0 \le \chi \le 1$ and $0 \le S_j \le \frac{1}{2}$ be defined as the *unit half-square*. It is easy to show that $S^{USS}_{LMenu}$, $S^{USS}_{UMenu}$, and $S^{\delta QD}_{LMenu}$ define negatively-sloped lines that curve through the interior of the unit half-square that intersect the point $\langle \chi = 0, S_j = \frac{1}{2} \rangle$ in its lower, righthand corner. All three lines intersect either the lefthand side (the $\langle S_j = 0 \rangle$ – axis) or the top side (the $\langle \chi = 1 \rangle$ – axis) of the unit half-square. We find:

- $S^{\delta QD}_{LMenu}$ intersects the $\chi = 1$ axis at $S_j = 0.2$
- $S^{USS}_{LMenu}$ intersects the $S_j = 0$ axis at $\chi = 0.968733$ (8.3.6)
- $S^{USS}_{UMenu}$ intersects the $S_j = 0$ axis at $\chi = 0.634012$

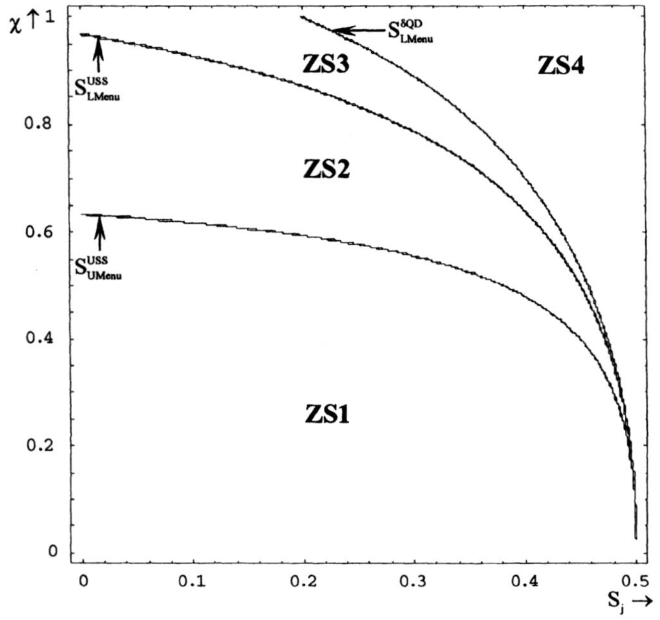


Legend:
$ZSx \equiv$ Zonal Scenario $x$, $x \in (1,2,3,4)$.
See Table 8.1 for the definitions of these Scenarios.

*Figure 8.1.* The Four Zonal Scenarios

Figure 8.1 illustrates the relative positions of these boundaries in the unit half-square. The upper internal boundary is $S^{\delta QD}_{LMenu}$, the middle internal boundary is $S^{USS}_{LMenu}$, and the lower internal boundary is $S^{USS}_{UMenu}$.

## 3.2 Manufacturer Profitability

We have seen in the three preceding Chapters that the manufacturer's profitability depends on the actual difference in retailer's fixed costs $(f_i - f_j)$. We know that the manufacturer can obtain all coordinated channel profit *if* $(f_i - f_j)$ lies in the interval $[L^{Menu^*}, U^{Menu^*}]$ (or at the point $\delta^{QD^*}$). Thus in this interval (or at this point), the menu (or the quantity-discount schedule) is the manufacturer-optimal strategy. What we must determine is the optimal wholesale-price strategy if $(f_i - f_j) \notin \{[L^{Menu^*}, U^{Menu^*}], \delta^{QD^*}\}$. To that end we focus our analysis on the set of $(f_i - f_j)$ – values that satisfy either $(f_i - f_j) < L^{Menu^*}$ or $(f_i - f_j) > U^{Menu^*}$. For expository purposes, we only discuss $Q_i^* > Q_j^*$.

Consider the situation for which $(f_i - f_j) < L^{Menu^*}$. From the Zonal Scenarios defined in (8.3.1), there are three possibilities regarding the other Zonal boundaries. In Scenarios 1 and 2, $L^{SS^*}$ is the *only* Zonal boundary less than $L^{Menu^*}$. In Scenario 3, both $L^{SS^*}$ and $U^{SS^*}$ are less than $L^{Menu^*}$, and in Scenario 4, $L^{SS^*}$, $U^{SS^*}$, and $\delta^{QD^*}$ are all less than $L^{Menu^*}$. Therefore, to identify the optimal pricing strategy when $(f_i - f_j) < L^{Menu^*}$, we analyze each of three sequences of Zonal boundaries: (1) $L^{SS^*} < L^{Menu^*}$, (2) $L^{SS^*} < U^{SS^*} < L^{Menu^*}$, and (3) $L^{SS^*} < U^{SS^*} < \delta^{QD^*} < L^{Menu^*}$.

Now consider $U^{Menu^*} < (f_i - f_j)$; in this case the required analysis is much simpler. We know that the channel-coordinating menu is optimal for all $L^{Menu^*} \leq U^{SS^*} < U^{Menu^*} \leq (f_i - f_j)$; thus, we only need to evaluate $U^{Menu^*} < U^{SS^*}$ to determine the optimal wholesale-price strategy.

### 3.2.1 Zonal Scenarios 1, 2 and 3: Manufacturer Profitability When $(f_i - f_j) < L^{Menu^*} < \delta^{QD^*}$

When $L^{SS^*} < L^{Menu^*} < \delta^{QD^*}$, we distinguish between $(f_i - f_j)$ – values that satisfy $(f_i - f_j) \leq L^{SS^*}$ and those that satisfy $L^{SS^*} < (f_i - f_j) < L^{Menu^*}$. (The inequality $L^{Menu^*} < \delta^{QD^*}$ eliminates the quantity-discount schedule from consideration.) When $(f_i - f_j) \leq L^{SS^*}$, changes in the retailers' fixed-cost difference have no impact on manufacturer profit under the sophisticated Stackelberg wholesale-price strategy or the menu of two-part tariffs $(d\Pi_M^{SS^*} / d(f_i - f_j) = 0 = d\Pi_M^{Menu^*} / d(f_i - f_j))$. By Observation 2 of Section 2.4, if the sophisticated Stackelberg tariff does not manufacturer profit-dominate at $L^{SS^*}$, it cannot be dominant at any $(f_i - f_j) \leq L^{SS^*}$. Conversely, if the sophisticated Stackelberg tariff is manufacturer profit-dominant at $L^{SS^*}$, then it is dominant at all $(f_i - f_j) \leq L^{SS^*}$. Henceforth we will write "SS – tariff" to denote the "sophisticated Stackelberg tariff" and we will write "MN – tariff" to denote the menu of two-part tariffs.

When $L^{SS^*} < (f_i - f_j) < L^{Menu^*}$, changes in the magnitude of $(f_i - f_j)$ alter manufacturer profit under the SS−tariff ($\$0 > d\Pi_M^{SS^*} / d(f_i - f_j) \geq -\$2$) but do not affect manufacturer profit with the menu ($d\Pi_M^{Menu^*} / d(f_i - f_j) = 0$). By Observation 3 of Section 2.4, if the SS−tariff does not manufacturer profit-dominate at $L^{SS^*}$, it cannot be dominant at any $L^{SS^*} < (f_i - f_j) < L^{Menu^*}$. However, if the SS−tariff does manufacturer profit-dominate at $L^{SS^*}$, then it dominates for all $(f_i - f_j) \leq E^{L,L}$, where $E^{L,L} \in (L^{SS^*}, L^{Menu^*})$ is the $(f_i - f_j)$−value at which the two pricing strategies generate equal manufacturer profits.[6] Of course, if the menu is manufacturer profit-dominant at $L^{SS^*}$, then the MN−tariff dominates at all $(f_i - f_j) \leq L^{Menu^*}$.

Given this summary, the key question is the optimal wholesale-price strategy when $(f_i - f_j) = L^{SS^*}$. Given this $(f_i - f_j)$−value, manufacturer profit under the sophisticated Stackelberg wholesale-price policy is:

$$\begin{aligned} \Pi_M^{SS^*}\left(L^{SS^*}\right) &\equiv \Pi_M^{SS^*}(\omega = 0) \\ &= \Pi_C^{SS^*}(\omega = 0) \\ &= R_C^{SS^*}(\omega = 0) - f_i - f_j - F \\ &= R_C^{SS^*}(\omega = 0) - L^{SS^*} - 2f_j - F \end{aligned} \tag{8.3.7}$$

The notation $\Pi_M^{SS^*}(\omega = 0)$ (or $\Pi_C^{SS^*}(\omega = 0)$) denotes manufacturer (or channel) profit under the sophisticated Stackelberg wholesale-price policy, evaluated at $\omega = 0$ (i.e., at $L^{SS^*}$). Similarly the notation $R_C^{SS^*}(\omega = 0)$ denotes channel net revenue at the same point under the same policy. To get from the next-to-last line to the final line of (8.3.7), we have made the substitution $L^{SS^*} = (f_i - f_j)$.

We evaluate the same point for manufacturer profit under the menu:

$$\begin{aligned} \Pi_M^{Menu^*}\left(L^{SS^*}\right) &= \Pi_M^{Menu^*}\left(L^{Menu^*}\right) \\ &= \Pi_C^{Menu^*}\left(L^{Menu^*}\right) \\ &= R_C^* - f_i - f_j - F \\ &= R_C^* - L^{Menu^*} - 2f_j - F \end{aligned} \tag{8.3.8}$$

Because $\Pi_M^{Menu^*}$ is constant at all $(f_i - f_j)$−values less than $L^{Menu^*}$, the first line of (8.3.8) states that the manufacturer's profit at $L^{SS^*}$ is equal to its profit at $L^{Menu^*}$. The second line recognizes that $\Pi_M^{Menu^*}$ is equal to channel profit at

$L^{Menu^*}$. Finally, to get to the last line of equation (8.3.8), we have made the substitution $L^{Menu^*} = (f_i - f_j)$. The notation $R_C^*$ denotes channel net revenue under coordination.

Subtracting (8.3.7) from (8.3.8) implies:

$$\begin{aligned} &\Pi_M^{SS^*}\left(L^{SS^*}\right) > \Pi_M^{Menu^*}\left(L^{SS^*}\right) \\ &\textit{iff} \qquad \left[L^{Menu^*} - L^{SS^*}\right] > \left[R_C^* - R_C^{SS^*}(\omega = 0)\right] \end{aligned} \tag{8.3.9}$$

The LHS of the second line in equation (8.3.9) is defined at equation (8.A.1); it is positive for $Q_i^* > Q_j^*$. The RHS of the second line may be rewritten as:

$$\Delta R_C^{(CC-SS)} \equiv \left[R_C^* - R_C^{SS^*}(\omega = 0)\right] = \left(\frac{(4b-3\theta)^2\left(Q_i^* - Q_j^*\right)^2}{2(b+\theta)(2b+\theta)^2}\right) > 0 \tag{8.3.10}$$

If condition (8.3.9) holds, the $SS-$tariff is manufacturer profit-dominant over the range $(f_i - f_j) < E^{L,L}$. However, if (8.3.9) does not hold, the channel-coordinating $MN-$tariff is manufacturer profit-dominant over the entire range $(f_i - f_j) < L^{Menu^*}$. In Section 4 of this Chapter we explore the factors that underlie inequality (8.3.9), but we postpone that analysis until we complete our exploration of the four Zonal Scenarios.

### 3.2.2 Zonal Scenario 3: Manufacturer Profitability When $(f_i - f_j) < L^{Menu^*}$ and $U^{SS^*} < L^{Menu^*} < \delta^{QD^*}$

In the last sub-Section we argued that, if the sophisticated Stackelberg tariff is not manufacturer-preferred at $L^{SS^*}$, then it cannot dominate the menu at any $L^{SS^*} \le (f_i - f_j) < L^{Menu^*}$. Thus the present case is relevant only when the $SS-$tariff is manufacturer-preferred at $L^{SS^*}$. We again distinguish between the $(f_i - f_j)-$values that satisfy $(f_i - f_j) \le L^{SS^*}$ and those that satisfy $L^{SS^*} < (f_i - f_j) < L^{Menu^*}$. We divide our analysis of this Scenario into two parts. First, when $(f_i - f_j) \le L^{SS^*} < U^{SS^*} < L^{Menu^*}$, we use the same analysis as in sub-Section 3.2.1. By Observation 2, if the $SS-$tariff does not dominate the $MN-$tariff at $L^{SS^*}$, then the menu is dominant at every $(f_i - f_j) < L^{SS^*}$. However, if the sophisticated Stackelberg strategy is manufacturer profit-dominant at $L^{SS^*}$, it will dominate at all $(f_i - f_j) \le L^{SS^*}$.

Second, when $L^{SS^*} < (f_i - f_j)$, the key question for the manufacturer involves the optimal strategy at the point $(f_i - f_j) = U^{SS^*}$. If the $SS-$tariff is *not* manufacturer-preferred at $U^{SS^*}$, then profit equality between the two strategies must occur in the interval $L^{SS^*} \leq (f_i - f_j) < U^{SS^*}$. (For details, see Appendix equation (8.A.12)). However, if the $SS-$tariff *is* dominant at $U^{SS^*}$, then it is dominant for *all* $L^{SS^*} < (f_i - f_j) \leq U^{SS^*}$ because decreases in $(f_i - f_j)$ raise (have no effect on) manufacturer profit under the $SS-$tariff (the $MN-$tariff) in this $(f_i - f_j)-$range. Thus, there exists an $(f_i - f_j)-$value, say $E^{U,L}$, at which the two wholesale-price strategies generate equal profits for the manufacturer. We define $E^{U,L}$, which must lie in the interval $U^{SS^*} \leq (f_i - f_j) < L^{Menu^*}$, in the Appendix at equation (8.A.22).

We now determine the optimal strategy at the point $(f_i - f_j) = U^{SS^*}$. Manufacturer profit under the sophisticated Stackelberg wholesale-price policy, evaluated at $(f_i - f_j) = U^{SS^*}$, is:

$$\begin{aligned} \Pi_M^{SS^*}\left(U^{SS^*}\right) &\equiv \Pi_M^{SS^*}(\omega = 1) \\ &= \Pi_C^{SS^*}(\omega = 1) \\ &= R_C^{SS^*}(\omega = 1) - f_i - f_j - F \\ &= R_C^{SS^*}(\omega = 1) - U^{SS^*} - 2f_j - F \end{aligned} \tag{8.3.11}$$

Manufacturer profit under the menu is:

$$\begin{aligned} \Pi_M^{Menu^*}\left(U^{SS^*}\right) &= \Pi_M^{Menu^*}\left(L^{Menu^*}\right) \\ &= \Pi_C^{Menu^*}\left(L^{Menu^*}\right) \\ &= R_C^* - f_i - f_j - F \\ &= R_C^* - L^{Menu^*} - 2f_j - F \end{aligned} \tag{8.3.12}$$

The menu expression is evaluated at $(f_i - f_j) = L^{Menu^*}$. Subtracting (8.3.11) from (8.3.12) implies:

$$\left[\Pi_M^{SS^*}\left(U^{SS^*}\right) - \Pi_M^{Menu^*}\left(U^{SS^*}\right)\right] > 0 \tag{8.3.13}$$

$$\textit{iff} \qquad \left[L^{Menu^*} - U^{SS^*}\right] > \left[R_C^* - R_C^{SS^*}(\omega = 1)\right] = \Delta R_C^{(CC-SS)}$$

The LHS of the lower line of (8.3.13) is defined at equation (8.A.3), while the RHS of the lower line is identical to equation (8.3.10). By definition both sides of (8.3.13) are positive.

When condition (8.3.13) is satisfied, the manufacturer prefers the SS – tariff to channel-coordination. When this condition is not satisfied, the manufacturer prefers the MN – tariff over the range $E^{U,L} \leq (f_i - f_j) \leq U^{SS^*}$.

### 3.2.3 Zonal Scenario 4: Manufacturer Profitability When $(f_i - f_j) < L^{Menu^*}$ and $U^{SS^*} < \delta^{QD^*} < L^{Menu^*}$

In Zonal Scenario 4 it is always true that the channel-coordinating quantity-discount schedule ("QD – schedule") manufacturer profit-dominates the MN – tariff when $(f_i - f_j) = \delta^{QD^*} < L^{Menu^*}$ because the manufacturer reaps coordinated-channel profit with the QD – schedule but not with the SS – tariff. To determine the manufacturer-optimal strategy in this situation, we divide our analysis into three parts. If $(f_i - f_j) \leq L^{SS^*}$, we see that $d\Pi_M^{SS^*}/d(f_i - f_j) = \$0$ and $d\Pi_M^{QD^*}/d(f_i - f_j) = \$0$. From Observation 2, if the manufacturer prefers the SS – tariff at $L^{SS^*}$, it will prefer this strategy at all $(f_i - f_j) \leq L^{SS^*}$. However, if the SS – tariff is sub-optimal at $L^{SS^*}$, it will be sub-optimal at all $(f_i - f_j) \leq \delta^{QD^*}$.

Second, if $U^{SS^*} \leq (f_i - f_j) < \delta^{QD^*}$, we know that $d\Pi_M^{QD^*}/d(f_i - f_j) = \$0$ and $d\Pi_M^{SS^*}/d(f_i - f_j) = -\$2$. By Observation 3, if the SS – tariff does not manufacturer profit-dominate the QD – schedule at $U^{SS^*}$, it cannot dominate anywhere in the range $U^{SS^*} \leq (f_i - f_j) < \delta^{QD^*}$. But if the SS – tariff does manufacturer profit-dominate the QD – schedule at $U^{SS^*}$, then it will be dominant throughout the range $L^{SS^*} < (f_i - f_j) < U^{SS^*}$; but, it will be dominant over only *part* of the range $U^{SS^*} \leq (f_i - f_j) < \delta^{QD^*}$. Thus there must exist a value of $(f_i - f_j)$, call it $E^{U,\delta}$, at which the two wholesale-price strategies generate equal profits for the manufacturer. (See Appendix equation (8.A.31) for a precise definition of $E^{U,\delta}$.)

Finally, when $L^{SS^*} < (f_i - f_j) < U^{SS^*}$, the optimal strategy depends on what happens at the two end points. If either the QD – schedule or the SS – tariff dominates at both endpoints, then it dominates at every point in between. However, if the SS – tariff manufacturer profit-dominates the QD – schedule at $L^{SS^*}$ but *not* at $U^{SS^*}$, then there is another $(f_i - f_j)$ – value, say $E^{L,\delta}$, at which the two strategies generate equal profits for the manufacturer. (For a definition of $E^{L,\delta}$, see Appendix equation (8.A.27).)

We now determine which strategy dominates in Scenario 4. Manufacturer profit under the SS – tariff, evaluated at $(f_i - f_j) = L^{SS^*}$ is given by equation (8.3.7) above, while profit evaluated at $(f_i - f_j) = U^{SS^*}$ is:

$$\begin{aligned}\Pi_M^{SS^*}\left(U^{SS^*}\right) &\equiv \Pi_M^{SS^*}(\omega = 1)\\ &= \Pi_C^{SS^*}(\omega = 1)\\ &= R_C^{SS^*}(\omega = 1) - f_i - f_j - F\\ &= R_C^{SS^*}(\omega = 1) - U^{SS^*} - 2f_j - F\end{aligned} \tag{8.3.14}$$

The notation $R_C^{SS^*}(\omega = 1)$ denotes channel revenue under the SS – tariff, evaluated at $\omega = 1$ (i.e., at $U^{SS^*}$). Note that, to get from the next-to-last line to the final line of (8.3.7), we have made the substitution $U^{SS^*} = (f_i - f_j)$.

Manufacturer profit under the QD – schedule is:

$$\begin{aligned}\Pi_M^{QD^*}\left(L^{SS^*}\right) = \Pi_M^{QD^*}\left(U^{SS^*}\right) = \Pi_M^{QD^*}\left(\delta^{QD^*}\right) &\equiv \Pi_C^{QD^*}\left(\delta^{QD^*}\right)\\ &= R_C^* - f_i - f_j - F\\ &= R_C^* - \delta^{QD^*} - 2f_j - F\end{aligned} \tag{8.3.15}$$

It is again a simple calculation to determine whether the SS – tariff or the QD – schedule dominates. At the point $(f_i - f_j) = L^{SS^*}$, the SS – tariff dominates the QD – schedule when:

$$\begin{aligned}&\left[\Pi_M^{SS^*}\left(L^{SS^*}\right) - \Pi_M^{QD^*}\left(L^{SS^*}\right)\right] > 0\\ &\textit{iff} \qquad \left[\delta^{QD^*} - L^{SS^*}\right] > \Delta R_C^{(CC-SS)}\end{aligned} \tag{8.3.16}$$

The LHS is defined at equation (8.A.5). Observe that, because the QD – schedule is channel-coordinating, it generates the same channel revenue as the menu $(R_C^*)$. The RHS of (8.3.16) is defined at (8.3.10).

Similarly, the manufacturer prefers the SS – tariff at $(f_i - f_j) = U^{SS^*}$ when the following condition holds:

$$\begin{aligned}&\left[\Pi_M^{SS^*}\left(U^{SS^*}\right) - \Pi_M^{QD^*}\left(U^{SS^*}\right)\right] > 0\\ &\textit{iff} \qquad \left[\delta^{QD^*} - U^{SS^*}\right] > \Delta R_C^{(CC-SS)}\end{aligned} \tag{8.3.17}$$

The LHS is defined at equation (8.A.6) and the RHS at equation (8.3.10).

In summary, when condition (8.3.16) is satisfied, the manufacturer prefers the sophisticated Stackelberg tariff to a channel-coordinating strategy over the range $(f_i - f_j) \leq E^{L,\delta}$. And, when condition (8.3.17) is satisfied, the manufacturer prefers the $SS-$tariff over the range $U^{SS^*} < E^{U,\delta} < \delta^{QD^*}$. When neither condition is satisfied, the manufacturer prefers (i) the $QD-$schedule over the range $(f_i - f_j) \leq E^{\delta,L}$ and (ii) the $MN-$tariff over the range $E^{\delta,L} \leq (f_i - f_j)$. (See equation (8.A.38) in the Appendix for details.)

### 3.2.4 Zonal Scenario 1: Manufacturer Profitability When $(f_i - f_j) > U^{Menu^*}$ and $U^{SS^*} > U^{Menu^*}$

We now return our attention to Scenario 1, in which $U^{Menu^*} < U^{SS^*}$. In this Scenario it is possible that, as $(f_i - f_j)$ approaches its maximum value, the manufacturer will prefer the $SS-$tariff. Again we divide our analysis into two parts.[7] When $U^{Menu^*} < U^{SS^*}$, changes in the retailers' fixed-cost difference have an equal impact on manufacturer profit under the $SS-$tariff and the $MN-$tariff because $d\Pi_M^{SS^*} / d(f_i - f_j) = -\$2 = d\Pi_M^{Menu^*} / d(f_i - f_j)$. From Observation 3, if the $SS-$tariff does not manufacturer profit-dominate at $U^{SS^*}$, it cannot be dominant at any $U^{SS^*} \leq (f_i - f_j)$. However, if the $SS-$tariff manufacturer profit-dominates at $U^{SS^*}$, it will be dominant at all $U^{SS^*} \leq (f_i - f_j)$.

When $U^{Menu^*} < (f_i - f_j) < U^{SS^*}$, an increase in $(f_i - f_j)$ produces a larger decline in manufacturer profit under the $MN-$tariff than under the $SS-$tariff because $d\Pi_M^{Menu^*} / d(f_i - f_j) = -\$2$ and $-\$1 > d\Pi_M^{SS^*} / d(f_i - f_j) > -\$2$. From Observation 3, if the menu is manufacturer profit-dominant at $U^{SS^*}$, it dominates at all $U^{Menu^*} \leq (f_i - f_j)$. However, if the $SS-$tariff manufacturer profit-dominates the $MN-$tariff at $U^{SS^*}$, it will be dominant only for the set of $(f_i - f_j)-$values that satisfy $(f_i - f_j) > E^{U,U}$, where $E^{U,U} \in (U^{Menu^*}, U^{SS^*})$ is the $(f_i - f_j)-$value at which the $SS-$tariff and the $MN-$tariff generate equal manufacturer profits. (See equation (8.A.17) for the definition of $E^{U,U}$.)

We now determine the optimal wholesale-price policy when $(f_i - f_j) < U^{SS^*}$. Manufacturer profit under the sophisticated Stackelberg wholesale-price policy is given by equation (8.3.14) when $(f_i - f_j) = U^{SS^*}$.

Using the same approach, manufacturer profit under the menu is:

$$\begin{aligned}\Pi_M^{Menu^*}\left(U^{SS^*}\right) &= \left\{\Pi_C^{Menu^*}\left(U^{Menu^*}\right)\right\} - 2\left[U^{SS^*} - U^{Menu^*}\right] \\ &= \left\{R_C^* - f_i - f_j - F\right\} - 2\left[U^{SS^*} - U^{Menu^*}\right] \\ &= R_C^* + U^{Menu^*} - 2U^{SS^*} - 2f_j - F\end{aligned} \tag{8.3.18}$$

Note that $[U^{SS^*} - U^{Menu^*}]$ is equal to the necessary fixed-fee adjustment in the menu when $(f_i - f_j) = U^{SS^*}$. Subtracting (8.3.14) from (8.3.18), we deduce:

$$\begin{aligned}&\left[\Pi_M^{SS^*}\left(U^{SS^*}\right) - \Pi_M^{Menu^*}\left(U^{SS^*}\right)\right] > 0 \\ \textit{iff} \qquad &\left[U^{SS^*} - U^{Menu^*}\right] > \Delta R_C^{(CC-SS)}\end{aligned} \tag{8.3.19}$$

Both sides of (8.3.19) are positive by definition (recall that the menu maximizes total net revenue in the channel, but the SS – tariff does not). The LHS is defined at equation (8.A.2), while the RHS is identical to equation (8.3.10), because $R_C^{SS^*}(\omega = 1) = R_C^{SS^*}(\omega = 0)$. When condition (8.3.19) holds, the manufacturer prefers the SS – tariff as long as $(f_i - f_j) > E^{U,U}$. However, when condition (8.3.19) does *not* hold, the manufacturer prefers the MN – tariff over the entire range $\langle \chi, S_j \rangle$.

## 3.3 Summary

Three important observations follow from our analyses in this Section. First, the nine Zones associated with our three wholesale-price strategies can be combined in only four ways—we called them Zonal Scenarios—across the fully comprehensive two-dimensional space defined by the intensity of competition and the magnitude of competition (i.e., the cross-price to own-price effect and the market shares). Second, channel non-coordination can be manufacturer profit-optimal in *every one* of these Zonal Scenarios, depending on the specific value of the difference in retailers' fixed costs $(f_i - f_j)$. Third, from the manufacturer's perspective, the quantity-discount schedule is attractive when retailers with roughly equal market shares experience a high degree of competition. However, when the degree of competition is not high, or when market shares are disparate, the menu of two-part tariffs out-performs the quantity-discount schedule.

# 4 THE MANUFACTURER'S CHOICE OF AN OPTIMAL WHOLESALE-PRICE STRATEGY: THEORETICAL EXTENSIONS

In the last Section we analyzed the relationship between the retailers' fixed-cost difference and the manufacturer's optimal wholesale-price strategy. We proved that there exist $(f_i - f_j)$ – values for which the manufacturer prefers the $SS$ – tariff to *both* channel-coordinating wholesale-price strategies. We have also seen that there are $(f_i - f_j)$ – values for which the manufacturer prefers the $QD$ – schedule, and values for which the manufacturer prefers the $MN$ – tariff. In this Section we examine the impact of the retailers' demand and variable-cost parameters on the manufacturer's choice of an optimal wholesale-price strategy. Because a purely mathematical analysis may obscure intuitive insight, we present our results in graphical form.

## 4.1 Dimensionality: a Basis for Comparison

As in sub-Section 3.1, we re-parameterize the profit comparisons of the previous Section in terms of *intensity of competition* $(\chi)$ and the *magnitude of competition* $(S_j)$.[8] The parameters $\chi$ and $S_j$ form a two-dimensional *unit-square*, within which we can map the manufacturer profit generated by each wholesale-price policy. Although the profit levels have been calculated in terms of $b, \theta, Q_i^*$ and $Q_j^*$, they are actually combinations of the demand and cost primitives $A_i, A_j, c_i, c_j, C, b,$ and $\theta$. This can be seen by writing out $S_j$:

$$S_j \equiv \left( \frac{Q_j^*}{Q_i^* + Q_j^*} \right) \equiv \left( \frac{A_j - b(c_j + C) + \theta(c_i + C)}{(A_i + A_j) - (b - \theta)(c_i + c_j + 2C)} \right) \tag{8.4.1}$$

The decentralized manufacturer's *endogenously*-determined profit under each wholesale-price policy can be expressed in abbreviated notation as a function of the *exogenous* parameters $S_j$ and $\chi$.

In addition to the aforementioned parametric values, fixed costs also influence manufacturer profit. The manufacturer's fixed cost (F) affects the profit derived from each price-policy equally; a \$1 increase in F shifts the manufacturer profit function down by \$1 under all three wholesale-price policies. Because changes in F cannot explain the manufacturer's preference for one wholesale-price strategy over another, we ignore F in the analysis that follows. In contrast, the retailers' fixed-cost difference has a complex impact on the manufacturer's decision, because changes in $(f_i - f_j)$ may alter the relevant Zone for one or more of the wholesale-price policies.

## 4.2 The Manufacturer's Optimality Conditions

We begin by determining the ways in which the manufacturer's choice of a wholesale-price policy varies with changes in $S_j$ and $\chi$. Figure 8.2 summarizes the manufacturer's optimal strategy under the assumption that $f_i = f_j$. This restrictive assumption provides a simple starting point for our analysis. Also, because the marketing science literature on distribution channels largely ignores fixed costs, this case provides the basis for a straightforward comparison with extant knowledge.[9]

Within the unit-half square we identify four Wholesale-Price Regions, each with its own, distinctive, manufacturer-optimal wholesale-price strategy. These Wholesale-Price Regions are defined in terms of the following three Conditions, which we phrase as questions.

**Condition M:** From the manufacturer's perspective, does coordination with a channel-coordinating menu of two-part tariffs *always* dominate the non-coordinating sophisticated Stackelberg tariff when $(f_i - f_j) < L^{SS^*}$?

**Condition SS:** From the manufacturer's perspective, does the sophisticated Stackelberg tariff *always* dominate the channel-coordinating menu when $U^{SS^*} < (f_i - f_j)$?

**Condition QD:** From the manufacturer's perspective, does coordination with a quantity-discount schedule *ever* dominate coordination with a menu of two-part tariffs?

As Table 8.2 illustrates, each Condition holds in one and only one Region.

*Table 8.2.* Wholesale-Price Regions

| | Condition M | Condition SS | Condition QD |
|---|---|---|---|
| Region SMS | No | Yes | No |
| Region SM | No | No | No |
| Region SQM | No | No | Yes |
| Region M | Yes | No | No |

See the text above for definitions of Conditions and Regions.

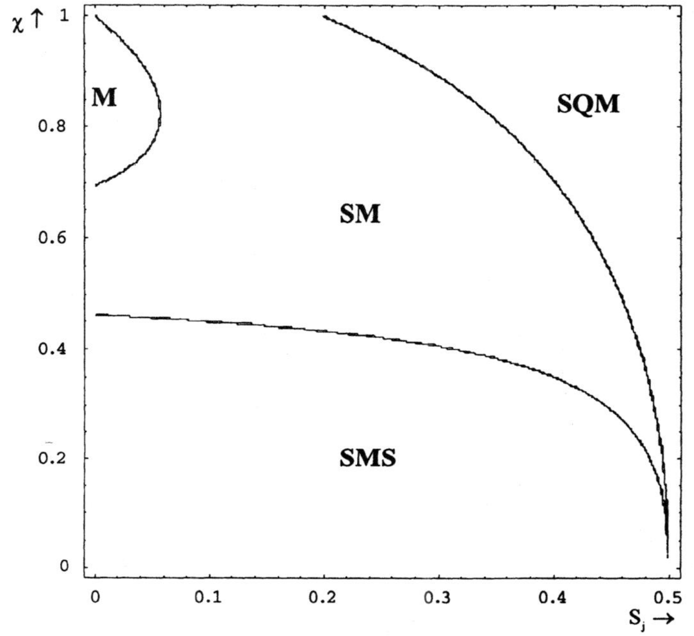


Legend:
As $f$ increases from 0 to 1, the manufacturer-optimal strategy in each Region changes in one of four possible sequences:
**SMS** ≡ Sophisticated Stackelberg Tariff, Menu, and then Sophisticated Stackelberg Tariff;
**SM** ≡ Sophisticated Stackelberg Tariff and then Menu;
**SQM** ≡ Sophisticated Stackelberg Tariff, Quantity-Discount Schedule, and then Menu; and
**M** ≡ Menu.
The Figure is drawn for zero fixed costs.

*Figure 8.2.* The Manufacturer-Optimal Wholesale-Price Policy

**Condition M:** This Condition holds when $\Pi_M^{Menu*} \geq \Pi_M^{SS*}$ for all $(f_i - f_j) < L^{SS*}$. To determine whether this Condition is satisfied, the manufacturer must compare its profit under the menu in Zone $Z_j^{Menu*}$ with the profit from the SS – tariff in Zone $Z_j^{SS*}$. These profit functions are equal when:

$$S_j = S_j^M(\chi) \equiv \left( \frac{16 - 16\chi - 32\chi^2 + 24\chi^3 + 17\chi^4 - 9\chi^5}{32 - 32\chi - 80\chi^2 + 32\chi^3 + 38\chi^4 - 14\chi^5} \right) \quad (8.4.2)$$

The curve $S_j^M(\chi)$, which defines a parabola in the unit half-square, intersects the $\langle S_j = 0 \rangle$ – axis at two points, $\chi = 1$ and $\chi = 0.694031$. Moreover, $S_j^M(\chi)$ assumes its maximum value, which is about 0.057, at $\chi = 0.823038$. Inside the unit half-square, Condition M holds for those $\langle \chi, S_j \rangle$ – pairs that lie inside the area that is bounded by $S_j^M(\chi)$ and the $S_j = 0$ axis. This area, which we label Region M, lies in the upper left-hand corner of Figure 8.2. In Figure 8.3 we have overlaid the Zonal Scenarios on top of the Regions. Notice that *most* of Region M lies in Zonal Scenario 2 (this area is labeled $M - ZS2$), with the remainder lying in Zonal Scenario 3 (labeled $M - ZS2$ and $M - ZS3$).

**Condition SS:** This Condition holds when $\Pi_M^{Menu*} < \Pi_M^{SS*}$ for every $U^{SS*} < (f_i - f_j)$. To determine if this Condition is satisfied, the manufacturer must compare its profit under the menu in Zone $Z_i^{Menu*}$ with its profit from the $SS -$ tariff in Zone $Z_i^{SS*}$. These profit functions are equal when:

$$S_j = S_j^{SS}(\chi) \equiv \left( \frac{16 - 16\chi - 48\chi^2 + 8\chi^3 + 21\chi^4 - 5\chi^5}{32 - 32\chi - 80\chi^2 + 32\chi^3 + 38\chi^4 - 14\chi^5} \right) \quad (8.4.3)$$

$S_j \equiv \left( Q_j^* / \left( Q_i^* + Q_j^* \right) \right) = 0.391$ defines a parabolic shape in the unit-half square that intersects the $\langle S_j = 0 \rangle$ – axis at $\chi = 0.462064$ and the $\langle \chi = 0 \rangle$ – axis at $S_j = ½$. Condition SS holds for those $\langle \chi, S_j \rangle$ – pairs that lie inside the area bounded by $S_j^{SS}(\chi)$, the $\langle S_j = 0 \rangle$ – axis, and the $\langle \chi = 0 \rangle$ – axis. This area, which we label Region SMS, lies in the lower left corner of Figure 8.2. Further, as depicted in Figure 8.3, it lies entirely within Zonal Scenario 1. (The relevant area is labeled $SMS - ZS1$).

**Condition QD:** This Condition holds when $\Pi_M^{Menu*} < \Pi_M^{QD*}$ for some $(f_i - f_j) < L^{Menu*}$. This Condition is satisfied if and only if $\delta^{QD*} < L^{Menu*}$, which is the Condition that defines Zonal Scenario 4. This area, which we label Region SQM, lies in the upper right-hand corners of Figures 8.2 and 8.3.

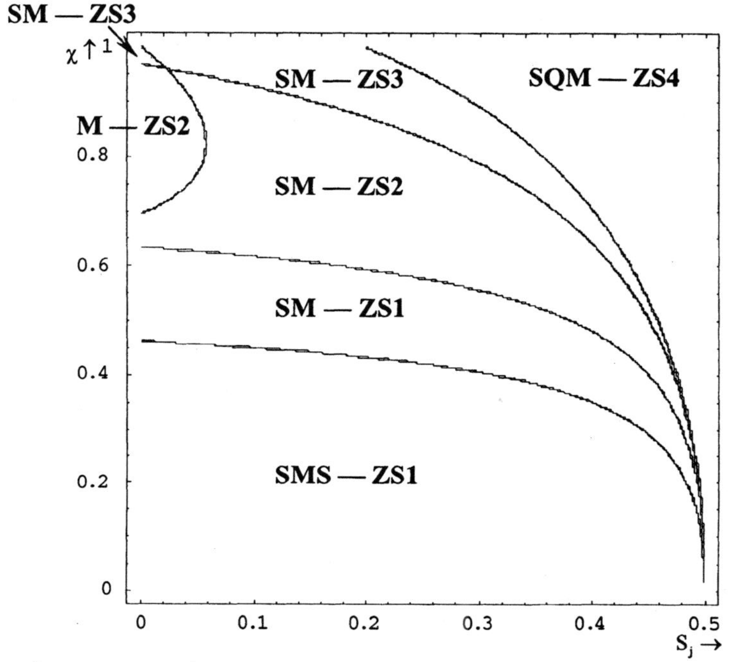


Legend:

The four Zonal Scenarios (ZS1, ZS2, ZS3, and ZS4) are defined in Table 8.1.

The wholesale-price sequences are denoted as:

**SMS** ≡ Sophisticated Stackelberg Tariff, Menu, and then Sophisticated Stackelberg Tariff;

**SM** ≡ Sophisticated Stackelberg Tariff and then Menu;

**SQM** ≡ Sophisticated Stackelberg Tariff, Quantity-Discount Schedule, and then Menu;

**M** ≡ Menu.

The order reflects the sequence of optimal strategies as $f$ increases from 0 to 1.

*Figure 8.3.* The Manufacturer-Optimal Wholesale-Price Policy across Four Zonal Scenarios

## 4.3 The Manufacturer's Optimal Wholesale-Price Strategy by Wholesale-Price Region

We now identify the manufacturer-optimal wholesale-price strategy within each of the Wholesale-Price Regions defined in Table 8.2. In each case we present a simple decision rule that summarizes the manufacturer's optimal wholesale-price policy.

### 4.3.1 Wholesale-Price Region SMS

**Region SMS**, which occupies the bottom of Figure 8.2, lies entirely inside Scenario 1. In this Region the manufacturer prefers the sophisticated Stackelberg tariff to the channel-coordinating menu for any $(f_i - f_j) > U^{SS*}$. Because Region SMS lies outside Region M, the manufacturer also prefers the sophisticated Stackelberg tariff when $(f_i - f_j) < L^{SS*}$. From Observation 1, the menu is dominant whenever $L^{Menu*} \le (f_i - f_j) \le U^{Menu*}$ because the channel-coordinating menu extracts all profits from both retailers.

In combination, these statements imply the existence of two distinct $(f_i - f_j)$ – values at which the sophisticated Stackelberg and the menu policies generate identical profits for the manufacturer; we call them $E^{L,L}$ and $E^{U,U}$. The former appeared in sub-Section 3.2.1; it denotes the critical value that lies in the interval $L^{SS*} < E^{L,L^*} < L^{Menu*}$ and that satisfies:

$$\left(f_i - f_j\right) = E^{L,L^*} \quad \Rightarrow \quad \Pi_M^{Menu^*} = \Pi_M^{SS^*}. \tag{8.4.4}$$

The critical value $E^{U,U}$, which was defined in sub-Section 3.2.4, lies in the interval $U^{Menu*} < E^{U,U^*} < U^{SS*}$; it satisfies:

$$\left(f_i - f_j\right) = E^{U,U^*} \quad \Rightarrow \quad \Pi_M^{Menu^*} = \Pi_M^{SS^*} \tag{8.4.5}$$

Using this notation, we summarize the manufacturer's optimal wholesale-price strategy in Region SMS as follows:

- If $\left(f_i - f_j\right) < E^{L,L}$ use the sophisticated Stackelberg tariff;
- If $E^{L,L} \le \left(f_i - f_j\right) \le E^{U,U}$ use the channel-coordinating menu of tariffs; and
- If $\left(f_i - f_j\right) > E^{U,U}$ use the sophisticated Stackelberg tariff.

"SMS" reflects the sequence of wholesale-price strategies (Stackelberg, Menu, Stackelberg) in this Region. We will illustrate this rule in Section 5.

### 4.3.2 Wholesale-Price Region SM

Region SM, which occupies the middle of Figure 8.2, includes most of Zonal Scenarios 2 and 3 and a portion of Scenario 1. In this Region *none* of our three Conditions hold. Specifically, because Region SM lies outside Region QD, the quantity-discount schedule never dominates the channel-coordinating menu. Thus the manufacturer's choice is (again) reduced to the menu or the sophisticated Stackelberg tariff. In addition, because Region SM lies outside Region M, the manufacturer prefers the sophisticated Stackelberg tariff to the channel-coordinating menu when $(f_i - f_j) < L^{SS*}$. Because, Region

SM is outside SMS, the manufacturer prefers the menu for all $(f_i - f_j) \geq L^{Menu^*}$.

Taken together, these statements imply the existence of a single, critical $(f_i - f_j)$ – value, located in the interval $(L^{SS^*}, L^{Menu^*})$, at which the two relevant wholesale-price policies generate equal profits for the manufacturer. This critical value is located in one of two possible places. In Zonal Scenarios 1 and 2, the critical value $E^{L,L}$ lies in the interval $L^{SS^*} < E^{L,L} < L^{Menu^*}$. (We define $E^{L,L}$ at Appendix equation (8.A.12).) In Scenario 3, the critical value may be (i) $E^{L,L}$, which lies in the interval $L^{SS^*} < E^{L,L} < U^{SS^*} < L^{Menu^*}$, *or* (ii) $E^{U,L}$, which lies in the interval $L^{SS^*} < U^{SS^*} \leq E^{U,L} < L^{Menu^*}$. (We define $E^{U,L}$ at Appendix equation (8.A.22)).

Let $E^{L^*}$ denote the relevant critical value $(E^{L,L}$ or $E^{U,L})$, depending on the underlying demand and cost parameters. Critical value $E^{L^*}$ satisfies:

$$\left(f_i - f_j\right) = E^{L^*} \quad \Rightarrow \quad \Pi_M^{Menu^*} = \Pi_M^{SS^*} \tag{8.4.6}$$

Using this compressed notation, we can summarize the manufacturer-optimal wholesale-price strategy in Region SM in two conditional statements:

- If $\left(f_i - f_j\right) < E^{L^*}$ use the sophisticated Stackelberg tariff; and
- If $\left(f_i - f_j\right) \geq E^{L^*}$ use the channel-coordinating menu of two-part tariffs.

"SM" reflects the sequence of wholesale-price strategies (Stackelberg, Menu) in this Region. We will illustrate this rule in Section 5.

### 4.3.3 Wholesale-Price Region SQM

Region SQM, which occupies the upper portion of Figure 8.2, coincides with Zonal Scenario 4. In this Region the manufacturer prefers the channel-coordinating quantity-discount schedule for some values of $(f_i - f_j)$. Three additional results are needed to fully describe the manufacturer's optimal wholesale-price strategy in this Region. First, because the manufacturer obtains all channel profit at $(f_i - f_j) = \delta^{QD^*}$, the QD – schedule is manufacturer-preferred at this point and at neighboring $(f_i - f_j)$ – points. Second, because Region SQM lies outside Region SM, the manufacturer prefers the MN – tariffs for any $(f_i - f_j) > L^{Menu^*}$. Third, the manufacturer prefers the SS – tariff for any $(f_i - f_j) < L^{SS^*}$.

Taken together, these statements imply the existence of two distinct $(f_i - f_j)$ – values at which the sophisticated Stackelberg and the channel-coordinating policies generate equal profits for the manufacturer. The critical value $E^{\delta,L^*}$ is located in the interval $\delta^{QD*} < E^{\delta,L^*} < L^{Menu*}$; it satisfies:

$$\left(f_i - f_j\right) = E^{\delta,L^*} \quad \Rightarrow \quad \Pi_M^{Menu^*} = \Pi_M^{QD^*} \tag{8.4.7}$$

The other critical value ($E^{\delta^*}$) lies in one of two possible locations that we label $E^{L,\delta}$ and $E^{U,\delta}$. The profit-equivalence point $E^{L,\delta}$, which is defined in the Appendix at equation (8.A.27), lies in the interval $L^{SS*} < E^{L,\delta} < U^{SS*} < \delta^{QD*}$. The profit-equivalence point $E^{U,\delta}$, which is defined in the Appendix at equation (8.A.31), lies in the range $L^{SS*} < U^{SS*} < E^{U,\delta} < \delta^{QD*}$. The relevant critical value $E^{\delta^*}$ (defined as either $E^{L,\delta}$ or $E^{U,\delta}$) is located in the interval $L^{SS*} < E^{\delta^*} < \delta^{QD*}$; it satisfies:

$$\left(f_i - f_j\right) = E^{\delta^*} \quad \Rightarrow \quad \Pi_M^{QD^*} = \Pi_M^{SS^*} \tag{8.4.8}$$

We can now summarize the manufacturer-optimal wholesale-price strategy in three conditional statements:

- If $\left(f_i - f_j\right) < E^{\delta^*}$ use the sophisticated Stackelberg tariff;
- If $E^{\delta^*} \leq \left(f_i - f_j\right) \leq E^{\delta,L}$ use the Quantity-Discount schedule; and
- If $\left(f_i - f_j\right) > E^{\delta,L}$ use the Menu of two-part tariffs.

"SQM" reflects this Region's sequence of wholesale-price strategies (Stackelberg, Quantity-Discount, Menu). We illustrate this rule in Section 5.

### 4.3.4 Wholesale-Price Region M

Region M, which occupies the half-oval shaped space in the upper left-hand corner of Figure 8.2, lies in Zonal Scenarios 2 and 3. In this Region the manufacturer prefers the menu to the sophisticated Stackelberg tariff when $(f_i - f_j) < L^{SS*}$. As this Region lies outside Region SMS, the manufacturer also prefers the menu when $L^{Menu*} < (f_i - f_j)$. Finally, because Region M lies outside Region SQM, the menu dominates the channel-coordinating quantity-discount schedule. Taken together, these results yield a very simple rule for the manufacturer in Region M: use the channel-coordinating menu of tariffs.

Region M exists only when the $S_j^*$ ratio is close to zero and the $\chi$ ratio is close to one.[10] To understand what this means, consider the special case of equal variable costs at retail ($c_i = c_j$). Under this assumption, inter-retailer differences arise solely from variations in the base levels of demand ($A_i$ and $A_j$). Numerical analysis indicates that parametric values that are consistent with Region M yield a peculiar result: the $i^{th}$ retailer sets a slightly higher price but sells a massively larger quantity, even though the retailers are nearly perfect competitors. We find it difficult to conceive of a real-world example that is compatible with these characteristics; thus we are inclined to regard Region M as a theoretical oddity with little practical relevance. This assessment is important, because Region M is the only Region within which channel coordination is optimal at all levels of the retailers' fixed costs. In fact, we will learn more about the relevance of Region M in Chapter 10.

## 4.4 Summary

We opened this Chapter by asking whether the manufacturer will prefer a non-coordinating wholesale-price strategy over one that coordinates the channel. The answer depends on the retailers' fixed-cost difference $(f_i - f_j)$, on the retailers' relative market shares $(S_j)$, and on the intensity of competition $(\chi)$. The pair $\langle \chi, S_j \rangle$ determines which Wholesale-Price Region is *relevant* for the manufacturer's decision, while the fixed-cost difference $(f_i - f_j)$ determines which wholesale-price strategy the manufacturer *prefers* within a specific Wholesale-Price Region.

# 5 THE MANUFACTURER'S CHOICE OF AN OPTIMAL WHOLESALE-PRICE STRATEGY: NUMERICAL ILLUSTRATIONS

We have proven that the manufacturer's choice of a wholesale-price policy depends on the difference in retailers' fixed costs $(f_i - f_j)$, the intensity of competition $(\chi)$, and the retailers' market shares $(S_j)$. In this Section we use several numerical examples to illustrate the nature of the manufacturer's choice. In the first sub-Section we consider one value of $S_j$ and five levels of $\chi$ in order to examine the impact of variations in the value of $(f_i - f_j)$. In the second sub-Section we consider two values of $S_j$ and two levels of $(f_i - f_j)$ in order to analyze the impact of changes in $\chi$. In the third sub-Section we consider three levels of $(f_i - f_j)$ to determine the manufacturer's optimal wholesale-price policy for all possible combinations of $S_j$ and $\chi$. On the basis of these analyses, we offer a qualitative observation on the practicality of coordination *versus* non-coordination in the final sub-Section.

## 5.1 Illustrations of the Effects of Changes in $(f_i - f_j)$

In this sub-Section we examine how changes in $(f_i - f_j)$ affect the manufacturer's choice of a wholesale-price policy at specific levels of competition. To keep our presentation manageable, we confine the numerical illustrations of this sub-Section to a single value of $S_j$. We work with the parametric values $A_i = 150$, $A_j = 100$, $c_i = c_j = C = \$10$ and $(b - \theta) = 0.5$. These parameters yield channel-coordinated outputs $Q_i^* = 70$ and $Q_j^* = 45$; thus the market share of the j[th] retailer is $S_j \equiv (Q_j^* / (Q_i^* + Q_j^*)) = 0.391$. This example, which constitutes a vertical "slice" of Figures 8.1, 8.2 and 8.3, runs through Wholesale-Price Regions SMS, SM, and SQM. An examination of this slice reveals several important consequences of changes in $\chi$ and $(f_i - f_j)$. Other slices would generate observations similar to those presented in this sub-Section, although a slice taken at an extreme market-share value ($S_j \cong 0$ or $S_j \cong 1$) would also pass through Region M.

To simplify our analysis we set $F = \$1{,}000$ and $f_j = \$0$, so that $(f_i - f_j) = f_i$. Table 8.3 catalogs five $\langle b, \theta \rangle$-Combinations that represent progressively higher levels of competitive intensity; this can be interpreted in terms of geographic space or customer service. Spatially, close retailer proximity implies a high degree of competition; all other things equal, retailers located in the same shopping mall are stronger competitors than they would be if they were located in different malls. Similarly, two retailers that supply comparable levels of customer service are stronger competitors than retailers that offer very different service levels (again, all other things held equal). Other marketing mix factors could be considered in the same vein.

*Table 8.3.* Five Scenarios to Illustrate the Manufacturer's Optimal Wholesale-Price Strategy

| Example | Scenario | Region | $S_j$ | b | $\theta$ | $\chi \equiv (\theta/b)$ |
|---|---|---|---|---|---|---|
| Table 8.4 | 1 | SMS | .391 | 0.7 | 0.2 | 0.286 |
| Table 8.5 | 1 | SM | .391 | 0.9 | 0.4 | 0.444 |
| Table 8.6 | 2 | SM | .391 | 1.0 | 0.5 | 0.500 |
| Table 8.7 | 3 | SM | .391 | 1.5 | 1.0 | 0.667 |
| Table 8.8 | 4 | SQM | .391 | 2.0 | 1.5 | 0.750 |

These five Combinations represent progressively higher levels of competitive intensity; this can be interpreted in terms of geographic space or customer service. In the spatial realm, close proximity of the retailers implies a high degree of competition. For example, all other things equal, two retailers located in the same shopping mall are stronger competitors than they would be if they were located in different malls. Similarly, two retailers that supply comparable levels of customer service are stronger competitors than retailers that offer very different service levels (again, all other things held equal). Other marketing mix factors could be considered in the same vein.

### 5.1.1 Zonal Scenario 1: A Low Degree of Competition

Table 8.4 illustrates the existence of Wholesale-Price Region SMS in Zonal Scenario 1. The optimal prices, quantities, and profits, are calculated under the assumption that $\chi = 0.286$. All profit results assume that $f_j = 0$, but the first profit column is calculated under the assumption that fixed costs for *both* retailers are zero ($f_i = f_j = 0$). Columns 2 and 4 report profits at the levels of $f_i$ that generate equal profits under the menu and the sophisticated Stackelberg strategies. Column 3 reports profits when $f_i$ lies exactly halfway between the $f_i$-values used to calculate profits in Columns 2 and 4. The final column reports profits when $f_i = U^{SS^*}$. Note that the *sum* of the i$^{th}$ retailer's fixed costs and profit of a fully coordinated channel (denoted as $\Pi_C^*$) is independent of the actual level of fixed costs in this and successive Tables, because a one dollar increase in the i$^{th}$ retailer's fixed costs always lowers channel profit by one dollar.

The results in Table 8.4 indicate that the manufacturer prefers the sophisticated Stackelberg strategy for all $0 \le (f_i - f_j) < \$3,567.61$ *and* for all $(f_i - f_j) > \$3,792.91$. Provided $(f_i - f_j)$ lies between these values, the manufacturer prefers the channel-coordinating menu of tariffs. The value $(f_i - f_j) = \$3,567.61$ is the manufacturer profit-equivalence point $E^{L,L}$ defined in equation (8.4.4), while the value $(f_i - f_j) = \$3,792.91$ is the profit-equivalence point $E^{U,U}$ from equation (8.4.5). In this example, because the chosen values of b and $\theta$ are incompatible with Condition QD, the quantity-discount strategy is never optimal for any $(f_i - f_j)$ – value. Table 8.4 indicates that, when competitive intensity is low, there is a low range *and* a high range of the retailers' fixed-cost differences that makes non-coordination desirable for the manufacturer.

*Table 8.4.* Sophisticated Stackelberg Tariff and Channel-Coordinating Menu: Zonal Scenario 1, Region SMS

| $f_i$ | *\$0.00* | *\$3,567.61* | *\$3,680.26* | *\$3,792.91* | *\$4,082.03* = $U^{SS^*}$ |
|---|---|---|---|---|---|
| Profit Ranking → | SS > M > QD | SS = M > QD | M > SS > QD | M = SS > QD | SS > M > QD |
| $\Pi_C^*$ | \$12,572.22 | \$9,004.61 | \$8,891.96 | \$8,779.31 | \$8,490.19 |
| $\Pi_M^{SS^*}$ | **\$9,217.19** | **\$8,998.49** | \$8,878.87 | **\$8,733.27** | **\$8,240.63** |
| $\Pi_M^{Menu^*}$ | \$8,998.49 | **\$8,998.49** | **\$8,891.96** | **\$8,733.27** | \$8,155.03 |
| $\Pi_M^{QD^*}$ | \$8,921.43 | \$8,921.43 | \$8,862.50 | \$8,637.20 | \$8,058.96 |

Note: We set parametric values $A_i = 150$, $A_j = 100$, $c_i = c_j = C = \$10$, $f_j = \$0$ and $F = \$1{,}000$, while holding $(b - \theta) = 0.5$. We also set $b = 0.7$ and $\theta = 0.2$. It follows that $Q_i^* = 70$, $Q_j^* = 45$, $p_i^* = \$148.89$ and $p_j^* = \$121.11$. Zonal boundaries are: $L^{SS^*} = \$3{,}105.47 < L^{Menu^*} = \$3{,}573.73 < \delta^{QD^*} = \$3{,}650.79 < U^{Menu^*} = \$3{,}746.87 < U^{SS^*} = \$4{,}082.03$. **Boldface** type denotes the manufacturer profit-maximum across the three wholesale-price policies for each level of the i[th] retailer's fixed cost.

### 5.1.2 Zonal Scenarios 1, 2 and 3: A Moderate Degree of Competition

Table 8.5 illustrates the existence of Wholesale-Price Region SM in Zonal Scenario 1. In this Table the degree of competition ($\chi = 0.444$) is slightly higher than in Table 8.4. Here the manufacturer prefers the sophisticated Stackelberg strategy when $0 \le (f_i - f_j) < \$2,633.31$; otherwise the manufacturer prefers the menu. The value $(f_i - f_j) = \$2,633.31$ is the critical value $E^{L,L}$ from equation (8.4.4). There is no fixed-cost difference above $E^{L,L}$ that will induce the manufacturer to switch back to the $SS$ – tariff.

Tables 8.6 and 8.7 represent Zonal Scenarios 2 and 3. Like the preceding Table, these Tables illustrate Wholesale-Price Region SM. As a result, all three Tables generate the same basic conclusion: (i) the manufacturer prefers the sophisticated Stackelberg strategy at "low" levels of $(f_i - f_j)$ and (ii) manufacturer prefers the menu at "high" values of $(f_i - f_j)$. Notice that the $Q_i^*$ – values and the $Q_j^*$ – values are the same for each of these Tables but the $p_i^*$ – values and the $p_j^*$ – values differ across Tables. This occurs because the values of b and $\theta$ change according to Table 8.3

Together, Tables 8.5-8.7 indicate that, at "moderate" competitive intensities (whether in Zonal Scenario 1, 2, or 3), non-coordination is prefered only for small or negative $(f_i - f_j)$ – values. The notion of a negative retailers' fixed-cost difference is quite plausible once we recognize that the $f_j$ – variable includes opportunity costs, rent, and other factors. If the smaller-quantity retailer is located in a mall, while the larger is not, the former might pay more for its retail space. Similarly, if the smaller retailer is an upscale boutique, while the larger retailer is a mid-market purveyor, then the former may have a greater opportunity cost than the latter. As these examples suggest, a negative value for $(f_i - f_j)$ is possible.

*Table 8.5.* Sophisticated Stackelberg Tariff and Channel-Coordinating Menu: Zonal Scenario 1, Region SM

| $f_i$ | *\$0.00* | *\$2,633.31* | *\$2,685.15* | *\$2,743.69* |
|---|---|---|---|---|
| Profit Ranking →: | SS > M > QD | SS = M > QD | M > SS = QD | M > SS = QD |
| $\Pi_C^*$ | \$12,465.38 | \$9,832.07 | \$9,780.23 | \$9,721.69 |
| $\Pi_M^{SS^*}$ | **\$9,972.93** | **\$9,823.38** | \$9,762.39 | \$9,681.00 |
| $\Pi_M^{Menu^*}$ | \$9,823.38 | **\$9,823.38** | **\$9,780.23** | **\$9,721.69** |
| $\Pi_M^{QD^*}$ | \$9,762.39 | \$9,762.39 | \$9,762.39 | \$9,681.00 |

Note: We set the following parametric values $A_i = 150, A_j = 100,\ c_i = c_j = C = \$10$, $f_j = \$0$ and $F = \$1,000$. We hold $(b - \theta) = 0.5$. In this Table we set $b = 0.9$ and $\theta = 0.4$. It follows that $Q_i^* = 70$, $Q_j^* = 45$, $p_i^* = \$144.62$ and $p_j^* = \$125.38$. The Zonal boundaries are:
$L^{SS^*} = \$2,355.37 < L^{Menu^*} = \$2,642.01 < \delta^{QD^*} = \$2,702.99 < U^{Menu^*} = \$2,815.04 < U^{SS^*} = \$2,871.90$.
**Boldface** type denotes the manufacturer profit-maximum across the three wholesale-price policies for each level of the i[th] retailer's fixed cost.

*Table 8.6.* Sophisticated Stackelberg Tariff and Channel-Coordinating Menu: Zonal Scenario 2, Region SM

| $f_i$ | *\$0.00* | *\$2,334.39* | *\$2,500.00* $= U^{SS^*}$ |
|---|---|---|---|
| Profit Ranking → | SS > M > QD | SS = M > QD | M > QD > SS |
| $\Pi_C^*$ | \$12,433.33 | \$10,098.94 | \$9,933.33 |
| $\Pi_M^{SS^*}$ | **\$10,225.00** | **\$10,087.65** | \$9,825.00 |
| $\Pi_M^{Menu^*}$ | \$10,087.65 | **\$10,087.65** | **\$9,933.33** |
| $\Pi_M^{QD^*}$ | \$10,037.50 | \$10,037.50 | \$9,829.17 |

Note: We set the following parametric values $A_i = 150, A_j = 100, c_i = c_j = C = \$10$, $f_j = \$0$ and $F = \$1,000$. We hold $(b-\theta) = 0.5$. In this Table we set $b = 1.0$ and $\theta = 0.5$. It follows that $Q_i^* = 70$, $Q_j^* = 45$, $p_i^* = \$143.33$ and $p_j^* = \$126.67$. Thus the zonal boundaries and their ordering are:

$L^{SS^*} = \$2,100.00 < L^{Menu^*} = \$2,345.68 < \delta^{QD^*} = \$2,395.83 < U^{SS^*} = \$2,500.00 < U^{Menu^*} = \$2,509.88$.

**Boldface** type denotes the manufacturer profit-maximum across the three wholesale-price policies for each level of the $i^{th}$ retailer's fixed cost.

*Table 8.7.* Sophisticated Stackelberg Tariff and Channel-Coordinating Menu: Zonal Scenario 3, Region SM

| $f_i$ | *\$0.00* | *\$1,493.33* | *\$1,515.63* = $U^{SS^*}$ |
|---|---|---|---|
| Profit Ranking →: | SS > M | SS = M | M > SS |
| $\Pi_C^*$ | \$12,350.00 | \$10,856.67 | \$10,834.37 |
| $\Pi_M^{SS^*}$ | **\$10,943.75** | **\$10,828.91** | \$10,787.49 |
| $\Pi_M^{Menu^*}$ | \$10,828.91 | **\$10,828.91** | **\$10,828.91** |
| $\Pi_M^{QD^*}$ | \$10,816.67 | \$10,816.67 | \$10,816.67 |

Note: We set the following parametric values $A_i = 150$, $A_j = 100$, $c_i = c_j = C = \$10$, $f_j = \$0$ and $F = \$1{,}000$. We hold $(b - \theta) = 0.5$. In this Table we set $b = 1.5$ and $\theta = 1.0$. It follows that $Q_i^* = 70$, $Q_j^* = 45$, $p_i^* = \$140.00$ and $p_j^* = \$130.00$. Thus the zonal boundaries and their ordering are:

$L^{SS^*} = \$1{,}359.38 < U^{SS^*} = \$1{,}515.63 < L^{Menu^*} = \$1{,}521.09 < \delta^{QD^*} = \$1{,}533.33 < U^{Menu^*} = \$1{,}641.41$.

**Boldface** type denotes the manufacturer profit-maximum across the three wholesale-price policies for each level of the i[th] retailer's fixed cost.

### 5.1.3 Zonal Scenario 4: A High Degree of Competition

Table 8.8 illustrates the existence of Wholesale-Price Region SQM, which is equivalent to Zonal Scenario 4. This is the only Zonal Scenario in which the quantity-discount schedule is manufacturer-optimal for some differences in the retailers' fixed costs. In this example the manufacturer prefers the $SS-$tariff when $(f_i - f_j) \leq \$1,094.47 = E^{U,\delta}$, where $E^{U,\delta}$ is the point of profit-equivalence from equation (8.4.8). The manufacturer prefers the $QD-$schedule when $\$1,094.47 \leq (f_i - f_j) \leq \$1,131.69$, this is a range of only \$39.22. When $(f_i - f_j) > \$1,131.69 = E^{\delta,L}$ ($E^{\delta,L}$ is the profit-equivalence value defined in equation (8.4.7)), the manufacturer prefers the menu.

The set of parametric values associated with Table 8.8 demonstrates the benefit to the manufacturer of a quantity-discount schedule: in some cases the defection costs are smaller than those generated by a menu of tariffs. Menu defection is more likely when the elements of the menu are similar, as is the case when there is a high degree of competition between the retailers. However, even when the level of competitive intensity is high, the manufacturer prefers the quantity-discount schedule over the menu only for a relatively small range of $(f_i - f_j)-$values. The point of indifference between the menu and the sophisticated Stackelberg tariff in this Table occurs at $(f_i - f_j) = \$1,096.69$. Without the quantity-discount schedule the point of indifference between coordination and non-coordination is $E^{U,\delta} = \$1,094.47$. Thus in this example the availability of the quantity-discount schedule extends the $(f_i - f_j)-$range within which coordination is manufacturer-optimal by only \$2.22.

*Table 8.8.* Sophisticated Stackelberg Tariff, Channel-Coordinating Menu and Channel-Coordinating Quantity-Discount Schedule: Zonal Scenario 4, Region SQM

| $f_i$ | *\$0.00* | *\$1,094.47* | *\$1,096.69* | *\$1,131.69* | *\$1,133.90* = $L^{Menu^*}$ |
|---|---|---|---|---|---|
| Profit Ranking : → | SS > QD > M | SS = QD > M | QD > SS = M | M = QD > SS | M > QD > SS |
| $\Pi_C^*$ | \$12,314.29 | \$11,219.82 | \$11,217.60 | \$11,182.60 | \$11,180.39 |
| $\Pi_M^{SS^*}$ | **\$11,282.85** | **\$11,184.82** | \$11,180.38 | \$11,110.39 | \$11,105.96 |
| $\Pi_M^{Menu^*}$ | \$11,180.38 | \$11,180.38 | \$11,180.38 | **\$11,180.38** | **\$11,180.38** |
| $\Pi_M^{QD^*}$ | \$11,184.82 | **\$11,184.82** | **\$11,184.82** | **\$11,180.38** | \$11,175.95 |

Note: We set the following parametric values $A_i = 150$, $A_j = 100$, $c_i = c_j = C = \$10$, $f_j = \$0$ and $F = \$1{,}000$. We hold $(b - \theta) = 0.5$. In this Table we set $b = 2.0$ and $\theta = 1.5$. It follows that $Q_i^* = 70$, $Q_j^* = 45$, $p_i^* = \$138.57$ and $p_j^* = \$131.43$. Zonal boundaries and their ordering are:
$L^{SS^*} = \$1{,}004.13 < U^{SS^*} = \$1{,}086.78 < \delta^{QD^*} = \$1{,}129.46 < L^{Menu^*} = \$1{,}133.90 < U^{Menu^*} = \$1{,}225.84$.
**Boldface** type denotes the manufacturer profit-maximum across the three wholesale-price policies for each level of the $i^{th}$ retailer's fixed cost.

## 5.2 Illustration of the Effects of Changes in the Intensity of Competition

To supplement the numerical examples discussed above, we provide several graphical examples that illustrate the effect of changes in the degree of competition on the manufacturer's profit for each wholesale-price policy. These examples provide some insight into the incremental change in manufacturer profit generated by switching from one wholesale pricing regime to another. We consider the impact of $\chi$ over four combinations of $S_j$ and $(f_i - f_j)$ which represent sharply different market shares and fixed costs:

| | $S_j^* = 40\%$ | $S_j^* = 10\%$ |
|---|---|---|
| $\mathit{f}_i = 0 = \mathit{f}_j$ | Figure 8.4 | Figure 8.6 |
| $\mathit{f}_i = .65 = \mathit{f}_j$ | Figure 8.5 | Figure 8.7 |

Recall that $\mathit{f}_k \equiv (f_k / R_k^*),\ \forall\ k \in (i,j)$, so $\mathit{f}_i = \mathit{f}_j$ does *not* imply that $f_i = f_j$; retailer fixed costs are equal (and are zero) only in the first row above.

Figures 8.4 and 8.5 illustrate the case in which the smaller retailer has a 40 percent market share, which is roughly equivalent to the $S_j$ value used in Tables 8.5-8.7 (where $S_j = 39.1\%$). Because the rivals in these two Figures have similar unit sales, we will refer to this case as "competition between near-equals." In Figures 8.6 and 8.7 the smaller retailer has a 10 percent market share. These Figures illustrate a "David *versus* Goliath" competition (i.e., a small apparel boutique *versus* a department store or a convenience food store *versus* a supermarket). We will term this case "competition between non-equals." In both cases we will show the manufacturer's profit-relationship between each wholesale-price policy at *every* possible degree of competition. In Figures 8.4 and 8.6 we follow widespread practice that retailers' fixed-costs are zero, while in Figures 8.5 and 8.7 we specify each retailer's fixed cost to be 65 percent of the net revenue generated by each retailer in a coordinated channel.

### 5.2.1 Competition between Near-Equals

When the rival retailers are nearly equal-sized, the manufacturer prefers the sophisticated Stackelberg tariff over both channel-coordinating wholesale-price policies at *all* degrees of competition. This dominance is relatively small at high $\chi$ – values, but becomes more significant at lower levels of competitive intensity, especially when fixed costs are substantial. At retailer fixed costs levels that are higher than shown in Figures 8.4 and 8.5, the menu and (sometimes) the quantity-discount schedule are manufacturer profit-optimal when there is also a ***high*** level of competitive intensity $\chi$. However, the sophisticated Stackelberg tariff generates at least 96 percent of the manufacturer profit generated by the optimal coordinating policy even when $f$ and $\chi$ are high. At *lower* levels of $\chi$, the sophisticated Stackelberg tariff outperforms the channel-coordinating policies by more than 10 percent.

We conclude that, when retail competition is between "near-equals" who have comparable fixed costs (i.e., fixed costs that are equal when expressed as a percentage of net revenue), the sophisticated Stackelberg wholesale-price policy—which cannot coordinate the channel—is robust, in the sense of generating manufacturer profits that are close to or higher than those generated by a channel-coordinating strategy. This robustness makes the sophisticated Stackelberg strategy particularly attractive when the precise degree of competition is unknown. It is the optimal policy over most of the relevant parametric space (i.e., the space in which competitors have roughly equal market share). When the sophisticated Stackelberg tariff is not optimal, it is an excellent alternative because it does almost as well as the channel-coordinating price policy. In contrast, when the coordinating schedules are non-optimal, they are often poor performers relative to the sophisticated Stackelberg tariff.

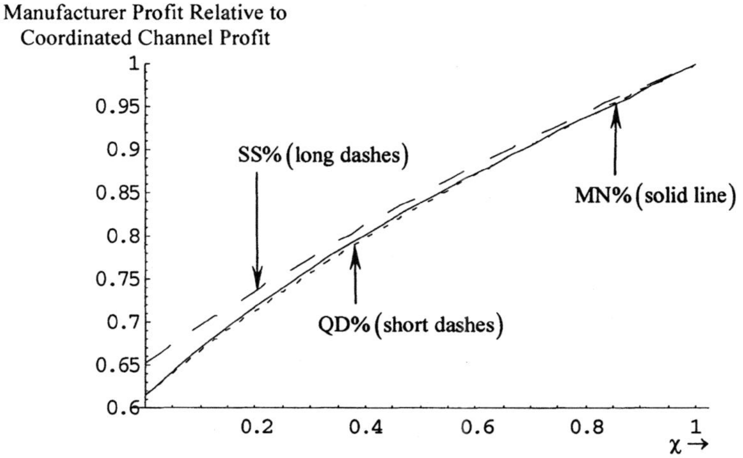


Legend:

$\chi \equiv (\theta / b)$ = Intensity of inter-retailer competition;

$SS\% \equiv \Pi_M^{SS*} / \Pi_C^*$ = Ratio of manufacturer profit under the non-coordinating sophisticated Stackelberg tariff relative to the profit earned by a vertically-integrated system (line with long dashes);

$MN\% \equiv \Pi_M^{Menu*} / \Pi_C^*$ = Ratio of manufacturer profit with channel-coordinating menu of tariffs relative to the profit earned by a vertically-integrated system (solid line);

$QD\% \equiv \Pi_M^{QD*} / \Pi_C^*$ = Ratio of manufacturer profit with the channel-coordinating quantity-discount schedule relative to the profit earned by the vertically-integrated system (line with short dashes).

Note: In this Figure the dotted QD line is obscured by the solid MN-line.

*Figure 8.4.* The Manufacturer-Optimal Wholesale-Price Strategy When $f = 0$ and $S_j = 0.4$

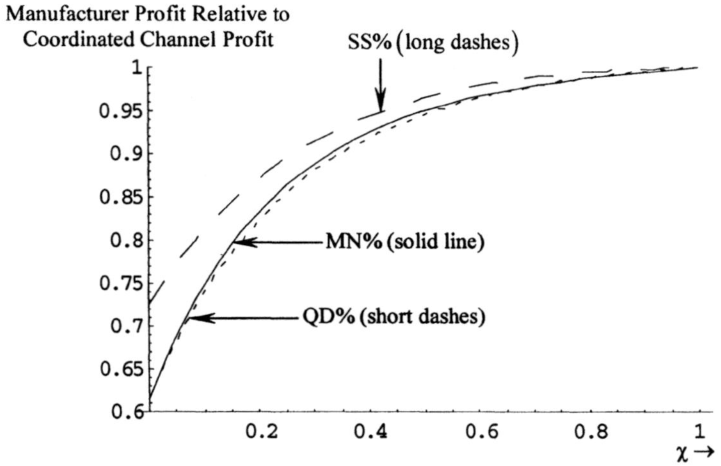


Legend:

$\chi \equiv (\theta / b)$ = Intensity of inter-retailer competition;

$SS\% \equiv \Pi_M^{SS*} / \Pi_C^*$ = Ratio of manufacturer profit under the non-coordinating sophisticated Stackelberg tariff relative to the profit earned by a vertically-integrated system (line with long dashes);

$MN\% \equiv \Pi_M^{Menu*} / \Pi_C^*$ = Ratio of manufacturer profit with channel-coordinating menu of tariffs relative to the profit earned by a vertically-integrated system (solid line);

$QD\% \equiv \Pi_M^{QD*} / \Pi_C^*$ = Ratio of manufacturer profit with the channel-coordinating quantity-discount schedule relative to the profit earned by the vertically-integrated system (line with short dashes).

*Figure 8.5.* The Manufacturer-Optimal Wholesale-Price Strategy When $f = 0.65$ and $S_j = 0.4$

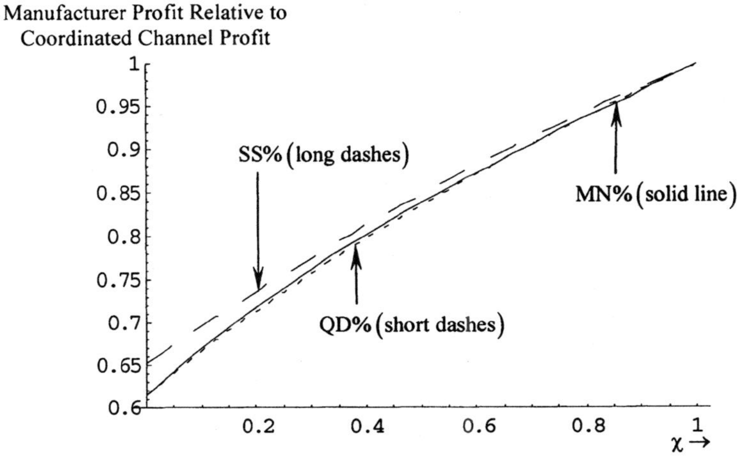


Legend:

$\chi \equiv (\theta / b)$ = Intensity of inter-retailer competition;

$SS\% \equiv \Pi_M^{SS*} / \Pi_C^*$ = Ratio of manufacturer profit under the non-coordinating sophisticated Stackelberg tariff relative to the profit earned by a vertically-integrated system (line with long dashes);

$MN\% \equiv \Pi_M^{Menu*} / \Pi_C^*$ = Ratio of manufacturer profit with channel-coordinating menu of tariffs relative to the profit earned by a vertically-integrated system (solid line);

$QD\% \equiv \Pi_M^{QD*} / \Pi_C^*$ = Ratio of manufacturer profit with the channel-coordinating quantity-discount schedule relative to the profit earned by the vertically-integrated system (line with short dashes).

Note: In this Figure the dotted QD line is obscured by the solid MN-line.

*Figure 8.4.* The Manufacturer-Optimal Wholesale-Price Strategy When $f = 0$ and $S_j = 0.4$

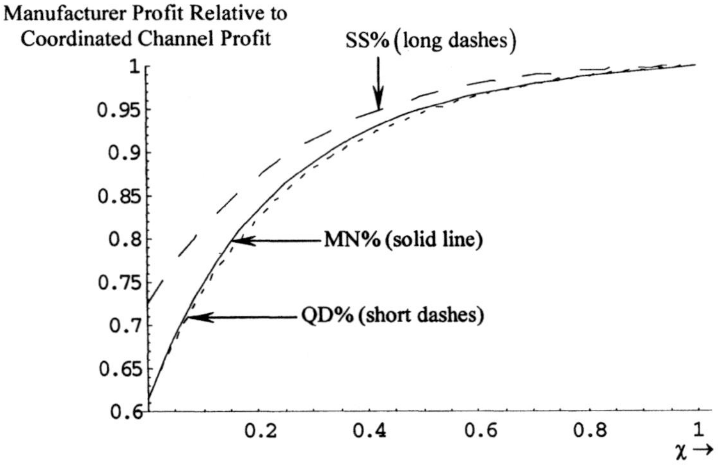


Legend:

$\chi \equiv (\theta / b)$ = Intensity of inter-retailer competition;

$SS\% \equiv \Pi_M^{SS*} / \Pi_C^*$ = Ratio of manufacturer profit under the non-coordinating sophisticated Stackelberg tariff relative to the profit earned by a vertically-integrated system (line with long dashes);

$MN\% \equiv \Pi_M^{Menu*} / \Pi_C^*$ = Ratio of manufacturer profit with channel-coordinating menu of tariffs relative to the profit earned by a vertically-integrated system (solid line);

$QD\% \equiv \Pi_M^{QD*} / \Pi_C^*$ = Ratio of manufacturer profit with the channel-coordinating quantity-discount schedule relative to the profit earned by the vertically-integrated system (line with short dashes).

*Figure 8.5.* The Manufacturer-Optimal Wholesale-Price Strategy When $f = 0.65$ and $S_j = 0.4$

### 5.2.2 Competition between Non-Equals

When the market shares of rival retailers differ significantly, the manufacturer prefers the sophisticated Stackelberg tariff to both of the channel-coordinating wholesale-price policies. This statement holds for every level of competitive intensity in Figures 8.6 and 8.7; thus channel-coordination is *never* in the manufacturer's best interest. Moreover, when the retailers' market shares differ substantially, and the level of competitive intensity is low, the sophisticated Stackelberg tariff significantly out-performs the two channel-coordinating wholesale-price policies. As competitive intensity increases (as $\chi \to 1$), the incremental benefit to the manufacturer of non-coordination declines.

The results in Figures 8.6 and 8.7 do not apply for all situations in which retailer market shares differ significantly. Specifically, when the level of competitive intensity is high and the market share of one retailer falls below 7 percent, the manufacturer may find itself in Wholesale-Price Region M (see Figure 8.2), where the menu *is* manufacturer-optimal. In this situation, our numerical analysis indicates that the sophisticated Stackelberg tariff generates about 99 percent of the profit yielded by the menu. Thus even in Region M, the sophisticated Stackelberg tariff is a robust pricing strategy.

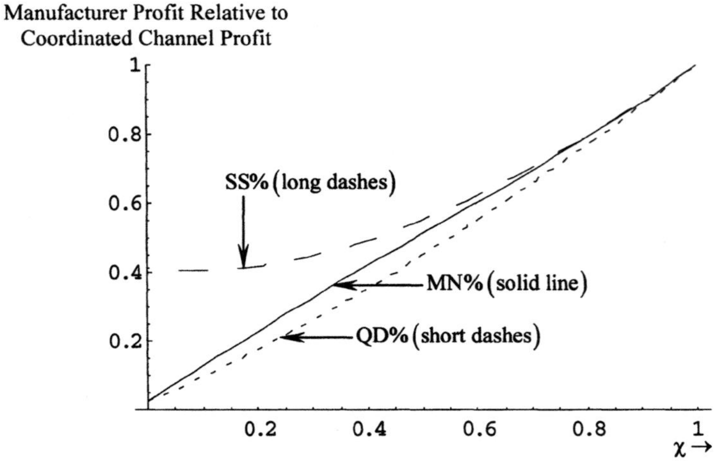


Legend:

| | | |
|---|---|---|
| $\chi \equiv (\theta / b)$ | = | Intensity of inter-retailer competition; |
| $SS\% \equiv \Pi_M^{SS*} / \Pi_C^*$ | = | Ratio of manufacturer profit under the non-coordinating sophisticated Stackelberg tariff relative to the profit earned by a vertically-integrated system (line with long dashes); |
| $MN\% \equiv \Pi_M^{Menu*} / \Pi_C^*$ | = | Ratio of manufacturer profit with channel-coordinating menu of tariffs relative to the profit earned by a vertically-integrated system (solid line); |
| $QD\% \equiv \Pi_M^{QD*} / \Pi_C^*$ | = | Ratio of manufacturer profit with the channel-coordinating quantity-discount schedule relative to the profit earned by the vertically-integrated system (line with short dashes). |

*Figure 8.6.* The Manufacturer-Optimal Wholesale-Price Strategy When $f = 0$ and $S_i = 0.1$

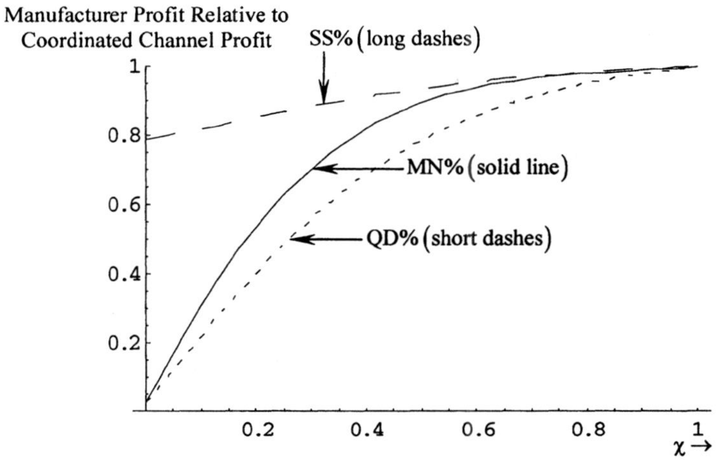


Legend:

$\chi \equiv (\theta / b)$ = Intensity of inter-retailer competition;

$SS\% \equiv \Pi_M^{SS*} / \Pi_C^*$ = Ratio of manufacturer profit under the non-coordinating sophisticated Stackelberg tariff relative to the profit earned by a vertically-integrated system (line with long dashes);

$MN\% \equiv \Pi_M^{Menu*} / \Pi_C^*$ = Ratio of manufacturer profit with channel-coordinating menu of tariffs relative to the profit earned by a vertically-integrated system (solid line);

$QD\% \equiv \Pi_M^{QD*} / \Pi_C^*$ = Ratio of manufacturer profit with the channel-coordinating quantity-discount schedule relative to the profit earned by the vertically-integrated system (line with short dashes).

*Figure 8.7.* The Manufacturer-Optimal Wholesale-Price Strategy
When $f = 0.65$ and $S_j = 0.1$

# 6 Commentary

Marketing scientists appear to believe that a properly-specified, channel-coordinating, wholesale-price policy is manufacturer-optimal. This belief is based on analyses of bilateral-monopoly and identical-competitors models. To ascertain whether coordination really is "all it's cracked up to be" requires an analysis of heterogenous, competing retailers. We established an optimal wholesale-price policy for a manufacturer that distributes through two competing, non-identical retailers that are comparably-treated. We considered the channel-coordinating quantity-discount schedule in Chapter 5, the channel non-coordinating sophisticated Stackelberg two-part tariff in Chapter 6, and the channel-coordinating menu of two-part tariffs in Chapter 7.

## 6.1 Commentary on the Manufacturer's Optimal Wholesale-Price Strategy

We proved that *any* of these three wholesale-price strategies can maximize the manufacturer's profit, depending on underlying demand and cost parameters (the Channel Environment). Our results make two critical contributions to the theory of distribution-channel structure. First, we found that a manufacturer's choice of an optimal wholesale-price policy depends on the retailers' fixed-cost difference, the intensity of inter-retailer competition, and the magnitude of competition (measured by market shares). Second, we proved that, over almost all intensities and magnitudes of competition, there are plausible values of fixed costs for which channel-coordination is *not* in the manufacturer's interest. Further, when coordination does benefit the manufacturer, it is typical for neither retailer to earn a positive profit. Thus, we conclude that *channel coordination is generally Pareto non-optimal.*

In terms of the questions raised in the Introduction of this Chapter, we provide the following answers. (1) The quantity-discount schedule dominates the sophisticated Stackelberg tariff in Wholesale-Price Region SQM, but only when the difference in the retailers' fixed-costs lies within specific bounds. The example of Table 8.7 indicates that these bounds are rather tight. (2) The quantity-discount schedule is a special case of the menu in Zonal Scenarios 1-3, although it does supplement the menu in Zonal Scenario 4, in the sense of extending the $(f_i - f_j)$ – range within which the manufacturer prefers channel coordination. (3) From the manufacturer's perspective, neither the menu nor the sophisticated Stackelberg tariff is dominant at all parametric values. Our examples highlight that the *non*-coordinating tariff can be in the best interest of the manufacturer. The sophisticated Stackelberg approach is attractive when the intensity of competition is not high and when retailers' fixed costs are a small share of net revenues.

## 6.2 Commentary on Three Channel Myths

In this Chapter we have again seen striking ways in which common modeling assumptions yield results that are not robust to the slightest relaxation of the assumptions. For example, assuming a Channel Environment that generates identical retailers[11] is sufficient to cause the manufacturer to prefer channel coordination over non-coordination. However, the manufacturer often prefers non-coordination when competitors are heterogeneous. To have faith that the manufacturer always prefers coordination is to believe in the *Channel-Coordination Strategic-Myth.* Further, to have faith that identical competitors behave like non-identical competitors is to believe the *Identical-Competitors Meta-Myth.*

We also found that fixed costs play an absolutely pivotal role in establishing the manufacturer's optimal wholesale-price strategy. Our discovery is in direct conflict with conventional wisdom (based on bilateral-monopoly and identical-competitors models) which holds that fixed costs have no impact on a manufacturer's wholesale-price policy. To have faith that "fixed costs don't matter" is to adhere to the *Fixed-Cost Modeling-Myth.*

## 6.3 Summary Commentary

Is channel coordination optimal for a manufacturer that sells through non-identical, competing retailers? The answer from marketing scientists has been "Yes." It has been reasoned that incremental channel profit generated by a channel-coordinating, wholesale-price policy can be re-distributed among channel members—manufaturers, retailers, and consumers—to the benefit of all. This logic, which dates back more than a century (Edgeworth 1881; Pareto 1906), has the easy charm of "something for nothing" because it implies that no one loses and everyone gains from channel coordination.

We have argued that this reasoning is flawed. Manufacturers rarely sell through a single retailer, or through identical competitors. The empirical evidence is that manufacturers typically market through multiple, differentiated competitors. Further, they commonly offer the retailers comparable wholesale-price treatment (Lafontaine 1990). In conformity with our Empirical-Evidence Criterion, our models incorporate comparable treatment of heterogeneous competitors.

Comparable treatment does not preclude channel coordination, as we proved with a quantity-discount schedule and again with a menu of two-part tariffs. But over a wide range of parametric values, comparable treatment imposes a "cost:" it limits the manufacturer's ability to extract profit from its retailers.

First, consider the channel-coordinating, linear *quantity-discount schedule.* Channel profit maximization requires that the per-unit fee induce each retailer to set its marginal revenue equal to the channel's marginal cost. The manufacturer maximizes its own profit by setting the fixed fee to extract all profit from the less-profitable retailer. The difference in retailer net revenues, relative to the difference in their fixed costs, determines this retailer's identity. The manufacturer obtains all channel profit only if the retailers' fixed cost difference is equal to their net revenue difference.

Second, consider the channel-coordinating *menu of two-part tariffs.* The manufacturer again maximizes its own profit by setting the fixed fee to extract profit from the less-profitable retailer, subject to the constraint that *neither* retailer defect to the tariff intended for its rival. While defection can always be prevented, there are parametric values for which the manufacturer must offer a reduced fixed fee, thereby leaving one retailer with a share of channel profit. When defection is not a potential problem, the manufacturer will prefer the menu to any non-coordinating strategy. However, when defection is a potential problem, the manufacturer often can increase its profit at the expense of channel profit by using a non-coordinating pricing strategy.

Third, consider the non-coordinating, *sophisticated Stackelberg two-part tariff* that is formed by the manufacturer recognizing that its choice of a per-unit wholesale price influences the level of retail profit. Maximization of the manufacturer's profit requires that the manufacturer's marginal revenue equal the manufacturer's marginal cost. The difference in retailers' net revenues, relative to the difference in retailers' fixed costs, determines the per-unit fee and the fixed fee that the manufacturer should charge. If these differences fall within certain bounds the manufacturer can obtain all channel profit, but it is a lower profit than is generated by a coordinated channel.

Although the implementation of any of these three wholesale-price strategies is straightforward, the manufacturer's choice between them entails assessing complex interactions across our three parametric dimensions (the intensity of inter-retailer competition, the difference in the retailers' fixed costs, and unequal market shares). The rigorous algebraic analyses required to make these assessments may block an intuitive grasp of the manufacturer's choice process. Thus, in the next Chapter, we provide a comprehensive, geometric evaluation of all possible combinations of our three parametric dimensions. We believe that the algebra of this Chapter and the geometry of the next Chapter will convincingly reveal that when evaluating channels of distribution, "the whole is more than the sum of its parts."[12]

# 7 APPENDIX

In this Appendix we define relationships between the zonal boundaries and manufacturer profits for all three wholesale-price policies. We also determine the $(f_i - f_j)$ – values at which these policies lead to an equal level of manufacturer profit.

## 7.1 Zonal Boundaries

We start by comparing the pair of two-part tariff policies. We use the boundary equations (6.2.4) and (6.2.5) for the sophisticated Stackelberg schedule and equations (7.3.4) and (7.3.5) for the menu. To ease our exposition we discuss the case of $Q_i^* > Q_j^*$. Algebraic manipulation yields:

$$\left(L^{Menu^*} - L^{SS^*}\right) = \psi_1\left(Q_i^* - Q_j^*\right)\left[\psi_2 Q_i^* - \left(\psi_2 - \psi_3\right)Q_j^*\right] \gtrless 0 \quad \text{as} \quad \frac{Q_i^*}{Q_j^*} \gtrless \frac{\left(\psi_2 - \psi_3\right)}{\psi_2} \tag{8.A.1}$$

$$\left(U^{SS^*} - U^{Menu^*}\right) = \psi_1\left(Q_i^* - Q_j^*\right)\left[\left(\psi_2 - \psi_3\right)Q_i^* - \psi_2 Q_j^*\right] \gtrless 0 \quad \text{as} \quad \frac{\left(\psi_2 - \psi_3\right)}{\psi_2} \gtrless \frac{Q_j^*}{Q_i^*} \tag{8.A.2}$$

$$\left(L^{Menu^*} - U^{SS^*}\right) = \psi_1\left(Q_i^* - Q_j^*\right)\begin{bmatrix}\left(\psi_3 - \left(\psi_2 + \psi_4\right)\right)Q_i^* \\ +\left(\psi_2 + \psi_4\right)Q_j^*\end{bmatrix} \gtrless 0 \quad \text{as} \quad \frac{Q_j^*}{Q_i^*} \gtrless \frac{\left(\left(\psi_2 + \psi_4\right) - \psi_3\right)}{\left(\psi_2 + \psi_4\right)} \tag{8.A.3}$$

where:

$$\begin{aligned}
\psi_1 &\equiv 1/\left(\left(b+\theta\right)^2\left(4b^2 - \theta^2\right)^2\right) > 0 \\
\psi_2 &\equiv \left(16b^5 - 8b^4\theta - 28b^3\theta^2 + 14b^2\theta^3 + 13b\theta^4 - 6\theta^5\right) \gtrless 0 \\
\psi_3 &\equiv 2\theta^2\left(b+\theta\right)\left(4b^2 - \theta^2\right) > 0 \\
\psi_4 &\equiv 2\theta\left(2b^2 - \theta^2\right)\left(4b^2 + 2b\theta - \theta^2\right) > 0
\end{aligned} \tag{8.A.4}$$

Given our expository assumption $Q_i^* > Q_j^*$, the boundary $L^{SS^*}$ always lies below $L^{Menu^*}$ while $U^{SS^*}$ may lie above $U^{Menu^*}$, between $U^{Menu^*}$ and $L^{Menu^*}$, or below $L^{Menu^*}$.

Now consider the relationship between the channel-coordinating quantity-discount schedule and the sophisticated Stackelberg two-part tariff. We use equations (8.2.3), (6.2.4) and (6.2.5) to obtain:

$$\left(\delta^{QD^*} - L^{SS^*}\right) = \left(Q_i^* - Q_j^*\right)\left[\frac{\left(\kappa_3 Q_i^* - \kappa_4 Q_j^*\right)}{\Delta^{SS^*}}\right] > 0 \tag{8.A.5}$$

$$\left(\delta^{QD^*} - U^{SS^*}\right) = -\left(Q_i^* - Q_j^*\right)\left[\frac{\left(\kappa_4 Q_i^* - \kappa_3 Q_j^*\right)}{\Delta^{SS^*}}\right] \gtrless 0 \quad \text{as} \quad \frac{Q_j^*}{Q_i^*} \gtrless \frac{\kappa_4}{\kappa_3} \tag{8.A.6}$$

where:

$$\begin{aligned} \kappa_3 &\equiv \left(8b^3 - 6b\theta^2 + \theta^3\right) > 0 \\ \kappa_4 &\equiv \left(8b^3 - 10b\theta^2 - \theta^3\right) \gtrless 0 \\ \therefore \quad & \kappa_3 > \kappa_4 \\ \Delta^{SS^*} &\equiv 2b(b+\theta)(2b+\theta)^2 \end{aligned} \tag{8.A.7}$$

Thus $U^{SS^*}$ can lie above or below $\delta^{QD^*}$, but $L^{SS^*}$ is always less than $\delta^{QD^*}$.

Finally, we turn to the relationship between the two channel-coordinating wholesale-price policies. We use equations (8.2.2), (7.3.4) and (7.3.5) to obtain:

$$\left(L^{Menu^*} - \delta^{QD^*}\right) = -\theta\left(Q_i^* - Q_j^*\right)\left[\frac{\left(\kappa_1 Q_i^* - \kappa_2 Q_j^*\right)}{\Delta^{Menu^*}}\right] \gtrless 0 \quad \text{as} \quad \frac{Q_j^*}{Q_i^*} \gtrless \frac{\kappa_1}{\kappa_2} \tag{8.A.8}$$

$$\left(U^{Menu^*} - \delta^{QD^*}\right) = \theta\left(Q_i^* - Q_j^*\right)\left[\frac{\left(\kappa_2 Q_i^* - \kappa_1 Q_j^*\right)}{\Delta^{Menu^*}}\right] > 0 \tag{8.A.9}$$

where:

$$\begin{aligned} \kappa_1 &\equiv \left(16b^5 + 8b^4\theta - 16b^3\theta^2 - 8b^2\theta^3 + 3b\theta^4 + \theta^5\right) > 0 \\ \kappa_2 &\equiv \left(16b^5 + 8b^4\theta - 8b^3\theta^2 + b\theta^4 - \theta^5\right) > \kappa_1 > 0 \\ \Delta^{Menu^*} &\equiv 2b(b+\theta)^2\left(4b^2 - \theta^2\right)^2 = (b+\theta)(2b-\theta)^2\Delta^{SS^*} \end{aligned} \tag{8.A.10}$$

The point of discontinuity $\delta^{QD^*}$ is always less than $U^{Menu^*}$, but it can lie above or below the lower boundary $L^{Menu^*}$.

Expression (8.A.2) is the ratio of a pair of fifth-order polynomials; it does not have a closed-form solution for parametric values for which the LHS is greater than the RHS. A fifth-order polynomial also characterizes relationships (8.A.3) and (8.A.8). Finally, the sign of expression (8.A.6) is determined by the ratio of a pair of third-order polynomials. To investigate these relationships further we conducted a numerical analysis using the substitutions $(S_j \equiv Q_j^* /(Q_i^* + Q_j^*))$ and $(\chi \equiv \theta / b)$. There are four "Zonal Scenarios:

$$\begin{array}{ll} \text{Scenario 1:} & L^{SS^*} < L^{Menu^*} < \delta^{QD^*} < U^{Menu^*} < U^{SS^*} \\ \text{Scenario 2:} & L^{SS^*} < L^{Menu^*} < \delta^{QD^*} \gtrless U^{SS^*} < U^{Menu^*} \\ \text{Scenario 3:} & L^{SS^*} < U^{SS^*} < L^{Menu^*} < \delta^{QD^*} < U^{Menu^*} \\ \text{Scenario 4:} & L^{SS^*} < U^{SS^*} < \delta^{QD^*} < L^{Menu^*} < U^{Menu^*} \end{array} \tag{8.A.11}$$

Figure 8.1 in Section 3 provides a representation of the relevant Scenario.

## 7.2 Manufacturer Profit Equivalence

In this sub-Section we identify the $(f_i - f_j)$ − value—provided one exists—at which the sophisticated Stackelberg two-part tariff generates the same manufacturer profit as does the relevant channel-coordinating wholesale-price policy.

**Zonal Scenarios 1-3:** Assuming the parametric values generate $\Pi_M^{SS^*} > \Pi_M^{Menu^*}$ at $L^{SS^*}$, we seek the $(f_i - f_j)$ − value at which the menu and the sophisticated Stackelberg strategies generate equal profits for the manufacturer. Let this value be $(f_i - f_j) = E^{L,L}$, where $L^{SS^*} < E^{L,L} < L^{Menu^*}$. We express $E^{L,L}$ in the context of equation (6.3.5) that defines $\omega$:

$$E^{L,L} = \omega^{L,L} U^{SS^*} + \left(1 - \omega^{L,L}\right) L^{SS^*} \tag{8.A.12}$$

The superscript $^{L,\ L}$ denotes this case. Manufacturer profit under the menu may be written as:

$$\begin{aligned} \Pi_M^{Menu^*}\left(\omega^{L,L}\right) &= R_C^{Menu^*} - f_i - f_j - F \\ &= \left\{R_C^{Menu^*} - L^{Menu^*} - 2f_j - F\right\} \\ &= \Pi_M^{Menu^*}\left(L^{SS^*}\right) \end{aligned} \tag{8.A.13}$$

We have used the substitution $(f_i - f_j) = L^{Menu^*}$ to eliminate $f_i$ in (8.A.13). This equation and equation (8.3.8) are identical, because $(f_i - f_j) < L^{Menu^*}$ and $R_C^{SS^*}(\omega = 1) = R_C^{SS^*}(\omega = 0)$ yield the same profit for the manufacturer.

Manufacturer profit under the sophisticated Stackelberg tariff is:

$$\begin{aligned}\Pi_M^{SS^*}\left(\omega^{L,L}\right) &= \left[R_C^{SS^*}(\omega=0) - f_i - f_j - F\right] + \omega^{L,L}\left(1-\omega^{L,L}\right)\beta_1 \\ &= \left\{R_C^{SS^*}(\omega=0) - L^{SS^*} - 2f_j - F\right\} - \left(\omega^{L,L}\right)^2 \beta_1\end{aligned} \tag{8.A.14}$$

The definition of $\Pi_M^{SS^*}(\omega^{L,L})$ in the first line of (8.A.14) comes from Table 6.2 and the definition of $\beta_1$:

$$\beta_1 \equiv \left(U^{SS^*} - L^{SS^*}\right) = \left(\frac{8(b-\theta)\left(Q_i^* - Q_j^*\right)^2}{(2b+\theta)^2}\right) \geq 0 \tag{8.A.15}$$

(The equality (8.A.15) holds for the trivial cases of bilateral monopoly and identical competitors.) To get from the first line to the second line of (8.A.14) we use expression (8.A.15) to write $\omega^{L,L}\beta_1 = (E^{L,L} - L^{SS^*})$. Making this substitution in conjunction with $(f_i - f_j) = E^{L,L}$ gives the final line of (8.A.14). Note that the {bracketed} expression duplicates equation (8.3.7).

Equating (8.A.13) with (8.A.14) and manipulating terms yields a simple expression for the profit-equating value $\omega^{L,L^*}$:

$$\left(\omega^{L,L^*}\right)^2 \beta_1 = \left[\left(L^{Menu^*} - L^{SS^*}\right) - \left(R_C^{Menu^*} - R_C^{SS^*}(\omega=0)\right)\right] \tag{8.A.16}$$

The RHS of (8.A.15) is positive, because it is the amount by which $\Pi_M^{SS^*} > \Pi_M^{Menu^*}$ at $L^{SS^*}$.

**Scenario 1:** Assuming the parametric values generate $\Pi_M^{SS^*} > \Pi_M^{Menu^*}$ at $U^{SS^*}$, we seek the $(f_i - f_j)$ – value at which profit equality between this pair of wholesale-price strategies is obtained. Let this value be $(f_i - f_j) = E^{U,U}$, where $U^{Menu^*} < E^{U,U} < U^{SS^*}$. For ease of presentation we first express $(f_i - f_j) = E^{U,U}$ in terms of $L^{SS^*}$ and $U^{SS^*}$ per equation (6.3.5):

$$E^{U,U} = \omega^{U,U} U^{SS^*} + \left(1 - \omega^{U,U}\right) L^{SS^*} \tag{8.A.17}$$

Manufacturer profit under the menu can be written as:

$$\Pi_M^{Menu^*}\left(\omega^{U,U}\right)=\Pi_C^{Menu^*}\left(U^{Menu^*}\right)-2\left[E^{U,U}-U^{Menu^*}\right]$$
$$=R_C^{Menu^*}-f_i-f_j-F-2\begin{bmatrix}\left(U^{SS^*}-U^{Menu^*}\right)\\-\left(1-\omega^{U,U}\right)\left(U^{SS^*}-L^{SS^*}\right)\end{bmatrix} \quad (8.A.18)$$
$$=\left\{R_C^{Menu^*}+U^{Menu^*}-2U^{SS^*}-2f_j-F\right\}+2\left(1-\omega^{U,U}\right)\beta_1$$

In the preceding equation we substitute for $E^{U,U}$ from equation (8.A.17) and set $(f_i-f_j)=U^{Menu^*}$. Note that the {bracketed} expression is the profit of the manufacturer under the menu, evaluated at $U^{SS^*}$; see equation (8.3.18).

Manufacturer profit under the sophisticated Stackelberg tariff is:

$$\Pi_M^{SS^*}\left(\omega^{U,U}\right)=R_C^{SS^*}(\omega=1)-f_i-f_j-F+\omega^{U,U}\left(1-\omega^{U,U}\right)\beta_1$$
$$=\left\{R_C^{SS^*}(\omega=1)-U^{SS^*}-2f_j-F\right\}+\left(1+\omega^{U,U}\right)\left(1-\omega^{U,U}\right)\beta_1 \quad (8.A.19)$$

Notice that $(f_i-f_j)=E^{U,U}$ in (8.A.19). The substitution incorporates the fact that $R_C^{SS^*}(\omega=1)=R_C^{SS^*}(\omega=0)$; this parallels the logic used in (8.A.14). The {bracketed} expression in (8.A.19), which is identical to equation (8.3.14), is the manufacturer's profit (evaluated at $U^{SS^*}$) under the sophisticated Stackelberg strategy. Equating (8.A.18) and (8.A.19), and manipulating terms, yields a simple expression for the profit-equating value $\omega^{U,U^*}$:

$$\left(1-\omega^{U,U^*}\right)^2\beta_1=\left[\left(U^{SS^*}-U^{Menu^*}\right)-\left(R_C^{Menu^*}-R_C^{SS^*}(\omega=1)\right)\right] \quad (8.A.20)$$

The RHS of (8.A.20) is positive by virtue of our assumption that the parametric values generate $\Pi_M^{SS^*}>\Pi_M^{Menu^*}$ at $U^{SS^*}$; indeed, the RHS is the amount by which $\Pi_M^{SS^*}>\Pi_M^{Menu^*}$ at $U^{SS^*}$.

**Scenario 3:** Assuming the parametric values generate $\Pi_M^{SS^*}>\Pi_M^{Menu^*}$ at $U^{SS^*}$, we seek the $(f_i-f_j)$– value at which profit equality is obtained. Let this value be $S_j=E^{U,L}$ where $U^{SS^*}<E^{U,L}<L^{Menu^*}$. For ease of presentation we convert $E^{U,L}$ using an expression that is inspired by (6.3.5):

$$1>\gamma^{U,L}\equiv\left(\left[\left(f_i-f_j\right)-U^{SS^*}\right]/\left[L^{Menu^*}-U^{SS^*}\right]\right)>0 \quad (8.A.21)$$

It immediately follows that:

$$E^{U,L}=\gamma^{U,L}L^{Menu^*}+\left(1-\gamma^{U,L}\right)U^{SS^*} \quad (8.A.22)$$

Manufacturer profit under the menu may be written as:

$$\begin{aligned}\Pi_M^{Menu^*}\left(\gamma^{U,L}\right) &= R_C^{Menu^*} - f_i - f_j - F \\ &= \left\{R_C^{Menu^*} - L^{Menu^*} - 2f_j - F\right\} \\ &= \Pi_M^{Menu^*}\left(U^{SS^*}\right)\end{aligned} \tag{8.A.23}$$

We have used the substitution $(f_i - f_j) = L^{Menu^*}$. Notice that this profit result duplicates equation (8.3.12).

Manufacturer profit under the sophisticated Stackelberg tariff is:

$$\begin{aligned}\Pi_M^{SS^*}\left(\gamma^{U,L}\right) &= R_C^{SS^*}(\omega = 1) - f_i - f_j - F - 2\left[E^{U,L} - U^{SS^*}\right] \\ &= R_C^{SS^*}(\omega = 1) - U^{SS^*} - 2f_j - F - 3\left[E^{U,L} - U^{SS^*}\right] \\ &= \left\{R_C^{SS^*}(\omega = 1) - U^{SS^*} - 2f_j - F\right\} - 3\gamma^{U,L}\beta_2\end{aligned} \tag{8.A.24}$$

We use $(f_i - f_j) = E^{U,L}$ in (8.A.24); and we define $\beta_2$ as:

$$\beta_2 \equiv \left(L^{Menu^*} - U^{SS^*}\right) \tag{8.A.25}$$

Equating expression (8.A.23) with (8.A.24) and manipulating terms yields a simple expression for the profit-equating value $\gamma^{U,L^*}$:

$$3\gamma^{U,L^*}\beta_2 = \left[\left(L^{Menu^*} - U^{SS^*}\right) - \left(R_C^{Menu^*} - R_C^{SS^*}(\omega = 1)\right)\right] \tag{8.A.26}$$

The RHS of (8.A.26) is the (positive) amount by which $\Pi_M^{SS^*} > \Pi_M^{Menu^*}$ at $U^{SS^*}$. The optimal value $\gamma^{U,L^*}$ is that profit difference divided by three times the $(f_i - f_j)$ distance between the lower boundary of Zone $Z_{ij}^{Menu^*}$ and the upper boundary of Zone $Z_{ij}^{SS^*}$.

**Scenario 4:** Assuming the parametric values generate $\Pi_M^{SS^*} > \Pi_M^{QD^*}$ at $L^{SS^*}$, we seek the $(f_i - f_j)$ – value at which profit equality is obtained. Let this value be $(f_i - f_j) = E^{L,\delta}$ where $L^{SS^*} < E^{L,\delta} < U^{SS^*} < \delta^{QD^*}$. We express $E^{L,\delta}$ in terms of $\omega$ as defined at equation (6.3.5):

$$E^{L,\delta} = \omega^{L,\delta}U^{SS^*} + \left(1 - \omega^{L,\delta}\right)L^{SS^*} \tag{8.A.27}$$

Manufacturer profit under the quantity-discount schedule may be written as:

$$\begin{aligned}\Pi_M^{Menu^*}\left(\omega^{L,\delta}\right) &= R_C^{QD^*} - f_i - f_j - F \\ &= \left\{R_C^{QD^*} - \delta^{QD^*} - 2f_j - F\right\} \\ &= \Pi_M^{Menu^*}\left(L^{SS^*}\right)\end{aligned} \tag{8.A.28}$$

We have used the substitution $(f_i - f_j) = \delta^{QD^*}$. Equation (8.A.28) duplicates equation (8.3.15).

Manufacturer profit under the sophisticated Stackelberg tariff can be written as:

$$\begin{aligned}\Pi_M^{SS^*}\left(\omega^{L,\delta}\right) &= R_C^{SS^*}(\omega=0) - f_i - f_j - F + \omega^{L,\delta}\left(1-\omega^{L,\delta}\right)\beta_1 \\ &= \left\{R_C^{SS^*}(\omega=0) - L^{SS^*} - 2f_j - F\right\} - \left(\omega^{L,\delta}\right)^2 \beta_1\end{aligned} \tag{8.A.29}$$

Notice that $(f_i - f_j) = E^{L,\delta}$ in (8.A.29).

Equating (8.A.28) with (8.A.29) yields the profit-equating value $\omega^{L,\delta^*}$:

$$\left(\omega^{L,\delta^*}\right)^2 \beta_1 = \left[\left(\delta^{QD^*} - L^{SS^*}\right) - \left(R_C^{QD^*} - R_C^{SS^*}(\omega=0)\right)\right] \tag{8.A.30}$$

The RHS of (8.A.30) is positive because it is the amount by which $\Pi_M^{SS^*} > \Pi_M^{QD^*}$ at $\delta^{QD^*}$.

**Scenario 4:** Assuming the parametric values generate $\Pi_M^{SS^*} > \Pi_M^{QD^*}$ at $U^{SS^*}$, we seek the $(f_i - f_j)$ – value at which profit equality is obtained. Let this value be $E^{U,\delta}$ where $U^{SS^*} < E^{U,\delta} < \delta^{QD^*}$. We first express $(f_i - f_j) = E^{U,\delta}$ in the context of equation (8.A.21). It immediately follows that:

$$E^{U,\delta} = \gamma^{U,\delta} L^{Menu^*} + \left(1-\gamma^{U,\delta}\right) U^{SS^*} \tag{8.A.31}$$

Manufacturer profit under the quantity-discount schedule can be written as:

$$\begin{aligned}\Pi_M^{QD^*}\left(\gamma^{U,\delta}\right) &= R_C^{QD^*} - f_i - f_j - F \\ &= \left\{R_C^{QD^*} - \delta^{QD^*} - 2f_j - F\right\} \\ &= \Pi_M^{QD^*}\left(\delta^{QD^*}\right)\end{aligned} \tag{8.A.32}$$

We used the substitution $(f_i - f_j) = \delta^{QD^*}$; the profit result duplicates (8.3.15).

Manufacturer profit under the sophisticated Stackelberg tariff is:

$$\begin{aligned}\Pi_M^{SS^*}\left(\gamma^{U,\delta}\right) &= R_C^{SS^*}(\omega=1) - f_i - f_j - F - 2\left[E^{U,\delta} - U^{SS^*}\right] \\ &= \left\{R_C^{SS^*}(\omega=1) - U^{SS^*} - 2f_j - F\right\} - 3\gamma^{U,\delta}\beta_3\end{aligned} \tag{8.A.33}$$

Note that $(f_i - f_j) = E^{U,\delta}$ in (8.A.33) and that we define $\beta_3$ as:

$$\beta_3 \equiv \left(\delta^{QD^*} - U^{SS^*}\right) \tag{8.A.34}$$

Equating (8.A.32) with (8.A.33) givess the profit-equating value of $\gamma^{U,\delta^*}$:

$$3\gamma^{U,\delta^*}\beta_3 = \left[\left(\delta^{QD^*} - U^{SS^*}\right) - \left(R_C^{QD^*} - R_C^{SS^*}(\omega = 1)\right)\right] \tag{8.A.35}$$

The RHS of (8.A.35) is the (positive) amount by which $\Pi_M^{SS^*} > \Pi_M^{QD^*}$ at $U^{SS^*}$. Thus the interpretation of this equation is similar to that of equation (8.A.26).

**Scenario 4 (Channel-Coordination Equivalency):** We now seek the $(f_i - f_j)$ – value at which the menu and the quantity-discount schedule equalize manufacturer profit in Scenario 4. We define this $(f_i - f_j)$ – value as $(f_i - f_j) = E^{\delta,L}$ where $\delta^{QD^*} < E^{\delta,L} < L^{Menu^*}$. Manufacturer profit with the menu is:

$$\begin{aligned}\Pi_M^{Menu^*}\left(E^{\delta,L}\right) &= R_C^{Menu^*} - f_i - f_j - F \\ &= \left\{R_C^{Menu^*} - L^{Menu^*} - 2f_j - F\right\}\end{aligned} \tag{8.A.36}$$

This expression replicates (8.A.23). Manufacturer profit with the quantity-discount schedule is:

$$\begin{aligned}\Pi_M^{QD^*}\left(E^{\delta,L}\right) &= \Pi_C^{QD^*}\left(\delta^{QD^*}\right) - 2\left[E^{\delta,L} - L^{Menu^*}\right] \\ &= R_C^{QD^*} - f_i - f_j - F - 2\left[E^{\delta,L} - L^{Menu^*}\right] \\ &= \left\{R_C^{QD^*} - \delta^{QD^*} - 2f_j - F\right\} - 2\left[E^{\delta,L} - L^{Menu^*}\right]\end{aligned} \tag{8.A.37}$$

Equating the equations (8.A.36) and (8.A.37) while recognizing that $R_C^{Menu^*} = R_C^{QD^*}$ gives the critical value $E^{\delta,L^*}$:

$$E^{\delta,L^*} = \left(L^{Menu^*} + \delta^{QD^*}/2\right) \tag{8.A.38}$$

This equation merely states that, under Scenario 4, the two channel-coordinating wholesale-price policies generate equal manufacturer profit at a value of $(f_i - f_j)$ that is halfway between Zone $Z_{ij}^{QD^*}$ (i.e., $\delta^{QD^*}$) and the lower boundary of Zone $Z_{ij}^{Menu^*}$ (i.e., $L^{Menu^*}$). Alternatively we may state that in Scenario 4 the manufacturer will offer the menu if $(f_i - f_j) \geq E^{\delta,L^*}$, or it will offer the quantity-discount schedule if $(f_i - f_j) < E^{\delta,L^*}$,both subject to the condition that $(f_i - f_j)$ is not so low as to induce the manufacturer to offer the sophisticated Stackelberg tariff.

# Notes

[1] An earlier version of this Chapter appeared, in combination with material from Chapter 7, in our *Journal of Retailing* paper "Is Channel Coordination All It Is Cracked Up to Be?" (Ingene and Parry 2000). This Chapter contains considerable material that has not appeared before. (New York University holds the *Journal of Retailing* copyright; our material is used with permission.)

[2] We explore a variation in channel breadth in Chapter 10.

[3] The labels "upper" and "lower" reflect our expository assumption $Q_i^* > Q_j^*$; this yields $U^{SS^*} > L^{SS^*} > 0$.

[4] These Scenarios apply when the SS-feasibility constraint $(Q_j^*(j) > 0)$ is satisfied. See Chapter 6, Section 5 for additional details.

[5] We detail this re-parameterization below, in sub-Section 4.1.

[6] The notation $E^{L,L}$ denotes manufacturer profit-equality between the two lower bounds: $L^{SS^*}$ and $L^{Menu^*}$. For a precise definition of $E^{L,L}$, see equation (8.A.12) of the Appendix.

[7] Recall that, if $L^{Menu^*} \leq (f_i - f_j) \leq U^{Menu^*}$, the channel-coordinating menu of two-part tariffs is always optimal. We have analyzed the case in which $(f_i - f_j) < L^{Menu^*}$ in sub-Section 3.2.1.

[8] The profit comparisons are given by the following inequalities: (8.3.9), (8.3.13), (8.3.16), (8.3.17) and (8.3.19). We define the intensity of competition as $\chi$ $(\equiv \theta / b)$ and the magnitude of competition as $S_j (\equiv Q_j^* / (Q_i^* + Q_j^*))$.

[9] Equal fixed costs are more general than zero fixed costs. Figure 8.2 is drawn for $f_i = 0 = f_j$. A fundamentally similar Figure is obtained for all $f_i = f_j < .66$. At higher fixed costs values Region M becomes more prominent. We detail these changes in Chapter 9.

[10] Specifically, the legs of the parabola intersect the $\langle S_j = 0 \rangle$ – axis at $.99 \geq \chi \geq .85$. The furthest extension of the parabola into the unit half-square is at $S_j \cong .07$.

[11] Equal cost, in conjunction with identical demand, is sufficient to cause the competitors to behave identically.

[12] The quotation is from Aristotle's *Metaphysica*, as translated by Apostle (1966).

Chapter 9

# Coordination *versus* Maximization: Graphical Analyses

*"I rarely think in words at all. A thought comes, and I may try to express it in words afterward."*

## 1 INTRODUCTION

We proved in Chapter 8 that any of our three wholesale-price policies can maximize the profit of a manufacturer that sells to competing, non-identical retailers that are comparably treated. The manufacturer-dominant strategy depends on three parameters that define the retail industry's structure: the intensity of competition, the magnitude of competition, and the retailers' fixed-cost ratio. To clarify the relationships among these parameters, we now present a set of three-dimensional graphs that identify the manufacturer's optimal wholesale-price strategy at *all* points in the unit-cube.[1] We also present a series of two-dimensional slices of the graphs in order to provide details at critical parametric values.

We address the same three questions analyzed in the last Chapter:

(1) Under what parametric values does the quantity-discount schedule manufacturer profit-dominate the sophisticated Stackelberg tariff?

(2) Under what parametric values (if any) does the quantity-discount schedule manufacturer profit-dominate the menu of two-part tariffs?

(3) Under what parametric values, if any, does the sophisticated Stackelberg tariff manufacturer profit-dominate the menu?

We saw in Chapter 8 that the answers to these questions involve higher-order polynomials that are functions of market shares, competitive intensity, and fixed costs. Because such functions provide little insight for some readers, in this Chapter we use graphical analysis to cast an intuitive light on our results.

We briefly review the dimensions of the unit-cube in Section 2. We compare manufacturer profitability under the quantity-discount schedule and the sophisticated Stackelberg tariff in Section 3. We contrast the menu of two-part tariffs with the quantity-discount schedule in Section 4, and in Section 5 we contrast the menu with the sophisticated Stackelberg tariff. In Section 6 we identify which of the three wholesale-price policies is optimal for the manufacturer; we also offer a commentary on our results.

# 2 BACKGROUND ASSUMPTIONS[2]

The re-parameterization of our model's cost and demand parameters involves three definitions:

$$\chi \equiv (\theta/b) \tag{9.2.1}$$

$$S_j \equiv Q_j^* / (Q_i^* + Q_j^*) \tag{9.2.2}$$

$$f_k \equiv (f_k / R_k^*) \quad \forall \quad k \in (i,j) \tag{9.2.3}$$

The *intensity of competition* variable $\chi$ must lie in the unit interval $(0 \le \chi < 1)$ for second-order conditions to be met; retailers compete more intensely as $\chi \to 1$. The *magnitude of competition*, which is the market share of the $j^{th}$ retailer, must lie in the unit interval $(0 \le S_j \le 1)$; competition increases as $S_j \to ½$. The $k^{th}$ firm's *fixed-cost ratio* must lie in the unit interval $(0 \le f_k \le 1)$; retailer profit is negative if this constraint is violated.

Because the market-share parameter and the fixed-cost ratios are functions of the original model parameters, our re-parameterization entails no loss of generality:

$$S_j \equiv \left( \frac{Q_j^*}{Q_i^* + Q_j^*} \right) = \left( \frac{A_j - b(c_j + C) + \theta(c_i + C)}{(A_i + A_j) - (b - \theta)(c_j + c_i + 2C)} \right) \tag{9.2.4}$$

$$f_j \equiv \left( \frac{bf_j}{(Q_j^*)^2} \right) = \left( \frac{bf_j}{(A_j - b(c_j + C) + \theta(c_i + C))^2} \right) \tag{9.2.5}$$

(To obtain the fixed-cost ratio of the $i^{th}$ retailer, reverse the $i^{th}$ and $j^{th}$ subscripts in (9.2.5)). We are able to reduce nine parameters to four dimensions because many combinations of the original model's demand and cost parameters are associated with the same point in $\langle \chi, S_j, f_i, f_j \rangle$ – space. We used this property in our tabular examples of Chapter 8 by changing b and $\theta$ in tandem, thereby varying $\chi$ while holding $S_j$ constant.[3] Our point is that *any acceptable values of the original parameters* can be mapped into $\langle \chi, S_j, f_i, f_j \rangle$ – space. It follows that an analysis of this reduced space leads to fully general conclusions.

Due to the inherent complexity of the profit comparisons we make in this Chapter, we further simplify our task by focusing on retailers who have equal fixed-cost ratios: $f_i = f_j \equiv f$. This is *not* the same as assuming equal fixed costs *except* in the special cases of identical competitors $(Q_i^* = Q_j^*)$ or zero fixed costs ($f_i = 0 = f_j$). Our approach is consistent with the presentation of the zonal boundaries in Chapters 5-7, but our graphical results are less general than the mathematical results that were presented in Chapter 8. The intricacy of our three-dimensional graphical analyses does not encourage an immediate extension to four dimensions; we leave that task for future research.

## 3 MANUFACTURER PROFITABILITY: THE QUANTITY-DISCOUNT SCHEDULE *vs.* THE SOPHISTICATED STACKELBERG TARIFF

We now compare the manufacturer profit generated by the channel non-coordinating, sophisticated Stackelberg two-part tariff (see Chapter 6) and the channel-coordinating, linear quantity-discount schedule (see Chapter 5). In both cases the manufacturer is limited to setting a fixed fee that extracts all profit from the less-profitable retailer. The difference in the retailers' fixed costs affects the manufacturer's profit and, in combination with the retailers' net revenues, it also affects the identity of the less-profitable retailer. Thus, manufacturer profit under each strategy can be characterized by three Zones that are defined in $\langle \chi, S_j, f \rangle$ – space.

Manufacturer profit with a sophisticated Stackelberg strategy is:

$$\begin{aligned} &\text{Zone } Z_j^{SS^*}: && (f_i - f_j) < L^{SS^*} && \Rightarrow \quad \hat{\Pi}_M^{SS^*}(j) \equiv \hat{\Pi}_j^{SS^*} \\ &\text{Zone } Z_{ij}^{SS^*}: && U^{SS^*} \geq (f_i - f_j) \geq L^{SS^*} && \Rightarrow \quad \hat{\Pi}_M^{SS^*}(\omega) \equiv \hat{\Pi}_{ij}^{SS^*} \\ &\text{Zone } Z_i^{SS^*}: && U^{SS^*} < (f_i - f_j) && \Rightarrow \quad \hat{\Pi}_M^{SS^*}(i) \equiv \hat{\Pi}_i^{SS^*} \end{aligned} \tag{9.3.1}$$

The first line of (9.3.1) defines Zone $Z_j^{SS^*}$ as the portion of the unit cube in which $(f_i - f_j) < L^{SS^*}$; we denote manufacturer profit in this area with the compressed notation $\hat{\Pi}_j^{SS^*}$.[4] Other lines of (9.3.1) have similar explanations. Note that the subscript symbolizes the zero-profit retailer; thus, Zone $Z_k^{SS^*}$ implies $\hat{\pi}_k^{SS^*} = 0$, and Zone $Z_{ij}^{SS^*}$ implies $\hat{\pi}_i^{SS^*} = \hat{\pi}_j^{SS^*} = 0$ for $k \in (i, j)$.

Manufacturer profit with the linear, channel-coordinating quantity-discount schedule is:

$$\begin{aligned} &\text{Zone } Z_j^{QD^*}: && \delta^{QD^*} > (f_i - f_j) && \Rightarrow \quad \Pi_j^{QD^*} \\ &\text{Zone } Z_{ij}^{QD^*}: && \delta^{QD^*} = (f_i - f_j) && \Rightarrow \quad \Pi_{ij}^{QD^*} \\ &\text{Zone } Z_i^{QD^*}: && \delta^{QD^*} < (f_i - f_j) && \Rightarrow \quad \Pi_i^{QD^*} \end{aligned} \tag{9.3.2}$$

Variables and labels are defined in a comparable manner to those in (9.3.1).

Because there are three Zones with each policy, simple enumeration seems to indicate a total of nine profit comparisons. However, because the manufacturer obtains all the profit from a coordinated channel in Zone $Z_{ij}^{QD^*}$, only six profit comparisons are necessary: the three sophisticated Stackelberg Zones ("$SS-$Zones") *vs.* the two remaining quantity-discount Zones ("$QD-$Zones"). In the first sub-Section we present, for each of the six possible cases, the difference in manufacturer profits under the two pricing policies. In the second sub-Section we set these differences equal to zero and graph the resulting *indifference surfaces*. We then explore the *precise details* of these surfaces for the manufacturer's wholesale-price decision.

## 3.1 An Analytical Comparison of the Quantity-Discount Schedule and the Sophisticated Stackelberg Tariff

To simplify our discussion, let $\Delta\Pi_{QD,k}^{SS,k}$ denote the iso-profit curve along which the sophisticated Stackelberg tariff (in $SS-$Zone $Z_k^{SS^*}$) and the quantity-discount schedule (in $QD-$Zone $Z_k^{QD^*}$) generate equal profit for the manufacturer. For the case of Zones $Z_j^{SS^*}$ and $Z_j^{QD^*}$ we have:

$$\Delta\Pi_{QD,j}^{SS,j} \equiv \left[\Pi_j^{SS^*} - \Pi_j^{QD^*}\right] = 0$$
$$= R_{QD}^{SS}\left(1-2S_j\right)\left[\left(1+\chi\right)\left(2-\chi\right)^2 - 2S_j\left(4-5\chi^2\right)\right] = 0 \qquad (9.3.3)$$

This expression contains no fixed-cost terms because the j[th] retailer is the less-profitable in *both* cases. In expression (9.3.3) we have employed the space-saving substitution:

$$R_{QD}^{SS} \equiv R_i^* \Big/ \left(2\left(1+\chi\right)\left(1-S_j\right)^2\left(2+\chi\right)^2\right) > 0 \qquad (9.3.4)$$

The term $R_i^*$ is defined as the net revenue of the i[th] retailer in a coordinated channel. This monotonic multiplier will be common to all our comparisons.

Because we concentrate on the unit half-cube, within which $S_j \le ½$, the $(1-2S_j)$ expression in (9.3.3) is positive except at $S_j = ½$. It follows that the sophisticated Stackelberg tariff (the "$SS-$tariff") and the quantity-discount schedule (the "$QD-$schedule") generate equal profit for the manufacturer when the retailers are identical. But, when $S_j \ne ½$, the [bracketed] expression in (9.3.3) determines which pricing policy generates more profit for the manufacturer. At no loss of generality we concentrate on $S_j < ½$ in our graphical analyses.

The difference between manufacturer profit in SS – Zone $Z_j^{SS^*}$ and in QD – Zone $Z_i^{QD^*}$ includes the fixed-cost ratio because the i[th] retailer is the less profitable in the QD – Zone, while in the SS – Zone the j[th] retailer fills that role. Setting their fixed-cost ratios to equality yields:

$$\Delta\Pi_{QD,i}^{SS,j} \equiv \left[\Pi_j^{SS^*} - \Pi_i^{QD^*}\right]\Big|_{f_i=f_j} = 0$$

$$= R_{QD}^{SS}\left(1-2S_j\right)\begin{pmatrix} +4(1+\chi)(2+\chi)^2 f \\ -\left(12+24\chi+15\chi^2+\chi^3\right) \\ -2S_j\left(4-5\chi^2\right) \end{pmatrix} = 0 \qquad (9.3.5)$$

In expression (9.3.6) we have used the definition:

$$\left(f_i - f_j\right) \equiv R_i^*\left(\left(1-S_j\right)^2 f_i - S_j^2 f_j\right)/\left(1-S_j\right)^2 \qquad (9.3.7)$$

With an equal fixed cost ratio ($f_i = f_j \equiv f$) definition (9.3.7) reduces to:

$$\left(f_i - f_j\right) = R_i^*\left(1-2S_j\right)f/\left(1-S_j\right)^2 \qquad (9.3.8)$$

We report the remaining profit comparisons in Table 9.1; they are calculated with the same approach as sketched in (9.3.3) and (9.3.5).[5]

The heart of our analysis lies in the observation that, in QD – Zone $Z_{ij}^{QD^*}$ the manufacturer obtains all profit from the *coordinated* channel with the QD – schedule; the SS – tariff does not have this property except at $S_j = \frac{1}{2}$. Thus, the manufacturer prefers the QD – schedule in this Zone. (To conserve space we write this as "$QD \succ SS$." The symbol "$x \succ y$" means "the manufacturer prefers *x* to *y*.") Because a small increase in the retailers' fixed-cost ratio lowers manufacturer profit only fractionally, it must also be true that $QD \succ SS$ in the *vicinity* of Zone $Z_{ij}^{QD^*}$.

*Table 9.1.* Manufacturer Profit Differences by Policy and Zone:
The Sophisticated Stackelberg Tariff *vs.* The Quantity-Discount Schedule

| Label | Definition | Multiplier | Core Value |
|---|---|---|---|
| $\Delta\Pi_{QD,j}^{SS,i}$ | $\left[\Pi_i^{SS^*} - \Pi_j^{QD^*}\right]\Big\|_{f_i=f_j} = 0$ | $R_{QD}^{SS}(1-2S_j)$ | $\left((1+\chi)(20+4\chi+\chi^2) - 2S_j(4-5\chi^2) - 4f(1+\chi)(2+\chi)^2\right)$ |
| $\Delta\Pi_{QD,i}^{SS,i}$ | $\left[\Pi_i^{SS^*} - \Pi_i^{QD^*}\right]\Big\|_{f_i=f_j} = 0$ | $R_{QD}^{SS}(1-2S_j)$ | $\left((4-7\chi^2-\chi^3) - 2S_j(4-5\chi^2)\right)$ |
| $\Delta\Pi_{QD,j}^{SS,ij}$ | $\left[\Pi_{ij}^{SS^*} - \Pi_j^{QD^*}\right]\Big\|_{f_i=f_j} = 0$ | $\left(\dfrac{R_{QD}^{SS}}{4(1-\chi)}\right)$ | $\begin{pmatrix} f(1+\chi)(2+\chi)^2\left[4(4S_j(1-\chi)+3\chi) - f(2+\chi)^2\right] \\ +4\left((1+\chi)(4-8\chi-4\chi^2-\chi^3) - 2S_j(1-\chi)\left[(8+12\chi+4\chi^2+\chi^3)+2S_j\chi^2\right]\right) \end{pmatrix}$ |
| $\Delta\Pi_{QD,i}^{SS,ij}$ | $\left[\Pi_{ij}^{SS^*} - \Pi_i^{QD^*}\right]\Big\|_{f_i=f_j} = 0$ | $-\left(\dfrac{R_{QD}^{SS}}{4(1-\chi)}\right)$ | $\begin{pmatrix} f(1+\chi)(2+\chi)^2\left[4(4S_j(1-\chi)-(4-\chi)) + f(2+\chi)^2\right] \\ +4\left((12+12\chi-5\chi^3-\chi^4) - 2S_j(1-\chi)\left[(8+12\chi+8\chi^2+\chi^3)-2S_j\chi^2\right]\right) \end{pmatrix}$ |

Note: $R_{QD}^{SS} \equiv R_i^* \Big/ \left(2(1+\chi)(1-S_j)^2(2+\chi)^2\right) > 0$

## 3.2 A Graphical Comparison of the Quantity-Discount Schedule and the Sophisticated Stackelberg Tariff

We now use this information to graph the profit relationships within the unit-cube. We begin with a set of three-dimensional diagrams. To simplify interpreting these graphs, we ignore the Region within which the sophisticated Stackelberg Tariff is infeasible ($Q_j^*(j) \leq 0$; see Chapter 6, Section 5 for details). Figure 9.1 illustrates *two* distinct surfaces along which the manufacturer is indifferent between the $QD-$schedule and the $SS-$tariff. (We write this in compressed notation as $QD \approx SS$; the symbol $x \approx y$ means that the manufacturer is indifferent between $x$ and $y$.) Because this three-dimensional graph is difficult to see in detail, we decompose it in Figures 9.2 and 9.3. Notice that all three Figures are drawn for $f \geq 0.65$. At lower $f-$values the $SS-$strategy is strictly preferred by the manufacturer.

The first surface appears in Figure 9.2 as a "curved wall" that intersects the $\langle \chi = 0 \rangle -$plane at $f = 1$ and the $\langle \chi = 1 \rangle -$plane at $f = {}^{25}\!/_{36}$. The manufacturer prefers the sophisticated Stackelberg tariff to the left of this indifference surface; it prefers the quantity-discount schedule to the right of the curved wall.[6] The second surface is presented in Figure 9.3. It forms a "cave" that exists above $f = .85$ and below $\chi = .75$. Inside the cave $SS \succ QD$; the reverse is true outside the cave.

Both indifference surfaces (curved wall and cave) are relevant for manufacturer decision-making. Their combination appears in Figure 9.1; $SS \succ QD$ to the left of the curved wall *and* inside the cave; elsewhere we find $QD \succ SS$. Clearly the channel-coordinating quantity-discount schedule is manufacturer preferred only at high levels of retailers' fixed costs. As $f$ rises the intensity of competition necessary for coordination to be preferred by the manufacturer declines.

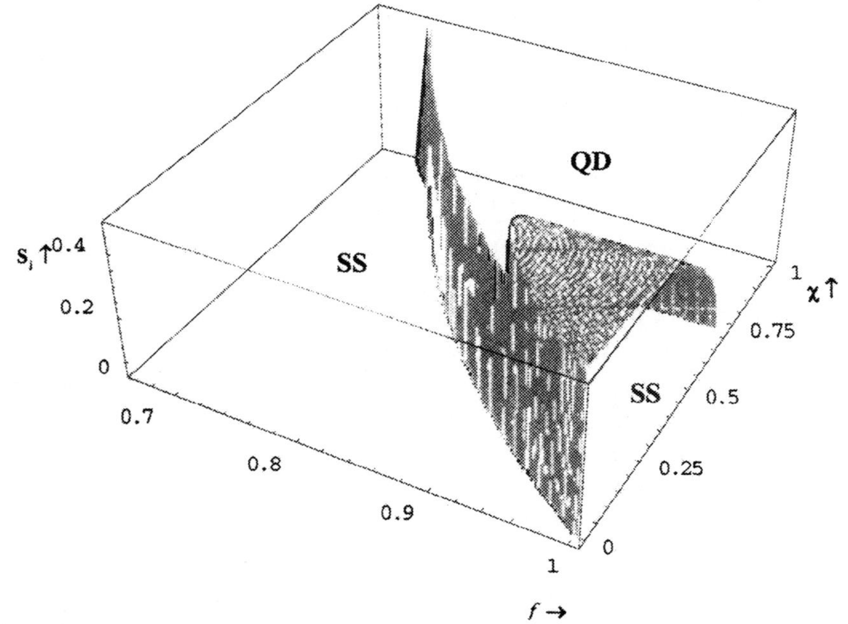


Legend:

**SS** ≡ The manufacturer prefers the sophisticated Stackelberg tariff, and

**QD** ≡ The manufacturer prefers the quantity-discount schedule.

*Figure 9.1.* The Two Indifference Surfaces for which Manufacturer Profit is Equal with the Sophisticated Stackelberg Tariff and the Quantity-Discount Schedule

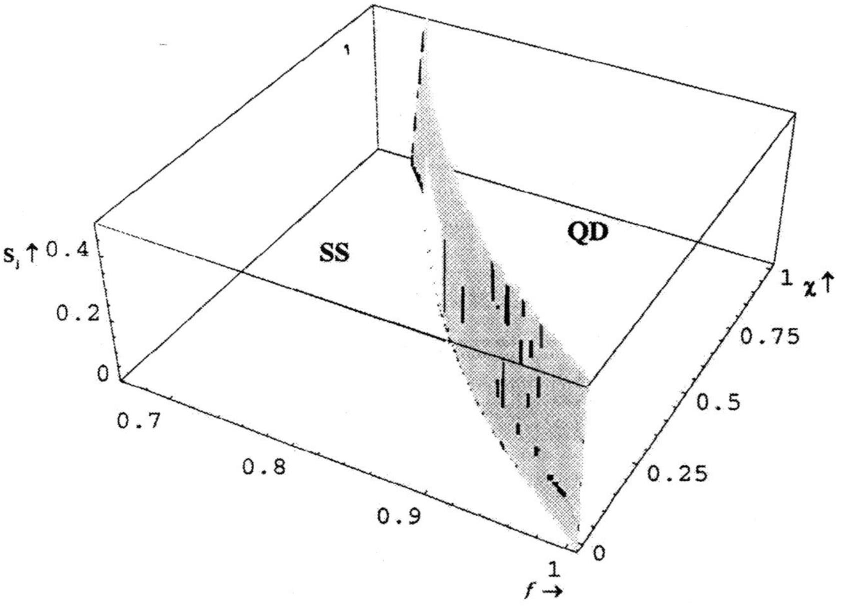


Legend:

**SS** ≡ The manufacturer prefers the sophisticated Stackelberg tariff, and

**QD** ≡ The manufacturer prefers the quantity-discount schedule.

*Figure 9.2.* A"Curved Wall" Indifference Surface for which Manufacturer Profit is Equal with the Sophisticated Stackelberg Tariff and the Quantity-Discount Schedule

Conceptually we can divide the unit-half cube of Figures 9.1-9.3 into three $f$ – Regions that are defined by their $f$ – values:

- $f$ – **Region 1:** $0 \le f < {}^{25}\!/_{36} \cong 0.69444$
- $f$ – **Region 2:** ${}^{25}\!/_{36} < f \le 0.838630$
- $f$ – **Region 3:** $0.838630 < f \le 1$

The indifference surfaces that appear in the three-dimensional unit-cube behave in different manners in each of these three $f$ – Regions. In order to succinctly depict the essence of each of these $f$ – Regions, we take two-dimensional slices of them at specific $f$ – values. This generates two-dimensional "indifference curves" within the unit half-square.

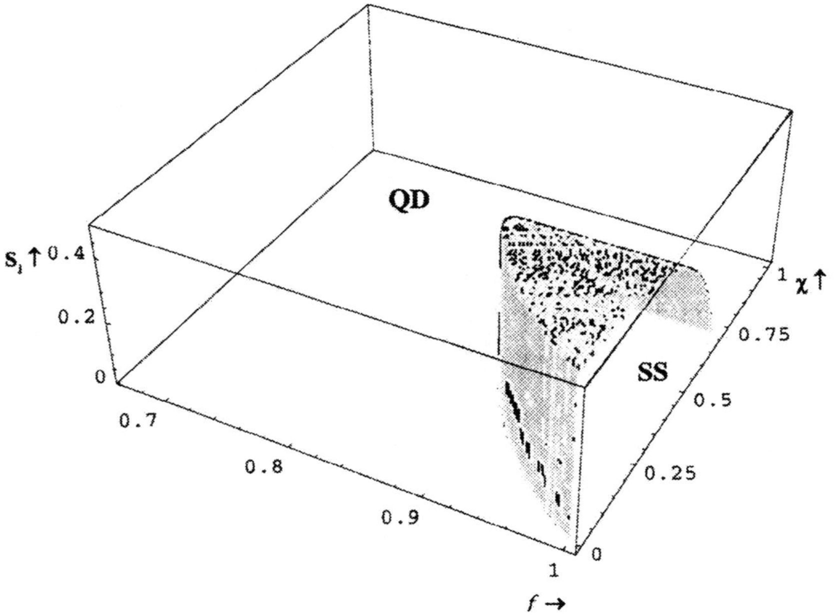


Legend:
**SS** ≡ The manufacturer prefers the sophisticated Stackelberg tariff, and
**QD** ≡ The manufacturer prefers the quantity-discount schedule.

*Figure 9.3.* A "Cave-like" Indifference Surface for which Manufacturer Profit is Equal with the Sophisticated Stackelberg Tariff and the Quantity-Discount Schedule

There is *no indifference surface* in $f$ – Region 1, so the manufacturer strictly prefers the sophisticated Stackelberg tariff whenever it is feasible (i.e., when $Q_j^*(j) > 0$). In contrast, $f$ – Region 2 incorporates much of the indifference surface of Figure 9.2, and $f$ – Region 3 includes both indifference surfaces depicted in Figure 9.1. We now fix $f$ at various values in order to examine the corresponding two-dimensional $\langle \chi, S_j \rangle$ – plane. This will enable us to provide further insight into these indifference surfaces.

$f$ – **Region 2**: Any vertical slice of Figure 9.1 that corresponds to a single value of $f$ generates a linear indifference surface that divides the unit half-square into two parts. The manufacturer prefers the channel-coordinating quantity-discount schedule in the area above the indifference curve and in the

$SS-$infeasible region (the area in which $Q_j^*(j) \le 0$). Elsewhere the manufacturer prefers the sophisticated Stackelberg two-part tariff. Within $f-$Region 2 we distinguish three sub-Regions:

- $f-$**Region 2a**: $25/36 \le f < 17/24 \cong 0.708333$
- $f-$**Region 2b**: $17/24 \le f < 0.716506$
- $f-$**Region 2c**: $0.716506 < f \le 0.838630$

We now develop the details on these $f-$Regions.

$f-$**Region 2a:** Figure 9.4 illustrates this $f-$Region for $f = 0.70$. As $f$ rises from $25/36$ to $17/24$ a triangular area forms and grows. We find $QD \succ SS$ inside the triangle in the upper left corner of Figure 9.4 and in the $SS-$infeasible region in the lower left of the Figure; everywhere else we find $SS \succ QD$. This indifference line (labeled $\Delta\Pi_{QD,j}^{SS,i}$) lies in $SS-$Zone $Z_i^{SS^*}$ and in $QD-$Zone $Z_j^{QD^*}$. As $f$ increases, its intersection with the $\langle S_j = 0\rangle-$axis declines from $\chi = 1$ to $\chi = 0.954196$ and its intersection with the $\langle \chi = 1\rangle-$axis increases from $S_j = 0$ to $S_j = 1/2$.

$f-$**Region 2b**: The indifference surface of the three-dimensional Figure 9.2 depicts a small l, hard-to-see triangular sub-Region at the top of the $\langle \chi, S_j\rangle-$axis; one side of this sub-Region coincides with the $\langle \chi = 1\rangle-$plane. As $f$ rises from $17/24$ to 0.716506, the intersection with the $\langle S_j = 0\rangle-$plane declines from $\chi = 0.954196$ to $\chi = 0.928203$ while the intersection with the $\langle S_j = 1/2\rangle-$plane falls from $\chi = 1$ to $\chi = 0.95378$. Inside this sub-Region, which lies entirely inside $SS-$Zone $Z_i^{SS^*}$ *and* $QD-$Zone $Z_j^{QD^*}$, we find $QD \succ SS$. Outside this sub-Region (and outside the $SS-$infeasible region), we have $SS \succ QD$. To conserve space we do not present a separate two-dimensional Figure to illustrate this sub-Region.

$f-$**Region 2c**: The indifference surface of Figure 9.2 still lies inside $QD-$Zone $Z_j^{QD^*}$ in this $f-$Region, but now it spans $SS-$Zones $Z_i^{SS^*}$ and $Z_{ij}^{SS^*}$. The indifference surface creates a rectangle at the top of $\langle \chi, S_j\rangle-$plane. The boundary defining this rectangle shifts toward the $\langle \chi = 0\rangle-$axis as $f$ increases. Figure 9.5 illustrates this $f-$Region for $f = 0.73$.

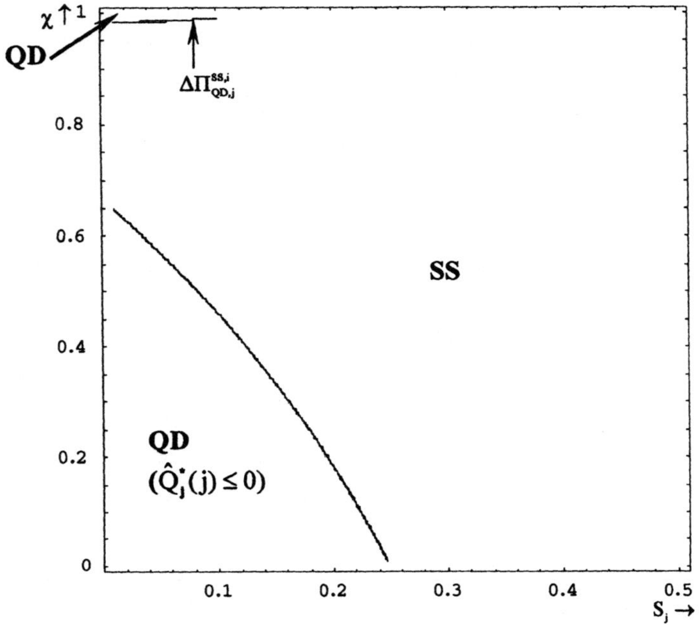


Legend:

**SS** ≡ The manufacturer prefers the sophisticated Stackelberg tariff;

**QD** ≡ The manufacturer prefers the quantity-discount schedule;

$\hat{Q}^*_j(j) < 0$ ≡ The region within which the sophisticated Stackelberg tariff is infeasible; and

$\Delta\Pi^{SS,i}_{QD,j}$ ≡ The boundary at which the sophisticated Stackelberg tariff and the quantity-discount schedule yield identical profits for the manufacturer. The symbol denotes a comparison of SS-Zone $Z^{SS^*}_i$ with QD-Zone $Z^{QD^*}_j$.

*Figure 9.4.* The Sophisticated Stackelberg Tariff *vs.* the Quantity-Discount Schedule When $f = 0.70$

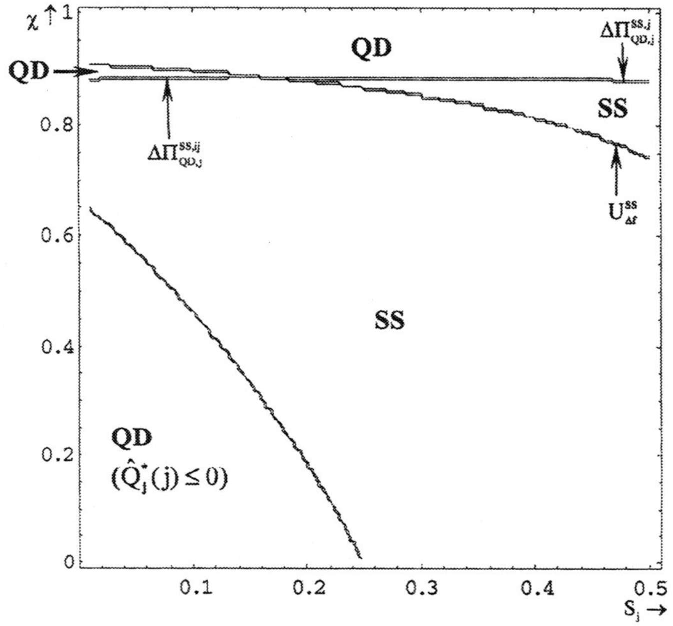


Legend:

**SS** ≡ The manufacturer prefers the sophisticated Stackelberg tariff;

**QD** ≡ The manufacturer prefers the quantity-discount schedule;

$\hat{Q}_j^*(j) < 0$ ≡ The region within which the sophisticated Stackelberg tariff is infeasible;

$U_{\Delta f}^{SS}$ ≡ The boundary that separates Zones $Z_{ij}^{SS}$ and $Z_i^{SS}$; and

$\Delta\Pi_{QD,j}^{SS,j}$ and $\Delta\Pi_{QD,j}^{SS,ij}$ ≡ Boundaries at which the sophisticated Stackelberg tariff and the quantity-discount schedule yield identical profits for the manufacturer. The former (latter) symbol denotes a comparison of SS-Zone $Z_j^{SS^*}$ with QD-Zone $Z_j^{QD^*}$ (SS-Zone $Z_{ij}^{SS^*}$ with QD-Zone $Z_j^{QD^*}$).

*Figure 9.5.* The Sophisticated Stackelberg Tariff *vs.* the Quantity-Discount Schedule When $f = 0.73$

$f$ – **Region 3**: *Both* indifference surfaces of Figure 9.1 are relevant. As $f$ increases from 0.83863 to 1, the point of intersection of the "curved wall" with the $\langle S_j = 0 \rangle$ – axis falls from $\chi = 0.429173$ to $\chi = 0$. Further, its point of intersection with the $\langle S_j = 0.5 \rangle$ – axis declines from $\chi = 0.422207$ to

$\chi = 0$. This indifference curve lies entirely inside SS – Zone $Z_i^{SS^*}$ and QD – Zone $Z_j^{QD^*}$; it is depicted by the lines labeled $\Delta\Pi_{QD,j}^{SS,ij}$ and $\Delta\Pi_{QD,j}^{SS,j}$ in Figure 9.6 and by the line labeled $\Delta\Pi_{QD,j}^{SS,ij} \big| \Delta\Pi_{QD,j}^{SS,j}$ in Figure 9.7.

In addition to the "curved wall" indifference surface shown in Figure 9.2, $f$ – Region 3 contains the cave-like indifference surface of Figure 9.3. A vertical slice of this Region generates a rectangle in $\langle \chi, S_j \rangle$ – space that is divided into four parts. We find QD $\succ$ SS in the part containing the point $(S_j = 0, \chi = 1)$ and in the SS – infeasible region. In the other two parts SS $\succ$ QD. One of these SS – areas is defined by the indifference surface of Figure 9.2; it lies entirely within QD – Zone $Z_j^{QD^*}$. The other SS – area is defined by the indifference surface of Figure 9.3; it lies entirely within QD – Zone $Z_i^{QD^*}$.

To illustrate the second indifference surface, we distinguish two sub-Regions within $f$ – Region 3:

- ***f* – Region 3a**: $0.838630 < f \le 0.886841$
- ***f* – Region 3b**: $0.886841 \le f < 1$

***f* – Region 3a**: The cave-like indifference surface lies entirely within the intersection of SS – Zone $Z_{ij}^{SS^*}$ and QD – Zone $Z_i^{QD^*}$. The indifference curve starts at the $\langle S_j = 0 \rangle$ – axis and moves toward the $\langle S_j = 0.5 \rangle$ – axis as $f$ increases. The curve intersects the $\langle S_j = 0 \rangle$ – axis twice. As $f$ increases, from 0.83863 to 0.886841, one intercept rises from 0.640915 to 0.719824, while the other intercept declines from 0.640915 to 0.31898. Inside the area defined by this surface we find SS $\succ$ QD. This indifference curve is represented by the curve labeled $\Delta\Pi_{QD,i}^{SS,ij}$ in Figure 9.6.

***f* – Region 3b**: The cave-like indifference surface lies in SS – Zones $Z_{ij}^{SS^*}$ and $Z_j^{SS^*}$. As $f$ rises from 0.886841 to 1, the part of the surface that lies in SS – Zone $Z_{ij}^{SS^*}$ intersects the $\langle S_j = 0 \rangle$ – axis at $\chi$ – values that range from 0.31898 to 0. The part of the surface that lies in SS – Zone $Z_i^{SS^*}$ intersects the $\langle S_j = 0 \rangle$ – axis at $\chi = 0.719824$ regardless of the value of $f$. This surface is represented by the line labeled $\Delta\Pi_{QD,i}^{SS,ij} \big| \Delta\Pi_{QD,i}^{SS,i}$ in Figure 9.7.

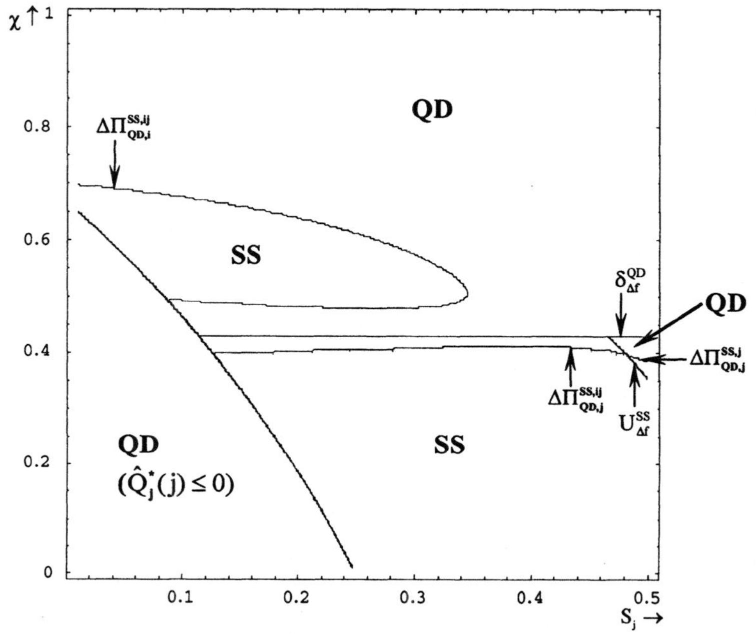


Legend:

**SS** ≡ The manufacturer prefers the sophisticated Stackelberg tariff;

**QD** ≡ The manufacturer prefers the quantity-discount schedule;

$\hat{Q}_j^*(j) < 0$ ≡ The region within which the sophisticated Stackelberg tariff is infeasible;

$U_{\Delta f}^{SS}$ ≡ The boundary that separates Zones $Z_{ij}^{SS}$ and $Z_i^{SS}$;

$\delta_{\Delta f}^{QD}$ ≡ The boundary that separates Zones $Z_j^{QD}$ and $Z_i^{QD}$; and

$\Delta\Pi_{QD,j}^{SS,j}$, $\Delta\Pi_{QD,j}^{SS,ij}$, and $\Delta\Pi_{QD,i}^{SS,ij}$ ≡ Boundaries at which the sophisticated Stackelberg tariff and the quantity-discount schedule yield equal profit for the manufacturer. The first symbol denotes a comparison of SS-Zone $Z_j^{SS^*}$ with QD-Zone $Z_j^{QD^*}$; the second compares SS-Zone $Z_{ij}^{SS^*}$ with QD-Zone $Z_j^{QD^*}$. The third symbol denotes a comparison of SS-Zone $Z_{ij}^{SS^*}$ with QD-Zone $Z_i^{QD^*}$.

*Figure 9.6.* The Sophisticated Stackelberg Tariff *vs.* the Quantity-Discount Schedule When $f = 0.85$

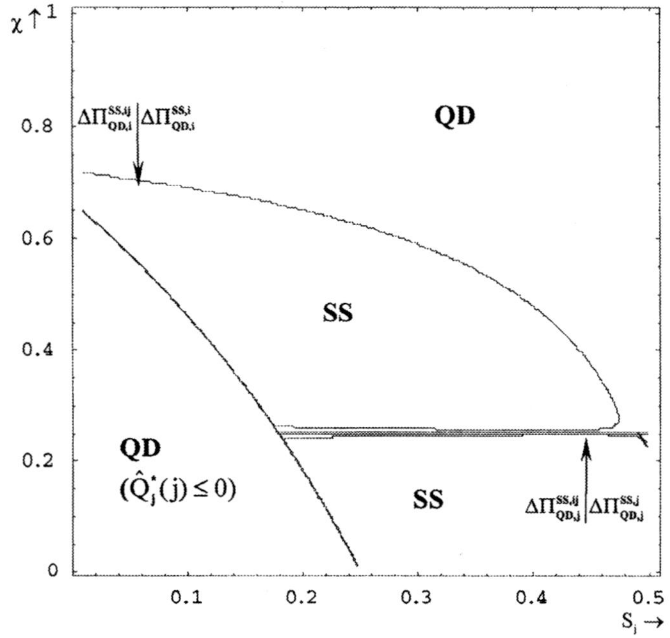


Legend:

**SS** ≡ The manufacturer prefers the sophisticated Stackelberg tariff;

**QD** ≡ The manufacturer prefers the quantity-discount schedule;

$\hat{Q}^*_j(j) < 0$ ≡ The region within which the sophisticated Stackelberg tariff is infeasible;

$U^{SS}_{\Delta f}$ ≡ The boundary that separates Zones $Z^{SS}_{ij}$ and $Z^{SS}_{i}$;

$\delta^{QD}_{\Delta f}$ ≡ The boundary that separates Zones $Z^{QD}_{j}$ and $Z^{QD}_{i}$; and

$\Delta\Pi^{SS,j}_{QD,j}$, $\Delta\Pi^{SS,ij}_{QD,j}$, and $\Delta\Pi^{SS,ij}_{QD,i}$ ≡ The boundaries at which the sophisticated Stackelberg tariff and the quantity-discount schedule yield identical profits for the manufacturer. The first symbol denotes a comparison of SS-Zone $Z^{SS^*}_{j}$ with QD-Zone $Z^{QD^*}_{j}$. The second symbol denotes a comparison of SS-Zone $Z^{SS^*}_{ij}$ with QD-Zone $Z^{QD^*}_{j}$. The third symbol denotes a comparison of SS-Zone $Z^{SS^*}_{ij}$ with QD-Zone $Z^{QD^*}_{i}$.

*Figure 9.7.* The Sophisticated Stackelberg Tariff *vs.* the Quantity-Discount Schedule When $f = 0.90$

# 4 MANUFACTURER PROFITABILITY: THE QUANTITY-DISCOUNT SCHEDULE *vs.* THE MENU OF TWO-PART TARIFFS

In this Section we compare the profit the manufacturer can obtain by utilizing the channel-coordinating, linear quantity-discount schedule (see Chapter 5) *versus* the channel-coordinating menu of tariffs (see Chapter 7). Although both wholesale-price policies maximize channel profit, it is not always possible for the manufacturer to acquire all the profit. As in the preceding section, we must ascertain the relevance of the Menu Zones (which we denote as $\text{MN}-\text{Zones}$) and the $\text{QD}-\text{Zones}$. For both policies there are three Zones. The quantity-discount Zones are defined by equation (9.3.2). The manufacturer's decision rule for the menu is:

$$\begin{array}{llll} Z_j^{\text{Menu}^*}: & (f_i - f_j) < L^{\text{Menu}^*} & \Rightarrow & \Pi_j^{\text{Menu}^*} \\ Z_{ij}^{\text{Menu}^*}: & U^{\text{Menu}^*} \geq (f_i - f_j) \geq L^{\text{Menu}^*} & \Rightarrow & \Pi_{ij}^{\text{Menu}^*} \\ Z_i^{\text{Menu}^*}: & U^{\text{Menu}^*} < (f_i - f_j) & \Rightarrow & \Pi_i^{\text{Menu}^*} \end{array} \tag{9.4.1}$$

Values of $L^{\text{Menu}^*}$ and $U^{\text{Menu}^*}$ are defined at (7.3.4) and (7.3.5) respectively. We have only four comparisons to make because the manufacturer earns all channel profit in Zone $Z_{ij}^{\text{Menu}^*}$ and Zone $Z_{ij}^{\text{QD}^*}$. We now address these comparisons.

## 4.1 An Analytical Comparison of the Menu of Two-Part Tariffs and the Quantity-Discount Schedule

Let $\Delta\Pi_{\text{QD},k}^{\text{MN},k}$ denote the iso-profit curve along which the menu (in $\text{MN}-\text{Zone } Z_k^{\text{MN}^*}$) and the quantity-discount schedule (in $\text{QD}-\text{Zone } Z_k^{\text{QD}^*}$) generate equal profit for the manufacturer. For the case of Zones $Z_j^{\text{Menu}^*}$ and $Z_j^{\text{QD}^*}$ we have:

$$\begin{aligned} \Delta\Pi_{\text{QD},j}^{\text{MN},j} &\equiv \left[\Pi_j^{\text{Menu}*} - \Pi_j^{\text{QD}*}\right] = 0 \\ &= R_{\text{QD}}^{\text{MN}}\left(1-2S_j\right)\chi\begin{pmatrix} 16+8\chi-16\chi^2-8\chi^3+3\chi^4+\chi^5 \\ -4S_j\left(2-\chi^2\right)\left(4+2\chi-\chi^2\right) \end{pmatrix} = 0 \end{aligned} \tag{9.4.2}$$

In this equation we have made use of the space-saving substitution:

$$\begin{aligned} R^{MN}_{QD} &\equiv R_i^* \Big/ \left(2(1+\chi)^2(1-S_j)^2(4-\chi^2)^2\right) \\ &= R^{SS}_{QD} \Big/ (1+\chi)(2-\chi)^2 > 0 \end{aligned} \tag{9.4.3}$$

As in the preceding Section, we have a monotonic multiplier that is common to all the profit comparisons in this Section.

The fixed cost terms in (9.4.2) cancel because the $j^{th}$ retailer is the less profitable under both strategies. That is not true with $\text{MN}-\text{Zone } Z_i^{Menu^*}$ *versus* $\text{QD}-\text{Zone } Z_j^{QD^*}$; the $i^{th}$ retailer is the less profitable in the $\text{MN}-\text{Zone}$ while the $j^{th}$ retailer is the less profitable in the $\text{QD}-\text{Zone}$. We find:

$$\begin{aligned} \Delta\Pi^{MN,i}_{QD,j} &\equiv \left[\Pi_i^{Menu^*} - \Pi_j^{QD^*}\right]\Big|_{f_i=f_j} = 0 \\ &= R^{MN}_{QD}(1-2S_j)\begin{pmatrix} (4+\chi-\chi^2)(16+24\chi-8\chi^3-\chi^4) \\ -4S_j\chi(2-\chi^2)(4+2\chi-\chi^2) \\ -4f(1+\chi)^2(4-\chi^2)^2 \end{pmatrix} = 0 \end{aligned} \tag{9.4.4}$$

To assess this profit relationship we use the fixed-cost definition (9.3.7). Other profit comparisons are made similarly; we detail them in Table 9.2.

*Table 9.2.* Manufacturer Profit Differences by Policy and Zone: The Quantity-Discount Schedule *vs.* The Menu of Two-Part Tariffs

| Label | Definition | Multiplier* | Core Value |
|---|---|---|---|
| $\Delta\Pi^{MN,i}_{QD,i}$ | $\left[\Pi_i^{Menu^*} - \Pi_i^{QD^*}\right]\Big\vert_{f_i=f_j} = 0$ | $R^{MN}_{QD}(1-2S_j)\chi$ | $\begin{pmatrix} (16+8\chi-8\chi^2+\chi^4-\chi^5) \\ -4S_j(2-\chi^2)(4+2\chi-\chi^2) \end{pmatrix}$ |
| $\Delta\Pi^{MN,j}_{QD,i}$ | $\left[\Pi_j^{Menu^*} - \Pi_i^{QD^*}\right]\Big\vert_{f_i=f_j} = 0$ | $R^{MN}_{QD}(1-2S_j)$ | $\begin{pmatrix} -\begin{pmatrix} 64+80\chi-8\chi^2-32\chi^3 \\ -4\chi^4+3\chi^5+\chi^6 \end{pmatrix} \\ -\ 4S_j\chi(2-\chi^2)(4+2\chi-\chi^2) \\ +\ 4f(1+\chi)^2(4-\chi^2)^2 \end{pmatrix}$ |

*Note: $R^{MN}_{QD} \equiv R_i^* \Big/ \left(2(1+\chi)^2(1-S_j)^2(4-\chi^2)^2\right) > 0$

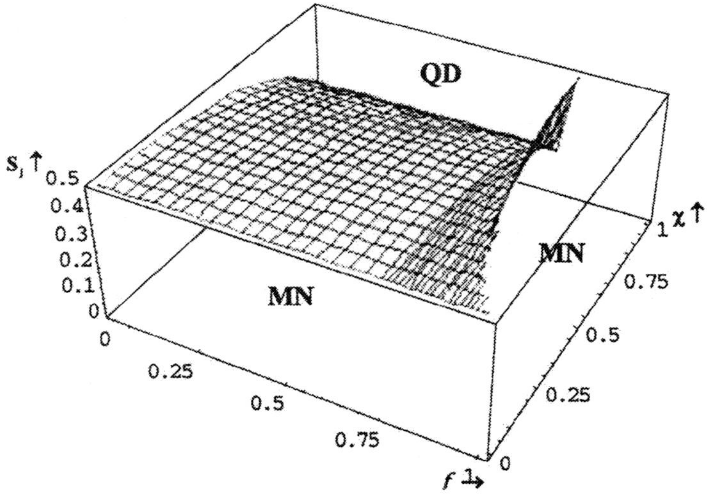


Legend:
**QD** ≡ The manufacturer prefers the quantity-discount schedule; and
**MN** ≡ The manufacturer prefers the channel-coordinating menu of tariffs.

*Figure 9.8a.* Channel Coordination: Comparing the Menu and the Quantity-Discount Schedule

## 4.2 A Graphical Comparison of the Menu of Two-Part Tariffs and the Quantity-Discount Schedule

The graphs in Figure 9.8a above and 9.8b (on the next page) illustrate the set of points at which the manufacturer is indifferent between the channel-coordinating quantity-discount schedule and the channel-coordinating menu of tariffs. (These Figures are two views of the same indifference surface.) Above the indifference surface the manufacturer prefers the channel-coordinating quantity-discount schedule, while below and to the right of this indifference surface the manufacturer prefers the channel-coordinating menu of tariffs.

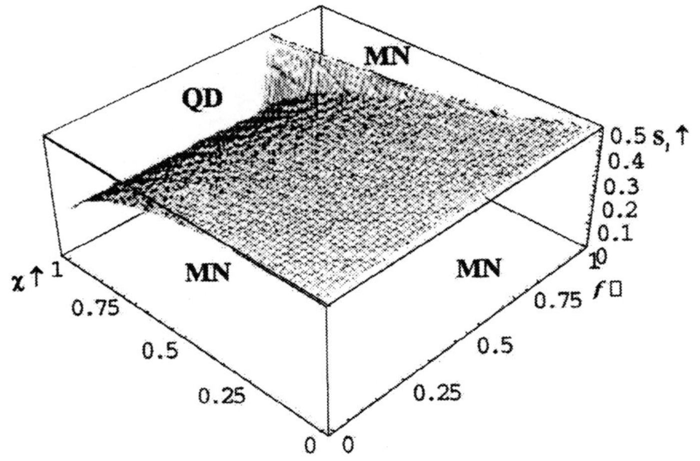


Legend:
**QD** ≡ The manufacturer prefers the quantity-discount schedule; and
**MN** ≡ The manufacturer prefers the channel-coordinating menu of tariffs.

*Figure 9.8b.* Channel Coordination: Comparing the Menu and the Quantity-Discount Schedule (Reverse View)

We divide the unit-half cube of Figures 9.8a and 9.8b into two $f$ – Regions:

- **$f$ – Region 1:** $0 \le f \le ¾$
- **$f$ – Region 2:** $¾ < f \le 1$

We now explicate the manner in which these $f$ – Regions are distinct.

**$f$ – Region 1:** In this $f$ – Region the indifference surface lies in MN – Zone $Z_j^{SS^*}$ and also in QD – Zone $Z_j^{QD^*}$. This surface intersects the $\langle\chi = 0\rangle$ – plane at $S_j = 0$ and the $\langle\chi = 1\rangle$ – plane at $S_j = 0.2$. We see that any vertical slices of Figure 9.8 that corresponds to a single $f$ – value divides $\langle\chi, S_j\rangle$ – space into two parts. As shown in Figure 9.9, QD $\succ$ MN in the part containing the point $(\chi = 1, S_j = 0.5)$, and in the remaining part we find MN $\succ$ QD.

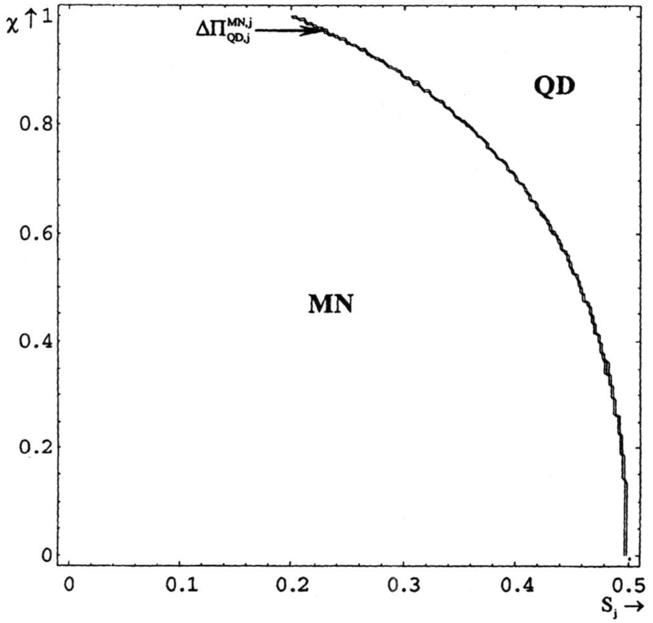


Legend:

**MN** ≡ The manufacturer prefers the menu of two-part tariffs;

**QD** ≡ The manufacturer prefers the quantity-discount schedule; and

$\Delta\Pi^{MN,j}_{QD,j}$ ≡ The boundary at which the menu and the quantity-discount schedule yield identical profits for the manufacturer. The symbol denotes a comparison of MN-Zone $Z_j^{Menu^*}$ with QD-Zone $Z_j^{QD^*}$.

*Figure 9.9.* Channel Coordination: Comparing the Menu and the Quantity-Discount Schedule When $0 < f < 0.75$

**$f$ – Region 2:** Within $f$ – Region 2 the indifference surface lies in both QD – Zones. The location of the surface within QD – Zone $Z_j^{QD^*}$ is identical to the location of the indifference surface in $f$ – Region 1, but in $f$ – Region 2 the surface is truncated by the boundary ($\delta^{QD}_{\Delta f}$) that separates QD – Zones $Z_j^{QD^*}$ and $Z_i^{QD^*}$. Figure 9.10 illustrates this truncation.

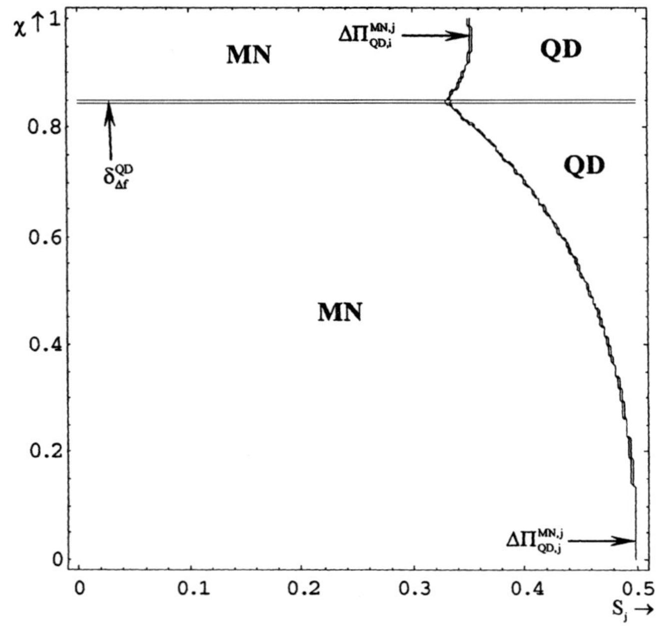


Legend:

**MN** ≡ The manufacturer prefers the menu of two-part tariffs;

**QD** ≡ The manufacturer prefers the quantity-discount schedule;

$\delta^{QD}_{\Delta f}$ ≡ The boundary that separates Zones $Z^{QD^*}_j$ and $Z^{QD^*}_i$; and

$\Delta\Pi^{MN,j}_{QD,j}$, $\Delta\Pi^{MN,j}_{QD,i}$ ≡ The boundaries at which the menu and the quantity-discount schedule yield identical profits for the manufacturer. The symbols denote a comparison of MN-Zone $Z^{Menu^*}_j$ with QD-Zone $Z^{QD^*}_j$ and QD-Zone $Z^{QD^*}_i$.

*Figure 9.10.* Channel Coordination: Comparing the Menu and the Quantity-Discount Schedule When $f = 0.770833$

Within QD – Zone $Z^{QD^*}_j$ (above the line labeled $\delta^{QD}_{\Delta f}$ in Figure 9.10), the indifference surface has one of three possible shapes, depending on the precise $f$ – value:

- ***f* – Region 2a**: $\frac{3}{4} < f \le 0.791615$
- ***f* – Region 2b**: $0.791615 < f \le \frac{19}{24} \cong 0.791667$
- ***f* – Region 2c**: $\frac{19}{24} < f \le 1$

*f* – **Region 2a**: The indifference surface lies in QD – Zone $Z_j^{QD^*}$. As *f* increases from ¾ to 0.791615, the point at which the indifference curve intersects the $\langle \chi = 1 \rangle$ – axis inclines from $S_j = 0.2$ to $S_j = 0.5$. This part of the indifference curve is represented by the line labeled $\Delta\Pi_{QD,i}^{MN,j}$ in Figure 9.10 above, which is drawn for $f = {}^{37}\!/_{48} \cong 0.770833$.

*f* – **Region 2b**: Here QD – Zone $Z_j^{QD^*}$ contains two indifference curves. The first of these curves intersects the $\langle \chi = 1 \rangle$ – axis *and* the $\langle S_j = \frac{1}{2} \rangle$ – axis. As *f* rises from 0.791615 to ${}^{19}\!/_{24}$, this curve collapses to the point $(\chi = 1, S_j = \frac{1}{2})$. The second of these curves *only* intersects the $\langle S_j = \frac{1}{2} \rangle$ – axis, and as *f* rises from 0.791615 to ${}^{19}\!/_{24}$, the point of intersection with the $S_j$ – axis decreases slightly from 0.98184 to 0.97025. Both these curves are illustrated in Figure 9.11 below for an *f* – value of 0.79164.

To clarify the curves corresponding to each surface, Figure 9.11 provides a *close-up* of one portion of the $\langle \chi, S_j \rangle$ – plane at $f = 0.79164$. Specifically, in Figure 9.11, the $\chi$ – value runs from 0.95 to 1 while the $S_j$ – value ranges from 0.49 to 0.5. Notice that the second sector is similar in shape to the QD $\succ$ MN sector shown in Figure 9.10.

*f* – **Region 2c**: Finally, in *f* – Region 2c, the indifference surface in QD – Zone $Z_j^{QD^*}$ forms a triangular-shaped area. As *f* increases from ${}^{19}\!/_{24}$ to 1, the point at which this surface intersects the $\langle S_j = 0.5 \rangle$ – axis decreases from 0.97025 to 0. This part of the indifference surface is represented by $\Delta\Pi_{QD,i}^{MN,j}$ in Figure 9.12 below.

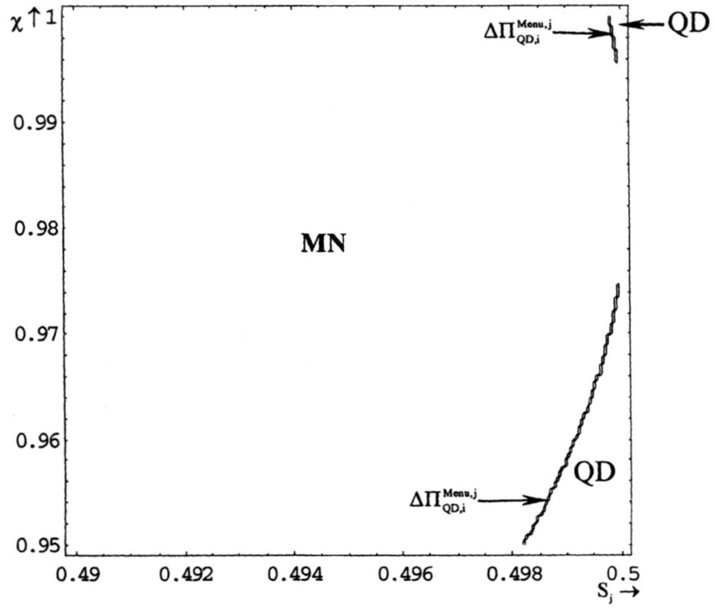


Legend:

**MN** ≡ The manufacturer prefers the menu of two-part tariffs;

**QD** ≡ The manufacturer prefers the quantity-discount schedule; and

$\Delta\Pi^{MN,j}_{QD,i}$ ≡ The boundary at which the menu and the quantity-discount schedule yield identical profits for the manufacturer. The symbols denote a comparison of MN-Zone $Z_j^{Menu^*}$ with QD-Zone $Z_i^{QD^*}$.

*Figure 9.11.* Channel Coordination: Comparing the Menu and the Quantity-Discount Schedule When $f = 0.79164$

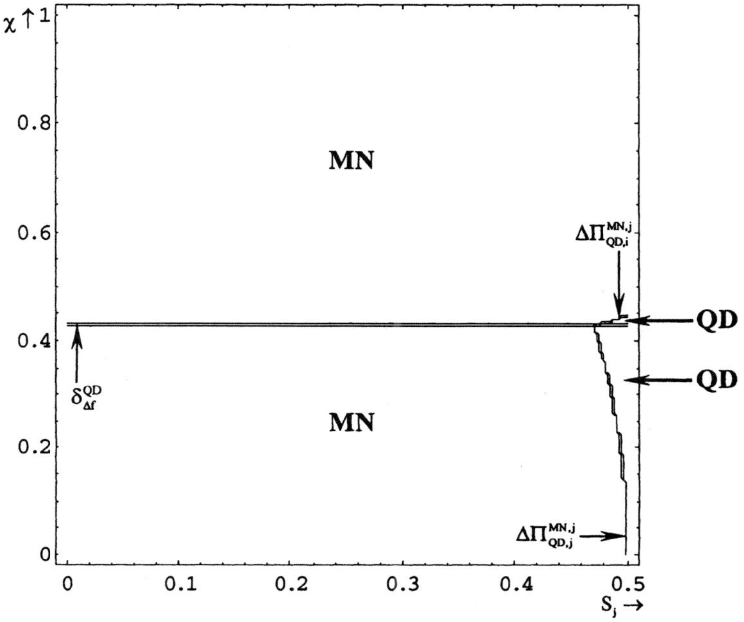


Legend:

**MN** ≡ The manufacturer prefers the menu of two-part tariffs;

**QD** ≡ The manufacturer prefers the quantity-discount schedule;

$\delta_{\Delta f}^{QD}$ ≡ The boundary that separates Zones $Z_j^{QD^*}$ and $Z_i^{QD^*}$; and

$\Delta\Pi_{QD,j}^{MN,j}$, $\Delta\Pi_{QD,i}^{MN,j}$ ≡ The boundaries at which the menu and the quantity-discount schedule yield identical profits for the manufacturer. The symbols denote a comparison of MN-Zone $Z_j^{Menu^*}$ with QD-Zone $Z_j^{QD^*}$ and QD-Zone $Z_i^{QD^*}$.

*Figure 9.12.* Channel Coordination: Comparing the Menu and the Quantity-Discount Schedule When $f = 0.85$

# 5 MANUFACTURER PROFITABILITY: THE SOPHISTICATED STACKELBERG TARIFF *vs.* THE MENU OF TWO-PART TARIFFS

In this Section we compare the profit the manufacturer can obtain by using either the sophisticated Stackelberg two-part tariff (see Chapter 6) or the channel-coordinating menu of tariffs (see Chapter 7). As in earlier Sections, this comparison can be simplified by screening the Zones that require explicit analysis (see expressions (9.3.1) and (9.4.1)). Because the manufacturer obtains all channel profit in Zone $Z_{ij}^{Menu}$, we know that no SS – Zone can earn a profit as great as $\Pi_{ij}^{Menu^*}$ for the manufacturer. Therefore, we have six comparisons to make: two MN – Zones *versus* all three SS – Zones.

## 5.1 An Analytical Comparison of the Sophisticated Stackelberg Tariff and the Menu of Two-Part Tariffs

Let $\Delta\Pi_{MN,k}^{SS,k}$ denote the iso-profit curve along which the sophisticated Stackelberg tariff (in SS – Zone $Z_k^{SS^*}$) and the menu (in MN – Zone $Z_k^{Menu^*}$) yield equal profit for the manufacturer. For Zones $Z_j^{SS^*}$ and $Z_j^{MN^*}$ we have:

$$\Delta\Pi_{Menu,j}^{SS,j} \equiv \left[\Pi_j^{SS^*} - \Pi_j^{Menu^*}\right] = 0$$
$$= R_{MN}^{SS}\left(1-2S_j\right)\begin{pmatrix}(1-\chi)\left(16-32\chi^2-8\chi^3+9\chi^4\right) \\ -2S_j\left(16-16\chi-40\chi^2+16\chi^3+19\chi^4-7\chi^5\right)\end{pmatrix} = 0 \quad (9.5.1)$$

In this equation we have made use of the space-saving substitution:

$$R_{MN}^{SS} \equiv R_{QD}^{MN} > 0 \quad (9.5.2)$$

Because the $j^{th}$ retailer is the less profitable in both cases, the fixed cost term cancels. This is not true with our evaluation of SS – Zone $Z_i^{SS}$ *versus* MN – Zone $Z_j^{Menu}$, because the identity of the less profitable retailer varies:

$$\Delta\Pi_{MN,j}^{SS,i} \equiv \left[\Pi_i^{SS^*} - \Pi_j^{Menu^*}\right]\Big|_{f_i=f_j} = 0$$
$$= R_{MN}^{SS}\left(1-2S_j\right)\begin{pmatrix}\left(80+80\chi-48\chi^2-32\chi^3+17\chi^4-\chi^5\right) \\ -4f\left(1+\chi\right)^2\left(4-\chi^2\right)^2 \\ -2S_j\left(16-16\chi-40\chi^2+16\chi^3+19\chi^4-7\chi^5\right)\end{pmatrix} = 0 \quad (9.5.3)$$

Notice that when $S_j = ½$ these wholesale-price strategies are equally effective in extracting all profit from the (identical) competitors. The remaining cases are calculated similarly. Table 9.3 reports their values.

*Table 9.3.* Manufacturer Profit Differences by Policy and Zone:
The Sophisticated Stackelberg Tariff *vs.* The Menu of Two-Part Tariffs

| Label | Definition | Multiplier* | Core Value |
|---|---|---|---|
| $\Delta\Pi_{Menu,i}^{SS,i}$ | $\left[\Pi_i^{SS*} - \Pi_i^{Menu*}\right]\Big\|_{f_i=f_j} = 0$ | $R_{MN}^{SS}(1-2S_j)$ | $\left((16-16\chi-48\chi^2+8\chi^3-21\chi^4-5\chi^5)-2S_j(16-16\chi-40\chi^2+16\chi^3+19\chi^4-7\chi^5)\right)$ |
| $\Delta\Pi_{Menu,j}^{SS,ij}$ | $\left[\Pi_{ij}^{SS*} - \Pi_j^{Menu*}\right]\Big\|_{f_i=f_j} = 0$ | $\left(\dfrac{R_{MN}^{SS}}{4(1-\chi)}\right)$ | $\begin{pmatrix} +f(1+\chi)^2(4-\chi^2)^2\left[4(4(1-\chi)S_j+3\chi)-(2+\chi)^2 f\right] \\ +16\left\{\begin{pmatrix} 4-8\chi-13\chi^2+5\chi^3 \\ +5\chi^4-2\chi^5 \end{pmatrix} - S_j(1-\chi)\begin{pmatrix} 2(8+4\chi-6\chi^2+\chi^3+3\chi^4-\chi^5) \\ +S_j\chi(16+12\chi-12\chi^2-7\chi^3+3\chi^4) \end{pmatrix}\right\} \end{pmatrix}$ |
| $\Delta\Pi_{Menu,i}^{SS,ij}$ | $\left[\Pi_{ij}^{SS*} - \Pi_i^{Menu*}\right]\Big\|_{f_i=f_j} = 0$ | $(R_{MN}^{SS}/4)$ | $\begin{pmatrix} -f(1+\chi)^2(4-\chi^2)^2\left[4(4(1-\chi)S_j-(4-\chi))+(2+\chi)^2 f\right] \\ -16\left(\begin{pmatrix} 12+16\chi-11\chi^2-15\chi^3 \\ +4\chi^4+4\chi^5-\chi^6 \end{pmatrix} - S_j(1-\chi)\begin{pmatrix} 2(8+20\chi+6\chi^2-11\chi^3-4\chi^4+2\chi^5) \\ +S_j\chi(16+12\chi-12\chi^2-7\chi^3+3\chi^4) \end{pmatrix}\right) \end{pmatrix}$ |
| $\Delta\Pi_{Menu,i}^{SS,j}$ | $\left[\Pi_i^{SS*} - \Pi_j^{Menu*}\right]\Big\|_{f_i=f_j} = 0$ | $R_{MN}^{SS}(1-2S_j)$ | $\begin{pmatrix} -(48+112\chi+32\chi^2-64\chi^3-21\chi^4+13\chi^5) \\ +4f(1+\chi)^2(4-\chi^2)^2-2S_j(16-16\chi-40\chi^2+16\chi^3+19\chi^4-7\chi^5) \end{pmatrix}$ |

*Note: $R_{MN}^{SS} \equiv R_i^* \Big/ \left(2(1+\chi)^2(1-S_j)^2(4-\chi^2)^2\right) > 0$

## 5.2 A Graphical Comparison of the Sophisticated Stackelberg Tariff and the Menu of Two-Part Tariffs

The graphs in Figure 9.13a and 9.13b illustrate the set of points at which the manufacturer is indifferent between the sophisticated Stackelberg tariff and the channel-coordinating menu of two-part tariffs. These points define two distinct *indifference surfaces*, each of which is continuous. We note that although limitations in our graphics software cause these surfaces to *appear* (incorrectly) as if they have jagged edges. Both indifference surfaces are shown in Figure 9.13a, while the perspective in Figure 9.13b reveals only one of the indifference surfaces. (For visual clarity, we have again ignored the SS – infeasible Region in our three-dimensional graphs.)

One surface in Figure 9.13a resembles a "cave" that opens onto the $\langle f=1\rangle$ – plane. The manufacturer prefers the sophisticated Stackelberg tariff inside the cave; outside the cave (and to the right of the indifference surface in Figure 9.13b) the manufacturer prefers the channel-coordinating menu.

The indifference surface that appears in both Figures resembles a vertical slice of a funnel, with the narrow opening intersecting the $\langle f=0\rangle$ – plane and the large mouth intersecting the $\langle f=1\rangle$ – plane. To the left (right) of this indifference surface, the manufacturer prefers the sophisticated Stackelberg tariff (the menu of tariffs).

The two indifference surfaces never intersect; a fact that may not be apparent from the graphs in Figures 9.13. For that reason, we now consider a series of two-dimensional slices of the graphs that collectively depict the following three Regions:

- $f$ – **Region 1**: $0 \leq f \leq \frac{2}{3}$
- $f$ – **Region 2**: $\frac{2}{3} < 0.916752$
- $f$ – **Region 3**: $0.916752 < f \leq 1$

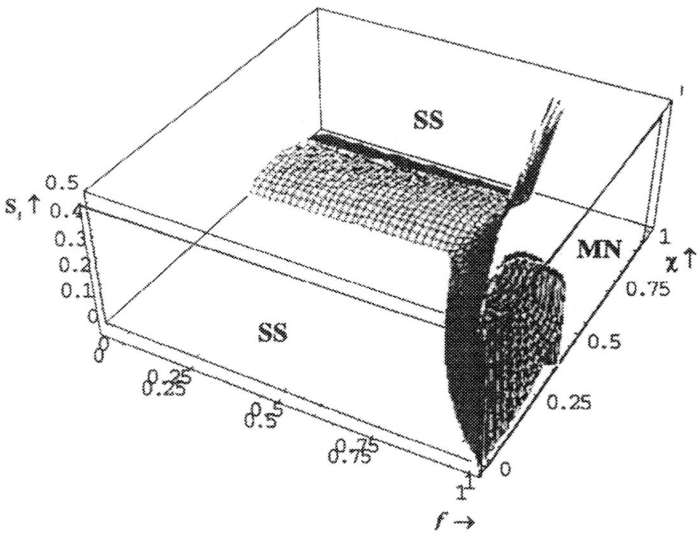


*Figures 9.13a.* The Sophisticated Stackelberg Tariff *vs.* the Menu of Two-Part Tariffs (A Two Indifference Surfaces View)

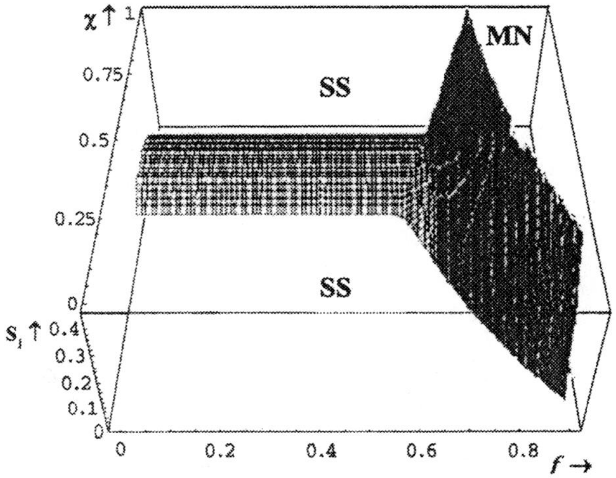


Legend:

SS ≡ The manufacturer prefers the sophisticated Stackelberg tariff

MN ≡ The manufacturer prefers the menu of two-part tariffs

*Figures 9.13b.* The Sophisticated Stackelberg Tariff *vs.* the Menu of Two-Part Tariffs (A One Indifference Surface View)

In $f$ – Region 1 the indifference surface lies entirely within the intersection of SS – Zone $Z_j^{SS^*}$ and MN – Zone $Z_j^{MN^*}$. In $f$ – Region 2, the indifference surface lies entirely within MN – Zone $Z_j^{MN^*}$, but spans two SS – Zones ($Z_{ij}^{SS^*}$ and $Z_i^{SS^*}$). The third $f$ – Region contains *two* indifference surfaces: one lies entirely in MN – Zone $Z_j^{MN^*}$, and the second lies entirely inside MN – Zone $Z_j^{MN^*}$.

The sector in $f$ – Region 1within which the manufacturer prefers the menu of tariffs resembles a "tunnel." We distinguish two sub-Regions:

- $f$ **– Region 1a**: $0 \le f \le 0.573753$
- $f$ **– Region 1b**: $0.573753 < f \le 2/3$

$f$ **– Region 1a**: In this sub-Region the indifference surface intersects the $\langle S_j = 0 \rangle$ – plane at $\chi = 1$ and at $\chi = 0.694031$. Inside the SS – infeasible Region *and* inside the indifference-surface "tunnel" the manufacturer strictly prefers the menu to the sophisticated Stackelberg tariff. We observe that $SS \succ MN$ in the rest of this sub-Region. This indifference surface is represented by the parabolic curve labeled $\Delta\Pi_{MN,j}^{SS,j}$ in Figure 9.14.

$f$ **– Region 1b**: A side of the tunnel intersects the $\langle S_j = 0 \rangle$ – plane at its $\langle \chi = 1 \rangle$ – edge, while the other side of the tunnel is a function of $f$; its intersection with the $\langle S_j = 0 \rangle$ – plane decreases from $\chi = 0.694031$ to $\chi = 0.565766$ as $f$ rises from 0.573753 to $2/3$. The height and width of the tunnel increase with $f$ within $f$ – Region 1b. To conserve space we do not present a separate Figure to illustrate this sub-Region.

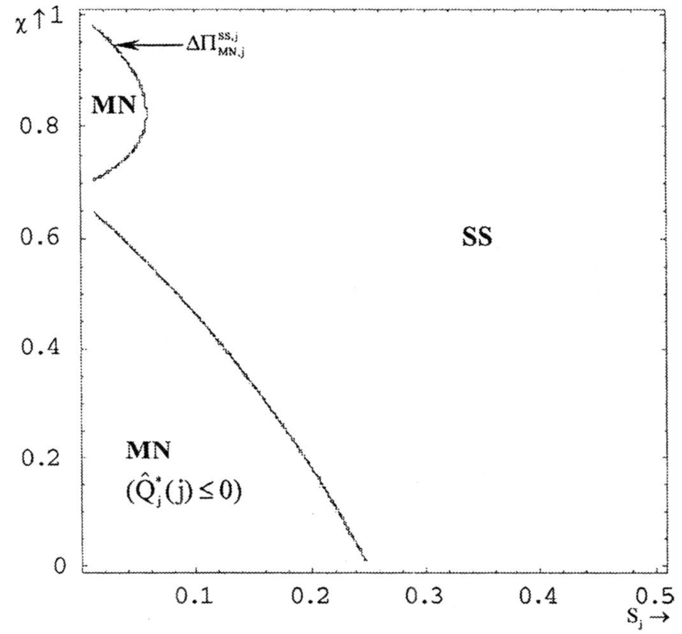


Legend:

**MN** ≡ The manufacturer prefers the menu of two-part tariffs;

**SS** ≡ The manufacturer prefers the sophisticated Stackelberg tariff;

$\hat{Q}^*_j(j) < 0$ ≡ The region within which the sophisticated Stackelberg tariff is infeasible; and

$\Delta\Pi^{SS,j}_{MN,j}$ ≡ The boundary at which the menu and the sophisticated Stackelberg tariff yield identical profits for the manufacturer. The symbol denotes a comparison of MN-Zone $Z_j^{Menu^*}$ with SS-Zone $Z_j^{SS^*}$.

*Figure 9.14*. The Sophisticated Stackelberg Tariff *vs*. the Menu of Two-Part Tariffs When $0 \leq f \leq 0.573753$

$f$ **– Region 2:** Any vertical slice of Figures 9.13 that corresponds to a single value of $f$ generates an area in $\langle \chi, S_j \rangle$ – space that is divided into three parts. The manufacturer prefers the channel-coordinating menu of tariffs in the SS – infeasible Region *and* in the part containing the point $(\chi = 1, S_j = 0)$, while in the remaining part $SS \succ MN$. To provide greater detail, we distinguish two sub-Regions:

- $f$ **– Region 2a:** $\frac{2}{3} < f \leq \frac{3}{4}$
- $f$ **– Region 2b:** $\frac{3}{4} < f \leq 0.916752$

$f$ **– Region 2a:** As $f$ rises from $\frac{2}{3}$ to $\frac{3}{4}$, the intersection of the indifference surface and the $\langle S_j = 0 \rangle$ – plane falls from $\chi = 0.565766$ to $\chi = 0.339338$ and its intersection with the $\langle \chi = 1 \rangle$ – plane rises from 0 to 0.5. This surface is represented by the curves labeled $\Delta\Pi_{MN,j}^{SS,ij}$ and $\Delta\Pi_{MN,j}^{SS,i}$ in Figure 9.15.

$f$ **– Region 2b:** As $f$ increases from $\frac{3}{4}$ to 0.916752 in this sub-Region, the indifference surface's intersection with the $\langle S_j = 0 \rangle$ – plane declines from $\chi = 0.339338$ to $\chi = 0.090907$ and the point at which it intersects the $\langle S_j = 0.5 \rangle$ – plane decreases from $\chi = 1$ to $\chi = 0.190834$. The points of indifference are represented by the curves labeled $\Delta\Pi_{MN,j}^{SS,ij}$ and $\Delta\Pi_{MN,j}^{SS,i}$ in Figure 9.16 below.

$f$ **– Region 3:** Here two indifference surfaces determine the choice of the sophisticated Stackelberg tariff versus the menu of tariffs. As $f$ rises from 0.916752 to 1, the indifference surface's intersection with the $\langle S_j = 0 \rangle$ – plane falls from $\chi = 0.090907$ to $\chi = 0$ and its intersection with the $\langle S_j = 0.5 \rangle$ – plane declines to $\chi = 0$ from $\chi = 0.190834$. This indifference surface is represented by the curve labeled $\Delta\Pi_{MN,j}^{SS,ij} | \Delta\Pi_{MN,j}^{SS,i}$ in Figure 9.17 below.

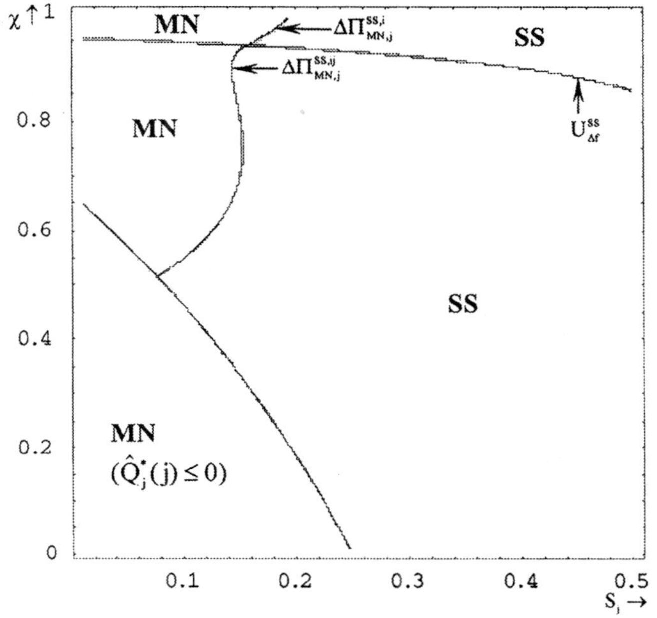


Legend:

**MN** ≡ The manufacturer prefers the menu of two-part tariffs;

**SS** ≡ The manufacturer prefers the sophisticated Stackelberg tariff;

$U^{ss}_{\Delta f}$ ≡ The boundary that separates Zones $Z_i^{ss^*}$ and $Z_{ij}^{ss^*}$; and

$\hat{Q}_j^*(j) < 0$ ≡ The region within which the sophisticated Stackelberg tariff is infeasible;

$\Delta\Pi^{SS,i}_{MN,j}, \Pi^{SS,ij}_{MN,j}$ ≡ The boundaries at which the menu and the sophisticated Stackelberg tariff yield identical profits for the manufacturer. The symbols denote a comparison of MN-Zone $Z_j^{Menu^*}$ with SS-Zone $Z_i^{ss^*}$ and SS-Zone $Z_{ij}^{ss^*}$.

*Figure 9.15.* The Sophisticated Stackelberg Tariff *vs.* the Menu of Two-Part Tariffs When $f = 0.70$

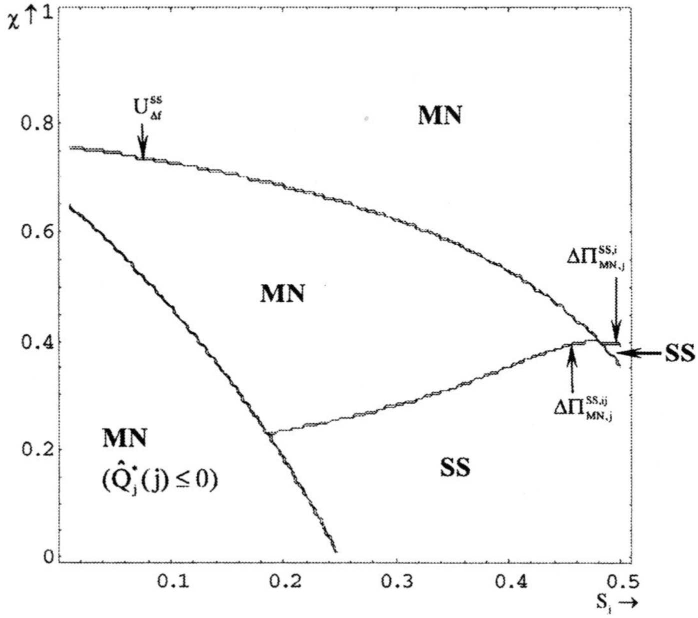


Legend:

**MN** ≡ The manufacturer prefers the menu of two-part tariffs;

**SS** ≡ The manufacturer prefers the sophisticated Stackelberg tariff;

$U^{ss}_{\Delta f}$ ≡ The boundary that separates Zones $Z^{ss^*}_i$ and $Z^{ss^*}_{ij}$; and

$\hat{Q}^*_j(j) < 0$ ≡ The region within which the sophisticated Stackelberg tariff is infeasible;

$\Delta\Pi^{ss,i}_{MN,j}, \Delta\Pi^{ss,ij}_{MN,j}$ ≡ The boundaries at which the menu and the sophisticated Stackelberg tariff yield identical profits for the manufacturer. The symbols denote a comparison of MN-Zone $Z^{Menu^*}_j$ with SS-Zone $Z^{ss^*}_i$ and SS-Zone $Z^{ss^*}_{ij}$.

*Figure 9.16.* The Sophisticated Stackelberg Tariff *vs.* the Menu of Two-Part Tariffs When $f = 0.85$

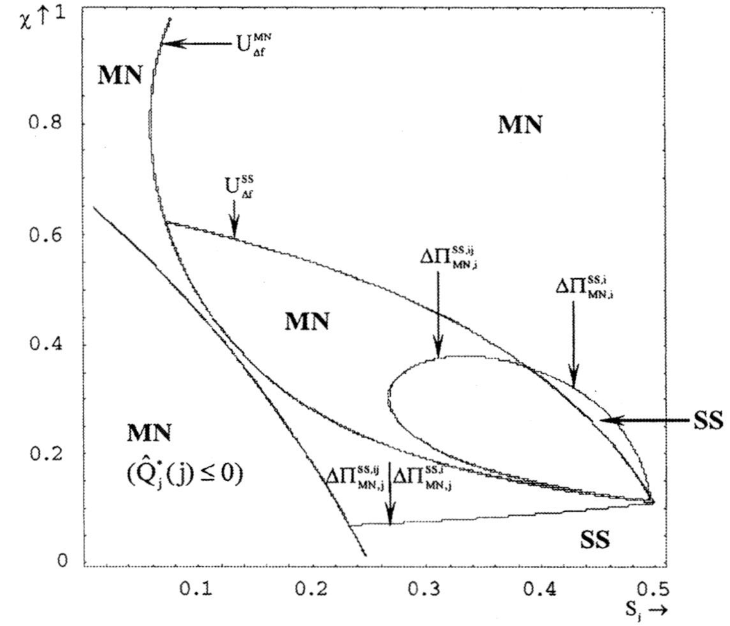


Legend:

**MN** ≡ The manufacturer prefers the menu of two-part tariffs;

**SS** ≡ The manufacturer prefers the sophisticated Stackelberg tariff;

$\hat{Q}^*_j(j) < 0$ ≡ The region within which the sophisticated Stackelberg tariff is infeasible;

$U^{SS}_{\Delta f}$ ≡ The boundary that separates Zones $Z^{SS^*}_i$ and $Z^{SS^*}_{ij}$;

$U^{MN}_{\Delta f}$ ≡ The boundary that separates Zones $Z^{Menu^*}_i$ and $Z^{Menu^*}_{ij}$; and

$\Delta\Pi^{SS,i}_{MN,i}, \Pi^{SS,ij}_{MN,i}, \Delta\Pi^{SS,ij}_{MN,j} \big| \Delta\Pi^{SS,i}_{MN,j}$ ≡ The boundaries at which the menu and the sophisticated Stackelberg tariff yield identical profits for the manufacturer. The symbols denote a comparison of MN-Zone $Z^{Menu^*}_i$ with SS-Zone $Z^{SS^*}_i$ and SS-Zone $Z^{SS^*}_{ij}$ and also MN-Zone $Z^{Menu^*}_j$ with SS-Zone $Z^{SS^*}_i$ and SS-Zone $Z^{SS^*}_{ij}$.

*Figure 9.17.* The Sophisticated Stackelberg Tariff *vs.* the Menu of Two-Part Tariffs When $f = 0.95$

# 6 COMMENTARY ON COORDINATION *vs.* MAXIMIZATION

Our final task is to determine the manufacturer's optimal wholesale-price strategy at *every* point in the unit half-cube. To do so we integrate our pair-wise comparisons from Sections 3, 4, and 5. Although we could present highly specific results, such a detailed approach would add little to what is already known from the preceding Sections. Thus, we develop a visual approach with the confidence that it will lead to a superior grasp of how the manufacturer's optimal strategy is shaped by the parametric values of cost and demand that are captured by the three dimensions of our unit half-cube. We present our results as a series of horizontal slices of the unit half-cube at various levels of the retailers' fixed-cost ratio ($f$). Our approach will reveal an intuitively appealing portrait of the manufacturer's optimal wholesale-price strategy. Because the literature is replete with models that assume *no* fixed costs, we begin our analysis at $f = 0$; then we examine the effect of increases in $f$. We also comment on four Channel Myths.

## 6.1 The Manufacturer-Optimal Wholesale-Price Strategy: Commentary on Zero Fixed Costs at Retail

The special case of zero fixed costs is presented in Figure 9.18. This is the bottom planar surface of our unit half-cube. The manufacturer prefers the channel-coordinating menu of two-part tariffs in two places: (i) inside the $SS -$infeasible Region and (ii) inside the small parabolic sector in the upper, left-hand portion of the unit half-square. Elsewhere the manufacturer generates higher profit for itself by utilizing the sophisticated Stackelberg two-part tariff. We conclude that, under the simple, realistic assumption of comparable treatment of competing, non-identical retailers, channel coordination is rarely in the manufacturer's interest. Indeed, the interests of the manufacturer and the channel coincide only under the extreme circumstance of high competitive intensity ($\chi > 0.69$) combined with very unequal market shares ($S_j < 0.07$).

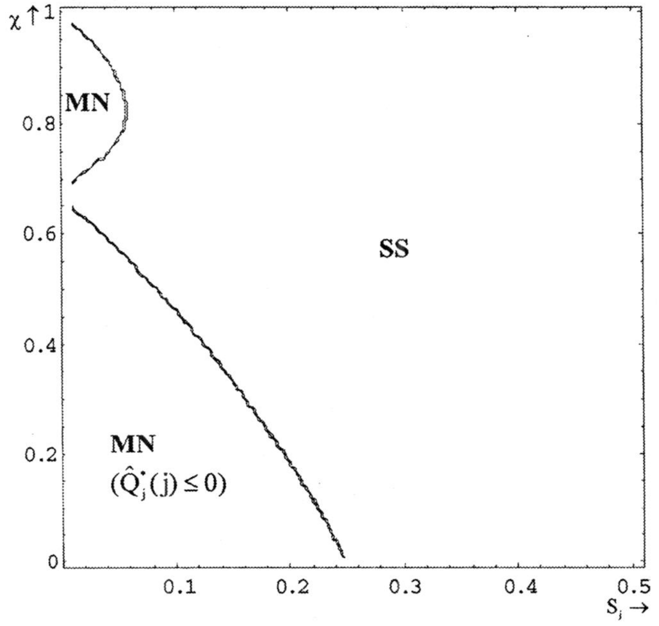


Legend:

**MN** ≡ The manufacturer prefers the menu of two-part tariffs;

**SS** ≡ The manufacturer prefers the sophisticated Stackelberg tariff; and

$\hat{Q}_j^*(j) < 0$ ≡ The region within which the sophisticated Stackelberg tariff is infeasible.

*Figure 9.18.* The Manufacturer's Optimal Wholesale-Price Strategy When $0 \leq f \leq 0.573753$

Results obtained in the absence of fixed costs generalize to any level of the retailers' fixed-cost ratio up to $f = 0.573753$. Above this $f$ – level the parabolic column discussed in Section 5 expands as $f$ rises. As we know from the earlier Sections of this Chapter, at higher $f$ – levels there are additional complexities associated with each of the three wholesale-price policies. Thus, to see the effect of further increases in $f$, we present a series of Figures taken at intervals of 0.05 from $f = 0.60$ to $f = 0.95$. These Figures are reminiscent of Section 5 (the menu *versus* the sophisticated Stackelberg tariff) because the quantity-discount schedule only comes into play above $f = 0.70$. We defer our discussion of any of these Figures until the complete set has been presented.

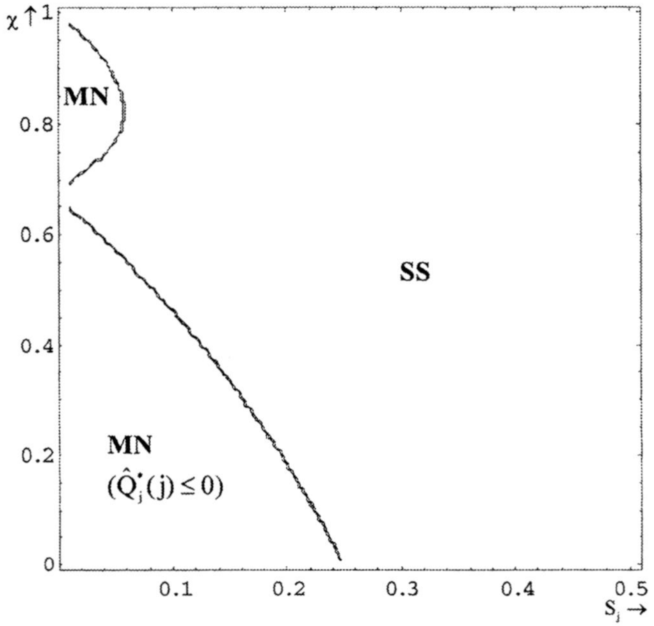


Legend:

**MN** ≡ The manufacturer prefers the menu of two-part tariffs;

**SS** ≡ The manufacturer prefers the sophisticated Stackelberg tariff; and

$\hat{Q}_j^*(j) < 0$ ≡ The region within which the sophisticated Stackelberg tariff is infeasible.

*Figure 9.19.* The Manufacturer's Optimal Wholesale-Price Strategy When $f = 0.60$

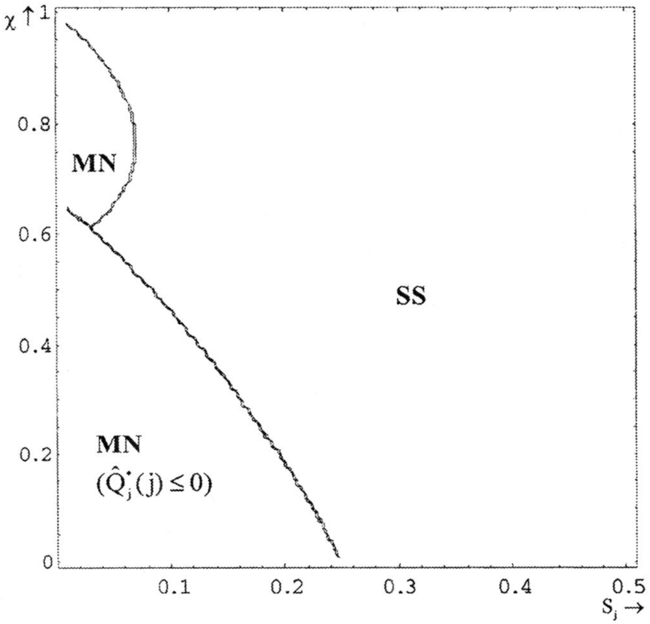


Legend:

**MN** ≡ The manufacturer prefers the menu of two-part tariffs;

**SS** ≡ The manufacturer prefers the sophisticated Stackelberg tariff; and

$\hat{Q}_j^*(j) < 0$ ≡ The region within which the sophisticated Stackelberg tariff is infeasible.

*Figure 9.20.* The Manufacturer's Optimal Wholesale-Price Strategy When $f = 0.65$

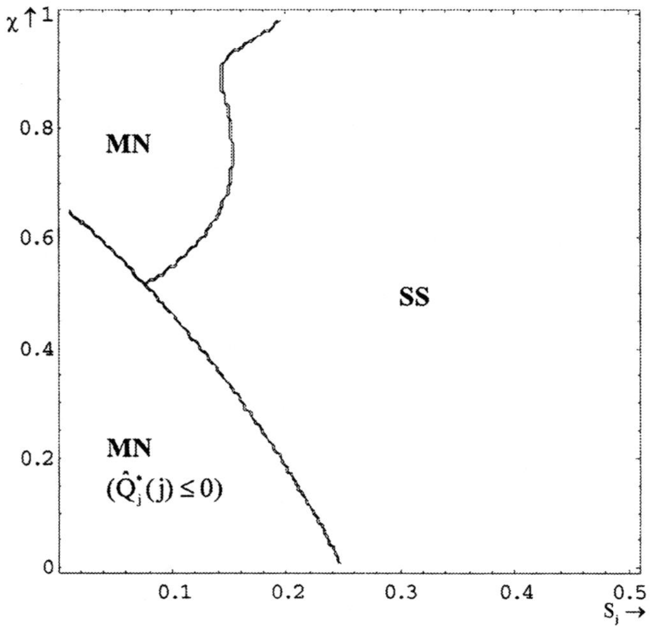


Legend:

**MN** ≡ The manufacturer prefers the menu of two-part tariffs;

**SS** ≡ The manufacturer prefers the sophisticated Stackelberg tariff; and

$\hat{Q}_j^*(j) < 0$ ≡ The region within which the sophisticated Stackelberg tariff is infeasible.

*Figure 9.21.* The Manufacturer's Optimal Wholesale-Price Strategy When $f = 0.70$

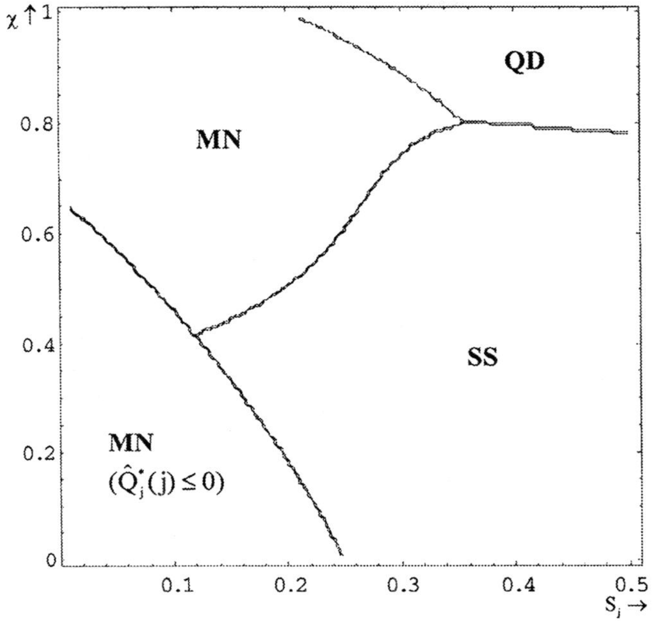


Legend:

**MN** ≡ The manufacturer prefers the menu of two-part tariffs;

**QD** ≡ The manufacturer prefers the quantity-discount schedule;

**SS** ≡ The manufacturer prefers the sophisticated Stackelberg tariff; and

$\hat{Q}_j^*(j) < 0$ ≡ The region within which the sophisticated Stackelberg tariff is infeasible.

*Figure 9.22.* The Manufacturer's Optimal Wholesale-Price Strategy When $f = 0.75$

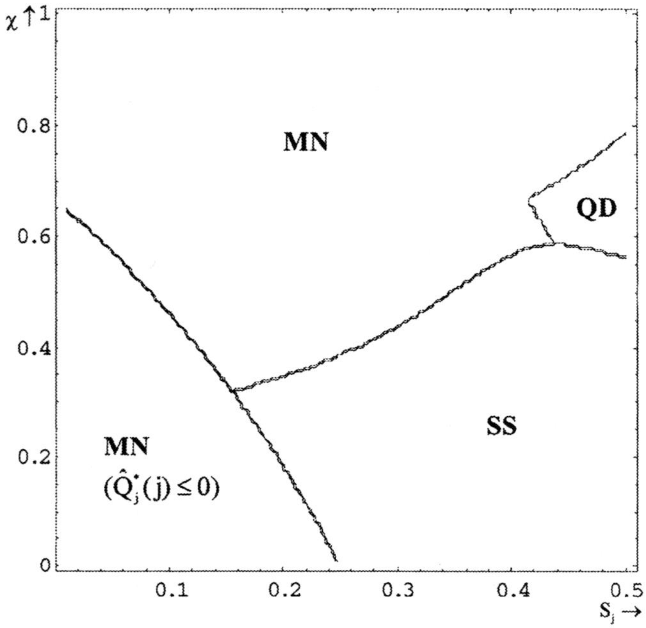


Legend:

**MN** ≡ The manufacturer prefers the menu of two-part tariffs;

**QD** ≡ The manufacturer prefers the quantity-discount schedule;

**SS** ≡ The manufacturer prefers the sophisticated Stackelberg tariff; and

$\hat{Q}_j^*(j) < 0$ ≡ The region within which the sophisticated Stackelberg tariff is infeasible.

*Figure 9.23.* The Manufacturer's Optimal Wholesale-Price Strategy When $f = 0.80$

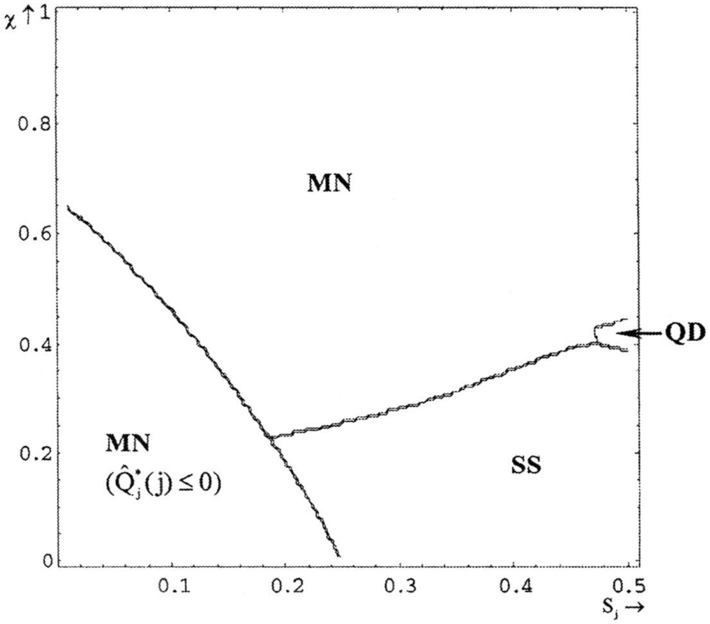


Legend:

**MN** ≡ The manufacturer prefers the menu of two-part tariffs;

**QD** ≡ The manufacturer prefers the quantity-discount schedule;

**SS** ≡ The manufacturer prefers the sophisticated Stackelberg tariff; and

$\hat{Q}_j^*(j) < 0$ ≡ The region within which the sophisticated Stackelberg tariff is infeasible.

*Figure 9.24.* The Manufacturer's Optimal Wholesale-Price Strategy When $f = 0.85$

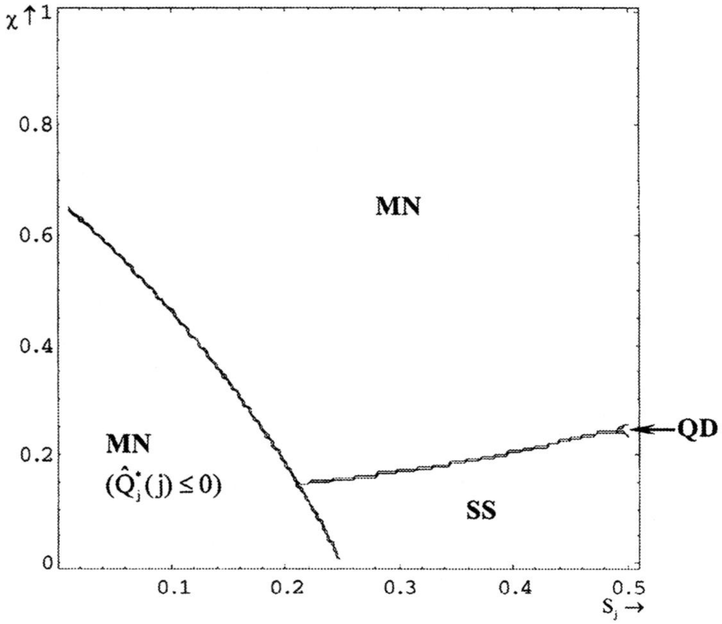


Legend:

**MN** ≡ The manufacturer prefers the menu of two-part tariffs;

**QD** ≡ The manufacturer prefers the quantity-discount schedule;

**SS** ≡ The manufacturer prefers the sophisticated Stackelberg tariff; and

$\hat{Q}_j^*(j) < 0$ ≡ The region within which the sophisticated Stackelberg tariff is infeasible.

*Figure 9.25.* The Manufacturer's Optimal Wholesale-Price Strategy When $f = 0.90$

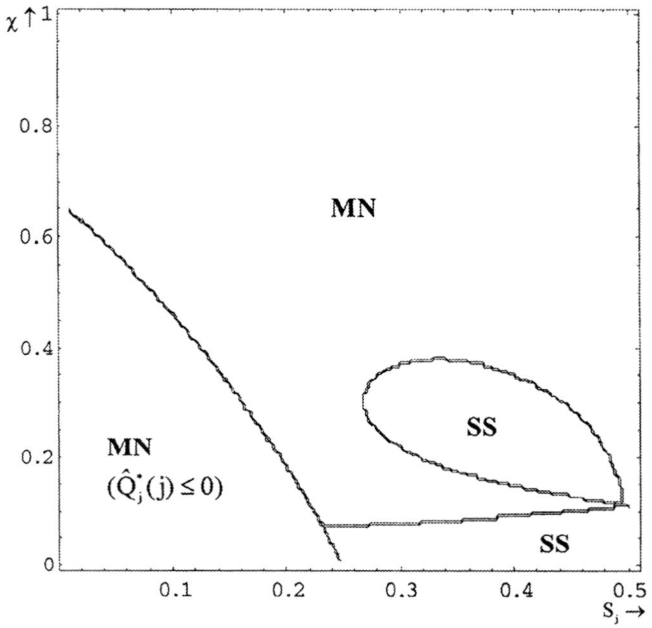


Legend:

**MN** ≡ The manufacturer prefers the menu of two-part tariffs;

**QD** ≡ The manufacturer prefers the quantity-discount schedule;

**SS** ≡ The manufacturer prefers the sophisticated Stackelberg tariff; and

$\hat{Q}^*_j(j) < 0$ ≡ The region within which the sophisticated Stackelberg tariff is infeasible.

*Figure 9.26.* The Manufacturer's Optimal Wholesale-Price Strategy When $f = 0.95$

## 6.2 The Manufacturer-Optimal Wholesale-Price Strategy: Commentary on Positive Fixed Costs at Retail

We derive three fundamental messages from a collective examination of the nine Figures for which $f > 0$. First, the menu's initial advantage (say at $.573753 < f < .694444$) is in the portion of the unit half-cube for which the intensity of competition is high, but the magnitude of competition is low. In this sector of the unit half-cube there is little problem with "defection."[7] The menu becomes progressively more attractive as fixed costs rise because defection becomes less likely. Ultimately, as $f \to 1$, the menu comes to dominate the manufacturer's wholesale-price strategy.

The second major message of this graphical series is that the quantity-discount schedule (the "$QD-$schedule") plays a boundary role. Although it appears to be of substantial consequence in the vicinity of $f = 3/4$, the reality is that almost all the area in the sectors labeled "QD" in Figures 9.22-9.25 would be assigned to the menu if the quantity-discount schedule were not available. And, at those parametric values for which the $QD-$schedule is optimal, it only *fractionally* increases the manufacturer's profit relative to either the menu or to the sophisticated Stackelberg tariff. Even this fractional increase is limited in scope, for the $QD-$schedule benefits the manufacturer only when the competitors are of roughly equal size. At $f = 3/4$ this is a large area at a high intensity of competition, but by $f = 4/5$ it is quite clear that the $QD-$schedule's boundary-spanning role is squeezed into a progressively thinner range of ever lower $\chi-$values as $f$ rises. Given the attention that the quantity-discount schedule has received in the literature, its limited value is astonishing.

The third important message is that the channel non-coordinating, sophisticated Stackelberg tariff (the "$SS-$tariff") has a tremendous appeal for the manufacturer whenever the retailers' fixed costs are below roughly 70 percent of their maximum permissible value. Although the $SS-$tariff fades in importance above $f = 0.70$, it still remains the dominant wholesale-price policy for the manufacturer at low levels of competitive intensity. Since competing retailers who are in different lines of trade are likely to be weak competitors, we infer that there is apt to be little reason for manufacturers to try to coordinate *across* lines of trade.

In summary, any of the three wholesale-price policies may be optimal for the manufacturer, depending on the specific parametric values of competitive intensity, the magnitude of competition, and the retailers' fixed-cost ratio. The overall message is that channel coordination is increasingly in the manufacturer's interest as the retailers' fixed-cost ratio ($f$) rises. Of course, total channel profit declines as $f$ increases. From the manufacturer's perspective, the optimality of channel coordination seems to be inversely related to total channel profit.

## 6.3 Commentary on Four Channel Myths

There are two special cases whose study has dominated the analytical, marketing science literature on distribution channels. They are the identical-competitors model and the bilateral-monopoly model. They are incorporated in our general model, as $S_j = ½$ and $\langle \chi = 0, S_j = 0 \rangle$ respectively. In terms of the unit half-cube, these are the entire right face ($S_j = ½$) and the vertical edge that joins the left face of the cube ($S_j = 0$) to its front face ($\chi = 0$). In terms of the unit-square, we reproduce Figure 1.1 from Chapter 1 as Figure 9.27. The unit half-square that we have focused on in Chapters 5-9 consists of the left half of this Figure. (Due to the detailed nature of the graphical material that we have presented, we "stretched" the unit half-square into what visually appears to be a full square.)

All three of our wholesale-price policies are functionally equivalent in these special cases; that is, all of them coordinate the channel, and they all enable the manufacturer to obtain the totality of channel profit. Thus, we again see that the *Bilateral-Monopoly Meta-Myth* (the belief that a bilateral-monopoly model generalizes to multiple competitors) and the *Identical-Competitors Meta-Myth* (the belief that an identical-competitor model generalizes to non-identical competitors) combine to dissuade researchers from analyzing the full complexity of the manufacturer's optimal wholesale-price strategy in the presence of competition. Conclusions drawn from analyses of the identical-competitors line in Figure 9.27 are very similar (and are often identical) to those deduced from the bilateral-monopoly point. Points—parametric values—located elsewhere in the unit-square are unlike these special-case points. Phrased differently, although most results of the bilateral-monopoly model generalize to an identical-competitors model, results of the identical-competitors model do *not* generalize to a model of multiple, non-identical competitors.

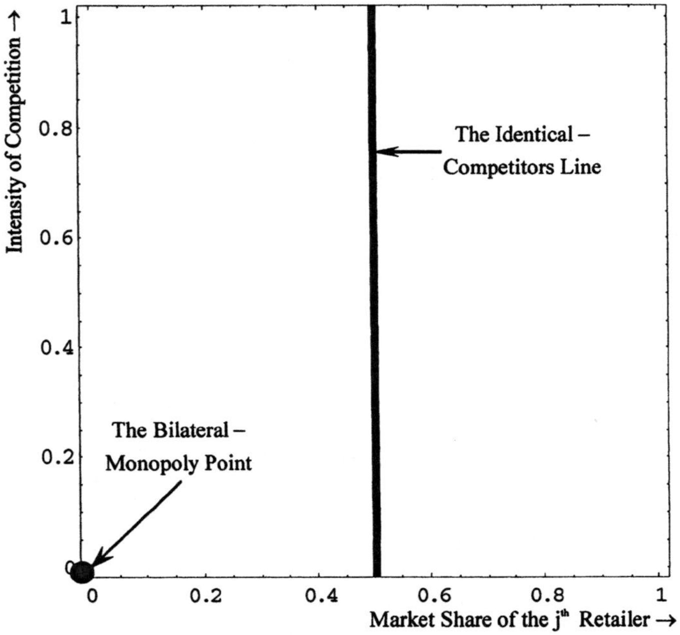


*Figure 9.27.* The Bilateral-Monopoly Model and the Identical-Competitors Model: Subsets of Our Model

We have seen in this Chapter, as we have throughout this monograph, that a belief that the manufacturer-optimal wholesale-price is independent of fixed costs at retail (the *Fixed-Cost Modeling Myth*) encourages marketing scientists to examine only the bottom planar surface of the unit half-cube; this is the simplest (and least interesting) slice of the multi-dimensional reality over which the manufacturer optimizes. Finally, our Empirical-Evidence Criterion has driven us to model the manufacturer's dealings with its channel members as being characterized by comparable treatment; this immediately leads to the realization that channel profit often *cannot* be allocated between channel members in a manner that makes them all better off. The belief that channel profit-maximization is Pareto optimal is clearly a myth that we term the *Channel-Coordination Strategic Myth.* It seems that an acceptance of this Myth has contributed to the scarcity of analyses aimed at endogenously ascertaining how a manufacturer *should* set its wholesale-price strategy.

## 6.4 Summary Commentary

In this Chapter we used graphical analysis to illustrate our answer to two nominally simple questions: "Should the manufacturer coordinate the channel, or should it not coordinate the channel? What wholesale-price strategy should a manufacturer use to maximize its profit when it sells to a pair of comparably-treated, non-identical retailers?" The bulk of the academic literature argues for coordination on the grounds that all channel members can benefit if they share the largest possible total profit. Implicit in this conventional wisdom is the implicit assumption that there are no limits to the distribution of channel profit. In fact, there is a tight restriction that is imposed by comparable treatment, for retention of both retailers as channel members limits the profit that the manufacturer can extract from either retailer in a coordinated channel. *Non*-coordination does not relax the channel participation constraints, but it does permit a per-unit wholesale price that shifts net revenue between retailers in a manner that benefits the manufacturer even though it harms the channel.

We have also seen that, in the absence of substantial fixed costs at retail, channel coordination is optimal for the manufacturer only if there are extreme differences in the retailers' market shares and/or a high intensity of competition (see Figures 9.18-9.21). But at ever *higher* fixed costs, coordination becomes more attractive at an ever *lower* competitive intensity (see Figures 9.22-9.26). There are two fundamental reasons for this relationship between the manufacturer-optimality of coordination, the intensity of competition, and the retailers' fixed-cost ratio. To understand this relationship, we begin with a reminder that the k[th] retailer's fixed-cost ratio is defined as its fixed cost ($f_k$) relative to its net revenue when the channel is coordinated ($R_k^*$): $\mathit{f}_k \equiv f_k / R_k^*$. (1) Quite clearly $\mathit{f}_k$ can range from zero to one in a coordinated channel. Because an uncoordinated channel generates less channel net revenue than does a coordinated channel, the uncoordinated channel cannot sustain $\mathit{f}_k = 1$ for both retailers without violating one retailer's participation constraint. Thus the higher is $\mathit{f}$, the lower is the attractiveness of non-coordination, *ceteris paribus*. (2) As partial compensation for this, as competitive intensity declines, total profit in an uncoordinated channel rises more rapidly than it does in a coordinated channel. From these two points it follows that coordination is more valuable to the manufacturer at high levels of competitive intensity and at high levels of fixed cost; non-coordination is the manufacturer's optimal strategy at low fixed-cost ratios and low levels of competitive intensity.

Although mathematical logic has aided our discoveries on the workings of distribution channels, such logic is not readily accessible to everyone. Thus, in this Chapter, we used graphical analysis to illustrate our theories. In taking this approach we are cognizant that some readers may be uncomfortable with mathematical and graphical analysis, and may even have a strong preference for a logic that is based on words rather than symbols. We wish we could accommodate all tastes, but we find that, in the words of Albert Einstein, "I rarely think in words at all. A thought comes, and I may try to express it in words afterward."[8] Our prejudices appear in the next Chapter as well. We use the rigor of mathematical logic with the beauty of graphical explication to analyze the even more complex problem of the manufacturer-optimal channel breadth, and the manufacturer-optimal wholesale-price policy, at every parametric value.

## Notes

[1] We use a numerical grid search that is sufficiently fine for our graphs to provide a close approximation to the precise characteristics of our model.

[2] We present this Section to make the Chapter self-contained; it largely replicates material from Chapters 5-8. Readers who are comfortable with our concept of a unit-cube may wish to skip this Section.

[3] Holding the magnitude of competition constant also requires $c_i = c_j$; we assumed this in our tabular presentations in Chapters 5-8.

[4] For ease of comparison we have changed notation. The left-hand profit symbol was used in Chapter 6; the right-hand one is used in this Chapter. The terms $L^{ss^*}$ and $U^{ss^*}$ are defined at (6.2.4) and (6.2.5). The ensuing term $\delta^{QD^*}$ that appears at (9.3.2) is defined at (5.A.3).

[5] Our mathematical analyses in Chapter 8 are predicated on four fundamental, parametric dimensions $(\chi, S_j, f_i, f_j)$ that form a unit *hyper*-cube; but our graphical analyses are based on three parametric dimensions $(\chi, S_j, f\ (\equiv f_i = f_j))$ that form a unit-cube. Does this dimensional-reduction distort our results? Our sense is that it does not. We have explored 3D-graphic "slices" of the unit hyper-cube for various $\langle f_i, f_j \rangle$ – combinations. Allowing the fixed-cost ratios to differ seems to generate "silly-putty" versions of the information reported in this monograph. That is, the general message—the manufacturer prefers different wholesale-price strategies at different points in the unit-cube (or the unit hyper-cube)—remains valid, although the precise iso-profit indifference surfaces do change, much as a picture impressed on silly-putty remains recognizable when the putty is stretched.

[6] Our graphics program samples a finite number of data points, thus giving the illusion that there are "windows" in the walls; in fact, the wall is solid.

[7] We proved in Chapter 7 that "defection" (a retailer selecting the element of the menu that is intended for its rival) can always be prevented, but only at the expense of the manufacturer obtaining a reduced share of channel profit.

[8] This quotation is cited by Eves (1977).

# Changes in Competition

*"A little spark is followed by a great flame."*

In Chapters 10-12 we address three types of change in competition. We concentrate on *optimal channel breadth* in Chapter 10. In previous Chapters we have established that, given a channel consisting of a single retailer, the manufacturer will coordinate the channel provided there is a single state-of-nature. We have also established that, given a channel consisting of two competing retailers, the manufacturer may or may not coordinate the channel.[1] In Chapter 10 we make the channel-breadth decision endogenous and ask whether the manufacturer should distribute its product through one retailer or through multiple, competing retailers. We solve for parametric values under which the manufacturer supplies only the $i^{th}$ retailer, both retailers, or only the $j^{th}$ retailer. We find that, when the fixed-cost ratio is low, channel breadth is primarily a function of relative market shares: as the share of the lower volume retailer approaches zero, the manufacturer should use exclusive distribution. When the fixed-cost ratio is high, both channel breadth and the optimal wholesale-price strategy depend on relative market shares and the intensity of inter-retailer competition. These results show that exogenously fixing channel breadth generates misleading conclusions about Channel Performance; that is, we refute the *Channel-Breadth Modeling Myth.*

Because the magnitude of fixed costs plays a key role in this deduction, we disprove the belief that fixed costs do not affect the manufacturer-optimal channel breadth (and the corresponding wholesale-price policy) is false; that is, we rebut the *Fixed-Cost Modeling Myth.* And, because the manufacturer is often better off without channel coordination, the belief that managers should coordinate the channel is false; that is, we reject the *Channel-Coordination Strategic Myth.*

In Chapter 11 we focus on the representative consumer's *willingness to substitute* purchases from one retailer for goods purchased from the other retailer. We begin by evaluating various methods of modeling a change in competition and identify important deficiencies in the two methods that have appeared in the literature. Our reasoning is tied to our rejection of the *Aggregate-Demand Modeling Myth*, which ignores the impact on aggregate demand of a change in the cross-price parameter of the retail demand curve. Having recognized this impact, we argue for an alternative method that focuses on the substitutability parameter in the representative consumer's utility function. We use this parameter as our metric for evaluating competitive change and obtain an elegant, intuitively appealing set of results: increased competition lowers prices, quantities, and channel profit.

In Chapter 11 we also show that the common modeling assumptions of equal demand intercepts and equal per-unit retail costs generate identical competitors. Only in this special case do all three of our wholesale-price strategies induce channel-coordination. Since coordination is often non-optimal for a manufacturer that sells through non-identical retailers, we rebuff the *Identical-Competitors Meta-Myth.*

We contemplate the *tools of competition* in Chapter 12 by addressing potential extensions of the meta-model investigated in this monograph. While our intention is to motivate research over a range of issues, we stress marketing-mix variables that might be investigated by future studies of inter-channel competition, inter-manufacturer competition, and inter-retailer competition. Our ideas are modest, but our hope is substantial, for they are offered in the spirit of Dante Alighieri, who wrote "A little spark is followed by a great flame"[2] We hope our suggestions will illuminate paths for exploration that will contribute to the creation of a Unifying Theory of Distribution Channels.

## Notes

[1] The sophisticated Stackelberg tariff will coordinate a bilateral-monopoly model or an identical-competitors model; it enables the manufacturer to extract all channel net revenue (apart from the retailer's fixed cost). A quantity-discount schedule will also coordinate such channels). A menu of two-part tariffs is meaningless in a bilateral-monopoly channel and is trivial in an identical-competitors channel.

[2] The quotation is from *Paradisio,* Canto I, Line 34; translated by Longfellow (1886).

Chapter 10

# The Competing-Retailers Model with Channel Breadth

*"Entities should not be multiplied unnecessarily."*

## 1 INTRODUCTION

In Chapters 5-8 we examined several wholesale-price policies under the assumption that the manufacturer distributes its product through two competing retailers. In this Chapter we evaluate the conditions under which the manufacturer prefers to distribute through a single retailer, even though a broader channel would generate greater channel profit. By serving a single retailer, the manufacturer can always extract *all* profit from the channel with an appropriate two-part tariff; therefore the manufacturer will set a wholesale price that maximizes channel profit.[1] In a channel with wider distribution, the manufacturer's profit-extraction capability is limited by the least-profitable retailer's participation constraint; thus a channel-coordinating wholesale-price strategy may not be in the manufacturer's best interest.[2] Intuitively, if market sizes are sufficiently divergent the manufacturer may benefit by extracting all profit from a single retailer rather than taking all profit from the marginally-profitable retailer and the same, small amount from its more profitable rival. We will show that the manufacturer's optimal wholesale-price strategy and its optimal channel breadth are influenced by the demand and cost parameters.

This Chapter will answer the following questions:

(1) If the manufacturer distributes through a single retailer, should it employ the $i^{th}$ or the $j^{th}$ retailer?

(2) If the manufacturer distributes through both retailers, should it use a wholesale-price strategy that will coordinate the channel?

(3) Should the manufacturer distribute through the $i^{th}$ retailer, or the $j^{th}$ retailer, or through both retailers?

Now consider how conventional wisdom would answer these questions. *If* the results of a single-retailer model generalize to the case of two competing retailers, we should find that:

1. In a single-retailer channel, the manufacturer will choose to serve the retailer that generates the larger unit sales, which is also the retailer that generates the greater net revenue.

2. In a two-retailer channel, the manufacturer will coordinate the channel by selecting a wholesale-price schedule that maximizes total channel profit.
3. Because a two-retailer channel generates more channel profit than a single-retailer channel, the manufacturer will prefer to serve two retailers.

These predictions are predicated on two implicit assumptions: (1) the irrelevance of modeling retailers' fixed costs and (2) the strategic optimality of channel coordination. Our previous discussions of the Fixed-Cost Modeling Myth and the Channel-Coordination Strategic Myth call these assumptions into question. In particular, we have seen that (i) unequal fixed costs can lead to profit rankings that diverge from revenue rankings and (ii) wholesale-price policies that induce coordination place limits on the manufacturer's rent-extraction capability.

To answer the strategic questions concerning channel breadth and optimal pricing, we must first answer four specific questions related to the parametric values of the intensity of competition, the magnitude of competition, and the retailers' fixed-cost ratios:

(A) For what parametric values does serving a single retailer yield greater manufacturer profit than does the quantity-discount schedule?

(B) For what parametric values does serving a single retailer yield greater manufacturer profit than does the sophisticated Stackelberg tariff?

(C) For what parametric values does serving a single retailer yield greater manufacturer profit than does the menu of two-part tariffs?

(D) For what parametric values does serving a single retailer yield greater manufacturer profit than does serving a two-retailer channel with *any* wholesale-price policy?

The relevance of these questions springs from the wholesale-price strategies investigated in earlier Chapters; each strategy was defined in terms of three Zones in $(f_i - f_j)-$space. The manufacturer obtains *all* channel profit in the "$Z_{ij}-$Zones," but in the other two Zones one retailer retains a non-trivial share of channel profit. As a result, in either the $Z_i-$Zone or the $Z_j-$Zone, the manufacturer might prefer extracting all profit from a single retailer to serving both retailers but not obtaining all channel profit.[3]

To illustrate, suppose retailers' fixed costs are zero and $\chi < 0.69$. Under these assumptions, Figure 9.18 indicates that the profit-maximizing manufacturer will use the sophisticated Stackelberg ("SS") tariff. How much does the manufacturer earn with the $SS-$tariff? The answer depends on the difference in retailer market shares. When market shares are equal, the manufacturer can extract all profit from both retailers.

Now consider how the manufacturer's actions change as market shares diverge. As the $j^{th}$ retailer's market share declines from $S_j = ½$, the fixed fee must decrease to retain the $j^{th}$ retailer as a channel member; thus the manufacturer's profit falls. But we know that as $S_j$ approaches zero, the j^th^ retailer's net revenue is a small fraction of that earned by the i^th^ retailer—who retains substantial profit after paying the fixed fee. In this simple scenario, there must be a critical market-share value (call it $S_j^{SO}$ where the superscript "SO" denotes a Single Outlet) below which reverting to a single retailer is in the manufacturer's interest. It is easy to see that $S_j^{SO}$ is a function of the retailers' fixed costs and the intensity of competition. An increase in the $j^{th}$ retailer's fixed cost decreases its profit, thereby forcing a reduction in the fixed fee (which lowers the manufacturer's profit); thus $S_j^{SO}$ is a function of $f_j$. Similarly, a change in competitive intensity alters the relative profitability of the retailers, so $S_j^{SO}$ is also a function of $\chi$. In short, each dimension of the unit half-cube analyzed in earlier Chapters is relevant to the determination of the manufacturer-optimal channel breadth.

We organize the Chapter as follows. In Section 2 we describe the proper method for modeling the demand curve facing a single retailer when the manufacturer has the option of serving two *competing* retailers. We also determine which retailer should be used for distribution. In Section 3 we compare the manufacturer profit generated by (i) serving a single retailer or (ii) serving two competing retailers with (a) a quantity–discount schedule, (b) a sophisticated Stackelberg tariff, or (c) a menu of two-part tariffs. In Section 4 we determine the manufacturer-optimal channel breadth and the manufacturer-optimal wholesale-price strategy by simultaneously comparing all three wholesale-price strategies with a Single-Outlet strategy. Concluding comments appear in Section 5.

## 2 THE DEMAND CURVE WITH A SINGLE OUTLET

In this Section we derive the demand curve for a Single-Outlet retailer. To ensure consistency in our comparisons of channel profits under different channel-breadth scenarios, we nest the single-retailer demand curve within the demand curve that applies when the channel consists of two competing retailers. We then determine the single retailer's performance measures: margins, output and channel profit. We also assess whether the manufacturer should distribute through the $i^{th}$ or the $j^{th}$ retailer.

### 2.1 Consistent Demand Curves: A Single-Outlet Retailer *vs.* Two Competing Retailers

We begin by deriving the demand curve facing the $i^{th}$ retailer in the absence of the $j^{th}$ retailer.[4] It *may appear* that the bilateral-monopoly demand curve of Chapter 2 should be utilized for the Single-Outlet retailer:

$$Q_i^{(1)} = A_i - bp_i . \qquad (10.2.1)$$

(The superscript $^{(1)}$ denotes that only one retailer is served.) This bilateral-monopoly demand curve implies the following aggregate demand curve:

$$\sum_k Q_k^{(1)} = \sum_k (A_k - bp_k) \quad k \in (i,j) \qquad (10.2.2)$$

However, aggregate demand (10.2.2) is *inconsistent* with the competing-retailers demand curve that we employed in Chapters 5-9. In those Chapters we used demand curve (5.2.1), reproduced here as:

$$Q_i = A_i - bp_i + \theta p_j \qquad (10.2.3)$$

Demand curve (10.2.3) generates the following alternative expression for aggregate demand:

$$\sum_k Q_k = \sum_k (A_k - (b-\theta)p_k) \quad k \in (i,j) \qquad (10.2.4)$$

Comparing equations (10.2.2) and (10.2.4) yields:

$$\left(\sum_k Q_k - \sum_k Q_k^{(1)}\right) = \theta \sum_k p_k > 0 \quad k \in (i,j) \qquad (10.2.5)$$

Equation (10.2.5) is zero only when $\theta = 0$; thus demand curves (10.2.1) and (10.2.3) are consistent *only* in the special case of non-competing retailers. When retailers do compete (when $\theta > 0$), demand curve (10.2.1) *underestimates* true demand because it fails to consider the following fact: if only the $i^{th}$ firm sells the product, then *some* customers who would have purchased from the $j^{th}$ firm will switch to the $i^{th}$ retailer. The reverse statement is also true: if we started with only the $i^{th}$ retailer, adding the $j^{th}$ retailer would result in some cannibalization of the $i^{th}$ retailer's output.

This insight leads us to the following conclusion: because equation (10.2.3) defines the $i^{th}$ retailer's demand when it competes with the $j^{th}$ retailer, the bilateral-monopoly demand curve of equation (10.2.1) understates the $i^{th}$ retailer's sales when channel breadth is narrowed. Intuitively, the relevant demand curve under the Single-Outlet strategy should reflect the influence of a potential retail competitor, an influence that is not captured by the bilateral-monopoly demand curve represented by (10.2.1).

To determine the demand for a Single-Outlet retailer we solve for the *minimum* price (call it $p_j^{SO}$) at which the $j^{th}$ retailer has zero sales; this value is the solution to $Q_j = 0 = A_j - bp_j^{SO} + \theta p_i$. Simple algebra reveals that $p_j^{SO} = (A_j + \theta p_i)/b$. An increase in the $i^{th}$ retailer's price or in the $j^{th}$ retailer's base level of demand ($A_k$) raises $p_j^{SO}$. Substituting $p_j^{SO}$ into demand (10.2.3) gives the Single-Outlet demand function when the $j^{th}$ retailer prices itself out of the market:

$$Q_i^{SO} = \left[bA_i + \theta A_j - (b^2 - \theta^2)p_i\right]/b \qquad (10.2.6)$$

Equation (10.2.6) is the Single-Outlet demand when the $j^{th}$ retailer is a latent competitor.

Note that we can rewrite (10.2.6) as:

$$Q_i^{SO} = \alpha_i - \beta_i p_i \tag{10.2.7}$$

where: $\alpha_i \equiv A_i + \chi A_j$

$\beta_i \equiv b(1-\chi^2)$

$\chi \equiv \theta / b$

The important point is that the bilateral-monopoly demand curve (10.2.1) and the Single-Outlet demand curve (10.2.7) should not be confused; they have different intercepts and distinct own-price terms.

In a similar fashion we can derive demand for the j[th] retailer under the assumption that the manufacturer does not sell through the i[th] outlet:

$$Q_j^{SO} = \left[\theta A_i + bA_j - (b^2 - \theta^2)p_j\right]/b \equiv \alpha_j - \beta_j p_j \tag{10.2.8}$$

It is *impermissible* to add equations (10.2.6) and (10.2.8) to compute industry demand because these demand curves were derived under different assumptions. Equation (10.2.6) assumes $p_j = p_j^{SO}$, while (10.2.8) assumes $p_i = p_i^{SO}$. The former equation applies when the manufacturer chooses to serve only the i[th] retailer, while the latter applies when the manufacturer chooses only to serve the j[th] retailer.

## 2.2 Channel Profit Maximization

We know from Chapter 2 that, given the decision to serve only one retailer, it is always in the manufacturer's interest to coordinate the channel. This conclusion also applies in the presence of a latent retailer. The optimization problem for the vertically-integrated, Single-Outlet system is:

$$\max_{p_i^{SO}} \Pi_C^{SO} = (p_i^{SO} - c_i - C)Q_i^{SO} - f_i - F \tag{10.2.9}$$

Maximization yields expressions for channel margin, output, and profit:

$$\mu_i^{SO^*} = \left[\frac{bQ_i^* + \theta Q_j^*}{(b^2 - \theta^2)}\right] \equiv \mu_i^* \tag{10.2.10}$$

$$Q_i^{SO^*} = (bQ_i^* + \theta Q_j^*)/b \equiv (Q_i^* + \chi Q_j^*) > Q_i^* \tag{10.2.11}$$

$$\Pi_i^{SO^*} = \left(\frac{(bQ_i^* + \theta Q_j^*)^2}{b(b^2 - \theta^2)}\right) - f_i - F \tag{10.2.12}$$

(Second-order conditions for a maximum are satisfied at these values.) These results can be replicated by an independent manufacturer/retailer dyad with a properly specified (i) two-part tariff, (ii) quantity-discount schedule, or (iii) sophisticated Stackelberg tariff.

The optimal channel margin in equation (10.2.10) is the same as the optimal margin when serving two retail outlets (see equation (5.3.4)). More importantly, the expression (10.2.11) for unit volume reflects the cannibalization argument discussed above: the i[th] outlet's unit volume is greater in the absence of the j[th] outlet, although it is less than the total output $(Q_i^* + Q_j^*)$ sold when both outlets are operated. The quantity $\chi Q_j^*$ is the incremental volume accruing to the i[th] outlet when the vertically-integrated system does not include the j[th] outlet. When $\chi = 0$, the i[th] outlet gains no sales from elimination of the j[th] outlet. In contrast, as $\chi \to 1$ the i[th] outlet gains an increasing share of the j[th] outlet's sales, because closing the j[th] outlet has almost no effect on aggregate demand. Alternatively, we can regard $\chi Q_j^*$ as a cannibalization measure; it is the volume that the i[th] outlet *loses* as channel breadth increases. As $\chi \to 1$, the volume-benefit of broadening the channel approaches zero.

Comparing total channel profit under the single-retailer regime (equation (10.2.12)) and the two-retailer regime (equation (5.3.10)), we obtain:

$$\Pi_C^* \gtrless \Pi_i^{so^*} \quad \text{as} \quad \left(\left\{(Q_j^*)^2/b\right\} - f_j\right) \equiv \left(\left\{R_j^*\right\} - f_j\right) \equiv g_j^* \gtrless 0 \qquad (10.2.13)$$

The terms $R_j^*$ and $g_j^*$ are the net revenue and profit, respectively, of the j[th] outlet when the two-retailer channel is coordinated. From the perspective of the vertically-integrated system, the j[th] outlet is worth opening if and only if it covers its fixed cost. This result is consistent with our analysis in Chapter 3, where we showed that, with non-competing outlets, a vertically-integrated system serves all outlets with a positive contribution.

Finally, given the decision to operate a Single-Outlet system, the i[th] outlet should be the distributor if:

$$\left(\Pi_i^{so^*} - \Pi_j^{so^*}\right) \equiv \left(R_i^* - f_i\right) - \left(R_j^* - f_j\right) \geq 0. \qquad (10.2.14)$$

Otherwise, the system should operate the j[th] outlet. Consistent with intuition, when the large-volume outlet has fixed costs that are no greater than those of the small-volume outlet, the vertically-integrated system will operate the large-volume outlet—as will an independent manufacturer/retailer dyad.

# 3 THE DECENTRALIZED MANUFACTURER'S CHANNEL-BREADTH DECISION

We now consider a decentralized manufacturer who has the choice of serving one or two retailers. In the former case the decentralized manufacturer earns a profit defined by (10.2.12).[5] In this Section we compare this profit with that earned by serving two retailers and offering (i) a channel-coordinating quantity-discount schedule, (ii) a sophisticated Stackelberg tariff, or (iii) a channel-coordinating menu of two-part tariffs (see Chapters 5-7 for the details of these wholesale-price policies). Our method is to assume a two-retailer, wholesale-price strategy and determine the manufacturer-optimal channel breadth given that strategy. Thus each of the following pair-wise comparisons focuses on the channel breadth decision within the context of a specified wholesale-price strategy. In the next Section we combine these analyses to determine the optimal combination of wholesale-price strategy and channel breadth.

Because all our comparisons involve three Zones that are defined in $\langle f_i - f_j \rangle$ - space, we use the same re-parameterizations that we employed in earlier Chapters:

$$\chi \equiv \left(\theta / b\right) \tag{10.3.1}$$

$$S_j \equiv \left( Q_j^* \Big/ \left(Q_i^* + Q_j^*\right) \right) \tag{10.3.2}$$

$$\mathit{f}_k \equiv \left(f_k / R_k^*\right) \quad \forall \quad k \in (i,j) \tag{10.3.3}$$

It follows that the profit of a Single-Outlet (the i[th]) retailer can be written as:

$$\Pi_i^{SO^*} = R^{SO}\left\{\left[1-(1-\chi)S_j\right]^2 - \left(1-S_j\right)^2\left(1-\chi^2\right)\mathit{f}_i\right\} - F \tag{10.3.4}$$

and the profit of a Single-Outlet (the j[th]) retailer can be written as:

$$\Pi_j^{SO^*} = R^{SO}\left\{\left[\chi+(1-\chi)S_j\right]^2 - \left(S_j\right)^2\left(1-\chi^2\right)\mathit{f}_j\right\} - F \tag{10.3.5}$$

In both these equations we define:

$$R^{SO} \equiv \left(R_i^* / \left(1-S_j\right)^2\left(1-\chi^2\right)\right) \tag{10.3.6}$$

The difference between the profit equations (10.3.4) and (10.3.5) is:

$$\left[\Pi_i^{SO^*} - \Pi_j^{SO^*}\right] = R^{SO}\left(1-\chi^2\right)\left[\left(1-2S_j\right) - \left(1-S_j\right)^2 \mathit{f}_i + \left(S_j\right)^2 \mathit{f}_j\right] \tag{10.3.7}$$

When $\mathit{f}_i = \mathit{f}_j \equiv \mathit{f}$ expression (10.3.7) reduces to:

$$\left[\Pi_i^{SO^*} - \Pi_j^{SO^*}\right]\Big|_{\mathit{f}_i = \mathit{f}_j} = R^{SO}\left(1-2S_j\right)\left(1-\chi^2\right)\left(1-\mathit{f}\right) \geq 0 \quad \forall \quad 0 \leq S_j \leq ½ \tag{10.3.8}$$

Inequality (10.3.8) is strictly non-negative in the unit half-cube, which is the portion of $\langle \chi, S_j, \mathit{f} \rangle$ - space satisfying $0 \leq S_j \leq ½$. Notice that this inequality is zero if $S_j = ½$ or if $\mathit{f} = 1$. In the latter case, channel profits are zero, and therefore the channel cannot exist. When $\mathit{f}_i = \mathit{f}_j$, the manufacturer serves only the i[th] retailer within the unit half-cube and serves only the j[th] retailer in the symmetric unit half-cube defined by $½ \leq S_j \leq 1$.

In the rest of this Section we adapt the approach used in Chapter 9 by performing a series of pair-wise comparisons between (i) the profit earned by the manufacturer from serving a Single-Outlet retailer as specified in equation (10.3.4) and (ii) the profit earned from serving two retailers. Because the manufacturer profit generated by a two-retailer channel depends on the manufacturer's wholesale-price strategy, we divide our analysis into three parts, one for each of the wholesale-price strategies discussed in Chapters 5-7. We combine our analyses to determine the manufacturer's optimal channel breadth in Section 4.

## 3.1 An Analytical Profit Comparison: the Single-Outlet Option *vs.* the Quantity-Discount Option

We begin with the channel-coordinating quantity-discount schedule. As in Chapter 9, we focus on the *unit half-cube*, which is the portion of $\langle \chi, S_j, f \rangle$ – space satisfying $0 \le S_j \le ½$. The relevant profit comparisons are:

$$\left[\Pi_i^{SO^*} - \Pi_j^{QD^*}\right] = \left(\frac{R_i^*(1-\chi)}{2}\right)\begin{pmatrix}(2+\chi)(1-2S_j) \\ -2(1+\chi)\begin{bmatrix}(1-S_j)^2 f_i \\ +S_j^2(1-2f_j)\end{bmatrix}\end{pmatrix} \tag{10.3.9}$$

$$\left[\Pi_i^{SO^*} - \Pi_i^{QD^*}\right] = \left(\frac{-R_i^*(1-\chi)}{2}\right)\begin{pmatrix}(2+\chi)(1-2S_j) \\ +2S_j^2(1+\chi) \\ -2(1-S_j)^2(1+\chi)f_i\end{pmatrix} \tag{10.3.10}$$

In these manufacturer-profit expressions the superscripts denote the models that are being compared ($SO^* \equiv$ single-outlet model, $QD^* \equiv$ two retailers purchasing from a quantity-discount schedule); the subscripts denote the identity of the single-outlet retailer (in (10.3.9) and (10.3.10) it is the $i^{th}$ retailer) or the relevant QD – Zone (Zone $Z_j^{QD^*}$ in (10.3.9) and Zone $Z_i^{QD^*}$ in (10.3.10)). There is no need for a comparison with QD – Zone $Z_{ij}^{QD^*}$ because the manufacturer obtains the full profit of a two-retailer channel in this Zone; no Single-Outlet strategy can dominate this result.

Notice that the $i^{th}$ retailer's fixed-cost ratio ($f_i$) appears in expression (10.3.10). The reason is that $f_i$ appears once in the Single-Outlet profit expression (10.2.12), but it appears twice in the profit expression for two retailers because it is a determinant of the fixed fee that is charged to both retailers. When $f_i = f_j \equiv f$, (10.3.9) becomes:

$$\left[\Pi_i^{SO^*} - \Pi_j^{QD^*}\right]\Big|_{f_i=f_j} = \left(\frac{R_i^*(1-\chi)}{2}\right)\begin{pmatrix}(2+\chi)(1-2S_j) \\ -2S_j^2(1+\chi) \\ -2(1+\chi)(1-2S_j-S_j^2)f\end{pmatrix} \quad (10.3.11)$$

We begin our description of the preferred channel-breadth strategy with a three-dimensional depiction of the regions within the unit half-cube that are associated with the SO – option and the QD – option.

### 3.1.1 A Three-Dimensional Overview

Figure 10.1 illustrates the set of points at which the manufacturer is indifferent between serving a Single-Outlet retailer (and extracting all channel profit) and serving two retailers by using the quantity-discount schedule. This *indifference surface*, which is defined as the set of parametric values for which (10.3.11) is equal to zero, slopes downward from both the $\langle f=0\rangle$ – plane and the $\langle f=1\rangle$ – plane; it contains a ravine that runs from the point $(f=3/4, \chi=1)$ to the point $(f=1, \chi=0)$. Above this surface the manufacturer prefers to serve both retailers with the quantity-discount schedule, and below the surface the manufacturer prefers to serve the Single-Outlet retailer with the larger unit volume. We write $SO \succ QD$ to mean "the manufacturer prefers the Single-Outlet strategy to the quantity-discount strategy." We denote an opposite preference as $QD \succ SO$.

The apparently jagged bottom to the ravine in Figure 10.1 reflects a limitation of Mathematica's three-dimensional graphics package; the bottom of the ravine actually touches the $\langle S_j = 0\rangle$ – plane. To prevent confusion, we present a set of two-dimensional slices of the unit half-cube that will clarify the points of manufacturer indifference between the Single-Outlet option and the two-retailers, quantity-discount option.

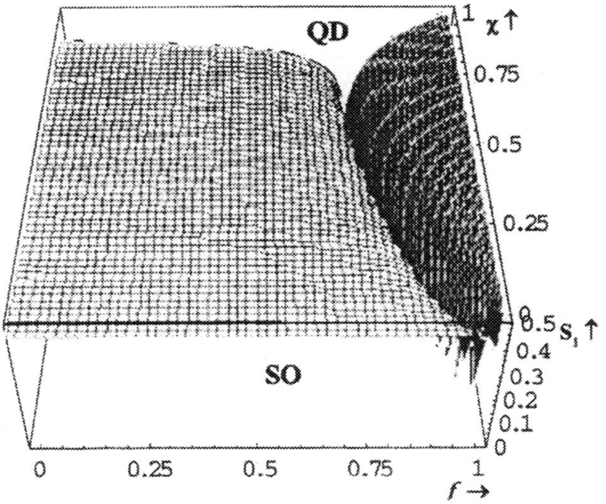


Legend:

**SO** ≡ The manufacturer prefers to serve a single retailer (the i[th]); and

**QD** ≡ The manufacturer prefers the quantity-discount schedule.

*Figure 10.1.* Channel Coordination:
Comparing the Single-Outlet Option with the Quantity-Discount Option

### 3.1.2 Two-Dimensional Perspectives

In this sub-Section we provide specific details that clarify the relationships embedded in Figure 10.1. We divide the unit half-cube of this Figure into two regions that are defined by their $f$ – values:

- **$f$ – Region 1**: $0 \leq f < \frac{3}{4}$
- **$f$ – Region 2**: $\frac{3}{4} \leq f < 1$

The reason for this division arises from the two-dimensional graphs created by vertically slicing the unit half-cube. In $f$ – Region 1 each $f$ – value generates a vertical slice that contains *one iso-profit curve* defined by the indifference surface presented as Figure 10.1. In contrast, in $f$ – Region 2 each $f$ – value generates a vertical slice that contains *two iso-profit curves* defined by the three-dimensional indifference surface. Slices taken in $f$ – Region 2 intersect a portion of the ravine depicted in Figure 10.1.

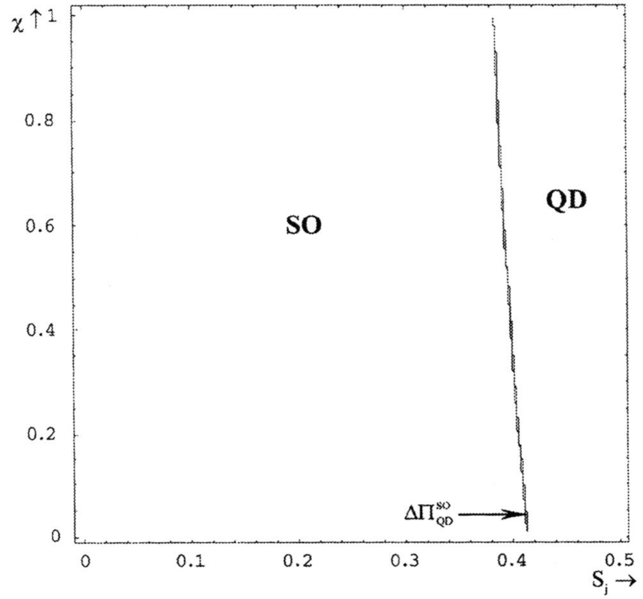


Legend:
**SO** ≡ The manufacturer prefers to serve a Single-Outlet retailer (the i$^{th}$);
**QD** ≡ The manufacturer prefers the quantity-discount schedule; and
$\Delta\Pi_{QD}^{SO}$ ≡ The indifference curve for which the manufacturer nets equal profit by serving either the i$^{th}$ retailer, or both retailers with the channel-coordinating quantity-discount schedule. This is located at the intersection of Zones $Z_j^{SO}$ and $Z_j^{QD}$.

*Figure 10.2.* Comparing the Single-Outlet Option with the Quantity-Discount Option When $f = 0.3$

$f$ – **Region 1**: The iso-profit curve intercepts the $\langle \chi = 0 \rangle$ – axis at $S_j = (\sqrt{2} - 1) \cong 0.412$ for all $f$ – values; it also intercepts the $\langle \chi = 1 \rangle$ – axis at an $S_j$ – value that declines from 0.395644 (at $f = 0$) to zero (at $f = 3/4$) according to the formula:

$$S_j^{\chi=1} = \left(-3 + 4f + \sqrt{21 - 52f + 32f^2}\right) \Big/ \left(4(1-f)\right) \tag{10.3.12}$$

This $f$ – Region is illustrated by Figure 10.2 (above) and Figure 10.3 (on the next page), which depict vertical slices of Figure 10.1 at $f = 0.3$ and $f = 3/4$. To the left of the iso-profit curves we find $SO \succ QD$ while to the right of these curves we observe $QD \succ SO$.

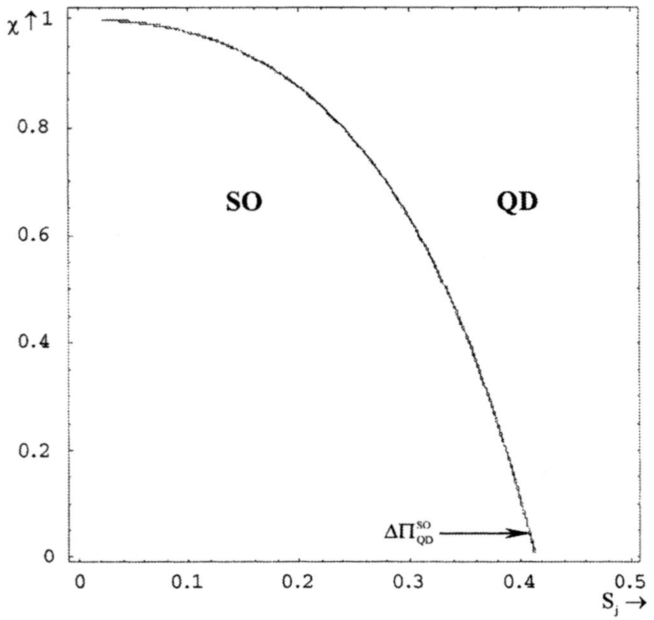


Legend:

**SO** ≡ The manufacturer prefers to serve a Single-Outlet retailer (the $i^{th}$);

**QD** ≡ The manufacturer prefers the quantity-discount schedule; and

$\Delta\Pi^{SO}_{QD}$ ≡ The indifference curve for which the manufacturer nets equal profit by serving either the $i^{th}$ retailer, or both retailers with the channel-coordinating quantity-discount schedule. This is located at the intersection of Zones $Z^{SO}_j$ and $Z^{QD}_j$.

*Figure 10.3.* Comparing the Single-Outlet Option with the Quantity-Discount Option When $f = 0.75$

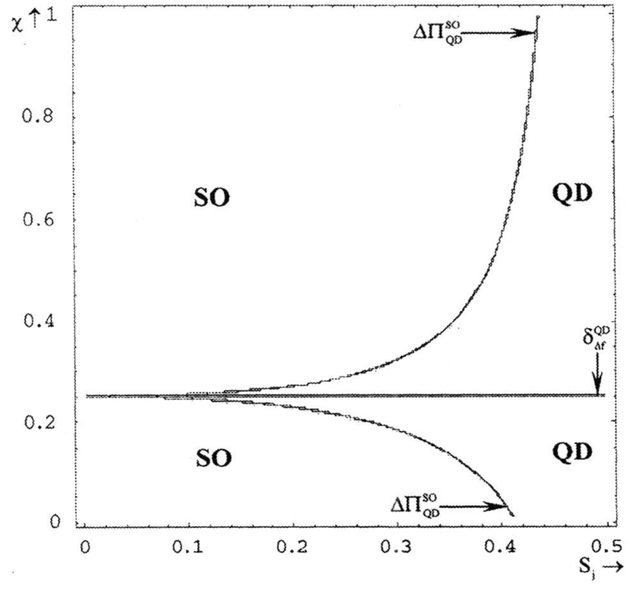


Legend:

**SO** ≡ The manufacturer prefers to serve a Single-Outlet retailer (the i[th]);

**QD** ≡ The manufacturer prefers the quantity-discount schedule;

$\delta^{QD}_{\Delta f}$ ≡ The boundary that separates quantity-discount Zones $Z^{QD}_j$ and $Z^{QD}_i$; and

$\Delta\Pi^{SO}_{QD}$ ≡ The indifference curves for which the manufacturer nets equal profit by serving either the i[th] retailer, or both retailers with the channel-coordinating quantity-discount schedule. The upper curve is located at the intersection of Zones $Z^{SO}_j$ and $Z^{QD}_i$. The lower curve is located at the intersection of Zones $Z^{SO}_j$ and $Z^{QD}_j$.

*Figure 10.4.* Comparing the Single-Outlet Option with the Quantity-Discount Option When $f = 0.9$

$f$ – **Region 2**: The zonal boundary $\delta^{QD}_{\Delta f} \equiv \{[\delta^{QD} - (f_i - f_j)] = 0\}$ defines a horizontal line that divides the unit half-square into two parts. Below this line the parabolic iso-profit curve intersects the $\langle \chi = 0 \rangle$ – axis at $S_j = (\sqrt{2} - 1) \cong 0.412$ and the $\langle S_j = 0 \rangle$ – axis where $\delta^{QD}_{\Delta f}$ intersects this axis. Above the horizontal line a different parabolic iso-profit curve intersects the $\langle S_j = 0 \rangle$ – axis at the same point as $\delta^{QD}_{\Delta f}$. The vertical intersection of the upper parabola ranges from 0 to ½ as $f$ increases from ¾ to 1. Figure 10.4 illustrates this $f$ – Region for $f = 0.9$.

## 3.2 An Analytical Profit Comparison: the Single-Outlet Option *vs.* the Sophisticated Stackelberg Option

Now consider the relative attractiveness to the manufacturer of the Single-Outlet option and the option of serving two retailers with the sophisticated Stackelberg tariff. We present the relevant profit comparisons (which involve $\Pi_j^{SO*}$, $\Pi_j^{SS*}$, $\Pi_i^{SS*}$, and $\Pi_{ij}^{SS*}$) in the Appendix. Given the complexity of these expressions, we turn to graphical analysis for insight.

### 3.2.1 A Three-Dimensional Overview

Figure 10.5 illustrates the manufacturer's points of indifference between serving a Single Outlet and serving two retailers with a sophisticated Stackelberg tariff. To simplify our presentation, we ignore the Area within which the sophisticated Stackelberg Tariff is infeasible ($Q_j^*(j) \leq 0$); we will illustrate this Area in the two-dimensional diagrams that follow. As in Figure 10.1, Figure 10.5 contains two indifference surfaces that curve downward from the $\langle f = 0 \rangle$ – plane and the $\langle f = 1 \rangle$ – plane. They create a ravine that runs approximately from the point ($\chi = 1, f = 0.7$) to the point ($\chi = 0, f = 1$). Above the indifference surface we see $SS \succ SO$, while below the indifference surface $SO \succ SS$. Given our graphical assumption of equal fixed-cost ratios, the manufacturer always selects the retailer with the larger unit volume (which is the i$^{th}$ retailer in the unit half-cube). To provide further insight, we turn to a series of two-dimensional slices of Figure 10.5.

### 3.2.2 Two-Dimensional Perspectives

In this sub-Section we provide specific details that clarify the relationships embedded in Figure 10.5. We divide the unit half-cube of this Figure into four regions that are defined by their $f$ – values:

- **$f$ – Region 1:** $0 \leq f < \frac{2}{3}$
- **$f$ – Region 2:** $f = \frac{2}{3}$
- **$f$ – Region 3:** $\frac{2}{3} \leq f < (\sqrt{3} - 1) \cong 0.732051$
- **$f$ – Region 4:** $(\sqrt{3} - 1) \leq f < 1$

All of these $f$ – Regions contain a single iso-profit curve that defines the manufacturer's preferred channel-breadth strategy.

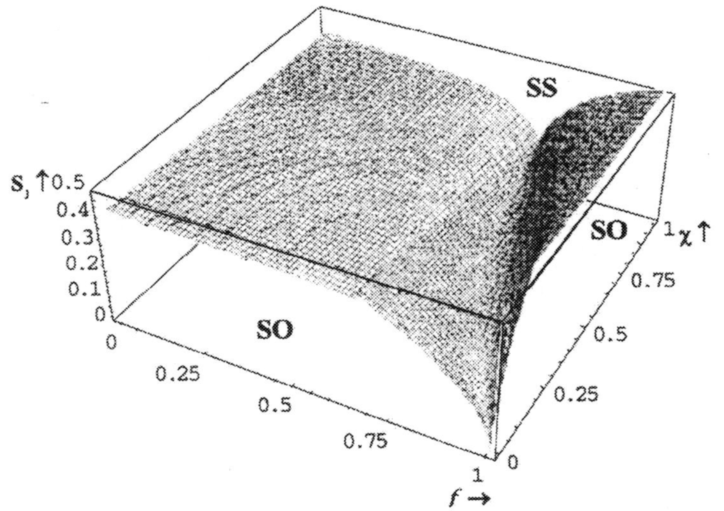


Legend:

**SO** ≡ The manufacturer prefers to serve a Single-Outlet retailer (the i$^{th}$); and

SS ≡ The manufacturer prefers the sophisticated Stackelberg tariff.

*Figure 10.5.* Comparing the Single-Outlet Option with the Channel Non-Coordinating, Sophisticated Stackelberg Option

$f$ **– Region 1**: Figure 10.6 (on the next page) illustrates this $f$ – Region for $f = 0.3$. To the left of the indifference curve we find $SO \succ SS$, while to the right of the indifference curve we see that $SS \succ SO$.

The manufacturer's iso-profit curve intercepts the $\langle \chi = 0 \rangle$ – axis at an $S_j$ – value that varies with $f$ :

$$S_j^{\chi=0} = \left( \frac{2f + \sqrt{2(3 - 7f + 4f^2)}}{2(3-f)} \right) \in \left(0.408248, 0.38673\right) \quad (10.3.13)$$

In this equation the first number inside the parentheses to the right of the "$\in$" symbol denotes the $S_j$ – intercept with the $\langle \chi = 0 \rangle$ – axis at the low end of the $f$ – range (here $f = 0$) and the second number denotes the $S_j$ – intercept with the $\langle \chi = 0 \rangle$ – axis at the high end of the $f$ – range (here $f = \frac{1}{3}$). As the value of $f$ rises from 0 to $\frac{1}{3}$, the $S_j$ – intercept with the $\langle \chi = 0 \rangle$ – axis falls from 0.408248 to 0.38673. Comparable values for the intersection of the iso-profit curve with the $\langle \chi = 1 \rangle$ – axis are given by the formula:

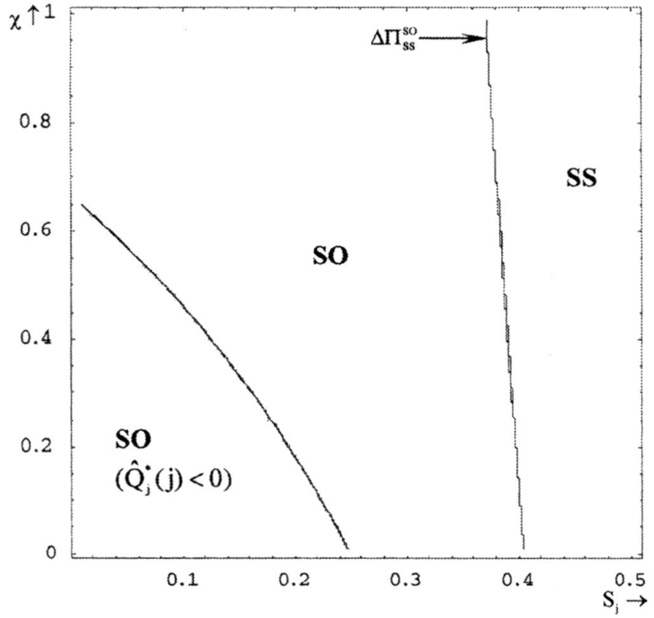


Legend:

**SO** ≡ The manufacturer prefers to serve the Single-Outlet retailer;

**SS** ≡ The manufacturer prefers the sophisticated Stackelberg tariff;

$Q_j^*(j) < 0$ ≡ The sophisticated Stackelberg tariff is infeasible; and

$\Delta\Pi_{SS}^{SO}$ ≡ The indifference curve for which the manufacturer nets equal profit by serving the i[th] retailer, or serving both retailers with the sophisticated Stackelberg tariff. This is located at the intersection of Zones $Z_j^{SO}$ and $Z_j^{SS}$.

*Figure 10.6.* Comparing the Single-Outlet Option with the Sophisticated Stackelberg Option When $f = 0.3$

$$S_j^{\chi=1} = \left( \frac{-13 + 18f + 3\sqrt{41 - 109f + 72f^2}}{2(8 - 9f)} \right) \tag{10.3.14}$$
$$\in \ (0.388086, 0.183013)$$

(Once again, the first number in the parentheses to the right of the $\in$ symbol is the value of the expression evaluated at the lower limit of $f$ and the second number is value of the expression assessed at the upper limit of $f$.) Thus we observe that an increase in $f$ decreases the value at which the iso-profit curve intersects the $\langle \chi = 1 \rangle$ − axis.

$f$ – **Region 2**: The indifference curve in this $f$ – Region intercepts the $\langle \chi = 0 \rangle$ – axis at $S_j = 0.38673$ and the $\langle \chi = 1 \rangle$ – axis at $S_j = 0.183013$. To the left of the indifference curve (labeled $\Delta\Pi_{SS}^{SO}$) we find $SO \succ SS$, and to its right we have $SS \succ SO$. Figure 10.7 depicts this $f$ – Region; we include the Zonal boundary $L_{\Delta f}^{SS}$ (previously shown in Figure 6.6) to illustrate that the iso-profit curve runs through two different SS – Zones.

$f$ – **Region 3**: Here the intersection of the manufacturer's iso-profit curve with the $\langle \chi = 0 \rangle$ – axis occurs over the range of $S_j$ – values defined by:

$$S_j^{\chi=0} = \left( \frac{2f + \sqrt{2(3 - 7f + 4f^2)}}{2(3-f)} \right) \in (0.38673, 0.366025) \quad (10.3.15)$$

The intercept of the iso-profit curve with the $\langle \chi = 1 \rangle$ – axis is defined by:

$$S_j^{\chi=1} = \left( \frac{11 - 18f + 3\sqrt{-7 + 11f}}{2(8-9f)} \right) \in (0.183013, 0.319124) \quad (10.3.16)$$

Figure 10.8 depicts this $f$ – Region for $f = 0.7$. To the left of the iso-profit curve we have $SO \succ SS$, and to its right we find $SS \succ SO$. This graph also depicts the SS – Zonal boundaries $L_{\Delta f}^{SS}$ and $U_{\Delta f}^{SS}$. We include these boundaries to illustrate the fact that, in this $f$ – Region, the iso-profit curve runs through three different SS – Zones.

$f$ – **Region 4**: The intersection of the manufacturer's iso-profit curve with the $\langle \chi = 0 \rangle$ – axis occurs over the range of $S_j$ – values defined by:

$$S_j^{\chi=0} = \sqrt{\frac{1 - 2f + f^2}{2(1-f)}} \in (0.366025, 0) \quad (10.3.17)$$

The intersection of the iso-profit curve with the $\langle \chi = 1 \rangle$ – axis is defined by:

$$S_j^{\chi=1} = \left( \frac{11 - 18f + 3\sqrt{-7 + 11f}}{2(8-9f)} \right) \in (0.319124, 0.5) \quad (10.3.18)$$

Figures 10.9 and 10.10 illustrate $f$ – Region 4 for $f = (\sqrt{3} - 1) \cong 0.73$ and $f = 0.9$, respectively. In both Figures the manufacturer serves one retailer when market shares are substantially different, but distributes through a broader channel with the SS – tariff when market shares are roughly equal.

The key difference between Figures 10.8 and 10.9 is in the bottom of the unit half-squares. In Figure 10.9 both the iso-profit curve *and* the boundary line separating SS – Zone $Z_j^{SS^*}$ from SS – Zone $Z_{ij}^{SS^*}$ intersect the $\langle \chi = 0 \rangle$ – axis at $(S_j = (\sqrt{3} - 1)/2 \cong 0.3665)$. Thus when $\frac{2}{3} < f < (\sqrt{3} - 1)$, the iso-profit curve runs through three SS – Zones; however, when $f > \sqrt{3} - 1$, the iso-profit curve only runs through two SS – Zones.

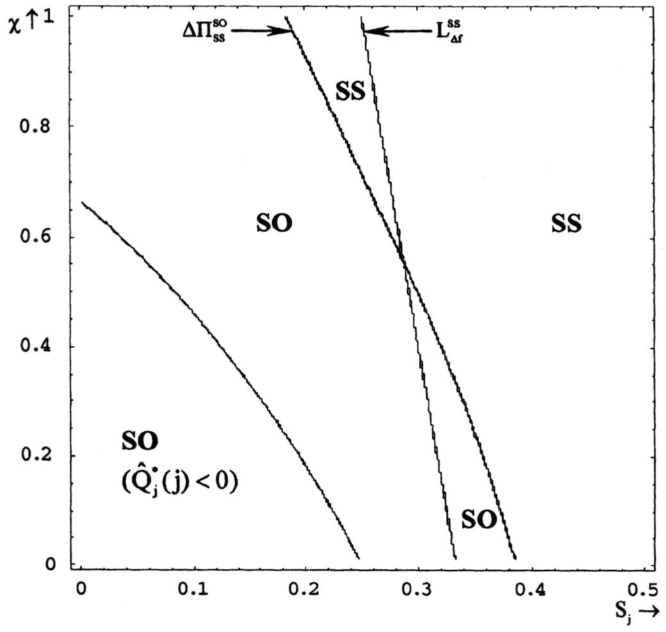


Legend:

**SO** ≡ The manufacturer prefers to serve a Single-Outlet retailer (the i[th]);

**SS** ≡ The manufacturer prefers the sophisticated Stackelberg tariff;

$Q_j^*(j) < 0$ ≡ The sophisticated Stackelberg tariff is infeasible;

$L_{\Delta f}^{SS}$ ≡ The boundary separating SS-Zones $Z_j^{SS}$ and $Z_{ij}^{SS}$; and

$\Delta\Pi_{SS}^{SO}$ ≡ The indifference curve for which the manufacturer nets equal profit by serving the i[th] retailer or by serving both retailers with the sophisticated Stackelberg tariff. This is located at the intersection of Zones $Z_j^{SO}$ and $Z_j^{SS}$.

*Figure 10.7.* Comparing the Single-Outlet Option with the Sophisticated Stackelberg Option When $f = \frac{2}{3}$

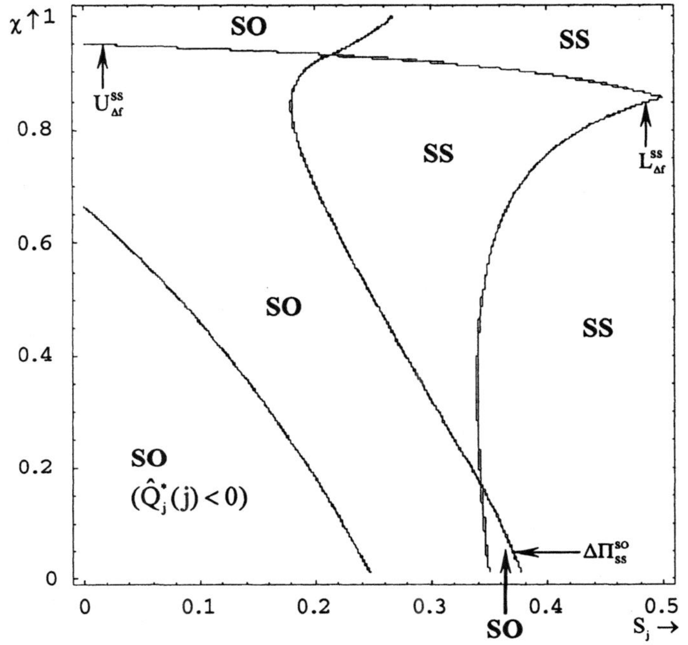


Legend:

**SO** ≡ The manufacturer prefers to serve a Single-Outlet retailer (the $i^{th}$);

**SS** ≡ The manufacturer prefers the sophisticated Stackelberg tariff;

$Q_j^*(j) < 0$ ≡ The sophisticated Stackelberg tariff is infeasible;

$L_{\Delta f}^{SS}$ ≡ The boundary separating SS-Zones $Z_j^{SS}$ and $Z_{ij}^{SS}$;

$U_{\Delta f}^{SS}$ ≡ The boundary separating SS-Zones $Z_{ij}^{SS}$ and $Z_i^{SS}$; and

$\Delta\Pi_{SS}^{SO}$ ≡ The indifference curve for which the manufacturer nets equal profit by serving the $i^{th}$ retailer, or by serving both retailers with the sophisticated Stackelberg tariff. Above $U_{\Delta f}^{SS}$ this is located at the intersection of Zones $Z_j^{SO}$ and $Z_i^{SS}$; between $U_{\Delta f}^{SS}$ and $L_{\Delta f}^{SS}$. It is located at the intersection of Zones $Z_j^{SO}$ and $Z_{ij}^{SS}$; below $L_{\Delta f}^{SS}$ it is located at the intersection of Zones $Z_j^{SO}$ and $Z_j^{SS}$.

*Figure 10.8.* Comparing the Single-Outlet Option with the Sophisticated Stackelberg Option When $f = 0.7$

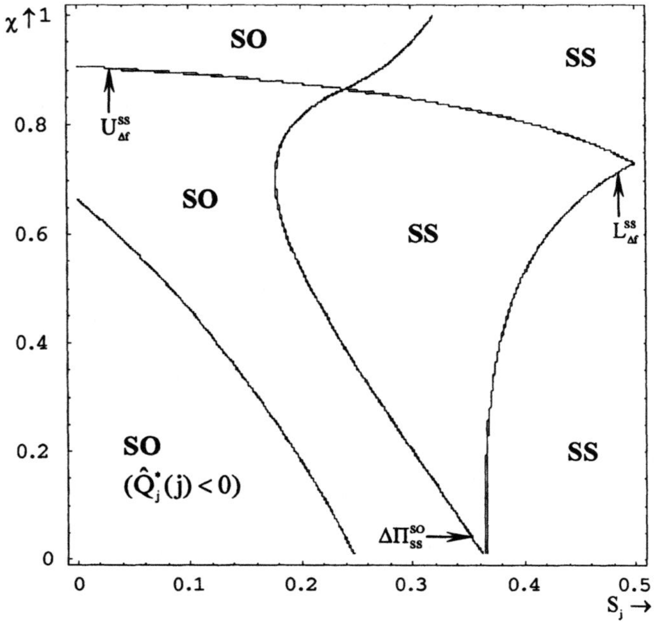


Legend:

**SO** $\equiv$ The manufacturer prefers to serve a Single-Outlet retailer (the $i^{th}$);

**SS** $\equiv$ The manufacturer prefers the sophisticated Stackelberg tariff;

$Q_j^*(j) < 0$ $\equiv$ The sophisticated Stackelberg tariff is infeasible;

$L_{\Delta f}^{SS}$ $\equiv$ The boundary separating SS-Zones $Z_j^{SS}$ and $Z_{ij}^{SS}$;

$U_{\Delta f}^{SS}$ $\equiv$ The boundary separating SS-Zones $Z_{ij}^{SS}$ and $Z_i^{SS}$; and

$\Delta\Pi_{SS}^{SO}$ $\equiv$ The indifference curve for which the manufacturer nets equal profit by serving the $i^{th}$ retailer, or by serving both retailers with the sophisticated Stackelberg tariff. Above $U_{\Delta f}^{SS}$ this is located at the intersection of Zones $Z_j^{SO}$ and $Z_i^{SS}$; below $U_{\Delta f}^{SS}$ it is located at the intersection of Zones $Z_j^{SO}$ and $Z_{ij}^{SS}$.

*Figure 10.9.* Comparing the Single-Outlet Option with the Sophisticated Stackelberg Option When $f = (\sqrt{3} - 1) \cong 0.732051$

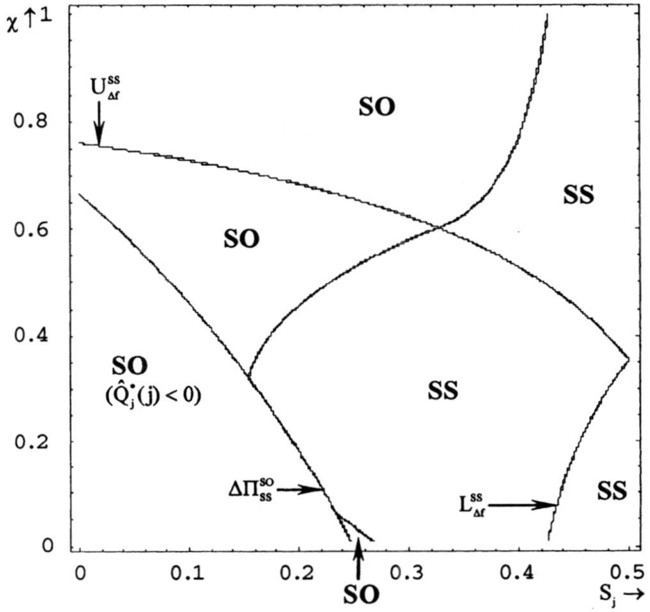


Legend:

**SO** ≡ The manufacturer prefers to serve a Single-Outlet retailer (the $i^{th}$);

**SS** ≡ The manufacturer prefers the sophisticated Stackelberg tariff;

$Q_j^*(j) < 0$ ≡ The sophisticated Stackelberg tariff is infeasible;

$L_{\Delta f}^{SS}$ ≡The boundary separating SS-Zones $Z_j^{SS}$ and $Z_{ij}^{SS}$;

$U_{\Delta f}^{SS}$ ≡ The boundary separating SS-Zones $Z_{ij}^{SS}$ and $Z_i^{SS}$; and

$\Delta\Pi_{SS}^{SO}$ ≡ The indifference curve for which the manufacturer nets equal profit by serving the $i^{th}$ retailer or by serving both retailers with the sophisticated Stackelberg tariff. Above $U_{\Delta f}^{SS}$ this is located at the intersection of Zones $Z_j^{SO}$ and $Z_i^{SS}$; below $U_{\Delta f}^{SS}$ it is located at the intersection of Zones $Z_j^{SO}$ and $Z_{ij}^{SS}$.

*Figure 10.10.* Comparing the Single-Outlet Option with the Sophisticated Stackelberg Option When $f = 0.85$

## 3.3 An Analytical Profit Comparison: the Single-Outlet Option *vs.* the Menu Option

We now consider the relative attractiveness to the manufacturer of the Single-Outlet option and the option of serving two retailers with the menu of two-part tariffs. When the parametric values place the channel in $\text{MN}-\text{Zone } Z^{\bullet}_{ij}$ (we use "MN" to denote the menu), the manufacturer obtains all channel profit whether it distributes either one or two retailers; thus it will prefer to distribute through the broader channel. A simple calculation confirms this:

$$\left[\Pi^{SO^{\bullet}}_{j} - \Pi^{MN^{\bullet}}_{ij}\right] = -R^{\bullet}_{i} S_{j}^{2} \left(1-\chi^{2}\right)\left(1-f\right) < 0. \qquad (10.3.19)$$

The real question is which option the manufacturer prefers when parametric values place the channel in $\text{MN}-\text{Zone } Z^{\bullet}_{j}$ or $Z^{\bullet}_{i}$. The relevant profit comparisons between $\Pi^{SO^{\bullet}}_{i}$, $\Pi^{MN^{\bullet}}_{j}$, and $\Pi^{MN^{\bullet}}_{i}$ are contained in the Appendix. Given the complexity of these expressions, we turn to graphical analysis for further insight.

### 3.3.1 A Three-Dimensional Overview

Figure 10.11 illustrates the set of points at which the manufacturer is indifferent between serving a single retailer (and extracting all channel profit) and serving two retailers with the menu of two-part tariffs. This graph has two indifference surfaces; one curves downward from the $\langle f=0\rangle$ – plane and the other curves downward from the $\langle f=1\rangle$ – plane. Together they create a ravine that runs approximately from the point $\langle \chi=1, f=0.7\rangle$ to the point $\langle \chi=0, f=1\rangle$; however, unlike the previous three-dimensional Figures in this Chapter, the walls of this ravine only meet at a single point of the unit half-cube, namely at $\langle \chi=0, S_{j}=0, f=1\rangle$.

The manufacturer prefers the menu of two-part tariffs (MN) above the indifference surfaces; below them the manufacturer prefers to distribute through one retailer (SO). Given our graphical assumption of equal fixed-cost ratios across retailers, the manufacturer always selects the retailer with the larger unit volume (which is the $i^{th}$ retailer in the unit half-square). To provide further insight we turn to a series of two-dimensional slices of Figure 10.11.

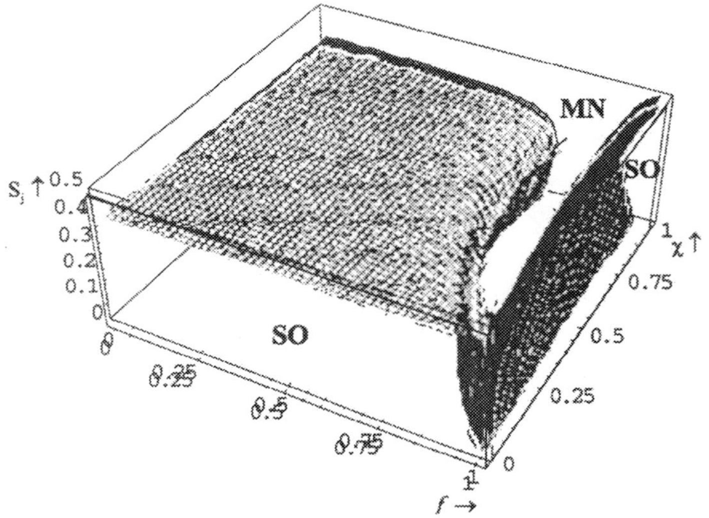


Legend:

**SO** ≡ The manufacturer prefers to serve only one retailer, and

**MN** ≡ The manufacturer prefers the channel-coordinating menu.

*Figure 10.11.* Channel Coordination:

Comparing the Single-Outlet Option with the Menu of Two-Part Tariffs Option

### 3.3.2 Two-Dimensional Perspectives

In this sub-Section we provide specific details that clarify the relationships embedded in Figure 10.11. We divide the unit half-cube of this figure into seven Regions that are defined by their $f$ – values:

- **$f$ – Region 1:** $0 \le f < 0.672572$
- **$f$ – Region 2:** $0.672572 \le f < {}^{25}\!/_{36} \cong 0.694444$
- **$f$ – Region 3:** ${}^{25}\!/_{36} \le f < 0.732471$
- **$f$ – Region 4:** $0.732471 \le f < {}^{10}\!/_{11} \cong 0.909091$
- **$f$ – Region 5:** ${}^{10}\!/_{11} \le f < 0.967638$
- **$f$ – Region 6:** $0.967638 \le f < {}^{35}\!/_{36} \cong 0.972222$
- **$f$ – Region 7:** ${}^{35}\!/_{36} \le f < 1$

All seven $f$ – Regions contain an iso-profit curve that intercepts the $\langle \chi = 0 \rangle$ – axis at an $S_j$ – value that is independent of the actual $f$ – value:

$$S_j^{\chi=0} = \left(\sqrt{2} - 1\right) \cong 0.414214 \tag{10.3.20}$$

In the discussion that follows we will identify a second intercept associated with this iso-profit curve. Because several $f$ – Regions contain an additional indifference curve, we will also identify the intercepts of this second curve, when it exists.

**$f$ – Region 1:** This $f$ – Region contains a single iso-profit curve that intercepts the $\langle \chi = 1 \rangle$ – axis at:

$$S_j^{\chi=1} = \left( \frac{10 - 18f - 3\sqrt{50 - 121f + 72f^2}}{2(9f - 14)} \right) \tag{10.3.21}$$

$$\in (0.400472, 0.338275)$$

(Recall that the first number in the parentheses to the right of the $\in$ symbol is the value of the expression evaluated at the lower limit of $f$; the second number is its value assessed at the upper limit of $f$.) The iso-profit curve that joins the points defined by (10.3.20) and (10.3.21) is a vertical line that is bowed slightly toward the $\langle S_j = 0 \rangle$ – axis. To the left of this iso-profit curve we find $SO \succ MN$ and to the right we observe $MN \succ SO$. Figure 10.12 illustrates this $f$ – Region for $f = 0.3$.

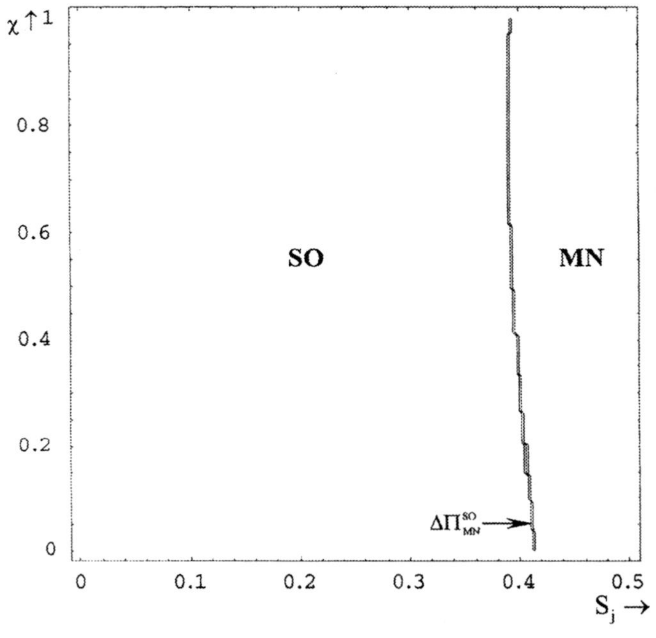


Legend:

**SO** ≡ The manufacturer prefers to serve a Single-Outlet retailer (the $i^{th}$);

**MN** ≡ The manufacturer prefers the menu of two-part tariffs; and

$\Delta\Pi^{SO}_{MN}$ ≡ The indifference curve for which the manufacturer nets equal profit by serving the $i^{th}$ retailer, or by serving both retailers with the menu of two-part tariffs. This is located at the intersection of Zones $Z^{SO}_j$ and $Z^{MN}_j$.

*Figure 10.12.* Comparing the Single-Outlet Option with the Menu Option When $f = 0.3$

$f$ – **Region 2**: In this $f$ – Region the SO and MN areas are defined by two iso-profit curves. One of these curves is a continuation of the curve sketched in Figure 10.12. It intercepts the $\langle \chi = 1 \rangle$ – axis at:

$$S_j^{\chi=1} = \left( \frac{10 - 18f - 3\sqrt{50 - 121f + 72f^2}}{2(9f - 14)} \right) \qquad (10.3.22)$$

$$\in (0.338275, 0.322581)$$

To the left of this iso-profit curve we have $SO \succ MN$ and to the right we find $MN \succ SO$.

The second iso-profit curve in this $f$ – Region has a parabolic form that visually appears to "take a bite" from the $\langle S_j = 0 \rangle$ – axis. Inside the bite we have $MN \succ SO$ and outside it $SO \succ MN$. We denote the two $\chi$ – values at which this second iso-profit curve intercepts the $\langle S_j = 0 \rangle$ – axis with the following notation:

$$\overline{\chi}^{S_j=0} \in (0.798223, 1) \qquad (10.3.23)$$

$$\underline{\chi}^{S_j=0} \in (0.798223, 0.579796) \qquad (10.3.24)$$

Expressions (10.3.23) and (10.3.24) are the upper and lower $\chi$ – values of the intercepts with the $\langle S_j = 0 \rangle$ – axis over the range of $f$ – values that define this $f$ – Region. (The upper value is signified by a super-bar and the lower value is denoted by a sub-bar.) The mathematical expressions for these intercepts are implicitly defined by the formula:

$$f\big|_{S_j=0} = \left( \frac{4 + 2\chi - \chi^2}{4 + 4\chi - \chi^2 - \chi^3} \right)^2 \qquad (10.3.25)$$

This formula also defines the lower $\chi$ – values in the remaining $f$ – Regions.

Figure 10.13 illustrates this $f$ – Region for $f = 0.68$. Inside the bite, the manufacturer's preference for serving both retailers with the channel-coordinating menu of tariffs reflects the underlying MN – Zones. The MN – Zonal boundary $L_{\Lambda f}^{MN}$, which separates MN – Zone $Z_j^{MN}$ from MN – Zone $Z_{ij}^{MN}$, lies just inside the $\Delta\Pi_{MN}^{SO}$ indifference curve. This curve lies so close to $L_{\Lambda f}^{MN}$ that the two boundaries appear as a single curve in Figure 10.13, but the distinction between them is apparent in Figure 10.14 below.

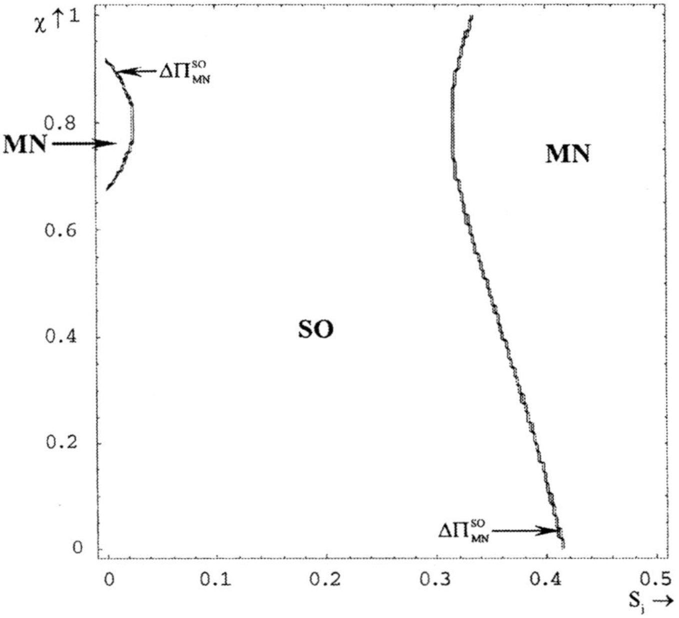


Legend:

**SO** ≡ The manufacturer prefers to serve a Single-Outlet retailer (the $i^{th}$);

**MN** ≡ The manufacturer prefers the menu of two-part tariffs; and

$\Delta\Pi^{SO}_{MN}$ ≡ The indifference curves for which the manufacturer nets equal profit by serving the $i^{th}$ retailer, or by serving both retailers with the menu of two-part tariffs. These are located at the intersections of Zones $Z_j^{SO}$ and $Z_j^{MN}$.

*Figure 10.13.* Comparing the Single-Outlet Option with the Menu Option When $f = 0.68$

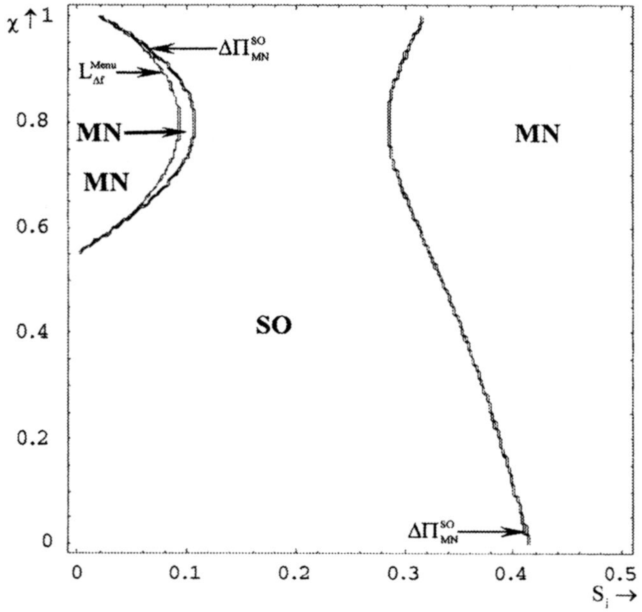


Legend:

**SO** ≡ The manufacturer prefers to serve a Single-Outlet retailer (the i[th]);

**MN** ≡ The manufacturer prefers the menu of two-part tariffs; and

$\Delta\Pi^{SO}_{MN}$ ≡ The indifference curves for which the manufacturer nets equal profit by serving the i[th] retailer, or by serving both retailers with the menu of two-part tariffs. These are located at the intersections of Zones $Z^{SO}_j$ and $Z^{MN}_j$.

*Figure 10.14.* Comparing the Single-Outlet Option with the Menu Option When $f = 0.7$

*f* − **Region 3**: The *right*-hand iso-profit curve intercepts the $\langle \chi = 1 \rangle -$ axis at:

$$\overline{S}_j^{\chi=1} = \left( \frac{-10 + 18f + 3\sqrt{50 - 121f + 72f^2}}{2(14 - 9f)} \right) \qquad (10.3.26)$$

$$\in (0.322581, 0.214942)$$

The *left*-hand indifference curve (the "bite") now intercepts the $\langle S_j = 0 \rangle -$ axis at lower $\chi -$ values that range from 0.579796 to 0.435582. The second intersection of the "bite" occurs on the $\langle \chi = 1 \rangle -$ axis at:

$$\underline{S}_j^{\chi=1} = \left( \frac{-10 + 18f - 3\sqrt{50 - 121f + 72f^2}}{2(14 - 9f)} \right) \qquad (10.3.27)$$

$$\in (0, 0.214942)$$

The enlarged area encompassed by this bite reflects the expansion of MN − Zone $Z_{ij}^{MN}$ that is located inside the bite. Figure 10.14 illustrates this *f* − Region for $f = 0.7$. Notice that the distinction between the iso-profit curve $\Delta\Pi_{MN}^{SO}$ and the zonal boundary $L_{\Delta f}^{MN}$ is now clearly visible.

*f* − **Region 4**: At $f = 0.732471$ both iso-profit curves that appeared in the previous *f* − Region intercept the $\langle \chi = 1 \rangle -$ axis at $S_j = 0.214942$. As *f* increases, the two iso-profit curves of *f* − Region 3 become a single indifference curve that intercepts (i) the $\langle \chi = 0 \rangle -$ axis at the constant value $S_j = 0.414214$ and (ii) the $\langle S_j = 0 \rangle -$ axis at:

$$\underline{\chi}^{S_j=0} \in (0.435582, 0.102928) \qquad (10.3.28)$$

(The value of this intercept is implicitly defined by equation (10.3.25); once again, the first number is the $\chi -$ value at the lower boundary of this *f* − Region (i.e., at 0.732471) while the second number is its $\chi -$ value at the upper boundary (i.e., at 0.909091)). Figure 10.15 illustrates this scenario for $f = 3/4$.

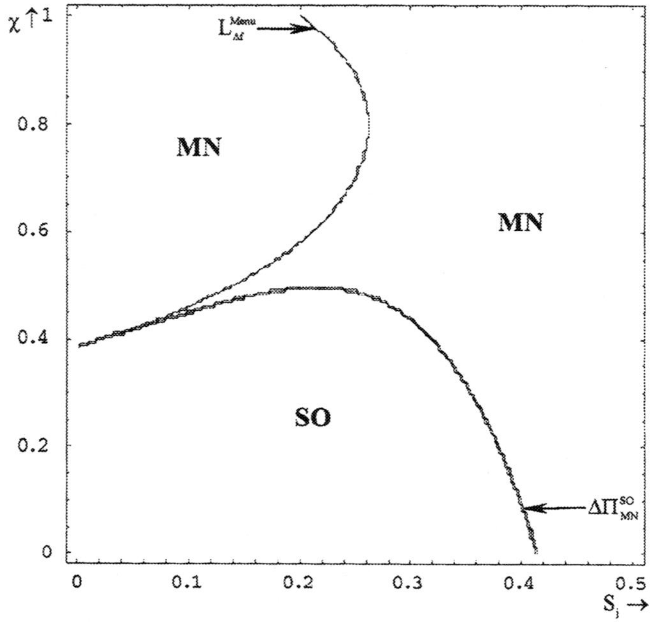


Legend:

**SO** ≡ The manufacturer prefers to serve a Single-Outlet retailer (the $i^{th}$);

**MN** ≡ The manufacturer prefers the menu of two-part tariffs; and

$\Delta\Pi_{MN}^{SO}$ ≡ The indifference curves for which the manufacturer nets equal profit by serving the $i^{th}$ retailer, or by serving both retailers with the menu of two-part tariffs. These are located at the intersections of Zones $Z_j^{SO}$ and $Z_j^{MN}$.

*Figure 10.15.* Comparing the Single-Outlet Option with the Menu Option When $f = 0.75$

$f$ – **Region 5**: The iso-profit curve intersects the $\langle S_j = 0\rangle$ – axis at:

$$\underline{\chi}^{S_j=0} \in (0.102928, 0.033739) \qquad (10.3.29)$$

(The value of this intercept is also implicitly defined by equation (10.3.25)). In addition, a new, parabolic-shaped iso-profit curve appears that intersects the $\langle \chi = 1\rangle$ – axis twice. Inside the parabola SO $\succ$ MN. To distinguish this indifference curve from the one that appeared in previous $f$ – Regions we use double-bars. The intercepts of this curve are defined by the equations:

$$\overline{\overline{S}}_j^{\chi=1} = \left( \frac{20 - 18f + 3\sqrt{11f - 10}}{2(14 - 9f)} \right) \in (0.3125, 0.471536) \qquad (10.3.30)$$

$$\underline{\underline{S}}_j^{\chi=1} = \left( \frac{20 - 18f - 3\sqrt{11f - 10}}{2(14 - 9f)} \right) \in (0.3125, 0.016537) \qquad (10.3.31)$$

The reason for the last result is that, when $f > 5/6$, $U_{\Delta f}^{Menu}$ takes a bite from the upper right-hand corner of the unit half-square. As $f \to 1$, $U_{\Delta f}^{Menu}$ shifts down and to the right; this increases the size of MN – Zone $Z_i^{Menu}$. This expansion enables the Single-Outlet option to dominate the menu option. Figure 10.16 illustrates this $f$ – Region for $f = 19/20$.

$f$ – **Region 6**: The *lower* iso-profit curve hits the $\langle S_j = 0\rangle$ – axis at:

$$\underline{\chi}^{S_j=0} \in (0.033739, 0.028785) \qquad (10.3.32)$$

The *upper* iso-profit curve, which intersected the $\langle \chi = 1\rangle$ – axis in $f$ – Region 5, now intercepts the $\langle \chi = 1\rangle$ – axis at the points:

$$\overline{\overline{S}}_j^{\chi=1} = \left( \frac{20 - 18f + 3\sqrt{11f - 10}}{2(14 - 9f)} \right) \in (0.471536, 0.47619) \qquad (10.3.33)$$

$$\underline{\underline{S}}_j^{\chi=1} = \left( \frac{20 - 18f - 3\sqrt{11f - 10}}{2(14 - 9f)} \right) \in (0.016537, 0) \qquad (10.3.34)$$

This curve also intersects the $\langle S_j = 0\rangle$ – axis at the points:

$$\overline{\overline{\chi}}^{S_j=0} \in (0.798223, 1) \qquad (10.3.35)$$

$$\underline{\underline{\chi}}^{S_j=0} \in (0.798223, 0.579796) \qquad (10.3.36)$$

These intercepts are implicitly defined by the formula:

$$f\Big|_{S_j=0} = \left( \frac{16 + 32\chi + 4\chi^2 - 16\chi^3 - 3\chi^4 + 2\chi^5}{(4 + 4\chi - \chi^2 - \chi^3)^2} \right) > 0 \qquad (10.3.37)$$

Notice that the $\chi$ – values that solve equation (10.3.37) are identical to the $\chi$ – values that solve equation (10.3.25)—see equations (10.3.23) and (10.3.24). Figure 10.17 illustrates this scenario for $f = 0.97$.

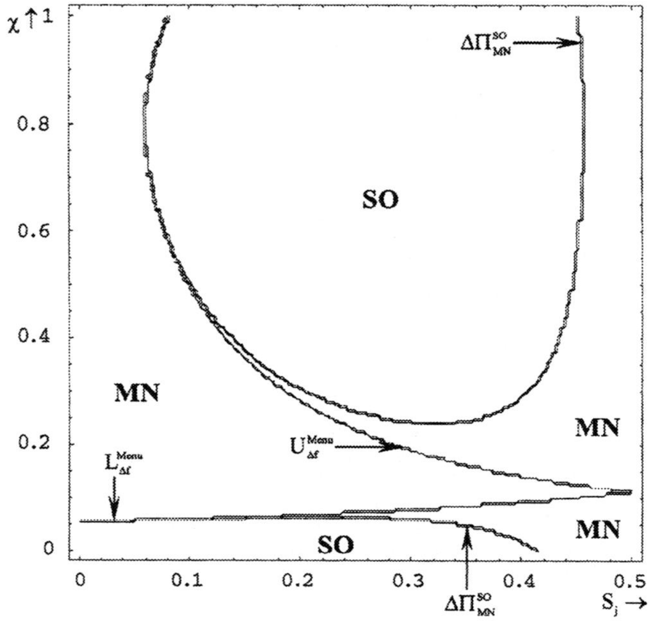


Legend:

**SO** ≡ The manufacturer prefers to serve a Single-Outlet retailer (the $i^{th}$);

**MN** ≡ The manufacturer prefers the menu of two-part tariffs;

$U^{MN}_{\Delta f}$ ≡ The boundary separating menu Zones $Z^{MN^*}_{ij}$ and $Z^{MN^*}_{i}$; and

$\Delta\Pi^{SO}_{MN}$ ≡ The indifference curve for which the manufacturer nets equal profit by serving the $i^{th}$ retailer, or by serving both retailers with the menu of two-part tariffs. This is located at the intersection of Zones $Z^{SO}_{j}$ and $Z^{MN}_{i}$ for the upper indifference surface and at the intersection of Zones $Z^{SO}_{j}$ and $Z^{MN}_{j}$ for the lower indifference surface.

*Figure 10.16.* Comparing the Single-Outlet Option with the Menu Option When $f = 0.95$

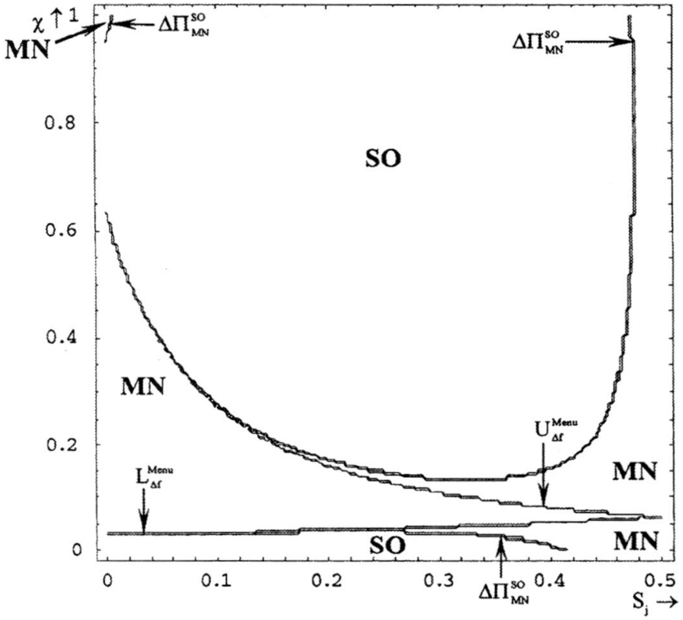


Legend:

**SO** ≡ The manufacturer prefers to serve a Single-Outlet retailer (the $i^{th}$);

**MN** ≡ The manufacturer prefers the menu of two-part tariffs;

$U^{MN}_{\Delta f}$ ≡ The boundary separating menu Zones $Z^{MN^*}_{ij}$ and $Z^{MN^*}_{i}$; and

$\Delta\Pi^{SO}_{MN}$ ≡ The indifference curve for which the manufacturer nets equal profit by serving the $i^{th}$ retailer, or by serving both retailers with the menu of two-part tariffs. This is located at the intersection of Zones $Z^{SO}_{j}$ and $Z^{MN}_{i}$ for the upper indifference surface and at the intersection of Zones $Z^{SO}_{j}$ and $Z^{MN}_{j}$ for the lower indifference surface.

*Figure 10.17.* Comparing the Single-Outlet Option with the Menu Option When $f = 0.97$

$f$ – **Region 7**: In this $f$ – Region, the *lower* iso-profit curve intersects the $\langle S_j = 0 \rangle$ – axis at:

$$\underline{\chi}^{S_j=0} \in (0.028785, 0) \qquad (10.3.38)$$

(The value of this intercept is implicitly defined by equation (10.3.25)). As before, this iso-profit curve appears to take a bite from the lower left-hand corner of the unit half-square. In addition, the *upper* iso-profit curve that intersected the $\langle \chi = 1 \rangle$ – axis in $f$ – Region 5 and $f$ – Region 6 intercepts the $\langle \chi = 1 \rangle$ – axis at:

$$\overline{\overline{S}}_j^{\chi=1} = \left( \frac{20 - 18f + 3\sqrt{11f - 10}}{2(14 - 9f)} \right) \in (0.47619, 0.5) \qquad (10.3.39)$$

This second iso-profit curve also intersects the $\langle S_j = 0 \rangle$ – axis at:

$$\underline{\underline{\chi}}^{S_j=0} \in (0.579796, 0) \qquad (10.3.40)$$

Visually the second iso-profit curve appears to take a bite from the upper left-hand corner of the unit-square. Inside both bites, we observe $SO \succ MN$; outside of them, we see $MN \succ SO$. Figure 10.18 illustrates this $f$ – Region for $f = 0.98$.

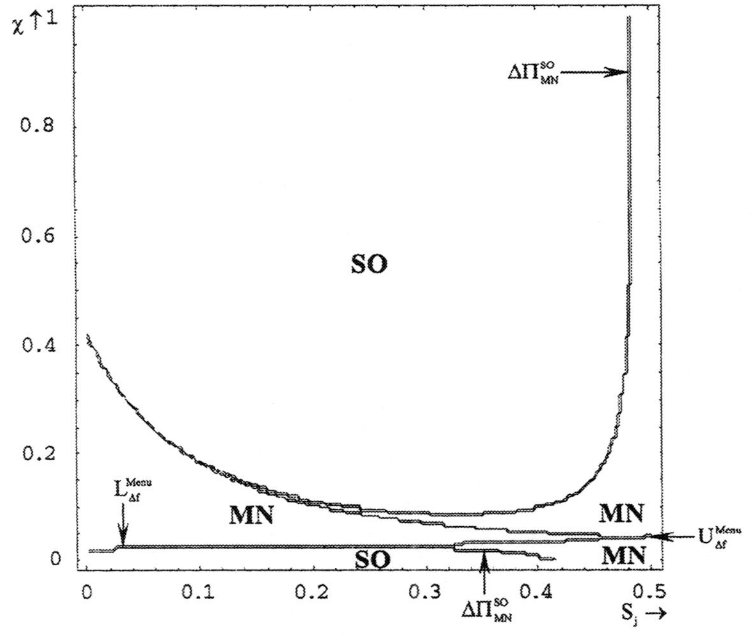


Legend:

**SO** ≡ The manufacturer prefers to serve a Single-Outlet retailer (the i[th]);

**MN** ≡ The manufacturer prefers the menu of two-part tariffs;

$U^{MN}_{\Delta f}$ ≡ The boundary separating menu Zones $Z^{MN^*}_{ij}$ and $Z^{MN^*}_{i}$; and

$\Delta\Pi^{SO}_{MN}$ ≡ The indifference curve for which the manufacturer nets equal profit by serving the i[th] retailer, or by serving both retailers with the menu of two-part tariffs. This is located at the intersection of Zones $Z^{SO}_{j}$ and $Z^{MN}_{i}$ for the upper indifference surface and at the intersection of Zones $Z^{SO}_{j}$ and $Z^{MN}_{j}$ for the lower indifference surface.

*Figure 10.18.* Comparing the Single-Outlet Option with the Menu Option When $f = 0.98$

# 4 COMMENTARY ON OPTIMAL CHANNEL-BREADTH AND OPTIMAL WHOLESALE-PRICE STRATEGIES

In this Section we identify the *manufacturer*-optimal wholesale-price strategy in $\langle \chi, S_j \rangle$ – space under the assumption that retailers have no fixed costs. We then vary the $f$ – value to ascertain how changes in the fixed-cost ratio affect the manufacturer's optimal strategy. To simplify our graphs, we only display the iso-profit curves; zonal influences on the indifference curves may be deduced from the Figures presented in the preceding sub-Sections.

## 4.1 Manufacturer-Optimal Channel Breadth: Commentary on Zero Fixed Costs at Retail

We depict the "zero fixed costs at retail" scenario in Figure 10.19, which consists of two graphs. On the left we reproduce the relevant Chapter 9 graph (Figure 9.14), which shows the manufacturer's optimal wholesale-price strategy when channel breadth is fixed at two competing retailers. On the right we present the graph that depicts the manufacturer-optimal wholesale-price strategy when channel breadth is a strategic-choice variable. In our discussion we initially focus on the right-hand graph and then discuss the differences between this graph and the one on the left-hand side of the Figure.

The iso-profit curve on the RHS of Figure 10.19 intersects the $\langle \chi = 0 \rangle$ – axis at $S_j \cong 0.408$ and the $\langle \chi = 1 \rangle$ – axis at $S_j \cong 0.388$. To the left of this iso-profit curve the manufacturer prefers to distribute through a single retailer, while to the right the manufacturer prefers a broader channel. This graph is important because a common modeling assumption is zero fixed costs at retail. We have now shown that, in the absence of such costs, *the manufacturer will not coordinate the channel when it serves both retailers.* Less obviously, because the sophisticated Stackelberg wholesale-price strategy coordinates a bilateral-monopoly channel, we have also shown that the sophisticated Stackelberg strategy is *always* manufacturer-optimal in the absence of retail-level fixed costs. Finally, a manufacturer that has the option of selling through one or two independent retailers prefers a narrower channel over roughly 80 percent of the model's parameter space.

The left-hand graph in Figure 10.19 (which replicates the previously discussed Figure 9.14) specifies the manufacturer's optimal pricing strategy when the manufacturer is modeled as serving both retailers. Notice that, when the manufacturer has no choice over channel breadth, the menu is manufacturer-optimal over a *portion* of the unit half-square. In contrast, when channel breadth is endogenous, the menu is *never* manufacturer-optimal. We now turn to the more realistic case of non-zero fixed costs.

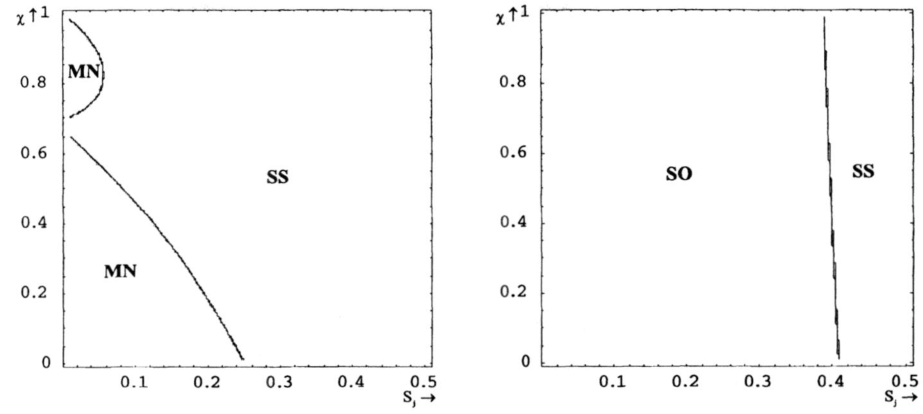


Legend:

**MN** ≡ The manufacturer prefers the ***channel - coordinating*** menu of two-part tariffs;

**SO** ≡ The manufacturer prefers to serve a Single-Outlet retailer (the $i^{th}$); and

**SS** ≡ The manufacturer prefers the sophisticated Stackelberg tariff.

*Figure 10.19.* Manufacturer-Optimal Strategies: Channel Breadth and the Wholesale-Price Strategy When $f = 0$

## 4.2 Manufacturer-Optimal Channel Breadth: Commentary on Positive Fixed Costs at Retail

In this sub-Section we show that variations in the retailers' fixed costs influence the manufacturer's optimal channel-breadth and wholesale-price strategies. This finding should be expected, given our discussions of fixed costs in earlier Chapters. What may be a surprise is that, until $f > 0.672572$, the retailer's fixed-cost ratio has a minimal impact on the conclusions drawn in the preceding sub-Section. For $0 < f < 0.672572$, variations in $f$ simply alter the size of the regions within which the manufacturer prefers (i) to serve a single retailer or (ii) serve two retailers using the sophisticated Stackelberg two-part tariff. In particular, an increase in the $f$ – value within the specified $f$ – range pivots the indifference curve of Figure 10.19 to the left about the point $\langle \chi = 0,\ S_j = 0.408248 \rangle$. As a result, the area within which $SS \succ SO$ increases. The Single-Outlet strategy, which is manufacturer-optimal over some 80 percent of the unit half-square when $f = 0$, is "only" optimal over about 60 percent of this parameter space as $f$ approaches $2/3$. (Figures 10.6 and 10.7 depict optimal channel breadth for $f = 0.3$ and $f = 2/3$, respectively, with the Single-Outlet option being manufacturer-preferred at more divergent market shares.)

There are fundamental changes in the nature of the manufacturer's optimal wholesale-price and channel-breadth strategies when the retailers' fixed-cost ratio exceeds $f = 0.672572$. First, coordination of a two-retailer channel becomes optimal in a portion of the unit half-square. Given the optimality of serving two retailers and coordinating the channel, the manufacturer simply relies on the menu of two-part tariffs when $f$ is close to 0.672572. However, as $f$ rises the quantity-discount schedule becomes an attractive option as well. Second, a narrower channel becomes progressively less attractive as $f$ increases. The portion of the unit half-square over which a Single-Outlet channel is optimal for the manufacturer declines from some 60 percent of the parameter space at $f = 2/3$ to about 15 percent at $f = 0.90$.

Third, the shift from a narrow to a broad channel, and from an uncoordinated to a coordinated two-retailer channel, does not follow a simple pattern; for instance, we showed in sub-Section 3.3.2 that the manufacturer prefers the menu option to the Single-Outlet option when competitive intensity is high and the magnitude of competition is low. Visually, this preference appeared in Figure 10.13 as a bite taken from the $\langle S_j = 0 \rangle$ – axis; inside the bite, the manufacturer prefers the menu to the Single-Outlet option. Figure 10.20 illustrates this phenomenon for $f = 0.70$. In this Figure there is another iso-profit curve; it intersects the $\langle\chi = 0\rangle$ – axis at $S_j = 0.381123$ and the $\langle\chi = 1\rangle$ – axis at $S_j = 0.256547$. To the right of the second curve the manufacturer prefers to distribute through both retailers while using the sophisticated Stackelberg tariff. Between the two iso-profit curves the Single-Outlet option is manufacturer-preferred.

To further clarify the effect of allowing channel breadth to be a strategic variable, we present a series of "side-by-side" graphs. Figures 10.20 to 10.25 illustrate the effect of increases in the retailers' fixed-cost ratio above $f = 0.672572$. These slices of the unit half-cube, taken at intervals of 0.05 from $f = 0.70$ to $f = 0.95$, graphically present the interrelationship between the manufacturer's optimal channel-breadth strategy and its optimal wholesale-price strategy. On the left of each Figure we reproduce the relevant Chapter 9 graph (Figures 9.21-9.26); these graphs show the manufacturer's optimal wholesale-price strategy when channel breadth is fixed at two competing retailers. The corresponding graph on the right depicts the manufacturer's optimal strategy when channel breadth is a choice variable. With this set of comparisons we are able to show how changes in $f$ affect channel breadth and the optimal wholesale-price policy. We defer our comments on these Figures until all of them have been displayed.

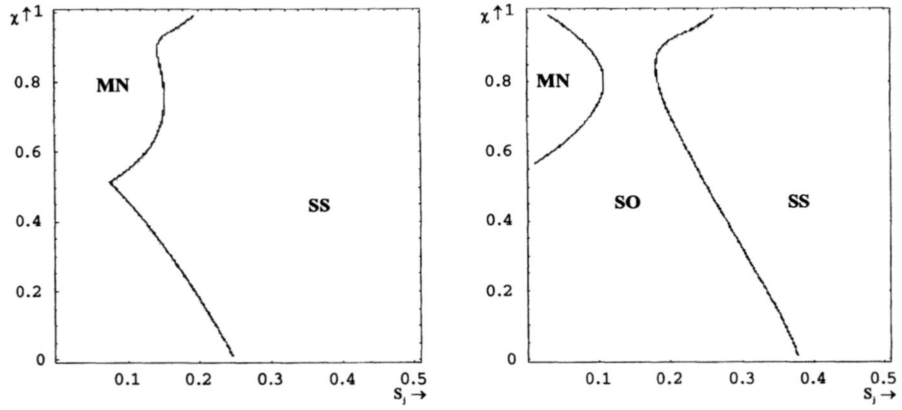


Legend:

**MN ≡ The manufacturer prefers the *channel - coordinating* menu of two-part tariffs;**

**SO ≡ The manufacturer prefers to serve a Single-Outlet retailer (the $i^{th}$); and**

**SS ≡ The manufacturer prefers the sophisticated Stackelberg tariff.**

*Figure 10.20.* Manufacturer-Optimal Strategies: Channel Breadth and the Wholesale-Price Strategy When $f$ = 0.70

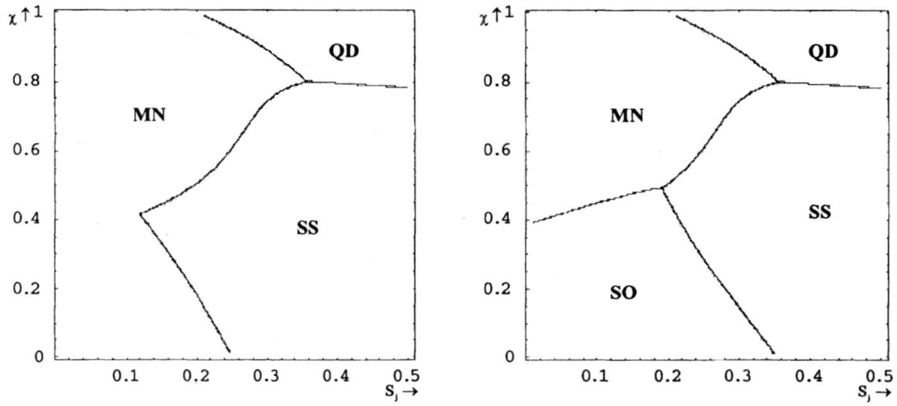


Legend:

**MN** ≡ The manufacturer prefers the *channel - coordinating* menu of two-part tariffs;

**QD** ≡ The manufacturer prefers the *channel - coordinating* quantity-discount schedule;

**SO** ≡ The manufacturer prefers to serve a Single-Outlet retailer (the $i^{th}$); and

**SS** ≡ The manufacturer prefers the sophisticated Stackelberg tariff.

*Figure 10.21.* Manufacturer-Optimal Strategies: Channel Breadth and the Wholesale-Price Strategy When $f$ = 0.75

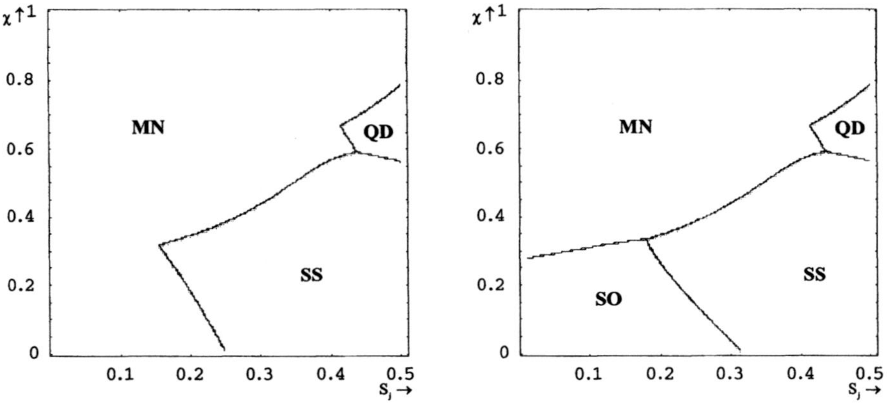


**Legend:**

**MN ≡ The manufacturer prefers the *channel - coordinating* menu of two-part tariffs;**

**QD ≡ The manufacturer prefers the *channel - coordinating* quantity-discount schedule;**

**SO ≡ The manufacturer prefers to serve a Single-Outlet retailer (the $i^{th}$); and**

**SS ≡ The manufacturer prefers the sophisticated Stackelberg tariff.**

*Figure 10.22.* Manufacturer-Optimal Strategies: Channel Breadth and the Wholesale-Price Strategy When $f = 0.80$

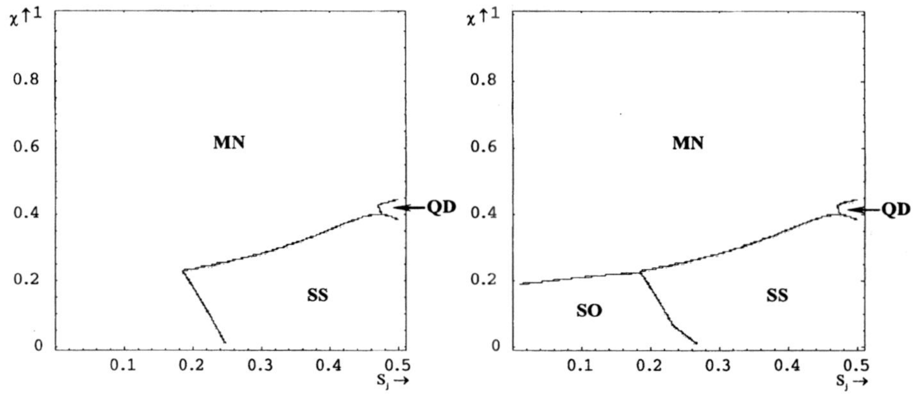


Legend:

**MN** ≡ The manufacturer prefers the *channel - coordinating* menu of two-part tariffs;

**QD** ≡ The manufacturer prefers the *channel - coordinating* quantity-discount schedule;

**SO** ≡ The manufacturer prefers to serve a Single-Outlet retailer (the $i^{th}$); and

**SS** ≡ The manufacturer prefers the sophisticated Stackelberg tariff.

*Figure 10.23.* Manufacturer-Optimal Strategies: Channel Breadth and the Wholesale-Price Strategy When $f$ = 0.85

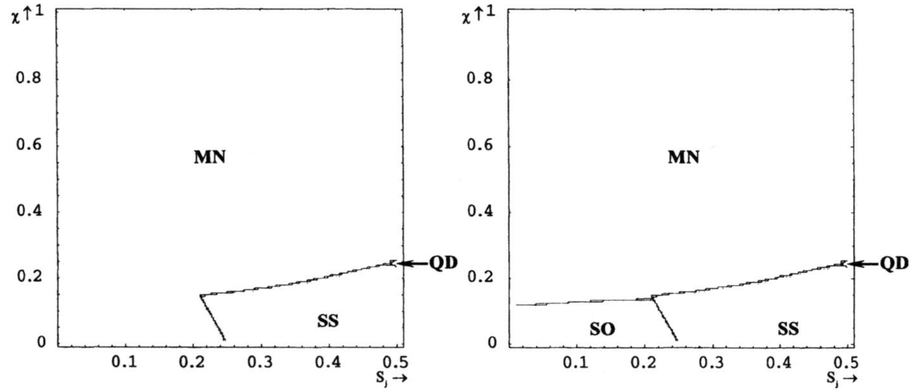


Legend:

**MN** ≡ The manufacturer prefers the *channel - coordinating* menu of two-part tariffs;

**QD** ≡ The manufacturer prefers the *channel - coordinating* quantity-discount schedule;

**SO** ≡ The manufacturer prefers to serve a Single-Outlet retailer (the $i^{th}$); and

**SS** ≡ The manufacturer prefers the sophisticated Stackelberg tariff.

*Figure 10.24.* Manufacturer-Optimal Strategies: Channel Breadth and the Wholesale-Price Strategy When $f = 0.90$

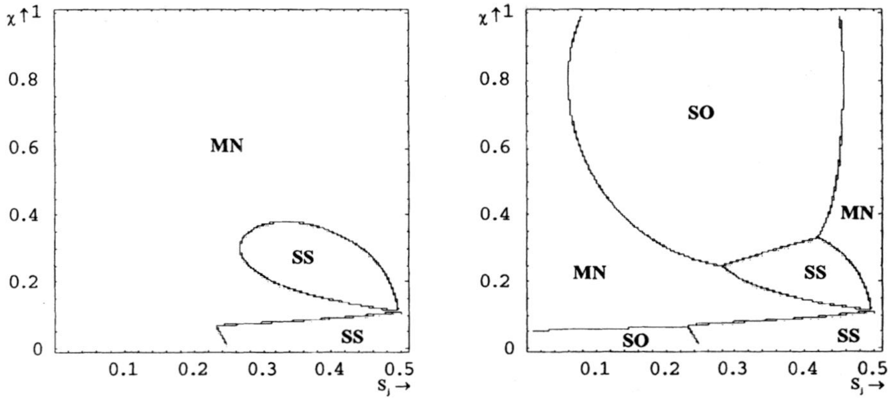


Legend:

**MN** ≡ The manufacturer prefers the *channel - coordinating* menu of two-part tariffs;

**QD** ≡ The manufacturer prefers the *channel - coordinating* quantity-discount schedule;

**SO** ≡ The manufacturer prefers to serve a Single-Outlet retailer (the $i^{th}$); and

**SS** ≡ The manufacturer prefers the sophisticated Stackelberg tariff.

*Figure 10.25.* Manufacturer-Optimal Strategies: Channel Breadth and the Wholesale-Price Strategy When $f = 0.95$

### 4.2.1 Changes in the Retailers' Fixed-Cost Ratio

We begin our discussion by examining Figures 10.20 to 10.24. These Figures cover the $f$ – range $[0.672572, 0.909091)$, although our Figures only provide detail in increments of 0.05 from $f = 0.70$ to $f = 0.90$.[6] These Figures collectively reveal how the manufacturer's channel-breadth strategy evolves with increases in the retailers' fixed-cost ratio. We start by concentrating on the changes in the right-hand-side graphs, which depict the manufacturer's optimal strategy when channel breadth is endogenous. Four basic messages appear from these graphs.

First, comparing Figures 10.20 and 10.21, we find that the Single-Outlet ("SO") portion of the unit half-square shrinks for three reasons as $f$ increases from 0.70 to 0.75. (1) The Menu ("MN") becomes more dominant over the SO – strategy at high $\chi$ – values combined with low $S_j$ – values. (2) The sophisticated Stackelberg strategy ("SS") becomes more superior to the SO – strategy at low $\chi$ – values combined with mid-range $S_j$ – values. (3) The Quantity-Discount schedule ("QD") becomes more preferred to the SO – strategy over a narrow range of $S_j$ – values at very high $\chi$ – values.

Second, the SS – portion of the unit half-square also shrinks. We find that SS is dominated by QD at high $\chi$ – values combined with $S_j$ – values that are near ½. SS is also dominated by the Menu at high $\chi$ – values combined with mid-range $S_j$ – values. The incremental area over which the SS – strategy is preferred to the SO – strategy is smaller than the areas that are "lost" to MN and QD. These downward trends in SO and SS continue as $f$ increases from 0.75 to 0.90.

Third, the attractiveness to the manufacturer of the Single-Outlet strategy is greatest when the competitors are very different in size and have sharply divergent market shares. To understand the reason for this result, fix the values of $f$ and $\chi$ and consider the profit implications for the manufacturer of serving both retailers. Because the less profitable retailer's participation constraint imposes a limit on the fixed fee that can be charged, the total rent the manufacturer can extract from the retailers diminishes as the retailers' market shares diverge. Thus the SO – strategy is more attractive to the manufacturer as $S_j \to 0$ (or $S_j \to 1$); that is, when few sales are sacrificed by not having a second retailer.

Fourth, the higher is the intensity of competition ($\chi$), the closer are total sales of an SO – strategy to the sales of a broader, coordinated channel; the reason is that $Q^{so^*} = (Q_i^* + \chi Q_j^*)$. At a constant level of fixed cost, the

SO – strategy generates greater profit at higher values of $\chi$. It is also true that higher $f$ – values increase the set of points for which the manufacturer can use the menu to extract all profit from both retailers; this means that the MN – strategy is more appealing at higher $f$ – values. An examination of Figures 10.19-10.24 reveals that as $f$ increases, the channel-broadening $f$ – effect dominates the channel-narrowing $\chi$ – effect; thus coordination of a broader channel with the Menu or the Quantity-Discount schedule becomes more desirable for the manufacturer as $f$ increases.

### 4.2.2 Changes in Channel Breadth

Now consider the differences between the left-hand and right-hand graphs in each Figure; that is, contemplate the effect on the wholesale-price strategy of introducing channel breadth as an endogenous decision. We again start our analysis with Figure 10.20 ($f = 0.70$). When we model the manufacturer as being able to choose its channel breadth, we find that the SO – strategy is a powerful alternative to the MN – strategy and the SS – strategy. When market shares are divergent, the manufacturer prefers to distribute through a single outlet over a wide range of parametric values.

Figures 10.20-10.24 reveal that, at high fixed-cost ratios, a *coordinated channel* is in the manufacturer's interest when competitive intensity is high, while an *uncoordinated channel* is in the manufacturer's interest elsewhere. The decision to treat channel breadth as endogenous reveals that the *coordinated, Single-Outlet channel* is more likely to be the manufacturer's optimal strategy at low levels of competitive intensity, at low fixed-cost ratios, and at divergent market shares. As a result, for many parametric values the manufacturer chooses between the Single-Outlet strategy and the sophisticated Stackelberg strategy. Because the latter policy cannot extract all profit from non-identical, competing retailers, the sophisticated Stackelberg strategy tends to be dominated by the Single-Outlet strategy when market shares are very different.

Now consider the highest levels of retailers' fixed cost ($f > 0.909091$). Figure 10.25, which illustrates this situation for $f = 0.95$, is dramatically different from its predecessors for two reasons. First, as we argued in our pair-wise comparison of a single outlet *versus* the menu option, when $f > {}^{10}\!/_{11}$ (shown in Figure 10.16) the Single-Outlet option takes a bite from the $\langle \chi = 1 \rangle$ – axis. Second, we demonstrated in Chapter 9 that, when $f > 0.916752$, a teardrop-shaped area arises in the lower right-hand corner of the unit half-square. Within this teardrop the manufacturer prefers the sophisticated Stackelberg tariff to the menu of two-part tariffs. Comparing the two graphs in Figure 10.25, we see that the Single-Outlet strategy that takes a bite from the $\langle \chi = 1 \rangle$ – axis also takes a bite from the upper left-hand corner of the teardrop-shaped area. As a result, we find that the manufacturer prefers the Single-Outlet strategy over roughly 50 percent of parameter space. It seems that, when the fixed-cost ratio approaches one, there is an incentive for the manufacturer to abandon its efforts to coordinate a broader channel in order to embrace the ease of coordinating a narrower channel.

## 4.3 Commentary on Three Channel Myths

In this Chapter we have explored the parametric values under which the manufacturer prefers to distribute through one retailer (a Single-Outlet strategy) rather than through two competing retailers. We began by specifying the demand curve facing one retailer when the other retailer does not participate in the channel. We used this demand curve to derive the Channel Performance of a vertically-integrated system that operates a single outlet. We then compared the manufacturer profit from a Single-Outlet strategy with that earned in a two-retailer channel under the three wholesale-price strategies derived in Chapters 5-7. Our results enabled us to describe the conditions under which the decentralized manufacturer chooses a narrower or a broader channel breadth.

Three important inferences follow from our analysis. First, our results reinforce the importance of fixed costs in any model of inter-retailer competition. We have shown that, when retailer fixed costs are zero, only two outcomes are possible: (i) the manufacturer will establish a narrower channel than does the vertically-integrated system or (ii) it will duplicate the channel breadth of the vertically-integrated system *but* it will utilize a wholesale-price strategy that does *not* maximize channel profit. In neither case is the Channel Performance of the vertically-integrated system reproduced. Thus the belief that the manufacturer-optimal wholesale-price policy is independent of fixed costs is false, which is why we call this belief the *Fixed-Cost Modeling Myth*. Second, over the entire three-dimensional parameter space we find that channel coordination often does not benefit the manufacturer relative to its best, non-coordinating alternative. As a result, the belief that managers should always coordinate the channel is also false, which is why we call this belief the *Channel-Coordination Strategic Myth*. Third, we have shown that determining a manufacturer-optimal wholesale-price strategy cannot be divorced from the analysis of channel breadth when retailers compete. Our analysis demonstrates that, for a wide variety of parametric values, the Single-Outlet strategy is manufacturer-preferred for over one-half the possible $\langle \chi, S_j, f \rangle$ – combinations. The belief that channel breadth can be ignored as a modeling issue is false, which is why we refer to this belief as the *Channel-Breadth Modeling Myth*.

## 4.4 Summary Commentary

We have shown that adding a competing retailer to a bilateral-monopoly channel may not increase manufacturer profit—even though the broader channel can be coordinated. This brings to mind the words of William of Ockham,[7] who noted that "entities should not be multiplied unnecessarily." We highlight Ockham's observation because we cannot know if, from a manufacturer's perspective, a distribution-channel model includes "unnecessary retail entities" unless we nest a single-retailer model within a multiple-retailers model. In moving from a bilateral-monopoly model to a multiple-retailers model we purposefully "multiplied entities;" we were thereby able to *endogenously* ascertain the manufacturer-optimal Channel Strategy. Our analysis unveiled a *Channel-Breadth Modeling Myth* and also a *Channel-Coordination Strategic Myth.* Our proof that the manufacturer-optimal wholesale-price policy depends on channel breadth reveals that the Nested-Models Criterion goes hand-in-hand with the Strategic-Endogeneity Criterion. We will return to the importance of these model-building criteria in Chapter 12, but first we explore the meaning and the implications of a change in competition.

# 5 APPENDIX

**In this Appendix we make a set of pair-wise profit comparisons between the manufacturer profit that is obtainable with the Single-Outlet strategy *versus* the manufacturer profit earned with (1) the sophisticated Stackelberg two-part tariff or (2) the channel-coordinating menu of two-part tariffs. (The Single-Outlet/quantity-discount comparison appears at (10.3.9)-(10.3.11).) To conserve space we only evaluate the Single-Outlet retailer being the i^th^ retailer (the case of the j^th^ retailer is symmetric).**

## 5.1 The Single-Outlet Strategy *versus* the Sophisticated Stackelberg Tariff

Manufacturer profit with a Single-Outlet (the $i^{th}$) retailer is denoted as $\Pi_i^{so^*}$. Manufacturer profit in the $k^{th}$ Zone with the sophisticated Stackelberg tariff is denoted as $\tilde{\Pi}_k^*$, $k \in (i, ij, j)$. We obtain:

$$\left[\Pi_i^{so^*} - \tilde{\Pi}_j^*\right] = \left(\frac{R^*(1-\chi)}{2(2+\chi)^2}\right)\begin{bmatrix}\left\{(2+3\chi)^2 + 4\chi(6+7\chi)S_j - 2\left(12+8\chi-5\chi^2+\chi^3\right)S_j^2\right\} \\ -2(1+\chi)(2+\chi)^2\left\{(1-S_j)^2 f_i - 2S_j^2 f_j\right\}\end{bmatrix} \tag{10.A.1}$$

$$\left[\Pi_i^{so^*} - \tilde{\Pi}_{ij}^*\right] = \left(\frac{R^*}{8(2+\chi)^2(1-2S_j)^2}\right)\begin{bmatrix} 8\left\{\begin{matrix}(2+4\chi+3\chi^2) - 2\left(4+4\chi+7\chi^2-\chi^3\right)S_j + 4\left(4+4\chi-7\chi^2-\chi^4\right)S_j^2 \\ +\left(4+12\chi+25\chi^2-6\chi^3+\chi^4\right)S_j^3 - 4\left(4+4\chi-5\chi^2-2\chi^3-\chi^4\right)S_j^3\end{matrix}\right\} \\ +(1+\chi)(2+\chi)^4\left\{(1-S_j)^2 f_i - S_j^2 f_j\right\}^2 - 4(1+\chi)(2+\chi)^3(1-2S_j)(1-S_j)^2 f_i \\ +4(2+\chi)^2\left\{(4+3\chi-\chi^2) - 6\left(2+\chi-\chi^2\right)S_j + 8\left(1-\chi^2\right)S_j^2\right\}S_j^2 f_j \end{bmatrix} \tag{10.A.2}$$

$$\left[\Pi_i^{so^*} - \tilde{\Pi}_i^*\right] = \left(\frac{-R^*(1-\chi)}{2(2+\chi)^2}\right)\begin{bmatrix}\{(12+12\chi-\chi^2)-4(8+6\chi-3\chi^2)S_j+2(12+8\chi-5\chi^2+\chi^3)S_j^2\} \\ -2(1+\chi)(2+\chi)^2(1-S_j)^2 f_i\end{bmatrix} \quad (10.A.3)$$

When $f_i = f_j \equiv f$, (10.A.1)-(10.A.3) become:

$$\left[\Pi_i^{so^*} - \tilde{\Pi}_j^*\right]\Big|_{f_i=f_j} = \left(\frac{R^*(1-\chi)}{2(2+\chi)^2}\right)\begin{bmatrix}\{(2+3\chi)^2+4\chi(6+7\chi)S_j-2(12+8\chi-5\chi^2+\chi^3)S_j^2\} \\ -2(1+\chi)(2+\chi)^2(1-2S_j-S_j^2)f\end{bmatrix} \quad (10.A.4)$$

$$\left[\Pi_i^{so^*} - \tilde{\Pi}_{ij}^*\right]\Big|_{f_i=f_j} = \left(\frac{R^*}{8(2+\chi)^2}\right)\begin{bmatrix}8\{(2+4\chi+3\chi^2)-2(1-\chi)\chi^2 S_j-(4+4\chi-5\chi^2-2\chi^3-\chi^4)S_j^2\} \\ +(1+\chi)(2+\chi)^4\{f-4(2+\chi)-2(1-\chi)S_j^2\}^2 f\end{bmatrix} \quad (10.A.5)$$

$$\left[\Pi_i^{so^*} - \tilde{\Pi}_i^*\right]\Big|_{f_i=f_j} = \left(\frac{-R^*(1-\chi)}{2(2+\chi)^2}\right)\begin{bmatrix}\{(12+12\chi-\chi^2)-4(8+6\chi-3\chi^2)S_j+2(12+8\chi-5\chi^2+\chi^3)S_j^2\} \\ -2(1+\chi)(2+\chi)^2(1-S_j)^2 f\end{bmatrix} \quad (10.A.6)$$

## 5.2 The Single-Outlet Strategy *versus* the Channel-Coordinating Menu of Tariffs

Manufacturer profit in the k[th] Zone with the menu of tariffs is denoted as $\Pi_k^{M*}$, $k \in (i, ij, j)$. We obtain:

$$\left[\Pi_i^{SO*} - \Pi_j^{M*}\right] = \left(\frac{(1-\chi)R^*}{(1+\chi)(4-\chi^2)^2}\right)\left\{\begin{array}{l}(4+2\chi-\chi^2)^2 - 2(16+8\chi-8\chi^2+2\chi^3+3\chi^4-\chi^5)S_j \\ -\{16+64\chi+24\chi^2-40\chi^3-15\chi^4+6\chi^5+\chi^6\} \\ -(4+4\chi-\chi^2-\chi^3)^2\left[(1-S_j)^2 f_i - 2S_j^2 f_j\right]\end{array}\right\} \tag{10.A.7}$$

$$\left[\Pi_i^{SO*} - \Pi_{ij}^{M*}\right] = -R^*(1-\chi^2)S_j^2(1-f_j) < 0 \tag{10.A.8}$$

$$\left[\Pi_i^{SO*} - \Pi_i^{M*}\right] = \left(\frac{-(1-\chi)R^*}{(1+\chi)(4-\chi^2)^2}\right)\left\{\begin{array}{l}(16+32\chi+4\chi^2-16\chi^3-3\chi^4+2\chi^5) \\ -2(16+40\chi+8\chi^2-22\chi^3-5\chi^4+3\chi^5)S_j \\ +(16+64\chi+24\chi^2-40\chi^3-15\chi^4+6\chi^5+\chi^6) \\ -(4+4\chi-\chi^2-\chi^3)^2(1-S_j)^2 f_i\end{array}\right\} \tag{10.A.9}$$

When $f_i = f_j \equiv f$, (10.A.7)-(10.A.9) become:

$$\left[\Pi_i^{SO^*} - \Pi_j^{M^*}\right]\Big|_{f_i=f_j} = \left(\frac{(1-\chi)R^*}{(1+\chi)(4-\chi^2)^2}\right)\left\{\begin{array}{l}(4+2\chi-\chi^2)^2 - 2(16+8\chi-8\chi^2+2\chi^3+3\chi^4-\chi^5)S_j \\ -\{16+64\chi+24\chi^2-40\chi^3-15\chi^4+6\chi^5+\chi^6\} \\ -(4+4\chi-\chi^2-\chi^3)^2(1-2S_j^2-S_j^2)f\end{array}\right\} \quad (10.A.10)$$

$$\left[\Pi_i^{SO^*} - \Pi_{ij}^{M^*}\right]\Big|_{f_i=f_j} = -R^*(1-\chi^2)S_j^2(1-f) < 0 \quad (10.A.11)$$

$$\left[\Pi_i^{SO^*} - \Pi_i^{M^*}\right]\Big|_{f_i=f_j} = \left(\frac{-(1-\chi)R^*}{(1+\chi)(4-\chi^2)^2}\right)\left\{\begin{array}{l}(16+32\chi+4\chi^2-16\chi^3-3\chi^4+2\chi^5) \\ -2(16+40\chi+8\chi^2-22\chi^3-5\chi^4+3\chi^5)S_j \\ +(16+64\chi+24\chi^2-40\chi^3-15\chi^4+6\chi^5+\chi^6) \\ -(4+4\chi-\chi^2-\chi^3)^2(1-S_j)^2 f\end{array}\right\} \quad (10.A.12)$$

# Notes

[1] The proof of this statement appears in Chapter 2.
[2] We proved this statement in Chapter 8 and illustrated it graphically in Chapter 9.
[3] Since the sophisticated Stackelberg tariff does not maximize channel profit, serving a single retailer may be manufacturer-preferred even in SS-Zone $Z_{ij}^{ss^*}$.
[4] The $j^{th}$ retailer's demand can be deduced from the following results by reversing the subscripts.
[5] For expository purposes, and without loss of generality, we will assume that if only one retailer is used for distribution, it will be the $i^{th}$ retailer.
[6] Recall that Figure 10.19 provides an excellent, first-order approximation over the $f$ – range $[0, 0.672572)$.
[7] By convention, the rule first developed by William of *Ockham* (1288-1347) is known as *Occam*'s razor. We have been unable to ascertain the reason for two spellings of his name. The quotation is from *Quodlibetal Questions*; the English translation is by Freddoso and Kelley (1991).

Chapter 11

# Modeling a Change in Competitive Substitutability

*"Truth is ever to be found in the simplicity, and not in the multiplicity and confusion of things."*

## 1 INTRODUCTION

In the last Chapter we investigated the channel-breadth decision of a manufacturer who had the choice of serving either one or two retailers. Our analysis required a formal specification of the way in which a *quantitative change in competition*—a change in the number of retailers—affected market demand. In contrast, a *qualitative change in competition*—which is commonly referred to as *a change in competitive substitutability*—involves a change in how the price of the $i^{th}$ retailer affects the demand facing the $j^{th}$ retailer. Marketing scientists have typically analyzed the latter type of change by interpreting the cross-price parameter of the demand curve ($\theta$) as a measure of competitive substitutability. We reject this interpretation because a change in $\theta$ alters the aggregate demand faced by the channel; this leads to counter-intuitive comparative static effects. Because modeling a change in competitive substitutability as a change in $\theta$ is so widespread, and because the consequences of this modeling technique are so egregious, we refer to this approach as the *Aggregate-Demand Modeling Myth*.

We also explore two alternative methods for modeling a change in competitive substitutability that rely exclusively on the information contained in the system of demand equations. We term these techniques a *compensating change in slopes*[1] and a *compensating change in intercepts*; both of them hold aggregate demand constant. The former approach simultaneously changes the own-price and cross-price terms (the slopes) of the demand curve. The latter method simultaneously changes the competitors' maximal demand quantities (the intercepts of the demand curves). While both measures eliminate the increase in units sold that characterizes the procedure that is common in the literature, we will show that both approaches have their own weaknesses that prevent them from being appropriate for assessing a change in competitive substitutability. In each of these cases the fundamental difficulty is that researchers have not recognized that (i) demand curves are derived from an underlying utility function or that (ii) this derivation imposes restrictions on the derived-demand curve.

Consumers maximize their utility from goods, and from the stores at which those goods are purchased, subject to their income, the prices they face, and their preferences for products and stores. By backward induction it is possible to deduce the utility function from which a system of demand equations was (implicitly) derived. We use the inter-retailer substitutability parameter from this underlying utility function as our core measure of substitutability. Thus, it is *consumer willingness to substitute a good available from one competitor for a good offered by its rival* that defines competitive substitutability. Our approach has three desirable characteristics. First, it demonstrates that the own-price and cross-price effects in the demand curves are affected by a change in consumers' willingness to substitute between retailers. Second, it also shows that the maximal demand quantities of rival stores are influenced by a change in competitive substitutability. Third, it generates results that possess substantial face validity.

The remainder of this Chapter is organized as follows. In Section 2 we explore three approaches to modeling competitive change: (1) a cross-price effect, (2) a compensating change in slopes, and (3) a compensating change in intercepts. Because each of these measures has its weaknesses, Section 3 presents the logic of a superior approach that is based on the underlying utility function. Section 4 utilizes this logic to investigate the impact of a change in competition on channel performance. In Section 5 we offer concluding comments on the effects of a change in competition on the manufacturer's optimal wholesale-price policy, including why the channel-coordinating menu largely dominates the non-coordinating sophisticated Stackelberg tariff at a high intensity of competition. Technical details appear in the Appendix.

## 2 POSSIBLE METHODS OF MEASURING A CHANGE IN COMPETITIVE SUBSTITUTABILITY

A widely-utilized approach for measuring a change in competitive substitutability is to employ the cross-price effect from the demand curve. We spell out the consequences of this technique in this Section. We then examine two alternative approaches that hold aggregate demand constant. One involves a compensating change in the own- and cross-price slopes of the demand curves. The other entails a compensating change in the intercepts of those curves.[2] We demonstrate that all three approaches lack face validity. As a consequence, we develop a theoretically-based measure of a change in competitive substitutability in the next Section that rectifies the shortcomings of the measures examined in this Section.

Our analysis is based on the linear demand curve (5.2.1) used in

Chapters 5-10. We reproduce that system of demand equations here:[3]

$$\left.\begin{aligned} Q_i &= A_i - bp_i + \theta p_j \\ Q_j &= A_j - bp_j + \theta p_i \end{aligned}\right\} \quad \text{s.t.} \quad 0 \le \theta < b \tag{11.2.1}$$

The parameters $A_i$, $A_j$, b, and θ are positive. Competitors are distinguished by the quantity intercepts, although equal demand ($A_i = A_j$) is embedded within our model as a special case. Summing individual retailer's demands gives aggregate demand:

$$\sum_k Q_k = \sum_k A_k - (b - \theta)\sum_k p_k; \qquad k \in (i, j) \tag{11.2.2}$$

As Equation (11.2.2) reveals, a well-behaved aggregate demand curve requires $b > \theta$. If $b = \theta$, demand is perfectly inelastic, while if $b < \theta$, the demand curve has a positive slope.

## 2.1 A Change in Competitive Substitutability Modeled with the Cross-Price Term θ

The existing channels literature typically has modeled a change in qualitative competition as a change in θ. The fundamental problem with this approach can be seen examining the impact of a change in θ on the $i^{th}$ retailer's demand:

$$\partial Q_i / \partial \theta = p_j > 0 \tag{11.2.3}$$

Equation (11.2.3) does *not* state that an increase in the $j^{th}$ retailer's price raises the $i^{th}$ retailer's sales. (The statement is true, but it follows from the expression $\partial Q_i / \partial p_j = \theta \ge 0$). Instead, equation (11.2.3) states that, as stores become closer substitutes (as $\theta \to b$), each retailer sells more. Because θ has symmetric effect on *both* retailers' demand curves, changing θ shifts aggregate demand:

$$\partial \sum_k Q_k / \partial \theta = \sum_k p_k > 0 \qquad k \in (i, j) \tag{11.2.4}$$

An increase in θ increases aggregate demand! Moreover, for any given change in θ, the higher are prices, the greater is the increase in demand. These results present immediate problems for those who interpret a change in θ as a change in competitive substitutability. Simple introspection should be sufficient to reveal that, as retailers become more readily substitutable in consumers' eyes, they compete more fiercely. Further, it seems highly unlikely that two very similar retailers can expand aggregate demand by becoming even more similar; that is, they should not be able to "grow the market" by becoming almost perfectly interchangeable.[4] The lack of an intuitive explanation for the increase in aggregate demand is our first indication that there is a problem with equating a change in competition with a change in the cross-price term. We will show that there are even stronger reasons for rejecting this modeling method.

## 2.2 The Effect of a Change in the Cross-Price Term θ on Channel Performance

A changing market size is one problem that arises from the interpretation of $\theta$ as a measure of competitive substitutability. A second problem arises in analyses linking competitive substitutability and channel performance. Recall from equation (5.3.4), reproduced here, that a coordinated channel has a channel margin at the $i^{th}$ store:

$$\mu_i^* \equiv \left(p_i^* - c_i - C\right) = \left(\frac{bQ_i^* + \theta Q_j^*}{b^2 - \theta^2}\right) \tag{11.2.5}$$

The channel margin increases as $\theta$ increases; in the limit (as $\theta \to b$) the denominator of (11.2.5) goes to zero—and the optimal price goes to infinity! In other words, increasing competitive substitutability increases the prices charged by each store. We obtain an equally absurd result by differentiating the coordinated outputs (equation (5.3.3)):

$$\frac{dQ_i^*}{d\theta} = \left(\frac{c_i + C}{2}\right) > 0 \tag{11.2.6}$$

$$\frac{d\sum_k Q_k^*}{d\theta} = \sum_k \left(\frac{c_k + C}{2}\right) > 0 \quad k \in (i,j) \tag{11.2.7}$$

The impact on the quantity sold of a change in $\theta$ depends on variable channel costs. The higher are the costs, the more rapidly unit sales increase as $\theta$ rises.

Given a finite number of units sold at a price that approaches infinity, it is unsurprising to find that channel profit also approaches infinity:

$$\Pi_C^* = \left(\frac{b\left(Q_i^*\right)^2 + 2\theta Q_i^* Q_j^* + b\left(Q_j^*\right)^2}{b^2 - \theta^2}\right) - f_i - f_j - F \tag{11.2.8}$$

$$\to \infty \quad \text{as} \quad \theta \to b$$

(This expression is reproduced from (5.3.10)). What drives these peculiar results is the fact that, as $\theta \to b$, aggregate demand (11.2.2) becomes utterly price-*insensitive*. The empirical evidence is that this is descriptively unrealistic of *any* market. We conclude that modeling a change in competitive substitutability as a change in $\theta$ is *not* the correct method of mathematically representing this phenomenon.

The preceding analysis assumes a coordinated channel, but similar results arise in the absence of coordination. The sophisticated Stackelberg price policy, which is the envelope of an infinite number of two-part tariffs, also generates infinite values for channel margins and channel profit as $\theta \to b$. This can be seen from the following expressions for margins and channel profit, which are reproduced from Table 6.1:[5]

$$\hat{\mu}_i^*(j) = \left( \frac{3(2b-\theta)Q_i^* - (2b-5\theta)Q_j^*}{2(b-\theta)(2b+\theta)} \right) \tag{11.2.9}$$

$$\hat{\mu}_j^*(j) = \left( \frac{Q_i^* + Q_j^*}{2(b-\theta)} \right) \tag{11.2.10}$$

$$\hat{\Pi}_C^*(j) = \left( \frac{\left(4b^2 + 8b\theta - 3\theta^2\right)\left[\left(Q_i^*\right)^2 + \left(Q_j^*\right)^2\right] + 2\left(4b^2 + 5\theta^2\right)Q_i^*Q_j^*}{2(b-\theta)(2b+\theta)^2} \right) - f_i - f_j - F \tag{11.2.11}$$

The denominators of (11.2.9)-(11.2.11) go to zero as $\theta \to b$.

In short, the decision to define a change in competitive substitutability as a change in the parameter $\theta$ automatically diminishes, and ultimately eliminates, price sensitivity from the demand curve. In the limit, prices and channel profit rise to infinity regardless of the manufacturer's wholesale-price policy. Because this result lacks face validity, we term the belief that a change in $\theta$ can be interpreted as a change in competitive substitutability the *Aggregate-Demand Modeling Myth.* We now examine two alternative approaches to measuring a change in competitive substitutability, each of which explicitly prevents fluctuations in aggregate demand.

## 2.3 A Change in Competitive Substitutability Modeled as a Compensating Change in Slopes

One method of holding aggregate demand constant is to vary the own-price parameter (b) as the cross-price parameter ($\theta$) changes. In this sub-Section we develop and discuss this methodology. We begin by totally differentiating aggregate demand to obtain:

$$d\sum_k Q_k = dA_i + dA_j - (db - d\theta)\sum_k p_k; \qquad k \in (i,j) \tag{11.2.12}$$

For aggregate demand to be constant requires $d\Sigma Q_k = 0$. Our first method of achieving this equality is to set $dA_i = 0 = dA_j$; this yields:

$$d\sum_k Q_k = 0 = (db - d\theta)\sum_k p_k; \quad dA_k = 0; \quad k \in (i,j) \tag{11.2.13}$$

Because $p_k > 0$, equation (11.2.13) implies $db = d\theta \neq 0$.[6] Formally we say that a change in $\theta$ is accompanied by a compensating change in b. To denote this compensation we use the notation:

$$\left( \frac{d\sum_k Q_k}{d\theta}\bigg|_{db=d\theta} \right) = 0 \tag{11.2.14}$$

Applying this constraint to both retail demand curves, we obtain:

$$\left( \frac{dQ_i}{d\theta}\bigg|_{db=d\theta} \right) = -\left( \frac{dQ_j}{d\theta}\bigg|_{db=d\theta} \right) = \left(p_j - p_i\right) \gtreqless 0 \tag{11.2.15}$$

An increase in $\theta$ increases the quantity sold by the low-price retailer and decreases the quantity sold by the high-price retailer. In the special case of identical competitors ($p_i = p_j$), an increase in $\theta$ has no effect on quantities.

## 2.4 The Effect of a Compensating Change in Slopes on Channel Performance

We now consider the implications of our $db = d\theta$ constraint for modeling intra-channel competition. We begin with an analysis of optimal channel margins. Differentiation of (5.3.4) reveals:

$$\left( \frac{d\mu_i^*}{d\theta}\bigg|_{db=d\theta} \right) = -\left( \frac{1}{(b+\theta)} \right) \left[ \frac{\left(Q_i^* - Q_j^*\right)}{(b+\theta)} - \left\{ \frac{dQ_i^*}{d\theta}\bigg|_{db=d\theta} \right\} \right] \tag{11.2.16}$$

This expression can be substantially simplified by substituting the definition of $Q_i^*$ (equation (5.3.3)); this yields:

$$\begin{gathered} \left( \frac{d\mu_i^*}{d\theta}\bigg|_{db=d\theta} \right) = \left( \frac{A_j - A_i}{2(b+\theta)^2} \right) = \left( -\frac{d\mu_j^*}{d\theta}\bigg|_{db=d\theta} \right) \\ \Rightarrow \frac{d\mu_i^*}{d\theta}\bigg|_{db=d\theta} \gtreqless 0 \quad \text{as} \quad A_j \gtreqless A_i \end{gathered} \tag{11.2.17}$$

Consequently:

$$\left( \frac{d\sum_k \mu_k^*}{d\theta}\bigg|_{db=d\theta} \right) = 0 \tag{11.2.18}$$

Thus when $db = d\theta$, an increase in $\theta$ raises the price obtained by the retailer with the *lower* base level of demand (the "less-attractive" or "lower-intercept" retailer), but has no effect on the unweighted *average* price paid by consumers.[7]

Now consider the impact of a compensating change in slopes upon the output levels of a coordinated channel. Differentiating (5.3.3) reveals:

$$\left(\left.\frac{dQ_i^*}{d\theta}\right|_{db=d\theta}\right)=\frac{(c_j-c_i)}{2}=-\left(\left.\frac{dQ_j^*}{d\theta}\right|_{db=d\theta}\right) \tag{11.2.19}$$

$$\left(\left.\frac{d\sum_k Q_k^*}{d\theta}\right|_{db=d\theta}\right)=0 \tag{11.2.20}$$

A compensating increase in the slopes raises the output level of the retailer with *lower* marginal cost. This gain comes entirely from the rival retailer, because aggregate output is constant. Notice that this result depends on the retailer's own per-unit costs and not on the wholesale prices paid by the retailers. We have already shown that the larger retailer pays the lower *marginal* wholesale price, but a retailer's own per-unit cost ($c_i$) may be of any magnitude relative to its rival's marginal cost ($c_j$).

It is important to recognize that the "compensating change in slopes" methodology is predicated on holding *aggregate demand* constant; thus it considers the parameters $A_i, A_j, b$ and $\theta$. What is *not* held constant is costs—as can be seen in the upper line of equation (11.2.19). The effect on the coordinated output of a retailer is non-constant because parameters $c_i$ and $c_j$ are typically unequal.

To find the effect of a compensating change in slopes on channel profit, we differentiate profit equation (5.3.10) to obtain:

$$\left(\left.\frac{d\Pi_C^*}{d\theta}\right|_{db=d\theta}\right)=\frac{(Q_i^*-Q_j^*)\{[A_j+(b+\theta)c_j]-[A_i+(b+\theta)c_i]\}}{2(b+\theta)^2}\gtrless 0$$

$$\begin{aligned}&\geq 0 \quad \text{if } Q_i^*\geq Q_j^* \text{ and } p_j^*\geq p_i^* \text{ or}\\ &\geq 0 \quad \text{if } Q_i^*\leq Q_j^* \text{ and } p_j^*\leq p_i^* \text{ or}\\ &<0 \quad \text{otherwise}\end{aligned} \tag{11.2.21}$$

The {bracketed} term in expression (11.2.21) is the condition that determines the sign of the *difference* in retail prices (see the discussion associated with equation (5.3.5)). It is positive (negative) if $p_j^*$ is greater (less) than $p_i^*$. Overall, an increase in slopes raises channel profit if and only if the larger retailer obtains the lower price.

The effect of a compensating change in slopes on the sophisticated Stackelberg variables is presented in the Appendix to this Chapter. Broadly speaking, the effects depend on the differences in coordinated quantities and the difference in per-unit costs. Although the effects may be of any sign, the *qualitative* message is consistent with that of equation (11.2.21) for channel-profit.

## 2.5 A Change in Competitive Substitutability Modeled as a Compensating Change in Intercepts

An alternative approach to modeling a change in competitive substitutability is to hold aggregate demand constant while varying the demand intercepts (and holding the own-price and cross-price terms constant). Because a constant aggregate demand entails $d\Sigma Q_k = 0$, we have:

$$d\sum_k Q_k = 0 = d\sum_k A_k \quad \rightarrow \quad dA_i = -\,dA_j \tag{11.2.22}$$

Formally, we say the change in $A_i$ is accompanied by a *compensating change in* $A_j$. To denote this compensating change we use the notation:

$$\left( \left. \frac{d\sum Q_k}{dA_i} \right|_{dA_i=-dA_j} \right) = 0 \tag{11.2.23}$$

We now consider how a change in competitive substitutability, measured as a compensating change in intercepts, affects channel performance.

## 2.6 The Effect of a Compensating Change in Intercepts on Channel Performance

Consider first the implications of our $dA_i = -\,dA_j$ constraint on channel margins. Differentiating equation (5.3.4) reveals:

$$\left( \left. \frac{d\mu_i^*}{dA_i} \right|_{dA_i=-dA_j} \right) = \left( \frac{1}{2(b+\theta)} \right) = -\left( \left. \frac{d\mu_j^*}{dA_i} \right|_{dA_i=-dA_j} \right) > 0 \tag{11.2.24}$$

An increase in a retailer's base level of demand raises the price it can charge, and lowers its rival's price. The unweighted *average* price paid by consumers is unaffected; of course, this reflects a constant aggregate demand.

The effect of a change in competition upon channel profit is found by differentiating profit equation (5.3.10) to obtain:

$$\left( \left. \frac{dQ_i^*}{dA_i} \right|_{dA_i=-dA_j} \right) = \left( \frac{1}{2} \right) = -\left( \left. \frac{dQ_j^*}{dA_i} \right|_{dA_i=-dA_j} \right) > 0 \tag{11.2.25}$$

The increase in the $i^{th}$ retailer's base level of demand increases units sold along with the price increase. Its competitor suffers accordingly.

Channel profit rises with increases in the attractiveness of the larger retailer and falls with an increase in the attractiveness of the less-profitable retailer. This can be seen by differentiating profit equation (5.3.10) to obtain:

$$\left(\frac{d\Pi_C^*}{dA_i}\bigg|_{dA_i=-dA_j}\right)=\left(\frac{Q_i^*-Q_j^*}{b+\theta}\right)\gtrless 0 \quad \text{as} \quad Q_i^*\gtrless Q_j^* \tag{11.2.26}$$

In the case of a sophisticated Stackelberg wholesale-price policy, examining the same variables yields the following results for Zone $Z_j^{ss^*}$ :

$$\begin{aligned}\left(\frac{d\hat{\mu}_i^*(j)}{dA_i}\bigg|_{dA_i=-dA_j}\right)&=\left(\frac{2}{2b+\theta}\right)>0\\ \left(\frac{d\hat{\mu}_j^*(j)}{dA_i}\bigg|_{dA_i=-dA_j}\right)&=0\end{aligned} \tag{11.2.27}$$

$$\left(\frac{d\hat{\Pi}_C^*}{dA_i}\bigg|_{dA_i=-dA_j}\right)=\left(\frac{4\theta\left(Q_i^*-Q_j^*\right)}{\left(2b+\theta\right)^2}\right)\gtrless 0 \quad \text{as} \quad Q_i^*\gtrless Q_j^* \tag{11.2.28}$$

Once again channel profit increases as the attractiveness of the larger retailer rises. Notice that the impact of a change in competitive substitutability on channel profit diminishes as the competitors become more alike. This is not a result that we would expect from a properly-specified model. Instead, we expect that increases in competitive substitutability would increase price competition and consumer surplus at the expense of channel profit.

## 2.7 Commentary on Current Methods of Measuring a Change in Competitive Substitutability

Table 11.1 catalogs our results for differentiations involving (1) changes in the cross-price term, (2) a compensating change in slopes, or (3) a compensating change in intercepts. We see that the first approach leads, in the limit, to infinite values for channel margins and channel profit. More importantly, all variables increase with what is supposed to be an increase in competition. Simply stated, the effect of an artificially induced change in aggregate demand overwhelms the results. We conclude that this approach is inappropriate for assessing the effects of a change in competition.

*Table 11.1.* The Directional Impacts of Various Measures of a Change in Competitive Substitutability

| | A Change in the Cross-Price Effect | A Compensating Change in Slopes | A Compensating Change in Intercepts |
|---|---|---|---|
| | $\theta$ | $db = d\theta$ | $dA_i = -dA_j$ |
| Coordinated Channel | | | |
| $\mu_i^*$ | $+ \rightarrow \infty$ | $\gtrless 0$ as $A_j \gtrless A_i$ | + |
| $Q_i^*$ | + | $\gtrless 0$ as $c_j \gtrless c_i$ | + |
| $\Pi_c^*$ | $+ \rightarrow \infty$ | + if $Q_i^* > Q_j^*$ and $p_j^* > p_i^*$<br>+ if $Q_i^* < Q_j^*$ and $p_j^* < p_i^*$<br>− otherwise | $\gtrless 0$ as $Q_i^* \gtrless Q_j^*$ |
| Sophisticated Stackelberg Tariff in Zone $Z_j^{ss^*}$ | | | |
| $\hat{\mu}_i^*(j)$ | $+ \rightarrow \infty$ | $\gtrless 0$ as $Q_i^* \gtrless Q_j^*$ * | + |
| $\hat{\mu}_j^*(j)$ | $+ \rightarrow \infty$ | 0 | 0 |
| $\hat{\Pi}_c^*(j)$ | $+ \rightarrow \infty$ | $\gtrless 0$ as $Q_i^* \gtrless Q_j^*$ * | $\gtrless 0$ as $Q_i^* \gtrless Q_j^*$ |

* Denotes that information on the difference in per-unit costs has been set aside in reporting the sign. See the Appendix for details.

The second approach models a change in competitive substitutability as a compensating change in slopes. One consequence of this approach is that, when competitors are identical, a change in competition has no impact on a Channel Performance. And, as market shares move toward equality, the effect of a change in competition diminishes. This result is inconsistent with economic intuition. The third approach models a change in competitive substitutability as a compensating change in intercepts. It also yields unsatisfying results: increased competition generally increases prices and quantities while having an effect on profits that diminishes as competitors become more alike.

# 3 A THEORETICAL BASIS FOR A CHANGE IN COMPETITIVE SUBSTITUTABILITY

In this Section we approach the issue of competitive substitutability by analyzing the utility function that underlies our system of demand equations. We show that this function imposes specific linkages among the demand curve's parametric values ($A_i$, $A_j$, b and $\theta$. These linkages enable us to define a change in competitive substitutability in an intuitively appealing manner; consequently, our conclusions are compatible with rational economic behavior. Because our results also pass the basic test of face validity when judged against *a priori* anticipations, we conclude that the method developed in this Section is the proper technique for modeling a change in competitive substitutability.

## 3.1 The Logic of Utility-Based Demand

Marketing scientists who engage in research on distribution channels often characterize consumer demand with a linear function. Indeed, when the intent is a game-theoretic analysis of duopolistic competition, linear demand curves are almost always chosen,[8] because they provide the analytical tractability necessary to obtain "closed form" solutions. Moreover, Lee and Staelin (1997) have proven that linearity induces no meaningful distortions relative to more complex demand curves that are compatible with positively sloped price-reaction functions. If one reasons that the $i^{th}$ firm's optimal response to a decrease in its rival's price is to lower its own price, then linear demand is a reasonable modeling choice.

Despite the widespread use of linear demand, we find little evidence that modelers regard their demand curves as being anything other than direct manifestations of consumer actions in the marketplace. In one sense this is not surprising, for much research is inspired by empirical analyses that measure actual purchase patterns.[9] However, the empirical justification for linear demand seems to have diverted attention from economic first principles, which state that a consumer's demand for goods is derived from constrained maximization of an underlying utility function. The utility function captures consumer preferences, while the constraint considers consumer income and the prices of all products.

Some modelers appear to believe that the choice is "either/or." *Either* demand is derived from individual utility theory *or* demand is based on the real-world characteristics of an industry. Most modelers choose the latter option for two reasons. First, distribution models typically focus on firm behavior, not on consumer behavior; thus modelers seem to conclude that the underpinnings of demand can safely be ignored.[10] Second, modelers seem to feel that "deriving an aggregate demand function from first principles . . . would lead to unnecessary complexity" (Kim and Staelin 1999, p. 64). We stress that we have heard this viewpoint expressed at conferences by *many* marketing scientists; it is by no means unique to those who have articulated it in print.

In our opinion the either/or argument misses a fundamental point: once we write out a demand curve, a utility function can be found (at least implicitly) from which that demand curve is derived. This statement is true regardless of whether the inspiration for the demand curve is a single consumer, a single market segment, or several market segments. Further, linear demand curves have *explicit* underlying utility functions. It makes no difference whether the modeler (1) starts with utility and derives linear demand, or (2) starts with empirical observation and assumes linear demand. Demand in case (1) is obviously utility-based. Demand in case (2) is also utility-based because there is a utility function of a representative consumer from which the assumed linear demand can be derived (we prove this statement in the next sub-Section). It makes no difference whether there is, in practice, a representative consumer. Just as statistical distributions—uniform, normal, bi-modal or whatever—have a mean value, so every linear demand curve (no matter how complex its non-price arguments) has an underlying utility function that describes the preferences of a representative (an average) consumer.

The idea of a representative consumer merits a few additional comments. We are not saying that a representative consumer necessarily corresponds to any specific "real" consumer. It may help to think of a bimodal distribution, in which every observation corresponds to one of two values. This distribution has a mean value, even though no single observation equals the mean value. In the same manner, a market comprised of mutually exclusive segments has a "representative consumer" who may not belong to any segment. But even a representative consumer[11] who is, in a real-world sense, a "phantom," does not prevent the formation of a utility function to generate the chosen demand curve.

We will show that the underlying utility function can be used to generate the information needed to calculate the impact of a change in competition on a channel's behavioral performance. We begin with a discussion of the utility function itself.

## 3.2 Derivation of a Utility-Based, Linear-Demand Curve[12]

To generate a system of linear demand curves, the representative consumer's utility function must have the following form:

$$\mathcal{U} \equiv \sum_{\kappa}\left(\mathcal{A}_{\kappa}Q_{\kappa} - \mathcal{B}_{\kappa}(Q_{\kappa})^2/2\right) - \mathcal{T}Q_iQ_j \quad \kappa \in (h,k),\ k \in (i,j) \quad (11.3.1)$$

In (11.3.1) the $Q_{\kappa}$ terms denote quantities purchased of the $\kappa^{th}$ product, $\kappa$ either the focal good (the $k^{th}$ product) or a composite commodity (the $h^{th}$ product); the $h^{th}$ and $k^{th}$ products are demand-*independent*. The terms $\mathcal{A}_{\kappa}$, $\mathcal{B}_{\kappa}$, and $\mathcal{T}$ are non-negative. Only function (11.3.1), or a monotonic transformation of it, is compatible with a linear demand system.

For this utility function, the marginal utility of the $k^{th}$ product bought from the $i^{th}$ retailer is $(\mathcal{A}_i - \mathcal{B}_iQ_i - \mathcal{T}Q_j)$ and the rate of change in marginal utility is $-\mathcal{B}_i < 0$. Thus total utility increases at a decreasing rate for the focal product when it is purchased from the $i^{th}$ retailer (the same is true for purchases from the $j^{th}$ retailer). The $i^{th}$ and $j^{th}$ retailers are demand-*interdependent* because our representative consumer is willing to purchase the $k^{th}$ product from either retailer; this interdependence is modeled by the inter-retailer substitutability term $\mathcal{T} > 0$. The more substitutable the retailers are, the larger is $\mathcal{T}$. Notice that it is not the fact of selling an identical product that defines interdependence; it is the consumer's *willingness to buy* from either retailer. Recall that in Chapter 3 all the retailers sold an identical product. Had we employed a linear-demand curve in that Chapter, the retailers' demand-*independence* would have been modeled by $\mathcal{T} = 0$.

Our representative consumer maximizes his/her utility subject to the budget constraint:

$$\max_{Q_h, Q_i, Q_j} \mathcal{V} \equiv \mathcal{U} + \lambda\left[Y - \sum_{\kappa} p_{\kappa}Q_{\kappa}\right] \quad \kappa \in (h,k),\ k \in (i,j) \quad (11.3.2)$$

The bracketed term in (11.3.2) is the consumer's budget constraint: Y is income, $p_{\kappa}$ is the per-unit price for the $\kappa^{th}$ product/$k^{th}$ retailer, and $\lambda$ is the marginal utility of income.

We take the requisite first-order conditions and solve them to obtain the demand system for the focal product:

$$
\begin{aligned}
Q_i &= \left( \frac{\left[\mathcal{B}_j\mathcal{A}_i - \mathcal{T}\mathcal{A}_j\right] - \lambda\mathcal{B}_j p_i + \lambda\mathcal{T} p_j}{\mathcal{B}_i\mathcal{B}_j - \mathcal{T}^2} \right) \geq 0 \\
Q_j &= \left( \frac{\left[\mathcal{B}_i\mathcal{A}_j - \mathcal{T}\mathcal{A}_i\right] - \lambda\mathcal{B}_i p_j + \lambda\mathcal{T} p_i}{\mathcal{B}_i\mathcal{B}_j - \mathcal{T}^2} \right) \geq 0
\end{aligned} \tag{11.3.3}
$$

Second-order conditions for a maximum are $\mathcal{B}_i\mathcal{B}_j > \mathcal{T}^2$. We also derive demand for the composite good:

$$
Q_h = \left( \frac{\mathcal{A}_h - \lambda p_h}{\mathcal{B}_h} \right) \geq 0 \tag{11.3.4}
$$

Because equation (11.3.4) represents a product that is demand-independent of the focal product, we do not discuss it further.[13]

## 3.3 Demand Simplifications

In conformity with the models presented throughout this book, we make two additional assumptions in order to simplify our analysis. First, we set $\mathcal{B}_i = \mathcal{B}_j \equiv \mathcal{B}$.[14] This equalizes the rates of change of the marginal utility of the $k^{th}$ product purchased from either the $i^{th}$ or the $j^{th}$ retailer. Because the product is the same at both retailers, this seems to be an innocuous assumption. By equating the rate of change of the marginal utility of the $k^{th}$ product across retail outlets, we equalize the own-price terms of the demand curves. With this assumption, the second-order conditions for utility maximization reduce to $\mathcal{B} > \mathcal{T}$. Second, we assume that the marginal utility of money ($\lambda$) is constant.[15] This ensures that changes in income or the price of the composite commodity do not affect demand for the focal product.

To simplify writing out the retail demand equations, we define the following four parametric substitutions:

$$
\begin{aligned}
A_i &\equiv \left(\mathcal{B}\mathcal{A}_i - \mathcal{T}\mathcal{A}_j\right) / \left(\mathcal{B}^2 - \mathcal{T}^2\right) > 0, \\
A_j &\equiv \left(\mathcal{B}\mathcal{A}_j - \mathcal{T}\mathcal{A}_i\right) / \left(\mathcal{B}^2 - \mathcal{T}^2\right) > 0, \\
b &\equiv \lambda\mathcal{B} / \left(\mathcal{B}^2 - \mathcal{T}^2\right) > 0, \text{ and} \\
\theta &\equiv \lambda\mathcal{T} / \left(\mathcal{B}^2 - \mathcal{T}^2\right) > 0
\end{aligned} \tag{11.3.5}
$$

With these substitutions we can rewrite demand equations (11.3.3) and (11.3.4) as:

$$Q_i = A_i - bp_i + \theta p_j$$
$$Q_j = A_j - bp_j + \theta p_i \tag{11.3.6}$$

Notice that the own-price coefficient is the same in both equations. This result follows directly from our assumption that the rate of change of the marginal utility of the $k^{th}$ product is constant across retail outlets.

We stress that we have used the system of demand equations (11.3.6) throughout Chapters 5-10. The analysis presented in earlier Chapters did not require an understanding of the definitions underlying the demand curve parameters. However, as we will show in the next Section, these definitions are necessary to determine the consequences of a change in competitive substitutability.

# 4 MODELING A CHANGE IN COMPETITIVE SUBSTITUTABILITY

The ideal term for modeling a change in competitive substitutability is the substitutability parameter from the utility function of the representative consumer ($\mathcal{T}$). There are several reasons. First, $\mathcal{T}$ is defined as the consumer's willingness to substitute a purchase of the $k^{th}$ product from the $i^{th}$ retailer for the same product from the $j^{th}$ retailer. This is important, for it focuses attention where it belongs: on the representative consumer's choice process. Second, $\mathcal{T}$ directly affects the cross-price term ($\theta$) of the system of demand equations. We cannot conceive of a legitimate method of measuring a change in competition that does not have this property. Third, $\mathcal{T}$ also directly affects the own-price term (b) of the demand curve. Fourth, $\mathcal{T}$ affects market shares via its impact on the demand intercepts ($A_i$ and $A_j$). We believe that a change in competitive substitutability generally has a differential impact on the retailers. The reason is that some consumers purchase from a store because it is different from its rival (perhaps on the basis of location or service). It is this differentiation that contributes to unequal demand intercepts. Fifth, aggregate demand is inversely affected by $\mathcal{T}$. This is as it should be; the more nearly identical are the retailers, the more likely are their sales to cannibalize each other. They are also more likely to shrink the market if they become even more similar. Conversely, the more distinct are the stores, the less price sensitive consumers are apt to be.

To establish these results formally, we differentiate definitions (11.3.5) and use the results in the demand system (11.3.6). We obtain:

$$\frac{dA_i}{d\mathcal{T}} = (\theta A_i - bA_j) \gtrless 0 \qquad \frac{db}{d\mathcal{T}} = \frac{2b\theta}{\lambda} > 0$$

$$\frac{dA_j}{d\mathcal{T}} = -(bA_i - \theta A_j) \gtrless 0 \qquad \frac{d\theta}{d\mathcal{T}} = \frac{(b^2 + \theta^2)}{\lambda} > 0 \tag{11.4.1}$$

A change in $\mathcal{T}$ affects *all parameters* of the demand system.[16] In particular, an increase in $\mathcal{T}$ increases own-price *and* cross-price sensitivity while lowering the aggregate attractiveness of the competitors, by which we mean the sum of the base demands facing the two retailers (i.e., $A_i + A_j$):

$$\left(\frac{dA_i}{d\mathcal{T}} + \frac{dA_j}{d\mathcal{T}}\right) = -(b - \theta)(A_i + A_j) < 0 \tag{11.4.2}$$

For completeness, we mention that a change in $\mathcal{B}$ also affects all terms of the demand system:

$$\frac{dA_i}{d\mathcal{B}} = \frac{-(bA_i - \theta A_j)}{\lambda} = \left(\frac{dA_j/d\mathcal{T}}{\lambda}\right) \gtrless 0$$

$$\frac{dA_j}{d\mathcal{B}} = \frac{(\theta A_i - bA_j)}{\lambda} = \left(\frac{dA_i/d\mathcal{T}}{\lambda}\right) \gtrless 0$$

$$\frac{db}{d\mathcal{B}} = \frac{-(b^2 + \theta^2)}{\lambda} = -\left(\frac{d\theta}{d\mathcal{T}}\right) < 0 \tag{11.4.3}$$

$$\frac{d\theta}{d\mathcal{B}} = \frac{-2b\theta}{\lambda} = -\left(\frac{db}{d\mathcal{T}}\right) < 0$$

In contrast, a change in the parameter $\mathcal{A}_i$ has a less comprehensive impact:

$$\frac{dA_i}{d\mathcal{A}_i} = \left(\frac{b}{\lambda}\right) > 0 \qquad \frac{dA_j}{d\mathcal{A}_i} = -\left(\frac{\theta}{\lambda}\right) < 0$$

$$\frac{db}{d\mathcal{A}_i} = 0 \qquad \frac{d\theta}{d\mathcal{A}_i} = 0 \tag{11.4.4}$$

Following common practice (see footnote 15), we set $\lambda$ equal to one and use the information contained in (11.4.1)-(11.4.4) to analyze the impact of a change in $\mathcal{T}$ on channel performance under various channel structures and wholesale-price policies.

## 4.1 The Effect of a Change in Substitutability $\mathcal{T}$ on the Performance of a Coordinated Channel

We start our analysis by focusing on those variables that are common across all methods of channel coordination. In the next sub-Section we address variables that are unique to a vertically-integrated channel. We then deal with variables that are unique to the quantity-discount and menu policies.

### 4.1.1 Variables Common to all Channel-Coordinating Strategies

The effect of a change in competition on the total output of a coordinated channel is:

$$d\left(Q_i^* + Q_j^*\right)/d\mathcal{T} = -\left(b-\theta\right)\left(Q_i^* + Q_j^*\right) < 0 \tag{11.4.5}$$

An increase in consumer willingness to substitute purchases from the i[th] retailer for goods from the j[th] retailer leads to lower *total* sales. However, this result need *not* affect both retailers equally. We find:

$$\frac{dQ_i^*}{d\mathcal{T}} = \left(\theta Q_i^* - bQ_j^*\right) \gtrless 0 \quad \text{as} \quad \chi \equiv \frac{\theta}{b} \gtrless \frac{Q_j^*}{Q_i^*} \equiv \frac{S_j}{\left(1-S_j\right)} \tag{11.4.6}$$

where the term $S_j$ denotes the market share of the j[th] retailer. Expression (11.4.6) offers a subtle insight into the relative success of the retailers. To see this we algebraically manipulate (11.4.6), while recognizing that second-order conditions require $(\theta/b) < 1$. We find that an increase in retailer substitutability *may* result in only one rival suffering a decline in demand:

$$\begin{aligned}
\frac{Q_j^*}{Q_i^*} > \frac{b}{\theta} > 1 > \frac{\theta}{b} \quad &\Rightarrow \quad \frac{dQ_i^*}{d\mathcal{T}} < 0 < \frac{dQ_j^*}{d\mathcal{T}} \\
\frac{b}{\theta} > 1 \gtrless \frac{Q_j^*}{Q_i^*} > \frac{\theta}{b} \quad &\Rightarrow \quad \frac{dQ_i^*}{d\mathcal{T}}, \frac{dQ_j^*}{d\mathcal{T}} < 0 \\
\frac{b}{\theta} > 1 > \frac{\theta}{b} > \frac{Q_j^*}{Q_i^*} \quad &\Rightarrow \quad \frac{dQ_i^*}{d\mathcal{T}} > 0 > \frac{dQ_j^*}{d\mathcal{T}}
\end{aligned} \tag{11.4.7}$$

What is *impossible* is:

$$\frac{dQ_i^*}{d\mathcal{T}} > 0 \text{ and } \frac{dQ_j^*}{d\mathcal{T}} > 0 \tag{11.4.8}$$

Both retailers cannot benefit from an increase in competitive substitutability, although the larger retailer *may* benefit.

The impact of a change in retailer substitutability on channel profit is:

$$\frac{d\Pi_C^*}{d\mathcal{T}} \equiv -2Q_i^* Q_j^* < 0 \tag{11.4.9}$$

As expected, an increase in the substitutability parameter lowers channel profit: As $\mathcal{T}$ rises sales are cannibalized, as can be seen from (11.4.5). And, the more similar are the retailers, the more dramatic is the decline in total purchases. What is interesting is that this profit decrease is precisely mirrored by the decline in total consumers' surplus:

$$\frac{d\sum_k CS_k}{d\mathcal{T}} = -2Q_i^* Q_j^* < 0 \tag{11.4.10}$$

Finally, the effect on the optimal channel margin is:

$$\frac{d\mu_i^*}{d\mathcal{T}} = 0 = \frac{d\mu_j^*}{d\mathcal{T}} \tag{11.4.11}$$

Thus the perceived similarity of the rival stores does not affect the prices paid by consumers.

### 4.1.2 Variables Unique to a Vertically-Integrated System that is Decentrally-Managed

In Chapter 5 we showed that a vertically-integrated channel can use a transfer-pricing scheme to maximize channel profits. Here we find that changes in $\mathcal{T}$ influence both the transfer price and the resulting retailer margin:

$$\frac{dT_i^*}{d\mathcal{T}} = \frac{\left(\theta Q_i^* + bQ_j^*\right)}{b} > 0 \tag{11.4.12}$$

$$\frac{dm_i^*}{d\mathcal{T}} = -\left(\frac{dT_i^*}{d\mathcal{T}}\right) < 0 \tag{11.4.13}$$

An increase in $\mathcal{T}$ shifts pricing power toward the manufacturing arm of the integrated system. Because channel margin is constant, the higher transfer price comes solely at the expense of the retail outlet. (Recall that the transfer prices are unique to each outlet.) Because the optimal transfer prices are identical to the optimal wholesale prices under a channel-coordinating menu of two-part tariffs, results (11.4.12) and (11.4.13) also hold with the menu.

The effect on the net revenue of the manufacturing arm is:

$$\frac{dR_M^*}{d\mathcal{T}} = 2Q_i^* Q_j^* > 0 \tag{11.4.14}$$

The higher transfer-price effect dominates the lower total-output effect. As a result, the manufacturing arm benefits from increases in retailer substitutability. Of course, both retail outlets experience lower net revenues:

$$\frac{dR_i^*}{d\mathcal{T}} = -2Q_i^* Q_j^* < 0 \tag{11.4.15}$$

Interestingly, even if a retailer experiences an increase in unit volume (see (11.4.7)), the lower retail margin dominates. Further, the differential effect on transfer prices for the $i^{th}$ and $j^{th}$ retailers precisely compensates for their unequal output-effects; both suffer equal losses in net revenue even though the retail outlets are not identical.

### 4.1.3 Variables Unique to a Quantity-Discount Schedule

The effect of a change in competition on the quantity-discount schedule depends on both the intercept ($W^{QD^*}$) and the slope ($w^{QD^*}$) of that schedule:

$$\frac{dW^{QD^*}}{d\mathcal{T}} = \frac{b\left(Q_i^* + Q_j^*\right)}{(b+\theta)} > 0 \tag{11.4.16}$$

$$\frac{dw^{QD^*}}{d\mathcal{T}} = \frac{(b-2\theta)}{2b} \gtrless 0 \qquad \text{as} \qquad \chi \equiv \left(\frac{\theta}{b}\right) \lessgtr \frac{1}{2} \tag{11.4.17}$$

Equation (11.4.16) indicates that the base price rises with $\mathcal{T}$, a result that is consistent with the transfer-price argument. In contrast, the intensity of competition $\chi$ determines whether the rate of quantity discount rises or falls with $\mathcal{T}$.

Despite this ambiguity, the effect on a retailer's margin is negative:

$$\frac{dm_i^{QD^*}}{d\mathcal{T}} = -\left(\frac{\left(b^2 + b\theta + \theta^2\right)Q_i^* + b(2b+\theta)Q_j^*}{2b(b+\theta)}\right) < 0 \tag{11.4.18}$$

We again find that an increase in substitutability lessens the per-unit margin at retail. Thus it is unsurprising that the retailers' net revenue declines with $\mathcal{T}$:

$$\frac{dR_i^{QD^*}}{d\mathcal{T}} = -Q_i^*\left(\frac{(b-\theta)Q_i^* + 2(2b+\theta)Q_j^*}{2(b+\theta)}\right) < 0 \tag{11.4.19}$$

The magnitude of this effect differs across retailers.

The manufacturer's net revenue rises because the per-unit margin effect is stronger than the quantity effect:

$$\frac{dR_M^{QD^*}}{d\mathcal{T}} = \left(\frac{(b-\theta)\left(Q_i^*\right)^2 + 4bQ_i^*Q_j^* + (b-\theta)\left(Q_j^*\right)^2}{2(b+\theta)}\right) > 0 \tag{11.4.20}$$

Although this is a nominally beneficial effect for the manufacturer, we must consider the fixed fee payment from the retailers. As retail revenues fall, the fixed fee must also fall. Taking the fixed fee payments into consideration reveals that the effect of a change in substitutability on the manufacturer's *profit* is equal to its effect on channel profit:

$$\frac{d\Pi_M^{QD^*}}{d\mathcal{T}} = -2Q_i^*Q_j^* = \frac{d\Pi_C^{QD^*}}{d\mathcal{T}} < 0 \tag{11.4.21}$$

Finally, we observe that the effect of a change in $\mathcal{T}$ upon the zonal boundary ($\delta^{QD^*}$) is:

$$\frac{d\delta^{QD^*}}{d\mathcal{T}} = -\left(\frac{(b-\theta)(Q_i^* + Q_j^*)(Q_i^* - Q_j^*)}{2(b+\theta)}\right) \gtrless 0 \quad \text{as} \quad Q_i^* \lessgtr Q_j^* \tag{11.4.22}$$

The value of this term pivots on the competitors' channel-coordinated market shares. Equation (11.4.22) states that, as $\mathcal{T}$ increases, the size of Zone $Z_j^{QD^*}$ decreases if $Q_i^* > Q_j^*$.

### 4.1.4 Variables Unique to a Menu of Two-Part Tariffs

The only additional information we need relates to zonal boundaries ($L^{Menu^*}$ and $U^{Menu^*}$) and the fixed fee adjustments needed to preclude defection ($B_i^{Menu^*}$ and $B_j^{Menu^*}$). Unfortunately the results do not lend themselves to easy interpretation. The effects of a change in $\mathcal{T}$ on the zonal boundaries are:

$$\frac{dL^{Menu^*}}{d\mathcal{T}} = -2(Q_i^* - Q_j^*)\left(\frac{(\upsilon_1 Q_i^* - \upsilon_2 Q_j^*)}{(b+\theta)^2(4b^2-\theta^2)^3}\right) \gtrless 0 \tag{11.4.23}$$

$$\frac{dU^{Menu^*}}{d\mathcal{T}} = 2(Q_i^* - Q_j^*)\left(\frac{(\upsilon_2 Q_i^* - \upsilon_1 Q_j^*)}{(b+\theta)^2(4b^2-\theta^2)^3}\right) \gtrless 0 \tag{11.4.24}$$

In expressions (11.4.23) and (11.4.24) we have made use of the definitions:

$$\begin{aligned}
\upsilon_1 &\equiv \left\{\begin{matrix} 32b^8 + 16b^7\theta - 48b^6\theta^2 - 20b^5\theta^3 \\ +30b^4\theta^4 + 10b^3\theta^5 - 5b^2\theta^6 \end{matrix}\right\} > 0 \\
\upsilon_2 &\equiv \left\{\begin{matrix} 16b^7\theta + 32b^6\theta^2 - 4b^5\theta^3 - 32b^4\theta^4 \\ -10b^3\theta^5 + 10b^2\theta^6 + 4b\theta^7 - \theta^8 \end{matrix}\right\} > 0
\end{aligned} \tag{11.4.25}$$

We use the information contained in the expressions (11.4.23) and (11.4.24) to determine how a change in $\mathcal{T}$ affects the width of Zone $Z_{ij}^{Menu^*}$:

$$\frac{d(U^{Menu^*} - L^{Menu^*})}{d\mathcal{T}} = \left(\frac{2(\upsilon_1 + \upsilon_2)(Q_i^* - Q_j^*)^2}{(b+\theta)^2(4b^2-\theta^2)^3}\right) > 0 \tag{11.4.26}$$

The width of Zone $Z_{ij}^{Menu^*}$ increases as competitive substitutability increases; that is, the area within which the manufacturer can extract all rent from both retailers expands. This is an intuitively appealing result. What is ambiguous is whether this increase comes via expansion into Zone $Z_j^{Menu^*}$ *and* Zone $Z_i^{Menu^*}$ or if one Zone shrinks while the other grows. To answer that question we turn to numerical analysis, which we present in Figure 11.1.

Figure 11.1 clarifies the range over which $dL^{Menu^*}/d\mathcal{T}$ is positive or negative for the *entire* unit-square.[17] On the left-hand side of the Figure, the lower bound of the menu is inversely related to a change in $\mathcal{T}$ except for a small, parabolic region above $\chi = 0.80$ in the vicinity of equal market shares ($S_j = ½$). On the right-hand side of Figure 11.1, the lower boundary responds positively (inversely) to a change in competitive substitutability in the lower (upper) triangular area that runs from $\{\chi = 0.80, S_j = ½\}$ to $\{\chi = 0, S_j = 1\}$. Because the upper and lower boundaries are mirror images, simply flipping Figure 11.1 about the $S_j = ½-$axis will yield the effect of a change in $\mathcal{T}$ on the upper boundary $dU^{Menu^*}/d\mathcal{T}$.

Finally, the affects of $\mathcal{T}$ on the fixed-fee adjustments needed to preclude defection are:

$$\frac{dB_i^{Menu^*}}{d\mathcal{T}} = -\left(\frac{dU^{Menu^*}}{d\mathcal{T}}\right) \gtrless 0 \qquad (11.4.27)$$

$$\frac{dB_j^{Menu^*}}{d\mathcal{T}} = -\left(\frac{dL^{Menu^*}}{d\mathcal{T}}\right) \gtrless 0 \qquad (11.4.28)$$

Unsurprisingly, these effects are the negatives of the zonal-boundary effects from a change in $\mathcal{T}$.

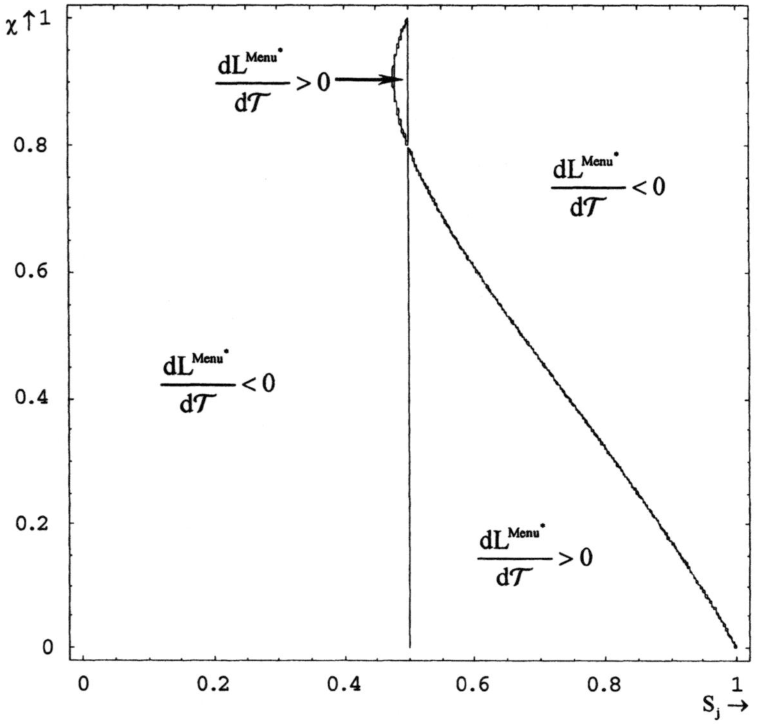


*Figure 11.1.* The Effect of a Change in Competitive Substitutability on the Upper ($dU^{Menu^*}/d\mathcal{T}$) and Lower ($dL^{Menu^*}/d\mathcal{T}$) Boundaries of the Menu

## 4.2 The Effect of a Change in Substitutability $\mathcal{T}$ on the Performance of a Sophisticated Stackelberg Channel

Now consider the impact of a change in competitive substitutability within the framework of the sophisticated Stackelberg two-part tariff developed in Chapter 6. Under this pricing policy the wholesale price is continuously variable over a bounded range of $(f_i - f_j)$ values. To conserve space we present our analysis only for Zone $Z_j^{SS^*}$. Results for Zone $Z_i^{SS^*}$ can be obtained by reversing the subscripts.[18]

Recall that the wholesale-price schedule is set to extract all profit from the $j^{th}$ retailer in Zone $Z_j^{SS^*}$; thus the effect of a change in $\mathcal{T}$ on channel margins differs by retailer:

$$\frac{d\hat{\mu}_i^{ss^*}(j)}{d\mathcal{T}} = \left(\frac{2b(b-\theta)(Q_i^* - Q_j^*)}{(2b+\theta)^2}\right) \gtrless 0 \qquad \text{as} \qquad Q_i^* \gtrless Q_j^* \tag{11.4.29}$$

$$\frac{d\hat{\mu}_j^{ss^*}(j)}{d\mathcal{T}} = 0 \tag{11.4.30}$$

If the i[th] retailer is larger (smaller) than its rival, its retail price will rise (fall) with an increase in $\mathcal{T}$. In contrast, the j[th] (the less profitable) retailer's price is unaffected by a change in $\mathcal{T}$.

In contrast to the clarity of the channel-margin results, the effect of a change in substitutability on the retailers' outputs is ambiguous:

$$\frac{d\hat{Q}_i^{ss^*}(j)}{d\mathcal{T}} = \left(\frac{\theta(4b^2+5b\theta+3\theta^2)Q_i^* - (8b^3+4b^2\theta-b\theta^2+\theta^3)Q_j^*}{2(2b+\theta)^2}\right) \gtrless 0 \tag{11.4.31}$$

$$\frac{d\hat{Q}_j^{ss^*}(j)}{d\mathcal{T}} = -\left(\frac{(4b^3+8b^2\theta+3b\theta^2-3\theta^3)Q_i^* + (4b^3-8b^2\theta-9b\theta^2+\theta^3)Q_j^*}{2(2b+\theta)^2}\right) \gtrless 0 \tag{11.4.32}$$

Notice that it is possible for the more-profitable (the i[th]) retailer's price and quantity to move in the same direction.

Summing expressions (11.4.31) and (11.4.32) yields the aggregate-demand effect:

$$\frac{d\sum\hat{Q}_k^{ss^*}(j)}{d\mathcal{T}} = -(b-\theta)\left(\frac{(2b^2+4b\theta+3\theta^2)Q_i^* + (6b^2+4b\theta-\theta^2)Q_j^*}{(2b+\theta)^2}\right) < 0 \tag{11.4.33}$$

Once again we see that an increase in competition diminishes total channel output, although there is a prospect that one of the retailers could experience enhanced sales.

The impact of a change in competitive substitutability on channel profit is negative:

$$\frac{d\hat{\Pi}_C^{ss^*}(j)}{d\mathcal{T}} = -\left(\frac{3\theta^2(2b-\theta)(Q_i^*)^2 + 3\theta^2(2b-\theta)(Q_j^*)^2 + 2(16b^3+24b^2\theta+6b\theta^2+5\theta^3)Q_i^*Q_j^*}{2(2b+\theta)^3}\right) < 0 \tag{11.4.34}$$

The decline in channel profit as competitive substitutability rises indicates that the possible margin increase (expression (11.4.29)) is more than offset by the decrease in total channel output (expression (11.4.33)).

Finally, the change in consumers' surplus is:

$$\frac{dCS_C^{ss^*}(j)}{d\mathcal{T}} \equiv \frac{\sum_k dCS_k^{ss^*}(j)}{d\mathcal{T}}$$

$$= -\left(Q_i^* - Q_j^*\right)\frac{\begin{pmatrix}\left(4b^3 - 2b^2\theta - 2b\theta^2 - 15\theta^3\right)Q_i^* \\ +\left(20b^3 + 14b^2\theta - 22b\theta^2 + 3\theta^3\right)Q_j^*\end{pmatrix}}{2\left(2b+\theta\right)^3} \gtrless 0 \qquad (11.4.35)$$

Notice that the consumers' surplus effect can be increased by $\mathcal{T}$ if $Q_i^* > Q_j^*$ and $\theta$ is large. (In Zone $Z_i^{ss^*}$ CS can be positive if $\theta$ is large and $Q_i^* < Q_j^*$.)

Turning to the SS boundary conditions, both the lower and the upper bounds are inversely related to $\mathcal{T}$, as is the size of Zone $Z_{ij}^{ss^*}$:

$$\frac{dL^{ss^*}}{d\mathcal{T}} = -2\left(b-\theta\right)\left(Q_i^* - Q_j^*\right)\left(\frac{\left(2b^2 + b\theta + 3\theta^2\right)Q_i^* + \left(2b^2 + 5b\theta - \theta^2\right)Q_j^*}{\left(2b+\theta\right)^3}\right) < 0 \qquad (11.4.36)$$

$$\frac{dU^{ss^*}}{d\mathcal{T}} = -2\left(b-\theta\right)\left(Q_i^* - Q_j^*\right)\left(\frac{\left(2b^2 + 5b\theta - \theta^2\right)Q_i^* + \left(2b^2 + b\theta + 3\theta^2\right)Q_j^*}{\left(2b+\theta\right)^3}\right) < 0 \qquad (11.4.37)$$

$$\frac{d\left(U^{ss^*} - L^{ss^*}\right)}{d\mathcal{T}} = -\left(\frac{8\theta\left(b-\theta\right)^2\left(Q_i^* - Q_j^*\right)^2}{\left(2b+\theta\right)^3}\right) < 0 \qquad (11.4.38)$$

The range of $(f_i - f_j)$ values over which the manufacturer can extract all rent from both retailers declines as $\mathcal{T}$ increases. In addition, the level of fixed-cost differences at which this Zone is relevant declines (see (11.4.36)).

Table 11.2 provides a summary statement of the effects of a change in competition (measured by a change in the substitutability parameter of the utility function) on key behavioral performance variables for the coordinated and sophisticated Stackelberg cases. We defer a discussion of some of its properties to the Commentary for this Chapter.

## 4.3 The Effect of a Change in Substitutability $\mathcal{T}$ on the Performance of a Single-Retailer Channel

In this sub-Section we address the effect of a change in retailer substitutability under the assumption that the channel consists of only one retailer, say the i[th]. Our analysis is based on the adjusted demand curve (10.2.6) used to analyze the channel-breadth decision in Chapter 10:

$$Q_i^{so} = \left( \frac{bA_i + \theta A_j - \left(b^2 - \theta^2\right) p_i^{so}}{b} \right) \tag{11.4.39}$$

A change in $\mathcal{T}$ has *no effect* on channel behavior or channel performance, as can be seen from the following differentiations:

$$\begin{aligned} &\frac{dM^{so^*}}{d\mathcal{T}} = \frac{dm_i^{so^*}}{d\mathcal{T}} = \frac{d\mu_i^{so^*}}{d\mathcal{T}} = 0 \\ &\frac{dQ_i^{so^*}}{d\mathcal{T}} = 0 = \frac{dCS^{so^*}}{d\mathcal{T}} \\ &\frac{dR_C^{so^*}}{d\mathcal{T}} = 0 = \frac{d\Pi_C^{so^*}}{d\mathcal{T}} \end{aligned} \tag{11.4.40}$$

What drives the initially surprising results of expression (11.4.40) is that the single-retailer case is effectively a bilateral monopoly in which the optimal wholesale price is equal to the marginal cost of production. The channel remains a bilateral monopoly when $\mathcal{T}$ changes, so $dM^{so^*}/d\mathcal{T} = 0$. It is also true that the optimal channel margin with one outlet is the same as the margin of the i[th] channel when both retailers are served (see (10.2.10)). Because this margin is invariant with $\mathcal{T}$ (see expression (11.4.11)), it necessarily follows that $d\mu_i^{so^*}/d\mathcal{T} = 0$. From these two points, the retail margin is unaffected by a change in $\mathcal{T}$. With no effect on channel margin (therefore no effect on price), quantity must also remain constant when $\mathcal{T}$ changes. Thus channel revenue, channel profit, and consumer's surplus are also invariant with respect to changes in $\mathcal{T}$.

The intuitive rationale for these results lies in the fact that a change in $\mathcal{T}$ alters the minimum price at which the j[th] retailer faces zero demand ($p_j^{so^*}$). Simple differentiation confirms this statement:

$$\frac{dp_j^{so^*}}{d\mathcal{T}} = -\left(A_i - bp_i + \theta p_j^{so^*}\right) < 0 \tag{11.4.41}$$

The RHS is two times the negative of the i[th] retailer's (unadjusted) demand, evaluated at $p_i^{so^*}$. The minimal price at which the j[th] retailer has no demand decreases as competitive substitutability increases. The intuition is that, when the two stores are almost perfectly interchangeable, only a slight price premium will eliminate demand at one of the stores. However, if the competitors are sharply differentiated, one store can maintain a significant price premium.

*Table 11.2.* Directional Impacts of a Change in the Substitutability Parameter $\mathcal{T}$ on Channel Performance

| | Coordinated Channel (*) | Sophisticated Stackelberg (Zone $Z_{ij}^{SS^*}$) |
|---|---|---|
| Channel Margin $\mu_i$ | 0 | $\gtrless 0$ as $Q_i^* \gtrless Q_j^*$ |
| Channel Margin $\mu_j$ | 0 | 0 |
| Transfer Price $T_k^*$ (**) | + | *NA* |
| Wholesale Margin M (***) | + | + |
| Quantity-Discount $w^{QD^*}$ | $\gtrless 0$ as $\frac{\theta}{b} \lesseqgtr \frac{1}{2}$ | *NA* |
| Retail Margin $m_k$ | – | – |
| Output $Q_k$ | $\gtrless 0$ as $\frac{\theta}{b} \gtrless \frac{Q_j^*}{Q_i^*}$ | $\gtrless 0$ |
| Total Output $\sum Q_k$ | – | – |
| Manufacturer Revenue $R_M$ | + | $\gtrless 0$ |
| Retail Revenue $R_i$ | – | – |
| Retail Revenue $R_j$ | – | $\gtrless 0$ |
| Channel Profit $R_C$ | – | – |
| Zonal Boundary $\delta^{QD^*}$ | $\gtrless 0$ as $Q_i^* \lesseqgtr Q_j^*$ | *NA* |
| Width of Zone $Z_{ij}^{X}$ $(U^X - L^X)$ | + | – |

(*) This column includes all coordinating policies: the vertically-integrated system, the quantity-discount schedule, and the menu of two-part tariffs.
(**) This term is also valid for the per-unit wholesale prices with the menu.
(***)This term is also valid for the base per-unit wholesale price $(W^{QD^*})$ with a quantity-discount schedule.
*Subscripts*: The subscript "k" indicates that the result applies to both the i[th] and the j[th] retailer.
*Superscripts*: The superscript refers to the quantity-discount schedule ($X \equiv QD^*$), the menu ($X \equiv Menu^*$), or the sophisticated Stackelberg policy ($X \equiv SS^*$).
*NA*: Not applicable.

The symbol $\gtrless 0$ indicates that the condition for signing the variable is very complex; see the Appendix or Section 4 for details.

## 5 COMMENTARY ON A CHANGE IN COMPETITIVE SUBSTITUTABILITY

Because markets are dynamic, it is essential to understand how a change in competitive substitutability affects the manufacturer's optimal wholesale-price strategy as well as how it influences Channel Performance. Marketers have traditionally interpreted a change in the cross-price parameter of the demand equations as a change in competitive substitutability. This interpretation confounds inter-retailer substitutability with an aggregate-demand effect. We examined two alternative approaches to disentangling these effects; they involved a simultaneous adjustment of two parameters in the retailer's demand equation.

Unfortunately, all three approaches generate results that are intuitively implausible. Specifically, when the retailers are not identical, an increase in competition generally either *raises*, or can raise, retail prices, units sold, and channel profit for all the wholesale-price policies which we have explored. Table 11.1 provides further details.[19] Common sense, as well as economic logic, strongly suggests that prices and profits should fall when competitive substitutability rises, and they most certainly should *not* go to infinity. Additionally, the impact of a change in competitive substitutability should have a greater impact when competitors are similar, yet all three approaches generate the opposite result. For these reasons, we concluded that all three techniques produce results that lack face validity.

Given these conclusions, we returned to "first principles" by stressing the utility function that underlies the system of linear demand curves used in Chapters 5-10. Embedded within the utility function is a substitutability parameter ($\mathcal{T}$) that measures consumer willingness to substitute purchases from one competitor for goods from its rival. It is a change in this willingness (a change in $\mathcal{T}$) that is the proper way to model competitive substitutability. This has the intuitive appeal of placing the consumer at the forefront of our analysis. We proved that using $\mathcal{T}$ links all the terms in the demand curve: a change in $\mathcal{T}$ induces a change in the demand intercept, own-price sensitivity, and cross-price sensitivity. We also showed that this approach generates results that are consistent with economic logic and with marketing intuition. Our results provide substantive support for the legitimacy of modeling a change in competition as a shift in the substitutability parameter of the utility function.

## 5.1 Commentary on the Effect of a Change in $\mathcal{T}$

The effect of an infinitesimal change in $\mathcal{T}$ is reminiscent of the Hicks-Slutsky approach to the impact of a change in the price of a product, say the $i^{th}$. Recall that an increase in $p_i$:

1. Lowers the consumer's utility ($\mathcal{U}$);
2. Increases the relative purchases of the $j^{th}$ product ($Q_j/Q_i$); and
3. Decreases the consumer's purchases of the $i^{th}$ product ($Q_i$).

A change in $p_i$, and the consequent change in purchase patterns, can be decomposed into an income effect and a substitution effect. The income effect reflects the fact that a price increase makes the consumer worse off by decreasing the quantity that the consumer can afford of *both* goods; this lowers $\mathcal{U}$. The substitution effect reflects the fact that an increase in $p_i$ makes the $i^{th}$ product relatively more expensive; this shifts consumption toward the $j^{th}$ product, thus increasing $Q_j/Q_i$. These two factors underlie the simple reality captured by a demand curve: an increase in the price of the $i^{th}$ product is associated with a decrease in the quantity demanded of that product.

In a similar manner, our analysis reveals that a change in competitive substitutability can be decomposed into a *market-share effect* and a *competitive-intensity effect.* Consider an increase in $\mathcal{T}$. The market-share effect reflects the fact that the relative sales of the lower-volume retailer decline. Using the information in expressions (11.4.1) reveals:

$$\frac{d\left(Q_j/Q_i\right)}{d\mathcal{T}} \gtrless 0 \quad \text{as} \quad S_j \gtrless ½ \tag{11.5.1}$$

To see the competitive-intensity effect in the case of a coordinated channel, we differentiate equation (5.3.3) with respect to $\mathcal{T}$:

$$\begin{aligned} &\frac{dQ_i^{\bullet}}{d\mathcal{T}} \gtrless 0 \quad \text{as} \quad \chi \gtrless \left( S_j \Big/ \left(1-S_j\right) \right) \\ &\frac{dQ_j^{\bullet}}{d\mathcal{T}} \gtrless 0 \quad \text{as} \quad \chi \lessgtr \left( S_j \Big/ \left(1-S_j\right) \right) \end{aligned} \tag{11.5.2}$$

Provided initial market shares are unequal, say $S_j < ½$, unit-sales of the larger-volume (the $i^{th}$) retailer rise or fall depending on competitive intensity ($\chi$) relative to the retailer's market share (see the upper line of (11.5.2)). Sales of the lower-volume retailer behave in the opposite manner (see the lower line of (11.5.2)). A similar (albeit more complex) set of relationships hold in the case of a sophisticated Stackelberg channel.

Finally, we note that if initial market shares are equal (if the RHS of (11.5.2) is equal to one), then the sales of both retailers decline in response to an increase in $\mathcal{T}$ because $\chi$ must be less than one. (The retailers' relative shares are invariant with changes in $\mathcal{T}$ for this case.) This is merely a statement that identical competitors respond identically to a parametric change.

## 5.2 Commentary on Coordination *versus* Maximization

Throughout this monograph we have focused on channel coordination *versus* manufacturer profit-maximization. We now have the information needed to explain why a channel-coordinating menu of two-part tariffs becomes more attractive to the manufacturer as competitive substitutability increases. We begin our explanation with four "refresher" points. First, we observe that *all* our wholesale-price policies steer all channel profit to the manufacturer in the Zones that are subscripted by an "ij." Second, the coordinating strategies maximize channel profit, the sophisticated Stackelberg strategy does not. Third, it immediately follows that whenever the difference in fixed costs ($f_i - f_j$) is compatible with Zone $Z_{ij}^{Menu^*}$ the manufacturer prefers the menu. Fourth, the best case scenario for the sophisticated Stackelberg tariff also occurs when $(f_i - f_j)$ places the channel in Zone $Z_{ij}^{SS^*}$.

We now consider equations (11.4.26) and (11.4.38). An increase in $\mathcal{T}$ increases the range of $(f_i - f_j)$ values (the "width") of Zone $Z_{ij}^{Menu^*}$ while simultaneously shrinking the width of Zone $Z_{ij}^{SS^*}$. It follows that, when competitive substitutability rises, the menu becomes more attractive to the manufacturer, while the sophisticated Stackelberg becomes less attractive.

It is also of interest to examine the effect of a change in retailer substitutability on channel performance under the channel-coordinating menu and the non-coordinating sophisticated Stackelberg wholesale-price strategy. A channel-profit comparison reveals:

$$\left(\left(\frac{d\Pi_C^*}{d\mathcal{T}}\right)-\left(\frac{d\hat{\Pi}_C^{SS^*}(j)}{d\mathcal{T}}\right)\right)=\left(\frac{3\theta^2(2b-\theta)\left(Q_i^*-Q_j^*\right)^2}{2(2b+\theta)^3}\right)>0 \qquad (11.5.3)$$

Expression (11.5.3) states that, as competitive substitutability increases, the decrease in the profit of a coordinated channel is less than the decrease in channel profit (in Zone $Z_j^{SS^*}$) under a sophisticated Stackelberg tariff.[20]

In terms of total channel output we find:

$$\left(\left(\frac{d\sum Q_k^{*}}{d\mathcal{T}}\right)-\left(\frac{d\sum \hat{Q}_k^{ss^*}(j)}{d\mathcal{T}}\right)\right)$$
$$=-\left(\frac{2(b+\theta)(b-\theta)^2\left(Q_i^{*}-Q_j^{*}\right)}{(2b+\theta)^2}\right)\gtrless 0 \quad \text{as} \quad Q_i^{*}\lessgtr Q_j^{*} \tag{11.5.4}$$

In Zone $Z_j^{ss^*}$ the quantity impact is greater with the menu if the $j^{th}$ retailer is larger than the $i^{th}$ retailer; the reverse is true in Zone $Z_i^{ss^*}$. Broadly speaking, a change in competition affects channel performance differentially across coordinating *versus* non-coordinating wholesale-price strategies.

## 5.3 Commentary on Two Channel Myths

This Chapter has provided clear evidence of two Myths that are widespread in the marketing science literature on distribution channels. First, modeling a change in competitive substitutability as a simple change in the cross-price parameter of the demand curve ($\theta$) generates results that lack face validity; we traced these unappealing results to the impact of change in $\theta$ on aggregate demand. We say that this erroneous approach to modeling competitive change is based on the *Aggregate-Demand Modeling Myth*.

Second, the combination of the common modeling assumptions of equal demand intercepts and equal per-unit retail costs is sufficient to ensure that the competitors are identical. In terms of our three-dimensional unit-cube (described in Chapters 7-10), only the $\langle S_j = ½\rangle$ − plane that defines equal market shares is relevant. In this special case, our three wholesale-price strategies (the quantity-discount schedule, the menu, and the sophisticated Stackelberg tariff) are unaffected by changes in competitive substitutability. Indeed, all three strategies induce channel-coordination. Yet this $\langle S_j = ½\rangle$ − plane is the only set of points in the unit-cube where these strategies yield identical results. Thus we have termed a belief in the appropriateness of assuming identical retailers a Myth—*the Identical-Competitors Meta-Myth*.

## 5.4 Summary Commentary

Marketing science researchers have evaluated the impact of a change in competition with a multiplicity of methods, such as employing a change in the cross-price term, or a compensating change in the own-price and cross-price slopes of the demand curves. Methodological variety comes at a price; inconsistency of analytical results across researchers suggests a collective confusion about the impact of a change in competitive substitutability on a Channel Performance and Channel Strategy. In this Chapter we have established that the correct approach is to return to the simplicity of first principles by rigorously deriving a system of demand curves that can be easily manipulated to assess the impact of a change in competitive substitutability upon all variables of interest for *any* system of demand curves, although our detailed focus was solely upon a linear-demand system. In developing our procedure we have followed the wisdom of Sir Isaac Newton who wrote, "truth is ever to be found in the simplicity, and not in the multiplicity and confusion of things" (1713, page 357).[21]

# 6 APPENDIX

In sub-Sections 6.1-6.4 of this Appendix we catalog the impact of various ways of calculating a change in competition on key variables under a *sophisticated Stackelberg* wholesale-price policy. We start with the three atheoretical methods; then we turn to the theoretically-justified parameter $\mathcal{T}$ of the representative consumer's utility function. Throughout we focus on Zone $Z_j^{ss^*}$ within which the j[th] retailer nets no profit after paying the fixed fee. Results for Zone $Z_i^{ss^*}$ can be found by reversing all the i[th] and j[th] subscripts. In sub-Section 6.5 we demonstrate the relationship between a change in competitive substitutability and the dimensions of the unit-cube that appeared in Chapters 5-10. Finally, in sub-Section 6.6 we evaluate the implicit effect that various methods of simplifying the demand curve for the original utility function.

## 6.1 A Change in Competitive Substitutability Modeled with the Cross-Price Term θ

In the case of equating a change in competition with a change in the cross-price term of the demand curve, we did not present the impact on output levels in Section 2. They are:

$$\frac{d\hat{Q}_i^*(j)}{d\theta} = \left(\frac{2b\left(Q_i^* - Q_j^*\right)}{(2b+\theta)^2}\right) + \left\{\frac{\begin{matrix}(2b+\theta)(2b+3\theta)(c_i+C)\\ +(4b^2-\theta^2)(c_j+C)\end{matrix}}{4(2b+\theta)^2}\right\} \gtrless 0 \qquad (11.A.1)$$

$$\frac{d\hat{Q}_j^*(j)}{d\theta} = \left(\frac{4b\left(Q_i^* - Q_j^*\right)}{(2b+\theta)^2}\right) + \left\{\frac{\begin{matrix}(2b+\theta)(-2b+3\theta)(c_i+C)\\ +(6b-\theta)(2b+\theta)(c_j+C)\end{matrix}}{4(2b+\theta)^2}\right\} \gtrless 0 \qquad (11.A.2)$$

$$\frac{d\sum\hat{Q}_k^*(j)}{d\theta} = \left(\frac{6b\left(Q_i^* - Q_j^*\right)}{(2b+\theta)^2}\right) + \left\{\frac{\begin{matrix}3\theta(2b+\theta)(c_i+C)\\ +(4b-\theta)(2b+\theta)(c_j+C)\end{matrix}}{2(2b+\theta)^2}\right\} \gtrless 0 \qquad (11.A.3)$$

In each case there is a relative-output effect ($Q_i^* - Q_j^*$) that is consistent across the three output measures. There is also a cost effect that is presented in {braces} for clarity. The cost effect is positive in equations (11.A.1) and (11.A.3), but in (11.A.2) it can be negative for low values of θ combined with $c_i$ very much greater than $c_j$. (This type of complexity prompted us to relegate these and other results to the Appendix.)

In Zone $Z_j^{SS^*}$ the j[th] retailer is the less-profitable retailer. If it is also the smaller-output retailer, then the output effect is uniformly positive: increased competition increases sales. This, of course, is the aggregate-demand effect. But, if the less profitable retailer is larger, then the output effect is negative. Clearly the indicated value of $dQ/d\theta$ from a small, negative output effect can be overturned by the cost effect for some values given by (11.A.1)-(11.A.3).

## 6.2 A Change in Competitive Substitutability Modeled as a Compensating Change in Slopes

We did not present any of the sophisticated Stackelberg values for this case in Section 2. The channel margin results are:

$$\left(\frac{d\hat{\mu}_i^*(j)}{d\theta}\bigg|_{db=d\theta}\right) = -\left[\left(\frac{6(Q_i^* - Q_j^*)}{(2b+\theta)^2}\right) + \left\{\frac{2(c_i - c_j)}{(2b+\theta)}\right\}\right] \gtrless 0 \qquad (11.A.4)$$

$$\left(\frac{d\hat{\mu}_j^*(j)}{d\theta}\bigg|_{db=d\theta}\right) = 0 \qquad (11.A.5)$$

Within Zone $Z_j^{SS^*}$ the price charged by the j[th] retailer is unaffected by this approach to measuring a change in competitive substitutability, while the margin of the i[th] retailer falls if it is the higher-cost, larger-volume competitor.

The output results are:

$$\frac{d\hat{Q}_i^*(j)}{d\theta}\bigg|_{db=d\theta} = \left[\left(\frac{2(b-\theta)(Q_i^* - Q_j^*)}{(2b+\theta)^2}\right) - \left\{\frac{\theta(c_i - c_j)}{(2b+\theta)}\right\}\right] \gtrless 0 \qquad (11.A.6)$$

$$\frac{d\hat{Q}_j^*(j)}{d\theta}\bigg|_{db=d\theta} = \left[\left(\frac{4(b-\theta)(Q_i^* - Q_j^*)}{(2b+\theta)^2}\right) + \left\{\frac{(2b-\theta)(c_i - c_j)}{(2b+\theta)}\right\}\right] \gtrless 0 \qquad (11.A.7)$$

$$\frac{d\sum\hat{Q}_k^*(j)}{d\theta}\bigg|_{db=d\theta} = 2(b-\theta)\left(\frac{3(Q_i^* - Q_j^*) + \{(2b+\theta)(c_i - c_j)\}}{(2b+\theta)^2}\right) \gtrless 0 \qquad (11.A.8)$$

The basic message here is the same as with equations (11.A.1)-(11.A.3).

Finally, the impact on channel profit is:

$$\left.\frac{d\hat{\Pi}_c^*(j)}{d\theta}\right|_{db=d\theta} = 2\left(Q_i^* - Q_j^*\right)\left(\frac{\begin{array}{c}(2b-5\theta)\left(Q_i^* - Q_j^*\right)\\ -2\theta(2b+\theta)\{(c_i - c_j)\}\end{array}}{(2b+\theta)^3}\right) \gtrless 0 \tag{11.A.9}$$

As can be seen, this effect is indeterminate.

## 6.3 A Change in Competitive Substitutability Modeled as a Compensating Change in Intercepts

Here we present the impact on output levels for Section 2. They are:

$$\left(\left.\frac{d\hat{Q}_i^*(j)}{dA_i}\right|_{dA_i=-dA_j}\right) = \left(\frac{\theta}{2b+\theta}\right) > 0 \tag{11.A.10}$$

$$\left(\left.\frac{d\hat{Q}_j^*(j)}{dA_i}\right|_{dA_i=-dA_j}\right) = -\left(\frac{2b-\theta}{2b+\theta}\right) < 0 \tag{11.A.11}$$

$$\left(\left.\frac{d\sum\hat{Q}_k^*(j)}{dA_i}\right|_{dA_i=-dA_j}\right) = -2\left(\frac{b-\theta}{2b+\theta}\right) < 0 \tag{11.A.12}$$

The results are clean, but we have argued in the body of the paper that the underlying methodology is flawed.

## 6.4 A Change in Competitive Substitutability Modeled by a Change in Substitutability $\mathcal{T}$

The channel margins presented in Section 4 can be decomposed into the wholesale price and the retailers' margins. For the manufacturer's margin we find:

$$\frac{d\hat{M}^{ss^*}(j)}{d\mathcal{T}} = \left(\frac{\begin{array}{c}\left(4b^3 + 11b\theta^2 + 3\theta^3\right)Q_i^*\\ +\left(4b^3 + 16b^2\theta - b\theta^2 - \theta^3\right)Q_j^*\end{array}}{2b(2b+\theta)^2}\right) > 0 \tag{11.A.13}$$

As in a coordinated channel, increased substitutability enhances the manufacturer's pricing power. From this fact we anticipate that retailer margins will fall as substitutability increases. This is the case:

$$\frac{d\hat{m}_i^{ss^*}(j)}{d\mathcal{T}} = -\left(\frac{\begin{array}{c}\theta\left(4b^2+11b\theta+3\theta^2\right)Q_i^* \\ +\left(8b^3+12b^2\theta-b\theta^2-\theta^3\right)Q_j^*\end{array}}{2b\left(2b+\theta\right)^2}\right) < 0 \qquad (11.A.14)$$

$$\frac{d\hat{m}_j^{ss^*}(j)}{d\mathcal{T}} = -\left(\frac{d\hat{M}^{ss^*}(j)}{d\mathcal{T}}\right) < 0 \qquad (11.A.15)$$

Note that the j[th] retailer's margin declines dollar-for-dollar in response to an increase in the manufacturer's margin in this Zone. The signs of these results conform to economic intuition: when two retailers become closer competitors, their power declines vis-à-vis the manufacturer. (In the limit they would be perfectly interchangeable and the manufacturer could decrease channel (fixed) cost by *not* selling through both retailers.)

We now turn to the effects of a change in competition on the net revenue of the retailers and the manufacturer. For the retailers we find:

$$\frac{dR_i^{ss^*}(j)}{d\mathcal{T}} = -\left(\frac{\begin{array}{c}3\theta^2\left(2b+3\theta\right)\left(Q_i^*\right)^2 \\ +2\left(8b^3+20b^2\theta+14b\theta^2-3\theta^3\right)Q_i^*Q_j^* \\ +\left(16b^3+8b^2\theta-10b\theta^2+\theta^3\right)\left(Q_j^*\right)^2\end{array}}{2\left(2b+\theta\right)^3}\right) < 0 \qquad (11.A.16)$$

$$\frac{d\hat{R}_j^{ss^*}(j)}{d\mathcal{T}} = \left(\frac{\begin{array}{c}\left(8b^3-4b^2\theta+2b\theta^2-21\theta^3\right)\left(Q_i^*\right)^2 \\ -2\left(8b^3+12b^2\theta+30b\theta^2-11\theta^3\right)Q_i^*Q_j^* \\ -\left(24b^3+20b^2\theta-34b\theta^2+5\theta^3\right)\left(Q_j^*\right)^2\end{array}}{2\left(2b+\theta\right)^3}\right) \gtrless 0 \qquad (11.A.17)$$

The i[th] (the more profitable) retailer is harmed by increased competition; the j[th] retailer *may* generate greater net revenue. The manufacturer's net-revenue effect is also unclear:

$$\frac{d\hat{R}_M^{ss^*}(j)}{d\mathcal{T}} = \left(\frac{\begin{array}{c}-\left(8b^3-4b^2\theta+2b\theta^2-33\theta^3\right)\left(Q_i^*\right)^2 \\ +2\theta\left(8b^2+38b\theta-19\theta^2\right)Q_i^*Q_j^* \\ +\left(40b^3+28b^2\theta-50b\theta^2+9\theta^3\right)\left(Q_j^*\right)^2\end{array}}{2\left(2b+\theta\right)^3}\right) \gtrless 0 \qquad (11.A.18)$$

The preceding results ignore the effect of fixed-fee payments. Taking these payments into account, we obtain the following profit impacts:

$$\frac{d\hat{\pi}_i^{ss^*}(j)}{d\mathcal{T}} = -2(b-\theta)\left(Q_i^* - Q_j^*\right)\left(\frac{\begin{array}{c}\left(2b^2+b\theta+3\theta^2\right)Q_i^* \\ +\left(2b^2+5b\theta-\theta^2\right)Q_j^*\end{array}}{2(2b+\theta)^3}\right) \gtrless 0 \qquad (11.A.19)$$

$$\text{as} \quad Q_i^* \lesseqgtr Q_j^*$$

$$\frac{d\hat{\pi}_j^{ss^*}(j)}{d\mathcal{T}} = 0 \qquad (11.A.20)$$

The $j^{th}$ retailer's profit is, by definition, fully extracted by the fixed fee in Zone $Z_j^{ss^*}$. The $i^{th}$ retailer's "take-home" profit rises (falls) if it has the smaller (larger) market share. Of course, in Zone $Z_j^{ss^*}$ the $i^{th}$ retailer will have the larger market share unless its costs are significantly greater than its rival's costs. Thus under "normal" conditions we would expect a decline in profit.

The effect on manufacturer profit is less clear:

$$\frac{d\hat{\Pi}_M^{ss^*}(j)}{d\mathcal{T}} = \left(\frac{\begin{array}{c}\left(8b^3-4b^2\theta+2b\theta^2-9\theta^3\right)\left(Q_i^*\right)^2 \\ -2\left(16b^3+16b^2\theta+22b\theta^2-3\theta^3\right)Q_i^*Q_j^* \\ -\left(8b^3+12b^2\theta-18b\theta^2+\theta^3\right)\left(Q_j^*\right)^2\end{array}}{2(2b+\theta)^3}\right) \gtrless 0 \qquad (11.A.21)$$

Recall that channel profit declines as $\mathcal{T}$ increases. With the $j^{th}$ retailer's profit held constant in Zone $Z_j^{ss^*}$ the manufacturer can only benefit if the $i^{th}$ retailer is worse off, although $d\hat{\pi}_i^{ss^*}(j) < 0$ is not sufficient for $d\hat{\Pi}_M^{ss^*}(j) > 0$. A distinct possibility is that both the manufacturer and the more profitable retailer are worse off in response to an increase in competition.

## 6.5 A Change in Competitive Substitutability and the Dimensions of the Unit-Cube

In this sub-Section we specify the effect of a change in the substitutability parameter $\mathcal{T}$ on the dimensions of our unit-cube. Recall that those dimensions are:

- The *intensity of competition*, measured as the ratio of the cross-price effect to the own-price effect of the demand curve $(\chi \equiv \theta / b)$. It must lie in the unit interval.

- The *magnitude of competition*, measured as the market share in physical units of the j[th] retailer ($S_j \equiv Q_j^* / (Q_i^* + Q_j^*)$). It must lie in the unit interval.
- The *fixed-cost ratio* of each competitor, measured as the ratio of fixed cost to net revenue ($f_k \equiv bf_k / (Q_k^*)^2$). As with the other dimensions, this one must lie in the unit interval.

We obtain the following results:

$$\frac{d\chi}{d\mathcal{T}} = b(1-\chi)^2 > 0 \tag{11.A.22}$$

$$\frac{dS_j}{d\mathcal{T}} = -b(1-2S_j) \gtrless 0 \quad \text{as} \quad S_j \gtrless ½ \tag{11.A.23}$$

$$\begin{aligned} \frac{df_i}{d\mathcal{T}} &= \frac{2bf_iS_j}{(1-S_j)} > 0 \\ \frac{df_j}{d\mathcal{T}} &= \frac{2bf_j(1-S_j)}{S_j} > 0 \end{aligned} \tag{11.A.24}$$

These equations merit two observations. First, although every dimension is economically meaningful, *no* dimension purely measures a change in competitive substitutability. Rather, a change in $\mathcal{T}$ implies a movement from an initial point in the unit-cube to a new point that, in general, has completely new coordinates. Second, although we have set $f_i = f_j \equiv f$, this is not the same as allowing $df_i / d\mathcal{T} = df_j / d\mathcal{T}$. The latter relationship is true only at $S_j = ½$. Given our assumption of equal fixed-cost ratios, a change of $f$ in our illustrative unit-cube does *not* depict a change in competitive substitutability. Nonetheless, our mathematics has been fully general throughout the monograph; it is only our illustrations that are of limited generalizability.

## 6.6 Commentary on Restricting the Parametric Values of the Demand Curves

The literature reveals several techniques that have been used to simplify a demand system such as (11.3.6). These simplifications place restrictions on own-price sensitivity ("b") or on the retailers' attractiveness (demand intercepts "$A_i$" and "$A_j$"). In this sub-Section we demonstrate that each simplification imposes specific restrictions on the underlying utility function (11.3.1) that limit the modeler's ability to evaluate a change in competitive substitutability.

First, it is common to assume $b_i = b_j \equiv b$; indeed, we have made this assumption throughout this monograph. This is equivalent to a utility function with parameters $\mathcal{B}_i = \mathcal{B}_j \equiv \mathcal{B}$. That is, the rate of change of marginal utility of the $k^{th}$ good purchased from the $i^{th}$ store must be the same as the rate of change of marginal utility of purchasing the same good from the $j^{th}$ store. Because the good is identical no matter the store at which it is purchased, assuming $b_i = b_j \equiv b$ is conceptually innocuous. It also has a minimal impact on the results that would be obtained with the more general model.

Second, one often sees the assumption $A_i = A_j \equiv A$ combined with the assumption $b_i = b_j \equiv b$; this leads to $\mathcal{A}_i = \mathcal{A}_j \equiv \mathcal{A}$. We write demand as:

$$\begin{aligned} Q_i &= A - bp_i + \theta p_j \\ Q_j &= A - bp_j + \theta p_i \end{aligned} \tag{11.A.25}$$

Only the price and quantity subscripts differ across retailers. In conjunction with the very common assumption of equal (or even zero) per-unit costs, the model of demand system (11.A.25) brings with it the difficulties associated with the *Identical-Competitors Meta-Myth.*

Third, it is not unusual to assume a unitary own-price slope ($b = 1$) combined with unique demand intercepts (Ingene and Parry 1995). This is a stronger assumption than it may appear, for it ties together the parameters of the utility function, a fact that echoes throughout the demand system. By manipulating definitions (11.3.5) we find the restricted values of the utility function and the demand system to be:

$$\begin{aligned} &\mathcal{T} = \sqrt{\mathcal{B}(\mathcal{B}-\lambda)} \\ \Rightarrow\ &\bar{\theta} = \sqrt{(\mathcal{B}-\lambda)/\mathcal{B}} \\ \Rightarrow\ &A_i = \left(\mathcal{A}_i - \bar{\theta}\mathcal{A}_j\right)/\lambda \end{aligned} \tag{11.A.26}$$

The term $\bar{\theta}$ denotes that the value of $\theta$ is restricted. The seemingly innocuous assumption $b = 1$ effectively strips a degree of freedom from the utility function; $\mathcal{T}$ cannot vary freely relative to the rate of change of marginal utility $\mathcal{B}$. Further, the value of the substitutability coefficient of the utility function now includes the marginal utility of money, although we could set $\lambda = 1$ to avoid this complexity. In any event, the *full effect* of a change in competitive substitutability cannot be measured.

Fourth, when the assumption $A_i = A_j \equiv A$ is combined with $b = 1$ (McGuire and Staelin 1983, 1986), we obtain an exaggerated version of the demand system (11.A.25) in which $\mathcal{T}$ is restricted to the value $\sqrt{\mathcal{B}(\mathcal{B}-\lambda)}$.

Fifth, the most extreme set of assumptions are $A = 1 = b$. We find that the underlying values of the utility function are now:

$$\begin{aligned} &\mathcal{T} = \sqrt{\mathcal{B}(\mathcal{B}-\lambda)} \\ &\Rightarrow \bar{\theta} = \sqrt{(\mathcal{B}-\lambda)/\mathcal{B}} \\ &\Rightarrow \mathcal{A} = \lambda/(1-\bar{\theta}) \end{aligned} \tag{11.A.27}$$

These assumptions lead to a single-parameter utility function; the rate of change of the marginal utility of the good ($\mathcal{B}$) determines the retailers' attractiveness *and* inter-retailer substitutability. Any investigation of the impact of a change in competition that is based on these demand curves is clearly restricted to an analysis of $d\bar{\theta}$—which inevitably raises the problems identified in our discussion of the *Aggregate-Demand Modeling Myth.*[22] Table 11.3 catalogs the implications of all these restrictions.

*Table 11.3.* Implications of Demand Curve Restrictions

| Demand Curve Restrictions | Demand Curve Definitions | Number of Utility Function Parameters | Utility Function Restrictions |
|---|---|---|---|
| none | $A_i \equiv (\mathcal{B}_j\mathcal{A}_i - \mathcal{T}\mathcal{A}_j)/(\mathcal{B}_i\mathcal{B}_j - \mathcal{T}^2)$<br>$b_i \equiv \lambda\mathcal{B}_j/(\mathcal{B}_i\mathcal{B}_j - \mathcal{T}^2)$<br>$\theta \equiv \lambda\mathcal{T}/(\mathcal{B}_i\mathcal{B}_j - \mathcal{T}^2)$ | 5 | none |
| $b_i = b_j \equiv b$ | $A_i \equiv (\mathcal{B}\mathcal{A}_i - \mathcal{T}\mathcal{A}_j)/(\mathcal{B}^2 - \mathcal{T}^2)$<br>$b \equiv \lambda\mathcal{B}/(\mathcal{B}^2 - \mathcal{T}^2)$<br>$\theta \equiv \lambda\mathcal{T}/(\mathcal{B}^2 - \mathcal{T}^2)$ | 4 | $\mathcal{B}_i = \mathcal{B}_j \equiv \mathcal{B}$ |
| $b_o = b_j \equiv 1$ | $A_i \equiv (\mathcal{A}_i - \bar{\theta}\mathcal{A}_j)/\lambda$<br>$b \equiv 1$<br>$\bar{\theta} \equiv \sqrt{(\mathcal{B}-\lambda)/\mathcal{B}}$ | 3 | $\mathcal{T} \equiv \sqrt{\mathcal{B}(\mathcal{B}-\lambda)}$ or<br>$\mathcal{B} \equiv \left(\lambda + \sqrt{\lambda^2 + 4\mathcal{T}^2}\right)/2$ |
| $A_i = A_j \equiv A$<br>& $b_i = b_j \equiv b$ | $A_i \equiv \mathcal{A}/(\mathcal{B} + \mathcal{T})$<br>$b \equiv \lambda\mathcal{B}/(\mathcal{B}^2 - \mathcal{T}^2)$<br>$\theta \equiv \lambda\mathcal{T}/(\mathcal{B}^2 - \mathcal{T}^2)$ | 3 | $\mathcal{A}_i = \mathcal{A}_j \equiv \mathcal{A}$ |
| $A_i = A_j \equiv A$<br>& $b_i = b_j \equiv 1$ | $A_i \equiv \mathcal{A}(1-\bar{\theta})/\lambda$<br>$b \equiv 1$<br>$\bar{\theta} \equiv \sqrt{(\mathcal{B}-\lambda)/\mathcal{B}}$ | 2 | $\mathcal{A}_i = \mathcal{A}_j \equiv \mathcal{A}$ and<br>$\mathcal{T} = \sqrt{\mathcal{B}(\mathcal{B}-\lambda)}$ or<br>$\mathcal{B} \equiv \left(\lambda + \sqrt{\lambda^2 + 4\mathcal{T}^2}\right)/2$ |
| $A_i = A_j \equiv 1$<br>& $b_i = b_j \equiv 1$ | $A_i \equiv 1$<br>$b \equiv 1$<br>$\bar{\theta} \equiv \sqrt{(\mathcal{B}-\lambda)/\mathcal{B}}$ | 1 | $\mathcal{A} = \lambda/(1-\bar{\theta})$ and<br>$\mathcal{T} = \sqrt{\mathcal{B}(\mathcal{B}-\lambda)}$ or<br>$\mathcal{B} \equiv \left(\lambda + \sqrt{\lambda^2 + 4\mathcal{T}^2}\right)/2$ |

Values of $A_j$ and $b_j$ may be found by reversing all subscripts.

# Notes

[1] Kim and Staelin (1999) have employed this technique to model a change in competition; however, the terminology is ours.
[2] These intercepts may be thought of as the "attractiveness" of each retailer, because they represent the amount each would sell if both firms set their prices equal to zero. In earlier Chapters we termed these intercepts the "base demand" of each retailer.
[3] A linear demand curve is common in the marketing science literature, albeit often in a less general form (e.g., $A_i = 1 = b$ is not unusual). We discuss the theoretical consequences of such restrictions in the Appendix of this Chapter.
[4] One can think of situations—increased word-of-mouth or more aggressive advertising—that would cause the market to grow, but these mechanisms are *not* present in equation (11.2.1).
[5] Recall that the parenthetical "j" denotes a value in Zone $Z_j^{SS^*}$; values in Zone $Z_i^{SS^*}$ are found by reversing the $i^{th}$ and $j^{th}$ subscripts, and switching the parenthetical i's and j's in equations (11.2.9) and (11.2.10).
[6] We used this approach to create the tabular examples in earlier Chapters of this monograph. By so doing we took a vertical slice of the unit-square at a constant magnitude of competition; that is, we held market shares constant. The logic of $db = d\theta$ also appears in Kim and Staelin (1999). Compatibility with a vertical-slice requires $c_i = c_j$; see equation (11.2.19) below.
[7] Recall that base demand ($A_k$) is not the same as the channel-coordinated output ($Q_k^*$); it is possible for the smaller retailer (say the $j^{th}$) to have a larger base demand ($A_j > A_i$) *provided* that it also has higher costs ($c_j > c_i$).
[8] The primary exception involves modeling demand as rectangular. This makes the amount of consumers' purchases price-independent so long as the reservation price is not violated. We find such models unappealing for an analysis of channel structure specifically because they banish price to the solitary role of what is the functional equivalence of a consumer's participation constraint. Clearly they do not permit a meaningful analysis of various wholesale-price strategies.
[9] We do not mean to belittle the importance of empirical inspiration; the second principle of Occam's razor specifies that a theory should be consistent with the evidence.
[10] Indeed, the origin of a demand curve *can* be safely ignored as long as modelers are not interested in assessing the effects of a change in competitive substitutability. For the modeler who wishes to examine such effects, assessment methods that ignore the utility basis of demand create serious difficulties—as we proved in Section 2 above.
[11] The term "representative consumer" is drawn from economics, had the concept been invented in marketing it might have been called a "theoretically average consumer."
[12] We express our appreciation to Professor Greg Shaffer for helpful discussions concerning derivation of a demand curve from the utility function of a representative consumer.
[13] Demand for this non-focal (the $h^{th}$) product is more commonly written as $Q_h = A_h - b_h p_h$ subject to $A_h \equiv \mathcal{A}_h / \mathcal{B}_h$ and $b_h \equiv \lambda / \mathcal{B}_h$.
[14] Had we not made this assumption, our "unit-cube" in Chapters 5-10 would have been four-dimensional, with the $\chi \equiv (\theta / b)-$ dimension split into the two dimensions $\chi_i \equiv (\theta / b_i)$ and $\beta \equiv (b_j / b_i)$. In this context we do not believe that the benefits of enhanced mathematical generality are sufficient to justify greater mathematical complexity.

[15] This conceptualization, which dates back at least as far as Marshall (1907), was used by Nash (1950) in generating an equal division of channel profit between bilateral monopolists. (See Chapter 2 for details.) It is common to set $\lambda = 1$, but any constant value will do.

[16] The elasticity of both "b" and "θ" with respect to λ is one. Thus $d(\theta / b)/d\lambda = 0$.

[17] The horizontal axis is the *magnitude of competition*, expressed in terms of the market share of the j[th] retailer; the vertical axis is the *intensity of competition*, expressed as the cross-price to own-price ratio $\chi \equiv (\theta / b)$.

[18] Because the results for Zone $Z_{ij}^{SS^*}$ are *very* complex, we do not present them.

[19] Holding aggregate demand constant does not freeze unit sales unless per-unit distribution costs are equal across retailers.

[20] Recall from equations (11.4.9) and (11.4.34) that an increase in $\mathcal{T}$ lowers channel profit whether the channel is coordinated or not.

[21] The translation is by Thorburn (1918).

[22] It does not help to return to the utility function to assess $d\mathcal{B}$.

Chapter 12

# Towards a Unifying Theory of Distribution Channels

*"What we know is not much. What we do not know is immense."*

## 1 INTRODUCTION

We noted in Chapter 1 that the analytical marketing science literature on competition in distribution channels has generated three research streams that address inter-channel competition, inter-manufacturer competition, and inter-retailer competition. Given the evolution of these streams, one might be tempted to conclude they are inherently separate. Such temptation must be resisted, for they are facets of a single phenomenon: the manner in which the distribution of goods and services is organized. While distinctive assumptions distinguish these research streams, they share four important features. First, all three streams originated as extensions of the bilateral-monopoly model, which was first developed by economists, and all three streams contain that original model as a special case. Second, manufacturers and retailers *cooperate vertically* in the distribution of goods. Third, manufacturers and retailers *compete vertically* over the distribution of channel profit. Fourth, channels, manufacturers, and retailers *compete horizontally* to distribute products to customers. These commonalities, which underscore the interconnectedness of the three research streams, suggest the possibility of future unification.

In this Chapter we present the case for creating an "integrated picture" of distribution-channels models that will illuminate both the commonalities and the differences in these and other, yet to be explored, research streams. We call our proposed "integrated picture" a *Unifying Theory of Distribution Channels*. To make our argument, we build on the research reported in Chapters 1-11. In Section 2 we review eight Channel Myths that have shaped the way in which marketing scientists envision distribution models. In our opinion, these Myths are responsible for the paucity of heterogeneous-competitors models, which should be a crucial component of a Unifying Theory of Distribution Channels. Many of the Myths arise from the bilateral-monopoly model, with its goal of channel coordination, and have been reinforced by the identical-competitors models that characterize much of the inter-channel and inter-manufacturer streams. We discuss the dynamics that have contributed to the persistence of Channel

Myths in Section 3. In Section 4 we offer four criteria for model construction that should facilitate the development of a Unifying Theory while lessening the likelihood that additional Myths will creep into the literature.

We believe that several research directions have the capacity to enrich the single-manufacturer meta-model used in this book;[1] we identify these opportunities in Section 5. In Section 6 we discuss a single-retailer meta-model that is the retail analogue of the single-manufacturer meta-model that has occupied our attention throughout this monograph. In Section 7 we present insights that we believe have the potential to move the field closer to the creation of a Unifying Theory of Distribution Channels. A Unifying Theory should reveal how Channel Structure and the Channel Environment affect Channel Strategy and Channel Performance. In Section 8 we offer concluding comments by summarizing modeling principles that we judge as essential for the development of a Unifying Theory of Distribution Channels.

## 2 CHANNEL MYTHS

We argued in Chapter 1 that the marketing science profession adheres to several erroneous beliefs about distribution channels; we call these beliefs "Channel Myths." Eight Myths have framed the analytical modeling of distribution channels and have shaped the strategic advice offered to managers. Many of these beliefs have a foundation in modeling devices and/ or managerial counsel that are perfectly appropriate within the narrow context in which they originated, typically the bilateral-monopoly model. The mythic elements in these beliefs can be traced to their inappropriate generalization to models of multiple retailers, manufacturers, or channels. Such errors of generalization are neither new nor unusual; to quote Plato, "Whenever . . . people are deceived and form opinions wide of the truth, it is clear that the error has slid into their minds through the medium of certain resemblances to that truth."[2]

The two most influential Channels Myths are the *Bilateral-Monopoly Meta-Myth* and the *Identical-Competitors Meta-Myth*. Each involves the belief that the Channel Performance obtained under a restrictive assumption (either no competitors or identical competitors) can be accurately generalized to situations involving competitors who are not identical. Neither of these beliefs is substantiated by the analysis of more complex models, nor are they supported by empirical evidence. In particular, when one models more than one retailer, the simple, intuitively appealing outcomes generated by the bilateral-monopoly model break down *except* when the retailers are identical. Because rivals in an identical-competitors model do not have different responses to the channel environment, or to the manufacturer's actions, their behavior is indistinguishable. Thus these Channel Myths reinforce each other in a manner that encourages scholars to infer that the results of a bilateral-monopoly model generalize to a multiple-retailers model. Phrased differently, marketing scientists appear to be unaware that what *seem* to be innocuous "modeling simplifications" produce a distorted perspective on distribution channels.

From a managerial perspective, prescriptive errors arise from the *Double-Marginalization Strategic Myth* and the *Channel-Coordination Strategic Myth*. The former Myth is a belief that a channel can be coordinated if only one channel member has a non-zero margin. This conviction, which is justified in bilateral-monopoly and identical-competitors models, is incorrect when there is even slight competition (or complementarity) between two or more non-identical retailers. Maximization of channel profits requires that the manufacturer *not* have a zero margin in its dealings with *any* competitor; wholesale margins must be unequal when there are competing retailers.[3] The latter Myth is a belief that maximizing channel profit enables all channel members to benefit through mutually acceptable profit redistribution. We have shown repeatedly that this belief is correct in a bilateral monopoly, or with identical competitors; but it is *often false* when there are comparably-treated, non-identical retailers—whether they are in competition or not.

Four other myths involve widely employed assumptions that simplify constructing distribution-channels models. According to the *Channel-Breadth Modeling Myth*, neither Channel Strategy nor Channel Performance depends on how many retailers participate in a multiple-retailers channel. Yet we have proven that, when channel breadth is a choice variable, the manufacturer can *often* net greater profit by increasing the number of retailers that distribute its product while simultaneously altering its wholesale-price policy. In Chapter 3 we demonstrated the validity of this statement when the retailers do *not compete*—switching from coordination to non-coordination enhanced manufacturer profit by encouraging an increase in channel breadth. In Chapter 10 we showed that, when bilateral monopoly is properly modeled, adding a second, *competing* retailer increases the manufacturer's profit over a wide range of parametric values. Further, it is *often* in the manufacturer's interest not to coordinate the broader channel. The general message is that, when channel breadth is a choice variable, the manufacturer often prefers to serve more retailers while foregoing channel coordination. Hence, the Channel-Coordination Strategic Myth and the Channel-Breadth Modeling Myth are mutually reinforcing.

The *Fixed-Cost Modeling Myth* states that it is acceptable to ignore fixed costs when building distribution-channels models. This simplification is understandable in a bilateral-monopoly model, or in a model with identical competitors, for in these models fixed costs only affect the participation constraints of channel members. But as we have shown in Chapters 5-10, when competitors are not identical the difference in the fixed costs of the retailers affects the optimal wholesale *price*, the ideal wholesale-price *policy*, the magnitude of consumers' surplus, the level of channel profit, and the distribution of channel profit. Fixed costs also influence the manufacturer's optimal wholesale-price policy in a bilateral-monopoly model when the channel faces multiple states-of-nature. Finally, fixed costs affect channel breadth, and the desirability of channel coordination, in a model of multiple, *non*-competing retailers.

According to the *Aggregate-Demand Modeling Myth*, the cross-price parameter in the retail demand curve can be interpreted as a measure of retailer substitutability. We proved that applying this interpretation yields utterly implausible results. Thus we developed a mathematical procedure for analyzing the impact of a change in retailer substitutability. We based our analysis on the utility function of a representative consumer; this is the same function that was used to derive our system of demand equations. Our method generates insights that comport with marketing intuition, yet that are clearly not obvious *a priori*.[4]

Finally, according to the *Multiple-Retailers/Multiple States-of-Nature Modeling Myth*, a multiple states-of-nature model is interchangeable with a multiple-retailers model. In Chapter 4, we showed the error in this logic. In a multiple-retailers model, *no* retailer participates in the channel unless it earns a non-negative profit. In a multiple states-of-nature model, the solitary retailer must earn a non-negative *expected* profit to ensure its channel participation. In addition, for distribution to occur in all states-of-nature, the retailer must not lose more than its fixed cost in the lowest-demand state. In short, the lowest profit retailer cannot lose any money, while the solitary retailer cannot lose too much money in the lowest profit state-of-nature. These are not the same thing.

The preceding Myths have generated a variety of observations that do not generalize beyond the narrow confines of bilateral monopoly and/or identical competitors. This statement raises two questions. Why have these Myths persisted? How can we lessen the chance of other Myths creeping into analyses in the future? We address these questions in the next two Sections.

# 3 THE PERSISTENCE OF CHANNEL MYTHS

We believe that three primary dynamics explain the persistence of these eight Myths in the marketing science literature. First, marketers tend to adhere to the time-honored tradition of borrowing theory from other disciplines, a point that seems to have first been made by Hawkins (1950).

Because channels commonly involve multiple participants at each level, he questioned the efficacy of uncritically using bilateral-monopoly models. Our own attitude toward borrowing is that, while there is little sense in re-inventing the wheel, we should not be surprised if a wheel developed for a bicycle-built-for-two works improperly on a multi-wheeled, multi-passenger vehicle. Theories need to be re-machined if they are to work properly in a new setting.

Second, marketers tend to accept generative work as authoritative. Yet there is a vital distinction between acknowledging an intellectual debt to the giants who developed a specialized field of study, and accepting received doctrine as flawless. Virtually all disciplines begin with analyses that are state-of-the-art for their time, but that are simple compared to the complexity of the real-world phenomenon being modeled. Jevons expressed this point at the end of his famous economic treatise:[5]

> [if] the admirers of a great author accept his writings as authoritative, both in their excellences and in their defects, the most serious injury is done to truth. In matters of philosophy and science, authority has ever been the great opponent of truth (1871, p. 260).

When the arguments of great authors achieve the status of conventional wisdom, the apparent clarity of that wisdom often interferes with an objective assessment of contrary ideas. The essence of our argument is not new, nor is it unique to mathematical modeling, as Locke's comment on philosophers makes clear: "New opinions are always suspected, and usually opposed, without any other reason but because they are not already common" (1690).

Third, marketing scientists tend to misidentify real-world scenarios as empirical support for the bilateral-monopoly model. In presentations in Australia, Europe, and North America, we have heard arguments that run something like this: "a firm employs a salesforce to provide individualized attention to each customer; further, each customer typically selects a different merchandise mix from the product line. Because each dyadic relationship has unique aspects, each should be modeled as a bilateral monopoly."

To illustrate the flaw in this logic, think of a barbershop that customizes haircuts, and conversations, for each customer. While our barbershop understands the importance of target marketing, what is relevant from a modeling perspective is that *all of its customers pay the same price* for a haircut. Even a salon, which charges different prices for haircuts and permanents, requires each customer to pay an amount that is listed on a menu of services offered to all who enter the salon. Customers are comparably treated by the barbershop (one price) and by the salon (a price-menu) even though products purchased and services received differ across customers.

The real issue is that when a price is constrained, for legal or practical reasons, to be the same for a set of customers, then the firm faces a single-variable optimization problem. Any managerial action that cannot be precisely targeted to one customer (whether end-user or retailer) induces an externality that affects other customers. As a result, no marketing-mix effort is sufficient to justify modeling a firm's relationships with its customers as a series of independent, bilateral monopolies; under comparable treatment, a multiple-retailers model (and/or a multiple-manufacturers and/or a multiple-channels model) is the accurate depiction of reality.

In sum, we are not saying that borrowing should end, that generative work should be forgotten, or that customer uniqueness should be ignored. We are saying that without appropriately modifying borrowed models, critically evaluating received wisdom, and carefully considering how we bring relevance to our models, other Myths may arise. Thus it is important to establish guidelines to ensure the enduring contribution of future research in distribution channels. We now turn to four proposed guidelines.

## 4 MODELING CRITERIA: TOWARD A UNIFYING THEORY OF DISTRIBUTION CHANNELS

While there has been considerable high-quality, analytical research on distribution channels, we see little evidence of an integration of the three main research streams that address competition: inter-channel, inter-manufacturer, and inter-retailer. We believe that combining these streams is essential to fully comprehend the impact of Channel Environment and Channel Structure on Channel Strategy and Channel Performance. We believe that the lack of integration has at least three severe consequences. First, the eight Channel Myths have constrained how marketing scientists conceptualize distribution models. As a result, much of what is known does not generalize beyond the model in which it was derived. Indeed, because some models rely on one or more Channel Myths, some of what we think we know is simply wrong. Second, the absence of a central organizing principle impedes cross-model comparisons—particularly when the models come from different parts of the analytical literature on distribution channels. Consequently, some research is redundant with work conducted under an alternative paradigm. Third, because papers typically differ on more than one assumption, it can be extraordinarily difficult to determine why models from the same paradigm produce discrepant results. This difficulty hinders comprehension and limits insights.

We believe the marketing science profession can do better. We believe that there is a need for a central organizing principle—a Unifying Theory—that will enable researchers to contribute to knowledge in a manner that enhances our common understanding and that enables us collectively to solve the puzzles of distribution research. We believe that rapid progress can be made provided that future models satisfy *four essential modeling criteria*. We first introduced these criteria in Chapter 1; we restate them here, adding details that reflect the analytical results reported in this monograph. We envision these principles as vital characteristics of a Unifying Theory of Distribution Channels.

1. *The First-Principles Criterion.* A Unifying Theory should be consistent with first principles; that is, decisions about the optimal level of any element of the marketing mix should be consistent with rational, maximizing behavior by economic actors. This Criterion should ensure that the elements of Channel Strategy are internally consistent and that Channel Performance is truly optimal. It should also facilitate comparisons across models, enabling marketing scientists to determine if differences in Channel Performance are due to variations in Channel Environment, Channel Structure, or sub-optimized Channel Strategy. This Criterion means that the demand curve facing consumer-oriented firms should be derived from a meaningful utility function and the demand curve facing business-oriented firms should be derived from the profit functions of their business customers'. Applying this Criterion is essential to the interpretation of changes in substitutability between retailers and between products. The First-Principles Criterion enabled us to solve the problems raised by the Aggregate-Demand Modeling Myth.
2. *The Empirical-Evidence Criterion.* A Unifying Theory should be in broad harmony with empirical evidence regarding the structure and operation of distribution channels. We used this Criterion to justify modeling *comparable treatment* of multiple competitors. This conceptualization was central to all our results. It led directly to our identification of the Double-Marginalization Strategic Myth, and it validated our decision to incorporate *fixed costs* at retail. Our models recognize that retailers incur expenses that are quantity-*independent*; such costs may be interpreted as non-trivial opportunity costs, or as out-of-pocket expenses. Heeding the Empirical-Evidence Criterion enabled us to identify the Fixed-Cost Modeling Myth.
3. *The Nested-Models Criterion.* A Unifying Theory should contain simpler models as special cases of more complex models; that is, the former should be "nested" within the latter (Moorthy 1993). Such nesting generates research that *systematically* builds on the literature, thereby simplifying the challenge of understanding how additional variables, or layers of complexity, alter Channel Performance and Channel Strategy. Nesting also facilitates assessing the robustness of

results to a relaxation of specific modeling assumptions. We used the Nested-Models Criterion as we constructed our models, so that the bilateral-monopoly model and the identical-competitors model were consistently embedded as special cases within our work. Nesting was critical to our identification of the Bilateral-Monopoly Meta-Myth and the Identical-Competitors Meta-Myth.

4. *The Strategic-Endogeneity Criterion.* A Unifying Theory should endogenously determine Channel Performance and Channel Strategy.
   - Channel Performance concerns the benefits that the channel delivers to its members and end-users. The elements of Channel Performance are:
     - The prices charged to, and the quantities purchased by, end-users and retailers;
     - The consumers' surplus obtained by end-users;
     - The total profit earned by the channel; and
     - The distribution of channel profit between channel members.

     Virtually all models determine prices, quantities, and channel profit; it is less common for the channel-profit distribution to be assessed endogenously; finally, marketing scientists rarely take consumers' surplus into account (though economists do assess it).
   - Channel Strategy entails the managerial decisions that directly or indirectly influence Channel Performance. The components of Channel Strategy are:
     - The optimal channel breadth from the perspective of the channel leader;
     - The optimal pricing strategy for each channel member;
     - The optimal level of all non-price elements of the marketing mix from the perspective of each channel member; and
     - The optimal category-management strategy from the perspective of each channel member.

   Many models exogenously impose some, or even all, elements of strategy. We intend this Criterion to encourage the *endogenous determination of Channel Strategy* by broadening the scope of channel analyses. The Strategic-Endogeneity Criterion enabled us to identify the Channel-Breadth Modeling Myth and the Channel-Coordination Strategic Myth. We evaluated the former by allowing channel breadth to vary; we discovered the latter by comparing models with coordinating and non-coordinating wholesale-price policies. This Criterion stimulated the research that we reported in Chapters 3, 4 and 10, where we proved that the distribution of channel profit is intertwined with channel (or temporal) breadth. More generally, Channel Performance depends on Channel Strategy.

On the basis of our research, we strongly believe that a consistent application of these modeling criteria will help to eradicate the eight Channel Myths from the marketing science literature; they will also help to prevent the emergence of new myths. We hope that these four criteria will facilitate the development of a Unifying Theory of Distribution Channels in two key ways. First, these criteria should illuminate opportunities for logically consistent extensions of existing models. Second, these criteria should clarify the potential for developing new models that will extend our knowledge of distribution channels in a substantive manner. In the next Sections we discuss ongoing efforts to implement these modeling criteria, including plausible extensions of our meta-model and other, analytical models of distribution channels. After completing these exercises we will return to the issue of a Unifying Theory.

# 5 OUR SINGLE-MANUFACTURER META-MODEL

We have argued that marketing scientists should seek a Unifying Theory of Distribution Channels specifically because it will permit a fuller understanding of the interrelationships between Channel Structure and the Channel Environment on one hand and Channel Strategy and Channel Performance on the other hand. We stress that our own work is *not* a Unifying Theory, although we believe that it contributes toward the creation of such a theory. In this Section we provide a synopsis of the models addressed in earlier Chapters, then we address plausible extensions of our meta-model. We organize our thoughts around our Channel Environment, Channel Structure, and Channel Strategy assumptions.

## 5.1 A Synopsis of Our Single-Manufacturer Meta-Model

We have analyzed several manifestations of the single-manufacturer meta-model in this monograph. In our models we considered one, two, or N retailers. When the number of retailers is determined *endogenously*, we can ascertain globally optimal channel breadth, as we showed in Chapter 3. When a specific number of retailers are *exogenously* assigned, a numerical increase changes the meaning of the model and raises its mathematical complexity. One retailer defines a monopsonistic buyer; this is the derived demand side of a bilateral-monopoly model. Two or more retailers are required to assess inter-retailer competition.[6] As we established in Chapter 10, with two retailers the manufacturer has three choices for its channel-breadth: it may sell to the $i^{th}$, to the $j^{th}$, or to both retailers. With three retailers the manufacturer faces seven channel-breadth evaluations; it could sell to the $i^{th}$, the $j^{th}$, the $k^{th}$, the $i^{th}$ and $j^{th}$, the $i^{th}$ and $k^{th}$, the $j^{th}$ and $k^{th}$, or to all three retailers. With any specific number of retailers, say $N_R$, there are $(2^{N_R}-1)$ channel-breadth evaluations. We believe that little insight will be gained in exchange for the considerable complexity associated with considering more than two retailers.

We also evaluated a states-of-nature model with one, two, or N states. A single state defines certainty; this assumption is typical of distribution models.[7] At least two states are needed to investigate uncertainty. N states-of-nature offers full generality, but seem to preclude closed-form solutions.

Table 12.1 catalogs the numbers of retailers and states-of-nature investigated in each Chapter. Notice that the "one retailer, one state-of-nature" cell contains two forms of bilateral monopoly. Chapter 2 evaluated the standard definition of one manufacturer facing one retailer; Chapters 10 and 11 explored an expanded definition of bilateral monopoly that included the possibility of competitive retail entry. We discuss the cells labeled $xR/y\Omega$ $(x,y \in (2,N))$ in the next sub-Section.

*Table 12.1.* Chapters Aligned with sub-Models of the Single-Manufacturer Meta-Model*

| | | Number of Retailers | | |
|---|---|---|---|---|
| | | **1** | **2** | **N** |
| Number of States-of-Nature | **1** | 2, 10, 11 | 5—11 | 3** |
| | **2** | 4 | $2\mathcal{R}/2\Omega$ | $N\mathcal{R}/2\Omega$ |
| | **N** | 4 | $2\mathcal{R}/N\Omega$ | $N\mathcal{R}/N\Omega$ |

Legend:
* $\mathcal{R} \equiv$ Retailers
$\Omega \equiv$ States-of-Nature
** $\equiv$ We only investigated $\theta = 0$

## 5.2 Extensions of Our Single-Manufacturer Meta-Model: Channel Environment

We have discussed three dimensions of the Channel Environment: demand, costs, and states-of-nature. We think that the only meaningful options for modeling demand within this meta-model are general demand (i.e., $Q = Q(p)$) and linear demand. Both have been used in this book. A constant-elasticity formulation is incompatible with solving models involving multiple players at the same level of the channel. We strongly believe that the results obtained from rectangular demand, which generates no price/quantity trade-off, fail the Empirical-Evidence Criterion; thus we see little value to channel models that feature rectangular-demand curves.

We have argued strenuously for the inclusion of positive per-unit variable costs and quantity-independent fixed costs at each horizontal channel level. Our own research incorporates these costs. However, we have concentrated on *constant* per-unit costs. Clearly one might investigate the impact of *non-constant* per-unit costs. Non-constant costs may ameliorate, or exaggerate, the effect of competitors having unequal market shares. It might be of interest to structure a model in which there are constant per-unit costs for each retailer, but increasing costs to the retail level. Phrased alternatively, we might model constant returns to scale for every store, but decreasing returns to the retail industry. The presence of negative externalities at a channel level could be motivated by competitive retailers that bid up the price of scarce resources. Theoretical studies of system externalities in the international trade literature could be a source of inspiration;[8] but, as we noted in Section 3, caution should be exercised in undertaking such borrowing.

Most of our models assume demand certainty but models featuring multiple states-of-nature are also worthy of investigation. The Empirical-Evidence Criterion encourages the study of uncertainty. Furthermore, certainty can be embedded within a model of uncertainty, thus satisfying our Nested-Models Criterion. Table 12.1 highlights opportunities for extensions of the single-manufacturer meta-model by adding uncertainty to models of multiple retailers—whether the retailers do or do not compete; these are the cells labeled $2\mathcal{R}/2\Omega$, $2\mathcal{R}/N\Omega$, $N\mathcal{R}/2\Omega$, and $N\mathcal{R}/N\Omega$ (our notation denotes x-retailers and y-states-of-nature, where $x, y \in (2, N)$).

## 5.3 Extensions of Our Single-Manufacturer Meta-Model: Channel Structure

We have detailed three dimensions[9] of Channel Structure that can be relevant in a single-manufacturer meta-model: vertical channel-relationships, horizontal channel-relationships, and horizontal product-resale assumptions. Only a *vertical Stackelberg leadership game* is consistent with a determinate distribution of channel profit when the wholesale-price policy is a two-part or three-part tariff, or a menu of such tariffs.[10] Our logic is that any wholesale-price strategy containing a fixed fee must assign a value to the fee. The Stackelberg leader sets the fee to extract all profit from one retailer—leaving it just willing to be a channel participant—other retailers realize a non-negative profit.[11] In contrast, the fee is arbitrarily chosen in a vertical Nash game. In short, we have serious reservations about any multiple-retailers model that is structured as a vertical Nash game.

We utilized a *horizontal Nash game* to assess models of competing retailers who purchase directly from the manufacturer. We believe that there is good reason *not* to model a horizontal Stackelberg game. Specifically, because the follower obtains lower sales than does the leader, and it is worse off than it would be in a Nash game, neither retailer is willing to be a Stackelberg follower. An alternative approach with more than two retailers would model a "dominant" retailer encircled by a "competitive fringe." Fringe players are typically modeled as *blindly matching* the dominant retailer's price without considering whether it is in their interest to do so. Similarly, the dominant retailer, which displays shrewd skills toward the manufacturer, ignores the existence of the fringe even though it clearly is not in its interest to do so. Although such models can be elegant, in our opinion they violate the Empirical-Evidence Criterion; we do not believe that models of fringe retailers are meaningful descriptors of reality. Nonetheless, there is an opportunity here to apply the Nested-Models Criterion to the competitive fringe model concept: nest the competitive fringe model within a model in which (i) small ("fringe") retailers do *not* match the dominant retailer's price and (ii) the dominant retailer does *not* ignore its small competitors, then determine the conditions under which the fringe players "match" and the dominant player "ignores." If no such conditions emerge, or if the conditions involve degenerate solutions, this would confirm our belief that competitive fringe models have no place in contemporary channels research.

We argued that allowing horizontal product-resale is equivalent to modeling sequential bilateral monopolies, because *only* the manufacturer makes money in this scenario. However, product-resale may be meaningful in a competitive fringe model if the dominant firm is restricted to a one-part tariff wholesale-price policy.

Finally, because assumptions concerning the existence and extent of inter-channel competition go to the heart of our call to unify the three parts of the marketing science literature on distribution channels, we defer our discussion of these assumptions to Section 7.

## 5.4 Extensions of Our Single-Manufacturer Meta-Model: Channel Strategy

We have discussed four dimensions of Channel Strategy: channel breadth, the wholesale-price policy, the category-management policy, and the non-price elements of the marketing mix. We noted in sub-Section 5.1 that, with a specific number of retailers $N_R$, there are $(2^{N_R}-1)$ channel-breadth evaluations to be made. Because we assess a one manufacturer meta-model in this Section, we have assumed away any questions regarding the optimal number of manufacturers; we address that issue in the next Section.

Our wholesale-price analyses have covered the known spectrum of wholesale-price policies that are compatible with closed-form solutions. Our sophisticated Stackelberg tariff is the envelope of all two-part tariffs that are manufacturer optimal for at least one possible value of the difference in retailer fixed costs. This tariff dominates any simple two-part tariff, including the naïve Stackelberg tariff that is so popular in the literature; however, the sophisticated Stackelberg tariff is incompatible with channel coordination except in the degenerate cases of bilateral-monopoly models and identical-competitors models. For this reason we designed a menu of two-part tariffs that ensures channel coordination. We also examined a channel-coordinating, linear quantity-discount schedule (a "three-part" tariff). In Chapters 8-10, we argued that this schedule is of little incremental value. Relative to the next best alternative, it adds less than 1 percent to manufacturer profit over the portion of parameter space where it is dominant. In retrospect, we think the linear quantity-discount schedule adds more complexity than insight; thus we see little value in the incorporation of a linear quantity-discount schedule into future analyses, at least when demand is modeled as linear. We stress, however, that when a general demand curve is used, a general quantity-discount schedule should be explored (as we showed in Chapter 3). We believe that a fruitful avenue for exploration could involve combining our two preferred policies into a menu of sophisticated Stackelberg two-part tariffs.

Because we concentrated on a one product meta-model, we could not investigate category-management. We address this issue in the next Section.

Most analytical channel models ignore non-price elements of the *marketing mix*; that is, the default value of these non-price variables is zero.[12]

We believe that there is a serious need to design and analyze heterogeneous-competitor models that incorporate at least one marketing-mix variable. A variable (say "service") could be explored in three veins. First, because service is a non-price form of competition, we might study the ways in which a higher-priced retailer can use service to overcome, or reverse, consumer price-resistance. Second, in a channel that is left uncoordinated by the wholesale price, we might assess the ability of a marketing-mix element to move that channel closer to coordination.[13] Third, we could introduce a tradeoff between categories of demand-enhancing, marketing-mix activities by adding an additional element to the mix (say "advertising"); this would enable us to gauge marketing-mix elements that operate within a retail store (e.g., service) and those that have an impact across stores (e.g., advertising).[14]

### 5.5 Extensions of Our Single-Manufacturer Meta-Model: Summary

We have shown that a single-manufacturer meta-model can be employed to delimit the attractiveness of channel coordination and to ascertain the ideal number of retailers that the manufacturer should utilize to distribute its product. We saw that the degree of inter-retailer competition, the market shares of the retailers, and their fixed costs interact to provide an answer to the coordination and channel-breadth questions. As outlined above, there are several extensions of the single-manufacturer meta-model that could lead to additional insights into distribution channels. Yet, despite its richness, this meta-model cannot be used to explore some of the extant models in the analytical distribution channels literature; examples include the two-manufacturers/one-retailer model (Choi 1991) and the two-manufacturers/two-retailers models (McGuire and Staelin 1983, 1986; Choi 1996). We now turn to meta-models that are relevant for analyzing these channel issues.

## 6 A SINGLE-RETAILER META-MODEL

In this Section we describe the single-retailer meta-model; this is the retail analogue of the one-manufacturer meta-model. We start by adding product-line breadth to the bilateral-monopoly model. Then we examine a meta-model of multiple-manufacturers, each selling one product; this meta-model contains the Choi model (1991) of two manufacturers with a common retailer as a special case. The final meta-model described in this Section consists of a single-manufacturer that sells multiple products and that contains our single-manufacturer/single-product model as a special case.

## 6.1 Extensions of a Single-Retailer Meta-Model: Bilateral Monopoly and the Number of Products

The bilateral-monopoly meta-model encompasses one manufacturer selling through one retailer, but places no restrictions on the number of products that are distributed or the number of states-of-nature that are relevant; special cases of this meta-model assume one product and demand certainty (Chapter 2), one product and two (or N) states-of-nature (Chapter 4), and two products and one state-of-nature. We focus on the third example, noting that many other examples could be given.

In a two-product, bilateral-monopoly model, issues of channel breadth have been assumed away. There are, however, issues of category-management strategy, because each channel member must choose between joint or individual product pricing. Moreover, each channel member has the option of making one product unavailable to consumers.[15] The subtlety lies in the fact that both the manufacturer and the retailer must decide whether to engage in product-line pricing (PLP)—jointly choose both prices to maximize the profits generated by the product line. A minor complication is that their decisions are mutually contingent: whether the retailer should use PLP depends on whether the manufacturer does, or does not, use PLP. Coughlan and Ingene (2002) have modeled this issue and have found that PLP is a unique, stable equilibrium for both channel members independent of the product-heterogeneity issue. However, unless the degree of inter-product competition is high, the manufacturer and the retailer are *both* better off when *neither* of them uses PLP. This counter-intuitive result, which reflects a prisoner's dilemma, occurs whether the vertical relationship is characterized by a Stackelberg or a Nash game. As provocative as the Coughlan-Ingene results are, they *may* reflect the absence of intra-level competition (we address this point in the next sub-Section). Only by extending their analysis to multiple-manufacturers and/or multiple-retailers models can we truly grasp the efficacy of product-line pricing for manufacturers, for retailers, and for the channel. These comments again highlight the need for a Unifying Theory, for without such a theory it would be easy to reach conclusions about channel practice on the basis of what *may* be an incomplete, or even an inadvertently misleading, model.

Another complexity can arise from product differentiation. Write the demand system for *two products* as:

$$\begin{aligned} Q_i &= A_i - b_i p_i + \gamma p_j \\ Q_j &= A_j - b_j p_j + \gamma p_i \end{aligned} \tag{12.6.1}$$

The $\gamma$-term signifies that competition exists between heterogeneous products, rather than between heterogeneous retailers (as in demand system (5.2.1)).

There is another important difference between these demand systems: in (12.6.1) we do *not* equalize own-price effects ($b_i \neq b_j$) because we can think of no good reason that the rate of change of marginal utility of the i[th] product and the j[th] product should be the same; that is, we allow $\mathcal{B}_i \neq \mathcal{B}_j$ in the representative consumer's utility function.[16] Without an assumption of equal own-price effects, the re-parameterization used in Chapters 9 and 10 that enabled us to offer a graphical illustration of our theories would have required four dimensions. The market-share and fixed-cost dimensions would be defined as before, while the $\chi$ – dimension would be delineated as $\chi_i\ (\equiv \theta / b_i)$. The final dimension would be defined as the ratio of own-price terms $\beta\ (\equiv b_j / b_i)$. Because one of the own-price terms must be smaller than the other, we arbitrarily set $b_j < b_i$. Thus $\chi_i$ and $\beta$ lie in the unit interval, as do the market share of the j[th] firm and each retailer's fixed cost expressed as a percentage of its coordinated net revenues. We realize that the thought of a four-dimensional ($\chi_i$, $S_j$, $f$, $\beta$) analysis is intimidating given the complexity of the three-dimensional ($\chi, S_j, f$) analyses presented in Chapters 8-10. While the task may appear daunting, we should keep in mind the words of Alfred North Whitehead. In explaining the results of an analysis that featured four-dimensional geometry, Whitehead said: "I do not apologize, because I am really not responsible for the fact that nature in its most fundamental aspect is four-dimensional. Things are what they are . . . ." (1920).[17]

Heterogeneous-product models merit the same perspective; the assumption $b_i = b_j \equiv b$ is problematic with non-identical products.[18] We are unaware of any channels model that includes the evaluation of unequal own-price effects, but it appears to be a promising direction for future research. In light of the Identical-Competitors Meta-Myth, we speculate that treating heterogeneous products as if they were homogenous may yield misleading results. Phrased differently, there *may be* an (as yet unproven) *Identical-Products* Myth that has points in common with the Identical-Competitors Meta-Myth.

## 6.2 Extensions of a Single-Retailer Meta-Model: Multiple Manufacturers and the Number of Products

The number of manufacturers in a multiple-manufacturers model ($N_M$) may be specified exogenously or endogenously. In either case, one issue to be resolved is the optimal channel breadth from the viewpoint of the single (monopolistic) retailer. When $N_M$ is modeled as endogenous, we may calculate the optimal number of manufacturers with whom the retailer trades. If $N_M$ is specified exogenously, then there are $(2^{N_M} - 1)$ channel-breadth evaluations to make and the optimal channel breadth cannot exceed $N_M$. But this statement masks a profound subtlety, for multiple manufacturers raises the question of how many products the retailer will sell. We consider the polar extremes: all manufacturers produce an identical product or each manufacturer produces a single, unique product.

When all manufacturers produce an identical product there are at least three reasons why a retailer would buy from more than one manufacturer. First, there may be decreasing returns to scale in production, so the inherent wholesale-price policy would be a quantity-surplus schedule. Avoiding a high price will cause the retailer to do business with as many manufacturers as possible. Second, there may be legal or technical constraints that limit the quantity that any one manufacturer can produce.[19] Third, the retailer may prefer multiple suppliers to limit a manufacturers' ability to extract economic rent in the form of fixed fees. We have not seen these reasons modeled in the channels literature. Rather, there is a tendency to discuss distinct products, but to model identical competitors. The result is that all manufacturers charge the same wholesale price and sell equal quantities. In effect, manufacturers produce identical products, no matter the verbiage used to "explain" the mathematics. We believe that, under normal circumstances, the decision to model multiple manufacturers should be inextricably intertwined with a decision by the retailer to carry multiple products.[20]

At the other extreme, if each manufacturer produces a unique product, the relevant question involves the appropriate category-management strategy, because channel breadth follows directly from the retailer's product-line decision. We believe a basic analysis of this phenomenon would parallel the approach taken in Chapter 3 (if the number of products is endogenous to the model) or Chapter 10 (if it is exogenous). A related issue involves the relative benefit to the retailer of pricing each product independently *versus* setting prices jointly (i.e., "product-line pricing" or "PLP"). Choi (1991) and Lee and Staelin (1997) have shown PLP to be retailer-optimal in a two-manufacturer/one-retailer model. This intuitively appealing conclusion requires a single comparison: PLP or non-PLP. But in a model with three manufacturers (A, B, and C), each producing one product, a retailer that carries all three products must make five comparisons; it may employ PLP with the product sets {A,B,C}, {A,B}, {A,C}, or {B,C}, or it may individually price all three products. As the number of products ($N_P$) increases, the number of category-management comparisons "explode" at the rate ($2^{N_P} - N_P$).

## 6.3 Extensions of a Single-Retailer Meta-Model: Multiple Products from Multiple Manufacturers

An interesting, but difficult, topic entails the modeling of two manufacturers (the $i^{th}$ and $j^{th}$), each producing related products (X and Y). As a result, the single retailer can choose to offer as many as four heterogeneous items ($X_i, X_j, Y_i$, and $Y_j$).[21] Suppose that the X's and Y's are distant substitutes, but that $X_i$ and $X_j$ are close substitutes, as are $Y_i$ and $Y_j$. (The X's may be sedans, say the Ford Taurus and Chevrolet Impala; the Y's may be trucks, say the Ford F-150 and the Chevrolet S-10.)

In this scenario, the retailer faces a channel-breadth decision, because there are fifteen possible product mixes: the retailer may carry all four products, three products (there are four possible combinations), two products (six combinations), or only one product (four combinations). The optimal channel-breadth decision depends in part on the category-management strategy, because for any particular channel-breadth decision, the retailer must determine whether to price any of the selected products jointly. (The number of category-management comparisons is 12, 5, 2, and 0 when the number of products is 4, 3, 2, and 1.)

Channel Strategy issues also arise, because each manufacturer must determine its optimal product-line length (sedan, truck, or both) and, if the decision is both, whether to use product-line pricing. Because there is only one retailer, the manufacturers' wholesale-price strategies are not constrained by "comparable treatment" in this model, although manufacturer power is limited by horizontal competition. A wholesale-price analysis (say sophisticated Stackelberg *versus* a menu) should allow channel coordination to be a potential outcome, but not a foregone conclusion. (If the model were restricted to a one-part tariff, the value of coordination could not be assessed.)

We surmise that this model's solution space will be significantly more complicated than the model presented in Chapters 8-10. We are convinced that a model of multiple products from multiple manufacturers will *require* a series of nested models to explore its full richness.

## 6.4 Extensions of a Single-Retailer Meta-Model: Summary

We believe that the single-retailer meta-model has the potential to be just as fertile for generating insights into distribution channels as the single-manufacturer meta-model has been. We have focused our spotlight on how this variation in Channel Structure may affect the channel-breadth and category-management elements of Channel Strategy. Although we have not discussed the marketing mix, it is certainly another legitimate, interesting, and relevant avenue for research.

## 7 COMMMENTARY ON A UNIFYING THEORY OF DISTRIBUTION CHANNELS

To create a Unifying Theory it is necessary to develop a meta-model that has sufficient flexibility to (i) incorporate existing channel models, (ii) meet the "Modeling Criteria" sketched in Section 4 of this Chapter and (iii) encompass the elements of Channel Environment, Channel Structure, and Channel Strategy. We believe that a unifying meta-model must allow at least two competing channels, each composed of two competing manufacturers, each selling to a pair of competing retailers. We will call this a "$2 \times 2 \times 2$ – meta-model," where the first value references the maximum number of channels ($N_C$), the second value refers to the maximum number of manufacturers in each channel ($N_M$), and the third value is the maximum number of retailers in each channel ($N_R$). This meta-model can have from one to four manufacturers ($N_C \times N_M$) and from one to four retailers ($N_C \times N_R$). Thus, with independent manufacturers and retailers, there are eight decision-makers in its most complete version ($N_C = N_M = N_R = 2$), and two decision-makers in its simplest variant ($N_C = N_M = N_R = 1$).

All the major models that have appeared in the marketing science literature are nested as sub-models in the $2 \times 2 \times 2$ – meta-model, including:

- The $1 \times 1 \times 1$ – bilateral-monopoly model that has two decision-makers (Jeuland and Shugan 1983);
- The $2 \times 1 \times 1$ – inter-channel competition model that has four decision-makers (McGuire and Staelin 1983);
- The $1 \times 2 \times 1$ – inter-manufacturer competition model that has three decision-makers (Choi 1991);
- The $1 \times 1 \times 2$ – inter-retailer competition model that has three decision-makers (Ingene and Parry 1995); and
- The $1 \times 2 \times 2$ – bilateral-duopoly model that has four decision-makers (Choi 1996).

Furthermore, the $2 \times 2 \times 2$ – meta-model and each of its sub-models can also be structured as a vertically-integrated system with a single-decision-maker in each channel.

Because the $2 \times 2 \times 2$ – meta-model incorporates a wide range of simpler sub-models, it meets the *Nested-Models Criterion*. As long as the researcher utilizes a demand curve that can be derived from an underlying utility function,[22] this meta-model meets the *First-Principles Criterion.* The *Empirical-Evidence Criterion* can be satisfied by designing a sub-model that is compatible with the Channel Environment and Channel Structure of whatever industry is under investigation.[23] The *Strategic-Endogeneity Criterion* can be met by completely analyzing Channel Strategy in any sub-model that is embedded in the $2 \times 2 \times 2$ – meta-model.

Finally, a modeler merely needs to spell out the elements of a channel's environment, structure, and strategy—and to determine strategic values endogenously—to ensure that the deduced Channel Performance is truly optimal. This is a point that we have repeatedly stressed, and demonstrated, throughout this monograph.

In sub-Section 7.1 we overview a *single-channel variant* of our proposed meta-model and discuss some of the shortcomings in the existing analyses of this $1 \times 2 \times 2$ – model. Then we review the $2 \times 1 \times 1$ – model of inter-channel competition and offer suggestions for its further development. In sub-Section 7.3 we briefly examine extensions of the $1 \times 2 \times 1$ – model of inter-manufacturer competition and the $1 \times 1 \times 2$ – model of inter-retailer competition. We then consider adding non-price marketing-mix elements to the model. In the final sub-Section we reflect on the scope of the fully developed $2 \times 2 \times 2$ – meta-model. In each sub-Section our purpose is not to be comprehensive, but to suggest possible models that can be developed.

## 7.1 The Single-Channel, Bilateral-Duopoly Model: A Basis for a Unifying Theory of Distribution Channels

We believe that an excellent *basis* for a Unifying Theory of Distribution Channels is provided by the model originally developed by Choi (1996) and extended by Trivedi (1998).[24] Two competing manufacturers distribute through a pair of competing retailers in this single-channel model. Thus the model treats channel breadth as exogenous but includes inter-manufacturer competition at the product level and inter-store competition at the retail level.

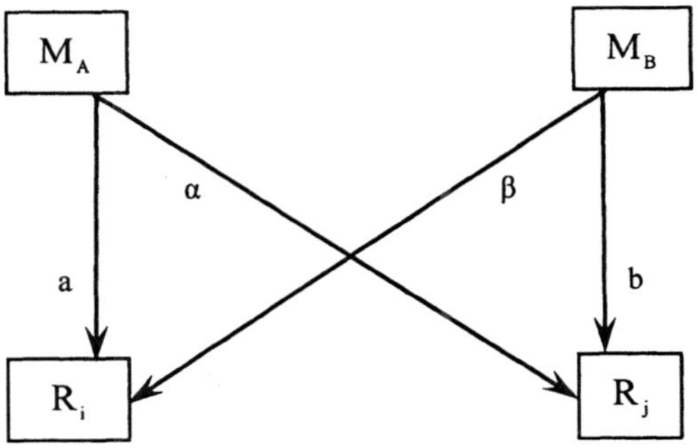


Legend:
$M_\kappa \equiv$ The $\kappa^{th}$ Manufacturer, $\kappa \in (A, B)$, and
$R_k \equiv$ The $k^{th}$ Retailer, $k \in (i, j)$.

*Figure 12.1.* The Single-Channel, Bilateral-Duopoly Model

Within this $1\times2\times2-$model, we say that manufacturers $M_A$ and $M_B$ fabricate products A and B, respectively. Two retailers ($R_i$ and $R_j$) provide distribution of both products; we label the $i^{th}$ ($j^{th}$) retailer's product mix as $A_i$ and $B_i$ ($A_j$ and $B_j$). Figure 12.1 depicts this bilateral-duopoly model (ignore the letters a, α, b and β for now).

Price is the sole marketing-mix element at either channel level. Each retailer jointly prices its products (i.e., it uses product-line pricing). Neither manufacturer faces category-management issues because each produces one product. Channel Structure is characterized by horizontal-Nash channel relationships while the Channel Environment features one state-of-nature, linear demand, and constant per-unit costs. There are no fixed costs.

Choi's analysis of his model includes a nice assessment of the three possible vertical-channel relationships: manufacturer Stackelberg leadership, vertical Nash, and retailer Stackelberg leadership. His use of a common demand curve across all three vertical-channel structures enables him to make legitimate cross-model comparisons. His core observations on Channel Performance are:

- Stackelberg leadership yields higher prices, and lower channel profit, than does a Nash game;
- The Stackelberg leader out-performs the Stackelberg follower;
- An increase in product differentiation raises the wholesale margin and benefits manufacturers; and
- An increase in store differentiation raises the retail margin and

benefits retailers.

The Stackelberg results do not differ from those that are obtained in a single-channel, bilateral-monopoly model. The product and store differentiation results are unsurprising, albeit not obvious *a priori*. In short, the standard conclusions *seem* to be reinforced by these results.

Unfortunately, three shortcomings limit this model's generalizability. We draw attention to these deficiencies because they must be rectified for the $1 \times 2 \times 2-$model to be understood as providing a firm basis for a Unifying Theory of Distribution Channels. First, a one-part tariff wholesale-price policy is inadequate, because it cannot coordinate a channel. As we now know,[25] coordination can be optimal in a single-manufacturer/dual-retailer model, just as it can be in a bilateral-monopoly model. There is little reason to think that adding a second manufacturer would rule out the potential optimality of coordination under some parametric values. Second, the $i^{th}$ and $j^{th}$ retailers are identical competitors—as are the two manufacturers. An identical-competitors model is embedded as a special case in the more general, heterogeneous-competitors model, and the results obtained from the former model may not generalize beyond that special case. Third, there are no fixed costs in this model. As we now know, fixed costs should be modeled because they are a critical input into the design of manufacturer-optimal two-part tariffs when there are multiple retailers. From these three points we conclude that there is a *potential* vibrancy to the single-channel, bilateral-duopoly model that is concealed by its shortcomings. The basis for our claim is that, throughout this monograph, we have consistently revealed a wealth of insights from a *truncated* version of this model. To identify more clearly the promise of the $1 \times 2 \times 2-$model, we briefly review its relation to the literature.

Table 12.2 catalogs five models that are nested in the single-channel, bilateral-duopoly model that is depicted by Figure 12.1. The major streams of the analytical literature on distribution channels can be summarized in the single-channel, bilateral-duopoly model. Each model is defined by various combinations of the lettered manufacturer-retailer connections (a, $\alpha$, b, and $\beta$).

Four of the models in Figure 12.1 have appeared in the literature: the bilateral-monopoly model, the inter-channel competition model, the inter-manufacturer competition model, and the inter-retailer competition model. The Figure also draws attention to what we term an "unbalanced-competition" model. This "new" model may be interpreted as (i) one manufacturer that serves a single retailer while the other manufacturer serves two retailers *or* as (ii) a retailer that has a narrow product assortment and another retailer that has a broad assortment—with one product being common across the retailers.[26]

*Table 12.2.* The Single-Channel Bilateral-Duopoly Model: Relationship to the Literature

| Channel Model | Illustrative Channel | Alternative Channels | Citation from the Literature |
|---|---|---|---|
| Bilateral Monopoly | **a** | **α** *or* **b** *or* **β** | Jeuland and Shugan (1983) |
| Inter-Channel Competition | **a & b** | **α & β** | McGuire and Staelin (1983) |
| Inter-Manufacturer Competition | **a & β** | **α & b** | Choi (1991) |
| Inter-Retailer Competition | **a & α** | **b & β** | Ingene and Parry (1995) |
| Unbalanced Competition | **a & α & b** | **a & α & β** *or*<br>**a & b & β** *or*<br>**α & b & β** | |
| Single-Channel Bilateral Duopoly | **a & b & α & β** | | Choi (1996) |

Note: See Figure 12.1 for a visual depiction of the illustrative and alternative channels.

## 7.2 Commentary on Bilateral-Monopoly Competition

The simplest multiple-channels model involves competition between the competing bilateral monopolies of a $2\times1\times1$-model; this is the well-known McGuire-Staelin model that played a vital role in encouraging mathematical modeling of distribution channels. The purpose of this model was to assess a "breakeven" level of competitive intensity above which a manufacturer would prefer *not* to coordinate a channel. However, its conclusions are less comprehensive than they appear on initial inspection.

While it was argued that the analysis applies to any distribution of market shares between the channels, the model is actually only compatible with *equal* market shares. The discrepancy between model and story has a simple technical explanation: the standardization procedure described in the paper involves two numeraires. This procedure is valid only with identical-competitors. As we have shown, results obtained when competitors are modeled as clones often do not extend to unequal market shares; it is easy to show that this lack of generality applies here. As a result, the detailed conclusions generated by this model—as analyzed thus far—hold only for the special case of equal market shares.

The original model evaluated whether manufacturer profit would be maximized (i) by vertically integrating and coordinating its channel or (ii) by selling through an independent retailer with a wholesale-price policy that does not coordinate the channel. At a suitably high level of competitive intensity ($\chi$), the manufacturer prefers naïve Stackelberg leadership with a one-part tariff over vertical integration. Thus there is a "breakeven" intensity level $\chi_{NS}$ that yields manufacturer profit-indifference between coordination and non-coordination (the subscript denotes the naïve Stackelberg tariff).

Although a one-part tariff cannot extract all rent from the retailer, a sophisticated Stackelberg two-part tariff allows the manufacturer to reap all profit earned by its own bilateral-monopoly channel, even in the presence of inter-channel competition. It follows that the manufacturer could raise its profit by shifting to a sophisticated Stackelberg two-part tariff. This will lower the breakeven intensity level (say to $\chi_{SS} < \chi_{NS}$). We stress that the logic sketched here was unavailable to the authors; the sophisticated Stackelberg two-part tariff was not developed until fifteen years after the publication of their seminal paper. Our point here is not to devalue the contribution of the original paper, but to identify opportunities for future research. We believe that there are two excellent reasons to revisit a $2\times1\times1-$model. The first is to introduce heterogeneous market-shares and the second is to evaluate the attractiveness of more sophisticated wholesale-price strategies.

## 7.3 Commentary on Competition Between Channels

There are many possible manifestations of multiple competitors in the $2\times2\times2-$meta–model. We briefly sketch two such models. Both involve competition between two channels and both have a real-world counterpart. First, consider two channels, each with a single manufacturer selling to two retailers. This $2\times1\times2-$model is a parsimonious depiction of competition that is both brand and store specific; an example is Pizza Hut *vs.* Wendy's. In this example the manufacturers (who are franchisors) are in product competition, while their retail franchisees are involved in product and locational competition. Conceptually this is a two-channel version of the model evaluated in Chapters 5-11.

Second, consider two channels, each with one manufacturer selling two products to one retailer; we call this a $2\times2\times1-$model;[27] this model is a two-product variant of the McGuire and Staelin model (1983, 1986). An example of the $2\times2\times1-$model is Ford *vs.* Chevrolet. Both manufacturers produce sedans and trucks and each dealer sells both products produced by its manufacturer.

We have already discussed in some detail the single-channel variants of these models; all our comments from the simpler context continue to apply. There can be no doubt that, in consumer-goods markets, there is competition between channels just as surely as there is competition between manufacturers and between retailers. Altering Channel Structure by introducing a second, competing channel will enable us to determine how assumptions regarding inter-channel competition affect Channel Strategy and Channel Performance.

## 7.4 Commentary on Models with Non-Price Elements of the Marketing Mix

An important direction for research involves the marketing-mix efforts—services—undertaken by channel members.[28] To be of interest, a service must be *demand-enhancing* and its level must be managerially discretionary. Services that do not enhance demand are mathematically uninteresting because they lower profit unless they are costless. Services whose level is non-discretionary are not the stuff of great insight, for they inevitably generate mathematical corner-solutions. Our discussion is restricted to services that are demand-enhancing and discretionary.

It is also important to distinguish between services that can only be efficiently provided by one level of the channel, and those that can be offered at either channel level. The later scenario raises the possibility of functional shifting, which has implications for how we model specific problems, and the questions that we ask within our models.

A discretionary service that can only be efficiently provided at one channel level, such as personalized service at the point of sale, raises one set of questions. What is the optimal amount of service? Is this amount affected by vertical channel-relationships (e.g., Stackelberg leadership *vs.* Nash)? Should the service performer bear the full cost of service or should costs be shared across channel levels, as happens with spiffs[29] and with slotting allowances? Our point is that, by asking these and other questions in the context of an inclusive meta-model, we can resolve a more complex question: Does channel breadth, at either level of the channel, affect our answers? Phrased alternatively, we cannot know if Channel Performance and Channel Strategy are dependent on Channel Structure and the Channel Environment unless we approach our questions from the perspective of a meta-model that facilitates identification of the boundaries within which particular results hold.

A discretionary service that can be efficiently provided at either channel level raises an additional question: Who should perform the service? The standard argument is that a service should be offered by the channel member who can do so at the lower cost (Bucklin 1966). While this response is correct for services that do not affect demand, many channel functions do influence demand. For example, define demand for the $i^{th}$ product as:

$$Q_i = A_i(s_i, s_j) - b_i p_i + \gamma p_j \qquad (12.7.1)$$

The demand intercept for the $i^{th}$ product is a function of the service that accompanies that product ($s_i$) and the service that accompanies the $j^{th}$ product ($s_j$). A product-based example is the warranty on durable goods, which can be offered by the manufacturer, the retailer, or both.[30] Within (say) a bilateral-monopoly model, the analysis would assign the service to one level of the channel and then to the other level. It is straightforward to ascertain the parametric values for which the manufacturer prefers to perform service or to have the retailer perform the service.[31] Of course, the retailer may have a different assessment, and the channel's best interest may not coincide with either of their views.

Knowing where service should be performed in a bilateral-monopoly model is only the first step toward acquiring a thorough, theoretical grasp of where service should be provided in a broader context; we must examine alternative channel structures. Within a $1 \times 2 \times 2$-model there are fifteen *specific* channel linkages when intra-level competitors are heterogeneous and six linkages when the competitors are identical (see Table 12.1). A comprehensive assessment of all options must precede a definitive statement regarding the conditions under which each channel member prefers to perform service and the conditions over which channel participants agree on this assessment. We strongly suspect that these conditions will depend on the Channel Structure.

In more complex analyses, the cost of service might be shared, or service provision might be shared, or the efficiency of service provision might differ according to who performs the service. The introduction of service can have strategic effects as well, because it may affect the retailers' or the manufacturers' decisions on whether to product-line price. That is, the service answer is almost certainly related to the category-management issue. Overall, adding service, or other marketing-mix elements, to any meta-model has the potential to enrich our understanding of distribution channels.

## 7.5 Commentary on the $2 \times 2 \times 2$-Meta-Model

In this sub-Section we detail the dimensionality of the $2 \times 2 \times 2$-meta-model with either an exogenous assignment, or an endogenous determination, of the number of channels and channel participants. Then we offer our views on adding other dimensions to the $2 \times 2 \times 2$-meta-model. Finally, we summarize the number of potential models.

### 7.5.1 An Exogenous Number of Channels and Channel Participants

A basic structural question is the number of channels to model. At least one channel is required, but there are situations in which two channels are meaningful, as demonstrated by the works of McGuire and Staelin (1983) and Coughlan (1985). We believe that there is little benefit to adding more than two channels to a model, although we admit that future research could prove us wrong. Accordingly, we think that a meta-model should allow the number of channels to be $N_C \in (1,2)$. It is equally important to determine the number of manufacturers ($N_M$) and retailers ($N_R$) to model. There seems to be no reason to evaluate more than two manufacturers or two retailers, especially in light of the resulting "complexity costs." Thus we believe a channel model should consider $N_M \in (1,2)$ manufacturers and $N_R \in (1,2)$ retailers.

These observations are the foundation of our call for a $2\times2\times2-$meta-model. We noted in Table 12.2 that, with heterogeneous competitors, a *single* channel composed of two manufacturers and two retailers contains six *distinct* channel structures. With two channels, there are 36 unique combinations of vertical-channel linkages to evaluate.

### 7.5.2 An Endogenous Number of Channel Participants

Because there is no decision-maker to assess the number of channels, we believe that it is unreasonable to consider the number of channels as being endogenous. In contrast, a manufacturer can determine its optimal number of retailers to distribute through ($N_R^*$), and a retailer can determine its optimal number of suppliers ($N_M^*$). Nonetheless, we have serious doubts about the feasibility of solving a model in which the number of manufacturers and the number of retailers is determined simultaneously. We *think* that $N_R^*$ can be found only when each channel is restricted to one or two manufacturers and that $N_M^*$ can be ascertained only when there are one or two retailers. This causes us to envision four models per channel; or sixteen models in total.[32]

### 7.5.3 Additional Modeling Dimensions

We believe that the range of potential models should be extended to incorporate at least three additional dimensions: states-of-nature, category-management decisions, and non-price elements of the marketing-mix. We address these dimensions sequentially. One state-of-nature is the default value that defines certainty. It is reasonable to investigate uncertainty with either two states-of-nature (Chapter 4) or N states-of-nature, *provided* channel participants have the option of not serving some states-of-nature.

There is a need for research into such category-management decisions as how many products to produce (or distribute) and how to price those products (i.e., non-product-line *versus* product-line pricing or PLP). The default is one product; two products immediately raise the issue of PLP. Three products raise the more subtle issue of whether PLP should apply to the entire product line or should be restricted to a portion of it. While there is no question that the number of products ($N^*$) can be endogenously determined, we seriously doubt that the optimal use of PLP can be assessed in such a model; this suggests that researchers should model $N_P \in (1,2,3)$ products. Finally, we note that the number of PLP combinations is $(2^{N_P} - N_p)$.

The default number of non-price elements of the marketing-mix is zero. It is straightforward to introduce a single element such as service. A more complicated model would involve two marketing-mix variables, one of that creates externalities at a level of the channel ("advertising") and one that does not ("shelf space"). To keep the problem manageable, we envision modeling a limited number of marketing-mix elements, so that $N_{MM} \in (0,1,2)$.

Table 12.3 catalogs the possibilities when the number of channels, manufacturers, retailers, states-of-nature, category-management decisions, and marketing-mix elements are assigned *exogenously*; the number of possible models totals 1,080. Using the same logic for *endogenously* determined values for the number of manufacturers and retailers reveals another 480 possible models. Of course, there is no real possibility that so many models will ever be explored, let alone published.

Nonetheless, we have two serious points in citing these numbers. First, there are enough models, and enough variety within models, to fruitfully occupy marketing scientists for many years. Second, and more importantly, we see in our own work the glimmerings of a *recurring regularity* across the models. We strongly believe that, as we work toward a far-reaching understanding of distribution within the context of a Unifying Theory of Distribution Channels, we will discover a handful of channel consistencies that are common to many models. When this occurs we will truly have an appreciation of the effects of Channel Structure and the Channel Environment on Channel Strategy and Channel Performance.

*Table 12.3.* Number of Modeling Combinations Nested in a $2 \times 2 \times 2$ – Meta-Model

| | Number of Options | | | | Number of Unique Channel Structures |
|---|---|---|---|---|---|
| | 0 | 1 | 2 | 3 | |
| Channels | | • | • | | 36 |
| Manufacturers | | • | • | | |
| Retailers | | • | • | | |
| States-of-Nature | | • | • | | 2 |
| Category-Management | | • | • | • | 5 |
| Marketing-Mix Elements | • | • | • | | 3 |
| Total Number of Unique Channel Structures: | | | | | 1,080 |

# 8 CONCLUDING COMMENTARY

We conclude this monograph by summarizing a set of modeling principles that we believe are essential ingredients for developing a Unifying Theory of Distribution Channels:

- Models of distribution channels must go beyond bilateral monopoly. We must model distribution channels as being competitive at the retail, or the manufacturer, or the channel level. We hope our discussion of the *Bilateral-Monopoly Meta-Myth* has clarified the consequences of focusing exclusively on a narrow model. However, a bilateral-monopoly model should always be embedded within a broader meta-model, so that authors and readers can determine the effects of introducing competition.
- Models of distribution channels must include heterogeneous rivals; that is, competitors must face different demands and costs. We identified the serious penalties associated with the assumption of homogeneous rivals in our discussion of the *Identical-Competitors Meta-Myth*. Nonetheless, it is important to embed the special case of identical competitors within a more general model so that authors and readers can ascertain the effects of differences in market shares.
- Models of distribution channels must explicitly incorporate fixed costs because we now know that these costs play a vital role in

assessing the optimality of various wholesale-price policies and in determining the distribution of channel profit. This principle flows directly from our discussion of the *Fixed-Cost Modeling Myth*. Of course, zero fixed costs must be embedded in models as a special case so that the effect of positive fixed costs can be assessed.

- Models of distribution channels must endogenously determine channel breadth. In our discussion of the *Channel-Breadth Modeling Myth* we observed that there are parametric values for which even a central decision-maker will prefer a broader channel and other parametric values for which it will prefer a narrower channel. The same attitude toward channel breadth holds for the leader in any Stackelberg game; we cannot legitimately assume a channel breadth.
- Models of distribution channels must not "normalize" to unity any demand or cost parameter without careful thought as to the consequences for being able to analyze the resulting model. We have illustrated the cost of violating this principle in our discussion of the *Aggregate-Demand Modeling Myth*. Consider, for example, the model examined in Chapter 5. If the demand intercepts are equalized and the own-price terms are normalized, this model becomes one of identical competitors; if the cross-price term is set to one it is impossible to evaluate the effect of a change in competitive intensity.
- Models of distribution channels must be designed for their intended application. When they are *uncritically* borrowed from another venue the results may not have the meaning that authors tend to assign. For example, the *Multiple-Retailers/Multiple States-of-Nature Modeling Myth* arose from a misapplication of a model outside its intended area. We have argued that the root cause of many Channel Myths has been a naïve borrowing from other disciplines, such as economics.
- Models of distribution channels must allow channel coordination to arise through an optimization procedure, but they must not impose coordination. This will generally require contrasting at least two specific wholesale-price policies, such as a channel-coordinating menu of two-part tariffs and a channel non-coordinating sophisticated Stackelberg two-part tariff. From our dialogue on the *Channel-Coordination Strategic Myth*, we understand that forcing coordination can lead to erroneous conclusions about Channel Strategy and Channel Performance.[33] The reason is that coordination can be non-optimal for a decision-maker *after* taking into consideration limits on its ability to extract profit from other channel members.
- Models of distribution channels must recognize that marginal-cost pricing by the Stackelberg leader is *not* equivalent to channel profit maximization. Our discussion of the *Double-Marginalization*

*Strategic Myth* proves that a non-zero markup by all channel members is required for channel coordination, except in the special cases of the bilateral-monopoly and identical-competitors models.

- Models must utilize a demand system that is derived from the utility (profit) function of a representative consumer (firm) for products sold to people (businesses). A consistent application of our *First-Principles Criterion* should help researchers to avoid inappropriate modeling simplifications that generate misleading implications.
- Models of distribution channels must be consistent with the nature of the industry being investigated. It is through the application of our *Empirical-Evidence Criterion* that we can minimize the chance of mathematically correct but managerially meaningless conclusions.
- Models of special cases must be contained within more general meta-models. It is only through a careful application of our *Nested-Models Criterion* that we can assess the true effect of adding a variable, altering a parameter, or convoluting a model. When this Criterion is properly applied, a reader will be able to determine the true effects by simple substitution. For example, in our work it is *always* possible to recover bilateral-monopoly results by setting $\theta = 0$; similarly, we can always recover the identical-competitor results by setting $Q_i^* = Q_j^*$.
- *Channel Performance* must be endogenously determined in models of distribution channels. No meaningful cross-model comparisons can be made if this aspect of our *Strategic-Endogeneity Criterion* is violated, for whatever the performance results that are obtained, they are inherently arbitrary.
- *Channel Strategy* must also be determined endogenously. If this component of our *Strategic-Endogeneity Criterion* is not heeded, managerial advice may be offered that is distinctly sub-optimal. This statement applies to optimal channel breadth, the optimal wholesale-price strategy, the optimal category-management decisions, and the optimal utilization of non-price, marketing-mix elements.
- All elements of the marketing-mix must be modeled as continuously variable in a distribution-channels context. The sole exception arises when there is empirical evidence that specific decisions are "either/or" rather than continuous. For example, marketing scientists often model a "yes or no" decision when it is transparent that firms actually make decisions about amounts. The interesting modeling (and real-world) question is *not* "Should we provide service?" The interesting and important question is "*How much* service should we provide?" Continuous-variable models are always superior to either/or models precisely because the "how much?" decision

includes zero as an option; that is, the "either/or" model is nested as a special case within a model of continuous variables.

We close with a cautionary note: as best as we can determine, it is not possible to nest vertical-channel relationships and horizontal-channel relationships in one model in a manner that allows the reader to alter the value of a single parameter to shift from one channel relationship to the other. Although any model based on linear or general demand can be analyzed under the assumption of (i) Stackelberg leadership by the manufacturer or the retailer or (ii) Nash equality, such relationships must be analyzed separately; only then can the results be compared.[34]

Researchers can build models that do not meet these principles, but w our opinion such efforts offer a minimal contribution toward an enhanced understanding of distribution channels. This is not to deny the potential elegance of such models, or the ability of their creators to offer meaningful insights into distribution practice. It is to state our belief, formed by a decade of mathematically modeling distribution channels, that to make progress toward a full grasp of complex phenomena by adhering to basic principles of model building. We have tried to set forth those principles in this sub-Section, with the sincere hope that they may be of benefit to scholars who approach research into distribution channels from an analytical perspective.

We have confidence that future analytical work by marketing scientists will ultimately be melded into a cohesive portrait of distribution channels through adherence to the Four Modeling Criteria. That is, we will collectively create a Unifying Theory of Distribution Channels that merges (i) the three research streams of the analytical channels literature, (ii) the bilateral-monopoly model, and (iii) other research streams that are as yet unexplored—such as the unbalanced competition model mentioned in Section 7. Toward this end we have highlighted several promising avenues for future research. Our roadmap is certainly incomplete. We have no doubts that valid arguments will emerge for additional dimensions to be explored, so that the task of fully explicating the mathematical nuances of distribution-channels models stretches far into the future. The enormity of this task brings to mind the words of the great mathematician Pierre-Simon Laplace, "What we know is not much. What e do not know is immense." [35] We hope our meditations and commentaries in this monograph will encourage other scholars to join with us in the collective pursuit of a Unifying Theory of Distribution Channels, thereby lessening the immensity of what we do not know about mathematical models of distribution channels.

# Notes

[1] We use the term *meta-model* to denote a set of strongly related models; our concept of a meta-model is akin to Moorthy's conception of a supermodel (1993). Meta-models help us organize our thoughts about the relationship between models; more importantly, they assist us in understanding how specific modeling differences affect the results that are obtained.
[2] The quotation is from a dialogue between Socrates (the question) and Phaedrus (the answer); it appears in Plato's *Dialogue Phaedrus,* section 262 (translated by B. Jowett 1871).
[3] Only if there is no competition is a zero margin compatible with channel coordination.
[4] If there were *a priori* obvious then marketing scientists would already have recognized the Aggregate-Demand Modeling Myth.
[5] Jevon's *The Theory of Political Economy* (1871) ignited the neo-classical revolution that introduced marginal analysis to economics, and thence to marketing science.
[6] A positive cross-price parameter is also required.
[7] There have been models of uncertainty, for example Desiraju and Moorthy (1997) and Jagpal (1999); but uncertainty is uncommon in the marketing science literature.
[8] There is considerable literature on the topic of non-constant costs and its dual: variable returns to scale. One example among many is Ingene and Yu (1991).
[9] The fourth dimension, inter-channel competition, appears to have no relevance in a single-manufacturer meta-model.
[10] A one-part tariff, which by definition has no fixed fee, is compatible with an endogenous determination of the distribution of channel profit irrespective of the vertical channel-relationship; however, it is incompatible with channel coordination. An ingenious method of ensuring coordination with a one-part tariff in a bilateral-monopoly channel was suggested by Rubenstein (1982): one firm makes an "all-or-nothing" offer; the other firm *must* either accept the offer or make a counter-offer. Offer/counter-offer continues until one firm accepts the other's offer. Introduction of a time-rate of discount is sufficient to ensure subgame-perfect equilibrium. However, it is not clear that this technique is compatible with comparable treatment of multiple, competing retailers. It is also not obvious that firms offer/counter-offer until reaching agreement; our reading of the empirical evidence is that firms often break off negotiations before a deal is reached.
[11] It is possible for several retailers to have zero profits after paying the same fixed fee with a two-part tariff wholesale-price policy, or after paying different fixed and per-unit fees with a menu of tariffs.
[12] Desiraju and Moorthy (1997) are a notable exception; they addressed service in conjunction with uncertainty.
[13] Desiraju and Moorthy (1997) have addressed this issue in a preliminary way.
[14] An alternative perspective would be to focus on the core services provided by a channel rather than thinking of the elements of the marketing mix (Bucklin 1966).
[15] The channel will distribute only one product if the manufacturer refuses to produce the second product *or* if the retailer refuses to distribute it. The same logic will eliminate the channel's existence if the first product is also abandoned.
[16] Chapter 11, Section 3 has details on the representative consumer.
[17] Whitehead was the senior author on *Principia Mathematica* (1910-1913), a three volume treatise co-authored with Bertrand Russell. Its stated purpose was to construct all of mathematics from first principles using as few axioms as possible.
[18] This comment applies, for example, to any generalization of the Choi (1991, 1996) or McGuire and Staelin (1983, 1986) models beyond the special case of identical competitors.
[19] During the 1980s the United States imposed an annual quota on apparel imports from many Asian countries. Since quota levels tended to be reached as the holiday season approached, retailers and distributors deliberately sought supply sources located in several countries.

[20] The converse need not be true; a retailer may carry multiple products from a single manufacturer, as we argued in the previous sub-Section.
[21] By heterogeneous we mean different production costs, distribution costs, or base levels of demand, or any combination of these three factors.
[22] With an industrial product demand should be derived from the profit function of a representative business customer.
[23] It is this Criterion that makes us leery of rectangular-demand curves; we find it almost impossible to conceptualize real-world products or services for which consumers are completely price-insensitive up to the reservation price. Even industrial products are unapt to have rectangular-demand curves for their inputs *unless* there is a fixed-proportions production process *and* all complementary inputs are purchased at a fixed price.
[24] We take inspiration from their research, noting that neither of them sought to create a meta-model, let alone a unifying theory.
[25] We stress "as we now know" because it is not clear that *anyone* was fully aware of these points in 1996.
[26] Choi noted that all these models (*except* the unbalanced-competition model) were embedded in what we are calling the bilateral-duopoly model; see his Figure 1 (1996, page 119).
[27] A $2\times1\times1-$ model has two manufacturers and two retail outlets. A $2\times1\times2-$ model has two manufacturers (e.g., Pizza Hut and Wendy's) and four retail outlets—two for each manufacturer. A $2\times2\times1-$ model has two manufacturers (Ford and Chevrolet), four products (Taurus, F-150, Impala, and S-10), and two retailers—one for each manufacturer. In the spirit of McGuire and Staelin (1983) we regard all these models as having two channels.
[28] We shall refer to marketing-mix efforts other than price as "services;" our terminology is merely shorthand for any channel function.
[29] A spiff is "a cash premium, prize, or additional commission for pushing or increasing sales of a particular item or type of merchandise" (Vargas). It is often paid by the manufacturer to retailers' sales personnel.
[30] In the durable goods arena, a manufacturer's warranty is common; retailers often offer an additional, extended warranty. A specific functional form for demand can be generated by maximizing a representative consumer's utility function, as we demonstrated in Chapter 11.
[31] Coughlan and Ingene are currently exploring this issue. By "parametric values" we refer to the intensity of competition, the representative consumer's valuation of service, and the degree of cost and effort sharing.
[32] We make the distinction "one, two, and a whole bunch" of players at a level of the channel to convey that:

- Models with one player exclude intra-level competition;
- Models with two players include intra-level competition, adding a *specific* number of additional players does *not* significantly alter the results; and
- Models with an unspecified number of players (N: "a whole bunch") enable the modeler to solve for the optimal number of players $N^*$.

[33] Of course, not allowing coordination can also lead to erroneous inferences.
[34] This fact does not impinge on creating a Unifying Theory. The situation described in the text is analogous to the fact that linear and constant-elasticity demand curves generate different results, neither of which can be derived from the other. What is relevant is that one of these curves represents vertical-strategic substitutability and the other represents vertical-strategic complementarity; their underlying theory (profit maximization) is the same, but the results play out differently.
[35] The quotation, allegedly Laplace's last words, appeared in de Morgan (1915). Our intent is that this monograph will not be our final word on the important and fascinating topic of mathematical models of distribution channels.

# REFERENCES

## Preface


Bartlett, John. (1968). *Familiar Quotations*, Boston: Little, Brown; (Herodotus. *The Histories*, Book VII, Chapter 10).

Donne, John. (1624). "Meditation XVII," In John Donne's *Devotions upon Emergent Occasions*, London: Thomas Jones; (Reprinted Cambridge: The University Press, 1923).

Doyle, Arthur Conan. (1890). "The Sign of The Four," *Lippincott's Monthly Magazine*, February.

Hoffmann, Paul. (1998). *The Man Who Loved Only Numbers: The Story of Paul Erdös and the Search for Mathematical Truth*, New York: Hyperion Press.

Keynes, John Maynard. (1935). *The General Theory of Employment, Interest, and Money*, New York: Harcourt, Brace.


## Chapter 1


Battacharyya, Sugato and Francine Lafontaine. (1995) "Double-Sided Moral Hazard and the Nature of Share Contracts," *Rand Journal of Economics*, 26: 761-781.

Bowley, Arthur. (1928). "Bilateral Monopoly," *Economic Journal*, 38:651-9.

Choi, S. Chan. (1991). "Price Competition in a Channel Structure with a Common Retailer," *Marketing Science*, 10:271-96.

Coughlan, Anne T. (1985). "Competition and Cooperation in Marketing Channel Choice: Theory and Application," *Marketing Science*, 4:10-29.

Coughlan, Anne T. and Birger Wernerfelt. (1989). "On Credible Delegation by Oligopolists: A Discussion of Distribution Channel Management," *Management Science*, 35:226-39.

Coughlan, Anne T. and Charles Ingene. (2002). "Product-Line Pricing in a Distribution Channel: Optimum or Pessimum?" (mimeo) Cornell University: Conference on Pricing Research.

Desiraju, Ramarao and Sridhar Moorthy. (1997). "Managing a Distribution Channel under Asymmetric Information with Performance Requirements," *Management Science*, 43: 1628-44.

Edgeworth, Francis. (1881). *Mathematical Psychics: An Essay on the Application of Mathematics to the Moral Sciences*, London: Kegan Paul; (Reprinted New York: Augustus M. Kelley, 1967).

Henderson, James and Richard Quandt. (1971). *Microeconomic Theory*, New York: McGraw-Hill.

Ingene, Charles and Mark Parry. (1995a). "Coordination and Manufacturer Profit Maximization: The Multiple Retailer Channel," *Journal of Retailing*, 71:129-51.

Ingene, Charles and Mark Parry. (1995b). "Channel Coordination When Retailers Compete," *Marketing Science*, 14:360-77.

Ingene, Charles and Mark Parry. (1998). "Manufacturer-Optimal Wholesale Pricing When Retailers Compete," *Marketing Letters*, 9:61-73.

Ingene, Charles and Mark Parry. (2000). "Is Channel Coordination All It Is Cracked Up to Be?" *Journal of Retailing*, 76:511-48.

Jeuland, Abel and Steven Shugan. (1983). "Managing Channel Profits," *Marketing Science*, 2:239-72.

Kennedy, John F. (1962). Quote from July 11, 1962, obtained from Quotes from a Collective Consciousness, http://www.10ac.com/darkside9.htm, accessed on July 11, 2002.

Lafontaine, Francine. (1990). "An Empirical Look at Franchise Contracts as Signaling Devices," (mimeo) Graduate School of Industrial Administration, Pittsburgh: Carnegie-Mellon University.

Lee, Eunkyu and Richard Staelin. (1997). "Vertical Strategic Interaction: Implications for Channel Pricing Strategy," *Marketing Science,* 16:185-207.

McGuire, Timothy and Richard Staelin. (1983). "An Industry Equilibrium Analysis of Downstream Vertical Integration," *Marketing Science,* 2:161-92.

McGuire, Timothy and Richard Staelin. (1986). "Channel Efficiency, Incentive Compatibility, Transfer Pricing and Market Structure: An Equilibrium Analysis of Channel Relationships," *Research in Marketing: Distribution Channels and Institutions*, Louis P. Bucklin and James Carman, eds., 8:181-223.

Monroe, Kent. (1990). *Pricing: Making Profitable Decisions,* New York: McGraw-Hill.

Moorthy, K. Sridhar. (1987). "Managing Channel Profits: Comment," *Marketing Science,* 6:375-9.

Moorthy, K. Sridhar and Peter Fader. (1988). "Strategic Interaction within a Channel," *Retail and Marketing Channels,* Luca Pellegrini and Srinivas Reddy, eds., London: Routledge.

Moorthy, K. Sridhar. (1993). "Theoretical Modeling in Marketing," *Journal of Marketing,* 57:92-106.

Morgan, James. (1949). "Bilateral Monopoly and the Competitive Output," *Quarterly Journal of Economics,* 63:371-91.

Oren, Shmuel, Stephen Smith and Robert Wilson. (1982). "Nonlinear Pricing in Markets with Interdependent Demand," *Marketing Science,* 1:287-313.

Pigou, Arthur C. (1908). "Equilibrium under Bilateral Monopoly," *Economic Journal,* 18:205-20.

Rey, Patrick and Jean Tirole. (1986). "The Logic of Vertical Restraints," *American Economic Review,* 76:921-39.

Spengler, Joseph. (1950). "Vertical Integration and Antitrust Policy," *Journal of Political Economy,* 58:347-52.

Stewart, Paul and J. Frederic Dewhurst. (1939). *Does Distribution Cost Too Much?* New York: The Twentieth Century Fund.

Wiseman, Anne and Peter Wiseman. (1980). *The Battle for Gaul/Julius Caesar: A New Translation,* Boston: D. R. Godine.

## Chapter 2

Bowley, Arthur. (1928). "Bilateral Monopoly," *Economic Journal,* 38:651-9.

Choi, S. Chan. (1991). "Price Competition in a Channel Structure with a Common Retailer," *Marketing Science,* 10:271-96.

Choi, S. Chan. (1996). "Price Competition in a Duopoly Common Retailer Channel," *Journal of Retailing,* 72:117-37.

Cournot, Augustin. (1838). *Recherches sur les Principes Mathematiques de la Theorie des Richesses,* Paris: Hachette; (English translation by Nathaniel Bacon, *Researches into the Mathematical Principles of the Theory of Wealth,* New York: Macmillan, 1897; Reprinted New York: Augustus M. Kelley, 1971).

Edgeworth, Francis. (1881). *Mathematical Psychics: An Essay on the Application of Mathematics to the Moral Sciences,* London: Kegan Paul; (Reprinted New York: Augustus M. Kelley, 1967).

Edgeworth, Francis. (1897). "Teoria Pura del Monopolio," *Giornale degli Economisti,* 15:13-31; (English translation by Francis Edgeworth, "Theory of Monopoly," Francis Edgeworth, *Papers Relating to Political Economy,* v. 1, London: Macmillan, 1925).

Fellner, William. (1947). "Prices and Wages under Bilateral Monopoly," *Quarterly Journal of Economics,* 61:503-32.

Gerstner, Eitan and Hess James. (1995). "Pull Promotions and Channel Coordination," *Marketing Science,* 14:43-60.

Hawkins, E. R. (1950). "Vertical Price Relationships," *Theory in Marketing,* Reavis Cox and Wroe Alderson, eds., Chicago: Irwin, 179-91.

Heath, Thomas. (1931). *A Manual of Greek Mathematics,* Oxford: Clarendon Press.

Jeuland, Abel and Steven Shugan. (1983). "Managing Channel Profits," *Marketing Science,* 2:239-72.

Jevons, William Stanley. (1871). *The Theory of Political Economy,* London: Macmillan.

Lafontaine, Francine. (1990). "An Empirical Look at Franchise Contracts as Signaling Devices" (mimeo), Graduate School of Industrial Administration, Pittsburgh: Carnegie-Mellon University.

Machlup, Fritz and Martha Taber. (1960). "Bilateral Monopoly, Successive Monopoly, and Vertical Integration," *Economica,* 27:101-19.

McGuire, Timothy and Richard Staelin. (1983). "An Industry Equilibrium Analysis of Downstream Vertical Integration," *Marketing Science,* 2:161-92.

McGuire, Timothy and Richard Staelin. (1986). "Channel Efficiency, Incentive Compatibility, Transfer Pricing and Market Structure: An Equilibrium Analysis of Channel Relationships," *Research in Marketing: Distribution Channels and Institutions*, Louis P. Bucklin and James Carman, eds., 8:181-223.

Monroe, Kent. (1990). *Pricing: Making Profitable Decisions,* New York: McGraw-Hill.

Moorthy, K. Sridhar. (1987). "Managing Channel Profits: Comment," *Marketing Science,* 6:375-9.

Moorthy, K. Sridhar and Peter Fader. (1988). "Strategic Interaction within a Channel," *Retail and Marketing Channels,* Luca Pellegrini and Srinivas Reddy, eds., London: Routledge.

Morgan, James. (1949). "Bilateral Monopoly and the Competitive Output," *Quarterly Journal of Economics,* 63:371-91.

Nash, John F. Jr. (1950). "The Bargaining Problem," *Econometrita,* 18:155-162.

Pareto, Wilfredo. (1906). *Manuale di Economia Politica,* Milano: Societa Editrice Libraria; (English translation by Ann Schwier, *Manual of Political Economy,* New York: Augustus M. Kelley, 1971).

Pigou, Arthur C. (1908). "Equilibrium under Bilateral Monopoly," *Economic Journal,* 18:205-20.

Spengler, Joseph. (1950). "Vertical Integration and Antitrust Policy," *Journal of Political Economy,* 58:347-52.

Tintner, Gerhard. (1939). "Note on the Problem of Bilateral Monopoly," *Journal of Political Economy,* 47:263-70.

Trivedi, Minakshi. (1998). "Distribution Channels: An Extension of Exclusive Retailership," *Management Science,* 44:896-910.

## Channels without Competition

Bacon, Francis. (1605). *The Advancement of Learning;* (Joseph Devey ed., New York: American Home Library 1902).

## Chapter 3

Battacharyya, Sugato and Francine Lafontaine. (1995) "Double-Sided Moral Hazard and the Nature of Share Contracts," *Rand Journal of Economics*, 26: 761-781.

Ingene, Charles and Mark Parry. (1995). "Coordination and Manufacturer Profit Maximization: The Multiple Retailer Channel," *Journal of Retailing*, 71:129-51.

Jeuland, Abel and Steven Shugan. (1983). "Managing Channel Profits," *Marketing Science*, 2:239-72.

Lafontaine, Francine. (1990). "An Empirical Look at Franchise Contracts as Signaling Devices" (mimeo), Graduate School of Industrial Administration, Pittsburgh: Carnegie-Mellon University.

Moorthy, K. Sridhar. (1987). "Managing Channel Profits: Comment," *Marketing Science*, 6:375-9.

Murphy, Michael. (1977). "Price Discrimination, Market Separation, and the Multi-Part Tariff," *Economic Inquiry*, 15:587-99.

Oi, Walter. (1971). "A Disneyland Dilemma: Two-Part Tariffs for a Mickey Mouse Monopoly," *Quarterly Journal of Economics*, 85:77-96.

Rey, Patrick and Jean Tirole. (1896). "The Logic of Vertical Restraints," *American Economic Review*, 76:921-39.

Smith, Adam. (1796). *An Inquiry into the Nature and Causes of the Wealth of Nations*, London: Strahan, Cadell, and Davies.

## Chapter 4

Blair, Benjamin and Tracy Lewis. (1994). "Optimal Retail Contracts with Asymmetric Information and Moral Hazard," *Rand Journal of Economics*, 25:284-96.

Cato, Marcus Porcius. (1934). *De agri cvltura* (English translation by William Hooper, *On Agriculture* Cambridge: Harvard University Press.

Crocker, Keith. (1983). "Vertical Integration and the Strategic Use of Private Information," *Bell Journal of Economics*, 14:236-48.

Desiraju, Ramarao and Sridhar Moorthy. (1997). "Managing a Distribution Channel under Asymmetric Information with Performance Requirements," *Management Science*, 43: 1628-44.

Jeuland, Abel and Steven Shugan. (1983). "Managing Channel Profits," *Marketing Science*, 2:239-72.

Rey, Patrick and Jean Tirole. (1986). "The Logic of Vertical Restraints," *American Economic Review*, 76:921-39.

## Channels with Competition

Battacharyya, Sugato and Francine Lafontaine. (1995) "Double-Sided Moral Hazard and the Nature of Share Contracts," *Rand Journal of Economics*, 26: 761-781.

Bernoulli, Jakob. (1713). *Ars Conjectandi.* Quote obtained from MacTutor History of Mathematics archive, www-gap.dcs.st-and.ac.uk/~history/ Quotations/ Bernoulli_Jacob. html, accessed on May 24, 2003.

Edgeworth, Francis. (1881). *Mathematical Psychics: An Essay on the Application of Mathematics to the Moral Sciences,* London: Kegan Paul; (Reprinted New York: Augustus M. Kelley, 1967).

Lafontaine, Francine. (1990). "An Empirical Look at Franchise Contracts as Signaling Devices" (mimeo), Graduate School of Industrial Administration, Pittsburgh: Carnegie-Mellon University.

Spengler, Joseph. (1950). "Vertical Integration and Antitrust Policy," *Journal of Political Economy,* 58:347-52.

## Chapter 5

Ingene, Charles and Mark Parry. (1995). "Channel Coordination When Retailers Compete," *Marketing Science,* 14:360-77.

Jeuland, Abel and Steven Shugan. (1983). "Managing Channel Profits," *Marketing Science,* 2:239-72.

Jeuland, Abel and Steven Shugan. (1988). "Competitive Pricing Behavior in Distribution Systems" *Issues in Pricing: Theory and Research,* Timothy Devinney, ed. Lexington: Lexington Books.

Lipsey, Richard and Kelvin Lancaster. (1956-57). "The General Theory of Second Best," *Review of Economic Studies,* 24:11-32.

McGuire, Timothy and Richard Staelin. (1983). "An Industry Equilibrium Analysis of Downstream Vertical Integration," *Marketing Science,* 2:161-92.

Moorthy, K. Sridhar. (1987). "Managing Channel Profits: Comment," *Marketing Science,* 6:375-9.

Ponomarev, Leonid. (1993). *The Quantum Dice.* (English translation by A. P. Repiev Bristol and Philadelphia: Institute of Physics Publishing).

Spengler, Joseph. (1950). "Vertical Integration and Antitrust Policy," *Journal of Political Economy,* 58:347-52.

## Chapter 6

Descartes, Rene. (1637). *Discours de la Méthode.* (English translation by Laurence Lafleur, *Discourse on Method,* New York: The Liberal Arts Press 1950).

Ingene, Charles and Mark Parry. (1998). "Manufacturer-Optimal Wholesale Pricing When Retailers Compete," *Marketing Letters,* 9:61-73.

## Chapter 7

Ingene, Charles and Mark Parry. (1995). "Channel Coordination When Retailers Compete," *Marketing Science,* 14:360-77.
Ingene, Charles and Mark Parry. (2000). "Is Channel Coordination All It Is Cracked Up to Be?" *Journal of Retailing,* 76:511-48.
Smith, Adam, *The Theory of Moral Sentiments*. London: 1759. (Facsimile, New York: Garland 1971)

## Chapter 8

Aristotle. (1966). *Metaphysica.* (Translated by Hippocrates Apostle, *Metaphysics,* Bloomington: Indiana University Press).
Edgeworth, Francis. (1881). *Mathematical Psychics: An Essay on the Application of Mathematics to the Moral Sciences,* London: Kegan Paul; (Reprinted New York: Augustus M. Kelley, 1967).
Ingene, Charles and Mark Parry. (2000). "Is Channel Coordination All It Is Cracked Up to Be?" *Journal of Retailing,* 76:511-48.
Lafontaine, Francine. (1990). "An Empirical Look at Franchise Contracts as Signaling Devices" (mimeo), Graduate School of Industrial Administration, Pittsburgh: Carnegie-Mellon University.
Pareto, Wilfredo. (1906). *Manuale di Economia Politica,* Milano: Societa Editrice Libraria; (English translation by Ann Schwier, *Manual of Political Economy,* New York: Augustus M. Kelley, 1971).

## Chapter 9

Eves, Howard. (1977). *Mathematical Circles Adieu: a Fourth Collection of Mathematical Stories and Anecdotes,* Boston: Prindle, Weber and Schmidt; Cited at Mathematical Quotations, math.furman.edu/~mwoodard/ascquote.html, accessed June 10, 2003.

## Changes in Competition

Alighieri, Dante. (1847). *La Divina Comedia: Paradiso,* Paris: Firmin Didot; (English translation by Henry Wadsworth Longfellow, *The Divine Comedy of Dante Alighieri,* Boston, New York: Houghton, Mifflin, 1886). Dante's original edition dates from 1321.

## Chapter 10

Ockham, William. (1991). *Quodlibeta Septem* (English translation by Alfred Freddoso and Francis Kelley, *Quodlibetal Questions,* New Haven: Yale University Press).

## Chapter 11

Ingene, Charles and Mark Parry. (1995). "Channel Coordination When Retailers Compete," *Marketing Science,* 14:360-77.
Kim, Sang Yong and Richard Staelin. (1999). "Manufacturer Allowances and Retailer Pass-Through Rates in a Competitive Environment," *Marketing Science.* 18:59-76.
Lee, Eunkyu and Richard Staelin. (1997). "Vertical Strategic Interaction: Implications for Channel Pricing Strategy," *Marketing Science,* 16:185-207.
Marshall, Alfred. (1907). *Principles of Economics,* 5th Ed., London: Macmillan.
McGuire, Timothy and Richard Staelin. (1983). "An Industry Equilibrium Analysis of Downstream Vertical Integration," *Marketing Science,* 2:161-92.
McGuire, Timothy and Richard Staelin. (1986). "Channel Efficiency, Incentive Compatibility, Transfer Pricing and Market Structure: An Equilibrium Analysis of Channel Relationships," *Research in Marketing: Distribution Channels and Institutions,* Louis P. Bucklin and James Carman, eds., 8:181-223.
Nash, John F. Jr., "The Bargaining Problem," *Econometrica,* 18:155-162.
Newton, Isaac. (1713). *Principia Mathematica,* 2nd Ed., Cambridge: University Press; (English translation by Andrew Motte, *Newton's Principia: the Mathematical Principles of Natural Philosophy,* New York: Daniel Adee, 1846).
Thorburn, W. M. (1918). "The Myth of Occam's Razor," *Mind* (new series), 27: 345-353.

## Chapter 12

Bucklin, Louis P. (1966). *A Theory of Distribution Channel Structure,* Berkeley: University of California, Institute of Business and Economic Research.
Choi, S. Chan. (1991). "Price Competition in a Channel Structure with a Common Retailer," *Marketing Science,* 10:271-96.
Choi, S. Chan. (1996). "Price Competition in a Duopoly Common Retailer Channel," *Journal of Retailing,* 72:117-37.
Coughlan, Anne T. and Charles Ingene. (2002). "Product-Line Pricing in a Distribution Channel: Optimum or Pessimum?" (mimeo), Cornell University: Conference on Pricing Research.
de Morgan, Augustus. (1915). *Budget of Paradoxes,* Chicago: Open Court Publishing.
Desiraju, Ramarao and K. Sridhar Moorthy. (1997). "Managing a Distribution Channel under Asymmetric Information with Performance Requirements," *Management Science,* 43: 1628-44.
Hawkins, E. R. (1950). "Vertical Price Relationships," *Theory in Marketing,* Reavis Cox and Wroe Alderson, eds., Chicago: Irwin, 179-91.
Ingene, Charles and Mark Parry. (1995). "Channel Coordination When Retailers Compete," *Marketing Science,* 14:360-77.
Ingene, Charles and Eden Yu. (1991). "Variable Returns to Scale and Regional Resource Allocation Under Uncertainty," *Journal of Regional Science,* 31:455-468.
Jagpal, Sharan. (1999). *Marketing Strategy and Uncertainty,* New York: Oxford University Press.
Jeuland, Abel and Steven Shugan. (1983). "Managing Channel Profits," *Marketing Science,* 2:239-72.
Jevons, William Stanley. (1871). *The Theory of Political Economy,* London: Macmillan.
Lee, Eunkyu and Richard Staelin. (1997). "Vertical Strategic Interaction: Implications for Channel Pricing Strategy," *Marketing Science,* 16:185-207.

Locke, John. (1690). "Dedicatory Epistle," John Locke, *An Essay Concerning Humane Understanding,* London: Thomas Basset.

McGuire, Timothy and Richard Staelin. (1983). "An Industry Equilibrium Analysis of Downstream Vertical Integration," *Marketing Science,* 2:161-92.

McGuire, Timothy and Richard Staelin. (1986). "Channel Efficiency, Incentive Compatibility, Transfer Pricing and Market Structure: An Equilibrium Analysis of Channel Relationships," *Research in Marketing: Distribution Channels and Institutions*, Louis P. Bucklin and James Carman, eds., 8:181-223.

Moorthy, K. Sridhar. (1993). "Theoretical Modeling in Marketing," *Journal of Marketing,* 57:92-106.

Plato. *Dialogues Phaedrus*. Quote obtained from Columbia World of Quotations, http://www.bartleby.com/66/35/54535.html accessed on April 7, 2003.

Rubenstein, Ariel. (1982). "Perfect Equilibrium in a Bargaining Model," *Econometrica,* 50:97-109.

Trivedi, Minakshi. (1998). "Distribution Channels: An Extension of Exclusive Retailership," *Management Science,* 44:896-910.

Vargas, Melody. Quote obtained from *About Retail Industry*, http://retailindustry.about.com/library/terms/p/bld_pm.htm, accessed on July 12, 2003.

Whitehead, Alfred North. (1919). *The Concept of Nature, Tarrner Lectures Delivered in Trinity College, November,* London: Cambridge University Press, 1920.

Whitehead, Alfred North and Bertrand Russell. (1910). *Principia Mathematica,* London: Cambridge University Press, 1910-1913.

# INDEX

Printed in the United States
71998LV00001B/3

9 781402 071638